THE HISTORY
AND SOCIAL INFLUENCE
OF THE POTATO

The Potato Eaters. 1885. By Vincent van Gogh.

THE HISTORY AND SOCIAL INFLUENCE OF THE POTATO

REDCLIFFE N. SALAMAN

WITH A CHAPTER ON

INDUSTRIAL USES

BY W. G. BURTON

REVISED IMPRESSION EDITED BY

J. G. HAWKES

Emeritus Professor of Plant Biology,
University of Birmingham

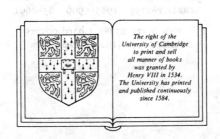

The right of the
University of Cambridge
to print and sell
all manner of books
was granted by
Henry VIII in 1534.
The University has printed
and published continuously
since 1584.

CAMBRIDGE UNIVERSITY PRESS

CAMBRIDGE

NEW YORK   PORT CHESTER

MELBOURNE   SYDNEY

Published by the Press Syndicate of the University of Cambridge
The Pitt Building, Trumpington Street, Cambridge CB2 1RP
40 West 20th Street, New York, NY 10011, USA
10 Stamford Road, Oakleigh, Melbourne 3166, Australia

First published 1949
Reprinted 1970
Reprinted, with a new introduction and corrections
by J. G. Hawkes, 1985
Reprinted 1986, 1987, 1989

Printed in Great Britain at Woolnough Bookbinding, Irthlingborough,
Northamptonshire

British Library cataloguing in publication data

Salaman, Redcliffe N.
The history and social influence of the potato.
– Rev. impression/edited by J. G. Hawkes
1. Potatoes – Social aspects – History
I. Title II. Burton, W. G. III. Hawkes, J. G.
394.1′2 SB211.P8

Library of Congress cataloging in publication data

Salaman, Redcliffe N. (Redcliffe Nathan), 1874–1955.
The history and social influence of the potato.

Bibliography.
Includes index.
1. Potatoes – History. 2. Potatoes – Social aspects.
I. Burton, W. G. (William Glynn). II. Hawkes, J. G.
(John Gregory), 1915–   . III. Title.
SB211.P8S255 1985 909 85–6691

ISBN 0 521 07783 4 hard covers
ISBN 0 521 31623 5 paperback

CONTENTS

NOTE. *In addition to the information given in the footnotes
further details will be found in the Bibliography*

INTRODUCTION TO THE
REVISED IMPRESSION

by J. G. HAWKES

This monumental work on the History and Social Influence of the Potato continues to show today, as it did when it was first published some thirty-five years ago, the unmistakable breadth of knowledge and vision of its author, Dr R. N. Salaman. Covering, as it does, an impressively wide field ranging through anthropology, archaeology, botany, potato breeding, agricultural history and economic and social history, it faces any present-day editor with a considerable problem, since no-one currently possesses the expert knowledge to cover the total range of disciplines that Salaman himself so brilliantly displayed.

Clearly after a period of thirty-five years, advances in knowledge, understanding and interpretation are bound to have occurred in a subject of this sort, and especially in the realms of archaeology and of agricultural, economic and social history, which have advanced very quickly in the post-war period. The temptation to re-write whole sections or even chapters incorporating such new knowledge and inter-pretation has been very strong. However, the constraints imposed by the publishers prevented this, and I have had to confine myself to the correction of small textual errors, the addition of footnotes (many of which are taken from Salaman's own manuscript notes deposited in the Cambridge University Library),[1] and the writing of this Introduction.

My own interests lie chiefly in the taxonomy of the potato and its wild relatives, its archaeological background and the history of its discovery and introduction into Europe. I am less well qualified in the social and economic history of the potato but I have been fortunate enough to be able to call on the professional expertise of Dr E. J. T. Collins, Director of the Institute of Agricultural History and Museum of English Rural Life at the University of Reading, in matters concerning English agricultural history. For Irish agricultural history I am grateful for the help of Dr Cormac O'Grada of the Department of Political Economy, University College, Dublin, and to Dr Austin Bourke for comments on the history of the potato in Ireland. Further reading lists kindly suggested by these authorities are given at the end of this Introduction. I should also like to pay tribute to my late friend Professor Kenneth Connell, whose work on the Irish potato famine is a classic of its type.

---

[1] My grateful thanks are due to Mr A. E. B. Owen, Keeper of Manuscripts at the Cambridge University Library, who kindly lent me five volumes of Salaman's

I have been fortunate again to enlist the help (as Salaman did in the first edition) of my friend and colleague Dr W. G. Burton, concerning the industrial uses of the potato (Chapter XXXI) and its nutritive value (pp. 121–5). To all these colleagues I offer my grateful thanks. I also wish to thank the author's sons Mr Raphael and Dr Myer Salaman for their friendly help and encouragement and for lending me his interleaved copy of the book containing useful notes and corrections.

Let us now turn to the book itself. This is so clearly a work of major scholarship that I fear that some of the comments and criticisms may appear to be somewhat carping. Nevertheless, certain points must be made and topics discussed because of the recent advances in knowledge and interpretation to which I have already referred.

The first four chapters deal with early man in the Andes of South America, his relationship to his environment, the domestication of his crops and, in particular, the prehistory of the potato. In this subject area there have been many advances during the last thirty-five years. Thus, although early man moved into the Andean zone from the tropical forests, either via the Amazon basin or, more probably, directly from the northern Colombian lowlands,[1] the idea that he was motivated by dread or terror is questionable. Probably all early men held the apparently inscrutable forces of nature in some dread; most of their religions incorporate attempts to propitiate these forces and at the same time to characterize or understand them, often by means of anthropomorphic or zoomorphic representation, or indeed by combinations of the two. Thus a certain amount of fear or dread of the known and unknown is normal to all primitive societies, and even in quite advanced ones, too.

Human hunter-gatherer groups undoubtedly arrived in South America, probably several millennia before the adoption of agriculture. Here they found an abundance of game and plentiful wild plants with edible seeds, stems, roots or tubers. We now have evidence for the cultivation of beans and squashes nearly 10,000 years ago,[2] and of potatoes some 8,000 years ago.[3] It is highly likely that other tubers such as oca (*Oxalis tuberosa*) and ulluco (*Ullucus tuberosa*) as well as the small grain crop Quinoa (*Chenopodium quinoa*) were also brought into cultivation at an early date. Thus several species of food plants were available at an early stage of agriculture in the central Andean zone of what are

[1] Clifford, P. (1983). Introduction. *In* Katz, L. (ed.), *Art of the Andes*, p. 7. The Arthur M. Sackler Foundation and The AMS Foundation for the Arts, Sciences and Humanities, Washington, D.C.

[2] Kaplan, L. (1980). Variation in the cultivated beans. *In* Lynch, T. F. (ed.), *Guitarrero Cave. Early Man in the Andes*. Academic Press, New York.

[3] Martins Farias, R. (1976). New Archaeological Techniques for the Study of Ancient Root Crops in Peru. Ph.D. Thesis, University of Birmingham.

now Peru and Bolivia. This area is now considered to be one of the four world nuclear centres of agricultural origins.[1] Hence the potato was, as Salaman states, almost certainly one of the important food plants of the high Andes and possibly the first to be domesticated in that area. Unfortunately, Salaman uses Mangelsdorf's theory on the origin of maize (p. 4) to add weight to his theory that early man reached the Andes directly from the eastern forests. There is now very strong evidence that maize was first domesticated in Mexico from wild ancestors that do not exist in South America,[2] and that it reached Peru very much later, probably some 3,500 years ago only.[3]

Salaman was of course fascinated, as we all have been, with the wonderful ceramics of the coastal peoples of Peru. A diverse series of styles exists, each with an overwhelming range of examples, those of chief importance to the botanist being Moche (formerly designated Mochica, Muchik, Proto-Chimú) and Chimú on the north coast, and Nazca on the south coast. It would seem that, particularly in Moche art, every aspect of human life and environment is depicted, so that to the palaeoethnobotanist a wealth of interesting examples is displayed. This includes not only potatoes but maize, peppers, many kinds of gourds and squashes, beans, peanuts, cassava, numerous fruits such as tree tomato, pepino (*Solanum muricatum*) and guanavana (*Anona muricata*), sweet potatoes, achira (*Canna edulis*) and many others. The Moche ceramics were produced from approximately 400 B.C. to A.D. 700, but actual food remains from the central Peruvian coast have been radiocarbon dated at least back to 4,500 years before present, and, as we have seen, potatoes date back to 8,000 and beans to 10,000 years ago. In the southern mountains urns of the type known as Robles Moqo style, at Pacheco (Huari culture), were made at about A.D. 1000 and bear representations of potato, oca, ulluco, mashua (*Tropaeolum tuberosus*), maize, quinoa and peppers.

Thus the potato is one of many crop plants depicted, and on the whole is not too frequently represented, contrary to Salaman's account which over-emphasises its importance. However, we must remember the potato was not grown on the coast since it was too hot there for its cultivation; thus it may possibly have been obtained only by barter from the highlands, or through transhumance.

Another matter that needs discussion here is Salaman's hypothesis

[1] Hawkes, J. G. (1983). *The Diversity of Crop Plants*. Harvard University Press, Cambridge, Mass.
[2] Beadle, G. W. (1980). The ancestry of corn. *Scientific American*, vol. CCXLII (1), 96–103.
[3] Bray, Warwick (1976). From predation to production: the nature of agricultural evolution in Mexico and Peru. *In* Sievking et al. (eds.), *Problems in Economic and Social Archaeology*, pp. 74–95. Duckworth, London.

that facial mutilations involving resection of the nose and lips were somehow associated with potato eyes in an attempt to indicate to the potato deity that strong sprouts growing from well marked 'eyes' (= nose and mouth of the human being) were required in order to ensure a good harvest. This hypothesis occurred to Salaman because of the presence of certain ceramics which showed a fusion of human and potato characteristics in one and the same pot. Figure 21, plate IX is particularly significant in this respect. It should be pointed out, however, that fanciful combinations of human/plant, human/animal, plant/animal and human/bird attributes are quite common, though the reasons for these combinations are unknown and generally thought to be of ritual or magic significance. It should also be pointed out that pots depicting human beings only, without potato attributes of any kind, and with the mutilations already referred to, also occur with about the same frequency. We may here be looking at some kind of punishment meted out to wrong-doers or enemies rather than the depiction of a religious rite or ceremony intended to increase agricultural production. Unfortunately, since there was no written language and this type of ceramic disappeared nearly one thousand years before the first Europeans arrived in Peru we shall probably never know the true significance of this or indeed any of the other mysteries of Moche ceramic art forms.

The Moche civilization was destroyed by Huari conquests spreading northwards from southern Peru in A.D. 700, and Huari was in turn replaced by the Chimú culture in about A.D. 900–1000. This style continued to develop until 1470 when the Chimú peoples were conquered by the Incas. From 1470 until the Spanish conquest in 1532 a distinctive Chimú-Inca style developed. Many of Salaman's figures (4–12) are of this late type.[1]

Before leaving the subject of Peruvian archaeology one other point should be mentioned. On page 16 Salaman reproduces a chronological table of Peruvian cultures, originally published by T. A. Joyce in 1920. This was completely out of date by the time of publication of the first edition in 1949 and is even more so in 1983. Newer, more useful schemes are given by Bushnell[2] and by Lanning.[3] A much better chronological sequence table, which includes reasonably accurate dating, is given by Rowe and Menzel,[4] and it is this one on which I have based my references to dates, cultures and styles, as well as to Katz's *Art of the Andes*, published in 1983.

[1] I am indebted to the late Geoffrey Bushnell for kindly helping me some years ago with the attributions of the Peruvian ceramics in Salaman's book.

[2] Bushnell, G. H. S. (1956; second edition 1963). *Ancient Peoples and Places: Peru.* Thames and Hudson, London.

[3] Lanning, E. P. (1967). *Peru Before the Incas.* Prentice-Hall, New Jersey.

[4] Rowe, J. H. and Menzel, D. (1967). *Peruvian Archaeology Selected Readings.* Peek Publications, Palo Alto.

Passing now to Chapter III, a number of errors were made in the first edition, which I have attempted to correct in the text or by means of footnotes. Salaman, unfortunately, never visited Latin America, and this is a pity, since he would undoubtedly have derived great advantages from his travels there. The history of the discovery and conquest of Peru and the other Andean countries has been dealt with by many Spanish chronicles, whose works have appeared in facsimile or edited publications, both in the original Spanish and in translation. Salaman draws on the translated accounts very freely, but makes the same error about Juan de Castellanos that I did until John Rowe in a personal communication kindly pointed out that the Castellanos who was a member of Jiménez de Quesada's expedition in New Granada (now Colombia) was not the person of the same name who published the account of the first mention of potatoes in South America—a very understandable error. For further details of the early published accounts of the potato in South America the reader is referred to two of my publications on the potato in its native land, its introduction into Europe and its early description.[1]

In his Chapter V, concerning the potatoes of America and the early European varieties, Salaman deals with the cultivated species and a number of their varieties, as well as several of the wild species. Knowledge of the evolutionary relationships and taxonomy of both cultivated and wild potatoes in Latin America has advanced greatly in the last thirty-five years. The reader is referred to the works of Correll[2] and Hawkes[3] for further information.

As Salaman rightly emphasized, the folk taxonomy of the potato has evoked some interest, since potatoes are given vernacular names in the two Indian languages still spoken in the high Andes, Quechua and Aymará, or in mixtures of these and Spanish. Each varietal name consists of a noun and a qualifying adjective, the latter generally referring to some definite or fanciful quality of the variety concerned. Two publications are available for further reading, by La Barre[4] and by Hawkes.[5]

[1] Hawkes, J. G. (1967). The history of the potato. Masters Memorial Lecture, 1966. *Journal of the Royal Horticultural Society*, vol. XCII, 207–24; 249–62; 288–300; 364–5; Hawkes, J. G. (1982). The history of the potato. In Harris, P. M. (ed.), *The Potato Crop. The Scientific Basis for Improvement*, pp. 1–14. Chapman and Hall, London (first published 1978).

[2] Corell, D. S. (1952). *The Potato and its Wild Relatives*. Texas Research Foundation Botanical Monographs, vol. IV. Renner, Texas.

[3] Hawkes, J. G. (1963). A revision of the tuber-bearing Solanums (2nd edn). *Scottish Plant Breeding Station Record*, 76–181; Hawkes, J. G. (1982). Biosystematics of the potato. In Harris, P. M., *op. cit.*, pp. 15–69.

[4] La Barre, W. (1947). Potato taxonomy amongst the Aymará Indians of Bolivia. *Acta Americana*, vol. V, 83–103.

[5] Hawkes, J. G. (1947). On the origin and meaning of South American Indian potato names. *Journal of the Linnean Society (Botany)*, vol. LIII (50), 205–50.

An error for which I am responsible was quoted by Salaman once or twice (see footnote to page 64). This concerns a report that I heard several times in Colombia and Ecuador that the Indians somewhere near Pasto in southern Colombia raised their potatoes from true seed. Although I was never able to locate the exact place where this was supposed to happen I heard the report from so many sources that I supposed it to be true. Later, however, I learned from some of my Colombian colleagues that the reports stemmed from the work of an amateur potato breeder living near Pasto but who had died some years before. Thus the facts grew and changed in the telling!

The variation of leaf type and plant habit in the tetraploid cultivated potato *Solanum tuberosum* and its Andean subspecies *andigen* (originally given species rank as *S. andigenum*) was a matter of considerable interest to Salaman and to me. In our joint and single-authored papers on this topic,[1] we were able to show that the two taxa did not differ fundamentally from each other and that their subspecific relationship provided the clue to the much debated origin of the European potato (see also Appendix v, p. 618).

The complex story of the introduction of the potato into Europe and the early botanical descriptions is dealt with by Salaman admirably and has not been much added to since the book was published. One extra point, however, emerges from a further scrutiny of the literature.[2] This is, that Sir Francis Drake was not instrumental in bringing the potato to England in 1586. This is because Gerard in his *Herball* stated that he obtained potatoes *after* 1588, the year in which they were first sent to the celebrated herbalist C. Clusius. Nevertheless there is evidence that Gerard was instrumental in bringing the potato to England round about 1590, though of course we cannot be completely certain of this. The fact remains, however, that neither Drake or Raleigh was responsible for bringing the potato to England.

In Chapter x on 'Potato varieties, past, present and future', Salaman mentions ten varieties which came into use in the last quarter of the eighteenth century and the early decades of the nineteenth century, namely, Howard or Cluster, Irish Apple, Manly, White Kidney, Ox Noble, Yam, Lumper, Cups, Ashleaf and Lapstone Kidney. Four of these, namely Ashleaf, Cups, Yams and Ox Noble, are listed by G. W.

---

[1] Salaman, R. N. (1946). The early European potato: its character and place of origin. *Journal of the Linnean Society* (*Botany*), vol. LIII, 1–27; Salaman, R. N. and Hawkes, J. G. (1949). The character of the early European potato. *Proceedings of the Linnean Society*, vol. CLXI, 71–84; Salaman, R. N. (1954). The origin of the early European potato. *Journal of the Linnean Society* (*Botany*), vol. LV, 185–90.

[2] See Quinn, D. B. (editor) (1955). *The Roanoke Voyages, 1584–1590*. Hakluyt Society, vol. CIV, CV. London; Hawkes, J. G. (1967). The history of the potato, *op. cit.*

Johnson in 1847[1] but he also includes a list of 116 early varieties and 35 late ones, possibly many of these being synonyms. It is interesting to note, however, that in his cultural notes he describes how to raise potatoes from true seed and to select for various characters, in particular for 'early ripeness'. This method described had, it seems, already been published in the *Gardeners' Chronicle* of 1844 (p. 806). Thus most of these varieties may indeed have been raised from seed by local plants-men.

Another point that needs to be discussed in Chapter x is Salaman's reference on p. 165 to the Reverend Chauncey Goodrich's importation into the USA in 1851 of a few samples of potato from the market in Panamá. One was named 'Rough Purple Chile', and Salaman felt that the name was misleading, since he considered that the so-called Panamanian tubers were *andigena* varieties, and had therefore come from the Andes and not Chile at all. It has seemed to me more probable that 'Rough Purple Chile' had in fact come from Chile, since all the really early European varieties in the latter part of the nineteenth century had been bred from 'Early Rose', the granddaughter of 'Rough Purple Chile'. They thus could have inherited the adaptation for yielding in the long summer days of southern Chile and, of course, northern Europe.[2]

It is interesting to notice in passing the change of importance of potato varieties over the years. In 1949 Salaman noted this fact (see pp. 169–71) and mentioned that 'Majestic' was at the time of publication the most widely grown late variety in Great Britain, with 'King Edward' a general favourite. The wheel of change has again moved on, for in 1983 the most widely grown Maincrop varieties planted by registered producers were 'Maris Piper', 'Desiree' and 'Record' (in descending order of importance).[3] 'King Edward' is placed seventh, whilst 'Majestic' is not mentioned at all amongst the fourteen varieties listed. Among the Second Earlies the varieties 'Wilja', 'Estima' and 'Maris Peer' take first, second and third place respectively, whilst the First Earlies list 'Pentland Javelin', 'Maris Bard' and 'Ulster Sceptre' in first, second and third places respectively. It is interesting to note in passing that of these nine varieties four were bred outside the United Kingdom.

The last part of this chapter presents a very interesting account of the potato breeding situation up to 1949. It is obvious that in thirty-five

[1] Johnson, G. W. (1847). *The Gardener's Monthly Volume: The Potato*. R. Baldwin, London.
[2] Hawkes, J. G. (1967). The history of the potato, *op. cit.*, p. 293.
[3] Potato Marketing Board (1984). *Potato Statistics Bulletin for the 1983 crop (and earlier seasons revises)*. PMB, London. I am grateful, also, to Dr R. M. J. Storey of the PMB for further confirmation of these facts.

years many more advances will have been made. Restrictions of space do not permit me to give details; for these the reader is referred to two works by H. W. Howard,[1] which deal with the older and the more recent problems confronting the potato breeder.

Another important advance during the last thirty-five years is the expanding use of wild potato species in breeding varieties with better resistance to pests and diseases. This point was of course mentioned by Salaman, but I am sure that if he were alive now he would be both surprised and gratified by the increase in the use of wild species in this field—a branch of research which he himself helped largely to begin and to promote. According to Ross,[2] writing in 1979, 49% of the cultivars of five European countries possess genes from the wild species, *Solanum demissum*, whilst at least 90% of the more than one million seedlings produced annually by West German breeders have wild species or primitive cultivars in their ancestry. The figures for 1985 would undoubtedly be higher still.

Finally, a word must be said about the development of potato breeding and research on a world scale, through the efforts of the International Potato Centre at Lima, Peru.[3] This Centre is funded by donor countries by means of aid funding for developing countries, and since its foundation in 1972 has made gigantic strides. Some of its more interesting work has involved the breeding of varieties adapted to the humid tropics, the promotion of breeding and research for growing potatoes from true seed and the development of lines resistant to frost, *Phytophthora*, viruses and cyst and root-knot nematodes. Another important function has been CIP's involvement in a programme of potato genetic resources conservation. Nearly all of CIP's activities include co-operation with scientists from both developed and developing countries.

In Chapters XI to XVIII Salaman deals in very considerable detail with the potato in Ireland. He brings out with startling and horrific clarity the tragedy of the famine years and the at times adverse socio-historical role that the potato assumed in that unfortunate country. The appalling poverty of the Irish people, exacerbated by the ease with which they could just exist on the potato crop until the onset of potato blight in the

---

[1] Howard, H. W. (1970). *Genetics of the Potato*, Solanum tuberosum. Logos Press, London; Howard, H. W. (1982). The production of new varieties. *In* Harris, P. M. (ed.), *The Potato Crop. The Scientific Basis for Improvement*, pp. 607–46. Chapman and Hall, London.

[2] Ross, H. (1979). Wild species and primitive cultivars as ancestors of potato varieties. *In* Zeven, A. C. and van Harten, A. M., *Broadening the Genetic Base of Crops*, pp. 237–45. Pudoc, Wageningen.

[3] CIP (Centro Internacional de la Papa – International Potato Centre) (1984). *Potatoes for the Developing World*. CIP, Lima, Peru.

mid-nineteenth century, is covered in considerable detail. Because new
facts and new interpretations have arisen in the last thirty-five years I
have asked Dr Cormac O'Grada and Dr Austin Bourke to comment on
the Irish chapters of Salaman's book and to provide further biblio-
graphical references (see the end of this Introduction). Dr O'Grada has
kindly allowed me to quote as follows from his unpublished letter:

It is true that Irish historians have criticized [Salaman's] findings over the
years but it is a book which is still held in high regard [in Ireland]. Bourke,
Cullen and Connell all take issue with Salaman about the chronology of
potato diffusion in Ireland. They disagree among themselves on other aspects,
however. Cullen's chapter in his recent monograph on the vagaries of Irish
diet over the centuries is fascinating, [whilst Mokyr attempts to] answer some
puzzles about diffusion [and] revises Bourke's guess at the maximum pre-
famine potato acreage downwards, though not substantially. Williams...uses
the absence of references to the potato in the first part of a seventeenth-
century work, coupled with several references in the second part, as a rough-
and-ready way of dating [the spread of the potato in Ireland].

These views echo the conclusions of Connell,[1] who, writing in 1950,
surveyed the information used by Salaman and concluded that 'on
reviewing the seventeenth- and eighteenth-century accounts of the
Irishman's food there is a strong case for regarding the generalization of
a potato diet as a more gradual process than Dr. Salaman would have
us believe. In place of the four or five decades into which his interpretation compresses the process it may well have been spread over
more than an additional century.' Further, he quotes (p. 134, footnote),
an interesting passage from Sir William Wilde's history of the potato in
Ireland, published in the 1851 Census, which states that the potato
'was grown in gardens as a rarity, used at table as a delicacy, and
described by herbalists as an introduced exotic; but we do not find any
warrant for believing that it was at all cultivated by the people as a
general article of food until from the end of the seventeenth to the
beginning of the eighteenth century'. Elsewhere, the same author says
'from the researches which I have made it would appear that the
cultivation of the potato was very irregular throughout the country;
some localities, especially in Ulster, having adopted it generally within
the memory of the past generation'.[2]
We now come to the comments made by Austin Bourke in a letter
and in his review of the 1970 reprint of Salaman's book:[3]

[1] Connell, K. H. (1950). *The Population of Ireland 1750–1845*. Clarendon Press,
Oxford, pp. 125–35.
[2] Cited by Connell (*op. cit.*, p. 134): Sir William Wilde (1853–7). The Introduction
and Time of general use of the Potato in Ireland. *Proc. R. I. Academy*, vol. VI, 360.
[3] Bourke, P. M. Austin (1970–1). *Irish Historical Studies*, vol. XVII, 410–13.

As regards the potato in Ireland, I will point out a few relatively minor errors and one major question of interpretation in which Salaman's deductions are difficult to justify. A new turn has been given to the familiar confusion between the Irish and the statute acre. O'Rourke,[1] on whose emotional account of the famine Salaman leans heavily as a 'classical work' (p. 300) had been puzzled to reconcile widely different estimates of the extent of the 1846 potato crop. *Thom's Almanac* had given a figure of 1,234,441 acres; the earl of Ross quoted the value as 2,100,000 and Father Matthew claimed that two million acres had been destroyed by blight. O'Rourke oddly failed to notice that the problem is resolved once one recognises that the first figure is in Irish acres, the popular unit of the period. Salaman (p. 321) compounds the confusion by accepting the lowest figure as the number of state acres under potatoes in 1846, and by arbitrarily assigning the larger figure to an earlier period. In an analogous error (pp. 318, 329) farm-sizes on the eve of the famine, expressed in Irish acres, are compared with post-famine figures in statute acres. This is, of course, a hoary old pitfall which continues to claim its regular quota of victims despite all warnings.[2]

Salaman follows Davidson[3] in the gross oversimplifications (p. 163) of regarding the Cup variety as a luxury potato and the food of the rich between 1810 and 1846. Even at the later date there were still parts of Ireland in which the Cup could be called 'the poor man's potato'.[4] On the eve of the famine, poorhouse guardians advertising for potato tenders often specified the Cup variety.[5]

Salaman (pp. 253, 278) was clearly taken by Evans's use[6] of the phrase 'blue month' for the period of mid-summer food scarcity between the old and new potato crops, although the adjective seems unlikely either in terms of nineteenth-century English or as a derivative from Irish. In a private letter, Professor Evans has said that he cannot now recall the origin of his usage, nor have I found any independent support for the phrase.

The major point of disagreement concerns Salaman's claim of the rapid adoption of the potato in much of Ireland: 'within fifty years of its introduction the potato had become the universal and staple article of the people's food in the greater part of the island' (p. 189). The dispute over this point is but an echo of a controversy which is over a hundred years old.

Thus the conclusions of Bourke, Connell, O'Grada and others do not agree with those of Salaman, that the potato was very rapidly adopted as a main article of diet until the latter part of the eighteenth century, though he quotes sources to the effect that it may have been more popular in the south. I shall comment on the botanical significance of

---

[1] O'Rourke, J. (1875). *See* Irish References.
[2] Bourke, P. M. A. (1959). *See* Irish References.
[3] Davidson, W. D. (1933). History of potato varieties. *Journal of the Department of Agriculture, Eire*, vol. XXXIII, 57–81.
[4] *Irish Farmers' Journal* (Dublin, 1846), p. 573.
[5] *Cork Constitution*, 26 July 1845. *Limerick Chronicle*, 27 September 1845.
[6] Estyn Evans, E. (1942). *See* Irish References.

these conclusions later, when the spread of the potato in other parts of the British Isles has been dealt with.

Chapters XIX and XXI deal with the potato in Scotland, and here I am afraid I have no authorities to guide me. It should be pointed out, however, that the Highland Line as defined by Salaman (p. 346) does not conform with the usual concept, namely, that it is a line following the Highland Geological Boundary Fault,[1] running roughly in a south-west/north-east direction from the Firth of Clyde to Stonehaven in Kincardineshire. So far as delimiting highland from lowland agricultural patterns is concerned, of course, Salaman's boundary is more or less correct, though he should not have confused it with the Highland Line.

We now come to the history of the potato in England and Wales, which Salaman covers in Chapters XXII to XXVII. As I mentioned above, Dr E. J. T. Collins has kindly let me have his views and comments on Salaman's book, and particularly on these chapters dealing with the potato in England.[2] He has also kindly provided a list of references for further reading on works of English agricultural history relevant to the potato (see list at the end of this Introduction). He writes as follows:

It would appear that very little published research has been done on the subject of potatoes, at least for England, in the modern period. But some important work has been done in agricultural and dietary history, and especially social history, and many of Salaman's statements, probably of the more general kind, will beed to be revised.... Salaman was much more interested in the potato in the pre-industrial era than in the nineteenth century when in Britain and elsewhere in Western Europe it became a staple food of the industrial workers and, for farmers, an important commercial crop cultivated on a field scale. He did not explain satisfactorily just why the potato took so long to become an integral part of the British diet, especially in Southern England and East Anglia where it was very little used before 1800. It is particularly disappointing that he did not give more effort to explaining the dietary but also the nutritional significance of the potato in terms of the niche which it occupied (it was never a perfect substitute for cereals) and as a source of energy, protein and vitamins.

I feel too that he could have said very much more about the agricultural history of the potato, especially after 1790. There is a large body of literature on the subject of the potato in the nineteenth century which is barely touched upon. Much more could have been said about varieties, methods of cultivation and especially the way in which it became integrated into arable farming systems as part of the rotation. His treatment of output and yields is very suspect and his use of statistics positively misleading. On p. 613, for

---

[1] *See* Frazer Darling, F. (1947). *Natural History of the Highlands and Islands*, p. 2. Collins, London.

[2] Collins, E. J. T. (1984). *Pers. comm.*

example, he makes the assumption that yields per acre were more or less static at c. 6 tons per acre between 1775 and 1914, which is untrue. I doubt also some of his estimates on wheat output and consumption (pp. 614–17)—in Great Britain as a whole but also in Scotland[1]—especially before 1850. This is very dangerous ground for, had he lived, he would have got nastily embroiled in the debate about the standard of living in the Industrial Revolution which exercised social and economic historians in the 1960s and 70s.

His view of British social and economic history in the late eighteenth and nineteenth centuries is based far too much on the Hammonds who took a fiercely pessimistic view of human progress during the Industrial Revolution. Had he read more widely and, at certain key points, rather more deeply, he might have produced a more balanced account. He was not, on his own admission, either an economist or historian and the pity is, I think, that he approached the subject so very broadly instead of concentrating on the agro-scientific and dietary aspects which he was best equipped to tackle.

Perhaps I sound too critical but at the time he was writing, in the 1940s, there was a sufficiently large body of secondary historical literature, scholarly and well-researched, on which he might have drawn, and, for the nineteenth century at any rate, a very useful and often remarkably perceptive contemporary literature. On the subject of working class diets, for example, he more or less ignored the splendid empirical surveys done by the food scientist, Edward Smith, in the 1860s.[2] He dealt with the post-1820 period in less than four pages.

Having said all that, I still regard the book as a major achievement and a monument of its kind. It is the work of a dedicated amateur written by a man of, I think, great honesty and broad horizons....As far as the British chapters are concerned he has made a most valuable and enduring contribution with regard to the sixteenth to eighteenth centuries for which he brought together a remarkable body of information drawn from the contemporary literature, including many scarce and relatively unknown texts.

So it would seem that as far as England itself is concerned Salaman's book is still the only detailed work directed to the social and economic history of the potato. Nevertheless, there is a major gap from the mid-eighteenth century onward, towards which future social and agricultural historians should turn their attention.

Before leaving the subject of the introduction and spread of the potato in the British Isles there is one clear point arising from the historical sources and modern commentaries quoted above. This concerns the speed of acceptance of the potato as a crop plant, which clearly seems to have been much slower than Salaman claimed—a process which may well have been due in part to the peasant farmers' reluctance to grow a quite unknown and alien crop, and in part to the open field system of

[1] See Collins, E. J. T. (1975). Dietary change and cereal consumption in Britain in the nineteenth century. *Agricultural History Review*, vol. XXIII (2), 97–115.

[2] See Collins, E. J. T. (1975), *op. cit.*, pp. 107, 108 etc.

agriculture which would prevent its cultivation as a late-maturing crop when the farm animals were allowed to graze over the stubble after the cereals were harvested in July to August.

The real reason, I believe, lies in the fact that the first potatoes brought to Europe were adapted to form tubers under a twelve-hour tropical day-length, and thus were not able to begin to form tubers until the end of September. Only in almost frost-free regions such as south-west Ireland were the potatoes of the Andes of South America able to yield a reasonable crop, and that by late October to early December. Gradually, the practice of growing from true seeds and selection for earliness changed the adverse photoperiodic reaction of the first introduced potatoes to a long-day adapted one. Evidence from Britain as well as from other European countries indicated that it took nearly two centuries for this adaptive process to have neared completion, and for this reason widespread field cultivation in all parts of Britain was not possible until the latter part of the eighteenth century.[1] The introduction of 'Rough Purple Chile' by Goodrich, very probably coming from Chile itself, reinforced the trend towards early maturing characteristics that now exist in our modern 'first early' varieties.

In the original edition of Salaman's book, Chapter xxxi on the Industrial Uses of the Potato was written by Dr W. G. Burton. He has kindly provided an appendix to the present Introduction, up-dating both his original chapter and also some aspects of Chapter viii, '"Vertues", Vices and Values'.

There is little more to be said about the final chapters. They form an important historical document and nothing short of a complete re-write would bring them up to date; this would in any case be inadvisable since they should in my opinion stand as they were written, as a fine example of the author's breadth of knowledge and understanding.

I should like to say, finally, that I have counted it as an honour and a privilege to edit this revised impression of a book written by a man I much admired and who gave me considerable help and guidance at the beginning of my career. If I have seemed to over-criticize him this is because, some thirty-five years on, knowledge and understanding of certain topics have clearly developed very materially. I can only end by quoting a passage from Austin Bourke's review,[2] with which I most heartily agree:

Every criticism is dwarfed by the stature of Salaman's work. For all its imperfections, the book remains a unique work of scholarship, by an author whose breadth of authoritative interest is unlikely to be matched in this field for a long time to come.

[1] Hawkes, J. G. (1967). The history of the potato, *op. cit.*, pp. 290–3.
[2] Bourke, P. M. A. (1970–1), *op. cit.*

ADDITIONAL REFERENCES

The Potato in Ireland

(Dr Cormac O'Grada and Dr Austin Bourke)

BOURKE, P. M. A. (1959). Uncertainties in the statistics of farm size in Ireland, 1841–1851. *Stat. Soc. Ire. Jn.* vol. XX 20–6

BOURKE, P. M. A. (1962). The scientific investigation of the potato blight in 1845–6. *Irish Historical Studies,* vol. XIII 26–32

BOURKE, P. M. A. (1964). Emergence of potato blight, 1843–46. *Nature,* London, vol. CCIII 805–8

BOURKE, P. M. A. (1965). The potato, blight, weather and the Irish famine. Ph.D. thesis, National University of Ireland

BOURKE, P. M. A. (1965). The agricultural statistics of the 1841 census of Ireland: a critical review. *Econ. Hist. Rev.,* 2nd series, vol. XXIII 376–91

BOURKE, P. M. A. (1965). Notes on some agricultural units of measurement in use in pre-famine Ireland. *Irish Historical Studies,* vol. XIV 236–45

BOURKE, P. M. A. (1968). The use of the potato crop in pre-famine Ireland. *Journal of the Statistical and Social Inquiry Society of Ireland,* vol. XII 72–96

BOURKE, P. M. A. (1970–1). Review of Salaman 2nd ed. *Irish Historical Studies,* vol. XVII 410–13

CONNELL, K. H. (1950). *The Population of Ireland, 1750–1845.* Clarendon Press, Oxford

CONNELL, K. H. (1951). History of the potato. *Economic History Review,* 2nd series, vol. III 388–95

CONNELL, K. H. (1962). The potato in Ireland. *Past and Present,* vol. XXIII 57–71

CULLEN, L. M. (1968). Irish history without the potato. *Past and Present,* vol. XL 72–83

CULLEN, L. M. (1981). *The Emergence of Modern Ireland.* London (ch. 7)

DWYER, GERALD P. and LINDSAY, COTTON M. (1984). Robert Giffen and the Irish potato. *American Economic Review,* vol. LXXIV 188–92

EDWARDS, R. D. and WILLIAMS, T. D. (eds.) (1956). *The Great Famine.* Dublin

ESTYN EVANS, E. (1942). *Irish Heritage.* Dundalk (p. 77)

MCNEILL, W. H. (1949). The introduction of the potato into Ireland. *Journal of Modern History,* vol. XXI 218–22

MOKYR, JOEL (1981). Irish history with the potato. *Irish Economic and Social History,* vol. VIII 8–29

O'GRADA, CORMAC (1984). Malthus and the pre-famine economy. *In* Antoin Murphy (ed.), *Economists and the Irish Economy.* Dublin, pp. 75–95

O'ROURKE, J. (1875). *The History of the Great Irish Famine of 1842.* Dublin.

WILLIAMS, NICHOLAS (ed.) (1981). *Pairlement Chloinne Tomais.* Dublin (p. 9)

WOODHAM-SMITH, C. (1962). *The Great Hunger.* London

The Potato in England
(Dr E. J. T. Collins)

BURNETT, JOHN (1979). *Plenty and Want: A Social History of Diet in England from 1815 to the Present Day* (1st edn, 1966; 2nd revised edn, 1979). Scolar Press, London

DRUMMOND, J. C. and WILBRAHAM, ANNE (1959). *The Englishman's Food*. Jonathan Cape, London

ODDY, D. J. (1976). A nutritional analysis of historical evidence: the working-class diet, 1880–1914. *In* D. Oddy and D. Miller (eds.), *The Making of the Modern British Diet*. Croom Helm, London. (N.B. See selected list of references in this work.)

APPENDIX
W. G. BURTON

Further Notes to Chapter VIII, '"Vertues", Vices and Values'

Salaman was correct in stating (p. 122) that the average dry matter of the potato is about 23 %, but often wrong in discussing the components of that dry matter. Starch usually amounts to about 70–5 % of the dry matter, rather than the 80–8 % he gave. An average value for sugars would be 1–3 %, rather than 3–6 %; and sugars, although very important in determining the quality of potatoes for processing, are not, as he states, one of the two main constituents of the dry matter. Citric acid, not mentioned by Salaman, is present in similar amounts, but both are normally exceeded by the fibre and much exceeded by the crude protein, amounting on average to some 10 % of the dry matter.

Salaman's view of the potato as a source of energy in the diet was probably biased by his studies of the potato in eighteenth- and nineteenth-century Ireland, where indeed it was the major source, though at the expense of a grossly excessive consumption. In present-day Ireland the potato provides less than 7 % of the energy in the diet (Elton, 1978), and still less in the rest of the EEC, in which the dietary energy supplied by the potato averages about 5 % (*ibid.*). This is equally true of the rest of western Europe, but in some countries of eastern Europe the proportion of the energy derived from potatoes is higher—e.g. about 10 % in Poland. The advantage to be gained from replacing present cultivars by those of higher starch content, as suggested on p. 122, would be minimal—particularly as the attainable starch content would be much less than stated on p. 122.

The potato, in common with most vegetable foods, provides a rather greater proportion of the requirement for dietary nitrogen than of the requirement for energy (see e.g. Burton, 1982). Salaman was thus in error in stating, on the one hand, that 'the importance of the potato as a source of calories cannot well be overestimated' and, on the other, that 'its value as a source of protein in the dietary of the people is inconsiderable'. At present levels of consumption it is not a major source of either energy or dietary nitrogen. At levels of consumption sufficient to provide an adequate supply of energy, the supply of nitrogen would also be adequate—as in fact shown by the extracts from Harriette Chick (1940) on pp. 124–5. It should be mentioned that the daily consumption of 2.6 kg of potatoes by a vigorous 75 kg man, quoted as giving a negative nitrogen balance, would probably have provided only some two-thirds (*c.* 9000 kJ) of the likely energy requirement.

Salaman rightly stressed the value of the potato as an antiscorbutic, probably its most important property in northern Europe at present consumption levels. It must be remembered, however, that the nutritive value can be much reduced by some methods of preparation and cooking. Too much weight should not be given to Salaman's comments on the effects of peeling, but cooking, and particularly processing, can markedly reduce the vitamin content. Particularly serious is the effect of keeping cooked potatoes for some hours and then re-heating. For some recent work on the effects of cooking and processing on nutritive value see Toma *et al.* (1978), Augustin *et al.* (1978) and Weaver *et al.* (1983).

Polyphenolases ('tyrosinase' on p. 125) are in fact of proved importance in catalysing the changes leading to one form of blackening after cooking—that associated with delay and exposure to air during preparation prior to cooking. The other main form of after-cooking blackening is non-enzymic, and involves the complexing of iron with phenolic compounds, particularly chlorogenic acid. Liability to its occurrence is a varietal characteristic dependent upon the content of the phenolic compounds and of citric acid, which competes for the iron and has a protective effect.

Further Notes to Chapter XXXI, 'The Industrial Uses of the Potato'

The overall conclusions in Chapter XXXI as to the suitability, or otherwise, of the potato as industrial raw material, and the economic factors which influence this suitability, are as valid now as in 1949. Much more is known of the constitution and properties of starch from various sources (see e.g. Greenwood, 1966) and there are uses for which potato starch is preferred—mainly for sizing and coating in the paper and textile industries (Treadway, 1975). This ensures its production to a limited extent, despite the inefficiency of the potato as a raw material. Starch production from potatoes is of greatest importance in the Netherlands, which has a long-established export trade in potato starch, and where, in 1979, 2.6 million tonnes of potatoes, over 40% of the crop, were used for its manufacture. No other country approaches this tonnage, although both Denmark and Finland use over a third of their much smaller potato production for starch manufacture (van Loon and Crosnier, 1982). Alcohol production in countries for which statistics are available (excluding the USSR) is of importance only in Poland and

West Germany (2.1 and 0.5 million tonnes of potatoes—5% and 6% of the crop—respectively in 1979).

Where Chapter xxxi is most out of date is in its treatment of the use of potatoes in the food processing industry. At the time the chapter was written the potato was still, as in the previous century, pre-eminently a cheap food providing a means of subsistence. The preceding twenty years had seen the farming slump of the 1930s, six years of warfare, and the years of austerity and, in many countries, food shortage following the war. The war had led to a great increase in the dehydration of potatoes in the combatant countries, as a means of reducing the bulk and extending the storage-life of supplies for the armed forces, and de-hydration found mention in the chapter. Whether dehydrated potato products would be readily acceptable in peacetime seemed problematical and on balance unlikely. The manufacture of other forms of processed potato was of little importance. Even in the USA, the home of potato processing by means other than dehydration, it was negligible prior to the war in forms other than potato 'chips' ('crisps' in the UK), and the production of these was comparatively small, using only about 100,000 tonnes of potatoes in 1939 (Talburt, 1975)—some 1% of the potatoes used as food—although by 1949 there had been a five-fold increase in this usage. Home freezers, and frozen foods in domestic packs, were practically unknown; even refrigerators were not common in most countries. All in all, in 1949 there was little to suggest a so-called 'affluent society' which would demand, and be prepared to pay for, 'convenience' foods, including many forms of processed potato, some requiring distribution and storage in the frozen state.

The post-war growth of the potato processing industry has been in fact phenomenal. By 1970 about half the potatoes used as food in the USA were processed, and of these almost half were frozen products. Potato crisps (US 'chips'), various forms of dehydrated and readily reconstituted potato, partially cooked and frozen chips (US 'French fries') and many other frozen products consisting wholly or partly of potato—mashed potato, patties, rissoles, dumplings, pancakes, to mention only a few—became important articles of commerce, and did much to stabilize, and indeed increase, the consumption of potatoes during a period which saw a marked decline in the demand for fresh potatoes. Weaver et al. (1975) in discussing the growth of the potato processing industry in the USA stated that 'approximately 70 per cent of all Idaho-grown potatoes and 80 per cent of all Washington-grown potatoes used as food are processed, with frozen potato products making up at least half of the food utilization of the Idaho crop'. Potato processing in the rest of the 'developed' world has not yet reached the proportions encountered in the USA, but it is nevertheless a major industry, particularly in Great Britain, West Germany and the Netherlands which by 1979 processed about 22%, 19% and 28%, respectively, of the potatoes used as human food (van Loon and Crosnier, 1982). In the developing world, industrial processing of potatoes occurs only on a minor scale in a few isolated cases, but may clearly develop in those countries in which the potato is, or becomes, an important crop.

References

AUGUSTIN, J., JOHNSON, S. R., TEITZEL, C., TRUE, R. H., HOGAN, J. M., TOMA, R. B., SHAW, R. L. and DEUTSCH, R. M. (1978). Changes in the nutrient composition of potatoes during home preparation. II. Vitamins. *Amer. Potato J.* vol. LV 653–62

BURTON, W. G. (1982). *Post-harvest Physiology of Food Crops.* Longman, London

ELTON, G. A. H. (1978). European diets in relation to standards of need. *In* J. Yudkin (ed.), *Diet of Man: Needs and Wants*, pp. 25–40. Applied Science Publishers, Barking

GREENWOOD, C. T. (1966). Physical and chemical characteristics of potato starch. *Proc. Pl. Sci. Symp., Campbell Inst. Agric. Res., Camden, New Jersey* 41–62

LOON, C. D. VAN and CROSNIER, J. C. (1982). 1955–1980, 25 ans de culture de la pomme de terre en Europe. *In* B. Schöber *et al.* (eds.). *EAPR. 25 Jahre Europäische Gesellschaft für Kartoffelforschung 1957–1982*, pp. 33–53. Wageningen

TALBURT, W. F. (1975). History of potato processing, chapter 1, pp. 1–10, of W. F. Talburt and O. Smith (eds.), *Potato Processing* (3rd edn). Avi Publishing Co., Westport, Ct.

TOMA, R. B., AUGUSTIN, J., ORR, P. H., TRUE, R. H., HOGAN, J. M. and SHAW, R. L. (1978). Changes in the nutrient composition of potatoes during home preparation. I. Proximate composition. *Amer. Potato J.* vol. LV 639–45

TREADWAY, R. H. (1975). Potato starch, chapter 15, pp. 546–62, of W. F. Talburt and O. Smith (eds.), *Potato Processing* (3rd edn). Avi Publishing Co., Westport, Ct.

WEAVER, M. L., REEVE, R. M. and KUENEMAN, R. W. (1975). Frozen French fries and other frozen potato products, chapter 11, pp. 403–42, of W. F. Talburt and O. Smith (eds.), *Potato Processing* (3rd edn). Avi Publishing Co., Westport, Ct.

WEAVER, M. L., TIMMS, H. and NG, H. (1983). Changes in nutritional composition of Russet Burbank potatoes by different processing methods. *Amer. Potato J.* vol. LX 735–44

PREFACE

Now that, after many years, a record of my studies on the history and economic repercussions, consequent on the introduction of the potato, is near completion, it may not be inopportune to give some account of how my interest in this otherwise inoffensive vegetable came about.

Indeed, there have not been wanting those who have regarded these activities with a shake of the head and an indulgent smile, indicating that nothing, short of mental instability, could excuse a lifelong attachment to the study of so banal a subject.

My career as a medical man and pathologist was brought by illness to a sudden close in 1903. Eight years had elapsed since I had left Cambridge: five strenuous and fruitful years had been passed in the laboratories and wards of the London hospital, and three more in a ceaseless effort to find time for research after the heavy claims on my time as administrator and teacher had been satisfied.

In the following year, I retired to what promised to be a life of ease and leisure in the beautiful village of Barley, in north Herts. In less than a couple of years my health was completely restored and I was able, once more, to lead a physically active life. Thirty-two years of age, happily married, free from financial cares, and devoted to hunting, one was unconsciously graduating for the part of a Jane Austen character. But I discovered, as I believe her men also would have done, had not their careers invariably terminated with their capture and mental sterilization at the altar, that 'respectability', even with a corresponding income, is not enough. It is not easy to identify, as one approaches the end of life's course, the motives which propelled one in any specific direction, in the days of one's early manhood. Not least was the fact that, whilst in the winter months I was sufficiently occupied with hunting, in the summer, having no liking for golf, tennis or cricket, I was at a loose end.

To pursue my interests in pathology was no longer possible, and none of the hobbies of my boyhood any longer made an appeal.

It was at this time that the study of heredity had taken on its new character and direction, following on the rediscovery of Mendel's epoch-making experiments. I was tempted to hope that within the field of the new science I might find an opportunity to satisfy my desire to do, as well as to learn.

In this connection, I was fortunate in knowing William Bateson, and it was at his suggestion that I enlisted as one of the small group of professionals and amateurs who, under his guidance, were building up the English school of Mendelian research.

With material supplied by Bateson, I set to work: in succession on butterflies, hairless mice, guinea-pigs, and Breda combless poultry. In my hands, all these adventures, I regret to say, were more or less complete failures. Loth to trespass further on Bateson's generosity and time, I decided that my next failure, if failure it was to be, should be in a field which, as far as I knew, had not been invaded by any of the new biologists.

Armed with this resolve, I confided to my gardener, Mr Evan Jones, that I felt it would be more becoming were I to confine my attention to some common kitchen-garden vegetable, and had he any suggestions to make? Jones was one of those men who, within the ambit of their own profession, feel themselves to be all but omniscient. His answer, prompt and to the point, remains fixed in my memory: 'If you want to spend your spare time on vegetables, then you had better choose the potato, for I know more about the potato than any man living.' This seemed a promising beginning, though not without its dangers, seeing that Jones was an autocrat and I was instinctively opposed to dictation by others. However, I asked him to procure for me two distinct varieties, one bearing red, the other white tubers, and said I would 'try my luck'. With a sweep of the hand towards the kitchen garden, Jones informed me that all that one could wish for, in the matter of red and white potatoes, was already at my disposal, and introduced me to two plants; one, a white tubered variety, he said was 'Ringleader', and the other, a red one, was 'Flourball'. With these two, in the year 1906, I embarked on an enterprise which, after forty years, leaves more questions unsolved than were at that time thought to exist. Whether it was mere luck, or whether the potato and I were destined for a life partnership, I do not know, but from that moment my course was set, and I became ever more involved in problems associated directly or indirectly with a plant with which I then had no particular affinity, gustatory or romantic.

After I had published a long paper in 1911 dealing with the inheritance of several characters of the potato, I discovered that my mentor, Jones, had, like Homer, nodded: both of the varieties on which the edifice of five years' work had been erected had been wrongly named by him. This error, whilst it in no way affected the value of the scientific results, such as they were, did more for me than confirm my distrust of the omniscient: it induced a punctilious, and some of my readers may perhaps think a pedantic, insistence on the verification of authorities.

Nor was Jones the only one to make mistakes: I had accepted the potato the more readily as my subject because I imagined that no one had as yet entered into that particular field of inquiry. I was wrong: before I had got far with my experimental work, I discovered that a distinguished biologist, Prof. Edward M. East, of Boston, U.S.A., had

anticipated me by a couple of years. By a curious coincidence, just as
I entered this particular field of research, East had been forced to retire
from it, owing to the destruction of all his equipment and records by
fire. For a few years to come I had no colleague at home or abroad
interested in the genetics of the potato.

In directing my faltering footsteps towards the potato, Jones may
have shown greater circumspection than even he was consciously aware
of. The potato is in many ways an ideal subject for biological research,
inasmuch as the individual plant, by reason of its perpetuation by tuber,
is immortal, whilst its sexual progeny can, without much difficulty, be
evoked at will. A great deal more might be said in its favour as a subject
for research, but here we are only concerned in its application and
influence as a foodstuff. In this respect also the potato can lay claim
to an exceptional status as compared with other staple foods.

Whilst the origin of wheat, barley, oats, rice and other important
cereals is lost in antiquity, the coming of the potato to the civilized world
can be dated within a few years. Moreover, it came to us at a time when
the use of the written and printed word was no longer the privilege of
the few, but was rapidly acting as an intellectual flux, allowing all classes
to share in and report on any new experience. Thus it is that the potato,
from the time it was first encountered by the Spaniards, acquired
written records; at first few and elusive; but many and strident when,
later, it became more intimately associated with those changes in the
social and economic structure of our country, known as the Industrial
Revolution.

The work at Barley, in which I was soon to be ably assisted by my
friend James W. Lesley, now Professor at the Citrus Experiment Station,
Riverside, California, grew apace, and in due course gave rise to reper-
cussions, foremost amongst which was the creation of the Potato Virus
Research Station at Cambridge, of which I had the honour to be the
Director for the first fourteen years of its existence.

Although for many years it was the genetics, morphology, and
pathology of the potato which in the main engaged my attention, it
was from an early date borne in on me that the potato—or rather its
employment as an article of diet—offered a unique opportunity for the
study of the social and economic reactions which might ensue from the
adoption by the masses of the people of a new, cheap, efficient and
easily produced foodstuff. Hence, alongside my studies in the laboratory
and field, the historical and economic aspects of the subject were never
absent from my mind.

Whilst the earlier problems required for their solution the limitation
of the field of experiment, excursions into sociology necessitated the
exploration of a great variety of data spread over large tracts of time

and space. Prior to the last quarter of the eighteenth century, the potato had never been seriously regarded as a factor capable of influencing the development of society. Hence to obtain material for its history, one must needs cast one's net widely and be guided by instinct as much as method, in one's search for information. After about 1775 the task becomes somewhat easier: agriculturists and politicians, faced by the food and social difficulties consequent on the American and Napoleonic wars, began to take an interest in the potato. Before long, thanks to the vision of Arthur Young, the potato won semi-official recognition. This was followed by its adoption as a subject worthy of official concern in the *Reports* of the Board of Agriculture from 1795 onwards.

It was not to be expected that officials or laymen realized that in urging the use of the potato they were calling into action an instrument charged with dynamic possibilities. That is the kind of discovery which is only made after the event.

The exploration of this field has necessitated the accumulation of a collection of material to the limits of which one can never ascribe finality, but whose reduction to book-form has consumed my leisure during the last nine strenuous years.

This study is primarily concerned with two problems: one comprises the history of the potato as a member of a genus of the botanical family Solanaceae, its adoption by man as a cultivated plant, and the record of its spread throughout the world. The other with the evaluation of the different reactions it induced, or the influence it may have indirectly exerted, on the social structure of those peoples who accepted it as a staple article of diet or an essential product of their economy. This second problem may be restated as the study of the reactions set up between a plant which, under cultivation, is relatively stable, and the social environment often unstable and variable, into which it has been introduced.

It is largely because of the variability of the human environment that it has been found advisable to limit the field of one's observations, in so far as the economic consequences of the adoption of the potato are concerned, to the United Kingdom.[1] During the major part of the period of time with which we are mainly concerned, viz. the eighteenth and nineteenth centuries, the political and cultural environments of England, the Lowlands of Scotland and, to a lesser extent, that of Wales were, at any one time, more or less alike. By which no more is implied than that they were more alike, for example, than would have been the environments of England, France and Bavaria. In respect to the tempo of their industrial development, however, these regions of the

---

[1] It is hoped that the material relative to other parts of the world, more especially Europe, may be published later.

United Kingdom differed very materially. Such differences allow one
to obtain some idea of the influence of industrial development on the
adoption of the potato as seen against a relatively uniform cultural
background.

The Highlands of Scotland, on the other hand, afford an opportunity
for the study of the influence of the potato in an environment whose
social and cultural status differed radically from that existing elsewhere
in Great Britain. The corresponding study of the role of the potato in
Ireland, introduces yet another divergent factor in the environment—
that induced by political and religious domination. An examination of
its career in Jersey, against a social and cultural background differing
from any mentioned so far, discloses the potato acting in yet another
but no less distinctive part in the lives of the people.

Outside the United Kingdom, I have included but two minor
excursions, one dealing with Tristan da Cunha, the other with St Helena.
In both, the potato performed different but essential duties in the two
very distinct environments, with consequences of great importance to
their inhabitants.

There have been several previous attempts to write the history of the
potato: the majority of authors have been contented to repeat, with
increasing inexactitude, the misstatements of their predecessors. To
these there are two outstanding exceptions, Roze's *Histoire de la Pomme
de Terre*, a classic of its kind, published in 1898, and still an invaluable
record of original and careful historical research, and a brochure by
Safford who, in 1925, first indicated the wealth of archaeological material
awaiting study in Peru. To him also belongs the credit for giving the
coup de grâce to some of the more misleading legends concerning the
potato which, till then, had masqueraded as history. Since that date it
has been my good fortune to have explored further avenues of approach,
as a result of which it should be possible to envisage the spread of the
potato and its influence on human society as phenomena in organic
relation with social history the world over.

Here then was a subject awaiting an author. For many years I waited
to see whether it would appeal to some professional student of history
or economics. As time went on it became increasingly unlikely that any
such, with a reputation to lose, would commit himself to a subject
deemed by the many as having no more scientific value or importance
than a cookery book; and by the few, as a subject lacking in precision and
beset with pitfalls. It was only after much hesitation that I determined
to make the attempt myself. Without training as economist or historian,
I am acutely aware of the lack of equipment for so difficult a task for
which my only credentials are a scientific training and an abiding interest
in my fellow-men.

It was some time before I realized how different my self-imposed task was from the type of scientific research to which I had been accustomed. Contrary to all previous experience, I discovered that in the study of social phenomena it was impossible to completely exclude the personal reaction. For this I offer no apology, realizing that no one, to-day, can pretend to live in a political vacuum. Indeed, one might argue that the reverse is true: if an author is so emotionally neutral as to be uninfluenced by the social implications of his own subject, might it not be held that he is either unfitted for the task or extremely unlikely to arouse in others that interest he has failed to evince in himself?

I take comfort, however, from the confession of a renowned master of the subject, in which I can at best claim to be but an amateur. Clapham, towards the end of the introduction to the 1939 edition of his *Economic History*, touches with great charm on this point when he writes: 'Five years ago I went through it [Arthur Young's *Travels in France*] again, to find that whenever Young spoke of a wretched Frenchman, I had marked him, but that many of his references to happy or prosperous Frenchmen remained unmarked. Sympathy with wretchedness is the sign of a generous mind. Let us hope that the attempt to record other things, in their due proportion, does not denote an ageing heart hardened by statistics.'

One is tempted to ask: Is there such a thing as a true interpretation of facts, divorced from the personality of its recorder and, if so, should we recognize it? I doubt it!

Throughout the prolonged gestation of this work I have received help from so many friends and correspondents, both at home and abroad, that it would be wellnigh impossible to name them all, a fact which in no way lessens my debt of gratitude. Some have given so much of their time and skill that it would be unthinkable to omit any record of my appreciation. Foremost amongst these, was my friend the late Sir John Clapham, who read and criticized the Irish section of the book. A like service was rendered by the Rt. Hon. Walter E. Elliot and Dr A. B. Stewart of the Macaulay Institute, in regard to the section on Scotland; and by Mr J. L. and Mrs B. Hammond, the eminent social historians, in respect to that dealing with the potato in England. Mr D. Simpson, Director of the States Experimental Station, Jersey, has read the chapter on that island. Sir John Mollett has read and advised on the chapter of 'The Potato in War-Time'. In writing the chapter on Nomenclature, I have had the advantage of the assistance of Prof. Sir E. H. Minns in regard to the terms for the potato in the Slavonic languages, and of Dr Isabella Massey who read the manuscript of this chapter. To Prof. Dover Wilson and to Mr Jack Isaacs my thanks are due for assistance in regard to references to the potato in the literature of the seventeenth and eighteenth centuries. To Miss E. H. Whetham I am indebted for much information on the war-time production and distribution of the potato, and to Mr K. H. Connell for valuable criticism, more especially of the Irish Section.

Whilst these eminent authorities have given me the benefit of their advice and criticism, I should be failing in my duty if I did not make it abundantly clear that they are in no way responsible for the conclusions which have been reached and recorded in the text.

In the accumulation of specific data, no less than in their evaluation, help has reached me from many other distinguished scholars. In regard to Irish evidence, I am deeply indebted to Prof. G. O'Brien, of Dublin, and Prof. Estyn E. Evans, of Belfast, and for that relating to Wales, to Dr E. G. Bowen, Dr A. H. Dodd, Dr F. T. Lloyd-Dodd, Prof. R. T. Jenkins, Dr I. C. Peate, Principal Sir J. R. Rees, Prof. Treharne, Dr G. J. Williams, and Prof. T. Whitehead. A like service in respect to the chapter on St Helena has been performed by Dr Philip Gosse. The chapter on 'Varieties' has been read by Mrs McDermott, the Supervisor of Potato Trials at the Nottingham School of Agriculture, Sutton Bonington, whose criticisms have been of great value. To Dr J. G. Hawkes I have turned for counsel in all matters relating to the wild potato, its species, varieties and cultivation in South America.

I am conscious that I have left many unnamed who have at various times either helped me spontaneously or responded to my enquiries. To all I tender my thanks and, not less sincerely, my apologies.

The name of one scholar, Mr Henry I. Burkill, I have left to the end, because his help, as generous as his erudition is extensive, has been asked for, and given, on so many different subjects, that it is difficult to thank him adequately.

To Mr H. R. Mallett I am indebted for the compilation of the Index, a task which has involved an immense amount of thought and time.

Not least is the pleasure it gives me to acknowledge my indebtedness to my secretary, Edith M. Hagger, who for nearly forty years has given me unstinted help in every branch of the work; and to my gardener, Martin Hayes, who for nearly as long has assisted me in the raising of the many thousands of seedlings used in the course of my research.

REDCLIFFE N. SALAMAN

BARLEY, HERTS
September 1948

TO

THE MEMORY

OF

A. DANIEL HALL

ILLUSTRATIONS

LIST OF PLATES

[1] This style is now known as Moche. – Ed.
[2] These are Chimú-Inca style. – Ed.

[1] These are Chimú-Inca style. – Ed.
[2] This style is now known as Moche. – Ed.

[1] These styles are now all known as Moche. – Ed.

[1] These styles are now known as Moche. – Ed.

XXXII. Fig. 101. Potato pot, Staffordshire ware; blue, glazed $7 \times 3\frac{1}{2} \times 2\frac{1}{2}$ in.

(The property of the author)

Fig. 102. Potato pot, Staffordshire ware; dull grey and brown, glazed; $6 \times 4\frac{1}{4}$ in.

(By permission of Messrs Berry & Co. of St James St., S.W.)

Fig. 103. Potato pot, British ware; cream glazed; $7\frac{1}{4} \times 5$ in.

(By permission of Messrs Berry & Co. of St James St., S.W.)

Fig. 104. An earthenware cup in the shape of a potato tuber

(By permission of the Director of the Brighton Museum)

LIST OF TEXT-FIGURES

DIAGRAMS, MAPS, ETC.

CHAPTER I

Immigrant Man and the Andean Potato

Just as it is impossible to discuss intelligently the history of the potato without a reference to those early agriculturists who won and fashioned it, so would it be futile were we to leave undescribed the peculiar setting in which both plant and man evolved their mutual understanding. For the early history of the potato was set on a stage dominated by the mysterious grandeur of the Andes, whose dread influence could never have been long absent from the thought and actions of the men who, thousands of years before the coming of Columbus, won for all mankind this and other priceless gifts from the recesses of nature's storehouse.

The problem is confined geographically to the continent of South America, by the fact that nowhere in Central or North America was the potato cultivated in pre-Columbian times. This is the more curious when we realize that as far north as Colorado various species of wild tuber-bearing *Solanums* are to be found.

Mexico, in particular, is so rich in such plants that Vavilov[1] regarded it as a definite focus of differentiation and dispersion. The tubers of some of these wild plants are at times eaten by the natives, but they are not, and apparently never were, cultivated. The same is reported from Guatemala. When later the potato gained an entry into Mexico after the Conquest, it was the Peru-Bolivian potato which was imported and grown there. The Navajo Indians of South Western United States still boil and roast the small tubers of the two wild species, *S. jamesii* and *S. fendleri*.[2] It seems possible that the people of these parts, especially in Mexico, were on the point of developing an independent culture of the potato when the coming of the Spaniards destroyed their civilization.

In South America, the immigrant peoples found a large variety of wild potatoes, but in contrast to those of North and Central America, they brought them into cultivation at an early stage of their settlement, possibly 2,000 years or more before the Spanish Conquest. Why people of the same original race should have behaved so differently on either side of the equator is a problem, the solution of which is almost certainly to be found in the extraordinary geographical and climatic conditions of the area into which the settlers penetrated.

In the warm regions of Mexico and Central America, the cereal maize, so easily grown and so bounteous in its returns, contended with the manioc or cassava for the first place in nature's bounty. On the high

[1] Vavilov, N. I. (1926). Studies on the origin of cultivated plants. *Bull. Appl. Bot. Genet. and Pl. Breed.*, vol. 16, 1–248. – Ed.
[2] Medsger, O. P. (1939). *Edible Wild Plants*, p. 200. New York.

tablelands of inner Colombia, Ecuador and Bolivia, where manioc is wanting and maize begins to fail, we may suppose that successive immigrant waves, searching for a staple food, eventually found it in the wild potato. These high altitudes, by reason of their isolation and their freedom from malaria and the diseases of the jungle, afforded a permanent home in which the immigrants attained for a time a level of culture only a little below that reached later on the Peruvian coast.

Of the vast continental mass of South America, it is only the western border which concerns us—that part whose physical character is dominated by the mountain chain which stretches in a north-south direction from the eastern end of the Isthmus of Panamá along the whole length of the continent to the Straits of Magellan.

The Andean range is folded along its length in such a manner that from the equator northwards it is broken up into a fan-shaped structure of three divergent ridges with intervening valleys and plateaux which, uniting at the equator, continue south of it as a double chain as far as Pasco (lat. 11° S.) only to diverge again into three parallel chains which converge on one another at Vilcanota (lat. 14° S.). Once more the range splits into two, between whose arms are held the great upland seas of Lake Titicaca and Lake Aullagas, more generally known as Lake Poopó, and the lofty plains of the Collao of Bolivia. The chain remains bifid until lat. 30° S., when it continues southward as a single ridge throughout the length of Chile, to fade out in Patagonia and the islands north of Cape Horn.

Although the main directions of the Cordilleras are north-south, they are buttressed along their length by mountain spurs running east to west; those on the west shepherd the scanty waters which fall on that side of the range, to the valleys which open on to the coast; those on the east, far more richly endowed, conduct their waters in ever-widening streams, ultimately to join the Amazon and discharge into the Atlantic Ocean. The peculiar formation of this mighty range, which extends from north to south some 4,000 miles, dominates not only the climate of the continent, the nature of its fauna and flora, but, above all, the character of its human occupants and their cultures.

That a great portion of the land we are discussing lies in the tropics and its neighbourhood, has not so important an influence on the variety of climate, as have the dazzling contrasts of altitude and humidity to be found at almost any latitude between areas lying but a relatively small distance apart in an east to west direction.

This becomes evident when we consider the variation of climate and geographical conditions along a line running west to east at a latitude of about 8° S. On the Pacific coast is a rainless desert leading to arid foothills and thence upwards to steep valleys, which at a height of about

10,000 ft. enjoy a moderate rainfall; the line then passes between mountains attaining a height of some 20,000 ft. to plateaux of 12,000–14,000 ft., intersected towards the east by deep canyons, where conditions are more or less tropical, such as that of the valley of the River Marañon, which drains eventually into the Amazon. Farther eastward are more high plateaux passing into the central range of the Cordillera, on the eastern side of which through lofty passes plateaux and river canyons are met again, such as that of the Huallaga, dividing the central from the eastern range. To the east of this the descent is rapid, passing through well-watered valleys in which tropical vegetation begins at an altitude of about 6,000 ft., and which lead down into the great rain-forests of the Amazon basin.

If man's material and psychological experience within a specific environment influences the structure of the society he builds, moulding the character, and colouring the reactions of the individuals who compose it, a thesis which to-day is not likely to be seriously disputed, then it is a matter of no small importance to determine how and from what direction the original immigrant natives, the first who cultivated the potato, reached the area we are discussing. This area comprises the countries Colombia, Ecuador, Peru, most of Bolivia, and the northern part of Chile, all of which, except Colombia, were united under the Incas before the Spanish Conquest.

Of the routes to the Peruvian coastlands, four come under consideration: one via the Isthmus of Panamá and down the north-west coast of Colombia and Ecuador, a second by crossing the sea from the Pacific coast of Central America, a third via the Magdalena or from some point on the north coast of Venezuela, and a fourth by migration up the great rivers debouching on the east coast. The first is an unlikely route as the dense rain-forests and broken country of these regions have proved an impenetrable barrier even to modern man.

Linne,[1] however, whilst admitting the great difficulties of movement in this region, says that there have been settlements of Indians from early times in these parts and that the natives do actually make their way through the forests, but that there seems no good reason for relating the people of these regions with those who cultivated the potato on the Andean plateaux.

The second route of migration, by sea, is of course always possible, and may be the one followed by the much earlier settlers, the fisher folk whose middens are found on the coast of Arica; whilst penetration by the third route, though quite possible, would afford a field of experience not materially different from that derived by the fourth route, an intrusion via the Orinoco and Amazon river-systems.

[1] Linne, *Nature*, 7 January 1939.

The importance of the question is apparent when we consider the dramatic contrast between the environment afforded by the rain-forest of the Amazon and that of the desert coast of Peru, one or other of which must have played the part of nursery to the people. If man came from the west via the sea, then he would have known nothing of the jaguar or the boa, the potato or the coca plant, till he encountered them as he penetrated eastward. In which case we should not expect that the dread of the former and the use of the latter would be already characteristic elements in the social system of the coast at an early archaeological date as, in fact, they were. The evidence would seem to point rather in the opposite direction, inducing us to accept the theory of the eminent Americanist, Tello,[1] that man reached the Peruvian area from the east. Without any pretence to expert archaeological knowledge, I reached a similar conclusion independently, from the study of the pottery of the coastal cemeteries.

Recently (1939), a new body of evidence, giving the strongest support to this view, has been published by Mangelsdorf and Reeves.[2,3] As an illustration of how genetical methods when allied with archaeological research can assist in the solution of one of the most difficult problems of plant evolution and agricultural practice, this work will assuredly take its place as a classic. In brief, they show that the original maize was a pod-corn and that such arose in the Savannas east of the Andes, probably somewhere in Paraguay, where botanists report that until recently primitive wild corn existed. From thence it was conveyed by man to the Andean valleys. In the Peabody Museum there exists a perfect representation of pod-corn from prehistoric times; it was found in the Peruvian highlands, and is made of clay. It was not cast in a mould, as was so much of the coastal pottery, but had been built up piece by piece. It is the view of the authors that the early migrants must have discovered, possibly by accident, that when this pod-corn[4] is heated, the hard stony seeds burst from their enclosing glumes and their flinty endosperm is converted to an easily masticated and palatable food. Although this variety of maize is no longer cultivated in the Andes, it does actually occur from time to time as a rogue but always in a heterozygous or hybrid form.

At some time in the historic past, subsequent to its adoption by man, a mutation of pod-maize to the glumeless type in use to-day presumably occurred, which the early immigrant native in his wisdom accepted and cultivated. The authors conclude that the original maize was a native of the eastern slopes and drier Savanna regions on that side of the Andes and not of the Brazilian rain-forests.

[1] Tello, J. (1922). Prehistoric Peru. *Inter-America*, p. 238 (1922).
[2] Mangelsdorf, P. C. and Reeves, R. G. (1939). The origin of Indian Corn and its relatives. *Bull. Tex. Agric. Exp. Sta.* No. 574.
[3] This view of the origin of maize is not at present generally considered to be correct. See Introduction. – Ed.
[4] This is pop-corn. – Ed.

Maize cannot be cultivated at heights above 12,000 ft. and indeed is rarely found above 11,000 ft., where it is a small and poor-yielding plant. Above these levels the staple foodstuff is the potato, helped out by *quinoa, oca* and various other crops.

Whether the discovery of the potato enabled man to bring the maize up and over the Andes, there to pursue its worldwide conquests, no less great in extent or importance than those of the potato itself, remains a matter of speculation.

It is suggested here that it was the potato which enabled the early immigrants from the east to maintain their hold on the bleak highlands, and it was only after they had succeeded in this, that they brought maize up from the eastern lowlands, initiated its cultivation and thus made good their hold on the lower valleys of the western slopes.[1] Such a sequence of events accords with the view expressed by these writers, that root cultivation, in which planting and harvesting are almost identical processes, invariably precedes that in which the sowing of seed and the reaping of its harvest are the dominant operations. It is of particular interest that the Peruvian maize is considered by these authors to have found its way to the Maya people from Peru and that in Central America it produced by natural hybridization with *Tripsacum*, the new genus *Euchlaena*. This latter, crossing naturally with the original maize parent, gave rise to the various Mexican and North American types of maize.

From Central America the culture of maize spread to the southwestern United States, thereby contributing the dominant character to the Cliff-dweller culture which succeeded that of the Folsom-man, the nomadic hunter who had never seen the maize plant.

If the general argument of Mangelsdorf and Reeves is correct, then we must conclude that the higher culture which gradually made its way from the south northwards in the North American continent took its origin from the Peru-Bolivian heights. This, it is suggested, was rendered possible by the antecedent discovery and cultivation of the potato.

We have numerous early Spanish accounts of expeditions into the montana which describe the eastern slopes of the Andes, the Brazilian forests, and the natives they encountered. The dense, impenetrable rain-soaked jungle through which a way must needs be hacked yard by yard, the only guide a network of rivers, the air swarming with savage insects, the land haunted by jaguar and boa constrictor, the waters infested by alligators and voracious fishes, all create a picture which is not merely one of hardship and difficulty, but one which inspired then, as it does to-day, a feeling of terror, even in the hardiest explorers. The Spanish found the natives adept in the use of poisoned arrows, invariably hostile, and at war with one another. That their chief source of meat, other than

[1] See footnote 3 on p. 4. – Ed.

fish and turtle, was human, was a source of dread both to the Spaniards and their native followers from the sierra, no less than to the forest tribesmen themselves. The savage hostility of some of the forest tribes is still a matter to be reckoned with, as many of the workers in the petrol companies' camps know to their cost. A recent writer, who observed the same overriding sense of fear and anxiety amongst those who live in the montana, no less than in those who merely visit it, remarks 'it is therefore not difficult to understand why it was generally not man who conquered the jungle, but the jungle which conquered man'.[1]

In general, the natives of the forest were well supplied with food: they cultivated small patches of manioc on clearings in the neighbourhood of the rivers; the potato they did not know, nor did they preserve food-stuffs, as did the natives of the sierra and the coast, for they had no occasion to insure against frost or loss of harvest.

Whether the original native immigrants to the forest experienced the feeling of terror which the forest inspired in the Spaniard, it is difficult to say, but we do know that the Djukas or African negroes who took to the bush in the seventeenth and eighteenth centuries in the Guianas, shared this feeling and restricted their settlements to clearings along the river banks.[2] There is abundant evidence that the native of the neigh-bouring sierra shared that feeling to the full, and one can only suppose that those who left the forest regions and settled on the inhospitable mountain plateaux were driven to do so as much by psychological, as material reasons.[4]

These views have received further support from a recent sociological inquiry into the life of the natives of the tribes of eastern Bolivia and western Matto Grosso.[3] In most of the tribes the jaguar plays an important part in their spiritual lives; one or two examples may suffice: speaking of the Guarayu:

'After shooting a jaguar, a man ran away, abandoning even his weapons, so as not to be overtaken by the animal's soul. If a man wounded a jaguar, his soul turned into a jaguar; such a person was served in isolation at drinking bouts. The Guarayu feared the cries of the night birds. They believed that certain sunset colors in clouds presaged death, which could be averted by throwing ashes into the air.'

Of the Itonama it says:

'Witches changed themselves into jaguars and killed their enemies without being detected.'

'The Mojo was so terrified of the jaguar spirit that Shamans easily persuaded

---

[1] Linke, Lilo (1944). *Andean Adventure*, p. 78. Hutchinson.
[2] De Leeuw (1935). *Crossroads of the Caribbean Sea.* Julian Messner: New York.
[3] Metraux, Alfred (1943). The Native Tribes of Eastern Bolivia and western Matto Grosso. *Bull. Bur. Amer. Ethn. Soc.* No. 134.
[4] See Introduction. – Ed.

people to bring them offerings of meat and food. If somebody killed a jaguar, all his belongings were exposed in front of his hut and henceforth were regarded as the rightful property of the animal. Those who had been wounded by a jaguar acquired high prestige and generally became Shamans.'

'A hunter who killed a jaguar took the name of the slain animal which was revealed to him by a Shaman; he also had to observe a special ritual and subject himself to a series of taboos. He had to fast, to cut off part of his hair, and seclude himself in the temple where the heads of the jaguars were kept and worshipped.'

'A jaguar's body was not taken to the village because it might cause an epidemic, but was eaten on the beach by the Chief and other people, who stayed away from the village, beating drums and drinking for many days.'

Metraux concludes:

'Archaeology shows that the contact between the Andean civilization and the Indians of the eastern valleys of the Andes and of the plains of the tributaries of the Amazon existed in the most distant past.'

Modern travellers, armed though they be with the sophistication of the West, often become as frightened children in the dark solitudes of the great forest. Here is the impression of a man who spent a year or two in the Bolivian Forest:

'During the next seven months I began to know that forest, and to understand the fiendish, callous power that underlay the calm exterior. Under the shadow of its leaves I was tired, elated, thirsty, hungry and afraid.... The silence of the forest is like none of these. It is alert, watchful, awake. It is the silence of the tiger's paw; the silence of the darting bat; the silence of the snake. It is not a bit restful, nor does it induce sleep. Rather it brings out all that is self-protective in man. It is the kind of silence that causes those that hear it, to refrain from glancing over their shoulders; the kind of silence that makes one cock a pistol in the sure knowledge that whatever comes will come too quick for thought. That night I entered into the spirit of Green Hell.'[1]

In this cultured European, the silent forest reawoke the nightmare terrors of his childhood. The writer has spoken to several friends who have travelled in the great rain-forests of the Amazon, and find that they were either possessed with a feeling of terror, or succumbed to a complete boredom. In the untutored savage it engendered a fatalism from the cradle to the grave, which induced such defensive and offensive reactions of body and mind as might enable him to survive in such an environment.

The native South American is, above all, an animist; he sees in every object of nature, whether living or not, some spirit. Rivers flowed, trees grew, the sun ruled by day and the moon by night, by reason of the spiritual beings which inhabited them. The forest, above all, was alive with spirits, mostly hostile. The boa, and particularly the puma and the

---

[1] Duguid, Julian (1931). *Green Hell*, p. 123. Jonathan Cape.

jaguar, were not merely animals capable of inflicting bodily harm, but potent spirits which could, and did, invade every aspect of his life. Tschudi[1] describing the Indian Bravos or natives of the Peruvian Montana, was greatly impressed by their all-pervading animism: 'In the animals, the plants, the stones, in everything, they trace these beneficent or demoniacal powers. Every idea, every action is with them a consequence of the influence of one of these two powers, and free will is impossible.' The spirits, moreover, of powerful medicine men were often transferred after death to the bodies of jaguars, and vice versa. The Djukas have evolved a similar spirit world.

The various accounts which the old Spanish writers have left us, whether they be friendly to the Indian as that of Garcilaso de la Vega,[2] or religiously prejudiced as that of Arriaga,[3] are identical in one respect with those of such modern writers as Bandelier[4] and Beals[5] who have studied the native Indian in those parts where he is least touched by European influences and find his spiritual life, though nominally Christian, in reality dominated by the traditional animism and ancient practices of his people. To all, the native mentality seems to be one in which fear, suspicion, cruelty, melancholy and resignation are the guiding forces.

It is in keeping with this psychological background that these people should exhibit to-day, as they did in pre-Inca times, a type of sensuality whose peculiarity is its divorce from beauty.

It may be urged that against this dark spiritual background, there stands in relief the highly developed legalistic attitude of the Peruvian towards justice, which reached its climax under the Incas. It is true that such a system of social law and justice did exist, but if we are to believe the chroniclers, its execution displayed what some would regard as a high degree of sadistic cruelty; others might more correctly attribute this to the complete suppression of any sense of humour, a not unnatural result of a reign of spiritual fear.

Franck, who travelled on foot almost the entire length of the Andes, gives many sketches of native life and character. He sees in the 'divine' autocracy of the Inca, with its consequent domination of every aspect of native life, the source of his fatalism and absence of initiative, and the ease with which even to-day he allows himself to be made a rightless slave, enduring with a sullen placidity the utmost rigours of his bleak

[1] Tschudi, J. von (1838–42). *Travels in Peru*, p. 413. London: D. Bogue, 1847.
[2] Garcilaso de la Vega (1609). *Royal Commentaries* (transl.). Hakluyt Series, 1869–71.
[3] Arriaga, Paul Joseph de (1562). *Extirpacion de la Idolatría de los Indios del Peru.* Edit. Collection de libres Historia del Peru, T. 1, 2a ser. p. 29. Lima, 1920.
[4] Bandelier, Adolph (1910). *Islands of Titicaca and Koati.*
[5] Beals, C. (1934). *Fire on the Andes,* p. 242.

and comfortless environment. Throughout his journey, his contacts with the Indian offer but little variation. Here is a vignette from Cuzco:[1]

The aboriginal. His stolidity passes all conception. He is native to, and of a piece with, the pampas, the bare, treeless upland world where the dreary expanse of brown earth and cold blue sky incites neither ambition nor friendliness, neither hopes nor aspirations. Hence his flat, joyless face with its furtive eyes suggests a soul contracted upon itself, an aridity of sentiments, an absolute lack of aesthetic affections. Passively sullen, morose, and uncommunicative, he neither desires nor aspires, and loves or abhors with moderation. The native language is scanty and cold in terms of endearment; I have never seen the faintest demonstration of affection between Indians of the two sexes, though plenty of evidence of bestial lust.

A recent writer[2] is more explicit:

Even in the short time I have spent in Peru, I have constantly been impressed by the profound melancholy of the race, not Spanish austerity, but an Indian pessimism and softness of fibre, springing, perhaps, from the consciousness of defeat....In Lima the Colisseo, with its rows of stolid spectators, staring in apathetic silence at two birds with enormous spurs trying to kill each other, is merely sordid and depressing. The Indian national dancing I have seen is little more than a dreary rhythmic shuffle of archaic interest, while their music has little to recommend it to those who are not charmed by the barbarous beating of drums, wailing of flutes, or primitive scratching of strings.

At the risk of being considered fanciful, I suggest that the mentality of the native of Peru and Bolivia has been conditioned by the terrors of the jungle which, like a miasma, spread over the plateau to the coast as the people migrated westward.

When the native escaping from the terror of the forest forced his way out of the montana up the eastern slopes, he would naturally have sought out favourable spots for settlements in the more secluded valleys and the more fertile portions of the high tablelands. A typical example of the latter is the Collao, the district to the west and south of the great inland sea of Lake Titicaca, the waters of which are some 12,500 ft., and the surrounding district between that and 15,000 ft., above sea-level.

On the plateaux there are no trees, the soil where not poisoned by borax is covered with a coarse *Stipa* grass. Here still abound the wild guanaco and vicuña (species of the llama tribe). At an early date, the native domesticated two varieties of the former, the common llama and the alpaca; both yielded him wool for his clothing, whilst the llama also acted as his beast of burden. These high plateaux, swept by driving rains, warm whilst the sun is overhead, cold and comfortless directly it goes down, enervating by reason of the altitude and shortage of oxygen, were

---

[1] Franck, H. A. (1917). *Vagabonding down the Andes*, p. 433. New York: Appleton.
[2] Sandeman, Christopher (1939). *A Forgotten River*, p. 27. Oxford.

never places for intensive settlement. Nor would such be a likely nursery ground for the cultivation of the aesthetic and more tender impulses of man's nature. A cold and pitiless environment could not be expected to evoke more than its counterpart amongst the human stock forced to seek therein a new home.

In such surroundings man had to shape his life anew. His former sources of food were no longer to hand; it was far too cold for the manioc, the staple food of the forest region, and maize, assuming that he had brought it with him from the eastern lowlands, would only grow in the more sheltered spots where the altitude was not above 12,000 ft., and even so the plants would be stunted and yield little. He must needs look for hardier food plants.

If a settlement was to be effected the immigrant had of necessity to provide himself with foodstuffs which would grow under these un-favourable conditions, and, at the same time, protect himself against the frequent destruction of his vegetable crops by frost. Perhaps one of the most remarkable of man's conquests of nature gave him the key to success.

On the Andean highlands, from Colombia in the north to Chile in the south, there grow many species of wild tuber-bearing *Solanums*, amongst them the parent stock of our domestic potato. Some forms are found practically on the snow-line, 15,000–16,000 ft. high, but these are of little value as human food; others, which grow at somewhat lower levels, are considerably more resistant to frost than European varieties and yield useful crops of tubers. At some very early stage the South-American native cultivated several types, amongst them a peculiar hybrid form which is relatively frost-hardy.

The researches of the Russian, English and other botanists who have visited Peru-Bolivia for the purpose of studying the potato, have shown that there exists a large number of potato types under cultivation which differ very widely between themselves. It is true that in the more culturally advanced districts, most of the varieties differ only in colour or shape from one another and are but forms of the species which is known as *S. andigenum*.[1] Others there are, however, which are either distinct species or hybrid forms between two species.

It would be a mistake to assume that the native Indian immigrant, either in the dim past, or to-day, made such hybrids himself. They were natural hybrids and man's part, no mean one, was that of the intelligent cultivator who selects the type which best suits his particular needs. It is to the great variety in the climatic and soil environment, resulting from the diversity of depth and direction of the mountain valleys, that we must ascribe the high degree of variation and differentiation which, aided by selection both natural and controlled, led to the establishment of specialized types.

[1] Now classified as *S. tuberosum* subspecies (or group) *andigena*. – Ed.

In view of man's insecurity and the shortage of food crops at these altitudes, the next step was to elaborate a method for the preservation of the potato. We know that such was in use at an early date, possibly 2,000 years ago, and the product known as *chuño* is to-day a common food throughout South America. It was probably here also, that man discovered how to preserve llama meat by sun-drying; the product was called *charqui* in the Quechuan tongue, which has become 'jerked' (meat) in English. Thus, by the discovery of the potato, the cultivation of frost-hardy types, and the preservation of foodstuffs, man solved the problem of how to live at great altitudes, and thereby attained the mastery of a continent.

Besides the potato, other useful local sources of food were found: *quinoa* (*Chenopodium quinoa*), whose seed is used in much the same way as oatmeal is in the Scotch Highlands, *oca* (*Oxalis tuberosa*), a tuber-bearing plant which is exceptionally hardy, and *ulluco* or *Papa lisa* (a species of Basellaceae), a tuberous plant, all of which grow on the alti-plano. But none of these plays a part at all comparable with that of the potato in the economic life of the peasant, with the exception of *quinoa* in the neighbourhood of Lake Titicaca.

It is curious that the native of these parts made so little use of the llama as a food, and none at all of its milk. Indeed, his chief source of animal nourishment was, and is the tame guinea-pig or cuy, which is allowed to run free in his dwellings.

Here on the high plateaux and in the lofty valleys the natives to-day live their lives in much the same way as they did before either Inca or Spaniard intruded upon them. On the plains, or perched on almost inaccessible heights overlooking them, are the low windowless thatched stone huts of the native and near by his small enclosed fields, or his carefully built-up terraces. As a consequence of the agricultural requirements dictated by potato-growing in a semi-sterile and frost-ridden environment, there grew up that peculiar communism which has existed for centuries in these distant outposts of man's dispersion, which may explain his continued existence under adverse conditions.

It was in such highland spots as the Collao that man first made use of the potato; we may go further and say that it was the potato which made residence on these plateaux possible. If man's progress to the coast was via the altiplano and Andean passes, then the great cultural developments of the coastland would also have been indirectly dependent on the association between the wild potato and man's pressing necessities.

One is tempted to speculate as to why the immigrant from the forest did not restrict his settlement to the more temperate valleys, such as the Yungas of Bolivia, which he would have encountered before he reached the altiplano. If, as is suggested, it was terror of the forest which drove him westward, it is unlikely that he would tarry in his flight till he found surroundings free from the dangers of his old home. Such would be the lofty if inhospitable altiplano. Here, one imagines, after exploiting the llama and potato as permanent sources of food and clothing, he later migrated to the inter-Andean valleys and thence to the coast, bringing with him his new-found allies, and, as we shall see, pregnant memories of the jaguar and boa, which he had known and feared in his original Amazonian home.

Notwithstanding the brilliant use to which man put the wild plants, life on the altiplano must at all times have been a severe struggle, holding out little material reward to cultivator or shepherd. Nor did the native create for himself a spiritual haven in which he might shelter; rather he allowed his subjective life to become enmeshed in a world of fantasy, peopled with innumerable malignant spirits, any of whom might be a potential enemy.

It is not surprising that a people who entered on life's adventure with so sombre and macabre a background should readily avail themselves of such relief as might strengthen their endurance or dull their pain. Fortunately, nature had not left them without opportunity, nor their own ingenuity without the means of making use of it. In the montaña there grows a small bush—the coca—the source of the alkaloid cocaine; it is to be found at a level of 5,000–6,000 ft., i.e. about half-way down the eastern slopes of the Cordillera in those parts of the montaña which are more readily accessible from the altiplano. When and how the natives discovered the hidden magic of this plant, or how they found out that to obtain its maximum effect it was necessary to add a pinch of ash or chalk before masticating it, neither history nor legend records. The early Conquistadores observed that every one they met, whether of high or low degree, had a wad of the leaves in his cheek, which they continually chewed. The Spanish chroniclers say that under the Incas, coca was rationed in quantity and only allowed to such as were engaged in specially arduous work. The finds in graves and representations on ceramics of the early Chimu period show that the people of the coast made the freest use of it. The modern traveller reports the same, and both ascribe, possibly rightly, the remarkable endurance of the native carriers and labourers, especially in the high altitudes, to this practice. How far the habit is responsible for the early ageing and short life-span of the native peasant is a question still awaiting an answer.

If the coca plant offered the sorely tried native a certain measure of escape, a dulling of the sense of pain, the discovery of alcoholic fermentation, which may be as old or older than that of coca, afforded him an opportunity for enjoyment, artificial and temporary perhaps, but nevertheless an escape from the sordid reality of life. From the earliest times he has brewed a drink, generally from maize, but also from *quinoa* and from the potato: this beer, or *chicha* as it is called in Quechua, was no temperance beverage; it was and still is consumed on every public occasion in great quantities, and with the desired effect. In some parts of the Peruvian sierra, notably Tarma, Beals[1] states that they distil a most potent drink from the potato which is called *chakta*.

The logical and systematized government of the Inca prescribed numerous festivals throughout the year, in which all participated, and which invariably developed into prolonged orgies of drunkenness. Similar feasts with dancing and unlimited drink are still observed to-day in the Collao of Bolivia and in every Andean town and village where the Church can stage a *Fiesta*. It is difficult to believe that without the numbing of the senses by cocaine, and the periodical release from reality by drunkenness, the Peruvian could have endured either the horrors of the spiritual or the hardships of the material world in which he lived.

[1] Letter to R.N.S. (4 Sept. 1935).

CHAPTER II

The Archaeological Record

I have referred to the great antiquity of potato cultivation in South America: it is desirable to examine the basis for this statement. The evidence as to the antiquity of the potato as a cultivated plant in South America, and the part it played in the life of the people, is largely based on archaeological data, more especially on the pottery which has been excavated in such profusion during the last forty years. The subject of exact dating and the sequence of cultures is a difficult one and outside my competence. It is therefore with especial pleasure that I acknowledge my indebtedness to that distinguished expert, the late Mr T. A. Joyce, for permission to reproduce extracts from his valuable résumé of the subject,[1] as well as for his advice and criticism in regard to the archaeological and anthropological aspects of the problem.

In dealing with archaeological problems in Peru, one is hampered by the absence of any form of writing or any system of dating, such as is exhibited by the Maya monuments. Joyce distinguishes between a highland culture, the Tiahuanaco, of which two phases are known, and two coastal cultures, a northern and a southern known respectively as the Proto-Chimú and Proto-Nazca.[2] Such knowledge concerning the potato as has so far come to us from the archaeological record, is derived from the pottery of the Chimú periods, and it is to those cultures that we must turn our attention.

At the end of the fourteenth century, the Inca imperial forces attacked and subdued the coastal area around Truxillo, then under the sway of a chief called Chimú—hence the name given to the cultures which developed in that district. Early Chimú, or the Proto-Chimú culture, was distinguished by its vast pyramids and other buildings, which were constructed out of great balls of clay moulded when wet and allowed to bake in the sun; very notable too, was the high development of textiles, but most characteristic, and for our purposes, the most significant, was the amazing wealth and excellence of their pottery. 'The Proto-Chimú pots', says Joyce, 'which are modelled in human and animal forms, are distinguished by a remarkable realism...only two slip colours were used, red and cream...it is obvious that these two coastal cultures (i.e. the Proto-Chimú and Proto-Nazca) had been in existence centuries before their suppression about the beginning of the third century A.D.'

[1] Joyce, T. A. (1920). *Catalogue of an Exhibition of Indigenous American Art* (Introduction). London: Burlington Fine Arts Club.

[2] Now spoken of as Moche and Nazca. - Ed.

Before very long, a new and vigorous civilization sprang up in the highlands, known as the Tiahuanaco II culture, which, after having influenced the coastal civilization by the extension of its empire, collapsed, leaving the autonomous chiefs to develop their states independently. The pottery of this somewhat decadent period is painted in red, white and black, and finally with simple black and white or white decoration. The Tiahuanaco II period, Joyce considers, came to an end about A.D. 800, at which time there was a great revival of the coastal arts, which are now spoken of as the Chimú and Nazca cultures. The pottery of the Chimú culture is again of the sculptured naturalistic style, 'but the ware typical of the revised art is black or dark grey, and though the vases are superior in technique to those of the earlier period, they are far inferior in artistic qualities'. The Chimú and Nazca periods extended from the eighth century till the conquest of the coastal lands by the Incas at the close of the fourteenth century.

The Inca people came out of the southern highlands in the neighbourhood of Lake Titicaca and settled in the valley of Cuzco at the commencement of the twelfth century, and for the next 300 years they consolidated their rule over the tribes immediately surrounding them. At the end of the fourteenth century the Inca state started out on a course of imperialistic expansion, which brought them to Truxillo, and by the time of the coming of the Spaniards they had reached the River Ancasmayu in Ecuador in the north,[1] and the River Maule in Chile in the south, as well as spreading south-easterly into Argentina.

In the late Inca period, 'many of the local arts practised by the subject peoples, such as the Chimú and Nazca, persisted. The tendency of the Inca system was to produce a greater social homogeneity, and the practice of transporting whole sections of the population from one part of the empire to another, in order to minimize the danger of revolt and to bring waste lands under cultivation, was highly conducive to this result'.[2]

It is in the pottery of the Proto-Nazca, Chimú and Inca cultural periods that we find the evidence of the existence of the potato to which allusion has been made. Joyce's table (p. 16) shows the relationship and the succession in time and space of the different phases of the main Peruvian cultures prior to the Spanish invasion.

The first representations of the potato occur in the Proto-Chimú period, in the second horizon of the Muchik pottery according to Tello; it is these which permit us to speak of the potato as a cultivated plant at least as early as the second century of the present era. The representations are of a symbolic character, implying that the potato had been a familiar article in the lives of the coastal people for many generations,

[1] In fact, further north, into southern Colombia. - Ed.
[2] Joyce, T. A. (1920). Ibid.

if not centuries, before they sculptured them on their pottery. How long the period was between the first attempt to cultivate the wild potato in the mountains and its acceptance and employment on the coast as a staple article of diet we do not know. It must have been some considerable time before it became not only an article of commerce but actually a cult object on the coast. This latter stage of its evolution we can date as being somewhere about the beginning of the Christian era. The prior phase must presumably have occurred several centuries, if not millennia, before that.

Scheme of Dating of the Principal Phases of Indigenous American Art[1]

[From T. A. Joyce, op. cit.]

Approximate date	Peru and Bolivia (Highlands)	Peru (Northern Coast)	Peru (Southern Coast)	Ecuador
A.D. 200	Tiahuanaco I	Proto-Chimú[2]	Proto-Nazca[2]	
A.D. 300	Tiahuanaco II	Tiahuanaco II, and derived styles ('Epigonal', etc.), degenerating		
A.D. 800	Period of degeneration	Chimú	Nazca	Pre-Inca probably related to Proto-Chimú
A.D. 1100	Early Inca			
A.D. 1400	Late Inca	Late Inca superimposed		
A.D. 1519–33	Spanish Conquest			

It is no exaggeration to say that the ceramic art of the northern coastlands of Peru from Trujillo to Nazca, i.e. roughly from lat. 8° S. to lat. 16° S., is amongst the finest in the world; for variety of design and realism in its execution the Proto-Chimú pots are unequalled. Quite different are the harmonious polychrome decorations of the Nazca ceramics which are rendered so outstanding by their peculiar stylistic beauty, their simplicity of shape, and the delicacy of their ware.

But what of the designs on these Proto-Nazca pots? They represent fearsome cat-gods, terrifying centipede-gods, complex nightmare combinations of man and jaguar, condor and serpent. Imagination seems to run riot in an atmosphere of fear and death in which unappeasable phantoms hound man on to his ineluctable fate. The stylistic treatment is evidence of the length and continuity in time of this strange sadistically cruel conception which makes of life a veritable hell on earth.

[1] Authorities are now agreed that the Proto-Chimú should be referred to c. A.D. 1000, and that subsequent pre-Spanish periods must also be advanced in date.

[2] Now known as Moche and Nazca. – Ed.

The early and late Moche styles differ profoundly from those of Nazca. Here we find marvellous sculptured portraits, rarely, one imagines, flattering, depicting men with a quiet sombre dignity but from whose faces, however young, youth's illusions have long since fled. Common are caricatures and grotesques of maimed beggars, of which we shall have more to say. Not much less so, are pots representing heads of men with single or double hare-lips, the faces elaborately ornamented with concentrically designed cicatrices or tattooing, all of which occur in the early and late Chimú periods.

In many of the designs the head of the jaguar or puma, with his mouth open and his canines bared, plays some symbolic part; but occasionally symbolism is dropped, and the tiger is seen devouring his victim, who may be bound and helpless, waiting for his end. In others we see masked men, or creatures with human heads and enormous threatening teeth, holding human heads in their hands; or it may be, a priest or other, with a short stone knife in hand, is deliberately decapitating some kneeling wretch. In very many there is displayed a macabre fascination for death. Still, not all is sombre and cruel in this vivid record which may be read on the sculptured and painted pots the early Peruvians have left us; thus, we meet with curiously outspoken scenes of sexual life, and others of perversions both with man and beast. A notable feature of this type of scene is that it is frequently represented as taking place in the presence of apparently uninterested witnesses. However, our business is not with man's failings, but with his foodstuffs, and in this connection we must turn to that class of pot which depicts for us *genre* scenes of home and farm, of the Indian's llama and his dog, and, above all, of the numerous plants he cultivated. Of these we find countless representations, including squashes, potatoes, beans, manioc, and maize. The spondylus shells, fishes, the llama, the monkey and the snake are all familiar designs, but more frequent than any are representations of maize and manioc amongst plants, the jaguar and puma amongst the animals. The latter may enter the designs in many ways, and though they frequently seem suggestive of terror, their association with the potato may possibly have a different symbolic meaning.

The *Yuca* (manioc) and the maize plants are occasionally represented on the early pots in close association with a human face; the latter, adorned with attributes of dignity in the headdress, probably represent the spirit of the plant, but these particular anthropomorphic pots are relatively rare and, as far as the writer's knowledge goes, are not associated with the representation of any physical deformity or mutilation. This latter fact makes, as we shall see, a definite and important distinction between the symbolic treatment accorded to the potato, and that extended to the other vegetable food plants in use.

As far as I know, the potato is not found as a motive whether in the design or in the decoration, of either the early or the late Nazca pottery. In the Proto-Chimú[1] vases, on the contrary, it is a frequent subject of the designer. We may divide all those pots which in one way or another portray the potato, into three groups:

Group 1. Includes those pots in which there is no association with the human figure, and in which the potato may be depicted either in a more or less realistic manner, or is in varying degree conventionalized, or even reduced to a mere symbol such as an incised or painted 'eye' or irregular tuber-like projections on the body of the vessel.

Group 2. Includes those pots in which the potato is represented either as a human being, or in some close relation to a human being: this group may be further subdivided into:

(*a*) Pots in which the human face is normal.

(*b*) Pots in which the human face is mutilated.

Group 3. Includes pots which present a design which is transitional between Groups 1 and 2.

The first group of potato pots, of which some thirty-five photographs are known to me, all belong to Tello's second and third epochs, i.e. the late Chimú, the pre-Inca, and the Inca periods, viz. to a epoch extending from about A.D. 800 to 1550.

It is easy to arrange the pots of this group in a graded series, so that those at one end are more or less vivid and realistic representations of potato tubers, whilst on those at the other, the potato as a motive is progressively reduced to a mere symbol. This may take the form of a few irregular swellings of the contour, with perhaps a suggestion of an 'eye', or there may be nothing to indicate the tuber itself but a few conventionalized 'eyes' introduced as part of a more or less formal design. The pots in which conventionalization of the potato has proceeded farthest, belong to the Inca and late Inca periods, whilst the more realistically designed at the Chimú-Inca period; Figs. 4–12 (Pls. II–V), illustrate the salient features of the series and are so arranged, that the latest in date are succeeded by those which are increasingly realistic and are thought to be progressively earlier in date. Amongst the pots of the early Chimú period, the writer has found one only which might, at first sight, be classed in this group. This pot (Pl. I, fig. 3) was originally described by Safford:[2] it represents twin tubers and, as such, has a special significance which probably does not apply to the twin pots represented in Figs. 11 and 12 (Pl. V). We know from the native folk-lore of to-day, that monstrous twin potato tubers are regarded as being endowed with special reproductive gifts; the Spanish chroniclers speak,

[1] For Proto-Chimú and early Chimú read Moche. – Ed.

[2] Safford, W. E. (1917). Food Plants and Textiles of Ancient America. *Proc. Nineteenth Internat. Congress of Americanists*, pp. 12–30.

too, of the magic value of twin maize cobs. Human twins were likewise
endowed with special powers, especially over the weather. In this particular pot (Pl. I, fig. 3), the schematic representation of the eyes, the
absence of buds within them, their clean-cut outline and dark colour as
contrasted with the very pale body of the tuber, all indicate that the pot
does not represent ordinary potato tubers, as Safford thought, but rather
those which have been converted into *chuño* of the *tunta* type. A comparison with Figs. 1 and 2 (Pl. I) in which both the common *chuño* and
the *tunta* type are represented, goes far to confirm this view. Regarded
thus, the pot is, in fact, highly realistic in its treatment, and in full
accord with the prevailing character of early Chimú[1] ceramics. It affords,
moreover, valuable evidence of the very early commerce in this manufactured highland product between the coast and the altiplano where
alone *chuño* could have been prepared.

Twin pots such as those in Figs. 11 and 12 (Pl. V) are a common
feature of the later Chimú-Inca period, but their design is perhaps to be
related to the whistle inside one of the spouts, which comes into play
when the water is poured out of its fellow, rather than to the symbolism
inherent in twinship.

Figs. 9 and 10 (Pl. IV), are both of Chimú-Inca period: the body of the
pot symbolizes the tuber, and in the treatment of the eyes considerable
realism is observed.

Fig. 7 (Pl. III), is a pot of the Chimú-Inca period, which is unusually
realistic and may well represent some favourite variety.

Figs. 6 and 8 (Pls. III and IV), are pots of the Chimú-Inca period: the
theme is the same as that in Fig. 9 (Pl. IV), but it is treated in a more
consistently conventional manner.

In Figs. 4 and 5 (Pl. II), both Chimú-Inca pots, the potato motif is
reduced to a few rather realistic 'eyes'.

Between the first and the second group of pots in which the human
form takes some part, we find examples, of Group 3, in which, whilst
the representation of the potato is realistic enough and related to the
monstrous twin-tuber type, the actual design derived from the com-
ponent tubers takes on an animal or human form of a conventionalized
type. In Fig. 13 (Pl. VI), we have such a pot, in which the head, body
and arms of a man are indicated by the appropriate combination of four
tubers beset with well-developed eyes.

Figs. 14 and 15 (Pl. VI) represent a type of pot of which several similar
examples are known. The general form of the pot is intended to represent
some small quadruped, which might be a dog or possibly a guinea-pig.
The eyes and ears of the creature, as well as the markings on its body,
may be intended to represent potato eyes, a view which is supported by
the tuber-like structure of the head and face. The actual 'eyes' are rather

[1] See footnote on p. 18. – Ed.

unduly schematic, but comparison with the other specimens, in which the design is slightly varied, gives some support to the view that they may be interpreted as potato eyes. An alternative, and perhaps, more likely explanation, is that the design is intended to represent beans.

The three pots of this intermediate series belong to a period which is not only pre-Inca, but one which is antecedent to the Chimú. Whether they belong to the Proto-Chimú[1] or, as the writer suspects, to a later epigonal period, is uncertain.

We now come to the second group of pots, those in which the dominant motive of the design is a human figure constructed in whole or in part from a potato tuber.

Group 2 (*a*). Thirteen different examples of pots of this group are known to me; in two of them, monkeys replace human figures, as in Fig. 18 (Pl. VIII). In several, the body of the pot represents the trunk of a man shaped from a tuber, from the top of which projects a human head. In Fig. 16 (Pl. VII), one sees secondary tubers at the level of the shoulders, which represent the arms. In one pot, Fig. 17 (Pl. VII), there projects from the belly of the figure a secondary tuber surmounted by another head, the whole being decorated with incised eyes.

A rather distinct type of pot (Pl. VIII, fig. 19), of which I possess photographs of four slightly varying examples, depicts a man in the squatting position, his whole body being decorated with potato 'eyes'. In one of them, Fig. 21 (Pl. IX), the artist has played one of those curious tricks occasionally to be found in Chimú pottery: the 'eyes', which are cut on cheek and forehead, are so placed that, if the pot be turned upside down, the upper part of the face and the forehead become a new head with the face looking downwards. A replica of this pot exists in which this 'trick' has not been played, showing that it was brought about after the pot had left the mould in which it was made.

Fig. 20 (Pl. VIII) portrays a pot in which a figure with a delicately, but stylistically sculptured head, lies prone with folded hands, and on one side of the body, another face is etched, and a few characteristic eyes are cut into the body of the pot. Similar in style is the pot seen in Fig. 22 (Pl. IX), where the spherical body of the pot represents a single male head and two small spherical heads are attached laterally, one looking forward, the other backward, with a potato 'eye' incised on the occiput.

The shape of the pots and the stirrup handles are common to the Proto-Chimú period; sophistication of design and restraint in its execution suggest that they belong to the end of an artistic period which once had been richer and more expansive in its expression.

We must return, for a moment, to the pot of the Moche type in the British Museum (Pl. VIII, fig. 18), in which there are four heads

[1] See footnote to p. 18. – Ed.

sprouting out of the main more or less cylindrical body of the jar. The central one, the biggest, is a normal male head with simple headdress, and a potato 'eye' on the crown; two lateral ones are simian, and a fourth, a female head, springs out of the body of the jar below the central head; on the crown of her head is a potato 'eye', and others are painted round the lower part of the jar near the base; the bodies of the apes are shown in outline on the body of the vase and the hands of both apes and men have only three fingers and a thumb. There is nothing to suggest that the missing little finger has been amputated. The arrangement of the figures on the pot strongly suggests a sexual relationship. So far, this is the only pot in which such has been observed in connection with the potato, unless that illustrated in Fig. 17 (Pl. VII) be so regarded. The fertility of the potato was invoked, as we shall see, by an entirely different and more appropriate symbolism.

Group 2 (*b*). This group, in which the potato is associated with a man and in one case a monkey, showing some mutilation of the face, is characterized by the diversity of the design and the early period to which most of the pots belong. Of the twenty-one examples of which there are photographs in my collection, four presented by Dr Tello are definitely assigned to the Muchik II[1] horizon, and date from the second to third century A.D. Most of the others are definitely of the Proto-Chimú period and their dates range somewhere between A.D. 200 and 800. None belongs to the Inca period.

A rough division of the pots may be made into:

(α) Those in which there are several human heads or whole bodies.

(β) Those in which there is a single more or less entire human form.

(γ) Those in which the pot is composed of a single head with potato elements impressed on it.

This subdivision is doubtless artificial, but it is of some interest that those pots which fall into division (α) contain all the really early Muchik and Chimu pots, and those of division (γ) almost certainly belong to a later period.

Division (α). Here the human form is represented as a body built up from a large tuber, with the head composed of a secondary tuber projecting from the main one. The pot may be of very irregular shape, with several projecting potato tubers each forming a human head (Pl. X, fig. 26); or, again, the pot may be of a sub-spherical shape with projecting heads in a low relief, with here and there a potato 'eye', and amongst these heads may occur that of a jaguar with exposed teeth (Pl. XIV, fig. 36). Finally, there are a few examples of pots in which several individuals are represented; one, reproduced by Tello,[2] but not included here, depicts one unmutilated figure and several mutilated

---

[1] For Muchik II read Moche II and see footnote to p. 18. – Ed.

[2] Tello, J. (1922). *Prehistoric Peru*, vol. XXII, pt. v.

heads, unmutilated corpses, and semi-skeletonized skulls. In another, Fig. 35 (Pl. XIV), a priest is conveying an unmutilated corpse together with some strange monster, while the body of the vase is covered with deeply incised potato eyes.

Division (β). Here we have pots in which the human figure is more or less complete, and in which the potato tuber is represented by an occasional adventitious outgrowth and several deeply incised 'eyes' scattered over the body.

There is a type of pot exhibiting slight variations, five of which are represented in my collection of photographs, which show a progressive deterioration of execution (Pl. XII, figs. 29, 30, 31). How far one is justified in regarding these as necessarily later in date than those in which the design is more realistic, it is impossible to say. In both Divisions (α) and (β) of this group, there is a tendency for the design to become conventionalized.

Division (γ). Here the jar represents a human head and the potato motive may be recognized only by the ornamentation taking the form of highly schematic 'eyes' (Pl. XIII, figs. 32, 33). In one jar of Tello's Muchik II[1] horizon period, which he refers to the second or third century A.D., there projects from the shockingly mutilated head great wen-like potato tubers (Pl. XIII, fig. 34).

It remains to consider the one character held in common by all the pots of Group 2: the mutilation of the face. This artificial deformity, when fully displayed, shows that the end of the nose and the upper or, in some cases, both upper and lower lips, have been cut away, so that the mutilated individual is made to appear like one who had been born with a double hare-lip.

The most exaggerated form of this mutilation was met with in a pot of black Moche ware, in which the figure is that of a monkey where the nose has been split and the two sides rolled back on to the cheek (Pl. X, fig. 23). In the Spanish wars of conquest in Chile, we read of natives being so treated and the sides maintained in position by the insertion of thorns through the flesh.

Occasionally, in pots which would appear to be somewhat later examples of the Proto-Chimú period, the mutilation itself has become conventionalized. The nose is more or less normal but the mouth is very large and so sharply outlined by a pigmented line that it suggests an artificially incised contour (Pl. X, figs. 25, 26). The second of these is a photograph of a pot recently found in an important burial of the late Moche or Huanesco Cultural period. The strikingly triangular form of the pigmented lips would appear to be symbolical of the oral mutilation of an earlier date.

When we regard these pots in their chronological order, it becomes

[1] See footnote to p. 21. – Ed.

evident that the earlier the pot, the more realistic is its representation of the potato, and the more outspoken the mutilation. As time went on, and probably several centuries before the Inca Empire became consolidated, both these characteristics became more and more conventionalized.

Prof. Tello, when lecturing in Cambridge in 1922, first called my attention to the mutilation of the face, for which he could then offer no explanation.

It was fortunate that when the problem of these potato pots was first encountered by me, examples of most of the types which have been discussed were to hand. Had only the late Chimú, and more particularly the Chimú-Inca pots, been under consideration, it would not have been unreasonable to regard the conventional potato symbolism as an aesthetic motive of no more importance than the decoration of a tea-cup with roses or the like. It is only when we regard the collection as a whole, that it becomes clear that these are derived from earlier types, in which the relation between the tuber and a human figure is the outstanding feature.

We have then to ask ourselves, what is the genesis and the meaning of this relationship: potato—man—mutilation, presented by these funeral pots? In order to see the problem clearly and as a whole, we may restate it as follows:

(*a*) Why was the potato so frequently represented in the burial pots throughout the whole range of pre-Columbian history?

(*b*) Why was the potato so often represented in close association with man?

(*c*) Why was the man so often depicted as mutilated, in such a way as to suggest an artificial double hare-lip?

(*d*) Why should the open-mouthed jaguar be also associated with the potato in many of these pots?

To these questions, the following answers are suggested, all of which are the natural deductions from a theory based on a fertility rite. The theory was put forward by me shortly after Prof. Tello's lecture.[1]

The answer to question (*a*) is to be found in the overwhelming importance to certain sections of the population of the potato as a food, and the facility with which from earliest times it had been converted into a conserved ration—*chuño*—valuable at all times, but especially so in times of famine and of war, to the people both of the coast and the sierra.

The answer to question (*b*), is that the human form depicted on these pots represents the spirit of the potato and that its more frequent association with the potato rather than with the other great food sources such as maize, is to be found in the answers given to questions (*c*) and (*d*). In the series of pots exhibiting mutilated figures, the monkey has

[1] Salaman, R. N. (1937). *J. Roy. Hort. Soc.* vol. LXII, pts. 2, 3, 4 and 6.

only once been found replacing a man. When there was no mutilation, such substitution occurred more often. It would seem significant that with rare exceptions only human beings were chosen for this rite.

The answer to question (c) is to be found in the consideration of the following. There exist in Peru and Bolivia to-day a great number of varieties of the potato, many of which have blood-red or deep purple coloured skins, and in not a few the flesh itself is similarly coloured; the suggestion of flesh and blood is obvious. Nearly all the native varieties have deeply incised 'eyes' and around the 'eye' in many is a bolster-like swelling which makes the 'eye' appear still deeper and bigger; from the bottom of these 'eyes' spring the buds which will give rise to the new plants in the following season. Finally, many of the native varieties are round and furnished with knobbly outgrowths, and are not cylindrical or kidney-shaped as our own are to-day.

If now, by a simple change of metaphor, we assume that the Indian regarded what we call an 'eye' as a 'mouth', then we see that all the common features of the tuber can be likened to those of a human being. The round tuber is the head, an elongated one the body, irregular outgrowths are limbs, the 'eye' becomes a mouth with well-defined lips, and the buds are teeth serrated like those of a tiger.

We have seen how intelligent an agriculturist the South American Indian was; at a very early date he must have learnt that the value of a seed tuber was to be measured by the vigour of its buds, i.e. by the size and strength of its teeth; the bigger, and more prominent the teeth, the greater the promise of the crop to come.

This thesis has received strong support since it was first propounded by the discovery of a pot in the great Wassermann Collection, reproduced by kind permission of the owner in Fig. 38 (Pl. XV). Here we have a human figure made up of a tuber; the nose and mouth have been mutilated, the body is covered with well-developed 'eyes' and from each of them springs three or four sprouts or shoots. As if to show that they represent the desired stage for successful planting, the man carries in his left hand a digging-stick. The pot is of the Proto-Chimú[1] period.

The next step would seem to follow logically. The potato, like everything living or non-living, was animated by a spirit, a god. The native of the altiplano, who knew only too well that the potato crop frequently failed, would naturally ascribe the failure to the incapacity or weakness of the potato spirit. It was essential, therefore, for the preservation of his own existence that the potato spirit's energy should be maintained at a high level. To reinforce that spirit he made a sacrifice, and, if necessary, an important sacrifice, a human sacrifice, the shedding and absorption of whose blood would be alone capable of imparting the required vigour. But mere sacrifice was not enough; there was too much

[1] Should be Moche. – Ed.

at stake; it was necessary to show the god exactly what was wanted in order to ensure a good crop. The prime prerequisite, as he well knew, was seed tubers with big mouths and prominent teeth. Hence by the means of a sacrificial mutilation, the cutting off of the end of the nose and the removal of the lips, the mouth was enlarged, the teeth made prominent, the god both strengthened and instructed, and the people eventually saved.

Question (d). The jaguar head with its open mouth and great serrated teeth may have served to reinforce the suggestion of a 'good mouth' already induced by the artificial hare-lip. There is the further reason that as the jaguar was identified with the creator god Viracocha, its participation in the ceremonial rite was but logical.

The sex of the mutilated figure is a matter of importance, but, unfortunately, one not readily determined. The great majority both of the full figures as well as of the heads, are most probably male, a few unmistakably so (Pls. IX, X, figs. 22, 24). It is said that females are very rarely depicted in Chimu pottery, and even on those pots where an infant is carried in the arms of an adult, the sex of the latter has been questioned.[1] It is on negative rather than positive grounds, that the sex of the figure can be determined. Women do not wear ear-ornaments or elaborate headdresses; they are not uncommonly dressed in a simple hooded cloak. On this basis, the great majority, if not all, of the figures represented in association with the potato must be regarded as male. Possible exceptions, however, are to be found in two pots of the series. In Fig. 20 (Pl. VIII), the head of the individual, judged both by its features and the hoodlike headdress, might possibly be intended for a woman, and still more likely is that represented in Figs. 30 and 31 (Pl. XII). In Figs. 27 and 28 (Pl. XI) there are two human figures represented; the larger one is clearly male and it is he who is mutilated, the smaller figure at his back wears only a bandeau around the head, displays no mutilation and might be intended to represent a female. The close association of potato, mutilation of the nose and mouth, and the male sex, is all the more peculiar in view of the following evidence of fertility rites of more recent date.

Both maize and potato were commonly invoked in field and store, in the form of specially decked corn cobs and potato tubers and these were adorned as women and addressed as *Sara-mama* or *Axo-mama*, the generative mother or spirit of the maize and potato respectively. Such customs persisted long into the Spanish period.

The association of woman and potato is found in an aboriginal people in North America. On the lower reaches of the Mississippi the women

[1] Montell, Gösta (1929). *Dress and Ornaments in Ancient Peru*, p. 93. Oxford University Press.

of the Chitimacha tribe who, in the main, are vegetarians, go out to collect nuts and what they term 'women-potatoes'—these latter are wild tuber-bearing *Solanums*.[1]

In the early graves on the coast, solid terra-cotta models of potatoes and maize cobs have frequently been found and these it may be assumed fulfilled a similar purpose. Payne[2] states that the 'stone' potato was planted in the field and a suitable invocation made to the spirit of the potato. The word *Acsu* is the equivalent for *papa* and these stone models, he says, were also known as *Papa-mama*.

It may be that it was regarded as a further advantage that the rite converted the sacrificial victim into a living hare-lipped individual. For the possessors of congenital hare-lips were sacrosanct and endowed with peculiar powers, particularly in relation to frosts. Their frequent appearance on pots suggests the possibility of an association of ideas between the success of the potato crop and the control of frosts.

The mutilations exhibited by the early pottery presumably represent the rite, as practised in the period in which such was made, and do not give us the full tale. It would seem almost certain that in its origin the rite was associated with cannibalism. Indeed, there is evidence that such was occasionally practised in many of the outlying parts of the foretime Inca Empire in the sixteenth century. Payne recalls how in 1611 Calancha states that he saw a woman in La Paz who was discarded as unfit for sacrifice. Hutton[3] is of opinion that cannibalism was common where the normal diet was mainly vegetarian and was to some extent induced by the desire for a flesh diet. He points out that its practice has been recorded among those peoples of South America who subsisted on the manioc and the potato. Indeed, Tschudi[4] mentions its occurrence amongst the manioc-eating[5] Chuncho of the Peruvian montaña, and Bandelier records the same, so late as the first decade of this century, amongst the potato-eating natives of the Titicaca region. Neither of these authors, however, connects the occurrence of cannibalistic practices directly or indirectly with the potato.

If the explanation which has been offered is the correct one, it might be expected that some memory, however faint and distorted, of such rites, might have been recorded by the early Spanish writers, or even observed to-day. We must not, however, expect to find any direct evidence of human sacrifice in relation to the potato, for we have seen that this type of sacrifice ceased to be recorded on the huaca pots long before the Inca period, which means that it probably had not been

---

[1] Swanton, John R. (1911). *Bull. Bur. Amer. Ethn.* No. 43.
[2] Payne, Ed. J. (1892). *History of the New World*, p. 414. Clarendon Press.
[3] Hutton, J. H. (1943). *Folk Lore*, vol. LIV, pp. 274–86.
[4] Tschudi, J. von (1847). Op. cit. p. 403.
[5] They also hunted and ate wild mammals and caught fish. – Ed.

current practice for six or seven centuries or more before the Spanish chroniclers appeared on the scene. Human sacrifice, however, had not entirely disappeared in the Inca Empire, even at its close.

The evidence of the persistence of sacrificial rites in connection with the potato at the time of the Spanish Conquest and later, comes from several sources.

Velasco[1] says that neither the kings of Quito, the Incas of Peru, nor the Spaniards were able to suppress the harvest festivals in southern Ecuador, where one hundred children annually were sacrificed. Potatoes in these parts were an important crop, and it is to be presumed that these ceremonies referred at least in part to them.

Cieza de Leon[2] gives a remarkable account of a scene observed by a priest in May 1547, and attested by him in Cieza's presence. It relates how a great gathering of Indians took place at the call of the drum in Lampa in the Collao and how, after the chiefs—who wore their best clothes—had seated themselves on richly embroidered mantles, there entered a procession of gorgeously dressed young boys, each carrying a weapon in one hand and a bag of coca in the other; these were accompanied by a similar group of young girls in grand robes with long trains held up by older attendants. The girls carried bags of rich clothing and gold and silver. Then followed native labourers with plough on shoulder succeeded by six pages, each with a bag of potatoes. After a ceremonial parade, and the labourers, holding the bags of potatoes high above their heads, had danced to the beating of the drums, there was brought in a one-year-old llama, 'all of one colour', and this was taken to the chief and then killed and its bowels withdrawn and given to the sorcerers. Then certain Indians collected all the blood they could from the llama and poured it on the potatoes in the bags. Unfortunately, at this critical moment an overzealous catechumen of only a few days' standing arrived on the scene and, having denounced them all, dispersed the gathering.

The original account of the ceremonial is well worth reading, and that it should have taken place seventeen years after the advent of the Spaniards, and near to the ancient capital of the empire, adds to its interest. But the great value of the narrative for us lies in the evidence it affords of the change from a human to an animal sacrifice, and the transference of the strengthening blood from the sacrificed animal direct to the seed potato. It is difficult not to see in this elaborate ceremony, in which young boys and girls play so prominent a part, a reminder of the part which children destined for sacrifice had played in earlier times,

[1] De Velasco (1789). *Historia del Reyno de Quito*, vol. II, p. 35.
[2] Cieza de León, Pedro de (1550). *The Chronicle of Peru*, p. 412 (trans. by C. Markham). Hakluyt Soc. 1864.

and to whom the most elaborate homage was paid as they passed in procession to the scene of the sacred rite.

Father Arriaga[1] tells us that all useful plants are animated by a divine being who causes their growth. Such are called *Sara-mama* (maize-mother), *Coca-mama*, and *Axo-mama* (potato-mother). He then describes an elaborate ceremonial in which puppets of maize or coca (potato is not mentioned specifically) are made and dressed as women, and kept as a sacred object or 'huaca', for the following year, and amidst much dancing, sacrifices were made to them. Especially large, or twin, or peculiarly coloured maize cobs, he says, have a certain religious value as fertility agents. 'Another superstition they have with them they call Axo-mama: for when two potatoes were found growing together they kept them in order to get a good crop of potatoes.'

Father Acosta,[2] who was in Peru from 1569 to 1585, describes the same type of rite in respect to maize and lays emphasis on the fact that the maize cob which was kept as a huaca was a particularly big one.

Tschudi[3] writing about 1847, says:

On the day of San Antonio, the natives of Acobamba (east of Lima) made a great feast; all the men assembled in the Plaza were divided into two parties, and began fiercely to fight, until some of them fell down wounded or dead. Now the women rushed forth amongst the men, collecting the flowing blood and guarding it carefully. The object of the barbarian fighting was to obtain human blood, which was afterwards interred in the fields with a view to securing an abundant crop.

Bandelier[4] tells a somewhat similar tale:

It may even be said, that no Indian festivity is satisfactory without one or more homicides. Feuds between neighboring haciendas are often fought out on such occasions, for the Indian often carries, besides his sling (for which the women provide round pebbles in their skirts) a dangerous weapon in the shape of a whip terminating at the upper end of the handle in a small tomahawk of steel. Whenever such fights take place it is not rare to see men swallowing the brains oozing out of the fractured skulls of the wounded, and women dipping *chuño* in the pools of blood, and eating it, when well soaked, with loathsome ferocity.

It is noteworthy that it is the women who eat the bloody *chuño*.

Recent evidence of sacrifice in relation to the potato in Peru has reached me from three different sources during the last twenty years. Prof. Tello informed me that when a group of natives were digging the potatoes, and one found a blood-red deep-eyed tuber, or a twin or

---

[1] Arriaga. Op. cit.
[2] Acosta, José de (1590). *Natural and Moral History of the Indies* (trans.), Bk. v, p. 374. Hakluyt Soc. 1880.
[3] Tschudi (1846). *Peru-Reiseskitzen aus den Jahren* 1838–42, vol. II, p. 358.
[4] Bandelier (1910). *Islands of Titicaca and Koati*, p. 114. New York.

other unusually shaped tuber, then if the finder were a man, he ran to the nearest woman, who ran away as fast as she could, till he caught her up and touched her gently with it. But if the finder were a woman, she ran up to the nearest man, who must stand his ground whilst she hit him as hard as she could on the face with the tuber. A very similar account of the same custom has been recently sent to me by Mrs Clarence Woods, the author of *High Spots on the Andes*, who adds that her native informant had no idea of what the custom meant.

There can indeed be little doubt that here we have a survival of the human sacrifice of former days. I am indebted to Mrs Woods for further information concerning ceremonies in relation to the potato. One of these would appear to be a variant version of the custom we have just described. It forms a feature of the first part of the harvest festival. The workers search for the biggest and most irregular tuber; when they have found one it is thrown at the owner of the farm, who, catching it, throws it as far as he can across the field. This procedure is thought to ensure that the whole of the field will in future produce similar large potatoes. The second part of the festival is given up to a religious service with dancing and drinking.

In May, in the high sierra, a service is held in the potato fields in which a burnt offering is made, composed of leaves of 'velacay', 'hancuir', the raw fat of the llama, 'huallpo', the raw fat of the vicuña, and alcohol, which is solemnly burnt while the owner prays that his potato crop may be productive. The ashes are then spread over the field, and dancing and drinking ensue. In August a similar ceremony takes place at the time of the cultivating of the potatoes; an altar is then set up in the field and mass said, followed by *chicha*-drinking and dancing.

In these latter ceremonies we see that a transference has taken place; instead of imparting fresh strength direct to the potato, its spirit is now given to the soil.

Mr Kenneth Grubb has told me how he has seen processions of natives going to the potato-planting in the highlands, carrying the image of some saint, Peter or Paul, but never one of the Virgin, who is not deemed a good fertility emblem; there is a great dancing and playing of flutes and pan-pipes, and the men are decked with coloured garters with bells hanging from them.

The following ceremony, which Mr Grubb personally witnessed, is a good example of the rationalization which follows the clash of two conflicting cultures:

A native small-owner was about to sow the first potato seed of the year; he took an old pointed digging-stick and made a hole in the ground, then, kneeling over the hole whilst he muttered a prayer, he put in it coca and potash, spat on the mixture and, placing the tuber on top, covered the hole. When he was asked why he did this, rather than open up a furrow with the one-handled ox-plough which he had on the farm, he explained that he had plenty of coca on the farm, there was no question of economy, but the plough (elementary in type as it was) was to him a symbol of the domination of the stranger, and he planted his first potato in this manner so as to preserve his free soul.

Bandelier describes a more elaborate ceremonial performed before commencing to prepare the land for the crop:[1]

The medicine-man repeated the formula of the afternoon and sprinkled wine and afterward brandy in the direction of each of the five Achachilas, (ancestral spirits), named, saying: 'All thy presents I have now brought.' With this, he counted out twenty balls one by one, each being counted as a *quintal*, or hundredweight, and adding: 'Thou hast to give me with all thy heart....The very things of the Inca thou hast to bring forth. Now, with thy permission we will take leave. Forgive me.'

Here, the primitive idea of compelling the 'spirits' to do their share in the work is manifested.

These accounts give grounds for the following suggestions:

(*a*) That the object of all these ceremonies was to fortify the innate spirit of the plant in order that it should exert its utmost activity—a fertility rite in the fullest sense.

(*b*) That the nature of the spirit was sometimes regarded as that of a sexually mature female.

(*c*) That departures from the normal, such as an over-large maize cob or a twin tuber, were regarded as being endowed with an extra gift of the spirit because they emphasized the type of reproductive activity desired.

It is interesting to note that there is no stress laid on the phallus as an emblem of fertility, as was so often the case in the Old World.

Before we leave the problem of sacrificial rites in relation to the potato, reference should be made to two groups of anthropomorphic pots, some of which are relatively common in collections of Moche pottery. In these pots human heads or whole figures, generally kneeling or squatting, are represented with nose and mouth mutilated in a manner similar to that already described, but in none is there any evidence of the potato. A second group of such figures display amputation of hands or feet, or both. I have collected a large series of photographs of these types of pots and feel confident that, so far as the facial mutilation is concerned, they represent a destructive ulcerative disease known as *uta* or *espundia*, a form of leishmaniasis.

[1] Bandelier (1910). Op. cit. p. 98.

The suggestion has been made that these representations of facial deformity were intended to portray the ravages of syphilis. Against this hypothesis it may be urged that, as the lesions are confined to the face, the nasal cartilage is always undamaged, and gummatous swellings are absent, the sculptured pots cannot well be interpreted as depicting syphilis. Apart from a differential diagnosis based on clinical lesions, the question arises as to whether syphilis was indeed present at all, in pre-Spanish South America. It is true that the weight of opinion, very recently endorsed by high authority,[1] is in favour of the view that Columbus and his men brought the disease to Spain in 1492, on their return from Haiti, but that cannot be accepted as evidence for its presence in Peru-Bolivia a thousand years earlier. The fact that Hrdlička[2] failed to find any evidence of syphilis in the ancient Peruvian mummies, strengthens the view that whilst the disease portrayed is unlikely to be due to syphilis, it may well represent the dire effect of an infection with the leishmaniasis.

There is, however, yet a further group of pots in which the victims display the same mutilation of mouth and nose, but in these it is associated with amputation of the legs below the knees; the victims are portrayed lying prone on their abdomens. In some of these pots large tumour-like swellings are seen on either side of the neck on which marks, suggestive of potato eyes, can sometimes be made out (Pl. XV, fig. 39). Before reaching any conclusion as to the meaning of these particular pots, it is necessary to compare a larger collection of them than has as yet been available, but the possibility that these particular neck swellings may represent potato tubers should not be disregarded, especially as sufferers from the *uta* disease do not develop such swellings as a consequence of their illness. On the other hand, somewhat similar protuberances, though generally neither so large nor so individual, are occasionally portrayed in the early pottery and in such cases are obviously intended to represent part of the coiffure. It may be that in these pots we see a fusion of two different ideas, the one a protection against a devastating disease, the other an agricultural fertility rite, whose only real relationship is the similarity of their symbolism, i.e. the mutilation of nose and mouth.[3]

Dietschy has suggested to me that it might be that the *uta* deformity originally gave rise to the idea of the potato spirit, and that only later was the condition induced by artificial means. If such were the case, we should expect to find some trace of a relationship between the disease

[1] Sherrington, Sir Charles (1946). *The Endeavour of Jean Fernel*, p. 129. Cambridge University Press.

[2] Hrdlička, A. (1918). *Bull. Bur. Amer. Ethn. Soc.* No. 34.

[3] Salaman, R. N. (1939). Deformities and Mutilations of the Face as Depicted in the Chimu Pottery of Peru. *J. Roy. Anthrop. Inst.* vol. LXIX, pt. 1.

and the potato. Poma de Ayala in 1613 described the great *Situa* festival, which was celebrated by the Incas every September in order to cleanse the nation of sickness, and to exorcize malignant disease-producing spirits; in addition, he sets out for most months of the year the diseases which may be expected to be most prevalent either in the coastal plain or in the mountain valleys. Dietschy[1] has commented on these passages, and to him I am indebted for the translations of the relevant passages.

In the Quechuan list of diseases, *uta* is spoken of as *acapana-ayapcha*, which means 'red fringed clouds', a reference to the walls of the ulcers. In Spanish the disease is called the disease of the valleys, or the Andean disease. The word *hutu* or *uta* in the early Spanish dictionaries of 1607–14 is said to mean 'chewed maize', both in the Quechuan and Aymara languages; but in 1772 it is said to mean a 'butterfly' whose bite causes the disease. So far there is no suggestion of the potato having any relation whatever to the disease.

Verruga, a dangerous disease common to the Andean valleys, is characterized by warty, corrugated, blood-stained excrescences, which appear all over the body and which, when elongated and thin, resemble a miniature maize cob; and when big and swollen, a potato tuber. De Ayala speaks of *verruga* in Quechuan as *Sara Papa Acoya*, i.e. the maize and potato evil, and in the Spanish list as *Zarnas carachas*, scabby eruptions. Men suffering from *verruga* are frequently depicted in the Moche pots, but in none is there any suggestion of the potato. We may therefore conclude, that although the lesions of *verruga* were occasionally likened to a potato tuber, the latter was not thought to have any significant relation to the malady.

There being therefore no reason to believe that the Peruvians related the mutilations of mouth and nose, which we find associated with the potato in the Moche pots, to any disease, we are strengthened in the opinion that they were designed, as already suggested, to further the success of the potato crop in the field.

It appears that the potato might itself be an active agent in the performance of magical rites. Tschudi[2] recounts how women fortune-tellers picked up pairs of tubers from a heap and if at the end none was left, the omen for the coming year was favourable, whereas if one odd tuber remained, the reverse was the case. Such divination was called piu-irute, or potato counting.

The sacrificial rites, bound up with the cultivation of the potato, as recorded in the ancient Peruvian pottery, carry the history of our subject back to at least the second century of this era. The folk-lore customs of

[1] Dietschy, H. (1944). *Acta Tropica*, vol. I, pp. 52–69.
[2] Tschudi, Johann J. (1891). *Beiträge zur Kenntniss der alten Peru*, p. 113.

PLATE I

Fig. 3. Pot, Moche period; representing twin tubers of *Tunta*.

Fig. 1. Potatoes after freezing and drying: the common *Chuño* of Peru and Bolivia.

Fig. 2. Specimen of *Chuño* of better quality, known as *Tunta*.

PLATE II

Fig. 5. Pot, Chimú-Inca period; black, polished, a tuber with deep 'eyes'.

Fig. 4. Pot, Chimú-Inca period; black polished, a potato tuber with conventionalized 'eyes'.

PLATE III

Fig. 6. Pot, Chimú-Inca period; black, polished,
a tuber with deep 'eyes'.

Fig. 7. Pot, Chimú-Inca period; a tuber of what
was probably a cultivated variety, with a great
number of 'eyes'.

PLATE IV

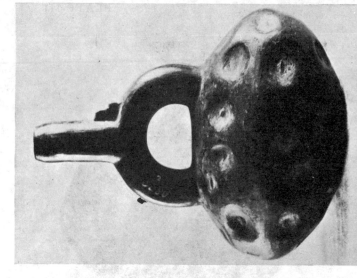

Fig. 10. Pot, Chimú-Inca period; black, polished, a tuber with unusually deep 'eyes'.

Fig. 9. Pot, Chimú-Inca period; tuber with deep 'eyes'. On the spout, a monkey.

Fig. 8. Pot, Chimú-Inca period; reddish brown ware, a deep-eyed tuber.

PLATE V

Fig. 11. Pot, Chimú-Inca period; two tubers linked by a bridge.
The figure on one spout is holding a jar of *Chicha*.

Fig. 12. Pot, Chimú-Inca period; twin tubers, similar to Fig. 11, but more
conventionalized. As water pours from one spout to the other, it whistles.

PLATE VI

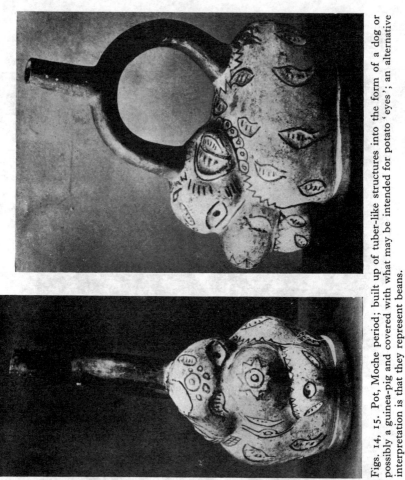

Figs. 14, 15. Pot, Moche period; built up of tuber-like structures into the form of a dog or possibly a guinea-pig and covered with what may be intended for potato 'eyes'; an alternative interpretation is that they represent beans.

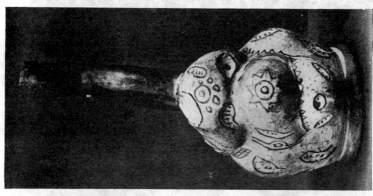

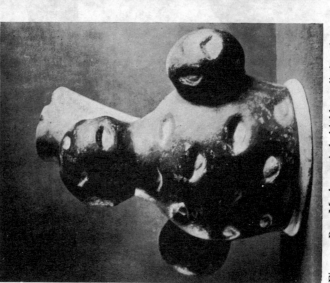

Fig. 13. Pot, Moche period; highly realistic tubers arranged to represent a human figure.

PLATE VII

Fig. 17. Pot, Moche period; figure of a man built up of tubers with 'eyes' cut on face and body; attached to the body are projecting tubers representing human heads. A sexual relationship may be intended.

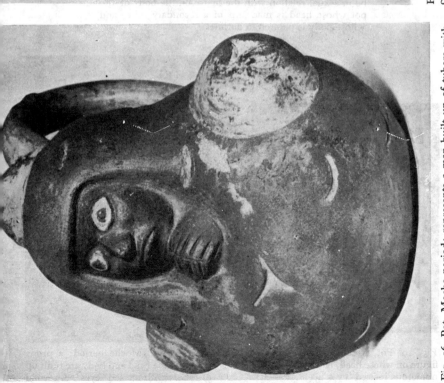

Fig. 16. Pot, Moche period; represents a man built up of tubers with conventionally incised 'eyes'.

PLATE VIII

Fig. 18. Pot, Moche period, body of pot is a tuber with conventionalized painted 'eyes', laterally are monkey heads. The central head is that of a man who appears to be in sexual relation with the figure on the body of the pot whose head is made up of a secondary tuber and whose body is painted in outline.

Fig. 19. Pot, Moche period; a man's figure on whose head, face and body are numerous incised 'eyes'.

Fig. 20. Pot, Moche period; a prone figure whose head and body are built up of tubers with incised 'eyes'. A second head, in relief, is cut on the hinder part of the main figure.

PLATE IX

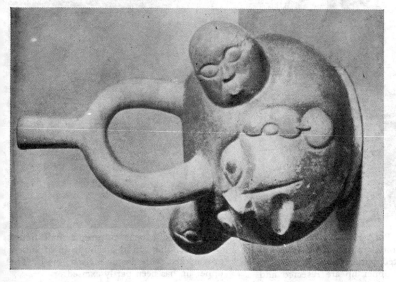

Fig. 22. Pot, Moche period; consisting of three human heads created out of tubers, with a few conventionalized incised 'eyes'. The main head is adorned with the large ear-rings of a headman.

Fig. 21. Pot, Moche period; a sitting figure whose head, face, and body are freely marked with incised potato 'eyes'. When inverted, a second face is seen on the same head.

PLATE X

Fig. 23. Pot, Moche period; black ware. A monkey whose head-dress is ornamented with small tubers. The nose and upper lip are resected and the sides rolled back.

Fig. 24. Pot, Moche culture; a male figure whose body and head are built up of tubers ornamented with deeply incised 'eyes'. The upper lip has been partly excised.

Fig. 25. Pot, Moche period; human head built up of a tuber with shallow 'eyes'. The mouth is outlined by a red band which suggests the excision of the upper lip.

Fig. 26. Pot, Moche period; two figures built up of tubers with large 'eyes'. The mouth is outlined in such a manner as to show the teeth and the absence of a properly developed upper lip.

PLATE XI

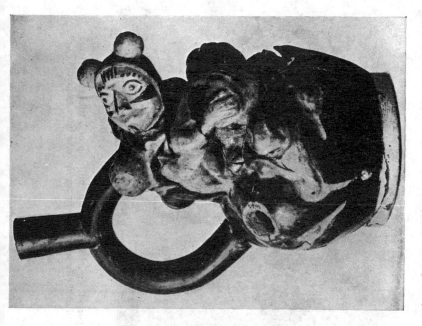

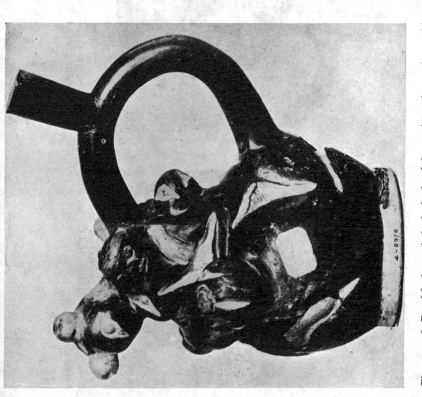

Figs. 27, 28. Pot, Moche period; the body of the pot is a tuber and out of it emerge other tubers modelled to represent human figures; the larger of them displays a nose whose end has been cut away and the upper lip excised. The figure at the rear would appear to be that of a woman, whose face has not been mutilated.

PLATE XII

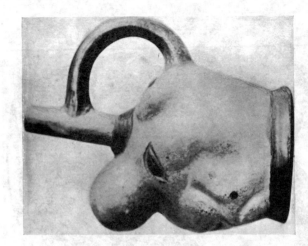

Figs. 30, 31. Pot, Moche period; figure of a woman, built up of a tuber with large incised 'eyes'. The end of the nose and the upper lip have been excised.

Fig. 29. Pot, Moche period; human figure built up of tubers with very prominent 'eyes'; the end of the nose and the upper lip have been excised.

PLATE XIII

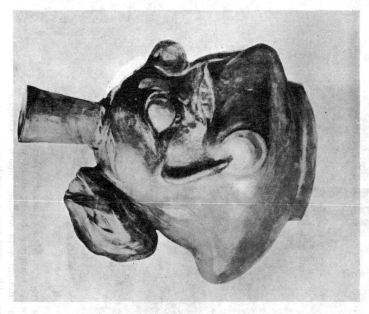

Fig. 34. Pot, Moche II Horizon of Tello; a male head built up of tubers with one on top of the skull suggesting a wen; extreme mutilation of all features of the face, including excision of the lips. A potato 'eye' is seen near the spout.

Figs. 32, 33. Pot, Moche period: human head, built up of tuber with large conventionalized 'eyes'. The end of the nose and both lips have been excised.

PLATE XIV

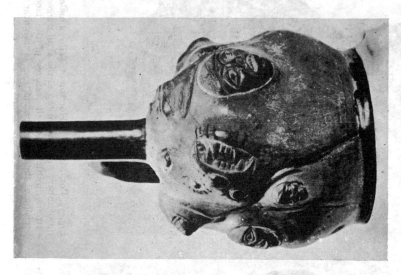

Fig. 36. Pot, Moche period; tuber from which emerge numerous heads, all of which display play mutilations of nose and mouth. A jaguar's head with gaping mouth in centre.

Fig. 35. Pot, Moche II Horizon of Tello; man carrying a corpse; both emerging from a tuber with deeply incised 'eyes'. A python-like monster is curled round the base.

PLATE XV

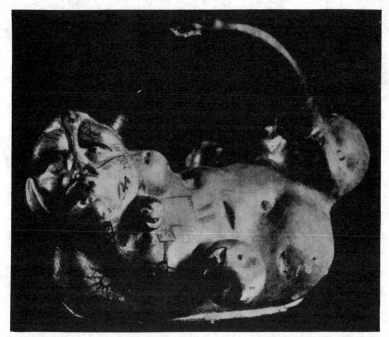

Fig. 37. Pot, Moche II Horizon of Tello; two large and several small heads, built up from secondary tubers emerging from one larger tuber representing a common body. All heads display mutilations of the nose and mouth.

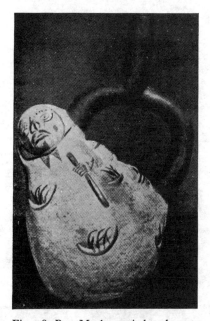

Fig. 38. Pot, Moche period; a human figure built up of a large irregular tuber; the nose and mouth have been mutilated. In the left-hand is a digging-stick. The whole is beset with large 'eyes' from which emerge well-grown sprouts.

Fig. 39. Pot, Moche period; a prone figure in which the feet have been amputated above the ankle; the end of the nose and the upper lip have been excised. The swelling on the shoulder may be meant to represent tubers.

the people of to-day testify to the reality and strength of those ancient rites. The history of a people's migration does not begin with the chronicler: its roots go back to an age whose only record to-day may be in the subconscious. It may well be that in the sacrificial rites themselves we have the sublimated expression of the fears and anxieties which harried man during the period of his early struggle with nature in his new environment, that struggle in which he must win the first round of the combat, or perish. How long that combat lasted we may never know, but when it was over, man had as his allies the manioc, the potato and the maize.

We have seen how the life of the pre-Columbian native of the highlands of Peru and Bolivia was largely conditioned by his cultivation of the potato; to-day in those parts where there are no mines or other intrusive European culture, the same holds good. Both Bandelier[1] and McBride,[2] who have independently made intensive studies of native life and customs in the Collao, confirm this; both point out how beneath the veneer of Christianity lies the primitive animism of the people. In order to understand the reason for this persistence, one must know something of the social system which reigned before the advent of the Spaniard.

[1] Bandelier. Op. cit.
[2] McBride (1921). *The Agrarian Indian Communities of Highland Bolivia.*

CHAPTER III

The Potato in Pre-Spanish Peru

Whether man migrated from the east westwards to the coast, or whether
the latter was reached independently by sea from the north, the fact
remains that at a very early date settlements were established at various
points along the coast. As the physical and climatic conditions of the
coastal plane and western slopes of the Andes differ so radically from
those of the montana and altiplano, we must pause to consider them in
their relation to our problem.

South of the equator the western coast of Peru is one broad belt of
arid desert intersected at a number of places by rivers disgorging from
the steep western mountain valleys, a few of which bring down sufficient
water to create oases, whose fertility is enhanced by the use of guano and
fish-manure. In pre-Columbian days the Incas and their predecessors
constructed elaborate aqueducts and channels so that a larger area of
the coast than now was cultivated. Then the main crop was maize; now
sugar-cane, introduced by the Spaniards, monopolizes these coastal
oases. It is more than doubtful whether the potato was ever grown on
the coast, the climate of which is too hot. Cieza alone of the early writers
makes a reference to potatoes growing near the coast, in the rainless
irrigated valleys of the foothills. The brothers Ulloa[1] writing in the
middle of the eighteenth century, have given us a survey of the local
products, imports and exports, of every part of the west coast of South
America from Panamá to Chiloé, with the exception of present-day
Colombia. Nowhere do they record the production of the potato outside
the higher mountain districts. Amongst modern authors, only one
mention of the potato in these regions has been found, and that probably
refers to a garden crop. Indeed, the potato was not known till recently
either wild or domesticated, until the higher valleys are reached, about
6,000 ft. above the sea, where it was and still is grown on the terraced
hills, some of which were irrigated.

Notwithstanding the absence of rain on the western coastal belt, and
the dependence of plant life on the *Garúa* or foggy mist which prevails,
certain wild potato species have been found in these regions. They are:
Solanum wittmackii ($2n = 24$),[2] *S. vavilovii* ($2n = 24$), and *S. medians*
($2n = 24$), none of which has any immediate economic value; the latter
two were described by the members of the Russian expedition as being

[1] Ulloa, George and Antonio (1760). *Voyage to South America*, 2nd edit. London.
[2] The numbers in brackets refer to the chromosome complement.

highly drought-resistant, but subsequent examination in Leningrad has shown that *S. Vavilovii* has no trace of such a quality and *S. medians* is probably not better endowed than the majority of other tuber-bearing species.

The coastal dwellers before the Spanish Conquest, although well provided with maize, squashes and other fruits, had no domestic animals of their own, barring the dog and the guinea-pig. Their dependence on the cultivators of the sierra for many articles of every-day use, whether as raw material or as manufactured, was a close one. The llama was needed for both meat and sacrificial rite; its wool, as well as that of the alpaca and the vicuña, was essential for the superb textiles woven in the lowlands and the infinity of robes made by the daughters of the Sun for the Inca, his family, and the priesthood. Fresh potatoes, and particularly the dried *chuño*, were probably as much in demand in the days of the Incas as they are to-day, which would account for it being so frequently found in the pre-Columbian graves on the coast.[1] All this implies the existence of a constant and close intercommunication between the coastal settlements and the highlands, a state of affairs which in fact existed at the time of the Conquest, and which was based on the interchange of commodities already referred to, on the one side from the highlands, and maize, fruit, textiles and pottery from the other. A dominating factor in this barter was the llama itself, which, driven in great flocks, conveyed the goods from altiplano to coast and back, each beast bearing a load from 75 to 100 lb. on its back.[2]

The small coastal states must themselves have been dependent on an adequate control of the sierra hinterland, if for no other reason than for the command of their water supply. These contacts were equally valuable to the upland peasant because his vital needs became in turn a matter of economic interest to the man of the coast, a fact which would suggest that the potato might have had an importance on the coastal economy over and above its value as an article of diet.

North of the equator conditions were quite different; from the Gulf of Guayaquil to the isthmus the mountains descend almost to the sea and, instead of a rainless desert which dominates the coast south of the equator, impenetrable rain-forests extend northwards to the isthmus. In the hinterland lie the northern part of Ecuador and the Republic of Colombia, where the deep valleys of the Atrato, the Cauca and the Magdalena lie between the folds of the Cordillera.

It was one of these valleys which witnessed the most important if less acclaimed of all the Spanish discoveries and conquests. It was in their struggle through the dense forest of the Magdalena valley that the

[1] Tschudi, J. von (1846). *Peru Reiseskitzen aus den Jahren* 1838–1842, vol. I, p. 262.
[2] Safford, W. E. (1925). *J. Heredity*, vol. X, p. 178.

members of Gonzalo Jiménez de Quesada's expedition[1] penetrated eastward to the high plateau, and in the native village of Sorocotá, about lat. 7° N., not far from the Spanish town of Vélez, made the first recorded encounter by Europeans with the potato.

I am indebted to Mr F. A. Kirkpatrick for bringing this very important and hitherto unrecognized reference to my notice. Castellanos,[2] who was a member of the party, describes how the natives fled on their approach, and that the Spaniards entered the houses and found in them maize, beans and 'truffles'. These 'truffles' he describes in detail: they were, in fact, potatoes. Plants with 'scanty flowers of a dull purple colour and floury roots', he says, 'of good flavour, a gift very acceptable to Indians and a dainty dish even for Spaniards'. A few months later, this same expedition of Quesada captured Bogotá,[3] the capital of the Chibcha kingdom, which occupied the lofty and salubrious plateau above the endless llanos that lay deep below to the east of the Cordillera. Here the Spaniards found that potato and maize were the staple foods of the people; Quesada comments on the abundant crops yielded by this truffle.[4]

It was but a little later, viz. in 1538, that Cieza de León, a private soldier on an expedition in the district of Popayán, about lat. 2° N., observed the potato and described it. Cieza's account,[5] published in 1550, has always been held to be the earliest record of the potato, but there seems no reason to doubt that Castellanos[6] has the right of priority, though his manuscripts remained unpublished till 1886.

In Colombia the potato, which was the staple food of the upland plateau, was unknown on the adjacent coast, a fact which may be correlated with the absence of the llama in these regions. This lack of intercommunication between coast and sierra probably accounts for the less-developed civilization of Colombia as compared with that of Peru.

The potato lands of Colombia lie between altitudes of 8,000 and 10,000 ft., and are generally on the mountains and high valleys, while the plains are devoted to pasture and cereals. Planting in one locality or

---

[1] The expedition left St Marta in April 1536, and the raid took place about ten months later, i.e. early in 1537. The commission authorizing Quesada's expedition was, however, dated 1537, and this has given rise to some confusion. Cunningham Graham was confident that 1536 is the actual date of their departure. See *Conquest of New Granada* (1922).

[2] According to John Rowe (pers. comm.), it was another Castellanos who wrote this account, not the member of the expedition. – Ed.

[3] Strictly, the city of Bogotá was the creation of Quesada, who founded it not far from the town in which Bogotá, the chief of the Chibchas, lived.

[4] Kirkpatrick, F. A. Communicated in a letter to R.N.S. 8 March 1935.

[5] Cieza de León, Pedro de (1562). *The Chronicle of Peru* (trans. by Markham). Hakluyt Soc. 1864.

[6] Castellanos, Juan de. *Historia del Nuevo Reino de Granada*. Publ. Madrid, 1886.

another may occur at any season of the year, the choice of season being regulated by the rainfall and not dictated by any fear of frost, except in the highest regions.

Besides the two extreme types of environment, the tropical luxuriant coastal oasis and the cold, bare upland in which man established himself in the Peru-Bolivian areas, there are temperate zones which intervene, and within which, separated by relatively short distances, a great variety of climate, soil and culture may be found. The district known as the Yungas, a belt of land extending on the eastern side of the Peruvian-Bolivian Cordillera, is a good example of the grading of one type into the other.

Jones[1] describes this region as follows: 'A narrow strip of deep valleys and high mountain spurs, the Yungas, stretches from the arid monte of northern Argentina to the major break in the eastern Cordillera just south of the Marañón. Bordered on the east by arid chaco, broad savannas and dense tropical forests, it extends from true tropical climes at about 2,000 ft., to cold areas near 10,000 ft. in the Cordillera.' In a few hours, he tells us, one may descend some steep, winding, treacherous trail, leaving behind the llama flock, the potato patch and thick-walled hut of the half-starved Indian on his cold, wind-swept plateau, to find oneself in a sweltering heat, tormented by insects and exposed to fevers in the forest home of the nomadic Indian, on whom in return nature has bestowed unlimited food.

In the temperate valleys are found not only extensive terraces reaching 1,000 ft. up the mountain-side, but also large levelled fields made up of alluvial soil which has been conveyed thither from the river beds and retained by stone dykes. These were probably constructed in Inca times and were used for growing crops, including the potato. In these regions the potato is still grown extensively but only assumes a position of commanding importance in the higher and colder valleys. The relation of the potato to the social economy of the various regions we have been considering may be briefly stated.

In the coastal area the potato was in no way essential as a food, but acquired a secondary importance due to the politico-economic relation which existed between coast and sierra. In the temperate areas the potato held no preponderant place in a dietary which included both a large number of nutritious roots and the cereal maize.

In the bleak highland plateaux the potato formed the daily and chief food of the people; its importance was further enhanced by the fact that, by a method of conservation, it became the safeguard against famine, following the destruction of the crops by severe frost.

It was in the highland districts that the potato, as Vavilov and his

---

[1] Jones, Clarence (1928). Agricultural Regions of South America. *Econ. Geog.* vol. V, p. 277. [He exaggerates the extent of the Yungas. – Ed.]

collaborators have shown, developed, probably in late geological times, the numerous species and varieties which are found wild there to-day, and which formed the raw material from which the early immigrant selected the plants he subsequently learned to cultivate.

In districts such as these, life is a more or less continuous struggle in a field in which man's action is in the main restricted by environmental factors over which he has no control: the temperatures of air and soil.

Most of the potato-growing areas lie between 7° N. of the equator and 43° S., which enables the native cultivator, if he wishes, to raise two or more crops each year,[1] the limiting factor being the danger of night frosts in the higher altitudes, as, for example, in the Puno region of Lake Titicaca, where there is reason to believe the earliest civilization took root. Here, severe night frosts are common, and the Indian cultivator is said to be fortunate if he secures one harvest out of five free from damage.

To meet this emergency, the natives cultivate certain species of potato which withstand several degrees Fahrenheit more frost than do our own. The Russian investigators[2] have identified and named these, of which the chief are *Solanum ajanhuiri* and *S. juzepczukii*. Both of these, though very similar to our own potato in external characters, differ by reason of their chromosome formulae; that of the first being $2n = 24$, and of the second $2n = 36$, as against $2n = 48$, the formula of the potato of Europe and of most of those in cultivation in South America. Both these species are sexually sterile, though *S. ajanhuiri* may occasionally function as a female. This latter species occurs as two cultivated varieties, one with white, the other with purple tubers. An important feature of these frost-resistant potatoes is that they are strictly adapted to the short-day environment of these latitudes.

There is good reason to believe that *S. juzepczukii* is a hybrid derived from a cross of two distinct species, one of which was *S. acaule*, a rosette type bearing few and small tubers but capable of withstanding 10° C. of frost. It is probable, as has already been suggested, that this cross took place in nature, but the fact that the hybrid offspring should have been selected and cultivated implies a high degree of intelligence on the part of the native cultivator as well as a sustained agricultural experience. Were we to assume, as indeed we have no right to do, that the original hybridizations were made by man, and the offspring selected, then we must needs picture a stage of agricultural development comparable with that of the nineteenth century in Europe. The bare facts are enough, construe them how we will: the native Indian cultivator did select certain

---

[1] Generally one crop is grown. – Ed.

[2] See particularly: Bukasov, S. M. (1930). The cultivated plants of Mexico, Guatemala and Colombia, Ch. 14, *Bull. Appl. Bot. Genet. and Pl. Breed.*, Suppl. 47, 191–226; Juzepczuk, S. W. and Bukasov, S. M. (1929). A contribution to the question of the origin of the potato. *Proc. USSR Congr. Genet. Pl. & Animal Breed.*, vol. 3, 593–611; Rybin, V. A. (1930). Karyologische Untersuchungen am einigen wilden und ein heimischen Kultivierten Kartoffeln Amerikas. *Z. indukt. Abstamm. u. Vererb.*, vol. 53, 313–54. – Ed.

weeds—for that is all the wild potatoes are in these lands—recognized their individual habits, and found that one might suit the conditions of a temperate valley, another that but little below the snow-line in the bleakest *puna*. Whatever our conclusions may be as to the general state of culture, mental and economic of the natives of the sierra, we are at least justified in assuming that pre-Columbian agriculture of Peru had attained a level sufficiently high to justify the assumption that very many generations must have elapsed since the first contact with the potato was made.

The frost-resistant species which we have mentioned and which are those mainly grown at the highest levels are insipid or bitter and are to-day reserved for the manufacture of *chuño*.

In order to enjoy palatable potatoes, the peasant to-day, as probably his forefathers for many centuries before him, cultivated other varieties, some closely akin to our own, and these were naturally given the more favoured locations. This may be regarded as the second stage in the evolution of the domestic potato.

One variety still grown, which is a great favourite, is *Solanum goniocalyx* or the *Papa amarilla*, a yellow-fleshed sort, of excellent flavour, with the chromosome formula $2n = 24$. We have evidence from the pottery found in the early tombs that this variety, or one very like it, was in use about A.D. 800, if not earlier.[1] This, again, must be regarded as a case of conscious selection, for the common potato of the Andes has the chromosome formula $2n = 48$. Of this type, the cultivated *Solanum andigenum* potato, there are some hundreds of varieties grown by native agriculturists to-day, differing one from another, as do our own at home, in colour, shape, season and taste. Mrs Clarence Woods, in her entertaining book, *High Spots on the Andes*, tells how recently at La Paz, at the Potato Fair, eighty-nine named varieties were exhibited, which illustrates the horticultural skill of the native cultivators no less than the great importance of the potato in their country. Because dependence on the potato led to outstanding improvements in its cultivation, we must not shut our eyes to the danger which such dependence on an easily raised staple crop may bring in its train. As in Ireland, where the peasantry had built up their whole economy on the potato, the blight of 1845 and 1846 brought about its collapse, with untold misery, so on the altiplano, failure of the crop frequently threatened the native with starvation or emigration.

Cieza tells us that the natives of the Collao on the uplands south of Cuzco, where in his day no maize was grown, were happy and contented when the potato harvest was good, but when it was bad their distress was great. The Indian, as we have seen, went far to solve the dilemma by making use of his worst enemy, the frost.

[1] Safford, W. E. (1925). The Potato of Romance and of Reality. *J. Heredity*, vol. XVI, pp. 113–84 and 217–30.

Chuño, a product which neither frost nor cold can injure, is made from potatoes, though the *oca* (*Oxalis tuberosa*) is occasionally treated in the same manner. The method in use to-day is precisely the same as that described by the early chroniclers. Actually the procedure varies somewhat according to the kind of *chuño* required. The potatoes are spread out on the ground and left there during the night to freeze. If they are making *tunta*, or white *chuño*, also called 'moraya', for which *Solanum ajanhuiri* is especially grown, then, before the sun rises, the potatoes are covered with a layer of straw; but if it is the common sort which is desired, they are left uncovered. In either case men, women and children turn out next day and 'tread' the tubers with their bare feet in order to squeeze the water out of them. The potatoes designed for *tunta* will again be covered during the day, the others left exposed to the sun. The whole process is repeated on four or five consecutive days. At the end of the period the ordinary *chuño* is dried off and stored; the *tunta* stock, however, is next put into a shallow pool of water and left for two months, after which it is dried off in the sun. 'Moraya', like the ordinary *chuño*, still retains the shape of the tuber, but it is snow-white and in comparison with the common *chuño*, very light in weight. From it a flour is made, which has been regarded from an early date with great favour by the Spanish housewife.

Throughout the ages, *chuño* has meant as much to the native as bread has to us. No *chupe*, or stew was, or is to-day thinkable without it, nor is a journey undertaken without carrying a supply of it.

But *chuño*, though essentially a product of cold regions, became from the earliest times an article of extensive domestic use in Peru, if we accept the evidence of the ancient tombs as a valid argument. Manufactured in the heights, it was carried down on the backs of the llamas to the lower valleys and to the coastal towns. The convoy which brought the *chuño* from the altiplano, presumably took also the long-stapled wool of the alpaca, and the precious silky fleece of the wild vicuña, all of which would be bartered—as they are still to-day—for maize and manioc, pots, and beautifully woven cloth, in the markets of town and village throughout the land.

Like many another of the gifts of nature or of man's own making, *chuño* acquired an anti-social side to its history directly contact was made between the ancient authoritarian but communist Inca state and the capitalistic economy of the Spaniards. One example may suffice. The silver mines of Potosí, discovered in 1545, were, of course, manned by native workmen, of whom, in the colonial period, untold thousands are said to have perished by reason of their ill-treatment in its deep and dust-laden galleries. These slave-workers were maintained almost exclusively on *chuño*, and bitter is the complaint raised by Cieza de León against the middlemen who swarmed out of Spain, bought *chuño* cheaply from the producer and, after selling it at a high price to the native workers, returned home with their ill-gotten fortunes. Potosí was no exception. Hans Sloane, after his return from the West Indies, informed the Fellows of the Royal Society[1] that this method of 'subsisting' slave labour had been adopted in all the Spanish mines in Peru and elsewhere.

[1] Royal Society, 1693. MSS. Journal, 6 December.

CHAPTER IV

The Inca Period

The Incas were an upland tribe living near the shores of Lake Titicaca, who gradually dominated their neighbours, and eventually established themselves in and around the town of Cuzco. In the course of a few decades this small but aggressive tribe launched out into a series of conquests radiating in all directions from Cuzco, building up an empire which eventually reached from Pasto in the north, to the River Maule in the south, and from the Pacific coastline to the jungles of the Amazon basin.

The Inca regime acted as an integrating force over a period of some 300 years, binding together a large number of states of varying degrees of culture into an imperial federation.

At its head was an autocrat, the Inca, to whom was ascribed an almost divine nature. Not even a federal prince, much less a humble subject, could enter his presence except he bore a burden, often represented symbolically by a roll on his shoulders. To this day no peasant, whatever his or her age, goes forth without some burden on the back, a memorial and a measure of the depth to which servility has cut its way into the unresilient and fatalistic spirit of the Indian.

Over each conquered and annexed province was a chief, usually one of the old reigning family. These and lesser chiefs, with the Inca blood royal, formed an aristocracy whose privileges, doubtless great as compared with those of the peasant, were, nevertheless, strictly limited by law.

The Inca autocracy from its inception inculcated an association amounting almost to an identification of themselves with the 'Sun', the chief of the pantheon and the pivotal point of their religious system. The Sun, through its earthly representative the priesthood, the head of whom was always a near relation of the reigning Inca, had a lien on one-third of the produce of all the land.

A vast number of the female population were segregated at an early age in convents for the service of the Inca and the Sun. From these were selected the Inca's own harem, as well as those ladies he presented to members of his family and others. In addition to this service, they wove the rich garments of the court, great collections of which were maintained in the government storehouses.

War and peace, the promulgation of laws, the control of public works, such as roads, temples, fortresses and the like, were all in the hands of the Inca. The executive was centralized in each province, which, in turn, was subject to supervision by higher imperial controllers from the capital.

An interesting custom, apparently invented by the Inca rulers, was that which provided that groups of natives called 'Mitimaes', taken from the more settled portion of the empire, were removed into those newly acquired, in exchange for a corresponding group of the conquered people. Like the planters in Ireland, they were intended to afford an element of loyalty, acting as foci from which Inca law and custom might radiate. Cieza was greatly impressed by this system and states how, by its means, barter of agricultural products was established, allowing the natives of the highland, who lived so largely on the potato, to obtain from their kindred, who had been settled in the lower valleys, supplies of maize and coca in exchange.

The Peruvians had no system of writing, but had developed a remarkable method of recording statistical information by means of an arrangement of knotted strings, called the 'Quipu' which Dietschy[1] states was constructed on a decimal system. Whether the passion for statistics begat the 'Quipu', or vice versa, would be a problem of interest, but however that may be, by means of the 'Quipu' the Inca converted his empire into a marvel of mathematically ordered and controlled well-being, over which ruled a horde of statisticians. The shepherds still use the 'Quipu' to keep count of their flocks.[2]

Law was brought to the people by judges, to whom no discretion of judgement was allowed, and who stood to lose their heads as readily as did the victims of their mechanical sentences, were they to deviate either from the path of statistical jurisprudence or, it is only fair to add, that of honesty. Punishment was prompt and severe, not to say brutal. Baudin[3] has drawn an interesting picture of the statistically run state, and has shown how closely its better aspects approximated, at least in intention, to the normal socialistic methods of an efficient modern government such as we enjoy to-day in England.

In such a system centralized control is brought into harmony with local and municipal independence. In the Inca empire, however, the former was for ever growing at the expense of the latter, a fault which did much to bring about the collapse of the empire.

The government of the Inca developed, nearly a thousand years ago, much of the social machinery which we are apt to think was created by Communist Russia, though in spirit it was more akin to Fascism.

Below the Inca class, all were equal; there were no slaves in the ordinarily accepted sense of the word; there was no money, no buying

[1] Dietschy. Die Heilkunst in Alten Peru. *Ciba Zeitsch.* pp. 1990–2017.
[2] A similar device was in use in China in the 4th century B.C.
[3] Baudin, L. (1929). *C.R. l'Acad. Sci. Morales et Politiques*, p. 445.

or selling, but controlled exchange and barter. All able-bodied people had to work, and adequate provision was made for the infirm and old. Marriages were controlled by the state. There were no taxes, but every man paid by service on the lands of the Inca and the Sun so much of his time as was ordained.

There were no famines, so at least it was claimed, for in every district were built great statistically controlled storehouses, and the excess of one district made good the deficiencies of another. Moreover, there were accurate statistics as to the number of the population, the size of their flocks, the area and output of their lands.

The central Incan authorities controlled the division of the land amongst the people, and under their control the vast system of terraces, the marvellously constructed irrigation canals, the recovered alluvial fields of the temperate valleys, and the system of roads from end to end of the empire were designed and developed.

If a war of conquest, or the suppression of revolt were on foot, all was prepared, we are told, 'to the last button'; the storehouses were filled with the necessary clothes, weapons and dried foods: potato, *chuño*, maize and *charqui*.[1] Were not the 'Quipu' records all filed at headquarters?

The picture of the Inca governmental system which I have attempted to sketch will be recognized as one of an autocracy of a fascist type which, like those of to-day, stole its fires from the communists. But the picture is not complete; the statistically and logically designed state which has been described was but an imposing facade on a primitive peasant communism which had existed since time immemorial and much of which exists to this day.

The people were grouped in small family communities, or 'Ayllus', corporations which held the land in common and distributed it amongst their fellows in a manner not unlike the old English strip system. The subdivision of the land each year probably arose from the necessity of giving the poor soils of the sierra and altiplano a long fallowing. It seems probable that the head of a family may have owned his own small house; otherwise there was no private ownership. It is not to be supposed that the Inca passion for statistical control left the 'Ayllu' untouched. Cieza tells us that the Huancas who lived to the east of Lima cultivated their valley as one piece, but afterwards Inca Huayna Capac marked out the land which was to belong to each lineage. It is probable that this illustrates a common tendency.

All the members cultivated the land in common, and if certain small portions, such as the gardens attached to the dwellings, were personally

---

[1] Vázquez de Espinosa, Antonio (*c.* 1628). Compendium and description of the West Indies. Trans. by C. U. Clark (1942). *Smithsonian Miscell. Collect.* publ. 3646, vol. 102, par. 1339.

owned, the 'Ayllu' made itself responsible for the cultivation of such as belonged to the aged and infirm. This system, with slight modification, persists to-day throughout all the highlands of Peru and Bolivia. The members of the 'Ayllu' display a passionate attachment to their land and have invariably offered the most desperate resistance to those who would dispossess them. The 'Ayllu' has, however, shown itself capable of adaptation, and in many places to-day it conducts co-operative marketing business for the benefit of its members.

Notwithstanding the almost serflike conditions of native labour on the haciendas, when left to his own devices the sierra Indian reverts to his native communist habits of life: as a young Bolivian artist[1] says: 'The Indian does not exist as an individual. He is and feels himself always a member of the community and, isolated, ceases to exist as a person.' Another authority,[2] commenting on the persistence of the prehistoric 'Ayllu', states that 'community members own and work the land in common, perform ritual to ensure their fertility, and struggle jointly to protect them'.

In any case, from pre-Inca days till now, the peasant members of the 'Ayllu' have cultivated their land in common, and the very tools they use are, as we shall see, silent witnesses to the system.

When the shock of the Spanish invasion occurred, a handful of men brought the statistically inspired governmental edifice, like a pack of cards, to the ground. In the matter of a score of years, nothing was left of the centralized government or its methods. Its granaries emptied, its treasure melted and borne away, the aqueducts destroyed, the terraces abandoned, in but a short time nothing material beyond the mighty ruins of temple, palace or fort, remained to bear witness of its great past. Wealth and glory, and the wisdom of the 'Quipu', all vanished before the stranger. Every conceivable injustice was done to the obedient and industrious units of this once statistical state. A population of some ten millions was decimated. Yet amidst all this ruin, the men of the 'Ayllu' and its organization persisted, clinging with a tenacious fury to their poor semi-barren patches of land beneath the eternal snows. These silent patient sons of the soil had not defied nature all through the centuries to be dispossessed by strange demented men, who preferred molten ingots to the beautiful vessels, which the Inca's skilled artificers had contrived, and who actually imagined that a small piece of gold was more to be desired than a handful of maize or a few potatoes when one was hungry. The men of the 'Ayllu' and the newcomers were worlds apart then, and have ever remained so. If man's initial success in winning a footing on the inhospitable Andean highlands may be attributed to the

[1] Goimbra, Gil (c. 1940). Quoted by Linke, op. cit. p. 245.
[2] Linton, Ralph (1945). The Science of Man, p. 299. Colombia Univ. Press.

potato, it is clear that to the culture of the potato the highland peasants of Peru-Bolivia owe that stabilization in their development which has characterized them throughout history, for the potato, by reason of its supreme importance as a foodstuff, dictated in no small measure the rhythm of their life.

The outstanding features of pre-Columbian Peruvian agriculture, as we have seen, were irrigation, terracing, the artificial reclamation of lands, the use of the guano deposits of the coast, and the planned cultivation by colonists of montana districts. All these necessitated or were themselves the outcome of a centralization, which the governmental system was particularly fitted to further. It is when we come down to the actual tillage of the soil that we find the old basic communistic organization still at work.

There was no plough, in the modern sense, in the pre-Conquest days, and llamas were not used to help till the soil or indeed as draught animals. Statements to the contrary have been made, but a re-examination of the data does not support them. The native labourer had as tools a variety of species of wooden spades or digging-sticks (Pl. XVI, fig. 40), some of which were occasionally furnished with a counter-weight at the handle (Pl. XVI, fig. 41), a sharp-pointed stick or dibbler, and stone knives for reaping; but his most efficient tool was the foot-plough, the Quechuan name for which is *chaqui-taclla*, which he uses in the traditional manner to this day. This instrument, made of the tough Quishuar wood of the highlands, is 5 or 6 ft. long, and 2 in. in diameter; the last 9 in. are bent at a slight angle upwards and the end, in the old days, was pointed, hardened by fire, or shod with copper. To-day an iron blade, 9 in. long and 3 in. wide, is fitted. On the shaft above the angle are bound two handle-like projections: the lower is for the foot, the higher for the hand. In the Puno district the grip for the left hand is a long stout pole lashed on to the main staff as in Fig. 46 (p. 48); there is, however, another type, in which the grip is attached lower down, just above the foot-rest. It is the former which is represented in the early seventeenth-century scenes depicted in Figs. 47–49 (Pl. XVII).

The *taclla* plough is driven deep into the soil by a thrust of the foot and the pressure of the hands. The long handle is then pressed downwards and, with a hand on the upper handle, the clod of earth is prised up. In actual practice the *taclla* is never used by one man working alone. It is essentially the working tool of a group. The description of its use by eyewitnesses as far apart in time as O. F. Cook[1] and Garcilaso,[2] who wrote nearly 300 years earlier, is the same. Groups of two to eight men

---

[1] Cook, O. F. (1918). Foot-Plow Agriculture in Peru. *Ann. Rept. Smithsonian Inst.* p. 487.
[2] Garcilaso. Op. cit.

each with his *taclla* work side by side, keeping time by the singing of a chant in which the word *Haylle* ('triumph') is repeated, as they pass down the field. They prise up the earth and, retreating after each united effort, the women and boys who advance in front of them turn the clod over on its back.

That the system still holds is shown by Tschiffely[1] in his account of the native agricultural method in practice at Tupiza in Bolivia about 100 miles south of Potosí; he describes how they all work in unison, singing weird songs the while and, when they have completed the ground of one of the tribe, pass on to that of another, so that the whole work is carried out on a communal basis.

This is probably the earliest example of tillage in which the sod is reversed and, it may be supposed, was devised to kill the coarse grass which covered the lands of the upland heights before planting the potato.

The *taclla* has a long history: it is represented in the Moche pottery. In the British Museum there is a pot which is fashioned to represent the 'business end' of the instrument, which is surmounted by a small corn cob which shows that its use was not confined to the cultivation of the potato. In the Poma de Ayala manuscript[2] there are drawings dating from the opening of the seventeenth century in which are shown the use of the *taclla* by groups of four men, the attendant women who turn the clods and the good wife who brings *chicha* to refresh the workers withal (Pl. XVII, figs. 47–49). In the corner of Fig. 48 (Pl. XVII) are the words:

As the men work they sing
A yau haylli yau—a yau haylli yau
Chai mi coya—chai mi palla.

Haylli is both the cry of the conqueror and that of rejoicing. The last sentence is the only one which has a particular application:

There it is *Coya* (mother)
There it is *Palla* (maiden)

a complimentary greeting to the matron in Fig. 48 as well as to the hunchback girl who is carrying the drink[3] (Pl. XVII, fig. 47).

The foot-plough now in use is rather shorter than that illustrated by Poma de Ayala, and is shod with a pointed iron shoe. Both the handles and the shoe are secured to the shaft by leathern thongs.

Mr E. K. Balls, who took photographs and careful field-notes of natives using the *taclla*, has kindly allowed me to reproduce a photograph

---

[1] Tschiffely, A. F. (1933). *Southern Cross to North Pole Star*, p. 53. Heinemann.
[2] Poma de Ayala, Felipe Guamán (c. 1613). *Neuva Corónica y Buen Gobierno*. Reproduced, Paris, 1936.
[3] Pietschman, Richard. Introduction to Poma de Ayala MSS., *Nueva Corónica*, p. 23.

(Pl. XVI, fig. 43), showing a pair of *taclla* men at work and two women advancing step by step in front of them, turning the great turves as they are prised up by the united efforts of the two men. The final result is to produce alternate ridge and furrow (Fig. 44): in the former, the two grass-covered surfaces of soil and turf are in contact.

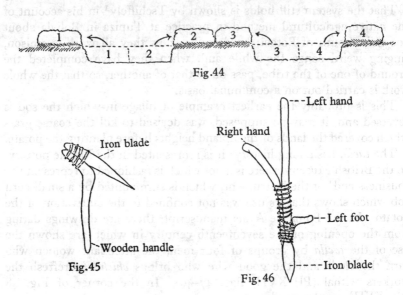

Fig. 44. Diagram showing how the earth is turned by a team of four men digging with the *taclla*. The clods cast up on either side of the two parallel trenches are turned so that the two grass-covered surfaces are in contact.

Fig. 45. A hand axe used for lifting the potato crop; it differs only from that employed in Inca times by the substitution of an iron for a stone blade.

Fig. 46. The *taclla* as in present use; the iron blade replaces the hardened wooden end formerly used.

The next step is for the women to break up the clods with a hand-pick (Fig. 45). In this condition the land is left all the winter. When sowing time comes, the seed tubers are dropped in between the two grass surfaces, which have now rotted down and make a suitable bed. When frost-resisting varieties are used, the ground is opened by the foot-plough, the seed tuber dropped in, and the turf replaced above it; later they are earthed up by raising a turf from either side by the *taclla* and placing it above them.[1]

The *taclla* is mentioned several times by Vazquez[2] who wrote about the same time as Poma de Ayala: he makes no reference to the attendant

[1] Vargas (1936). *El Solanum tuberosum altravés del desenvolvimiento de las actividades humanas*. Doctoral Thesis. Lima. Imprenta del Museo Nacional.

[2] Vázquez de Espinosa, Antonio (*c*. 1628). Op. cit. vol. 102, par. 1727.

PLATE XVI

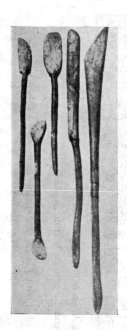

Fig. 40. Early Peruvian digging-sticks.

Fig. 42. *Tacllas* in foreground and 'ploughed' land behind, workers standing by.

Fig. 41. Wooden spade from Nazca, with counterweight.

Fig. 43. Men digging in pairs, with *tacllas*: in front of each pair is a woman who turns the upliftedsod.

PLATE XVII

Digging and harvesting of potatoes in Inca times, from the Poma de Ayala MSS. reproduced by the Institut d'Ethnologie.

Fig. 47. Incan *taclla* diggers with kneeling women who turn the sods, behind a woman bearing *chicha*.

Fig. 48. The diggers are resting whilst being given *chicha*.

Fig. 49. Man raising the potato crop with *taclla*; a woman breaking the clod with a hook, and another carrying the tubers to store.

women who turned over the sods. He notes that the weeding was done with a special stick called *caucanas*.

The *taclla* is now only used in a few districts, notably those in the region of Cuzco, and in the department of Apurimac. Where the potato is cultivated on the high mountain slopes or terraces and in small enclosed spaces, the hand-pick is used. The same tool is employed by the Indian generally for harvesting. This latter instrument was in use at the time of the Spanish occupation as shown by Pl. XVII, fig. 49, reproduced from the early seventeenth-century document already referred to, but in those days it was not supplied, as now, with an iron blade, Fig. 45 (p. 48).

In a later chapter, it will be seen how close a parallel exists both in regard to the tools used, and the method of tillage, between the system of potato cultivation in South America and those which prevailed till recently in Celtic countries.

To-day, as in the sixteenth century, the work of the field is shared between the men and women, though the heavier work with the *taclla* is the man's job. But this does not appear to have been always the case. In the neighbourhood of Quito, Cieza tells us, all the agricultural work was done by the women, whilst, to his disgust, the men were left to weave and sew. In central Peru the transference of field-work to men had already taken place, as we know from Garcilaso.

Frazer[1] points out that whilst in South America generally, agriculture was the women's department, in Peru we see a transitional stage. The ancient custom of relegating the field-work to women finds an explanation in some of the customs to which we have referred, which seem to have their basis in the belief that the generative spirit of the plant is female. That in Peru this important step in social evolution had taken place at an early date is not surprising seeing that its people had developed methods of plant selection and cultivation which entitle them to a high rank amongst the agriculturists of the world.

For the history of Chile south of the River Maule, lat. 35°, we have no pre-Conquest data, and very little for anything north of it. All we know is that the potato was grown and eaten in the Andean regions of north Chile, and that it was cultivated on the eastern side of the Isle of Chiloé, where there are very fertile and well-watered lowlands, as well as on the opposite mainland. We know, further, that in Chiloé in the eighteenth century the natives grew some thirty varieties and raised heavy crops.

No archaeological data bearing on our problem have been reported from Chile, and it is therefore not possible to say how far back the cultivation of the potato goes.

The Chilean tribes were never brought into the Inca system, and at

[1] Frazer, J. G. *Golden Bough* (enlarged edit.), vol. VII, p. 120.

the time of the Spanish incursion they were themselves in the process of evolving a series of more or less democratically controlled local tribal units in which, although there were appointed war chiefs, the individual retained a very considerable degree of independence. The Chilean had no special food problem to solve, such as had the peasant of Peru and Bolivia, and there is no reason to suppose that the potato played as important a part in his life and cultural development as it did in that of his northern neighbour.

Vázquez[1] who wrote in 1628, at a time, it is true, when much of northern Chile had been ravaged by war, states that in the Santiago area, whilst other vegetables were abundant, potatoes were but scantily grown, and around the city of Castro in Chiloé, he tells of much cereal and bean culture, but makes no mention of the potato.

[1] Vázquez de Espinosa. Op. cit. pars. 1936 and 1937.

CHAPTER V

The Potatoes of America and their Relation to the Early European Varieties

In the last chapter it was seen how strongly entrenched the potato had become in the lives of the Inca's subjects, and how the Spanish conquerors had accepted it as a fundamental necessity for the sustenance of the subjugated native population. In succeeding chapters we shall attempt to trace its progress in Europe during the ensuing 300 years. It remains, however, to fill in at least some of the gap between the two epochs of its history as a people's food, the age-long period of its dominance in the New, and the time when it was to become one of the controlling factors in the lives of the people of the Old World.

It is a curious fact that the merits of the potato as a food for the people were not recognized in the rich semi-industrialized western fringe of Europe for the best part of a hundred years. Earlier than that, it is true, one hears from time to time the voice of some far-seeing virtuoso urging its claim as a protection against the ever-recurrent famines of the countryside, or that of the economic adventurer who saw in it a source of cheap food, and hence of cheaper labour.

The records of the potato in the early decades of its settlement in Europe, are at the best scanty, and fail us entirely when we seek to discover its immediate place of origin, or the means by which it reached Europe.

For nearly two and a half centuries it was commonly accepted that the potato had reached England from Virginia, where it was supposed to be native; this unfortunate error was due entirely to the statement made by Gerard in his *Herbal*, to which further reference will be made in chapter VI. It has been generally recognized during the last fifty years, that Virginia, a land in which the potato was entirely unknown in the sixteenth and seventeenth centuries, does not enter the picture.

The more enlightened commentators from the latter half of the nineteenth century onwards, adopted the view that the European potato had been exported from Peru, but from what part, in what year, or how, were matters of conjecture rather than of knowledge. In this unruffled pool of nescience, there was suddenly dropped a bomb whose effect, not unsuspected by its authors, was to seriously shake our honest beliefs no less than our cherished legends, on these points. It did more than disturb our scientific complacency; it gave rise to a flood of research, directed to important problems in relation to the natural history and the adaptive capacities of the plant, many of which had been long neglected, the fruits of which are yet to be garnered.

The bomb was the result of certain conclusions reached by a band of Russian scientists, inspired and led by the eminent geneticist, Vavilov, and presented by Drs S. M. Bukasov and S. W. Juzepczuk.[1] During the years 1925–33 these latter made an exhaustive search of the entire American continent south of the U.S.A., for both wild and cultivated species and varieties of the potato. The feature of their discoveries which concerns us will be best understood if we express the facts underlying the important new knowledge which has been won, in terms of the hereditary structure of the material which they have discovered.

Prior to the Russian expedition, our knowledge of the potato family, or, to speak scientifically, of the genus, was scanty, but by no means negligible. A small number of wild tuber-bearing species was known, but their relation to each other and to our European potato was largely a matter of conjecture. With the advance of the new science of heredity (genetics), it came to be recognized that every variety of living thing, plant or animal, was endowed with a definite apparatus which was primarily concerned with the inheritance of parental characters and their distribution and development in the offspring. In essentials, this apparatus is very much the same in all: the nuclei of the sex cells, i.e. the eggs and sperm, are furnished with a number of elements known as chromosomes which, in the preparation for, and in the process of, fertilization, go through a remarkable and orderly series of movements. These chromosomes are known to contain the organized elements, or genes, which are concerned in bringing about the development, in the fertilized egg, of the structures and properties inherited from the parents. The nuclei of the sex cells of each member of a species have a definite number of such chromosomes, but the nuclei of the cells of the body of the plant or animal, commonly spoken of as somatic cells, which have resulted from the union of the male and female sex cells, have twice as many.

Different species in a family of related plants or animals may, but do not necessarily, have different numbers of chromosomes. If we use the symbol 'n' as expressing the number of chromosomes in the sex cell, then '$2n$' represents that in the ordinary body cells, and if we know, as we now do, the value of 'n' in any particular species of plant or animal, we can go further, and say that it has a somatic chromosome formula: $2n$ = some definite number. We know also that in families of plants and animals, there is a definite minimum basic number of chromosomes, and the different species may be furnished with different multiples of this basic number. In the potato family, this number is 12.

As a result of the Russian work, we now know a large range of potato

[1] See footnote 2, p. 38.

species, whose chromosome formulae fall into one or other of the following series: $2n = 24$; $2n = 36$; $2n = 48$; $2n = 60$; and $2n = 72$.

In its original South American home, several distinct species of potatoes have been cultivated by the natives.[1] Although to-day the great majority of the varieties grown belong to the *Solanum andigenum*[2] species $2n = 48$, Hawkes found that whilst these preponderated in the more northerly parts, in Peru-Bolivia the cultivated sorts were not only more variable but included a larger number of distinct species and varieties of the same. It is obvious that continuous specialization, consequent on man's selection of types yielding the largest crops of the most palatable tubers, a process which has gathered impetus during the last hundred years, has led to an accumulation of *S. andigenum* varieties in Ecuador and Colombia, to the more or less complete exclusion of those derived from other species. On the other hand, these latter still play an important part in the central Peru-Bolivia regions and may be the dominant ones in areas where the environmental conditions demand special consideration. It must, however, be remembered that the distinction between cultivated and wild species was neither in the past, nor is it to-day, a hard and fast one. In the more isolated districts where small-scale native cultivation preponderates, not only are the varieties grown in a particular plot frequently mixed, but all around, and even in the potato fields themselves, 'wild' potatoes occur as weeds, and these are often collected and eaten.[1] Hence one finds examples of the $2n = 24$ and $2n = 36$ species, both as cultivated varieties and as weeds, in many Andean areas, more particularly in the central ones.

The problem is complicated by the fact that in the far-distant past, and to some extent to-day, new species and new varieties have arisen without the direct intervention of man. This has been brought about by several means, as for example, the doubling of the chromosome outfit during meiosis, i.e. the process by which the chromosome number of the germ-cell is reduced by half preparatory to fertilization; by the cross-pollination of species with different chromosome numbers through the agency of insects, and finally by mutation.

It is generally agreed that the evolution of the potato in South America, and the formation of the great variety of species which occur there, took place in relatively recent, i.e. Pleistocene time, and that the foundation species was one with the chromosome formula $2n = 24$. The species *S. stenotomum* $2n = 24$ which is regarded as a possible ancestral type, is to be found cultivated throughout the Andes of Peru and Bolivia, though far more commonly in the central region. By the doubling of its chromosomes, the $2n = 48$ potatoes represented by the species *S. andigenum*,

---

[1] The story of the South American potato varieties has been dealt with in great detail by J. G. Hawkes (1944). Potato Collecting Expeditions in Mexico and South America. ii. *Imp. Bur. Pl. Breed. & Genetics, Cambridge.*

[2] Now known as *S. tuberosum* subsp. *andigena*. – Ed.

were presumably brought into existence. This latter by reason of its bigger crop, and its great plasticity, as evidenced by its innumerable varieties differing, often widely, in their morphological and physiological qualities, has afforded the native cultivators opportunities of which they have made full use, with the result that it is by far the most widely grown species in South America. Nevertheless, S. *andigenum* is, so to speak, a fair-weather plant; highly susceptible to frost and blight (*Phytophthora infestans*): it needs a relatively humid atmosphere, though it does not flourish in marshy ground. Both it and the *Solanum tuberosum* varieties of the Chilean region are unable to maintain themselves as wild plants, even in those parts where they are not exposed to the ravages of virus infection, to which they are both very susceptible.

Some of the more primitive $2n = 24$ species, if possessed of some quality which enables them to hold their own where *S. andigenum* varieties fail, are still actively cultivated. Examples are to be found in *S. ajanhuiri* ($2n = 24$), which is relatively frost-hardy, and is tolerant both of moisture and drought: it is cultivated in the highlands of Bolivia, where its tubers are used for the manufacture of *tunta*, a much sought-after brand of *chuño*. *S. goniocalyx* ($2n = 24$), on the other hand, is susceptible to frost, yields very well, and is esteemed for its eating qualities; it is grown in the high valleys of central Peru. *S. phureja* ($2n = 24$) is grown in the mountain valleys of Bolivia to Colombia at altitudes far lower than most potatoes, viz. from 2,500 to 3,000 ft. It is early and bears a fairly good crop. Another of the $2n = 24$ species which has survived and is grown in Colombia, is *S. Rybini*:[1] its particular merits are that it is an early and, because of its very short dormancy, can be grown twice in the same year.

Hybridization, in nature, between species of the $2n = 24$ and the $2n = 48$ species, has given rise to several new species of the $2n = 36$ type. Most of these are to be found in the central Andean region. The $2n = 24$ parent may have been *S. stenotomum* or a kindred species, but the $2n = 48$ parent has not always been a variety of *S. andigenum*. A distantly related species which is not a member of the section Tuberosa known as *Solanum acaule*, has acted in this capacity. This latter species is a very distinct type: it has a low growing rosette form, and is found both wild and as a weed. At the highest altitudes at which potatoes will grow, i.e. up to 15,000 ft. *S. acaule* is highly resistant to frost, withstanding as much as 8° to 10° C. of frost, equal to a temperature of about 15° F. Though itself economically useless, some of its hybrids with the $2n = 24$ species, which have arisen naturally, are of great importance.

Foremost amongst these is a species known as *S. juzepczukii*, of which there are several varieties. Whether these latter are the consequence of as many different crosses between *S. acaule* and distinct $2n = 24$ varieties, or whether they are all mutational forms from one original hybrid is, in

---

[1] Now classified as part of *S. phureja*. – Ed.

Hawkes's opinion, an open question. These $2n = 36$ species, known to the natives in the pre-Spanish period as Luki, are themselves quite infertile, and their continuity is dependent on vegetative, i.e. tuber proliferation, which, over a long period of centuries, has been effected by man. *S. juzepczukii* is highly resistant to frost, and it is for this reason that it has been cultivated as one of the main sources of food by the natives living on the high Andes, even in the region of 'eternal snow'. The tubers are of a bitter taste, but this is of no matter as they are converted into *chuño*.

S. acaule has most probably been involved in yet another cross which has resulted in the creation of a species with economic value, *S. curtilobum*, having the chromosome formula of a pentaploid, i.e. $2n = 60$. The second parent involved must have been one of the $2n = 48$ class, and there is good reason to think it was one of the *S. andigenum* varieties. *S. curtilobum*, which is grown in the highlands of Peru and Bolivia, is a particularly hardy type displaying a considerable degree of resistance to frost. The tubers of most of its varieties are bitter and are mainly used for *chuño*. It is known in Bolivia as *Ch'oque pitu* and *Poco toro*, and in Peru as *Utucuri* and *China malcco*. This pentaploid type is the only one of its sort to occur either as a wild or cultivated species in South America. In Mexico, wild pentaploids are not very common either.

The Chilean potato area, including that of the Isle of Chiloé, is separated from that of the Andean, which extends from Colombia in the north to the province of Jujuy in Argentina in the south, by snow-covered mountains and the great coastal desert of Atacama, but here all the cultivated potatoes possess the same chromosome formula as the *S. andigenum* varieties of the Andean Region, viz. $2n = 48$.

The Russians have pointed out that there are considerable differences of habit, and some of form, between the Chilean group and the Andean, and that the former closely resemble the European potato, and hence should be given the same specific name, *Solanum tuberosum*. The latter were, in their opinion, quite distinct, and should be looked on as a separate species, to which they gave the name *S. andigenum*. Notwithstanding the distinction between the two species, it was recognized by both Russian and other experts that the two could be freely crossed one by the other; in fact, that there was no trace of any sterility between them, as so commonly occurs between different species of the same genus, in both plant and animal worlds. So strongly did the Russians hold the view of the distinction between the two species of potato, that they declared emphatically, that only from Chile could the European potato have been derived, and that all the tales which connected Drake, Raleigh and other claimants with its introduction from the Spanish Main must, in view of its assured Chilean origin, be regarded as worthless legends.

In 1939 an expedition organized by the Imperial Bureau of Plant Breeding and Genetics, and financed by the United Kingdom, the Dominions, and India, was sent under Mr E. K. Balls to South America, with Dr J. G. Hawkes as the expert on potatoes. A large collection of potato species and varieties resulted, and amongst them a representative collection of cultivated varieties of *S. andigenum* was obtained. Tubers were sent to England and herbarium specimens preserved on the spot. This material, of which I was the curator during the expedition's absence abroad, and of which I have been allowed to make full use, contained about 150 different varieties of *S. andigenum* collected throughout the distribution areas of the species (see Map I, p. 57), at heights from 8,000 to 13,000 ft. An account of the analysis of this material, its variations as regards types of foliage, their distribution and bearing on the problem of the provenance of the European potato, has been published.[1] The conclusions reached have a direct bearing on the question under discussion, and will be briefly referred to.

The Russian authorities never under-estimated the degree of variation in the *S. andigenum* species, but they had not taken any steps to study it in detail. In the paper referred to, an analysis of the collection was made on the basis of the development and character of the leaf. This allows of the recognition of six distinct groups with intergrading forms. Examples of the types are shown in Figs. 50–58. Here it must suffice to point out that the leaves from Group I are small and simple; that those of Group II are somewhat larger and exhibit a greater development of secondary leaflets; Group III includes forms with leaves which are not merely bigger in area but are long and frond-like, with the leaflets mounted on long petiolules or stalks, between which the secondary leaflets are generally well developed. In Group IV we find large leaves built up of leaflets broader than those in the preceding groups, and with large secondary leaflets which are not, however, generally numerous. In Group V are varieties with large more or less polygonal shaped leaves, whose leaflets are broad and often overlap, and whose development of secondary leaflets is generally considerable. The leaves of this latter group cannot be distinguished by any single characteristic, or combination of such from the leaves of the generality of our European domestic varieties. The only feature of the plant which does so differ, is their habit of growth. Owing to the greater number of rather thin and woody secondary stems, and their tendency to fall over, the plants assume a dense and bushy development, which contrasts to a greater or lesser extent with the type of European potato to which we are accustomed, one which has a few strong, thick and rather fleshy upright stems.

Occasionally, however, one finds plants in the *S. andigenum* collection

---

[1] Salaman, R. N. (1946). *J. Linn. Soc. Bot.* vol. LIII, pp. 1–27.

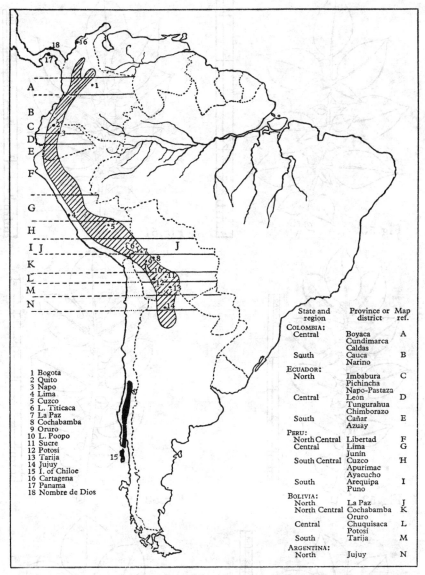

State and region	Province or district	Map ref.
COLOMBIA:		
Central	Boyaca	A
	Cundimarca	
	Caldas	
South	Cauca	B
	Narino	
ECUADOR:		
North	Imbabura	C
	Pichincha	
	Napo-Pastaza	
Central	León	D
	Tungurahua	
	Chimborazo	
South	Cañar	E
	Azuay	
PERU:		
North Central	Libertad	F
Central	Lima	G
	Junín	
South Central	Cuzco	H
	Apurímac	
	Ayacucho	
South	Arequipa	I
	Puno	
BOLIVIA:		
North	La Paz	J
North Central	Cochabamba	K
	Oruro	
Central	Chuquisaca	L
	Potosí	
South	Tarija	M
ARGENTINA:		
North	Jujuy	N

1 Bogota
2 Quito
3 Napo
4 Lima
5 Cuzco
6 L. Titicaca
7 La Paz
8 Cochabamba
9 Oruro
10 L. Poopo
11 Sucre
12 Potosí
13 Tarija
14 Jujuy
15 I. of Chiloe
16 Cartagena
17 Panama
18 Nombre de Dios

Map 1. A map of South America. The hatched portion represents the distribution area of *S. andigenum* corresponding to the 8,000 ft. contour of the Andean range. The blackened portion represents the distribution area, according to Bukasov, of *S. tuberosum* in Chile and Chiloé. The letters A to N refer to the regions in which the collections were made (see text, p. 60). The dotted lines represent State boundaries.

From Salaman, R. N. (1946). *J. Linn. Soc. Bot.* vol. LIII.

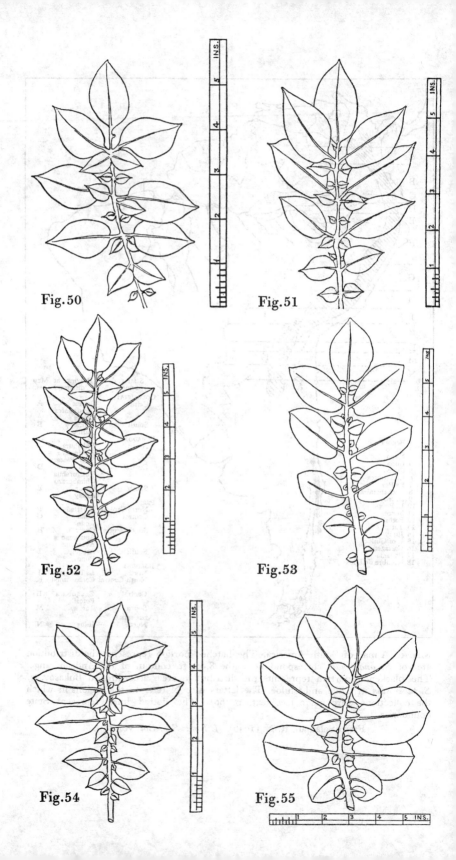

Fig. 50

Fig. 51

Fig. 52

Fig. 53

Fig. 54

Fig. 55

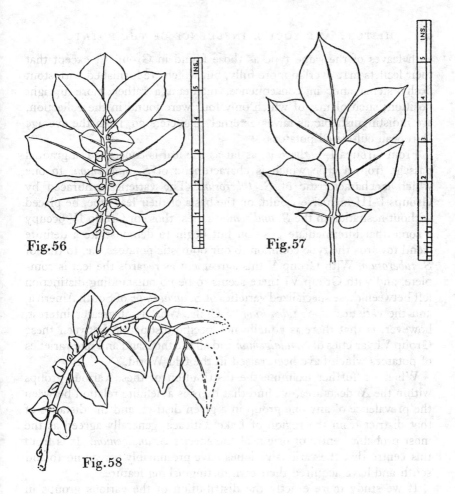

Fig. 56

Fig. 57

Fig. 58

Fig. 50. A variety from Paucartambo, near Cuzco, Peru. An example of Group I type of leaf.

Fig. 51. A variety *Puca Imilla* (red girl), from Cochabamba, Bolivia. An example of the Group II type of leaf.

Fig. 52. A variety *Sabanera*, from Central Colombia. An example of the Group III type of leaf.

Fig. 53. A variety *Arbolona*, from Sota, Boyacá, Colombia. An example of the Group IV type of leaf.

Fig. 54. A variety *Pali*, from Sucre, Bolivia. An example of the Group IV type of leaf.

Fig. 55. A seedling of *Argentina* from Caldera, Cundinamarca, Colombia. An example of the Group V type of leaf.

Fig. 56. A variety *Lanta Mari*, from Puno, Peru. An example of the Group VI type of leaf.

Fig. 57. A seedling of *Abundance × Flourball*, devoid of all secondary leaflets, and exhibiting the completely 'open' leaf.

Fig. 58. A leaf from the reproduction of the aquarelle made in 1589 of the plant grown from tubers sent to Clusius by Philippe de Sivry, 26 January 1588. From the Frontispiece to Roze's *Histoire de la Pomme de Terre*.

with leaves of the same type as those found in Group V, except that their leaflets may overlap more fully, but which are furnished with stout fleshy stems and, in consequence, maintain a rather more upright position; such plants, of which only four were found in the collection, are indistinguishable as far as external characters go, from the average European cultivated potatoes.

From Groups I–V there is, as far as the leaf is concerned, a gradual passage from a type which is characteristic of *S. andigenum*, to one which is characteristic of *S. tuberosum*. The varieties embraced by Groups I–III inclusive would, on the basis of their leaf type, be placed without hesitation in the *S. andigenum* series; those of Group IV occupy a somewhat intermediate position but begin to demonstrate a definite trend towards the type common to our domestic potatoes, i.e. to that of *S. tuberosum*. With Group V this agreement as regards the leaf is complete, and with Group VI there seems to be no outstanding distinction left between these specialized varieties of *S. andigenum* of South America, and the varieties of *S. tuberosum* of Chile. What is of greater interest, however, is that there is equally no specific distinction between these Group VI varieties of *S. andigenum* and all the thousand and one varieties of potatoes which have been raised in the Old World.

When we further examine the distribution of these various groups within the Andean area, we find that there is a definite relation between the prevalence of any one group in a given district, and the distance of that district from the region of Lake Titicaca, generally agreed as the most probable centre of origin of the species *S. andigenum*. It is from this centre that the various varieties have presumably spread north and south and have acquired their own distinguishing features.

If we study more exactly the distribution of the various groups in relation to the regions (A–N, Map I, p. 57) from which they were collected, it will be observed that the early groups are commoner nearer the Titicaca region, and that the higher grades become more common, the further removed they are from it. This distribution is shown graphically in Fig. 59. If we divide the whole collection into two, viz. those of Groups I–III, and those of Groups IV–VI inclusive, i.e. into those whose foliage and habit are admittedly *S. andigenum*-like, and those which are to a varying degree *S. tuberosum*-like, then the relation between plant type and distance from the centre of distribution becomes both obvious and striking, see Fig. 60.

The majority of Groups V and VI types occur in Ecuador and Colombia, some 1,500 miles from Titicaca. Exactly 1,500 miles to the south of the lake, we find in Chile and the Isle of Chiloé another group of potatoes, all of which are claimed by the Russian authorities to be of the *S. tuberosum* type, with leaves which fit into our Groups V–VI. In the Empire Collection there are only a few varieties from Chile, but one, a native variety called 'Pichuna', was found to correspond in all respects to those included in Group IV.

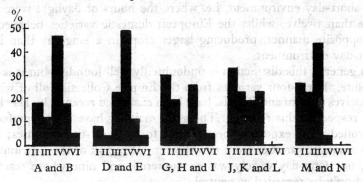

Fig. 59. A graph showing the incidence of the varieties of *S. andigenum* in Groups I–VI in the different regions, whence the Empire Collection acquired them.

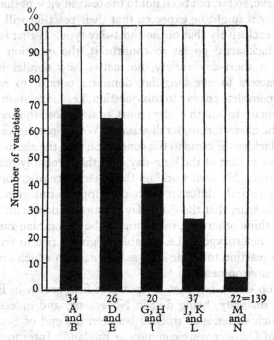

Fig. 60. A graph showing the incidence of the varieties of *S. andigenum* in Groups I–III white, and Groups IV–VI black.

So far, we have only discussed the external or morphological differences and similarities between the *S. andigenum* varieties and those of *S. tuberosum* as represented by the domestic cultivated potatoes, but there are others—physiological ones—which may well be more important. The Russian scientists pointed out that the *S. andigenum* varieties flourished best, and produced a greater crop, in a shorter period, when they grew in a short-day environment, i.e. where the hours of daylight were not more than twelve, whilst the European domestic varieties behaved in the opposite manner, producing larger crops in a long-day than in a short-day environment.

In general, this distinction is undoubtedly well founded, but it is not absolute. Forty-four varieties from the Empire Collection all of which are natives of Peru and Bolivia, have been examined recently by Hawkes[1] with respect to this reaction. The great majority have, under perfectly controlled light exposure, been found to be short-day varieties; but even amongst varieties from this the central region of the distribution area, one long-day variety was encountered, and nine whose reaction could only be regarded as neutral.

The varieties from Ecuador and Colombia included in the Empire Collection have, so far, not been put to the test; in view of their proximity to the equator it might be expected that their reaction will be found to be wellnigh exclusively that of the short-day type. If that is so, and the results of Hackbarth[2] go far to confirm it, the question arises: is it possible for a short-day variety, no matter how similar in regard to foliage characters to our long-day domestic potato, to be its direct ancestor? A complete answer to this question, i.e. the relation of tuberization in the potato to length of day, must await a more thorough genetical analysis of the characters under discussion. We are not, however, without guidance; Hackbarth[2] came to the conclusion that the short-day reaction was dominant to that of the long-day, and that probably more than one gene is involved. My own work[3] on the inheritance of cropping, though arrived at by entirely different methods, supports this view.

If then it is true, that the short-day reaction is dominant and there is no reason to think otherwise, then some of the Colombian varieties might very well be heterozygous, i.e. capable of giving rise to seedlings with a favourable reaction to a long-day, as well such which are adapted to a short-day environment.

There is no doubt but that the potatoes first grown in Europe were of very late maturity, being dug in November; and indeed for a long time only such varieties as ripened between the end of September and the middle of October were common in England. Interpreted from the

[1] Driver, C. M. and Hawkes, J. G. (1943). Photoperiodism in the Potato. *Imp. Bur. Pl. Breed. & Genetics, Cambridge.*

[2] Hackbarth, J. (1935). *Versuche ü. Photoperiode bei Südamerikanischen Kartoffelklonen. Züchter,* vol. VII, pp. 95–104.

[3] Salaman, R. N. (1928). The Inheritance of Cropping in the Potato. *Zeitschrift f. induktive Abstammungs- und Vererbungslehre,* 1928.

standpoint of photoperiodism, this means that the varieties in use were short-day or neutral in their reaction. In support of this, is the fact that in Basutoland, such English varieties as were introduced prior to 1845, have, as might be expected, behaved in their new home as short-day varieties.[1]

That most, if not all, the Chilean varieties, fall into the foliage Group VI, and that at the opposite end of the continent a high proportion of the cultivated varieties fall into the related Groups of IV, V and VI, invites two questions: In what manner did the potato reach Chile, and what are the influences responsible for bringing about this peculiar distribution of potato types? To neither question can we give a completely satisfactory answer, but we are certainly in a better position to-day than we were ten or twelve years ago, to offer a tentative one.

How the potato reached the Chilean area is still an open question. Wight's view[2] that it was brought there by man in the relatively recent Inca times is, as Hawkes[3] has shown, unlikely, seeing that the Araucanian name for a potato, *Pogni*, differs completely from either the Quechuan *papa* used by the Incas, or the old Aymara term *choque*. Hawkes thinks, and I fully agree with him, that the forty-eight chromosome potato of the Chilean region was introduced by man long before, possibly thousands of years before, the Inca period, and that it there underwent a process of selection in regard to its photoperiodic reaction and cropping capacity, resulting in a high degree of uniformity of its physiological and associated morphological characters. This process was rendered possible by the strict geographical isolation of the district which, cut off by the Atacama desert on the west, and the Andes on the north, could only be approached by high and difficult mountain passes on the east.

Hawkes further points out that, whilst it is almost certain that the original $2n = 48$ *Solanum andigenum* species arose from the doubling of one or more of the $2n = 24$ species in the Lake Titicaca region, such as *S. stenotomum*; in Chile and Chiloé there are no representatives of the $2n = 24$ group of species at all; hence its $2n = 48$ varieties must have been derived from the pool of potato material to the north.

The further question arises as to what were the forces which were responsible for the specific patterns of distribution of the cultivated *S. andigenum* varieties described above, a distribution in which the more *S. tuberosum*-like leaf types represented in Groups IV–VI tend to separate out at either fringe of the distribution area. I have suggested

[1] Plank, J. E. van der (1946). Origin of the first European Potatoes and their Reaction to Length of Day. *Nature, Lond.* (20 April), vol. CLVII, p. 503.

[2] Wight, W. F. (1917). Origin, Introduction and Primitive Culture of the Potato. *Proc. Potato Assoc. America* (1916), pp. 35–52.

[3] Hawkes, J. G. (1944). Potato Collecting Expeditions in Mexico and South America. *Imp. Bur. Pl. Breed. & Genetics*, vol. II. Systematic classification, p. 107.

that the bigger, more developed leaf character of these groups may well have a selection value in both the north and south of the area, because it is better adapted to the heavier rainfall and moister atmosphere encountered in these regions. Hawkes looks to man as the main and perhaps the sole agent responsible for the pattern of distribution and, in support, adduces ample evidence to show that in the past, and to a much greater extent in recent times, cultivators have made a practice of growing these large-leafed types in Colombia and Ecuador because they are better yielders and possess in greater degree than the others the qualities they desire.

Further support for this view is the fact that in certain districts in the north of Ecuador, viz. El Quinche in the Province Pichincha, the true seeds from the berry are sown, the resultant tubers, known as *Papa Chimbale* (berry) are replanted the next season, and the crop then harvested is used for normal consumption. Hawkes, to whom the author is indebted for this information, was informed that a similar practice obtained in the southern parts of Colombia around Pasto.[1]

Whether the peculiar distribution of the types is independent of man, or results from a happy coincidence of man's desires and nature's dictates, the result is the same; a sorting out of a specialized *Solanum tuberosum*-like type of potato at either end of the South-American continent.

We may now turn to consider what were the characters of the original potato introduced into Europe, and from whence did it derive.

In Table I there are set out the characters, so far as they can be ascertained from the accounts which have come down to us, of the potato varieties known and described by botanists and others between the years 1588, the date on which Clusius received his first tubers from the Papal Legate, and 1651, when J. Bauhin's *Historia* was published. It will be seen that four were vigorous growers, the stems often attaining 5 or 6 ft. in length; all tend to sprawl and form a bushy growth. The flower colours are white, heliotrope or purple, all of which are common to the *S. andigenum* varieties.

Of the leaf we learn that the number of primaries was variable, as was the development of secondaries; the latter, however, seem to have been neither numerous nor large enough to attract much attention.

When one turns to the contemporary illustrations of the haulms that have come down to us, it is obvious that the woodcuts of Clusius, Gerard, Bauhin and Parkinson are all schematic and conventionalized, and are of little value from a taxonomic point of view. There is, however, one most important exception. As we shall learn, Clusius received his potato tubers from Phillip de Sivry whilst he was in Vienna but they were grown at Frankfurt-on-Main. In the following year de Sivry sent

[1] No clear evidence in favour of this statement has been found, however. – Ed.

Clusius an aquarelle (Pl. XIX, fig. 63) of a branch of the potato (see chapter VI, p. 90), which is preserved in the Plantin Museum.[1] It is evident that we are dealing here with no conventional figure, but a realistic work of art.

The plant has a stout stem, bearing a long pedicel surmounted by a group of heliotrope flowers, very similar in shape and colour to that found in the variety 'Up-to-date'; attached to the inflorescence is a spherical berry. Three leaves are represented, and although the distal end of the apical leaflet in each case is cut off by the margin of the drawing, the character of the leaf, as a whole, as well as its details, are readily appreciated. A tracing of one of the leaves is reproduced in Fig. 58 (p. 59).

It will be observed that its leaf is composed of four pairs of primary leaflets, between which are two pairs of small, broad, rounded, sessile secondary leaflets. The primary leaflets are rather narrow, and their apical processes scarcely developed. More important is the fact that the primary leaflets are inserted widely apart on the rachis, and that there is no suggestion of overlapping. The whole leaf is long and narrow, and widely 'open', by which is meant that the leaflets, both primary and secondary, fail to fill the space included in the general outline of the leaf as a whole and, in consequence, open spaces are developed on either side of the rachis of the leaf, as well as between the primary leaflets. According to the classificatory scheme here adopted, such a leaf would undoubtedly be placed in Group IV and, as such, differs considerably from the *S. tuberosum* type of leaf to which we are accustomed. Indeed, the leaf bears a strong resemblance to varieties grown in Colombia, such as *Arbolona* in the Boyacá, and *Lizaraza* in the Cundinamarca departments, both of which are included in this group.

That the stem and rachis of Clusius's specimen are represented as short and fleshy, whilst in the majority of *Solanum andigenum* varieties they are thin and rather woody, does not exclude it from the *S. andigenum* species. It is recorded in the field-book of Dr Hawkes that in eight of the *S. andigenum* varieties encountered in this expedition, the growing specimens had remarkably thick stems. Three examples occurred in Group III, four in Group IV, and one in Group VI. Five of the eight come from the northern and one from the southern end of the distri-bution area; the remaining two were found in south-central and southern Bolivia respectively. It would appear that this 'tuberosum-like' feature also tends to be commoner at the periphery of the species' habitat.

When attention is turned to the underground parts of these early

---

[1] I am indebted to Mr Savage, Secretary of the Linnean Society, for permission to reproduce this interesting record. The coloured plate in Roze's *Histoire de Pomme de Terre* is an accurate copy of the original aquarelle.

TABLE I

Author and date of publication	Habit of haulm	Length of stem	Division of leaf	Secondary leaflets	Colour of flower	Shape of tuber	Colour of tuber	Number of tubers	Maturity	Variety
(1) G. Bauhin (1596)	Vigorous, sprawling	Usually 2–3 ft., may be 5–6 ft.	Six or eight primary leaflets, of which one is terminal	Regularly placed between the leaflets, one-sixth the size	Bluish purple, anthers reddish	Irregular, round, knobbly	Brown or reddish black	—	Late	'B'
(2) M. Chmielecius (1596)	Like a spreading shrub	—	Compared with parsnip	—	White	No tubers	—	—	A very late seedling	'A'
(3) J. Gerard (1597)	Sprawling	5–6 ft.	Compared with parsnip	Probably present	Heliotrope	Round to oval, knobbly	Brown, i.e. a dirty white	Many	Main crop	'C'
(4) O. de Serres (1600)	Sprawling	—	Five to seven, one being terminal	—	White	—	Light brown	—	Late	'D'
(5) C. Clusius (1601)	Sprawling	6–7 ft.	Five to seven, one being terminal	Present between the primaries	'Pale purplish', ?heliotrope	Variable, knobbly	Reddish purple	40–50	Late	'D'
(6) J. Hogeland (1601)	—	—	—	—	White	No tubers	—	—	A very late seedling	'D'
(7) G. Bauhin (1620)	Bushy and sprawling	2 ft. 8 in. to 4 ft., sometimes to 6 ft.	Six to eight, one terminal	A pair between each pair of leaflets	Blue or purple with reddish yellow anthers	Very irregular, knobbly	Black or red	40–50	Late	'B' and 'D'
(8) J. Parkinson (1629)	Sprawling	—	Many primary leaflets	Secondaries probably present	Pale bluish purple, dove colour, ?heliotrope	Irregular, knobbly	Light brown	—	—	'A'
(9) R. Dodoens (1644)	Thick	8 ft. or more	Two or three pairs and terminal	Present	Purple upper-surface, whitish under-surface, some white	Small, up to 2 oz. in weight	Red or purple, sometimes purple inside	50 or more	Very late	'D'
(10) J. Bauhin (1651)	—	3 ft. to 4 ft. 6 in. and more	Three pairs	Second and ? tertiary present	Pale to purple, some white	Large, irregular	Black to red	—	—	'B'

(1) Bauhin, G. (1596). *Phytopinax.*
(2) Chmielecius, G. (1596). See Bauhin, G.
(3) Gerard, J. (1597). *The Herbal.*
(4) de Serres, O. (1600). *Théâtre d'Agriculture.*
(5) Clusius, C. (1601). *Rariorum plantarum historia.*
(6) Hogeland, J. (1601). See Clusius.
(7) Bauhin, G. (1620). *Prodromos, etc.*
(8) Parkinson, J. (1629). *Paradisi in Sole, etc.*
(9) Dodoens, R. (1644). *Cruydt Boeck.* (B. Mordtus ed.)
(10) Bauhin, J. (1651). *Historia plantarum, etc.*

potatoes, we find several interesting features which differentiate them, in degree rather than in kind, from present-day European varieties. They are all late, indeed extremely late, varieties; two seedlings amongst them never came to tuberization at all. In the early accounts it is frequently stated that it is desirable to leave the potatoes in the ground till the tops are cut down by frost, which implies that tuberization was generally slow and did not take place until the days grew shorter. In fact, these early varieties were what we now speak of as short-day varieties, and behaved as do all the *S. andigenum* potatoes which grow in our country. It was not till considerably later, that early and maincrop varieties came to be developed in Western Europe.

Another feature of the early sixteenth-century European varieties was the length of their stolons: this is often mentioned in the writings of the period, and is invariably shown in the illustrations. Driver and Hawkes[1] point out that the *S. andigenum* short-day varieties, when grown in a long-day environment, develop long stolons. In Europe breeders have steadily eliminated long-stolon plants, and by so doing have brought their new seedlings into harmony with the correct tuber-bearing reaction necessary for good cropping in their new environment.

All these characters which distinguish the earliest introductions from the potato of to-day were, in fact, the reactions of a short-day plant, doing its best to survive in a long-day environment.

A constant feature of the early introductions is the irregular 'knobbly' appearance of the tubers, and the great depth of their eyes. Both these characters are extremely common to-day amongst the typical *S. andigenum* varieties. The large, smooth, handsome tuber we expect to-day is a relatively recent acquisition which has been obtained by breeders consciously working to that end.

Once the potato was established in Europe, its propagation by tuber was the recognized method of reproduction, but that did not exclude the raising of seedlings by persons specially interested. So soon as this occurred, it is obvious that those seedlings which failed to form tubers would be discarded, and those which did, and whose tubers were of a goodly size and shape, would be selected and grown. In this way, maincrop varieties arose which gradually replaced the very late croppers of the first fifty years. Before very long it must have been obvious that early varieties could, by selection of suitable seedlings, also be secured. Such early selections were undoubtedly based on families raised from naturally self-set seed, and hence the wider variations, which cross fertilization renders possible, did not make their appearance until the potato had won its place in the dietary of the people, and demands for specific types for specific purposes came to be expressed.

[1] Driver, C. M. and Hawkes, J. G. (1943). Op. cit. p. 10.

It might be thought that it would take many generations of breeding, if neither hastened by hybridization nor by purposive selective breeding, to convert a Group IV *S. andigenum* plant, with its appropriate foliage and habit, into one of Groups V and VI, but such is not the case. Some *S. andigenum* varieties when self-fertilized, give rise to families of seedlings which vary widely in respect to their foliage, flower colour and tuber characters, so that a parent belonging to a lower foliage group will, and does, give rise to seedlings which fall into a higher one. Thus, there is no inherent obstacle which would prevent an *S. andigenum* variety of any of the Groups IV–VI, being converted by one or two generations of selective breeding into the European potato which our forefathers got to know in the latter half of the seventeenth century.

An unexpected support for the *S. andigenum* origin of the European potato is to be found in recent work on the nature of 'bolters'.[1] A bolter is a plant which differs from the standard type of the variety to which it belongs, by being about a foot taller than its fellows, flowering much more freely, and by a retarded maturity of both haulm and tubers. The latter are elongated, coarser, and are borne on long stolons. Bolters occur spontaneously in most varieties and in some, e.g. 'Eclipse', they have all but replaced the original type. Evidence is accumulating that bolters are plants which have changed their long-day habit to that of short-day. In other words, the potato in its northern long-day home is continually reverting by somatic mutation to the original short-day type, natural to it in its tropical home.

We must now consider the historical and political data which are relevant to the problem under discussion. The first step is to ascertain as nearly as possible the date of the introduction of the potato in Europe. We are on safe ground in assuming that this took place in Spain, the only country which enjoyed any contact with the western parts of South America between the critical years of 1550 and 1570.

In 1564 Clusius visited Spain for the purpose of describing the rare plants to be found there, and published his results in 1576.[2] In that work there is no mention of the potato. From this we may conclude that it was not there in 1564, and that between then and 1576, its cultivation, if any, must have been but local and insignificant, or it would scarcely have escaped the attention of so careful and industrious a savant as Clusius.

I have, in an earlier publication,[3] told how the potato was being eaten in the wards of the Sangre Hospital at Seville in 1573[4] and,

[1] Hawkes, J. G. (1946). Potato Bolters. *Nature, Lond.* (23 March), vol. CLVII, p. 375.
[2] Clusius, C. (1576). *Rariorum aliquot stirpium per Hispanias observatarum historia.* (Quoted from Laufer: *Field Mus. Nat. Hist.* vol. XXVIII, no. 1, 1938.)
[3] Salaman, R. N. (1936). Masters Lect. *J. Roy. Hort. Soc.* vol. LXII.
[4] Further reference, in more detail to this incident, is to be found in Ch. IX.

assuming, as there is good reason to do, that the stocks were raised locally, then it may be accepted that the potato must have reached Seville at the latest in 1570 and that it must have left South America not later than 1569.

If the Russians are correct in their view that the potato of Europe must have been introduced from the Chilean area, and that a Peru-Bolivian source is unthinkable, then it is necessary to inquire into the possibility of such being effected in 1569, or a year or two earlier.

No journey was made from Chile direct to Europe via the Magellan Straits till 1579, so it could not have come that way, even had Sarmiento not been completely cleared out of stores before he left the Straits. It could not have been taken from south Chile till that part of the country was reached by Mendoza in 1559, when Chiloé was first sighted. This island was not occupied, however, till 1565. From 1559 till 1565 there was ceaseless warfare between Spaniard and Araucanian on the mainland north of Chiloé, and no real progress was made southward although the Spaniards founded the town of Valdivia over 100 miles to the north of Chiloé in 1553. From 1565 onwards their held on the country was tenuous in the extreme, fighting for every inch of land, losing it one day to recover it the next; the war continued till 1568, when, after a disastrous defeat, the Spaniards called a truce which lasted till 1572. In 1570 occurred the great earthquake which destroyed Concepción and most of the southern settlements. From 1572 the fighting was spasmodic, but taken up in earnest again in 1576. After 1576, internecine warfare broke out again, and lasted, off and on, for the next 200 years; but Spain already had the potato growing, and the patients of the Sangre were enjoying them in 1573.

The potato apparently did not appeal to the Spanish conquerors in Chile as a food substitute during Valdivia's leadership, 1541–54. In a letter to Charles V dated 1551, Valdivia mentions the potato as one of the crops grown by the natives, yet when his own forces were in the direst want of food, and the daily ration measured by a few score grains for each man, neither then, nor later when he grew crops of maize and wheat for his army's needs, does he make mention of the potato.

It is not claimed that it was impossible for a man to have put a potato in his pocket in Chiloé and to have brought it back to the more settled country in the north during this period, but it was, to say the least, no very happy time for the *curioso* to roam an enemy country for botanical specimens, especially as he had all the potatoes he needed in the settled hill country around Lima. But assuming that someone did deliberately export potato tubers from the Chiloé region at some date during the critical period we are discussing, how would the journey to Spain have been made?

The tuber would have been harvested in Chiloé in April and forwarded by boat to Lima—when such happened to be available. The sea voyage would take about two weeks. At Lima it would be a thousand chances to one that it got no further, for, from the time of Valdivia's invasion in 1541 till well into the eighteenth century, Chile was regarded as a mere appanage of Peru and had no direct relation, official or commercial, with the outer world; its exports were consigned to the merchants of Lima, where, presumably, they were merged with the produce of Peru. If, however, some tubers did get forwarded after change of ship and only a couple of weeks delay, they would have reached Panamá two weeks later and then would have been carried by porters and mules a three days' journey across the isthmus to Nombre de Dios. The arrival in Nombre de Dios might possibly have taken place as early as the end of June if all the connections had been promptly made. Were a ship ready to start at once, the tuber might be landed at Seville before the end of September; too late, however, to be planted in the same year.

Assuming finally that the precious tuber had been kept as cool as possible during its journey through the tropics, and its long sea voyage through the warm waters of the gulf, and had, on arrival in Spain, been placed in a cool cellar till planting time in April, it would still have been out of the ground for about twelve months, a very long time for a tuber, even under the most favourable conditions.

It is not to be denied, however, that such a tuber might still give rise to a plant capable of yielding some sort of a crop, or a crop might have been raised from the secondary tubers which would have formed on the stolons arising from the outgrowing sprouts; in either case the problem would have been solved. But the chances of the tuber ever surviving such a journey or, indeed, arriving at all in Spain under the prevailing conditions, are so slender as to be scarcely worth considering. Potatoes were regularly exported in sailing ships from Falmouth to Buenos Ayres in 1826[1], but this was an easier, if longer journey.

What then, are the alternatives to a Chilean origin, with its wellnigh insuperable transport difficulties?

Potatoes were an everyday article of commerce and consumption in Lima and the northern ports of Peru and New Granada such as Payta, Tumbez and Buenaventura and, owing to the variety of climatic conditions at any one latitude, they could be grown at practically any time of the year. The journey from Lima to Nombre de Dios could be made in about seventeen days and so arranged that the tubers might be taken on board at once; in this way they could have arrived in Spain in time to be planted in the early summer.

[1] Head, Sir Francis (1826). *Journey across the Pampas, etc.* 4th edit. 1846, p. 162. John Murray: London.

Another, and more likely route is for potatoes to have reached Cartagena in Colombia on the north-west Atlantic coast from the Bogotá district. Already by 1549 a regular route had been opened between this port and the interior, and the journey from Bogotá was accomplished in about twelve days. Every ship which sailed from Nombre de Dios en route for Spain, called at Cartagena and stayed there ten days, to receive the royal revenues and await the Margarita patache. It is possible that potatoes might have been taken on board at Cartagena as ships' stores for the journey home, although this was normally done at the next port, Havana.

The difficulties both of transit and season would, of course, have been surmounted, at one stroke, by any one who had the genius to send home the true seed from the potato-berry, instead of tubers. Such seed might have come from a stray fruit in Chile, Peru, Bolivia or Colombia, and we have no proof that it was not so transmitted. There is, however, very good reason to doubt it. Had the potato come over as true flower seed, it is almost certain that for some time at least this method of propagation would have been pursued as the normal one for growing crops, but of such practice there is no evidence.

Indeed, against such a theory is the fact that neither Clusius nor any of the great herbalists make mention of it. It is true that Clusius sent true seed to his friend Hogelandius, but it will be recalled that the result was not very happy, as the seedling produced no tubers.

It is interesting to compare the date and manner of arrival of the sweet-potato to Europe, with that of the common potato. Specimens of the former were brought over by Columbus to Spain within twelve months of the discovery of Haiti, and may well have been planted in some garden near to the court. From 1493 onwards, the sweet-potato was an invariable ships' store for all vessels coming from Haiti and the west, and in that way must have gained an entry to the districts around the ports of Barcelona, Palos and Bayona. We are on surer ground with regard to a variety of the sweet-potato which was discovered in Darien, imported to Hispaniola some time after 1508 and established in Spain prior to 1516.[1] The potato did not make its appearance in Spain till about thirty-five years after its discovery.

Clearly the delay in regard to our potato must have been on the Pacific, not the Atlantic, side of the route. It is suggested that it was not till the potato could reach an Atlantic port by a land or river route, that its export was undertaken. Such a combination did not occur till the Colombian potato fields were connected to the Atlantic at Cartagena by a service of boats on the Magdalena.

[1] I owe this information to Mr I. H. Burkill, who generously placed at my disposal his manuscript of an unpublished article on the sweet-potato.

The evidence from contemporary history, which demonstrates the well-nigh insuperable difficulties of transporting Chilean potato stocks to Europe, in the period under discussion, thus adds material strength to the views which have been presented here, based on a study of the Andean varieties of to-day, viz. that the potato which reached Europe in the latter half of the sixteenth century might, and possibly did, come from the northern end of the Andean area of distribution of the species *S. andigenum*. We may go further, and say that the most likely port of departure would have been Cartagena, and the most probable source of the seed tubers, the varieties cultivated by the natives near Bogotá, which belong to the Groups IV, V and VI, as described in this chapter.[1]

What may be called the literary arguments against a Chilean origin for the European potato, may be concluded with a reference to the name of the potato in the language of the Araucanian natives of northern Chile and Chiloe. They referred to the bitter wild potato, which has no part in the ancestry of our potato, as *Maglia*, and the edible cultivated potato they called by the borrowed Peruvian name of *Papas*, although the Araucanian name, *Pogni* exists. Moreover, they cultivated the potato, even so late as 1830, when Tschudi visited Chiloé, with a foot-plough which seems not only to have been identical with the Peru-Bolivian *taclla*, but to have been used in a similar manner. It is difficult to dismiss the suggestion that, as man trekked southward, he brought both the potato and the instrument of its cultivation with him.

[1] Further evidence as to the character of the early European potato has recently come to hand, an account of which will be found in Appendix V.

CHAPTER VI

Early Descriptions of the Potato in Europe

Our knowledge of the arrival and the characters of the first potatoes grown in Western Europe is derived from the descriptions of the plant that are to be found in the Herbals of the period. The herbal literature can boast an ancient lineage. During the 2,000 years and more of its existence, it acquired a specific style and a well-defined outlook.

Essentially the Herbal was a hand-book designed for the collector of 'Simples' or individual constituents of the various medicines, or 'Compounds', as these unholy hotch-potches were called. The recipes for these compounds had, through the ages, acquired an ever-increasing complexity. Taking their origin in the common experience of the people, and hallowed by tradition, such medicines were originally decoctions of herbs to which specific properties were often correctly assigned; as the art of medicine became increasingly professional in character, these herbal preparations became more complex, and to them a variety of bizarre accessories were added. It is, in the main, these accessories which the profession has gradually shed during the last 200 years. How grateful we have reason to be, may be recognized when we remember that not a few potions of merit contained some part of a toad, an extract of worms, the dried horn of a deer, and, last but not least, some animal excreta. To these, if the disease and the patient's pocket warranted it, might be added a powdered pearl, some red coral, and even a sapphire or ruby.

But it was the extract of the herb which was, both in theory and fact, the essential ingredient; hence the necessity that layman, doctor and apothecary alike, should be in a position to recognize the medicinal plant they were seeking and be aware of its properties or, as they were called, its 'vertues'. From the earliest times, the Herbal was designed to fulfil these two functions. From the sixteenth century onwards, these dual purposes tended to become increasingly differentiated till they ultimately separated and acquired in their own rights the title and dignity of independent sciences, botany and pharmacology.

Although signs of the separation of the two functions may be recognized throughout the whole herbal literature, yet an apparent synthesis was maintained by the superposition of an impressive cloak of legend, pseudo-philosophy and astrological extravagances, which had accumulated throughout the Middle Ages and from which medicine did not free itself till well into the seventeenth century. Even to-day, medicine displays in the literature, its professional terminology, and its prescriptions, the unmistakable stigmata of its unregenerate past.

The history of the evolution of the Herbal is one of the most fascinating chapters in the bypaths of scientific literature, and it has been fortunate in finding so worthy an interpreter as Mrs Agnes Arber; to her personally, and to her delightful book *Herbals*[1] I am much indebted. The Herbal, so far as it is a description of plants and their uses, can be traced back to the great father of biology, Aristotle (382–322 B.C.); for it was to his pupil Theophrastus (*b.* 370 B.C.), who inherited his library and was nominated his successor, that the first work of the kind has been ascribed.

In its present form the work is entitled *The Enquiry into Plants*. It is thought that it is possibly a compilation from a student's notes of lectures given by Theophrastus, in which he described the plants of Greece and the Mediterranean region. Actually, he subdivided plants according to the character of the locality where they are to be found, and in so doing foreshadowed the modern ecological attitude. The progress of the Herbal was carried a step further by Nicolaus Damascenus, who was in the service of Herod the Great: he combined the work of Aristotle and Theophrastus in a book known as *De Plantis*. His main claim to consideration to-day lies in the fact that his work formed the basis upon which the botanical knowledge acquired during the later Middle Ages was grafted, and thus brought into relation with that which had been garnered in the classical world. The most outstanding figure of this latter age was the famous scholar, Albert of Bollstadt, Bishop of Ratisbon (1193–1280), better known as Albertus Magnus; he composed a botanical treatise *De Vegetabilibus* about 1256. Albertus regarded, even by those who, like Roger Bacon, disagreed with him, as the greatest scholar of his age, devoted himself to the task of incorporating the teaching of Aristotle into the general religious and philosophic thought of his day. Although he had original and valuable ideas on the morphology of plants, his influence on the progress of botany as a science, no less than that on medicine, was hampered by his rigid adherence to the Aristotelian attitude on the subject which, as Mrs Arber points out, 'suffered from one serious handicap—an inadequate basis of actual fact'. But that was not the only influence which hampered medicine; still stronger fetters, golden fetters though they may have been in their day, had been wrought for the enslavement of both medieval and renaissance botanical knowledge, as well as for applied medicine, by virtue of the remarkable work of a Greek scientist at the beginning of our era.

During the first century A.D., there flourished a certain Pedanios Dioscorides who, born in Asia Minor, had travelled widely in the Mediterranean region, probably in the capacity of an army doctor. He

---

[1] Arber, Agnes (1938). *Herbals*. Cambridge University Press.

compiled a great work known as *De Materia Medica Libri Quinque,* in which he described about 500 species of plants. A sixth-century manuscript copy of this work, with numerous and remarkably accurate drawings of plants, thought by Dr Charles Singer to be early copies of contemporary originals, was, before the war, extant in Vienna. Dioscorides's work became the basis on which all subsequent Herbals were founded, whilst his conclusions as to the uses of herbs as medicines were accepted as valid and, indeed, incontrovertible for the next 1,600 years.

During the Dark Ages, the early sources were relatively few, and were accessible only in Latin translations which had been made generally from the Arabic. The Greek tradition had been preserved through the Dark Ages by Arabic and Jewish scholars of the Near and Middle East, but it was not till after the thirteenth century that the translations made by these scholars and the study of the ancient Greek philosophers in the original, created that interest in travel and that passion for the literature of antiquity which ushered in the Renaissance. At the same time, the development of printing, together with the new art of illustration by means of woodcuts, powerfully reinforced the activity of the learned, and awakened the latent intellectual appetite of the rising middle classes. These forces, in turn, reacted on the further development of the Herbal. In the fifteenth century, herbal literature took on a new and vigorous growth: old manuscripts were recovered, rewritten and printed; such were the *Herbarium* of Apuleius Platonicus, probably of the fifth century, the Latin *Herbarius* (1484), the German *Herbarius* (1485) and, derived from this, the *Hortus sanitatis* (1491). In all of these the virtues of the plants were evaluated on the basis of the theory laid down by the ancients and incorporated into medicine by Hippocrates. The theory maintained that there exist four elements and four principles of nature, from which all matter, including living organisms, were created. The elements were fire, air, water, earth, and these were qualified by the four principles hot, cold, dry, moist. To these Hippocrates added the four correlated humours of living bodies, viz. blood, yellow bile, black bile and phlegm. In the early English *Herbal* known as *The Grete Herball* (1526), which was a translation from the French *Le Grand Herbier* (1500), itself a version of the *Hortus sanitatis*, we find this philosophy in full swing. Mrs Arber has reproduced an interesting passage from the Herbal which illustrates this point and the scholastic attitude of the times which dogged the progress of medicine for nearly another 300 years. It reads as follows:

Considering the great goodness of Almighty God, creator of heaven and earth, and all things therein comprehended to whom be eternal laud and praise....

Considering the course and nature of the four elements and qualities whereto the nature of man is inclined, out of the which elements issueth divers qualities infirmities and diseases in the corporate body of man, but God of his goodness that is creator of all things hath ordained for mankind (which he hath created in his own likeness) for the great and tender love which he hath unto him to whom all things earthly he hath ordained to be obedient for the sustentation and health of his loving creature mankind which is only made equally of the four elements and qualities of the same, and when any of these four abound or hath more dominion, the one than the other it constrains the body of man to great infirmities or diseases, for the which the eternal God has given of his abundant grace, vertues in all manner of herbs to cure and heal all manner of sickness or infirmities to him befalling through the influent course of the four elements beforesaid, and of the corruptions and venomous airs contrary to the health of man. Also of unwholesome meats or drinks, or wholesome meats or drinks taken intemperately which are called surfeits that bring a man soon to great diseases or sickness, which diseases are too numerous and impossible to be rehearsed, and fortune as well in villages where as neither surgeons nor physicians be dwelling nigh by many a mile, as it does in good towns where they be ready to hand. Wherefore brotherly love compelleth me to write through the gifts of the Holy Ghost showing and informing how man may be helped with green herbs of the garden and weeds of the fields as well as by costly recipes of the apothecaries prepared.[1]

As Mrs Arber points out, the whole atmosphere of the *Herbal* is thoroughly medieval and she suggests it may be no coincidence that one finds so many prescriptions against melancholy in its pages, no uncertain measure, she thinks, of the miserable condition of life in those days.

On the other hand, it is only fair to state that merriment could apparently be as readily induced:

Take four leaves and four roots of Vervein (Verbena) in wine, then sprinkle the wine all about the house where the eating is and they shall be all merry;

and to ensure domestic harmony, one should place the lesser Mugwort (*Artemesia vulgaris*) under the door of the house whereby 'man nor woman can annoy this house'.

A very considerable advance was made by the group of natural philosophers known as 'The German Fathers of Botany': Brunfels (*d.* 1534), Bock (1498–1554), Fuchs (1501–66) and Cordus (1515–44), scholarly writers who, though basing their work firmly on the older Herbals, from which they reproduced much of the traditional myth, did introduce many original and accurate descriptions of plants and illustrated them with much greater accuracy than their more immediate predecessors had done. Nevertheless, their horizon was still limited by the *Flora* of Dioscorides.

One of the most outstanding botanists of his day, who, in his commentary on Dioscorides embodied all the known information on plants, was Pierandrea Mattioli, known as Matthiolus (1501–77). His work came

---

[1] The spelling is modernized by R.N.S.

to be accepted as the standard of descriptive botany by all subsequent authors till Gaspard Bauhin, to be followed nearly a hundred years later by Ray's *Historia Generalis Plantarum* (1686), opened up the new era of systematic botany.

Another of the botanical masters of the period, whose work *Cruyde-boeck* indirectly impinges on our subject, is Rembert Dodoens (1517–85), a Belgian physician: his books were published by the famous house of Plantin in Antwerp. Dodoens was translated into French by Charles de l'Écluse, of whom we shall have more to say directly, and into English by Henry Lyte in 1578.

As the object in sketching the history of the Herbal has been to bring those herbalists who first described the potato, into correct perspective, mention must be made of Jacob Bergzabern (?1520–90), better known as Tabernaemontanus, a pupil of Brunfels, who published a Herbal known as the *Neuw Kreuterbuch* (1588), for it is the woodcuts from his book which were employed by Gerard for his Herbal.

We have now reached that point in the history of the Herbal when we might hope to find some record of the potato in Western Europe. Yet the one book in which one could with good reason have expected to find this is curiously silent. I refer to the work of Nicolas Monardes[1] (1493–1588) on the animals, plants, medicinal and others, which had been introduced from the Americas to Europe. This was first published in 1569 and 1571 and again in 1574. In none of the editions is there any reference to the potato. Mention, too, must be made of William Turner[2] (d. 1568), a physician and divine who is generally regarded as the father of British botany. He published his Herbal in parts between 1551 and 1562. Although he had travelled extensively in Europe, had studied medicine at Ferrara and Bologna, he appears never to have encountered the potato. Nor is it likely that it was even known to him as a rare luxury, for as personal physician to Protector Somerset he would assuredly have encountered it and have recorded the fact.

Turner thus provides us with a datum line before which we may be reasonably certain that the potato was unknown in Europe.

At this stage it will be best to pursue a chronological order, rather than one in accord with the originality or importance of the author's contribution, keeping in mind, however, that even in the opening years of the seventeenth century, the Herbal writers were still largely under the spell of the traditional atmosphere of their profession.

The first recorded mention of the potato in print that we know of, is that by John Gerard in the *Catalogue* he published in 1596[3] of the plants

---

[1] Monardes, Nicolas (1569, 1571). Trans. by Jhon Frampton, 1577, under the name *Joyfull newes out of the newe founde world....* Tudor Translation Series, 1921.

[2] Turner, William. *The Nature of Herbs* (1551 edit.), and *A New Herbal* (1568 edit.).

[3] Caspar Bauhin also mentioned the potato in his *Phytopinax* in the same year (1596). See p. 84. – Ed.

in the gardens under his control in Holborn which, incidentally, is the earliest known catalogue of growing plants. It is laconic: 'Papus orbiculatus'. In 1599 he produced a second edition, and here we find it entered as 'Papus orbiculatus, Bastard potatoes'. I will not here discuss the nature of the terms used, as the subject of nomenclature is dealt with in another chapter. The next published mention of the potato in England is again to be put to the credit of Gerard: it is to be found in the first edition of his famous *Herball*, published in December 1597, where the potato is given a chapter to itself. In this, Gerard made certain statements as to the original home of the potato which misled historians for the best part of 300 years, in consequence of which he has been subjected to much adverse criticism.

A short sketch of Gerard's life and personality may help to evaluate his responsibility in this matter, as well as his part in the introduction of this *enfant terrible* amongst plants, to the people of the Old World.

John Gerard was born at Nantwich in 1545: he was educated at Willaston, after which he studied medicine and then travelled widely in Europe. Later he was apprenticed as a barber-surgeon and retained his connection with this Livery Company of the City of London all his life, becoming its Master in 1607. For twenty years he maintained his own garden in Holborn, which Wheatley[1] considers to have been at the Holborn corner of Fetter Lane.

In addition to this garden, Gerard controlled two important gardens on behalf of the first Lord Burghley, Elizabeth's Lord High Treasurer. One was in the Strand, and attached to Burghley's residence, Cecil House; the other was at Theobalds, a palace which the second Burghley, the Earl of Salisbury, was forced by James I to exchange for the palace at Hatfield. Whatever may be thought as to Gerard's competence as a scientific botanist, there can be no doubt as to his intense interest in gardening as an art, and in the introduction of new plants from the Americas, though he does not appear to have taken any steps to assist in their distribution throughout the country. Gerard, as we should expect from his training, never lost sight of the medicinal value of herbs, and he persuaded the Barber-Surgeon Company to found a garden of herbs of its own. Under his guidance, a plot of land was selected at Smithfield, but the project was ultimately abandoned.

The origin of Gerard's *Herball*, and its preparation, tells us as much about the author as it does of the book itself. Queen Elizabeth's printer (John Norton, *d.* 1612) commissioned Dr Priest to translate Dodoens' work, *Pemptades*, published 1583, from the Latin into English; this was nearing completion when Priest died, and Gerard acquired the manu-

---

[1] Wheatley, Henry B. (1877). Note on Norden's 1593 Map of London in Furnivall's edit. of Harrison's *Description of England*.

script; how, we do not know. Benjamin Jackson, who produced a critical edition of Gerard's *Catalogue* in 1876, suggests that he deliberately rearranged the text so that it accorded with that of de l'Obel, in order that it should not be recognized as a mere translation of Dodoens. Mathias de l'Obel (1538–1616), who was born at Lille, spent most of the active years of his life in England, where he died. His best known work was the *Stirpium adversaria nova*, commonly referred to as the *Adversaria* (i.e. Memoranda). De l'Obel's contribution to botanical science was his determined effort to introduce an objective classificatory system, and this he did, founding it on the character of the leaf. Norton had provided the illustrations for Priest's projected translation, by purchasing the woodcuts with which Tabernaemontanus had illustrated his *Eicones* (published 1590). With this substantial aid, Gerard set to work, but unfortunately, either through carelessness or ignorance, he ascribed the wrong text to a number of the figures. Before publication, however, James Garnet, an apothecary of London and a friend of Charles de l'Écluse, intervened and, in consequence, John Norton brought in de l'Obel himself to straighten out the muddle. This proceeded for a while till Gerard, becoming impatient, declared that de l'Obel was insufficiently acquainted with English, and that in any case an adequate degree of accuracy had been obtained. This did not interrupt the old friendly relations between the two men for some years, but later de l'Obel wrote in bitter terms of Gerard and accused him of making use of his *Adversaria* without acknowledgement. Gerard's book itself is furnished with a preface and a collection of laudatory letters. The former reads as follows:

To the Courteous and well-willing Readers.

... The drift whereof is a readie introduction to that excellent Art of Simpling, which is neither so base nor contemptible, as (perhaps) the English name may seeme to intimate; but such is it, as altogither has been a studie for the wisest, an exercise for the noblest, a pastime for the best....

Nothing of the kind has been done since Dr Turner's work...after which time Master Lyte a worshipful Gentleman, translated Dodonaeus out of French into English; and since that Doctor Priest, one of our London Colledge, hath (as I heard) translated the last edition of Dodonaeus, which meant to publish the same; but being prevented by death, his translation likewise perished: lastly, my selfe one of the least among many, have presumed to set foorth unto the view of the world, the first fruits of these mine owne labours, which if they be such as may content the reader, I shall think myself well rewarded, otherwise there is no man to be blamed but my selfe to performe so great a work....

From my house in Holburne within the Suburbs of London, this the first of December 1597.

It is obvious from this, that Gerard was well aware of the importance of his subject and had persuaded himself of the originality of 'the first fruits of these mine owne labours'.

Much has been made of the passage concerning Dr Priest and at first sight it certainly appears to be a deliberate attempt to mislead. A somewhat different view of the matter is reached when one turns to the congratulatory letter from St Bredwell, a London physician, which Gerard himself caused to be published in his prefatory pages. After saying how much we owe to those who have recorded the wisdom of the ancients, he proceeds:

Dr Priest, for his translation of so much as Dodonaeus, hath thereby left a tombe for his honourable sepulchre. M. Gerard, coming last, but not the least, hath in many waies accommodated the whole work unto an English Nation: for the Historie of Plants, as it is richly replenished by those five men's labours laied together, so yet could full ill have wanted that new accession he hath made unto it.[1]

Had Gerard been consciously guilty of deliberately and fraudulently filching the fruits of another man's work, he would assuredly have suppressed St Bredwell's letter rather than accord it a prominent place in his introductory pages. It would appear rather to afford evidence of his *naïveté* and vanity, seeing how perfunctory is the praise allotted him, and how full and genuine that bestowed on Priest. Thomas Johnson (*d.* 1644) who edited the second edition 1633, was severely critical of Gerard's treatment of Dr Priest, and flatly accused him of fraud and ignorance.

Looking back over 300 years we may be permitted a more charitable estimate. Gerard was an amateur botanist who lived under the patronage of the most powerful man in England; he had, in consequence, acquired considerable social status, and had adopted the coat of arms belonging to a family of the same name, to which he may have been distantly connected. He is depicted in the portrait which adorns the first edition, as a man of elegance and courtly carriage (Pl. XVIII, fig. 61). That he was vain, is obvious, and I think we shall not be wrong in regarding him as probably inclined to be ostentatious. If it was for such reasons as these that he chose to display his exclusive knowledge of the potato in English circles, by causing his portrait to be executed with a spray of potato foliage with flower and berry in his hand, we have no reason to complain. That he was incorrigibly careless and hence inaccurate, we shall see directly, but I very much doubt whether he was consciously guilty of misleading his readers, for he had so thoroughly misled himself.

---

[1] The five names are given in the margin: Turner, Dodonaeus, Pena, L'Obelius, Tabernaemontanus.

But most of these errors were venial and were corrected in the next edition. Far different has it been with his statement that he had 'received roots hereof from Virginia', a matter to which we shall return.

Gerard's description is preceded by that of the sweet-potato, of which he says 'this plant (which is called by some Sisarum Peruvianum, or Scyrrets of Peru), is generally of us called Potatus or Potatoes'. He then passes to his next chapter (335), which reads as follows:

Potatoes of Virginia: Virginia potatoes hath many hollowe flexible branches trailing uppon the grounde, three square uneven, knotted or kneed in sundrie places at certaine distances; from the which knots cometh foorth one great leafe made of divers leaves, some smaller, & others greater, set togither upon a fat middle rib by couples; of a swart greene colour tending to rednes. The whole leafe resembling those of the Parsnep in taste at the first like grasse, but afterwards sharp and nipping the toong: from the bosome of which leaves come foorth long rounde slender footstalks, whereon do grow very faire and pleasant flowers, made of one entire whole leafe, which is folded or plaited in such strange sort, that it seemeth to be a flower made of sixe sundrie small leaves, which cannot easily be perceived except the same be pulled open. The colour whereof it is hard to expresse. The whole flower is of a light purple colour, stripped down the middle of every folde or welt, with a light shew of yellownes as though purple and yellow were mixed togethir: in the middle of the flower thrusteth foorth a thicke fat pointell, yellow as gold, with a small sharp greene pricke or point in the midst thereof. The fruite succeedeth the flowers, round as a ball, of the bignes of a little bullesse or wild Plum, greene at the first, and blacke when it is ripe; wherein is contained small white seede lesser than those of Mustarde. The roote is thicke, fat and tuberous; not much differing either in shape, colour, or taste from the common Potatoes, saving that the roots hereof are not so great nor long; some of them round as a ball, some ovall or egge fashion, some longer, and others shorter: which knobbie rootes are fastened unto the stalks with an infinite number of threddie strings....

The Place. It groweth naturally in America, where it was first discovered, as reporteth C. Clussius, since which time I have received rootes hereof from Virginia, otherwise called Norembega, which growe and prosper in my garden as in their owne native countrie.

The Time. The leaves thrust foorth of the ground in the beginning of May: the flowers bud foorth in August, the fruite is ripe in September.

The Names. The Indians do call this plant Papus (meaning the roote) by which name also the common Potatoes are called in those Indian countries. We have the name proper unto it mentioned in the title. Bicause it hath not onely the shape and proportion of Potatoes, but also the pleasant taste and vertues of the same, we may call it in English, Potatoes of America, or Virginia.

To this description there is attached a woodcut in the text (see Pl. XVIII, fig. 62). From the woodcut one gets some idea of the character of the tubers; they seem to be for the most part borne on long stolons and to be knobbly, although in the text he describes some as being as round as balls. What the colour of Gerard's tubers were, it is difficult to say. That they were not strongly coloured—deep red or purple—may be taken for granted, for otherwise he would have been sure to mention it. Personally, I think they were of the yellowish brown type we speak of as being 'white', but which the seventeenth-century authors described as 'brown'.

The statement that the stems were flexible and trailed on the ground might arouse the suspicion that his stocks were already infected with mosaic, for that is a common result of the chronic form of the milder types of infection; but such is, I think, excluded by the fact that all the early authors speak of the trailing habit, and most of them of the great length and vigour of the stems, whereas, although the virus-infected potato stem sprawls, yet it is always below the normal length. The condition here described, is very common amongst *Solanum andigenum* varieties from South America, and the same habit occurs very frequently in seedlings of our domestic potatoes. In some cases the sprawling habit is genetic in origin, and pure prostrate varieties can be raised which have, perhaps, some potential value in dry climates.[1]

We turn now to consider Gerard's statement as to the provenance of his potato tubers. All the evidence, including, as we shall see, the personal testimony of Clusius, is that Peru was the native home of the potato. Nevertheless, Gerard says he received them from Virginia. This statement allows of two interpretations, the one that they grew in Virginia and had thence been conveyed to him, a conclusion which is almost inescapable when one remembers the name he proposed for his new plant—'Potatoes of America or Virginia'; the other interpretation being, that the tubers merely came to him via Virginia. If this latter interpretation, which may, in fact, well be the truth, is not what Gerard meant, we must attempt to discover how the confusion came about.

It is not difficult to see how Gerard may have fallen into error. In 1585 Harriott accompanied Sir Richard Grenville on the second expedition to Virginia, or rather to the Island of Roanoke, planned and financed by Sir Walter Raleigh. A year later, Hariot and most of his companions were taken off by Sir Francis Drake and brought back to Plymouth. In 1588 Hariot[2] wrote an account of the Virginia Settlement and the 'commodities there found and to be raysed'. Amongst these, he described three different edible roots under their native Alonquin names—*Openauk*, *Okeepenauk* and *Kaishcucpenauk*. The latter is our Jerusalem

---

[1] Salaman, R. N. and Lesley, J. W. (1920). The Inheritance of an Abnormal Haulm Type. *J. Genetics*, vol. v, no. 1.
[2] Hariot (1588). *A Brief and True Report...etc.* Frankfurt: De Bry, 1590.

artichoke and the second, identified as the truffle-like fungus *Pachyma Fries*,[1] was not favoured by the settlers and only eaten by the natives when other 'bread' was scarce. It is with the first-named root that we are concerned. The description given by Hariot runs: 'a kind of root of round form and of the bignes of walnuts, some far greater, which are found in moist and marish grounds growing many together, one by another, in ropes or as they were fastened with a string. Being boiled or sodden they are very good meat.'

These roots are the well-known *Glycine apios*, a staple food of all native tribes in eastern North America from the Gulf of Mexico to the St Lawrence River. The French likening them to a rosary, called them *Chapelets*. The English spoke of them as Indian potatoes, bog potatoes or ground nuts.

Clusius in his account of the potato (*Solanum tuberosum*) remarks that 'not wholly dissimilar there appear to be those roots which the Virginians named *Openauk*—a perfectly correct and legitimate remark. It may be that Gerard, either in that same year or a little later, had received a tuber of the potato from Clusius or, as is suggested in chapter IX, Harriott may have given him in addition to his Virginian specimens a potato tuber from the cookhouse stores of Drake's ship. In either case he would doubtless have planted both in his Holborn garden. It is probable that the *Glycine apios* or *Apios tuberosa* failed to grow but the plant which flourished was the common potato.[2] This might well have been accepted as one of Harriott's Virginian collection. It is not impossible that Gerard was the more readily confused by his desire to ingratiate himself with Elizabeth by being able to announce that this new food plant, the importance of which he had the good sense to recognize, was the first fruit of the colony which had been established at so great a sacrifice by her favourite Raleigh and named after the Virgin Queen herself.

Unfortunately, Gaspard Bauhin in his *Prodromos*, 1620, made matters worse: he supports Gerard by the statement: 'They were transplanted from the Isle of Virginia to England, then to France and other countries', but adds—'The tubers of this plant are described under the name of *Openauk*, as one learns from the author of its history.'

Roze[3] in a note observes: 'One might almost entertain the suspicion that this statement has been written in bad faith, for G. Bauhin knew

[1] Gray and Trumbull (1877). *Amer. J. Sci.* vol. LXIII, p. 352.

[2] *Glycine apios* has been grown at Kew. It needs a sunny spot and a light sandy soil; it is a climbing plant and a poor yielder compared with the potato. [Salisbury, E. J. (1945). Communicated by letter to R.N.S.]

The Pilgrim Fathers in their first hard winter 'were forced to live on ground nuts', and during colonial days, the Swedes on the Delaware ate them for want of bread. [Winslow. Quoted by Medsger, O. P. (1939). *Edible Wild Plants*, p. 188.]

[3] Roze. Op. cit. p. 97, n.

the *Rariorum plantarum Historia* of Clusius, for his own description recalls in part that of the latter author.' However this may be, through Gerard's lack of precision and Bauhin's blunder it came about that for the next 250 years the honour of being the birthplace of the potato was ascribed to Virginia.

Jackson's complaint that Gerard was 'inaccurate to a degree', will be seen to be justified in this short account of the plant of which he was so proud. He describes the corolla as appearing as if it were made up of 'sixe sundrie small leaves', whereas, it is built up of five such segments. In the woodcut, a flower is shown and it is correctly furnished with a five-lobed corolla, but the flower which he carries in his hand, in the frontispiece portrait, has a six-lobed corolla. The cone of anthers is described in the text as if it were a single indivisible block, whilst in the woodcut it is clearly made up of separate anthers, of which there are apparently six instead of five. As Mrs Arber says, the description may seem vague to a twentieth-century botanist, but it is not to be despised, seeing that Gerard had no knowledge of the function or the relations of the structure he described. That Gerard does not distinguish between the true fibrous roots and the stolons or underground stems on which the tubers are borne, should equally not be held to be a fault, as the distinction had not been recognized by far better men, including Clusius himself. If the most misleading of Gerard's statements is that in which he ascribes a Virginian origin to the potato, that by which he would have us believe that the 'common Potatoes', by which he means the sweet-potato, *Ipomoea batatas*, are known in 'those Indian countries' as *Papas*, is little less so. The sweet-potato was known by its native name of *Camote*, and by its Spanish name of *Batata*. His views as to its virtues are discussed, with those of others, in chapter VII.

Contemporary with Gerard's notice of the potato in the *Catalogue*, is that by Gaspard Bauhin, in his *Phytopinax*, published in 1596. There were two brothers Bauhin, sons of Jean Bauhin of Amiens, who, as Mrs Arber tells us, having adopted the protestant faith as a result of reading the Latin translation of the New Testament by Erasmus, and being, in consequence, exposed to the danger of persecution, removed with his family to Geneva, where the brothers Jean and Gaspard were born. Jean (1541–1612) wrote the *Historia Plantarum Universalis*, which was not published till 1651, when it was edited by Chabrey. To this we shall refer later.

Gaspard Bauhin (1560–1624) was twenty years younger than Jean, and a more distinguished scholar than his brother. Though in his case, too, his main work the *Theatrum Botanicum* was not published during his lifetime, the *Phytopinax* (1596), the *Prodromos Theatri Botanici* (1620), and the *Pinax Theatri Botanici* (1623), were all produced during his life.

The outstanding contributions of Gaspard Bauhin were the creation of a great herbarium of specimen plants, and the development in his *Pinax*, or chart, of a system of nomenclature which, as Mrs Arber says, 'introduced a complete and methodical concordance of the names of plants. It brought order out of chaos, and its author has been held in honour as "legislateur en botanique"'. The *Pinax* did, in fact, form the basis on which Ray, Linnaeus and others, erected the taxonomic structure of modern botany. To us, Gaspard Bauhin's work has a special appeal, for it was he who first gave the potato its botanical name, viz. *Solanum tuberosum esculentum*, the last term of which was omitted by Linnaeus in order to fit it in with his binomial system. In point of fact, Bauhin in the *Phytopinax*, called the potato *Solanum tuberosum*; it was a quarter of a century later, in his *Prodromus*, that he extended the name into *Solanum tuberosum esculentum*.

The chapter in the *Phytopinax* which deals with the potato and is reproduced below, is a translation of Roze's French version of the original Latin:

This plant has a stem which is from one and a half to two coudées long [i.e. about 2 to 3 ft.], which, like that of the tomato, is almost round though striate and slightly hairy, full of juice, green and slightly branched; occasionally it extends to the height of a man and then it is very branched in its growth; such a development does not occur when it is grown in a pot. The leaves are longer than a palm's breadth [more than 4 in.] in length, almost completely hairy, pale green, subdivided into six or eight or more small segments as if they were cut up into separate leaflets, of which one is always terminal. These are oblong and rounded, entire, seldom disposed [exactly] opposite one another and between them one finds interspersed two others one-sixth of the size. The branches commonly divided into two pedicels, each of which supports a number of flowers a few in buds and three or four expanded; they resemble the flowers of the Aubergine, and are large and a bluish purple in colour, and resemble a chalice which remains undivided at its base; they terminate in five pointed lobes, traversed by five yellow lines which appear to divide them into two halves. In the centre one finds four[1] reddish stamens similar to those in the Aubergine. The flowers are followed by round fruits suspended separately, one after the other, from long pedicels like grapes, just as one sees them on the common Morelle[2] but these fruits are bigger, equal in size to a walnut, whilst others are no bigger than hazels; they both display certain smooth grooves as does the tomato. At first green, they become black and when ripe reddish-black and are full of small seeds, flat round and brown, resembling those of Belladona. The root [tuber] is of an irregular round shape; it is either brown or reddish-black, and one digs them up in the winter lest they should rot, so full are they of juice. One puts them in the earth once more in spring: should it happen that one leaves them in the

---

[1] This in the *Prodromus* is corrected to five.
[2] *Morelle vulgaire* = *Solanum nigrum*.

sun, in the springtime they will sprout of themselves. Further, at the base of the stem close to the roots there spring long fibrous radicles on which are borne the very small round roots. The root itself [mother tuber] generally rots when the plant is fully developed.

We have judged it our duty to call this plant *Solanum* by reason of the resemblance of its leaves with that of the tomato, and its flowers with those of the Aubergine, its seed with that of *Solanums*, and because of its strong odour which is common to these latter. I received some of the seed of the plant which is called by some the *Pappas* of the Spanish and by others the *Pappas* of the Indies; sown in our gardens it grows into a sort of branching bush; it did the same in the garden of Dr Martin Chmielecius, with whom it produced a white flower. The illustrious Dr Laurent Scholtz, a physician of Breslau (in whose well-kept garden it was grown) sent to me as a token of our friendship a coloured drawing, but this displayed neither fruit nor tubers.

We have further learnt that this plant is also known under the name of *Tartuffoli*, doubtless because of its tuberous root, seeing that this is the name by which one speaks of Truffles in Italy, where one eats these fruits [i.e. potato tubers] in a similar fashion to truffles.

The tubers of Bauhin's potato are described as brown and reddish-black. It might well be that he had under consideration two distinct varieties; I am inclined to think that, in fact, he was dealing with two seedlings. He tells us that the anthers are reddish; now reddish-black tubers are closely correlated with a dark 'orange' or 'old gold' coloured anther which could be called reddish; whilst blood-red anthers have frequently occurred in such of my cultures where a black-tubered variety called Congo—almost certainly a *Solanum andigenum* type—was introduced. In that case, the brown tubers might be regarded as belonging to a seedling which had not flowered.

The next publication to deal with the potato does not belong to the herbal literature: it is that of the celebrated French agriculturist, Olivier de Serres, who devotes a chapter to the potato in his *Théâtre d'Agriculture et Mesnage des Champs*, published in 1600. Olivier de Serres lived on his estate of Prudel near Villeneuve-de-Berg, a small town in the Vivarais district of Languedoc, a region which to-day forms part of the Department of the Ardèche, and it was there he grew his potatoes. That his observations are trustworthy is apparent from the account itself; he is, however, specially commended by Albrecht von Haller (1708–77), the famous Swiss naturalist, for his simplicity, and for the fact that he wrote of his own personal experience. The chapter dealing with the potato is here translated from the original.[1]

This shrub, called Cartoufle, bears a fruit of the same name comparable to truffles, and is so called by some. It came from Switzerland to the Dauphine,

---

[1] Serres, Olivier de (edit. 1619). *Théâtre a' Agriculture et Mesnage des Champs*, ch. x, livre VI.

a short time ago. The plant only lives for one year, so that it is necessary to renew it each year. One grows it from seed, that is to say by the fruit [tuber] itself, putting it into the ground at the commencement of Spring after the heavy frosts, the moon being on the wane, four fingers breadths deep; it needs good soil, light rather than heavy, well manured and moderately airy. It is desirable to sow it well spaced out as for example three by three feet or four by four feet apart so as to allow room for the branches to grow and be layered. From each tuber there arises a stem which develops many branches, which attain a height of five or six feet, if they are not held back by layering. But for the sake of the fruit, one layers the stem together with all its branches, when they have attained a height of two feet, leaving a few inches free at the ends in order to continue their growth; and one relayers whenever they are fit to do so and continues so to do till the month of August, at which time the shoots cease growing actively and come to making white flowers which are useless from every point of view. The fruits [berries] grow, as do the buds, from the axils of the nodes, like acorns. It [the plant] grows and dies in the earth from whence one recovers it [the tubers], by pulling out the layered branches at the end of the month of September by which time they have attained complete maturity. One keeps them during the winter in sand—in a cool cellar, taking good care that they are out of the way of any rats for they find such food so dainty that if they can get at them, they would eat the lot in no time. Some do not trouble to layer this plant, but let it grow and fruit at its will, harvesting the crop in due season, but the tubers do not do so well in the air as in the ground, thus conforming to the habit of true truffles, which the cartoufle resembles in shape, though not so well in colour, as they are lighter than truffles! The skin not being rough but smooth and moveable. That is the difference between these fruits. As to the taste, the cook so dresses all of them that one can recognize but little difference between them.[1]

The *Théâtre* of de Serres was reprinted in 1805, and edited by Parmentier who claims that the passage refers to the Jerusalem artichoke. The context itself sufficiently disposes of such an interpretation, apart from the fact that the Jerusalem artichoke was not introduced into Europe until about ten years later. Parmentier's influence in the past stood so high on the Continent, that several authorities have been led to share the same erroneous opinion.

The colour of de Serres's tuber was presumably a light brown, or, what potato-growers in England would call 'white'. He says it is lighter than a truffle which, when fresh, is brown, without any red or purple coloration. The further remark that the skin is loose, suggests that the variety must have been very late indeed, seeing that even in the French Midi it was not mature by the end of September.

Following closely on de Serres's account, comes that of Clusius (1526–1609), who devotes a most informative chapter to the potato in

[1] It is of interest that Viviers and Villeneuve are in a district famous for its truffles.

his *Historia* (*Rariorum plantarum historia*), published by Moretus of the Maison Plantin in Antwerp in 1601.

Jules Charles de l'Écluse was born in Arras, and studied at Montpellier under Guillaume Rondelet, where he met many of the most distinguished botanists of the time. The family of l'Écluse were protestants, as were indeed nearly all the botanical writers who have been mentioned, and many paid dearly for their liberty of conscience. The l'Ecluses, in fact, suffered very considerably, losing by confiscation their estates. Jules devoted all his money to helping his father, and was never able to free himself from the burden of poverty or, indeed, of ill health, both of which clung to him throughout his long career, yet neither could ever quench his courage or his passion for work. He travelled widely in Europe, and composed Floras of Spain and Hungary. England he visited several times, and made contact with Sir Philip Sidney and Sir Francis Drake in 1581. It was from the latter that he received some plants, and learnt of more, from the west coast of the New World, about which he published a small book in the following year, but in it the potato finds no place. Mrs Arber says:

De l'Écluse had a reputation for versatility scarcely inferior to that of his contemporary, the 'Admirable' Crichton. In addition to his botanical knowledge, he is credited with an intimate acquaintance with Greek, Latin, Italian, Spanish, Portuguese, French, Flemish, German, law, philosophy, history, cartography, zoology, mineralogy, numismatics and epigraphy. His gift for languages was of great service in the diffusion of botany, for, besides translating the Flemish, he made Latin versions of the Portuguese work of Garcia de Orta, and the Spanish writings of Christoval Acosta and Nicolas Monardes.

Harrison, his contemporary, writing in 1577, of the wonders which the horticulturists of his day had done in perfecting fruits and herbs says:

The chief workman, or as I may call him the founder of this device, is Carolus Clusius, the noble herbarist, whose industry hath wonderfully stirred them up unto this good act. For albeit Matthiolus, Rembert, Lobell, and others have travelled very far in this behalf, yet none hath come near to Clusius, much less gone further in the finding and true descriptions of such herbs as of late are brought to light. I doubt not but if this man were in England but one seven years, he would reveal a number of herbs growing with us, whereof neither physician nor apothecaries as yet have any knowledge.[1]

In this generous appreciation we see that the master was in the main valued for the influence his knowledge would have on medicine; his skill as a botanist was but ancilliary to that end.

Between 1573 and 1587 Clusius served the Emperor Maximilian II in Vienna and was employed in the Imperial gardens. Some time later

[1] Harrison, William (1577). *A Description of England, Britain, etc.*, p. 329. Edit. Frederick Furnivall. New Shakespeare Soc. 1877.

he accepted a professorship in Leyden, and it was there that he composed the *Historia*.

As a scholar and scientist, Clusius was almost in a class apart: his breadth of outlook and his colossal industry raised him above all his contemporaries. As regards knowledge of the potato, it will be seen that in reality he both antedated and far surpassed Gerard; nor was he content to describe a novelty: he did much to spread its culture throughout Europe. To his credit also, is the bulb culture in Holland. Indeed, it was said of him by his friend Marie de Brimen, Princess de Chimay, as Mrs Arber tells us, that he was 'Le père de tous les beaux Jardins de ce pays'.

The description of the potato occurs in Book IV, p. lxxix, of the original 1601 edition of the *Historia*, and is literally translated below from the Latin:

Arachidna Theoph forte Papas Peruanorum.

The root of this new plant, only known a few years ago in Europe, is edible; in my judgement it was unknown to the ancients as will appear from the evidence to be produced.

First a bulb, which is usually sown with us not earlier than April, puts out leaves, within a few days of sowing, black, purplish and hairy, which having opened out, later take on a green colour, five, seven or more growing on the same wing, not very different from the leaves of Raphanus [Horseradish] always in uneven numbers, with other small leaves in between, with the odd one always occupying the end of the wing. The stalk, the thickness of one's thumb,[1] is angular, woolly, five or six cubits in length, with many shoots and divided into many branches which are long and weak and unless sustained with a rod or other means, are bent to the ground by their own weight and scatter themselves far and wide; from the axils of the thick branches there issue angular pedicels a foot long bearing the twelve or more elegant flowers, about one inch or more across, made up of one leaf but so folded that it appears as if it were five distinct leaves; the colour is white to purplish on the outer side and purplish on the inner, with five herbaceous rays coming out from the umbel like a star and with the same number of yellow stamens coming together in a boss, with a greenish style projecting beyond the flowers which give off a scent like the flowers of a Lime tree. Later these develop rounded apples not unlike the fruit of a mandragora but smaller, at first they are green, later white and full of a humid pulp containing numerous small seeds no bigger than those of a fig. It has roots, either a single one or two or three thick and straight ones, going down as far as possible and branching to a certain extent. Then appearing from the extreme end of these roots are others thinner and white, which spread sideways and emerge sometimes above the ground some distance from the mother plant, here they put out leaves or form new plants. These plants have hanging from them long thick fibres and when after the first frosts the plant itself comes out of [the ground] in the month of November,

---

[1] Compare Hawkes's description of some of the *S. andigenum* types with thick stems which he encountered in Colombia.

there are to be found attached tubers of varying but unequal size beset with certain marks [eyes] from which in the following year buds will emerge. Now of the tubers of which I recollect collecting more than fifty from the same stem (so fruitful is it), some are larger so that they weigh one or even two ounces and on the outside their skin is reddish or verging on purple, others are smaller as though not yet matured, and have a skin for the most part white, but which is in all the tubers very thin, whilst the flesh itself is firm and white. Now all these tubers, whether together with the fibres to which they are attached or freed from them, should be laid in an earthenware pot, or other vessel full of dry earth, and put under cover of a roof in the hope of sowing the same in the next year; they can however be kept bare in a dry but warm place; but the roots go rotten if retained in the garden unless in somewhat warmer regions and when dug up, and the earth removed from them, they become dried and are rendered useless. From the tuber alone is the conservation of the race to be expected. I have never made the experiment of raising plants from the seed but I have learnt from others that such have produced flowers in the same season which have differed in colour from those of the mother plant. Certainly my friend the distinguished Johannes Hogelandius wrote to me that stocks he had raised from seed which I had sent him had borne flowers wholly white and that when he had dug them up at the same time as those raised from tubers he discovered that they had formed no tubers, the stocks perhaps being as yet insufficiently matured. I have noticed, however, that the tuber from which the plant had sprung was when dug up, sometimes empty and useless, at other times firm and sound.

It flowers in July and until the autumn, or it may not stop bearing flowers, and fruit right up till the first frosts, by which it is readily damaged.

The first mention which I have received of this plant is from Philippe de Sivry, Lord of Walhain and Prefect of the City of Mons, in Hanovia [Hainault] of Belgium, who sent two tubers with fruit to me in Vienna in Austria towards the beginning of the year 1588, and in the following year he sent me a picture of a branch of it with flowers. [See Pl. XIX, fig. 63.] He wrote that he had received it from a certain friend of the Papal Legate in Belgium under the name of *Taratouffli*. Following that, Jacobus Geratus Junior sent a picture of the whole plant to me at Frankfurt but I did not desire to exhibit either of these here, but rather another which I had made as two woodcuts from the living plant, the one representing the flowers and the fruit, the other the roots and the tubers adhering to their fibres. [See Pl. XIX, fig. 64.]

The Italians do not know whence they first obtained it, but it is certain that they got it either from Spain or America. But it is indeed to be wondered at, that knowledge of the plant has come so late to us, although it was so common and frequent in certain parts of Italy, for it is said that they used to eat the tubers of it cooked with mutton in the same manner as they do with turnips and the roots of carrots. They actually employed it for fodder for pigs.[1] Nevertheless it is still more remarkable that it was unknown at Padua. But

---

[1] I find that in the *Hortus Siccus* (1606) of Gregory of Reggio in Emilia neither sweet nor common potato are included, hence the possibility that Clusius was misinformed. See Druce, G. C., Hist. of Botany, *Pharmaceut. Journ.* 1899, p. 538.

now it has become sufficiently common in many gardens in Germany since it is so fecund.

There is no doubt that it is the same plant which Petrus Cieza describes in Chapter XL of the First Part of his *Chronicle* in the Spanish tongue. I have rendered it thus in Latin [translated]:

In the neighbourhood of Quito besides Maize the inhabitants have two other things with which for the most part they sustain life, namely *Papas* roots, which are almost like truffles though they have no firm envelope and these when cooked have a soft pulp like a cooked chestnut; when dried by the sun they are called *Chuño* and are stored for use. This fruit produces a plant like a poppy, this comparison may be pardoned in a soldier. The other [foodstuff] is *Quinoa*, a plant equal in height to that of a man with leaves like those of the *Blettum mauritanicum* [a species of *Amaranthus* as 'love-lies-a-bleeding'], with a small white or red seed from which they prepare after cooking it a porridge, or else eat it as we do rice.

In certain other works I remember seeing references to it. Augustus Çarate as well as Gomara in his general *History of the Indies,* also mentions *Papas.* From which it likewise appears that the root which the Virginians call *Openauk* is not wholly dissimilar.

Now one must consider whether this plant has been known to the ancients. Theophrastus, Book I, *Hist. Plant,* Cap. XI, gives information concerning Arachidna which seems to me to agree very well with this, especially in relation to the history of the root. For, says he, the Arachidna and that which resembles the *Aracus* bears fruit no smaller than that which is borne on the upper part of the plant and it has one thick fleshy root which goes vertically down, others (on which there are fruits) are thinner at a level of the ground and are scattered widely. But he [Theophrastus] says that neither of them have leaves nor anything akin to leaves but seem to produce, he says, as it were a fruit in both places, which is marvellous.

But I could readily persuade myself that Theophrastus, in considering his subject, has not given the account of each plant with sufficient accuracy. Even in the first chapter of the same book, he places it amongst those plants which bear fruit underground. But let those more skilled than I weigh the matter carefully and it may be that they will come to the same opinion as myself.

Twenty-four years after the appearance of his *Phytopinax,* the younger brother, Gaspard, published his *Prodromos Theatri Botanici* and under the caption *Solanum Tuberosum Esculentum* he wrote as follows [translated from the Latin]:

This plant has a stalk which may be two or three cubits in height more rarely rising to that of a man, it is thick, angular, furrowed, lightly hairy, bushy with many weak branches which lean down to the ground unless held up by a support. From the axils there issue pedicels, which are short and angular and bear flowers; the leaves, which are at first produced, are akin to those of Berbaria [Winter-cress or Yellow Rocket] as the figure illustrating all parts of the plant which I have supplied to my edition of Matthiolus'

Commentaries as well as to this book clearly shows; they are blackish purple and almost covered with hairs. The other leaves [later ones] are pale green, arising from a pedicel a span [length of the hand] long; it is divided into six to eight parts, more or less, which hang down from the one [central] rib, they are rounded oblong and symmetrical, between each [pair] is interposed six times, the smaller [leaflets], and always a single segment is added to the end of the leaf, a seventh or ninth larger than the rest. The flowers are elegant, on the outer side white to purple, on the inner purple or blue. (In Austria they are said to occur with double flowers), ten, twelve or more in a bunch, some closed and fewer open. They are large and similar to that of the *Malum Insanum* [egg-plant] composed of a single leaf [furnished] with five angles and five lines or rays of a yellowish green which run outwards the whole length. From the middle projects the small reddish or yellow stamens usually five in number, with a greenish style protruding. These flowers give rise to an odour resembling that of *Tilia* [Lime]. Following on these, are rounded fruits, several clustered together hanging down from a long pedicel as in *Solanum vulgare* [*S. nigrum*] some of which are as big as walnuts, others as hazels. Others which are smaller and miniature are blackish green; when mature they [the berries] become black and reddish or more rarely white streaked, and are filled with a damp white pulp filled with numerous seeds, small, flat, somewhat rounded and of the shape of those of *Solanum somniferum fecundum* [Belladona].

The root is tuberous, these are sometimes the size of one's fist, sometimes they are oblong and at others very small, more rarely shaped as a single membrum virilis [penis], the surface is uneven with numerous marks [eyes] from which buds will emerge in the following year. They are covered with dark skin which may be black or red, the marrow or flesh is firm and white: sometimes when the tuber from which the plant grew is dug up, it is found to be flabby and useless. [Pl. XX, fig. 66.]

At the base of the stalk are many fibrous roots, oblong white and scattered through the earth, sometimes going deep down; on these the tuberous roots [tubers] are borne so that when the plant has been dug up towards winter, we have observed more than forty (others have noted as many as fifty) tubers of different size which many people dig up so that they may not rot through the winter, and store them in a dry but somewhat warm place, others put them in a vessel full of dry earth and in springtime again commit them to the earth. The Burgundians have the habit of bending down branches and covering them with soil in order to make buds and thus acquire more tubers. They flower with us in June and often continue till autumn, they are damaged by the first frosts. The plant was brought from the Island of Virginia to Britain, thence to France and other regions.

The roots are called *Openauck* in Virginia as the author of its history [Clusius] tells in his *History*.

Petrus Cieza in his *Chronicle*, and Gomara in his *General History of the Indies*, write that it is called '*Papas*' in places about Quito. Benzoni calls it '*Papa*', and Joseph Acosta in the *History of India*, '*Papas*'; hence it is called *Papus Indorum or Hispanorum*, by Italians it is called *tartoffoli*, a name they also apply to the tubers, by the Germans it is called *Grübblingsbaum*, that is, 'the tree of truffles'.

When in the year 1590 I had received a drawing of the plant in its natural colours from Dr Scholtzius under the name *Papas Hispanorum* and could find it described by nobody, I described it in my *Phytopinax* under the name *Solanum tuberosum*, and in my edition of Matthiolus as *Solanum tuberosum esculentum* with a figure annexed, and I sent this drawing to Dr Clusius. I called it *Solanum* on account of the similarity of its leaves with those of *Lycopersicum* [tomato], of its flowers with that of the unsound apple [*Aubergine*], of its fruits with that of *Solanum vulgare*, and of its seed with almost all the *Solanums*, finally on account of the smell of the whole plant it has a further affinity with the *Solanums*.

Was it known to the ancients? The most noble Cortusus thought it was the same as the *Pycnocomon* of Dioscorides, driven to that opinion by the consideration of Diascorides's text and figure; certainly *Diascorides Pycnocomi* does correspond with it, so far as flower and tuber are concerned, but not so in respect to flower and seed. Clusius, in his *History*, thinks the Arachidna of Theophrastus is its counterpart, but he calls the plant *Papas Peruvianorum*.

It is rather pathetic to watch two such outstanding scholars, as Clusius and Bauhin, struggling against their reason to fit the potato into the accepted scheme of things as laid down by the masters of the classical age. It affords some measure of the persistent strength of medieval tradition that they should even have attempted it, seeing that both knew full well that only in the New World had the potato ever been seen. In their treatment of the 'vertues', all the herbalists of the seventeenth century adhere, as we shall see, more or less closely to the medieval interpretation of natural philosophy.

The history of the potato in England is resumed in 1629, when Parkinson takes up the tale, but prior to that, we find one of those ambiguous references to the potato which occur so often in the early decade of the seventeenth century, and which are difficult to assess correctly. I refer to the remarks of Dr Venner in 1620, chapter XXIII, p. 424.

John Parkinson (1567–1650) was, as Mrs Arber points out, one of the last in the strict lineage of herbalists. Like Gerard, he also cultivated a London garden. His, however, was in Long Acre and he, too, was made herbarist to the Crown. He has left us two works: the first appeared under the title '*Paradisi in Sole Paradisus Terrestris*. A garden of all sorts of pleasant flowers which our English ayre will permitt to be noursed up; together with the right orderinge planting and preserving of them and their uses and Vertues.' He dedicated the book to Queen Henrietta Maria, begging her to accept this, 'the speaking garden'.

Like Gerard, Parkinson was not above adopting the work of others as his own.[1] Dr William Howe, who published in 1665 the *Stirpium* illustrations of Mathias de l'Obel, accuses Parkinson of appropriating l'Obel's observations *en masse*, 'whose volumes', he says, 'were compleat, the Title, the Epistle and Diploma affixed'. He certainly made the fullest use of Bauhin's *Phytopinax*; his book, however, was, as Mrs Arber says, a garden guide rather than a herbal, and it is in this capacity that we find an account of the potato under the heading Kitchen Garden. It runs as follows:

The Potatoes of Virginia, which some foolishly call the apples of youth, is another kinde of plant, differing much from the former [the sweet-potato], saving in the colour and taste of the roots, having many weake and somewhat flexible branches, leaning a little downwards, or easily borne down with the winde or other thing, beset with many winged leaves, of a dark grayish greene colour, whereof divers are smaller and some greater than others; the flower grows many together upon a long stalke, every one severally upon a short foot-stalke, somewhat like the flower of tobacco, for the forme being one whole leaf six cornered at the brimmes but somewhat larger, and of a pale blueish purple colour, or pale dove colour, and in some almost white, with some red threads in the middle, standing about a thicke gold yellow pointele, tipped with greene at the end: after the flowers are past, there come up in their places small round fruit, as big as a Damson or Bullises, greene at the first, and somewhat whiteish afterwards; with many white seeds therein, like unto Nightshade: the rootes are rounder, much smaller than the former [sweet-potato] and some much greater than others, dispersed under ground by many small threads or strings from the roots, of the same light browne colour on the outside and white within, as they, and near of the same taste but not altogether so pleasant.

Parkinson's account is not impressive and seems to have been largely inspired by Gerard, with whom he shares the same error as to a six-pointed corolla; the stigma is not credited with being an independent structure but is simply a tip to the 'pointele' of the anthers which he appears to regard as undivided. When he deals with the uses (see chapter VII), he again seems to be merely reproducing Gerard.

The figure of the potato which Parkinson has left us (Pl. XX, fig. 65), suggests the habit of a tree; it is, in fact, an adaptation of that employed by Gaspard Bauhin in his *Prodromos*. It might be thought that neither had much personal knowledge of the plant, but inasmuch as the same figure appears in the 1656 edition of Parkinson's Herbal, and a very similar one in his *Théâtrum* published in 1640, it would doubtless be an unsafe deduction to make. The tree-like appearance is very probably suggested by the name the potato temporarily acquired in western

---

[1] The *D.N.B.*, Howe, William: states that Howe's attack on Parkinson was vindictive and unfair as Parkinson had paid for the plates.

Germany, *Grübblingsbaum*, or truffle-tree. In the later book, Parkinson only speaks of the uses of various roots in which our potato is included, together with the sweet-potato and the Manihot; he excuses himself from describing them in detail as he says he has already done so in the *Paradisus*. Whether it was indifference or ignorance which delayed his correcting the discrepancies between the description in the text and the appearance in the figure, one can only suppose that gardeners could have had but little acquaintance with or interest in the potato, for otherwise such blunders would have injured his reputation, which we know was not the case.

In 1633 Thomas Johnson (*d.* 1644), a botanist and apothecary, was commissioned by Gerard's publishers to supervise a new edition of his *Herbal*. Although, as Mrs Arber tells us, he improved the Herbal in many ways, he interfered but little with the description of the potato which Gerard had given. He corrects the statement that the corolla was six-pointed; omitting that the colour of the flower is hard to express, he states that it is of a light purple, and instead of describing the tubers as being attached by an 'infinite number' of threads, he substitutes the word 'indefinite'. Johnson's reaffirmation of the flower may possibly be taken as evidence that at the time he was writing he knew of only one variety in England, and that the same as Gerard had described over thirty years before.

The woodcut he uses was derived from l'Obel's *Plantarum seu Stirpium Historia* (1581), the plates of which were subsequently reproduced as an album by Plantin without any text, after they had already been used to illustrate the *Herbals* of Dodoens and Clusius. Hence it is that the illustration to the chapter on the Potato in the second edition of Gerard, is identical with that in the *Historia* of Clusius.

Although Jean Bauhin died in 1612, his *magnum opus*, the *History of Plants*, was not produced till 1651, when Chabraeus edited it. The description of the potato there given is translated from the Latin and runs as follows:

The stems are two to three and even more cubits in height [say 3 ft. to 4 ft. 6 in. and more], somewhat thick, fleshy, rounded, striated, rather hairy, of a green colour with numerous red spots, hollow, branching, uneven owing to the existence of membraneous wings which are often crinkled and may be black or purple in colour and which are continuous from the pedicels of the leaves upwards on the stem. The leaves are a palm and a half in length, composed of three pairs of leaflets and one larger than the rest which closes the leaf [terminal leaflet]; in addition there are single hairy leaflets of irregular origin which do not however distort the leaf which is so much longer than it is wide; they [the leaves] are blackish green and shiny above, below they lack both the glaze and the intensity of green colouring. Other rounded smaller leaflets [folioles] are interposed between each pair almost as is seen in *Lentus* [Lentil] or *Lupinus* which are equally irregular both in their place of origin and their distribution. The branching stems give rise to smaller ones and these to pedicels which are numerous and hairy and articulated to such an extent that the upper part with its flower can easily or spontaneously fall. Each plant consists of a green calyx of five divisions [from which issues a corolla] equal in size to the larger flowers of the *Malva sylvestris* [common mallow]; on the outside they are somewhat pale and hairy but on the inside they are pale to purple, sometimes white, all [the flowers are] in one piece with five blunt apical processes on the circumference; in the centre there is a green style surrounded by five yellow fibres [anthers]. Towards each apical process there runs a green ray. I have observed that out of the same [central] region of the flower may arise certain smaller leaves of the same colour as the flower which suggest that Nature is laying down the rudiments of a double flower.

An equal number of berries succeed the flowers, each with the circumference of a chestnut, but spherical, blackish green, and containing many small smooth seeds like those of the *Solanums*.

The root is bulbous, thick, the length of a palm to a palm and a half [4–6 in.], others are of much less size, on the outer side they are black to red, on the inside pale or white; one tuber may put forward [give rise to] many branches and send out many fibres [stolons] from which may hang other tubers both large and small. They are insipid. The plant extends and propagates itself freely. [Pl. XX, fig. 67.]

Bengo says there is a kind of root amongst the Peruvians which they call *Pape*—it is a kind of truffle of little taste. Concerning it Thomas Henreiotus [Hariot] says the *Openauk* is a root common to Virginia; they are round, hang together like knots [on a string]; and when cooked are fit for food. But Peter Cieza says of the roots called *Papas* that when cooked they have a tender flesh like boiled chestnuts; when dried in the sun they are known as *Chuño*.

In the mountain ranges of Peru (Lib. I, de rar. var. Ch. III), J. Cardon (1557) says: Papas is a kind of tuber which they use for bread, it is produced in the earth, thanks to the universal wisdom of nature; they are dried and then called *Chuño*, and certain men have enriched themselves by this sole merchandise of bringing it to the province of Potossi.

This root has as they say a green top like *Argemone* [prickly poppy]; in form like a chestnut but more pleasant to the taste. It is also found amongst other nations of the Archipelago and equally among the inhabitants of the province of Quito.

Bauhin ends his account by quoting from Clusius and enters a caveat against calling the potato a *Grübblingsbaum* or tree of tubers, and expresses his opinion that the tuberous roots which were prohibited by the Burgundians (see chapter VII), differ very much from either the *Papas Americanus* or his own *Solanum tuberosum esculentum*.

Jean Bauhin's description is of particular interest because it shows that his editor had acquired an increased acquaintance with the potato as a garden plant since Gaspard Bauhin described it in 1596. It is possible that he was conversant with three varieties, one with blue-purple flower and dark purple tubers, another with pale bluish purple or heliotrope flower and red tubers, and a third with white flowers and presumably red tubers; his remark that the flower may be white is evidence that his cultures contained more than one variety.

Another point of interest is the reference to the abscission of the flower buds, a feature common to our potatoes to-day, but which is here mentioned for the first time.[1] This, together with the larger size of the tubers, may indicate perhaps that selection for better crops was already taking place.

Here, too, we find for the first time a description of the calyx, and more exact details in regard to the disposition of the folioles.

Gerard's blunder in regard to the Virginian origin is seen to be casting its shadow forward, although Bauhin has not himself fallen into the trap, yet he is prepared to see a relationship founded rather in a community of use than botanical affinity, between the potato and Hariot's Virginian *Openauk*. He creates, however, a new difficulty when he talks of a root with a top like *Argemone*, which is common both to Quito and the Archipelago, by which he presumably refers to Haiti and Cuba. In these latter places, we have no evidence that the potato proper was grown, and indeed it is extremely unlikely that it would prosper there sufficiently to make it a food for the 'nations' of those parts.

With this, the formal description of the potato as a botanical novelty may be said to have come to an end, but before the century closed, there are a few more references to it which are of interest.

John Tradescant, junior (1608–62), gardener to Charles I, gathered together a collection of plants, flowers, shells and other objects of interest, and in 1656 he published a catalogue of his Museum. In it, he mentions two varieties of the potato, one with white, and the other with purple flowers. It was the Tradescant collection which formed the basis of the Ashmolean Museum, following on its gift to Oxford in 1683 by Elias Ashmole, who had purchased it in 1659.

Chabrey, better known under his latinized name Dominicus Chabraeus, who edited Jean Bauhin's *Historia*, published his *Stirpium Icones et Sciagraphia* in 1666. In the 1667 edition of this work, the potato is described as *Papas Americanum, Pyconoconium, Openauk Insulae Virginiae radix*; *chuño*, and the plate which is a reproduction of that in Jean Bauhin's *Historia*, is described as 'Virginiae insulae Incolis Planta dicitur Openauk et est hodie in Europaeorum Hortis cognita', indicating that Gerard's blunder had made considerable progress.

Dr Christopher Merrett (1614–95), in his *Pinax rerum naturalium*

---

[1] This feature has proved of value in the classification of the section Petota of the genus *Solanum* by taxonomists.

Britannicarum 1667, also describes two varieties, one with white, the other with ash-coloured flowers, which I think may be regarded as pale heliotrope.

John Ray in his *Historia Plantarum* (1686), under the title *Solanum tuberosum*, reproduces Bauhin's and Clusius's description, and makes an interesting allusion to its use as a drink, which is referred to in chapter 1, p. 13.

Robert Morison (1620–83), who was Professor of Botany in Oxford from 1669 onwards, in the second volume of his *Plantarum Historia Universalis*, published posthumously in 1699, is the first to cast doubt on the Virginian origin of the potato. His acquaintance with the potato dated at least from 1661, when he wrote from Blois, where he was Curator of the Royal French Gardens, to the well-known botanist, William Cloy, asking amongst many other things, that he might be sent tubers of *Battata Virginiana* from Cloy's garden at Stubbers, North Oakington, Essex.[1]

He says of the potato [translation from the Latin]:

From Virginia called Openauck or Apenauk, it was brought into England and thence it was scattered throughout Europe. Dr John Banister, who lived for twelve years in Virginia, made it perfectly clear in his writings that he never found it here nor can it be discovered whether it is a native of any other American or Spanish province. In our garden it flourishes quite naturally.

Banister (*d.* 1692), was a missionary: he sent his collection of Virginian plants to John Ray, who published a list of them in his *Historia* in 1686, the year in which he received them; the potato was not included.

Zwinger, in the *Neu Vollkomen Kraüter-Buch* (1696) describes the potato, which he says has knobbly 'roots' with forty to fifty tubers to a plant.

The last description to be quoted here is that of William Salmon, in his *Herbal* published in 1710.

Salmon was a gifted and supremely energetic man; he professed himself an alchemist and peddled in horoscopes; sold pills of his own concoction which cured all diseases, at 3*s.* per box; in short, he lived by his wits and on other people's follies. Besides the *Herbal*, he wrote a book on medicine, embodying the teachings of all the ancients, as well as that of Paracelsus; one on domestic medicine, another on surgery; nothing seems to have been alien to him; he wrote a treatise on transubstantiation, and a book on drawing and the art of engraving. One should not, therefore, be surprised if his treatment of the potato is more imaginative than accurate. Salmon distinguishes three kinds of potatoes, the Spanish, which is the *Battata* or sweet-potato, the Virginian or *Pappas vel*

---

[1] Gunther, R. W. T. (1922). *Early British Botanists*, p. 354. Oxford.

Battata Virginiana, which is our potato, and which he asserts 'grows wild not only in Virginia but almost everywhere thro' the whole continent of Florida', and '*Pappa seu Battata Anglicana seu Hiberniana*, the English or Irish potato, which grows in vast plenty in many of our English gardens so that now the roots are sold by bushels in our London Market'. These English and Irish potatoes, he tells us, 'are only nurst up in gardens in England and Ireland where they flourish and come to perfection, prodigously encreasing to a vast plenty'.

Salmon, besides creating a rich crop of new errors, has reaped the full harvest of the blunders engendered by Gerard, as will be seen from the descriptions he gives of the two latter of these so-called types of potatoes; it is to be regretted that he only provides an illustration of the sweet-potato; one would have been intrigued to have seen how he differentiated the Virginian from the Irish.

The second, or Virginian Potato. The Root of this is nothing like the former [the Spanish Potato], neither in form, magnitude, color, nor taste, nor resembles it in any thing but the solid, compact, uniform Substance thereof. The Roots are small, some about the bigness of Wall-Nuts, green and all, some lesser by much, and others greater; some of them almost round, some oval, some of a long round, and almost pointed at each end, some smooth, others knobby, all of them being tuberous, of a dirty brown whitish color on the out side, and white within; not of a pleasant sweet Taste, as the Spanish are, but rather of a Flatulent, or insipid Taste, which yet being boiled, baked or roasted; and eaten with Butter, Salt, Vinegar, and a little Sugar, are most admirable Food, and not much inferior to those of the Spanish Kind, (both sorts of them, as also the English following, being very mealy when they are drest, for which reason they require a great deal of Butter). It has many weak and somewhat flexible Branches, leaning a little downwards, or easily born down with the Wind or other things, beset with many Winged Leaves, of a dark grayish green color, whereof divers are smaller, and some greater than others. The Flowers grow many together upon a long Stalk, coming forth from between the Leaves and the great Stalks, every one severally, upon a short foot Stalk, somewhat like to the Flowers of Tobacco for the form, being one whole Leaf, six cornered at the brims, but something larger, and of a pale blewish purple color, or pale Dove color, and in some almost white, with some red Threads in the middle, standing about a thick Gold-yellow Pointel, tipt with green at the end. After the Flowers are past, there comes up in their places small round Berries or Fruit, as large as a Damson, or Bully, green at the first, and something whitish afterwards, with many white Seeds therein like to Night-shade; from the likeness of which Bauhinus upon Matthiolus calls it *Solanum tuberosum esculentum*.

The third, or English, or Irish Potato. This is a round tuberous Root sometimes smooth, sometimes knobby, of various magnitudes from the smallness of a Filbert, to bigger than a large Fist doubled; it is solid, compact, and of one uniform Substance, white within, and reddish without, having a Cuticula or Scarf Skin, over the principal Skin, not sweet in Taste, like those of the Spanish Kind, but of a more flatulent or insipid Taste, which being thoroughly boiled, baked or roasted, are mealy like the others. They are dispersed under the Ground by many small Threads or Strings, from the Head of the Root, and one from another, each encreasing in its tuberous bulk, in its station or place where it lyes, without running deeper into the Ground, as long Roots usually do.

This is the first reference I have encountered in which the potato is called the Irish potato, a designation which was to become general in the United States of America.

NOTE. An interesting article on the characters of the early potato which reached the continent of Europe, was contributed some fifty years ago by Roze,[1] who clearly differentiated between the potatoes of Gerard and Clusius, to both of which he ascribed a Peruvian origin. Later varieties he regarded as being due to the influence of improved cultivation. In the same essay he deals, somewhat inconclusively, with the question of nomenclature, discussed in chapter VIII.

[1] Roze, E. (1896). Les deux premières variétés de la Pomme de terre. *Jour. d. l. Soc. Nationale d'Hortic. de France.* 3e Série, T. XVIII, pp. 146–53. Paris.

CHAPTER VII

'Vertues', Vices and Values

'Prejudices' might perhaps have been a better title to this chapter, were it to be used in its more literal sense, implying a premature, hasty, or ill-founded judgement rather than in its more usual connotation of an adverse or biased one. But so difficult is it to dissociate this word from the suggestion of like or dislike of an individual or a group, their ideas or their persons, that one hesitates to use it here.

The arrival of the potato in Western Europe at a time of unprecedented literary and intellectual activity, has been of great advantage to its historian, for, unlike other important but much earlier of man's adventures in dietetics, its characteristics, real or imaginary, were not left unchronicled. This activity reflected a social and spiritual upheaval which, breaking with much of the past, completed the foundation on which the structure of modern society has been built.

The seventeenth century saw the birth both of modern inductive science and the early efflorescence of the capitalist system, two streams of human endeavour which between them have shaped the world of to-day. The present crisis appears to promise, like Pharaoh's dream, continuity and ever growing success to the one, and increasing feebleness to the other. Both movements, but more especially capitalism, have played their part in determining the policy of the ruling caste towards the masses and this, in turn, has reacted on the adoption of the potato, the only new foodstuff of first-class importance, other than maize, which has permeated Western Europe in the last 300 years. It took several years before it was recognized that the adoption of the potato might have peculiar social and economic repercussions, but towards the middle of the seventeenth century in England, and earlier in some parts of the Continent, a few far-sighted statesmen and men of science began to realize this possibility.

It is of interest to observe that the Spanish Conquistadores who first encountered the potato, immediately realized its economic importance and at once relegated it as a food for slaves. This was not surprising when we remember that their outlook on the New World was that of a superior race dominating and exploiting the persons and property of an inferior one, whilst reserving their souls as a sin offering to Rome. Even when the conquest was complete, and the so-called colonial period super-vened, they assumed a relationship to the country closely resembling that of the feudal overlords in their native Spain; they never became colonists in the sense that the English and French did in North America. Hence the potato was essentially a food for the natives rather than one for the poorer classes. In Ireland, for like reasons, a rather similar attitude towards it ensued.

The assessments of the potato's merits which have come down to us from the sixteenth and seventeenth centuries were generally favourable, but its adoption met with considerable opposition from the common folk, and this was based, as we shall see, on a variety of grounds, most of them fallacious.

The Spanish conquerors of South America speak, in general, most favourably of the new vegetable. Castellanos[1] (1536) writes: 'It is a gift very acceptable to the Indians, and a dainty dish even for the Spaniards.' Cieza de León[2] (1538): 'The potato when boiled is as tender as a cooked chestnut.' At a later date he observes that many Spaniards have amassed fortunes by selling potatoes for the use of the native workers at the Potosí Silver Mines. López de Gómara[3] (1554), referring to the inhabitants of the Collao or uplands of Peru, states that 'men live to the age of a hundred and more years, not having maize, they use the potato as their food'. Jerome Cardan[4] (1557) thinks the flavour of the potato is superior to that of chestnuts, and adds: 'these papas are a kind of truffle, which one uses instead of bread.... It is thus that Nature wisely provides for all our wants'. This latter speculation, we shall see in another chapter, is a very common prelude to its recommendation as a food for the working classes. Christoval de Molina[5] (c. 1570) transcribes a native prayer, which he says was offered at the Situa feast in Cuzco: 'O Creator! Lord of the ends of the earth! Oh most merciful! Thou who givest life to all things, and hast made men that they may live, and eat and multiply. Multiply also the fruits of the earth, the papas [potatoes] and other food that thou hast made, that men may not suffer from hunger and misery. Oh preserve the fruits of the earth from frost, and keep us in peace and safety.' It is more than possible that Molina has adjusted this invocation to his own Christian outlook, but the reference to the loss by frost rings true to native thought and experience. Acosta[6] (1590) records that potatoes are the mainstay of the people of the highlands around Cuzco and the natives rejoice exceedingly when the harvest is good and escapes frost; he adds: 'there is a great trade in this *chuño* [dried potatoes] which is

[1] Castellanos, Juan de (1536). Op. cit.

[2] Cieza de León, Pedro de (1554). Op. cit.

[3] Gómara, López de (1552). *Historia General de las Indias.*

[4] Cardan, Jerome (1557). *De Rerum Varietate* (quoted from Roze, p. 5).

[5] Molina, Cristóbal de (1573). *An Account of the Fables and Rites of the Incas*, p. 173. Trans. Clement Markham. Hakluyt Soc. 1873.

[6] Acosta, José de (1590). Op. cit. p. 259.

conveyed to the Mines of Potosi'. Antonio de Herrera[1] (1601) emphasizes the importance of the potato to the highland people and says they are very nourishing. Antonio Vázquez de Espinosa,[2] describing Peru and New Granada between the years 1612–21, notes how the potato in the diocese of Quito is becoming the food of the Spanish no less than the native. In some parts of the country, as in the Collao district, the potato is the principal foodstuff grown, and often much is preserved as *chuño*.

In the following fifty years one encounters several references to the potato as a crop, but without further comment. Its position had become established.

Thus we see that the Spanish chroniclers recorded the plain facts as they found them, viz. that the potato was an indispensable food for the highland natives; a little later they seized on the fact that it was an invaluable agent in the exploitation of native labour in the Potosí Mines, and it is not surprising that this should be followed by the Spaniards themselves adopting the new food and proving its value in their own domestic economy. Although 1620 is the date of the first reference to this effect, Spaniards in South America seemed ready to accept it as part of their own dietary within a few years of encountering it.

Bernabé Cobo[3] (1653) devotes a whole chapter to the potato, describing its cultivation and its many uses, including the preparation of *chuño*, from which 'the Spanish women make a flour more white and fine than that of wheat, from which they make starch, sponge cakes, and all delicacies which they usually make from almonds and sugar; and with the cooked green potatoes they make the most delicious fritters'.

In the seventeenth century, references to the use of the potato begin to accumulate. The herbalists did more than furnish us with the description of the plants which have been recorded in chapter VI: they gave us their views as to its merits in the first place as a herb and a potential 'simple', and only secondarily as an article of diet.

Just as in their descriptions of the potato as a plant, they are prone to reproduce or adapt the views of others, so in regard to the 'vertues' we find a somewhat monotonous repetition of the tale of its properties, much of which was founded rather in the fertile brains of the herbalists than in the tissues of the plant.

Gerard (1597) records his appreciation of the potato under the intriguing title 'The Temperature and Vertues'.

The temperature and vertues are referred unto the common Potatoes [i.e. the sweet-potato], being likewise a foode, as also a meate for pleasure,

---

[1] Herrera, Antonio de (1601). *The General History of the Vast Continent and Islands of America*, vol. IV, pp. 221 and 282. Trans. Stevens.

[2] Vázquez de Espinosa, Antonio (c. 1628). Op. cit. pars. 1110 and 1615.

[3] Cobo, Bernabé (1653). *Historia del Nuevo Mundo*, ch. 13.

equal in goodnesse and wholesomenesse unto the same, being either roasted in the embers, or boiled and eaten with oile, vinegar and pepper, or dressed any other way by hand of some cunning in Cookerie.

Clusius (1601) discussing its virtues, tells us that the Papal Legate used them cooked like carrots or parsnips for the sake of his health. 'Nevertheless they are flatulent, and therefore some use them for exciting Venus.' He tells us that he tried them himself:

I used to take them boiled, stripped of their epidermis rather than in their skin, for it comes off very easily, and soaked between two dishes with a rather fat broth of mutton, turnips or radishes: and in truth I thought them no less tasty and agreeable to the palate than turnips themselves, but when raw I think they are excessively rough and flatulent.

Gaspard Bauhin, in *The Prodromos*, 1619, writes:

Our own people [of the city of Basle] sometimes roast them under embers in the manner of Tubers [truffles] and having taken off the cuticle eat them with pepper: others having roasted them and cleaned them cut them up into slices and pour on fat sauce with pepper and eat them for exciting Venus, increasing semen: others regard them as useful for invalids since they believe them to be good nourishment. They nourish no less than chestnuts and carrots and are flatulent.

Jean Bauhin (1651) describes the potato in his great work on the *History of the Plants of the World* but speaks only of its use in the New World as a substitute for bread and flour. Dr Tobias Venner, who was a well-known physician of Bath, wrote a delightful book called *Via Recta ad Vitam Longam*, which first appeared in 1620, and incidentally, contains the first reference in English to the Jerusalem artichoke under that name. Its relationship to the herbal literature is a close one, but it deals in greater detail, and with more authority, on the uses of the various food-stuffs, plant and animal, that were available in his day. It is in this connection that we find an estimate of the worth of the potato which may surprise many of us who have consumed this apparently innocent root two or three times daily, no less than did the discovery that he had been talking prose all his life, surprise Molière's 'Bourgeois Gentilhomme'.

Potato roots are of a temperate qualitie and of strong, nourishing parts. The nutriment which they yield is, though somewhat windie, verie substantiall, good and restorative, surpassing for nourishment of all other roots and fruits, they are diversely dressed and prepared, according to every man's taste and liking, some use to eat them, being roasted in the embers, sopped in wine which way is specially good, but in what manner soever they be dressed, they are very pleasant to the taste and doe wonderfully comfort, nourish and strengthen the bodie, and they are very wholesome and good for every age and constitution, especially for those that be past their consistent age.

This last remark, taken literally, means those in whom growth has ceased and decay not yet begun; we may assume, I think, that the worthy doctor thought it a highly suitable food for the aged. In the next edition, published two years later, Venner repairs what was a notable omission in those days, 'that it incites to Venus'!

It is well to remember that when the writers of the early seventeenth century speak of the 'common potato' they, like Gerard, had in mind the sweet-potato. So late as 1637 the horticulturist, John Goodyer who, when on a visit to his brother-in-law William Yalden's home at Sheet in Hampshire, records that he saw *Battata Hispanorum* (the sweet-potato) or 'common potato' growing there and that the tubers 'howsoever they may be dressed, they comfort nourish and strengthen the body procuring bodily lust and that with greediness'.[1] It was a simple case of transference to a synonymous newcomer of an attribute which had been enjoyed by its predecessor.

This acquired reputation was, in its more restricted sense, slow to die; but its corollary that it induced large families, had a much longer life, and was held by some serious writers so late as the end of the last century. A very sober eighteenth-century agricultural expert,[2] after recounting how great a help the potato was to the poor in dear times, declares that it has also a special claim on the consideration of the 'great'. 'It is favourable to population; for it has been observed, that in the western parts of Ireland where it is almost the only diet of the labouring poor, it is no unusual thing to see six, seven, eight, ten and sometimes more children, the issue of one couple, starting almost naked out of a miserable cabin, upon the approach of an accidental traveller' and, he adds, reassuringly, it 'also creates a vigorous population.'

The aphrodisiacal reputation of the sweet-potato suffered a sharp revival in France and in the French Empire after Napoleon's marriage with Josephine. The latter, being a Creole, was from her youth very fond of the root, and although they had gone completely out of cultivation in France, she caused them to be grown at Malmaison and later at Saint Cloud, whence they were served at the court banquets. It soon became the fashion for courtesans to regard the sweet-potato, a dish patronized by the highest, as the one best suited to their endeavours, and market gardeners responded by growing it in quantities. The fashion died out once more when the market had become glutted and the price had fallen away.[3]

Parkinson (1629) in his *Paradisi in Sole*, does not think our potato

[1] Gunther, R. W. T. (1922). Op. cit. p. 75.
[2] Henry, David (1771). *The Practical Farmer or The Complete English Farmer*, p. 275.
[3] Gibault, G. (1912). *Histoire des Légumes*, p. 242.

as pleasant as the sweet-potato; he then proceeds to tell us how the sweet-potato is used:

The Spanish Potatoes are roasted under the embers, and being pared or peeled or sliced, are put into sacke with a little sugar, or without, and is delicate to be eaten. They are used to be baked with marron, sugar and other things in Pyes, which are a dainty and costly dish for the table. The comfit makers prefer them, and candy them as divers other things, and so ordered is very delicate, fit to accompany such other beautiful dishes.

He adds:

The Virginia Potato's being dressed after all these waies before specified, maketh almost as delicate meat as the former.

This latter may, I think, be taken as conclusive evidence that the potato in his day was still a rarity and had not begun to make its way into the dietary of the people.

Nearly a century later, we have an estimate of its virtues from William Salmon, whose work has already been referred to. He distinguishes between 'Qualities' and 'Virtues'. Of the former he tells us:

The Leaves of Potato are manifestly hot and dry in the beginning of the second Degree, as manifestly appear by the Taste. But the Roots are temperate in respect to heat or cold, dryness and moisture: They Astringe, are moderately Diuretick, Stomatick, Chylisick, Analeptick, and Spermatogenetick. They nourish the whole Body, restore in Consumptions, and provoke Lust.

The preparations of the potato he advises are: (1) boiled, baked or roasted roots, (2) the broth, (3) *sanguis*, the blood. Salmon then describes the 'Virtues':

The Prepared Roots. They stop Fluxes of the Bowels, nourish much, and restore in a pining Consumption: Being boiled, baked or roasted, they are eaten with good Butter, Salt, Juice of Oranges or Limons, and double refined Sugar, as common Food: they encrease Seed and provoke Lust, causing Fruitfulness in both Sexes: and stop all sorts of Fluxes of the Belly.

The Broth of the Roots. They are first boiled soft in fair Water, then taken out and peeled, afterwards put into the same Water again, and boiled till the broth becomes as thick, as very thick Cream, or thin Hasty Pudding: some mix an equal quantity of Milk with it, and so make Broth; others after they are peeled, instead of putting them into the Waters they were boiled in, boil them only in Milk, till they are dissolved as aforesaid, and the broth is made pleasant with sweet Butter, a little Salt and double refined Sugar, and so eaten. It has all the Virtues of the Roots eaten in Substance, nourishes more, and restores not only in an Atrophia, or pining Consumption, but also in a Phthisis or Ulceration of the Lungs.

Sanguis, or the Blood of Potato's. It is made as the Blood of Satyrion, Parsneps, Eddo's Comfrey, and other like Roots. It may be taken to a Spoonful or two, Morning, Noon, and Night, in a glass of choice Canary, Tent, Alicant, old Malaga, or other good Wines. It restores in deep Consumption of all Kinds, nourishes to admiration, is good against Impotency in Men and Barrenness in Women, and has all the other Virtues of both the Prepared Roots and Broth.

Extravagantly absurd as Salmon's estimate of the potato's merits appears, one must not conclude that he held the potato in any special regard. Equally prodigal claims are made by him for foods which were common at every man's table, such as parsnips and carrots. Indeed, the latter's virtues put those of the potato to shame: it is

Aperitive, Attractive, Digestive, Carminative, Diuretick (increasing the flow of urine), Cephalick (good for brain troubles), Stomatick, Nephitick, Hysterick (operative on the womb), Lithontriptick (capable of breaking up stones in the bladder), Alterative (affecting nutrition and adjusting it to the normal), Alexipharmick (acts as an antidote to poisons), and Spermatogenetick (productive of lust).

Those who are interested in the history of early medicine and dietetics will miss one name in the list of authorities so far quoted, that of Nicholas Culpeper (1616–54), who wrote several works on pharmacology, all of which were inspired by an ardent belief in astrology, and an intense contempt for the College of Physicians. It is a comment on our intellectual standards that his teachings are to-day being financially exploited.

In addition to all the reputed medicinal herbs, Culpeper describes all the known foodstuffs, the common cereals, orchard fruits, and all the vegetables of the kitchen garden of his day. Thus we find an account both of the growing plant and its properties, of asparagus, artichokes, beans, beets, cabbages, carrots, cucumbers, leeks, onions, parsnips, radishes, rhubarb and skirrets.

Culpeper's neglect of the potato, sixty years after its introduction to this country, cannot be dismissed, out of hand, as of no importance. It is true that he is equally silent about the turnip, a plant which had been grown in English gardens, as opposed to field cultivation, for centuries. If we look at his account of the turnip's near relatives, the cabbage family, which are included under the heading 'Cabbages and Coleworts', he has very little to say in their favour as curative agents. Indeed, he pours out his choicest pieces of sarcasm on them:

He [Cato] appropriates them to every part of the body, and to every disease in every part; and honest old Cato, they say, used no other physic. I know not what metal their bodies were made of; this I am sure, Cabbages are extremely windy, whether you take them as meat or as medicine: yea, as windy meat as can be eaten, unless you eat bag-pipes or bellows, and they are but seldom eaten in our days; and Colewort flowers are something more tolerable, and the wholesomer food of the two. The Moon challenges the dominion of the herb.

We may therefore presume that the turnip was discarded for lack of merit. The potato is in a different category; it is omitted in company with two other plants, the Jerusalem artichoke and the tomato which reached these shores at about the same time as itself. We know that all three had a very restricted culture for a considerable time, although the Jerusalem artichoke was, during the latter part of the first half of the seventeenth century, imported from Terneuzen in Holland, and sold in the streets of London; the other two were confined to the private gardens of a few large houses. We may, I think, safely assume that not one of the three plants was sufficiently accessible as to be worth discussing in a book primarily intended for the use of the ordinary intelligent householder. Indeed Culpeper's omission of the potato may be regarded as almost conclusive evidence that it was not cultivated in the Home Counties as late as 1653.

We must now return to a remark which we find in the second edition of Gerard's *Herball*, at the end of his description of the potato. It runs thus:

Bauhine saith that he heard that the use of these roots was forbidden in Burgundy (where they call them Indian artichokes) for that they were persuaded the too frequent use of them caused the leprosie.

The statement is, in fact, to be found in nearly identical words in Gaspard Bauhin's *Prodromos* published in 1620.

I am told that the Burgundians are forbidden to make use of these tubers, because they are assured that the eating of them causes leprosy, and they call them the artichokes of the Indies.

The edict must have been issued prior to 1620, at the latest one might presume in 1619. Jean Bauhin, his brother, at the end of his article on the potato in the *Historia* (1651) refers to this statement: 'That plant which he [i.e. Gaspard Bauhin] says the Burgundians call "Indian artichoke", differs very much from *Papas Americanus* or from his *Solanum tuberosum esculentum*.' Roze, commenting on this, suggests that the tuber which was under such grave suspicion was the Jerusalem artichoke. As the climate of Burgundy does not admit of the sweet-potato being grown, we need only consider whether it was the potato or the Jerusalem artichoke to which the edict applied.

Although it is impossible to determine with certainty to which of the two the statement refers, the probability is that it was to our potato. The Jerusalem artichoke had been introduced into France at the earliest in

1607. By 1616 this root had become sufficiently well established in some parts of France as to be fed to animals, although but a few years prior to that, it had been a luxury on the tables of the rich. In the year 1615 it was known in French-speaking countries under two names, either as 'La Truffe du Canada', or by its recently acquired nickname 'Topinambour'.[1] It must be admitted that there is no adequate reason to think that in 1619 Gaspard Bauhin would not have been well aware of the difference between these two very distinct new tuberous food plants. But even if the exact identity remains in some doubt, the problem as to why such an interdict should have been issued against an apparently harmless tuber, remains to be solved, and the solution suggested would apply equally to either. In the sequel, it is the statement of Gaspard Bauhin that it was the potato to which he referred, which is accepted.

In favour of the proscribed plant being the potato, is the persistent legend that this root was definitely forbidden by the Parliament of Besançon in 1630. The order is said to read as follows:

Attendu, que la Pomme de terre est une substance pernicieuse et que son usage peut donner la lepre, defense est faite, sous peine d'une amende arbitraire de la cultiver dans le territoire de Salins.

Roze, quoting an historian of that town, J. Tripard, shows that no parliament sat in Besançon at that date, and a search amongst the muniments of Doubs of the edicts of that year, failed to find any such document. It is, however, unlikely that so circumstantial a tale is altogether without foundation; it may well be that the place and date have been incorrectly recorded. Thirty-three years later, we hear the same note of alarm in a book devoted to housewives: 'If too frequently eaten, they are thought to cause Leprosie.'[2]

So late as 1761 Turgot, who was then Intendant of the Généralité of Limoges, found it necessary to combat the prejudice felt by the people against the potato for its alleged part in inducing leprosy, by causing it to be served at his own table and distributing tubers to the members of the Agricultural Society.[3]

Had the potato been arraigned on some more general grounds, such as encouraging flatulence or lust, even in the improbable case that such would lead to its prohibition, it would have been no great cause for astonishment in an age where superstitions were wont to run riot and harmless old women were burnt as witches. But here the indictment is

---

[1] For a full account of the introduction and naming of the Jerusalem artichoke, see Salaman, R. N. (1940). *J. Roy. Hort. Soc.* vol. LXV.
[2] Lovell, Robert (1659). *The Compleat Herbal*, 2nd ed. 1665, p. 347. Oxford. (1st ed. 1659.)
[3] Clos (1874). *Quelques documents pour l'histoire de la Pomme de terre.* Quoted from Roze.

absolutely specific, and the alleged crime the most heinous conceivable. To solve a problem such as this, one must look for a cause embodying both authority and logic and this, I believe, is to be found in the teaching of the Doctrine of Signatures.

The origins of the 'Doctrine' doubtless reach back to the earliest strata of human folk-lore, seeing that its basic principle is the conception that like cures or effects like, which is the very essence of primitive magic. As examples may be cited the belief that the juice of a red beet is good for anaemic women, and that yellow celandine is the cure for jaundice; both are to be found in widely scattered districts amongst countryfolk, who had never heard of the 'Doctrine' as such; indeed, the early Egyptians dedicated the celandine to the sun because of its likeness thereto.[1] These two examples illustrate the principle at work, so to speak, in either direction. In the first, that which is to be desired, a good ruddy complexion, is induced by consuming the blood-red beet; in the other, that which is hurtful and undesirable, the yellow complexion of jaundice, is combated and removed by the consumption of that which is like it, the yellow celandine.

The existence of a mystical relation between man and the mandrake with its forked two-legged root, was an established belief in the earliest Biblical times. The procreative affinity of the plant is impressed and patent in its form. Rachel, so long barren, begs Leah to let her have the mandrake that her son has brought in from the field. 'Is it a small matter that thou hast taken away my husband? and wouldest thou take away my son's mandrakes also?' replies Leah. And then follows the amazing bargain: Rachel can have the mandrakes if she allows Jacob to sleep that night with Leah.

A notable example of the persistence of this trend of thought is to be found amongst the womenfolk of the lower and middle classes, in the widespread belief that the use of dark red wine, especially port, invigorates the blood. Indeed, there are well-known patent concoctions which have made fortunes for their authors out of this particular fantasy. However primitive its origins, the 'Doctrine' took definite form as a philosophy early in the sixteenth century. To like cures like, was added the belief that everything in nature, animal, plant, or mineral, either bore on its own person, so to speak, or exhibited by its properties, its specific character. But that in itself is merely a self-obvious proposition, and brought one no further unless that character was related to man, the ruler under God, of the earth and all that is in it. This relationship was established by the embodiment in the 'Doctrine' of another and very ancient principle, that man and the world bore to each other the relation-

---

[1] Quelch, Mary T. (1941). *Herbs for Daily Use in Home, Medicine and Cookery.* Faber and Faber, pp. 35 and 60.

ship of microcosm to macrocosm where, in the one, was always to be found the counterpart of the other. This agglomeration of primitive ideas received definite shape and form and, above all, a degree of authority, at the hands of its first 'prophet', Paracelsus. Theophrastus von Hohenheim (1493–1541) was born at Einsiedeln in the Canton of Schwyz, near the southern end of the Lake of Zürich: his contempt for the teaching of Galen and the Arabian masters of medicine, led him to call himself Paracelsus, after one of the early Roman fathers of the art, whilst his unbounded arrogance, and the intemperate defence of his own theories against that of accepted medicine, led his colleagues to dub him 'Bombastus', a name which has clung to his memory for four hundred years. Paracelsus was himself a mystic, a student of Cabbala, and a believer in astrology. Agnes Arber, in her book on *Herbals* (1938) describes how Paracelsus, in order to determine the virtues of plants, elaborated the guide which was known as the Doctrine of Signatures, to which, however, he attached a further principle, teaching that all bodies contained, in varying proportions, sulphur which induced change, combustibility, volatilization and growth; salt, which endowed it with stability, and non-inflammability; and, finally, mercury, which gave fluidity. These fanciful theories, bizarre as they are, were not entirely fruitless, for in formulating his views on the composition and properties of living things in chemical terms, he pointed the way to curative methods, based likewise on chemical bodies, and thus helped to overthrow the Galenic pharmacopoeia which, prescribing mixtures of heterogeneous herbs and odd fragments of animals, not excluding their excreta, disfigured the practice of medicine up till the end of the eighteenth century, and even later.

Paracelsus was followed by Giambattista Porta of Naples, in his *Phytognomonica*, published in Naples in 1588. The following example of his teaching is quoted, but not verbatim, from Agnes Arber:[1] Long-lived plants lengthen, and short-lived ones shorten man's life. Herbs with yellow sap heal jaundice; those with a rough surface heal diseases that destroy the normal smoothness of the skin. The resemblance of certain plants to animals, opened up a whole new field of speculation and dogmatism. Those like butterflies, cured insect bites; those whose roots or fruits had a jointed appearance, and thus remotely resembled a scorpion, must necessarily be remedies against scorpion sting. The maidenhair, because the leaf stalks are bare, is a cure for baldness; Aroides, with their spotted stalks, are like snakes; pomegranates, with seeds exposed, are human teeth. Porta linked the doctrine up with astrology, by his teaching that the planets had an influence on the virtues of plants.

[1] Arber, Agnes (1938). Op. cit. p. 251.

In England, the Doctrine of Signatures found its main exponents in William Coles, who wrote *Adam in Eden*, and his contemporary, Nicholas Culpeper. Cole offers us, perhaps, the most perfect example both of the principle and of the fatuity of the Doctrine, though to his credit it should be remembered that he repudiated the influence of the planets on plants, for the convincing reason that plants were created on the third day, and planets on the fourth. 'The Wallnut is a cure for troubles of the brain.' The reason is obvious: its outer, green, fleshy husk represents the scalp, its hard shell the bony skull, the inner skin the meninges and pia mater, whilst the convoluted, bisected kernel represents the hemispheres of the brain itself. The 'Doctrine' necessarily led to the transference of the known or supposed qualities of one plant to another, similar in form, which might or might not be botanically akin. Thus the assumed windiness and lust-propelling 'vertues' of the *Battata* or sweet-potato, were straightway fastened, and for generations stuck, to its equally innocent namesake and proxy, the potato; similarly, the true resemblance of the flowers of the poisonous nightshades and bitter-sweet, themselves members of the same family of *Solanums*, led to the belief that the potato itself was poisonous, a view long held and as we shall see, revived by Ruskin.

To return to Bauhin's report of the edict against the potato in Burgundy: it must be remembered that the potato was the first edible plant in Europe to be grown from tubers and not from seed, and that till then, no similar plant in north-western Europe was grown which bore on underground stems numerous white or flesh-coloured nodules; both the cultivation, the behaviour and the habits of the plant were unusual.

Such a stranger in the midst of an unsophisticated countryfolk excited both interest and suspicion. The question which presented itself to the doctors of the day would be: What signature, veiled or patent, did this newcomer bear, and what warning did it convey? I suggest that the answer was obvious to those anxious to find one. The 'signature' of the potato was hidden in its tubers, and how irregular these tubers of the early potatoes were, has already been shown. The white nodular tubers, with bulbous finger-like growths, may well have recalled the deformed hands and feet of the unfortunate leper, the dreaded outcast of the Middle Ages and the Renaissance. A superbly engraved plate of the potato, made in the first decade of the seventeenth century,[1] may be cited in support of this thesis.

The supposed likeness between a plant, and the external manifestation of a disease, was frequently made use of by the followers of Paracelsus;[2] the drooping flower of the lily-of-the-valley suggested the picture of

---

[1] Besler, Basil (1613). *Hortus Eystettensis* (Norimberg).
[2] Wooton, A. C. (1910). *Chronicles of Pharmacy*, p. 183. Macmillan.

PLATE XVIII

Fig. 62. Woodcut of the haulm and tubers of the 'Potatoes from Virginia', from the first edition of Gerard's *Herball*, 1597.

Fig. 61. Portrait of John Gerard.
Frontispiece to the first edition of the *Herball*, 1597.
The left hand is holding a leaf and flowers of potato.

PLATE XIX

Fig. 63. Photograph of the Aquarelle which Clusius caused to be made, now in the Plantin Museum, Antwerp. On it is inscribed: Taratoufli à Phillip de Sivry acceptum Viennae 26 Januarii 1588 Papas Peruänum—Petri Ciecae.

Fig. 64. Woodcuts illustrating the potato in Clusius' *Historia*, 1601.

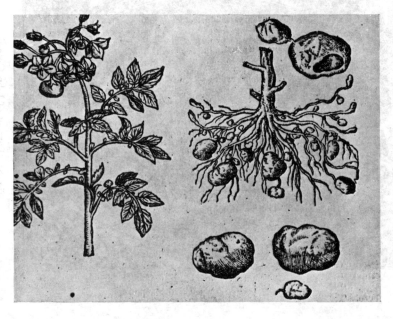

PLATE XX

Fig. 65. Woodcut illustrating the potato
in Parkinson's *Herbal*, 1629.

Fig. 67. Woodcut illustrating the
potato in Jean Bauhin's *Historia*,
1651.

Fig. 66. Woodcut illustrating the potato in Gaspard Bauhin's *Prodromus*, 1620.

a man with apoplexy, Paracelsus likened the date to a cancerous tumour and claimed it as a specific cure. The suggestion that the potato, so far from being a cure for leprosy, was itself the cause, is, it must be confessed, a reversal of the above principle. But it should be remembered that the potato came on the scene after the chief exponents of the 'Doctrine' had passed away, and its condemnation was the outcome of popular sentiment rather than the teaching of esoteric philosophers. It may be said that the theory advanced is no more artificial and forced than most of the deductions made in the name of the Doctrine. It is a sobering thought when discussing these extravagantly absurd arguments, that the final result may, by sheer chance it must be confessed, be sometimes right. Because the willow so it was argued, thrives best in wet and boggy districts, where men suffer most from rheumatism, an extract of the willow should relieve the disease; nonsensical of course, but as a matter of fact, it does so, and because of it, our pharmacopoeia became enriched by the drug salicin, and at a later date, indirectly, by the salicylates and aspirin.

Thomas Tryon,[1] a devotee of the simple life and an ardent vegetarian was, in addition, a firm believer in the Doctrine of Signatures, of which he says: 'The outward body or signature does in all particulars manifest and shew the inward nature of each thing to the enlightened and sagacious Naturalist whom God and Nature have made capable of such sublime learning.' Thus armed, he combated the evil opinion held of the potato on the following grounds: 'Turnips and Potatoes etc., that grow almost on the top and surface of the earth are better than other roots and more familiar to our natures than such as grow deeper in the ground, because they participate more of the influences both of the air and sun than the others.' In 1688 he visited the West Indies and found that sugar and spices 'with the help of bad diet and other uncleanliness doth cause Botches, Boils and various sorts of Leprous diseases'. This vindication of the potato by the transference of its guilt to other foods, was not sufficient to dissipate the prejudices of the peasantry, though it indicates some change in the popular judgement.

Robert Burton[2] says very little in favour of any roots, the continuous use of which makes men mad, but admits that some people approve of parsnips and potatoes. It must be confessed that it is not certain that even this grudging acknowledgement does not, in fact, refer to the sweet-potato.

The opposition to the potato, which preceded its general acceptance in nearly every country of Europe, seems often formless and irrational, but it may well be that deep down, there existed a pseudo-philosophic basis to it, allied to this same Doctrine of Signatures. Thus, as leprosy

[1] Tryon, Thomas (1683). *The Way to Health*, p. 213.
[2] Burton, Robert (1621). *The Anatomy of Melancholy*.

disappeared in Western Europe, the potato was called on to bear the burden of another of the people's banes, scrofula.

Daniel Langhaus,[1] a Swiss physician writing in 1768, is more precise than most:

The scrofulous are common in Switzerland, where the people support themselves above all on potatoes. I am persuaded, myself, that the scrofulous troubles which prevail in our Cantons are entirely the result of this harmful dietary and the absence of exercise. The proof of which is that they are extremely rare in Countries where the potato is unknown.

So late as 1813 we find the great naturalist, Cuvier,[2] in his elegy on Parmentier, saying how 'he looked forward to seeing full use made of the potato in France, notwithstanding the fact that some of the old-fashioned doctors still renewed the accusations of the seventeenth century against it. It was not of leprosy now, but of "fever" they complained. The famines in the south had produced epidemics, and these they had attributed to the one thing (the potato), which had proved the only means of preventing these disasters'. This feeling was as widespread amongst the peasantry of Western Europe as it often was vague in its expression. Even the mind of so practical a person as the agriculturist, de Serres,[3] was evidently not easy on the subject: it will be remembered that he advised that the tubers should be planted in a waning moon, a measure evidently devised to avoid some malevolent influence.

Johannis Royer,[4] writing about 1651, advises, on the other hand, that they should be planted in full moonlight, a measure still advocated a century later.[5]

It may be an echo in a rationalized guise of these same mystic warnings reverberating down the ages which we meet in the advice tendered by an authority mentioned by Munster[6] in his work on the 1845 outbreak of Blight: 'Plant early in the morning, because the tuber planted in the afternoon carries the disease with it into the earth.'

The intelligentsia of eighteenth-century France, as represented by Diderot and his colleagues, looked on the problem from a different angle. In the first edition of the great *Encyclopaedia* the article on the potato ends thus: 'This root, however one cooks it, is insipid and starchy. One cannot reckon it amongst the more pleasant foods for those who only look to it to maintain themselves. One blames, and with reason, the

---

[1] Langhaus, Daniel (1768). *L'Art de guerir soi-même*, vol. II, p. 78. Quoted from Roze, p. 146.

[2] Cuvier, Leopold (1813). *Éloge de Parmentier*. Quoted from Roze, p. 162.

[3] De Serres (1600). Op. cit.

[4] Royer, Joh. (? *c.* 1651). *Beschreibung des fürstlich Braunschweigischen Gartens in Hessen*... 1607–1651. (Quoted from Fuess, *Die Ernährung d. Pflanze*, 1935, Bd. XXXI, p. 291.)

[5] Zedler, J. H. (1744). *Lexicon Universalis*. Leipzig.

[6] Munster, Julius (1846). *Die Krankheiten der Kartoffeln*, p. 153. Berlin.

potato for its windiness; but what is a question of wind to the virile organs of the peasant and the worker?' In the 1777 edition, the potato was dealt with by the distinguished agriculturist, Samuel Engel (1762–84), who vigorously combats the widely held views of its unwholesomeness and points out that in Ireland, where it is the chief food of the people, not only are the diseases of which it is supposed to be the cause, very rare, but the peasantry are strong and peculiarly liable to beget twins. His final argument is that it is a sovereign cure against famine. It was because of famine in 1772, that he induced the people of Nyon, Lake Geneva, to adopt the potato as a staple article of their diet. A few years later they presented him with a medal in token of their gratitude.[1]

As late as 1771, the potato was so much under suspicion that the government appealed to the Medical Faculty of Paris for their considered judgement on its merits. Their verdict was that the potato was a good and healthy food, in no way injurious to health, and of great utility.

In Prussia, where the belief that the potato gave rise to scrofula, rickets, consumption, and doubtless many other evils, was so strongly held, it needed all the influence of Frederick the Great to break this down. When Frederick sent a waggon-load of tubers to Kolberg in 1774 after the famine, in the hope that the people might grow potatoes for themselves all the answer he got was—'The things have neither smell nor taste, not even the dogs will eat them, so what use are they to us?' This opposition was only overcome by sending a Swabian gendarme who, by persuasion and example, showed the peasants how to grow and use them.[2]

Rumford[3] so late as 1795 tells much the same tale in regard to Munich. All sorts of subterfuge were resorted to, in order to get the inmates of his beloved House of Industry to taste the soup made from them. A few years later, the prejudice was overcome, and they were adopted generally.

That the fears which were entertained by the peasantry of Great Britain and Western Europe were without foundation, did nothing to discount their deterrent effect, and but little to shorten their hold on the people. In Ireland they appear either not to have been developed, or else very rapidly to have been overcome. The latter view is almost certainly the more correct, as will be shown in chapter XIV, which deals with the Irish scene; there the pressure of want was strong enough to break down all opposition. But even to-day there are folk-customs with a semi-religious sanction which seem to suggest that in the subconsciousness of the people it is felt that certain dangers need to be avoided and that suitable

[1] Engel, S. *Biographie Universelle.*
[2] Bruford (1935). *Germany in the Seventeenth Century*, p. 116.
[3] Rumford, Count. *Collected Works*, vol. IV, p. 414.

ceremonial action must be taken to that end. These 'dangers', as we have seen, are incurred as a result of eating the new food, and have been brought to the surface of consciousness and rationalized under such titles as 'Leprosy' and 'Scrofula'. If this suggestion is true, then we must beware of accepting such reasons at their face value. It would seem more probable that the basic trouble lay in the fact that the potato was in every sense a new type of food, the like of which had not been seen previously in Europe. To eat of it, was not merely a venture in dietetics, but an audacious break with common tradition, a tradition which in Europe was permeated through and through by the Bible. To eat the new food was akin to eating the forbidden fruit of Eden, a sinful act which, even if its effects were physically harmless, was bound to create a feeling of personal guilt, which demanded some kind of expiation lest the individual be smitten with some dreaded disease.

What evidence, it may be asked, have we, which would support such a theory? There are two avenues of approach: that which deals with the beliefs, and that with the practices of the people. To the former, reference has already been made, and to that should be added the significant fact that throughout the Highlands and, to a lesser extent, amongst the Highland Scottish of Ulster, definite objection was taken to the potato because it was not mentioned in the Bible, and hence was not a food designed for man by God.

A much more pronounced reaction to what would seem to be the same line of thought, is to be found in Russia. When the Old Believers, following on Patriarch Nikon's reforms, broke away from the Russian Orthodox Church in 1667, the more powerful group of schismatics known as the *Bozpopovschini*, or the 'Priestless', regarded certain foods and the like as abominations. Chief amongst these were sugar, tobacco and potatoes, none of which, it will be noted, are mentioned in the Bible. Cane-sugar, a luxury in England, must have been a great rarity in Russia in those days; tobacco and potatoes, both new arrivals, were not only rarities but, sharing the primal curse of the *Solanums*, were considered to be generated by some peculiar botanical form of incest and were in consequence regarded as the incarnation of the evil thing (see chapter VIII).

Fantastic as such taboos seem, there is no need for surprise. There is scarcely any absurdity which was not raised to the rank of a religious sanction in the Russia of the eighteenth century. Reverting to the fact that the three forbidden articles are not mentioned in the Bible, it is noteworthy that many of the schismatics returned to a type of Judaism and added pork to their other taboos.

As regards folk-lore customs, there is a considerable wealth of material, most of which is associated with the planting and harvesting of the potato.

In County Mayo, the seed potatoes were dressed during planting, with a pinch of salt and human excrement. This may be a purely pagan rite of a protective character resembling that existing in Bolivia to-day, referred to in chapter II; or it may originally have had some such purpose but have been modified to deal with the guilt of growing a strange food. More suggestive was the almost universal practice of planting potatoes on Good Friday. So intimate was this relationship, that when Good Friday fell as much as a month later than is customary, potato-planting was commonly postponed to synchronize with it. In Ireland so essential was it that the two events should coincide, that it was a commonly held view, especially in the west where these ancient customs tended most to persist, that if the planting proper could not be done, at least one 'sgiotan', i.e. a chitted tuber set, should be put in the ground as a token of planting. Seed potatoes in Ireland were also frequently sprinkled with holy water by the priest. This relation between Good Friday and the potato, owes its origin in the first place to the fact that in the West, Easter-time is, in fact, a suitable time for planting, but the close and insistent linkage to Good Friday itself must assuredly have some deeper meaning, something suggestive of the expiation which this day commemorates. In Galway, it was considered unlucky to plant potatoes on a Cross Day, i.e. on any fourth day following Christmas, counting Christmas Day as the first of the four. Again it would seem to come back to a subconscious feeling of 'guilt'. It is not to be expected that such practices have but one form, even if the underlying motive is essentially the same: other and non-Christian influences may have been at work in their formulation. Thus in Kerry a piece of cypress was stuck into the ridge on planting day, and on harvesting a branch of the same was burnt.

During the season, the potato crop in some parts of Ireland was assisted by Church ritual, the use of magic, or a combination of both. On Ascension Day, holy water was sprinkled on the growing crop. On the eave of the Feast of St John, midsummer fires were lit, and a burning faggot from them thrown into the potato plot; moulding up was always done on St John's Day itself. The potato harvest also had its rites: Garland Sunday, being the last in July, was in Galway the day on which the first digging was permitted. In Kerry the date was 7 July, the day of the local patron saint. In Cork, some potatoes, however few, should always be dug on 29 June. In Mayo, in every home the end of the potato harvest was celebrated by a feast. In Tipperary, when new potatoes first appeared on the table, it was usual for each to say to the other: 'May we all be alive and happy this time twelve months.'

Elsewhere, on the Continent, there exists a custom, ancient and pagan, which in the seventeenth century was transferred from the corn harvest to that of the potato. At the end of harvest, the labourers speak of the killing of the 'potato dog', and at Epinal they go out, not to harvest the wheat, rye and potato, but to kill the wheat, rye, or 'potato dog'. The woman who carries home the last sheaf, or the last basket of potatoes, is known throughout the year as the 'corn' or 'potato dog'.[1] According to Frazer, the spirit of the plant is embodied in the animal which, in ages past, was killed at the ingathering of the last sheaf.

A German version of this custom, which is said to be directed against the Kartoffel wolf, takes the following form: at the end of the potato harvest, a mannequin is dressed up and is taken with due ceremony to the house of the farmer, when the following is recited:

> We have come to you with the Potato-man
> Who no longer can maintain himself in the field
> Seeing how cold and wet it now is
> He demands a feast of bacon and pancakes.[2]

In day-to-day folk-lore of peasant people, the potato acquired a more individual and intimate position. A few examples may suffice.

A dried tuber carried in the pocket or suspended from the neck, is a sure protection against rheumatism.[3]

A 'pealed' potato, if carried in the pocket of the same side as an aching tooth, will cure the latter as soon as it itself is reduced to crumbs.[4]

Pregnant women should avoid potatoes, especially at night, if they desire their child to have a small head.[4]

The laying of the skin of a potato on May the first at a maiden's door, is an expression of contempt for her.[4]

In addition to what one might call legitimate folk-lore customs and beliefs, one also finds 'how short the way to fairyland' is, especially in Ireland. But what surprises one most is that these airy figments of the folk-mind should be interested in so recent a newcomer as the potato. The death of a child, i.e. its removal from this world by the fairies, is recorded by them, by the turning red of the flesh of the seed potato.[5] The Blight in Ulster was caused by the defeat of the local fairies by those from other parts. The importance of St John's Day, already referred to, is due to the fact that on that day the fairy bands of each province wage war with each other, and the potatoes of the territories of the vanquished suffer accordingly. When the Blight reached Skye, the peasantry demanded that the Fairy Banner should be unfurled.[6]

[1] Frazer, Sir J. (1912). The Spirits of the Corn and the Wild. The Golden Bough, vol. I, 3rd ed.; vol. VII, p. 270.
[2] Gubernatio, A. de (1882). La Mythologie des Plantes, T. II, p. 300. Translation by R.N.S.
[3] Bergen, Fanny (1899). Animal and Plant Lore. Boston.
[4] Rolland, Eugène. Flore populaire, T. VIII, pp. 110–11.
[5] Synge, J. M. (1907) (The Arran Islands, p. 4, Lond.) gives a first-hand account of the myth.
[6] See chapter XX, p. 376.

Occasionally the potato became involved in a secondary capacity. Thus two hundred years after the battle of Aughrim, 12 July 1691, 'fort field', the burial-place of the French and Irish dead was ploughed and planted with potatoes. The farmer was warned of the impiety of his act, but persisting, died before the crop was harvested. The field was never cultivated again.[1]

The prejudice which attached to the potato was not all of its own begetting. The herbalists had recognized its relationship to the Solanaceae family, and the evil repute in which many of its members stood in the estimation of both peasant and philosopher, was not allowed to be forgotten. The berries of the Henbane (*Hyoscyamus niger*), the Bittersweet (*Solanum dulcamara*), the Thorn-apple (*Datura stramonium*), the Deadly Nightshade (*Atropa belladonna*), and the ubiquitous Garden Nightshade (*Solanum nigrum*), are all poisonous and were regarded with fear by the peasantry all over Europe where many of the group are more or less common weeds. The potato for this reason came under a certain amount of suspicion from the very start, but it was entertained by the learned rather than the common people, to whom it spread later. Phillips,[2] who spoke with authority in his day, thought that many people were prejudiced against it on the grounds of it being a species of nightshade, and hence narcotic. Linnaeus, according to a modern herbalist,[3] for some time raised objections to its use, on account of its relation to Deadly Nightshade and Bittersweet.

In the potato famine period, we meet the objection again: one of tne many pamphleteers of the day writes:

We also know that the potato has qualities pertaining to it of an impure nature—in short, that the genus *Solanum* is the actual type of a powerful narcotic family such being the case, and valuable no doubt as the root in question certainly is, still we ought rather to desire the pure and wholesome cereal food.[4]

The basis of this pseudo-scientific heresy hunt was widened, and the controversy brought into the open field of English letters by Ruskin[5] who in *The Queen of the Air* attempts to reinterpret what he calls the early Grecian philosophic outlook on nature, as exemplified in myth and symbol, though it is more than doubtful whether he is justified in foisting the ideas he elaborates on the Greeks. Both animal and plant are regarded as possessed of a vital spirit which expresses itself symbolically in the form and colour of the organism. This spirit has reciprocal

[1] Walton, Clifford (1894). *History of the British standing Army*, p. 162 n. Harrison and Sons: London.

[2] Phillips, H. (1822). *History of Cultivated Vegetables*, vol. II, p. 87. London.

[3] Grieve, M. (1931). *A Modern Herbal*, vol. II, p. 655. Jonathan Cape.

[4] Niven, N. (1846). The Potato Epidemic, etc., A letter to His Grace the Duke of Leinster, Dublin.

[5] Ruskin, John (1869). *Queen of the Air*. London.

affinities with the vital spirit of man, by which means an ethical relationship is established between man and all created living things. 'Whatever the origin of species may be, or however those species, once formed, may be influenced by external accident, the groups into which birth or accident reduce them have distinct relation to the spirit of man.'

How strongly Ruskin was influenced by this aesthetic valuation of nature may be gathered from the following: 'The flower is the end or proper object of the seed, not the seed of the flower. The reason for seeds is that flowers may be; not the reason of flowers that seeds may be. The flower itself is the creature which the spirit makes; only in connection with its perfectness is placed the giving birth to its successor.'

Plants were noble or lowly; the most beautiful, however, might suffer degradation and induce it in other creatures. 'The star-group, of the squills, garlic and onions, has always caused me great wonder. I cannot understand why its beauty, and serviceableness, should have been associated with the rank scent which has been really amongst the most powerful means of degrading peasant life and separating it from that of the higher classes.'

One need not be surprised that, imbued with these views, he has no good word for the unfortunate *Solanums*.

The spirit of evil is also represented, and it has found its lodgment in one group of plants above all others—the accursed family of the *Solanums*. Not even the potato can escape the family bane: 'Next in the potato, we have the scarcely innocent underground stem of one of a tribe set aside for evil, having the deadly nightshade for its queen, and including the henbane, the witch's mandrake, and the worst natural curse of modern civilization—tobacco.'

Ruskin in a note adds: 'Some two out of a hundred and fifty species of *Solanums* are useful to man. It is not easy to estimate the demoralizing effect on the youth of Europe of the cigar, enabling them to pass their time happily in idleness.'

The potato's popularity was delayed to some extent by the fact that in the seventeenth century it had been a luxury food enjoyed only by the court and the nobility, so that in the next century when, for economic reasons, the ruling classes were anxious that the working classes should adopt it as their main food, the latter from time to time raised a humble remonstrance that this was a food 'not for the likes of them'.

In some counties, notably Suffolk, and to a lesser extent Sussex, the prejudice of the working class against a new food seriously delayed its adoption. At Lewes, the feeling against it was so high that at an election about 1765 the popular slogan was: 'No Potatoes, No Popery'.[1]

[1] Moore, Rev. Giles (1848). *Journal and Account Book of Sussex Archaeological Collection*, vol. I, p. 97.

We also find the reverse side of the social pattern playing its part, when it was thought somewhat degrading that English people should be consuming so much of a food which was, in fact, only fit for the despised Irish peasant.[1]

Finally, within the domain of the potato itself, social distinction in Ireland occasionally came to be based on the variety of potato eaten. In the late eighteenth and early nineteenth centuries, the poor ate 'Lumpers' and the rich 'Gregors Cups'. It must be nearly a hundred years ago when a boy beaten in an examination at school by a lad called Laughlin explained that no merit attached to the latter's success, seeing that Laughlin was luxuriating each day on good 'Cups', whilst he himself was merely kept alive on 'English Reds'.[2]

The Values

The dietetic value of the potato, its worth as a food, has long since been established by experience, but only in recent years has popular verdict been approved by scientific experiment.

How curiously discerning mass opinion may be, is illustrated by the respective fates of the potato and the Jerusalem artichoke. Introduced at almost the same date, the latter presumably offered as many advantages as did the potato. Pleasant to the taste as it is, easy, and in so far as labour and manure are concerned, possibly cheaper to grow, nearly as heavy in yield, far less subject to disease both in field and in store than the potato, yet for every hundredweight of the latter, not a pound of the former is consumed. Nor did it take many years for the masses to arrive at their verdict. They decided against the Jerusalem artichoke[3] long before the scientists were aware that inulin, its carbohydrate, was far less digestible than the starch of the potato, that is to say, it has 25 % less energy value than a similar quantity of potato starch. The decision, so overwhelmingly in favour of the potato, though resting ultimately on its superior digestibility, was no doubt strengthened by the fact that its taste, being less pronounced, did not cloy, and that it allowed of a greater range of uses in the economy of the household. Ultimately the supremacy of the potato over its competitors must rest on its composition, and to that, attention will now be turned.

Analysis shows that the main constituents of potato tubers, when ascertained at the same period after harvesting, vary widely in quantity as between different varieties, as they do to a lesser extent within the same variety. This latter source of variation is, in its turn, dependent

[1] Garnier, Russell M. (1895). *Annals of the British Peasantry*, p. 307.

[2] Kennedy, Pat (1875; first written in 1856). *The Banks of the Boro*, p. 5. Macmillan.

[3] Salaman, R. N. (1940). Why Jerusalem Artichoke? *J. Roy. Hort. Soc.*, vol. LXV, p. 348.

on the character of the soil on which they are grown, the manurial treatment which it has received, and the season, wet or dry, hot or cold, in which the crop was raised.

Its value as a staple food must therefore be gauged by the average values of the various constituents as they are found in the potatoes commonly grown and put on the market. Thus defined, about 77% of the potato tuber consists of water, leaving some 23% of solids, the two main constituents of which are starch, which accounts for about 80–88%, and sugar, on the average, for 3–6% of the total dry weight.

As it is the starch of the potato which has won it pre-eminence, it is of interest to note that recent expert opinion is in favour of ranking it above that of the cereals; not because of its richness in this respect, but because of its quality. The starch of potatoes, owing to the tuber's poverty in phytic acid, does not fix the calcium in the diet to the same extent as does that derived from cereals. Hence the daily use of potato as a food, so far from leading to the deterioration of the teeth, so commonly seen amongst people who depend largely on oatmeal and the like for their supplies of carbohydrates, actually tends to their perfect development in youth and their preservation in advanced life.[1]

It is the starch of the tuber which in the main determines its caloric value as a food, but the quantity of starch present is subject to such wide varietal differences that it would be possible, in the course of years, for those responsible for the food of the nation to adjust the calorie output of the crop in the interest of the people, by encouraging the growing of varieties with higher starch content.[2] In this country there is a tendency to cultivate varieties which produce heavy yields, rather than those which are richer in starch, and this will continue to be, so long as price and bonus depend on quantity rather than quality. In Germany, varieties such as 'Industrie' and others where the percentage of starch may be as high as 25–40% of the total weight, have been produced in response to the demand for varieties suitable for commercial starch production.[3]

The importance of the potato as a source of calories cannot well be overestimated, especially in the less advanced communities. The position can best be gauged when we remember that its value when boiled, is equal to at least one-third that of the best white bread, whilst the cost per calorie in normal times, is not more than half.

Next in importance to starch, is the amount of nitrogen-containing substances: in all, they average about 2% of the total weight, one-half of which is 'tuberin', a good protein, and the remainder a collection of

---

[1] See chapter XXVIII, p. 544.
[2] For more on this subject, see chapter X, p. 159.
[3] Lampitt, L. H. and Goldenberg, N. (1940). The Potato as Food. *Chemistry and Industry*, vol. LIX, p. 748.

amino-acids and organic bases. Though the quality of the nitrogenous content is good, its quantity is but small; hence, unless the potato is eaten in very large amounts, as it used to be in Ireland, its value as a source of protein in the dietary of the people is inconsiderable.

The potato also contains useful and assimilable quantities of the more important mineral elements; iron about 0·01 %, calcium about 0·05 %, magnesium about 0·1%, sulphur 0·15%, and chlorine 0·2%, whilst potassium is present to the extent of 2·0% and more of the dry weight of the tuber. Of the trace elements, i.e. copper, boron, silicon, manganese, fluorine and iodine, which in very small quantities are necessary for health, all are present in the potato.

The general use of the potato amongst urbanized communities has done much to abolish scurvy, a fact recognized by Mustel nearly 200 years ago.[1] One pound of cooked new potatoes contains about 75 mg. ascorbic acid, the anti-scurvy vitamin C, the minimum quantity regarded as adequate for the daily needs of an adult by the League of Nations Commission of 1939. It should be noted, however, that the longer potatoes are stored, the greater the loss of ascorbic acid which, after five months, may be reduced to one-third of its original strength. Inasmuch as the average pre-war consumption of potatoes per person in England is not less than 12 oz. per day, and is usually considerably higher in the households of the poor, it alone affords sufficient protection against scurvy. How important has been the part which the potato has played in this respect, is referred to elsewhere,[2] but it may be recalled that in the two great wars, it was our sheet-anchor against vitamin C deficiency,[3] and that in 1916 when the crop failed, cases of scurvy soon appeared in our towns.

Aneurin, the anti-beriberi vitamin B_1, is present to the extent of between 30–60 international units per 100 g., so that 14 oz. of boiled potatoes will supply about 180 of the 500 units required by an adult in his daily diet. Riboflavin, a vitamin of the B_2 group, is also present in the potato in the same ratio as in equal quantities of wheat, meat or fish. Nicotinic acid, the anti-pellagra vitamin B_2, on the other hand, is said only to be present in amounts insufficient to protect; nevertheless the disease is unknown in those countries where the potato is freely eaten.[4]

Against these many and substantial advantages, which the potato offers as a staple article of diet, must be placed the fact that it is deficient in

[1] Mustel, G. F. le chevalier (1767). Address to the Roy. Soc. Agric. Rouen. *Abst. Rev. Hort. Suisse* (Sept. 1942), p. 220.

[2] See chapter XVI, p. 304.

[3] Olliver, M. (1941). From a paper read before the Food Group of the Soc. Chemical Industry, 9 April.

[4] Harris, Leslie (1940). Communication to the author.

two of the most essential vitamins, viz. carotene or vitamin A, and the anti-rachitic vitamin D. In lands where the potato is almost the sole food of the masses, as it was in eighteenth-century Ireland and in parts of Poland before the war, these deficiencies are made good by the drinking of milk, which is generally available in the poorer agricultural communities. Potatoes normally contain an alkaloidal glucoside, solanin, which may be harmful when absorbed in large quantity. It is more plentiful in the unripe than in the mature tubers, and although exposure to the light greatly increases the amount of solanin in the tuber, the effect is to make the latter unpalatable rather than harmful. There is, indeed, no incontrovertible evidence that its presence has ever caused trouble.

The digestibility of the potato, and its capacity to act if necessary as a 'sole diet', is a subject which cannot be neglected in post-war Europe, where the total supply of food is insufficient and its variety restricted. The following paragraphs from an article by Dr Harriette Chick throws much light on these matters:

Many human experiments among the most notable of which are those of Rubner, have shown that only about 5 % of the total calories [of the potato] remain undigested; the loss in nitrogen was greater and varied from 15 % to 30 %.[1] In experiments made by Rubner with the finest white flour, there was a loss of only 6 % of the ingested nitrogen in the faeces, but with 'whole' meal (95 % extraction in the milling), the loss was about 30 %, similar to that suffered with the nitrogen of the potato.[2]

To what extent the potato alone can support life, is another problem which has received serious attention. Dr Chick has summed up the position as follows, more especially in respect to the value of the nitrogenous constituents:[3]

The lengthy experiments by Hindhede (1913) are the best-known example; on a diet consisting only of potato and margarine, taken for periods of 100 days and more, the body weight was nearly maintained and positive nitrogen balances were reported, when the daily intake of 'digestible nitrogen' was as low as 3–4 g.—corresponding to 11–15 g. protein with the additional non-protein nitrogen referred to above. The subject was a man of 27 years old, of body weight 70 kg. (11 stone) who consumed 3000 calories daily and led an active life. These experiments and the conclusions drawn have been the subject of lively controversy. In a carefully controlled experiment carried out by Rubner and Thomas (1918) lasting 6 days, upon a vigorous man of 75 kg. weight (11 st. 11 lb.) the diet consisted solely of potato; 2600 g. (5 lb. 11 oz.) were consumed daily, with a little salt, the average daily nitrogen intake was 8·7 g. and the average daily nitrogen excretion in urine and faeces 10·6 g.,

[1] Rubner, M. and Thomas, K. (1918). *Abt. Physiologie-Jahg.* 1.
[2] Rubner, M. (1918). *Arch. Anatomie Physiol., Abt. Physiologie-Jahg.* 53.
[3] Chick, Harriette (1940). Nutritive Value of the Potato. *Chemistry and Industry*, vol. LIX, p. 738.

showing a negative balance amounting to about 2 g. nitrogen. Other observations, however, showed equilibrium and even a positive balance (Rubner and Thomas, 1918). Abderhalden (1915) and his colleagues reported nitrogenous equilibrium on an intake of 4·5 g. N daily derived from potato, and Rose and her co-workers (1917) a similar result with a woman subject of 50 kg. (8 stone) weight, who derived the nitrogen of her diet, 4·97 g. daily, from 1500 g. potatoes (3½ lb.).

The above account of the more valuable properties of the potato by no means exhausts the consideration of all its best-known constituents.[1] There is one substance constantly found in the potato which should be mentioned, and that is the enzyme known as 'tyrosinase': it is this substance, harmless in itself, which for long has been believed to be responsible for the blackening of the potato after cooking. This view has been strongly criticized of late and the cause of blackening has been ascribed to the existence of a protein and ferrous iron complement which is held to occur in the tuber in quantities which differ materially in different varieties.[2]

Before taking leave of the 'values', a word must be said as to the distribution throughout the tubers of the two most important constituents, viz. starch and protein. Those parts of the potato nearest the skin, which are removed by peeling with a knife, contain the highest proportion of starch and, incidentally, of solanin, whilst the inner and more watery layer of the tuber is richest in all the nitrogenous constituents. It is obvious therefore that the best method of cooking potatoes is that which leaves the skin, or at least the subepidermal layer, intact.

In the process of cooking, much that is of value, more especially the ascorbic acid, may be greatly reduced. In general, it may be said that the more rapidly the potato is cooked, and the less time which is allowed to elapse between cooking and consumption, the less is the loss of essential values. The common habit of leaving peeled potatoes to soak in water, is equally to be eschewed if loss of vitamins by leaching is to be avoided.

[1] For an exhaustive account of the constituents of the potato, see Lampitt, L. H. and Goldenberg, N. *Chemistry and Industry*, vol. LIX, pp. 748–62 and *The Nation's Food*, 1946. Soc. Chem. Ind. Lond.
[2] Robinson, Ursula (1941). *Nature, Lond.*, vol. CXLVII, p. 717.

CHAPTER VIII

Names and Aliases

A study of the familiar names as opposed to the botanical, by which the potato has been known in different countries and at different times, has a wider interest than that presented by the etymology of the words themselves, though that is not inconsiderable. The associations of the names with other objects, together with their country of origin, are valuable guides towards the discovery of the paths and the agencies by which the potato spread amongst the peoples of the world.

The early sixteenth-century Spanish invaders of South America, when they encountered the new root in Colombia, spoke and wrote of it as 'Papa' or, as was more usual, by the plural form 'Papas', a word which all authorities agree they found current in Peru.

Castellanos[1] (1886), who mentioned potatoes, which were seen in 1537 both growing and on the table of the natives in Colombia, described them as truffles. Cieza,[2] who encountered them in the following year in the district of Popayán in Ecuador, compared them to truffles but speaks of them by the native name, *Papas*. Gomara[3] in 1552, and Herrera[4] in 1601, describing the potato of the Collao a thousand miles farther south, both use the same word, *Papas*.

Ondegardo[5] (c. 1560), who has much to say about the potato being used in discharge of tribute, refers to it always as *Papas*. The corregidor, Bricegno[6] (1586), who was probably the first white man publicly to recommend that potatoes should be cultivated in order to combat famine, particularly in Spain, speaks of them as 'truffles' and 'papas' alternatively. Cardan[7] (1557), does the same. Benzoni,[8] who had no very high opinion of the potato, speaks of it only as a sort of 'truffle'. One could quote other sixteenth-century authorities in support of the view that the Spaniards generally likened the potato to a kind of truffle but at the same

---

[1] Castellanos, Juan de (1886). Op. cit.
[2] Cieza de León, Pedro (1550). *The War of Quito*. Madrid, 1886. Trans. C. R. Markham. Hakluyt Soc. 1913.
[3] Gómara, López de (1552). Op. cit.
[4] Herrera, Antonio de (1601). Op. cit. vol. v, p. 187.
[5] Polo de Ondegardo, J. (c. 1560). Report. Trans. C. R. Markham. Hakluyt Soc. 1873.
[6] Bricegno, Diego Dávila (1586). *Relat. Geograph. d. Indes*. Quoted from E. Heckel, *Ann. de la Faculté des Sciences de Marseilles*, 1906, tome xvi, fasc. N.
[7] Cardan, Jerome (1557). Op. cit.
[8] Benzoni, Girolamo (1565). *History of the New World showing his travels from 1541–1556*. Venice, 1565. Hakluyt Soc. 1857.

time recognized it as distinct and unlike anything they had previously encountered. The retention of the native name, which happened to be an easy one to pronounce, was assured, at least in its own homeland.

There is no doubt that 'Papa' is Peruvian, and neither a borrowed word nor one invented by the Spaniards; in fact it was at the time of the Conquest the official native term for the potato. In the prayers for the potato recorded by Molina,[1] which were recited, in the days of the Incas, at the annual Situa Ceremonial at Cuzco, when representatives from all parts of the empire were gathered in the capital, it was the 'Papas' for which they prayed.

Guamán Poma de Ayala[2] who, an Inca on his mother's side and a Spaniard on his father's, might well be expected to employ a term which would be familiar to both nations, speaks frequently of 'Papas' in his great book.

The word itself is said to be of Quechuan origin, i.e. it derived from the language spoken by the Incas, their immediate clansmen and the official classes, a language which eventually became the *lingua franca* of the empire. The meaning of the word is strictly 'tuber' and in the vernacular it is said to be used for any tuber, whether of a *Solanum* or other genus, always excepting such cultivated tubers as the 'Oca'.

It has been suggested that 'Papa', far from being a native Quechuan, is a Latin word, meaning nourishment and derived from the sucking sounds of an infant. Such a foreign origin is obviously untenable, for the word was established long before the Spaniards arrived in South America, as witness the name of the Peruvian village Papamarca (*marca* = village), so called because of its importance as a potato-raising centre, which Garcilaso[3] mentions as being visited by the Inca Tupac Yupanqui on one of his imperial expeditions in the middle of the fifteenth century. Similarly, a high mountain area of the Province of Cauca, Colombia, is known as the 'Páramo de las Papas'. That it is primarily imitative in origin, is equally improbable, seeing that the potato is neither a juicy fruit nor one eaten uncooked.[4]

There are other native and distinct names for the potato[5] in the Quechuan and the Chibchan tongues, as well as in the Aymaran

---

[1] Molina, Cristóbal (1573). Op. cit.
[2] Poma de Ayala, Felipe Guamán (c. 1613). Op. cit.
[3] Garcilaso de la Vega (1609). *Royal Commentaries*, vol. II, p. 328 (ed. 1723).
[4] It is not inconceivable that the pre-Columbian Peruvians in the long-distant past, as they trekked up from the Amazonian forests, borrowed the name of the fruit of the *Carica papaya*, the papaw, and applied it to the new-found tubers of *Solanum tuberosum*. In the Caribbean languages, the fruit is called 'papay', which Europeans sometimes spoke of as 'papa' [*Oxford English Dict.* See 'Papaw'.] The papaw is a large fruit with a fleshy rind surrounding a soft pulp containing numerous seeds, in view of which it would not be extravagant to infer an onomatopoeical origin to the various forms of its name, such as *papay, papa, papaw, papaya* and *paupau*.
[5] See also Hawkes (1947) quoted in the Introduction. – Ed.

language which was spoken by all the peoples conquered by the Incas in the neighbourhood of Lake Titicaca. None of these alternative names would have been likely to have held their own against a word with an onomatopoeical origin in its own right.

Markham, in his Quechuan vocabulary, gives 'Acsu' = Petticoat, and 'Ascu' = *S. tuberosum*. Wight[1] points out that whilst the Dictionary of Antonio Ricardo, 1586, supports the former, it knows nothing of 'Ascu' and gives 'Papa' for the potato; he goes on to say that 'Akso' or 'Acsu', meaning potato, is unknown amongst the Quechuans to-day, though he records the fact that Jean de Figueredo (1754) in his vocabulary of the language of Chinchaisuyo in the Province of Junin, gives 'Acsu' = Papas. This latter is confirmed by Tschudi[2] who, however, knows of no Quechuan word for the potato. Recently my friend, Dr J. G. Hawkes, has received two varieties from this Peruvian district bearing the names 'Suito Acczu' = long potato, and 'Yana Acczu' = black potato, which bears out the contention of both Wight and Hawkes that the Quechuan term 'Acczu', though rare, does occur. The Chibchan term 'Iomsa' or 'Iomuy' was once used in the Bogotá district.

The Aymaran names for the potato are 'Amca' and 'Choque': the literal meaning of the latter is said by Laufer[3] to be 'testicle'; the former has become obsolete.[4]

In Chile, the Araucanians who throughout the seventeenth century were in constant, if hostile, contact with the Spaniards, employed the word 'Pogni' or 'Poñi' for the cultivated potato, whilst they called the wild potato 'Malla',[5] a word which reappears in our name for the wild species, *S. maglia*. Writing prior to 1787, Molina[6] states that the cultivated potato is known in Chile under the names 'Pogny' and 'Papa'. The use of the latter has been held as evidence that the potato reached Chile from Peru-Bolivia.[7]

According to Tschudi[8] the Quechuan language has no word for the potato, but in the Chinchay dialect, which was spoken all along the coast, it is called 'Acsu' which is, of course, the same word as other authorities have asserted is Quechuan. In view of the fact that there were several terms for the potato in current use in the day of the empire of the Incas, it is a matter of surprise and congratulation that only one of them,

---

[1] Wight, W. F. (1917). *Proc. 3rd Ann. Meeting, Potato Assoc. America* (1916), pp. 35–52.

[2] Tschudi, J. J. (1846). *Peru-Reiseskitzen*, p. 262 n.

[3] Laufer, B. (1938). American Plant Migration, pt. 1, The Potato, p. 102. *Field Mus. Nat. Hist.* vol. xxviii, No. 1.

[4] Dr Cardenas, a Bolivian biologist and Quechuan scholar, tells me that he is not in agreement with Laufer.

[5] Pogni and Poñi are respectively the Italian and Spanish transliterations of the Indian word that in English would be written as Ponyi; similarly Maglia, Malla (Malya). – Ed.

[6] Molina, Ignatius (1787). *History of Chile*.

[7] Wight, W. F. (1917). Op. cit.   [8] Tschudi (1847). *Travels in Peru*, p. 178 n.

viz. 'Papa', was adopted by the Spaniards and, still more, that it has held its own throughout all Latin America.

When we turn to the Spanish homeland, we find that except in the provinces of Andalusia and Estremadura, 'Papa' as a designation for the potato disappears, nor does it recur elsewhere. That it should have penetrated into these two provinces is presumably due to the importance of Cadiz as the port for the South American trade and the route thence to the capital. The objection which was felt to its use doubtless lies in its identity in form and pronunciation with *papá*, a father, and *Papa*, the Pope.[1]

The name, however, was not dropped without a struggle: Clusius (1601) invented the latinized name *Papas Peruanorum*; Gaspard Bauhin in 1596 and 1620 that of *Papas Indorum vel Hispanorum*, and his brother, Johannes, *Papas Americanum*, but great as these authorities were they were yet unable to attach to the potato the one name which was its own by right of priority.

For the source of some of the more widespread names of the potato we must go back once more to the Spanish conquistadores: it will be remembered that they described it as being a kind of truffle, or 'turma de tierra' which means literally an earth-testicle. This likeness to a testicle may perhaps appear somewhat far-fetched, but it may have been suggested by the Aymara name 'choque' which it is claimed stood equally for a potato tuber or a testicle.[2] Although the term 'turma de tierra' did not persist for long in Spain, it soon obtained a firm foothold in Italy, where the truffle as early as 1584 was known as 'tartufi' and 'tartufoli',[3] and the potato as 'tartuffo' and 'tartuffolo'. Clusius inscribed in his own hand the word 'taratoufli' on the aquarelle of the potato plant which he received in 1588 (Pl. XIX, fig. 63). Thus was initiated one of those successful aliases the adoption of which has characterized the nomenclature of the potato throughout its career of conquest.

'Tartufflo' was converted by the Frenchman, Olivier de Serres in his *Théâtre d'Agriculture*, published in 1600, into 'Cartoufle', which suffered a further change into 'Kartoffel', as the potato made its way into German-speaking Western Europe during the eighteenth century.

Following the migration of this particular synonym, we find it reappearing in those Slavonic lands, where the potato was introduced from Germany.[4] In both Russian and Polish, the potato is called 'Kartofel'.

[1] The potato is, however, feminine (*la papa*) whereas father and Pope are masculine (*el papa*). – Ed.

[2] Dr Hawkes does not agree with Laufer's view, and doubts whether in any case it influenced the European terminology.

[3] Durante, Castore (1584). *Herbario Nuovo Venezia*. (Quoted from Laufer.)

[4] I am indebted for much of the information which follows to the work of Berthold Laufer, as well as to the learning of Mr I. H. Burkill, and Prof. Sir E. Minns, the fruits of which have been so generously placed at my disposal.

Numerous variations of the name have crept in, in different districts, such as the diminutive 'Kartoska' and the dialectal form 'Kartopha,' 'Kartocla' and 'Kartovka' in Russian; 'Karrofla' and 'Karczofle' in Polish; as well as the eighteenth-century 'Taretofl', this last harking directly back to the original Italian. In Lettish one finds 'Kartupelis', in Bulgarian 'Kartof', and in Serbian 'Krtola'.[1]

Whilst all the above forms are directly derived from 'tartoufle', there exists in the Welsh language a word for the potato, 'Cloron', which though having the same literal meaning as 'tartoufle', has its origin in the root *clor*, meaning an earth-nut.

In southern Russia, the German introduction of the potato is again made evident by the use of the terms 'Mandybúrka' and 'Gardybúrka', which embody the old Czech word 'Bramburk', i.e. Brandenburg; in the Czech language it is known as 'Brambor' which means Prussian. In Roumania, derivatives from both Tartoufle and Brandenburg reappear, the first under the names 'Cartofla', 'Cartofa', 'Cartof', and the latter as 'Bandraburca'.

In Poland the Brandenburg influence is seen in the words 'Panbowka' and 'Perka'; in Finnish we meet it as 'Peruna'.

Once more we must return to the Americas for perhaps the most successful of all the potato's aliases, the name 'Potato' itself, but in doing so, confusion will be avoided if, during the remainder of this chapter, we refer to the different plants involved, by their Linnaean names, as given below:

    Solanum tuberosum, i.e. *S. tuberosum* = the common potato.
    Ipomoea batatas, i.e. *I. batatas* = the sweet-potato.
    Helianthus tuberosus, i.e. *H. tuberosus* = the Jerusalem artichoke.
    Dioscorea opposita, i.e. *D. opposita* (and other species) = the yam.
    Colocasia esculenta, i.e. *C. esculenta* = the taro.
    Potentilla anserina, i.e. *P. anserina* = silver weed.
    Manihot utilissima, i.e. *M. utilissima* = the manioc, cassava, or yuca.
    Cyclamen europaeum, i.e. *C. europaeum* = the common cyclamen or sow-bread.

The sweet-potato, *Ipomoea batatas*, was known some hundred years before the discovery of America. It is thought to have reached the Marquesas Islands some time in the thirteenth century, and was recorded by several of the early voyagers during the fourteenth and fifteenth centuries. Columbus and his followers found the sweet-potato established as a familiar food throughout the West Indies; in Peru it had been known for hundreds, possibly thousands, of years, prior to the coming of the Spanish, for dried specimens have been frequently recovered from the earliest tombs. It was brought back to Spain at an early date, so that it was in general cultivation there in suitable districts early in the

---

[1] Salaman in a manuscript note adds 'Kaltuvag' in Prince William Sound, Alaska, derived no doubt from the Russian. – Ed.

sixteenth century. As the sweet-potato needs a warm climate, it never spread to Northern Europe, though it was grown for a short time in some parts of southern France; it was, however, a common import to London, where it was regarded as a delicacy. Its appearance as a rarity in a garden in Hampshire in the early seventeenth century, has already been referred to.[1]

Columbus encountered 'sweet-potatoes' on his first journey to Hispaniola in 1492, and referred to them as looking like yams and tasting like chestnuts. On his return he made a triumphal progress to the court of Ferdinand and Isabella at Barcelona. There he exhibited his ten Indian natives and a variety of animals, fruits, and ornaments of gold. López de Gómara states that amongst the fruits were 'ajíes'[2] and maize. It was therefore with 'ají' that Columbus first introduced *Ipomoea batatas*. On the second voyage, Columbus was accompanied by a surgeon called Diego Alvarez Chanca, and a priest Father Roman Paul. The latter wrote a Memoir on the religious beliefs of the natives of Hispaniola in which he refers to this same root as 'age'.[5]

Peter Martyr the historian, who served on the Council of the Indies in 1526, sent home a series of Memoirs between 1511 and 1521 and states, on information derived from the surgeon Chanca, that in Hispaniola they grew a considerable quantity of a root like a turnip, with an excellent flavour, for whith the Arawak name was 'age'.[5] Peter Martyr, however, adheres to the form 'age'. Later in the same work, he again describes the sweet-potato under the name of 'patatas', of which he says there are several varieties. In Jamaica he finds no less than eight varieties of 'patatas' and remarks what pleasure it would have given him to send some to the Pope.[3]

Oviedo[4] went to the Indies twenty years later: he speaks of the same root (*Ipomoea batatas*) as 'aje',[5] and thought so highly of it that he brought some back to Avila in Spain. He tells how a quite similar plant, the 'Batatas', is the chief food of all the Indians in Hispaniola, and that whilst it looks exactly like the 'aje', it is, in his opinion, more delicate, has a thinner skin, is more easily digested and of a better taste, and compares favourably with marzipan. He mentions several varieties of 'batata' between which the expert can discover differences in quality. Peter Martyr, writing in 1514, to some extent inverts the position, saying that it is the 'botato' which grows wild in Darien, and that the 'age' is like a turnip or the 'great puffe' of Milan. At Darien the natives eat both 'batatas' and 'age'.[5]

---

[1] Chapter VII, p. 101.
[2] 'Ají' is a Peruvian word applied to-day to the peppers (*Capsicum* spp.).
[3] Martyr, Peter (1516). *De Orbe Novo*, p. 589. Trans. Paul Gaffarel, 1907.
[4] Oviedo y Valdés (1557). *Historia de las Indias*, vol. I, p. 272, ed. 1851.
[5] There may have been a confusion here between *ají* (*Capsicum*), *ajipa* (*Pachyrrhizus*) which has a tuberous root, and sweet potatoes, which are called *batatas* by Gómara. – Ed.

Mr Burkill thinks that it was the starchy types of *Ipomoea* which were spoken of generally as 'aje', and that the sweet varieties were known as 'batatas', a view which falls into line with Clusius's statement after his visit to Spain, that 'batatas' were like 'ages' but smaller and sweeter.

The early navigators encountered the sweet-potato in Central America: they added to the names already known, the native terms 'camotes' and 'amotes'. The former has been transferred without change into Spanish, but neither 'aje' nor 'camote' became established as terms for either type of potato in Europe, with one possible exception. In the patois of the Vosges, the common potato is known as 'Quemotte',[1] doubtless a derivative of 'Camote', which is the more likely, seeing that Franche Comté, which included part of the Vosges, was under Spanish rule throughout the sixteenth and most of the seventeenth centuries.

It was as the 'batatas' that the *Ipomoea* became generally known.[3]

There is some doubt as to what the origin of this word is: Lord Hepburn,[2] one of the outstanding authorities on, and advocate for, the use of the potato during the latter quarter of the eighteenth century, quotes an unnamed French author as saying that 'they, i.e. our common potatoes, *Solanum tuberosum*, were discovered at a village called Patata in some island in the South American sea', and hence the name. One wishes that one could be as readily satisfied as was this eminent lawyer. The *Oxford Dictionary* regards it as an Hawaiian word. Whatever its origin, 'batata' as the name for the sweet-potato became firmly established, and has held its own for 400 years. It was, one may suppose, the superficial likeness between the tubers, rather than any similarity in the habits of growth of *S. tuberosum* and of *Ipomoea batatas*, that led the average Spaniard of that day to designate the newcomer, *Solanum tuberosum*, by the same name as that of the sweet-potato, *Ipomoea batatas* he had known and enjoyed for more than half a century. The result is that in Spain to-day, 'batate' retains its original connotation *I. batatas*, and its closely allied form 'patate' has become identified with the common potato *Solanum tuberosum*. It may be said that from the early part of the seventeenth century, the name used for *S. tuberosum* throughout the Spanish-speaking world, is one form or another of the word 'batata'.

In the Philippines, *S. tuberosum* is known both as 'papas' and 'patatas'; in Portugal and the Portuguese-speaking countries, 'batata' or variations of the name, hold sway; whilst the sweet-potato is spoken of as 'batata doce'. In Brazil and the Cape Verde Islands this becomes 'battata-Ingleza', a token of the predominant part England took in the develop-

[1] Haudricourt, André and Hédin, Louis (1943). *L'Homme et les Plantes Cultivées*, p. 196. Paris.

[2] Hepburn, G. Buchan (1808). *Communications to the Board of Agriculture*, vol. II, p. 138.

[3] But not in Latin America where 'Camote', 'Papa dulce' or 'Kumara' are the usual names in the Spanish-speaking countries and 'batata doce' in Brazil. – Ed.

ment of Brazil after the Portuguese royal family had migrated there in 1808. In the Portuguese enclave of Goa in India, it is known as 'batata-Surrata', indicating its introduction through the trading factory at Surat, 120 miles north of Bombay, founded by the English early in the seventeenth century.

The track of the sixteenth century and subsequent Portuguese explorers and traders can be recognized by the names adopted by the natives for the *Ipomoea batatas*. Thus we find 'patas' or 'patat' in Wolof, Senegambia 'matata' in Sobo, south Nigeria; 'libala' in Ifumu; 'mbala' in Kongo; 'i. batata' and 'lwe-batata' in the Kaffir language. In Timor the Malays speak of 'batata', the Alfur tribes of Amboyna of 'patatas', and those in north-east Celebes, of 'watala'.

In the English-speaking world, the use of the name 'potato' has become general. In Scandinavia it reappears as 'potatis' in Sweden, and 'potet' and 'potetes' in Norway. In Greece, 'patata' is one of the names applied to *Solanum tuberosum*.

This partial promise of a consistent system of nomenclature, even if founded on an originally erroneous identification of the common with the sweet-potato, was soon to be belied.

During the seventeenth century the potato, which was grown but very little anywhere in France, was spoken of as 'truffe' and 'truffe rouge'. The term 'cartoufle' used by de Serres disappeared. A name derived from 'batata' was used for the potato only in Brittany where, under English influence it took the form of 'patate'. Elsewhere in France this name was reserved for the *Ipomoea batatas*.

Perhaps the most remarkable of the aliases assumed by the potato is that represented by the term 'Pomme de terre' and its various mutations. Its history in brief is as follows: In the spring of 1613, a French adventurer, Claude Delaney, seigneur of Razilly, brought back from the island of Maranhão, which lies in the delta of the River Grajahu in Brazil, some of the native warriors of the Guaranís, who were known as Topinambous. He introduced them to the queen-mother and she, possibly seeing in them a tangible token of France's claims against the Portuguese to the eastern coast of Brazil, made much of them at the court, where the Topinambous were spoken of as 'allies and confederates of our nation'. In a very short time these strange visitors became the 'rage' in Paris. The king acted as godparent at their baptism, and suitable marriages were arranged for the three who survived the excitement of their journey and public reception. Before long, partly as a result of the interest aroused by these strange savages, and partly owing to the satire of writers such as Malherbe, the Parisians reacted by coining a new word 'Topinambour' which came to mean someone or something gross, absurd, or bizarre.

It was at this critical moment that a tuberous vegetable, *Helianthus tuberosus*, introduced from Canada by Champlain and Lescarbot, began to appear in the markets of Paris. It was something quite new; unlike anything encountered before, peculiar in taste, ungainly in shape; in short, something foreign to the cultured Frenchmen, and hence a little absurd, rather 'topinamboue', in fact; and as 'Topinambour', the tubers were hawked through the streets of Paris. How the same tubers came to be known in England as Jerusalem artichokes is another tale, not so romantic but equally irrational.[1]

The new root became popular in France, Holland, Italy and, to some extent in England, but its vogue, especially in Britain, was not for long. On passing to Holland it acquired the name of 'erdappel' (earth apple), and on reaching Burgundy this was translated into French as 'Pomme de terre'. The term 'erdappel' was annexed from the Common Cyclamen, *Cyclamen europaeum*, whose tuber for centuries had been valued as a source of medicine and occasionally eaten as a food. The cyclamen had acquired various local names: 'sow-bread' in England and 'erdappel' in Holland. When the *Solanum tuberosum* reached Burgundy, it was this borrowed name put into French, which it was given, and thus we get the familiar 'Pomme de terre'. The *Helianthus tuberosus* was also known as 'Erdbirn' and this likewise became 'Poire de terre' which in Zedler's *Lexicon* (1735) is mentioned as an alternative name to 'Topinambour'.

During the eighteenth century in France, the Jerusalem artichoke seems to have been more widely grown than was the potato, and when in 1713 a conflict broke out in the Vosges between the peasants and the tithe-owners as to the propriety of tithing roots, the term used throughout was 'Pomme de terre'. In most cases it was probably the *H. tuberosus* and not *Solanum tuberosum* which was involved, because the main defence of the peasants was that inasmuch as the crop regenerated itself spontaneously, it should be exempt. Both crops, of course, could be so 'regenerated', but whilst it was the rule in regard to the *Helianthus tuberosus*, it was the exception in the case of the *Solanum tuberosum*.

As the century progressed, the balance of popularity began to tip in favour of *S. tuberosum*, which gradually came to monopolize the term 'Pomme de terre'. At the same time, the less popular titles 'Poire de terre', 'Poirette' and 'Pomette', passed into oblivion. *S. tuberosum* had successfully acquired and monopolized yet another alias, but not without increasing the confusion already reigning in the minds of those who had neither need nor desire to consume the new food.

[1] Prain, Sir David (1923). The Story of Some Common Garden Plants. *Trans. South Eastern Union Scientific Soc.* pp. 38–59.
    Salaman, R. N. (1940). Why Jerusalem Artichoke? *J. Roy. Hort. Soc.* vol. LXV, pp. 338–82.

Misson[1] writing in 1697 says of the people of Ireland that 'they are mighty lovers of Potatoes...an earth apple, a kind of Topinambour'. And so late as 1826 the *Dictionnaire des Sciences Naturelles*, under 'Pomme de terre' gives both *Helianthus tuberosus* and *Solanum tuberosum*. Engel[2] in 1777 jokingly refers to the confusion of names which dogged the progress of the potato, and illustrates it by the adventures of a consignment of tubers from Ireland to Lyons. Leaving Ireland as 'potatoes', they arrived in Bordeaux as 'patatas' and left there as 'truffes rouges', or 'truffes blanches', reached the Customs at Lyons, where they were dubbed 'truffe-sèches' and, as such, duly assessed for duty. On taking them to his own garden, they were spoken of as 'truffières', whilst he himself insisted on calling them 'pommes de terre'.

The German term 'Erdappel' retained its new meaning and, as 'Aardappel', represents the Dutch term for *S. tuberosum*. Derivatives of the name appear in the Far East, where Dutch influence is or has been paramount. Thus in Malay and Ceylon it appears as 'Artappel'. In the Ainu language, *S. tuberosum* is called 'Appura', which Laufer[3] claims to be derived from 'Aardappel'. Elsewhere it has been used in a translated form: thus in Persia, *S. tuberosum* is spoken of as 'sib-i-Zamini' (earth apple), but it is also known as 'alu-i Malkam' (Sir John Malcolm's tuber).

'Alu', the sanskrit for tuber, is employed in Hindi for the potato, whilst the Bengali form is 'bilati aloo' (the English tuber). 'Alucha' from the same root, in Persian, means a plum.

In the Roumanian province of Transylvania, *S. tuberosum* is known as 'Mere de pamint': 'mere' is derived from Malum, an apple, and 'pamint' is the earth. In Finnish it is also spoken of as an earth-apple, 'Maaomena'. In the Czech, Polish and Ukrainian languages the words 'zamnak', 'zemniak', and 'zemnyak', all meaning earth-apple, are employed. In modern Greek 'geó-melon', the earth-apple, follows the same tradition.

It was mentioned above that the terms 'birne' and 'poire' (a pear) had both served as names for *Helianthus tuberosus*: one of these, 'birne', still lives on, though its allegiance was transferred in the eighteenth century to *Solanum tuberosum*. In Germany we find it as 'Grundbirne,' and in dialect forms as 'Grummbire'; in Bavaria as 'Krumbeer'; and as 'Gruntpirn', 'Grumper' and 'Krumpir' in Kärnten.

Grundbirne as a root term for *S. tuberosum* has spread beyond the Reich along the Danube and into the Balkans. In the Bulgarian tongue

---

[1] Misson, François (1697). *Memoirs and Observations, etc.* Trans. by W. Ozell, 1719.
[2] Engel, Samuel. Author of the article 'Pomme de terre' in the 1777 edition of *La Grande Encyclopédie*.
[3] Laufer, Berthold (1938). Op. cit.

it appears as 'Krumpir', and 'Gombiri' with the plural form 'Gombelki'; in the Serbian as 'Krompir' and 'Krumpir'; in Slovenian as 'Krompir'; in Czech as 'Krumpir' and 'Krumple'; in Moravian as 'Grumbir'; Slovakian as 'Krumpla', and in Polish as 'Kompery', 'Kumpery', 'Krompele' and 'Kraple'; in the Lithuanian as 'Klumberis'; in the Hungarian as 'Krumpli', and in the Roumanian as 'Crumpira', 'Crumpena' and 'Grumciri'.

I have to thank Prof. E. H. Minns for introducing me to a further group of names for the potato, which take their origin from the Greek 'βυλβος', Latin 'Bulbus'; a word used in both languages for any swollen root or tuber, especially of vegetables. The names so derived all occur amongst the Slavonic peoples in the easternmost parts of Europe.

The use of an imported word of Greek origin for a vegetable, which only reached those parts towards the end of the eighteenth century, may be accounted for by the fact that throughout the Turkish empire trade was carried on at that time by itinerant Greek and Jewish merchants. The former served the more eastern portions, especially Bessarabia; the latter had more influence in Wallachia and Moldavia.

In Ukrainian, 'bulbos' occurs as 'Bulba', 'Barabolya'[1] and 'Garabola'. In Czech as 'Barabol'. In Serbian as 'Baraboj' and 'Garabola'; in Bulgarian as 'Baraboj' and 'Bruboj';[1] in Yiddish as Boulbés and in Russian as 'Barabolya', 'Bulba', 'Bunba', and 'Gulba'.

The last-mentioned, Gulba, has a peculiar origin. In chapter VII attention is drawn to the fact that the Old Believers of Russia regarded the potato as something evil and sexually tainted. In this word they found expression for their feelings. For whilst 'Gulba' is a valid transformation from 'Bulba', its use was, in fact, an intentional play on words. 'Gulba' really means a promenade, but one with a sinister bias of a sexual character; hence a 'going astray', a reference to the potato's alleged tarnished ancestry.

From Zedler's *Lexicon*[2] one obtains a reliable synopsis of the nomenclature which prevailed in the first half of the eighteenth century in Western Europe in respect to the various immigrant American roots and the home plants to which they were likened:

Solanum tuberosum, the common potato, is described as *S. tuberosum esculentum*, *Papas Peruanorum*, and colloquially as 'Tartuffeln'.

Helianthus tuberosus, the Jerusalem artichoke, is described under the title *H. tuberosus* and also under 'Erdbirne', 'Poire de terre' and 'Topinambour'.

---

[1] These two latter terms for *S. tuberosum* are given by Laufer as derivatives of 'Bramburk', Czech for Brandenburg and Bramboa, the Serbian for Prussia.
[2] Zedler, J. H. *Lexicon Universalis*, 1732–1750. Leipzig.

Ipomoea Batatas, the sweet-potato, appears as 'Battata', 'Camote', 'Zuckerwurzel', and 'English potatoes' which, in view of the description of the plant, cannot refer to *Solanum tuberosum*. All that seems to be implied is that in England the 'battata' is called a potato, which was a fact. It may be recalled that *Ipomoea batatas* in England was often spoken of as the 'Spanish potato'.

Cyclamen europaeum, the cyclamen, is called 'Erdappfel', 'Pomum terrae', 'Schweinbrod', and 'Hirschbrunst'. This latter term refers to its supposed power of inciting rutting amongst deer.

Truffles are described as 'Erdnüssen', but are also spoken of as 'Erdappeln'.

The following terms are not mentioned: 'Patate', 'Potato' (except as applied above), 'Cartoufle', 'Kartoffel', 'Pomme de terre', and 'Jerusalem artichoke'.

When the *Solanum tuberosum* reached lands far away from Europe, the names which attached themselves to the immigrant tuber depended to a considerable extent on the state of civilization of the people and the national and linguistic characteristics of the Europeans who introduced it. Thus, when it impinged on the ancient civilization of China, the names employed for it were Chinese in origin and were formed on the 'alias' principle. Two models existed, the yam and the taro. The yam, *Dioscorea opposita*, the form grown from time immemorial in China and there known as 'shu', led to *Solanum tuberosum* being called 'yang shu', 'foreign yam'. 'Shu' is a generic name for tuber and implies a bulky tuber and needed a qualifying term when applied to a yam. Originally, *Dioscorea opposita* was known as 'shu-yi', but as this happened to be the personal name of an Emperor of the Tang Dynasty, in order to avoid disrespect, the yam was altered to 'shu-yu'.

The taro, *Colocasia esculenta*, a popular source of food, is called in Chinese 'yu', and *Solanum tuberosum* 'yang yu', 'foreign taro'; it is also spoken of as 'yam shan yu', the 'foreign mountain taro'.

In Tibetan, besides 'p'an sù', derived from the Chinese 'fan shu' which Laufer says means 'foreign tuber', *S. tuberosum* is also known as 'rgyra gro', a name which is derived from 'gro-ma', the name given to the plant *Potentilla anserina*, and 'rgya' which may refer either to India or China. The name 'skyiu' = sikkim, though originally applied to the yam, was also used for the potato, as 'p'i-lin skio', English yam.

Whether Laufer, from whom this statement is derived, is correct in equating 'gro-ma' with *P. anserina* I am unable to say, but it is a fact that in the Scotch Hebrides and Highlands, *P. anserina*, under the name 'brisgein', was much used as a food before the introduction of the potato.[1]

[1] Carmichael, Alex. *Carmina Gadelica*, vol. IV, p. 119.

In Arabic the potato is known as 'kalkas firenze', the 'taro' of the Franks.

In Japan, besides the term 'bareisho', they speak of *Solanum tuberosum* as 'jagatara imo'; Jakarta is the place where, in 1619, the Dutch made their first Javan settlement, and is the equivalent of Batavia, i.e. the Batavian tuber; another name of the same pattern is 'orando imo', the 'Holland tuber', and 'Ryukyo imo', the 'tuber from Ryuku Islands'; this latter, however, refers probably to the *Ipomoea batatas*. In Malay, besides the name 'artappel' already referred to, we have others denoting its origin, viz. 'Ubi Wolanda', the Holland yam, 'Ubi Europa', and 'Ubi Benggala', the European and Bengal yams 'ubi' meaning, simply, tuber. In Java the *Dioscorea opposita* is 'Kentang' which is a Batavian term meaning any kind of tuber, and *Solanum tuberosum*, having borrowed the name of its rival, is known as 'Kentang Welonda', the Holland yam, or 'Ubi Kentang', the yam tuber. In the neighbouring Island of Sunda, the *Manihot utilissima* is used as the model for another alias for *Solanum tuberosum*, so that 'huwu Wolanda' stands both for 'Dutch manihot' and 'Dutch potato.'

The use of the yam as an alias for the potato is not peculiar to the Far East. The sweet-potato was called by the followers of Columbus, 'nyame', which was also spelt and pronounced as 'igname' and 'inhame'. Salmon (1710), who never missed an opportunity of confounding confusion, grouped all potatoes, i.e. *S. tuberosum*, *Ipomoea batatas* and what he called the Irish potato, which was of course just *Solanum tuberosum* as grown in Great Britain, under one head, and to that he gives a list of names including 'Batata', 'Potato', 'Camotes', 'Pappus', 'Ignames' and 'Inhames'. The two last were the Spanish and Portuguese variants respectively of a West African native term applied to various kinds of tubers, more especially to a species of *Dioscorea*. Burkill[1] has shown that the name was introduced by the slaves imported in the fifteenth century into Portugal, to denote *Colocasia esculenta*, on which they were largely subsisted, a plant long known to the Middle East, which the Arabs had brought to the Peninsula in the tenth century.

The Maoris of New Zealand have several names for the potato, one of which may further illustrate the alias principle: it is 'parareka', 'para' an edible fern, and 'reka', sweet. Mr Burkill is of opinion that the word 'parareka' is related to the Tahitan forms 'patara', 'paraara', and 'panaura', all of which refer to the yam, *Dioscorea pentaphylla*, and that the connection with the fern is a secondary one resting rather on the fact that both were used as foodstuffs than on any likeness between the two.

[1] Burkill, I. H. (1938). The contact of the Portuguese with African food plants which gave words such as 'yam' to European languages. *Proc. Linn. Soc.* (Sess. 150), pp. 84–95.

In countries like Ireland, and to a lesser degree England and Wales, where the potato has become a staple article of food, it has drawn on itself a certain number of nicknames, some of which are of interest. Chief amongst these is the word 'Pratie' which, though claimed to be Gaelic, is almost certainly derived via 'prata' from 'patata', and is in common use throughout Ireland. The word 'fata' has a considerable and long-standing vogue in Ireland: it, too, is probably a derivative of 'patata'. 'Taters', a term very common in Wales, is yet another variation of the same. 'Murphy' is a slang term frequently used in Ireland: it is but one example of the employment of personal names to denote the potato, a practice which in some cases may commemorate some particularly successful local grower. Thus, 'Gleeson's potato' and 'O'Brien's potato' were household words. If the word 'potato' is omitted as superfluous, then the personal name comes to be used as a synonym for the potato itself. An example in the literature is that of 'Crokers', which is said to have been in use as early as 1640.[1]

There is, however, a term for the potato used in the western Hebrides which, if not purely Gaelic in origin, has at least acquired its final form under Gaelic influences. It was the custom for the co-partners of a Runrig farm of any 'town' to set aside a piece of land whose produce was devoted to the support of the poor.[2] If the land was bearing oats, then it was known as 'Faoch Araia', and if potatoes, as 'Faoch Buntata'. This latter word obviously suggests the original form 'batata' but the introduction of an 'n' creates a difficulty. Cameron[3] disregards this, a view confirmed by Prof. Angus Matheson.[4] Reference to a fanciful derivation of the word is to be found in Armstrong's *Gaelic Dictionary*, 1825: 'Bun-taghta, a potato; literally a choice root. For this ingenious rendering the Gaelic language is indebted to the late Sir John Mac-gregor Murray, Bart.' (1745–1822). From this it would appear that the introduction of the letter 'n' was either a concession to folk etymology, or, as Matheson points out, a deliberate attempt to gaelicize the word, in the belief that Gaelic was the 'root' of all things. It is of interest to observe that the word 'buntàta' must have been derived from 'bătātă' before it became anglicized to 'bătētă'.

In England, and particularly in Scotland, the term 'spud' is a wide-spread and familiar term; the word originally meant some kind of spade or digging-fork, more particularly the three-broad-pronged fork commonly used to raise the potato crop. 'Spuddy' is a slang term used for a man who sells bad potatoes.

[1] This matter is discussed in chapter IX, p. 152.
[2] A very similar custom was practised by the communal workers of the Ayllu under the Incas in Peru. See p. 44.
[3] Cameron, John (1883). *Gaelic Names of Plants.*
[4] Matheson, Angus. Letter to R.N.S. 17 May 1947.

The word 'potato' has been used as a slang term, in reverse, since the last part of the eighteenth century. One finds expressions such as potato-jaw[1] and potato-trap,[2] and even potato-nose[3] used as derisory terms by writers of distinction.

The names assumed by the potato in Europe, it will be observed, neither belong to, nor are borrowed from, any of the well-known root or bulbous food plants in use at the time, whether skirret, carrot, turnip or onion. The fact that, unlike them, it was not raised from seed, and that the tubers were dispersed in the soil at a distance from the plant, may have excluded the idea of such an association. On the other hand, these strange, often darkly coloured, isolated tubers lying within a radius of perhaps 3 ft. from the parent plant, were, in fact, not unlike truffles. Nor was it less logical to call them 'apples of the earth', for their distribution beneath the ground suggests that of the fallen fruit of an apple tree above it. It is true that the word 'erdappel' was already in general use for the cyclamen or sow-bread, but it was not confined to this plant; it was employed as a name for the mandrake, as well as for the water-melon. In fact the term seems to have had no narrow specific limitation, but rather to be a descriptive and picturesque designation for the less well-known vegetable food types other than those of the cabbage family.

The *batatas* group of names, though botanically resting on no sounder foundation than the others, has a secure basis in tradition. The *Ipomoea batatas* had come from the Americas to Spain and spread thence eastwards; it was a many-tubered 'root'; it could be propagated like *Solanum tuberosum*; it was cooked in the same manner; and the flavour of the cooked 'roots' were not dissimilar.

The restricted use of the 'bulbos' group of names, points clearly to the economic route by which it reached the Slav peoples who adopted the term. In its favour is the fact that its use was entirely non-committal.

Some indication of the route by which the potato reached the various parts of Europe, can be to some extent gathered from the names. In England we obtained our sweet-potatoes from Spain and used their name-root 'Batata' for the new root from America. When the potatoes from Great Britain were introduced to the English colonists on the American mainland they were, and still are, spoken of as Irish potatoes. In France the name first used came from Italy, as did its first tubers. In Germany the most widely used name, 'Kartoffel', indicates the passage of the new vegetable from Burgundy into Alsace. The wide use in the Slavonic-speaking countries of the 'Brandenburg' root-name is

---

[1] Mme d'Arblay. *Diary*, 4 June 1791: '"Hold your potato-jaw", cried the Duke [of Clarence], patting her [Mrs Schwellenberg].'

[2] Grose (1785). *Dict. of the Vulgar Tongue*: 'Shut your potato-trap.'

[3] Braddon, Eliz. (1881). *Asphodel*, vol. 1, p. 119: 'You wouldn't love a man with a potato-nose.'

indicative of the flood-like influence of the Prussia of Frederick the Great's day on Eastern Europe.

In the Far East, where people were accustomed to the yam and the taro, both producing tubers in a manner similar to that of the potato, there was no need to go outside their own immediate experience to find a suitable name; well-known plants were inevitably taken as models, and the immediate source of the new plant indicated by the use of such terms as 'Foreign', 'Dutch' or 'English'.

The variety and character of the root-names which have been borrowed to furnish out suitable titles for the potato in Europe afford us some measure of the interest which its advent aroused, and foreshadow the importance of the part it was to play in the destiny of most of its peoples.

CHAPTER IX

The Introduction to Europe: The Raleigh and other Legends

In the preceding chapters argument has been confined to the botanical type of the early European potato and its country of origin. Here it is proposed to deal with the oft-raised problem as to who was actually responsible for introducing the potato into Europe. Although it is common throughout history to link great events, whether social, economic, literary or religious, with the name of some individual, in very many cases such are, in truth, but eponymous heroes. It is to the clash between widely different social traditions, of which history knows no more impressive or tragic example, than that which occurred between the Europe of the sixteenth century, and the Inca and Aztec civilizations, that we must look for the creation of many of the new ideas and activities which emerged. Though such are, in the main, the offspring of the storm and strain of the struggle, they are associated in the public mind with the names of a few outstanding personalities who have themselves become more or less legendary. Thus the introduction of an important novelty such as the potato, is automatically ascribed to a Drake or a Raleigh, and the same accepted without further question.

The introduction of the potato has, it is true, proved to be one of the major events in man's recent history but, at the time, it was a matter of relatively little moment, and called forth no immediate public comment. In this respect it fared no worse than the vast majority of plants which have been brought into Europe in the last 2,000 years. In one respect, however, it had an advantage over all others, for it came to Europe not as one whose appeal was based on the delight of the eye or the palate alone, but with a long-tried record of economic worth which the more far-thinking of that adventurous generation were not slow to realize.

It also shared, but to a greater degree than any other of the botanical novelties which poured into the Old World at that time, the advantage of coming on to the European stage at a time when actor and recorder in the great dramas of the New Capitalism and the birth of Empire were, if not combined in one person, never far removed spiritually from one another.

From Clusius's account we learn that prior to 1588 the tuber was an established garden vegetable in certain parts of Italy, which implies that it must have arrived there from Spain at least five or more years earlier, and that it could not therefore have reached Spain much later than 1580.

This, however, is but guessing, and, till recently, 1588 has been our earliest fixed date.

With the help of Prof. E. Hamilton[1] one is able to improve on that date by fifteen years. He mentions that the account books of the Hospital de la Sangre at Seville show that they bought potatoes as part of their normal housekeeping in 1576. Recently Prof. Hamilton has written to me that he found mention of such a purchase in the fourth quarter of 1573, and thinks there may be still earlier ones.

It is interesting to note that prior to 1584 the hospital bought its potatoes by the pound, but that at the later date they were purchased by the 'arroba' (a unit of 25 lb.); moreover, all the purchases took place in the fourth quarter of the year, which is good evidence that they were grown in Spain and eaten freshly harvested. They were probably regarded as luxuries up till 1584.

The new evidence permits us to put the date of introduction of the potato into Spain at least as early as 1570, which would allow of three years for its multiplication to the stage when it could be marketed profitably. This means that the original seed tubers could not have been gathered in South America later than in the previous year, 1569.

That the potato had not made much headway in Spain at this date, is shown by a passage in a document written in 1586 by Diego Davilla Bricegno, who spent forty-five years in Peru and was corregidor in Guarocheri for the last thirteen years of that time. Bricegno's article is entitled 'Descripción y Relación de la Provincia de los Yauyos', a department in the sierra south-east of Lima. It was reproduced in a book entitled *Relación Geográfica de Indias* written about 1700 but not published till 1881. The passage is quoted by Jiménez de la Espada in a footnote to his edition of Bernabé Cobo's *Historia del Nuevo Mundo*, written in 1653, but not published till 1915. It runs thus:

And in the heights skirting the said rivers (in the vicinity of Lima) are sown and gathered the seeds of the potato, which like cold ground. These are one of the best provisions which the Indians have in this said province, they are like truffles: *and if we were to cultivate them in Spain in the manner they do there it would be a great help in years of famine, for the seed is the same.*[2]

The italicized passage allows of two different interpretations: it can be read as implying that if the cultivation of the potato were to be introduced into Spain, where it is not at present, it would be a great help, etc., or: If only the potato which is already in Spain, were cultivated as we do it here, then it would be, etc. On the whole, the second reading seems the more likely, and this view is strengthened by a sentence in the

[1] Hamilton, E. (1934). American Treasure and the Price Revolution in Spain, 1501–1650. *Harvard Economic Studies*, vol. XLIII, p. 196, n. 2.
[2] My italics.

Bricegno document which follows immediately: 'and the occa also grows with these potatoes where they are sown: the cavi is there, as also other roots, very good and of much substance.'

With regard to these latter plants he makes no suggestion as to their cultivation in Spain. Unlike the potato, they had presumably not reached Spain. If this is the correct reading, we may assume that the potato in 1586 had been grown, on a small garden scale, in most parts of Spain for a considerable time.

Although 1570 may be regarded as the earliest reliable date for the introduction of the potato into Europe, several statements occur in the literature which suggest that this may have happened at a considerably earlier date.

It has been said that John Hawkins brought the potato back with him after the visit, in 1565, of his ship the *Jesus of Lubeck* to Santa Fé in Venezuela, where he received, as a present from the natives, hens, pine-apples and potatoes 'the most delicate that may be eaten'. These latter, Safford[1] concludes were sweet-potatoes, as this was 'a region where *Solanum tuberosum* was quite unknown at the time of Hawkins' visit'— this may be, and possibly was true, but wild potatoes do, in fact, occur in Venezuela, as has been reported by Kern.[2]

There are several places in the Americas called Santa Fé: the one here referred to is near Cumana, in the province of Sucre, where the potato has not, so far, been reported as an indigenous plant; but even had they been our potatoes and had been brought to England as early as 1565, it is unlikely that we should have had to wait till 1596, when they are mentioned in Gerard's Catalogue, before we heard anything of them. Henze[3] and Courtois-Gérard[4] both assure us, though without the slightest evidence, that Hawkins brought the potato to Ireland: the former says in 1545, a date at which Hawkins was but thirteen years old, and the latter in 1563, and proceeds to credit Drake with having introduced it to England in 1568. Hawkins we may acquit of having introduced the potato to Europe; would that the same could be said of him in regard to the trading of negro slaves to the Americas!

Malpeaux[5] improves on these authors by asserting that Hawkins introduced the potato into Ireland in 1635, but that the culture was soon abandoned. He states that Drake introduced it into England in 1586

[1] Safford, W. E. (1925). The Potato of Romance and of Reality. *J. Heredity*, vol. XVI, pp. 113–230.

[2] Kern, Frank D. Visiting Venezuela. *Scientific Monthly* (Feb. 1937), pp. 101–16.

[3] Henze, Gustave (1886). *Notice sur l'Introduction et la Propagation de la Pomme de Terre en Europe et en France.*

[4] Courtois-Gérard (?1894). *Du Choix et de la Culture des Pommes de Terre*, p. 2. Paris.

[5] Malpeaux (1899). *Culture de la Pomme de Terre*, p. 20. Paris: Masson et cie.

THE SOUTHWELL FAMILY

THE SOUTHWELL FAMILY

[d. = daughter.   d. = died.   b. = born.   m. = married.]

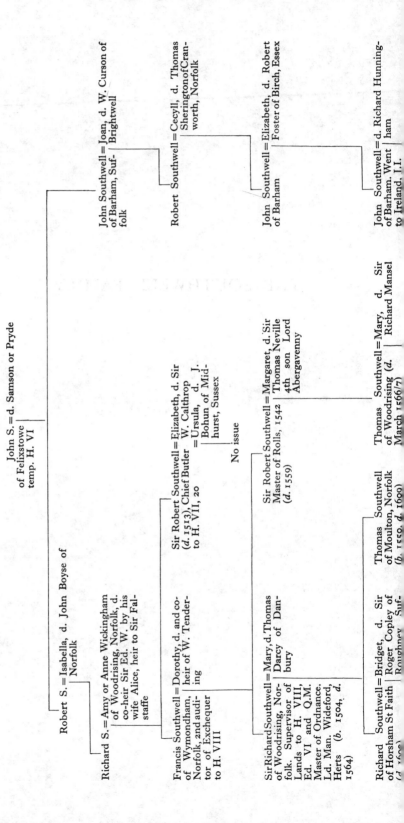

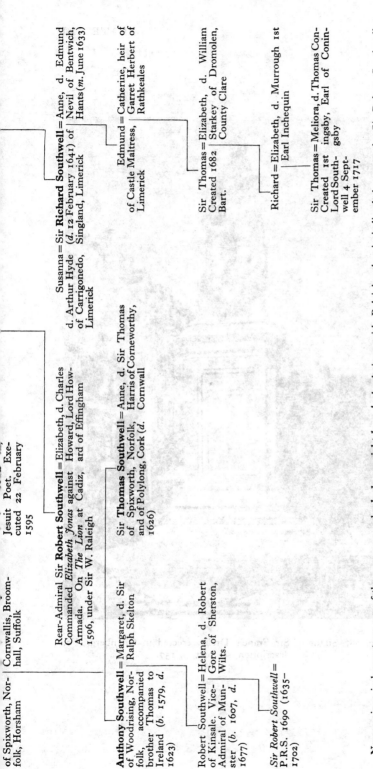

of Spixworth, Norfolk, Horsham

Cornwallis, Broomhall, Suffolk

Jesuit Poet. Executed 22 February 1595

Rear-Admiral Sir **Robert Southwell** = Elizabeth, d. Charles Commanded *Elizabeth Jonas* against Howard, Lord Howard of Effingham Armada. On *The Lion* at Cadiz, 1596, under Sir W. Raleigh

Susanna = Sir **Richard Southwell** = Anne, d. Edmund d. Arthur Hyde (*d.* 12 February 1641) of Nevil of Bentwich, of Carrigonedo, Singland, Limerick Hants (*m.* June 1633) Limerick

Anthony Southwell = Margaret, d. Sir of Woodrising, Norfolk, accompanied brother Thomas to Ireland (*b.* 1579, *d.* 1623)

Sir **Thomas Southwell** = Anne, d. Sir Thomas of Spixworth, Norfolk, Harris of Corneworthy, and of Polylong, Cork (*d.* Cornwall 1626)

Edmund = Catherine, heir of of Castle Maltress, Garret Herbert of Limerick Rathkeales

Robert Southwell = Helena, d. Robert of Kinsale. Vice-Admiral of Munster (*b.* 1607, *d.* 1677)

Sir Thomas = Elizabeth, d. William Created 1682 Starkey of Dromolen, Bart. County Clare

Sir Robert Southwell = P.R.S. 1690 (1635–1702)

Richard = Elizabeth, d. Murrough 1st Earl Inchequin

Sir Thomas = Meliora, d. Thomas Coningsby, Earl of Coningsby Created 1st Lord Southwell 4 September 1717

Names given in heavy type are of those persons who had, or might have had relations with Raleigh; that in italics belongs to the Sir Robert Southwell who first referred to such a connection.

PLATE XXI

Fig. 68. Statue of Sir Francis Drake, erected in Offenberg. For
description, see text, p. 157.

(which may well be correct), and Raleigh made a further introduction in 1623. As Raleigh had then been dead five years, one is not surprised to learn that 'cette introduction eut d'heureuses consequences et Raleigh fut regarde comme le véritable importateur de la pomme de terre en Europe'. Notwithstanding, Malpeaux says that Ravius introduced the potato into Spain in 1553. It has not been possible to further examine this latter claim.

The name of Jerome Cardan, physician, mathematician and astrologer, is not infrequently mentioned as the one responsible for the introduction of the potato into Italy. Putsche,[1] an otherwise reliable author, states that he did so in the year 1580, that is, four years after his death! What may have given rise to the legend is that in his book *De Rerum Varietate*, published in 1557, he mentions the potato as serving the Peruvian Indians in place of bread. It is clear, however, that he had no personal acquaintance with the plant as he states that the top is said to be like that of *Argemone*, the prickly poppy which, however, according to Sanders' *Encyclopaedia of Gardening*, was not introduced into Europe till 1592. Had Cardan had first-hand acquaintance with the potato, he would surely have likened it to the common weed *Solanum nigrum*, rather than to a poppy.

Another account which alleges that the introduction occurred in 1565, has a show of circumstantial truth far in excess of its intrinsic reliability. It is contained in a statement made by Mellado in his *Diccinario Universal*, published in Madrid 1854, which runs as follows:

The Catholic King Phillip II, paid homage to the pope, perhaps on account of the resemblance in the name [*Papas*], with some of these tubers which the Spaniards at that time brought to Europe from America, which, thanks to certain tonic [aphrodisiac] properties which were attributed to them, were to restore the health of the holy father. He divided the King of Spain's gift with a valetudinarian cardinal who was at that time Legate in the Netherlands, and this cardinal in his turn, also by way of medicine, gave some of these tubers to Philip of Sivry, Governor of Mons, calling them 'tartufoli', by which name they were known in Italy for a long time.

Finally in 1638, Philip of Sivry sent two of these 'tartufoli' to the celebrated French botanist Lécluse, who at that time lived in Vienna. Instead of eating them Lécluse planted them and was the first man who in his *Rariorum Plantarum Historia* described the vegetable which he had obtained in this way, in which he immediately found some resemblance to the ground pistachio.

Mellado is obviously in error when he states that the tubers were given to Clusius in 1638, seeing that the latter died in 1609 and that he received his tubers in 1588. Moreover, Bauhin and Gerard were the first to publish descriptions of the new plant. Although Mellado's

---

[1] Putsche, C. (1819). *Versuch einer Monographie der Kartoffelen*. Weimar.

original statement has recently been reproduced abroad as an 'historically proved fact',[1] and the date 1565 ascribed to it, no evidence whatever of its truth has been advanced, unless it be the fact that Pope Pius IV died in December of that year. The chief archivist of the Vatican has been kind enough to make certain investigations, and has informed me that after a lengthy research he has been unable to find any evidence bearing on the matter. One can only say that 1565 is not an unlikely date for the introduction of the potato into Italy via Spain and might account for Clusius's statement that in some parts of Italy it was in 1588 already being used as cattle fodder.[2]

Father Magazini of Vallambroso, in his book Dell' Agricultura Toscana, 1623, says that the potato reached Tuscany from Spain and Portugal by the hands of the bare-footed friars, but gives no date.

Another theory is that Clusius himself secured tubers when he was in Spain in 1564 and disseminated them through northern Italy and southern Germany, but had this been so, there is no reason why he should not have mentioned it in his very full account of the potato (see chapter VI).

So far, we have been proceeding on the assumption that there was but one introduction, and that it reached Spain first, not later than 1569. There is, however, good reason to think that the potato described by Gerard (chapter VI), which is clearly distinct from that of Clusius's, was derived independently. This, which we may call the second introduction, Gerard received and grew in his garden for several years before the publication of the Catalogus in 1596. It is of course in the reference to this potato in his Herball (1597) that Gerard loosed the hare which has led so many to follow a false scent. 'It groweth naturally in America', he says, 'where it was first discovered as reports C. Clusius, since which time I have received roots thereof from Virginia, otherwise called Norembega, which grow and prosper in my garden as in their native country.'

This has been critically examined in a previous chapter, and the suggestion advanced that Gerard's tuber was derived from Hariot, Raleigh's agent, and that he may have obtained it from the cook's store on Drake's ship; Drake having taken potatoes on board at Cartagena.

A rather similar theory was put forward fifty years ago by Pink[3] but in this Drake collected the tubers in the West Indies (where they do not grow), and gave them to Raleigh who planted them at Youghal. Raleigh asked his gardener to bring him a dish of the new plant, was presented with a plate of bitter berries, and accordingly ordered his gardener to

[1] Fuess, W. (1935). Die Urheimat der Kartoffel. Die Ernährung der Pflanze, Bd. XXXI, Ht. XVII.
[2] See supra, p. 90, n. 1.
[3] Pink, James (1879). Potatoes and How to Grow Them. London: Crossley Lockwood.

root them up. Unfortunately, our author then adds: 'Had he known the potato first hand, he would have realized that it was the tubers that were eaten. Hence he never saw them in Virginia where they are not indigenous.' As Voltaire said: 'Et voilà justement comme on écrit l'histoire.'

Drake left Cartagena on 30 March, and after picking up Hariot and the Virginian settlers, reached Plymouth on 26 July 1586. These later dates would have allowed for the successful planting in England of potato tubers, should he have brought any with him. According to Mason,[1] the expedition had been a failure, notwithstanding the 110,000 ducats which Drake had secured as a ransom for Cartagena. The failure of course lay in the fact that the Plate Fleet, laden with bullion, was missed by a mere twelve hours' sailing. What an irony of history if Hariot, the scientist, by reason of a few odd tubers secured from the cook's galley, had won for his country and mankind a fortune far greater than that carried by all the Spanish fleets that ever left the Spanish Main!

That Clusius, who was on friendly terms with Drake and stayed with him in 1581, makes no mention of the potato in England at that date, is good evidence that Drake had not introduced it earlier.

Drake himself had long been aware of the existence of the potato and of its value as ships' stores. He had first come across the potato in the Isle of Mocha off the coast of Chile on 28 November 1577, on his tour round the world: 'We being on land, the people came down to us to the water side with shew of great curtesie, bringing to us potatoes, rootes and two very fat sheepe....'[2]

Ten years later, Master Petty, who recounted the tale of the Voyage of Thomas Cavendish, tells how they called at St Mary's Isle off Concepción in Chile, where he reports: 'Cases of straw filled with potato rootes, which were very good to eat, ready made up in the store houses for the Spanish against they should come for this tribute.'

Both these references are of interest as showing that the potato was used as ships' stores and was assessed as tribute to be shipped elsewhere by the Spaniards, but they afford no evidence as to the problem of the original homeland of the early European introductions. Drake did not reach Plymouth for another two years, and Cavendish, making his way through the East Indies, did not return home till a further twelve months had elapsed. In neither case would any seed tubers have survived so long a journey in tropical waters.

Although legend has never ceased to link Raleigh's name with the introduction of the potato, amongst scientific writers there has been a growing tendency to deny him any credit in the matter. This is mainly due to the influence which Safford's excellent treatise, *The Potato of*

---

[1] Mason, A. E. W. (1941). *Life of Drake*. Hodder and Stoughton.
[2] Drake's *World Encompassed*, 1628. Hakluyt Soc. (1854), pp. 97 and 238.

Romance and of Reality,[1] has exerted. Safford pointed out that Raleigh never went to Virginia, and that if he had, he would not have found the potato there. Incidentally, of the five expeditions he financed, only one, the fourth, ever touched at Ireland on its return journey, and that at Smerwick, County Kerry, on 16 October 1587, when it is possible that they were short of food, for it is stated that they 'obtained fresh water, wine and other fresh meats'.[2] Safford also called attention to the fact that the charming tale of Raleigh and his gardener at Myrtle Grove was retold 120 years ago—*mutatis mutandis*—of Drake, by the German scholar Putsche.[3] In a second version of the legend, Raleigh is supposed to have brought the tubers from Quito, but, here again, Safford points out, he never was within a thousand miles of the spot. Recently, the late Prof. Paul Murphy[4] of Dublin, a distinguished authority on the diseases of the potato, and his colleague, the late W. D. Davidson[5] both, independently, dismiss the supposed connection between Raleigh and the potato as purely legendary.

Davidson concludes his discussion on the problem by saying: 'It is not known in what year the potato was introduced into Ireland, or to whom the country is indebted for its introduction. There is no evidence that the potato was introduced by Sir Walter Raleigh, and nothing can be gained by surmising by what means it reached Ireland in the absence of credible information.' This notwithstanding, the case for Raleigh cannot be dismissed so lightly.

Davidson argues that the Raleigh legend does not appear in literature till John Houghton's article[6] in 1699, and that because it is there stated that Raleigh brought the potato from Virginia, the tale is *ipso facto* disproved. For the same reason he dismisses Southwell's evidence. In my opinion both deductions are unjustified. The intimate relation of Sir Walter Raleigh to Virginia was common knowledge. Although Raleigh never went to Roanoke and his early attempts to effect a settlement were a failure, the colony was re-established and reformed in 1607, and after a few years of struggle, so prospered that its name became synonymous in the people's mind with the most characteristic development of the time. It was England's first attempt at colonization as opposed to conquest, and Raleigh was the first Englishman who entertained the dream of empire. He, moreover, was the most active and

---

[1] Safford, W. E. (1925). Op. cit.

[2] Brushfield, T. N. (1898). *Raleghana*. Trans. *Devonshire Assoc.* vol. xxx.

[3] Putsche, C. (1819). Op. cit.

[4] Murphy, Prof. Paul (1936). *Report of Speech in the Weekly Irish Times*, Saturday, April 26.

[5] Davidson, W. D. (1936). The History of the Potato and its Progress in Ireland. *J. Dept. Agric. Saorestat Eirean*, vol. xxxiv, pp. 3–24.

[6] Houghton, John (1699). Houghton's *Collection*, vol. II, p. 469. Friday 15 Dec. 1699. See p. 149.

far-seeing of that small band of adventurers, who, scholarly soldiers and greedy courtiers though they were, dominated the period by the sheer force of their intelligence and personality. All that was new in the realm of thought and action gravitated towards Raleigh, or sprang from his fertile imagination. New plants and the like, found in him a welcome, and a patron; to him we owe the sweet-smelling yellow wallflower from the Azores, and the Assane cherry from the Canaries, both of which were established first at Assane and later at Dromona near Youghal on the Blackwater.[1] He also is held responsible, on evidence of some weight, for having planted the great open-air Orangery at Beddington, near Croydon, over which a movable cover was placed in the winter months.[2]

But apart from his ambitious imperial schemes, Raleigh was an outstanding and discriminating patron of the new learning in all its forms. He assisted in the publication of books of travel both here and abroad; he paid for the production of coloured illustrations of Florida scenery painted by the French artist, Jacques de Morques,[3] but, beyond and above all this, he remained the improving landlord, and it is in this capacity that he may well have played the part that tradition has ascribed to him. Bagwell[4] states that Raleigh planted a large number of English families on his estate with a view to its rapid development, and that he instituted many improvements in the Mallow district. Unfortunately, all the good work done was destroyed in the 1598 revolt, and that probably accounts for the very low price Raleigh obtained from Boyle for the estate. Cobbett[5] who hated Raleigh and all that he stood for, when speaking of 'Ireland's lazy root', tempers justice with venom when he says: 'It was one of the greatest villains upon earth (Sir W. Raleigh) who, they say, first brought the root into England.'

The suggestion that Raleigh's right-hand man, Hariot, added the potato to his collection of plants from the stores on Drake's ship, if true, implicates his master, indirectly, as being instrumental in bringing the tuber to these shores. But the claim, which has been specifically made, that he personally introduced it on to his lands at Youghal in Ireland is, on the whole, more cogent. The claim was specifically made in 1699 by Houghton[6] who published the following in his weekly bulletin:

The Potato is a bacciferous herb, with esculent roots, bearing winged leaves and a bell flower.

[1] Hennessy, Sir John Pope (1883). *Sir Walter Raleigh in Ireland*. London: Kegan Paul.
[2] Oldys, W. (1736). Life of Sir Walter Raleigh. Preface to Raleigh's *History of the World*, p. 72.
[3] Hume, Martin (1906). *Sir Walter Raleigh*, p. 115. Fisher, Unwin.
[4] Bagwell, R. (1885). *Ireland under the Tudors*, vol. III, pp. 108 and 304.
[5] Cobbett, W. (1830). *Rural Rides*.
[6] Houghton, J. (1699). Op. cit., see supra, p. 148.

This I have been informed was brought first out of Virginia by Sir Walter Raleigh, and he stopping at Ireland, some was planted there, where it thrived well and to good purpose, for in three succeeding wars, when all the corn above ground was destroyed, this supported them; for the soldiers, unless they had dug up all the ground where they grew, and almost sifted it could not extirpate them; from whence they were brought to Lancashire, where they are very numerous, and now they begin to spread all the kingdom over.

Houghton's statement would have been forgotten had it not been repeated, without acknowledgement, by Smith, in his *History of Water-ford*, 1745. In his later work on Cork, 1750, Smith tells the tale how the gardener thought the plant had been grown for the sake of the small green and bitter berry, and his surprise, on digging the ground in pre-paration for another crop, at finding the tubers beneath the soil. All this is located at Myrtle Grove, Raleigh's home in Youghal. It is perhaps significant that Oldys, a discriminating but very sincere admirer of Raleigh, whilst giving much prominence to the part he is supposed to have played in connection with the introduction of tobacco, makes no mention at all of the potato.[1] From that time till recent years, the Raleigh legend has been repeated with embellishments but without any critical analysis, in most works which touch on the potato.

Raleigh's connection with Youghal came about as follows: When the rising of Desmond was suppressed, the Earl was attainted and his estates confiscated to the Crown. On 3 February 1585–6 a warrant under the Privy Seal granted to Sir Walter Raleigh three and a half seignories in Waterford and Cork, an area of 42,000 acres. This gift was confirmed by Elizabeth on 28 February 1586. Included in the grant was the small town of Youghal, in which was situated the collegiate buildings known as the New College of the Blessed Virgin. This establishment possessed a separate house for the Warden, and tradition has it that it was here that Raleigh took up his residence which later became known as Myrtle Grove.

Orpen[2] is of opinion that Raleigh's first contact with Youghal was in 1588, and that he did not have legal possession of the College till 1602, to which there never was a Warden House but only the College House. Dorothea Townshend[3] on the other hand, says Raleigh rented the Warden's House from the College and lived there when he visited his estates, and that it is this house which is now shown as his home. Orpen thinks Myrtle Grove was one of the four messuages or tofts in the town

---

[1] Oldys, W. (1736). Op. cit.

[2] Orpen, Goddard (1903). Raleigh's Home at Youghal. *J. Roy. Soc. Antiq. Ireland*, vol. XXXIII, p. 345.

[3] Townshend, Dorothea (1904). *The Life and Letters of the Great Earl of Cork*, pp. 120 and 125.

conveyed to Raleigh who lived there and possibly built the house. In 1616, according to Hayman[1] the well-known authority on the local history of Youghal who, incidentally, is a firm believer in the introduction by Raleigh, Sir Lawrence Parsons, Recorder of Youghal for the first Earl of Cork, took over this house, which came to be known as Parson's House. It was only later that, owing to the fine myrtles in the garden, which are still there, the house acquired its present name.

We find ourselves on more solid ground in 1588, for both in this year and in the following one, Raleigh was Mayor of Youghal. Notwithstanding Raleigh's engagements as Lord Lieutenant of Cornwall, Lord Warden of the Stanneries, his consuming interest in the threatened attack from Spain against which he was responsible for raising 2,000 men in the west, he, nevertheless, went to his estate in Ireland and took up his office as Mayor. He did not stay long, but hurried back to the west to complete the preparations against the Armada, which arrived off The Lizard on 20 July. Raleigh's mayoralty was served by proxy. In 1588 he appointed William Magner his Deputy, and in 1589 John Forrest and John Gitto acted as his bailiffs. How much of this time Raleigh spent in Ireland before he sold his Irish estates to Richard Boyle, later Lord Boyle (1616) and Earl of Cork in 1620, it is difficult to say, but the transaction does not seem to have been completed till 1604.[2] Hume[3] says that at this period 'he was intensely absorbed in his plans at Lismore, in the misgovernment of Ireland, and in the pipe-stave enterprise on his Irish estates'.

Raleigh's interest in the Cork estates did not cease with their sale. Financial difficulties, as well as technical ones concerning the title to various properties, took several years to surmount, during which time his friendship with Sir Richard, now Earl of Cork, was maintained. Indeed, his deep interest in Ireland, and in the Youghal district in particular, never flagged.

In March 1617, Raleigh, after fourteen years' confinement in the Tower, had bought his provisional release by a rash promise to bring great treasure from Guiana without doing violence to Spain. In July of the same year he sailed once more into Kinsale harbour on this last and ominous venture, to await certain of his ships which had been scattered by storm. He immediately got into contact with Lord Boyle,[4] who lent him £100 in cash, and sent six barrels of Spanish wine and a hogshead of salmon as a present to him. On 28 July Sir Walter was engaged with

---

[1] Hayman, Rev. Samuel (1856). Ecclesiastical Antiquities of Youghal. *J. Roy. Soc. Antiq. Ireland*, vol. IV, p. 25.
[2] Maxwell, Constantia (1923). *Irish History from Contemporary Sources*, p. 252. London.
[3] Hume, Martin (1906). *Sir Walter Raleigh*, p. 138. London.
[4] Harlow, V. T. *Raleigh's Last Voyage*, 1932, p. 53. London: Argonaut Press.

Boyle in clearing up outstanding difficulties about title deeds.[1] He spent
seven weeks in Youghal and the neighbourhood, leaving Cork harbour
on 20 August 1617. On his return from Guiana, Raleigh landed at
Kinsale in May 1618, in order to rid himself of the mutinous members
of his crew, and made a last short visit to Youghal before he proceeded
to Plymouth, to be betrayed by his friend, sold by his king, and sacrificed
on the scaffold for an ideal which gave England her empire.

A writer signing himself 'G.M.', and who was probably George Moore,
states[2] that potatoes were ordinary food in the south of Ireland before
the time of the Commonwealth, and quotes a few lines from a popular
song which runs as follows:

> The brave Walter Raleigh, Queen
> Bess's own knight
> Brought here from Virginia
> The root of delight.
> By him it was planted
> At Youghal so gay;
> An' sure Munster praties
> Are famed to this day.

This song, known as the 'Pratie Song', will be found in Crofton
Croker's Collection.[3] 'G.M.' goes on to say that about the year 1640
'potatoes were called "Crokers" from having been first planted in
Croker's field at Youghal'; this he presumably learnt from the history
of the potato to be found in the same volume of Crofton Croker, who
refers to an undated manuscript in the Southwell papers which he
believes to have been written in 1640, in which potato roots are spoken
of as 'Crokers' for the reason given. He suggests that this may be the
same spot as is spoken of by Lord Castlehaven in his *Memoirs* when he
camped before Youghal in 1645 and ordered Major-General Butler to
take up a position 'towards the sea near Croker's works'.

Who, then, was this 'Croker'? In a letter to the *Cork Examiner* of
25 May 1936, a correspondent who signs himself 'Donal', says that he
read in an issue of the *Cork Historical Journal* that Raleigh leased land
at Tallow to a Mr Croker. Tallow is about twenty miles north of Youghal.
Miss Mary Aher, a highly qualified authority on local Irish history, and
a lifelong resident of Youghal, states that the Crokers settled in Youghal
as colonists under the aegis of Sir Robert Boyle, who made over to
Richard Croker a parcel of land called Norries Land, and half a plowland
called New Aughundan.

---

[1] *Lismore Papers*, vol. I, p. 138.
[2] *J. Cork Hist. and Archaeol. Soc.* 1920, vol. XXVI, p. 56.
[3] Croker, Crofton (1886). *Popular Songs of Ireland.*

In 1612 the sale of Boyle's Balliregan Woods to Mr Croker of Lismore is recorded in the *Lismore Papers*[1] as well as further dealings in 1617 in relation to the shipping of timber.

Following up a letter in the *Cork Examiner* on 7 May 1936, asking for information in respect to the use of 'Croker' as a synonym for 'potato', a letter from H. F. Longfield of Cork appeared on 14 May 1936. In it he says that a field known as Croker's Garden exists near Mallow, twenty miles north of Cork; it is not near any residence new or old, and it has been known by this name for over 100 years. The word 'Garden' suggests that it has generally been used for growing potatoes, as fields thus employed are commonly called gardens. This field is still used for growing potatoes.

Another link between Raleigh and the potato is to be found in the following entry from the Manuscript Journal of the Royal Society under the date 13 December 1693: 'The President [Sir Robert Southwell] related that his grandfather brought potatoes into Ireland, who had them from Sir Walter Raleigh after his return from Virginia.' This oft-repeated statement has, as far as I know, never been critically examined.

With the invaluable help of the late Lord Southwell, Mr A. T. Butler, Windsor Herald, the Admiralty Librarian and others, an attempt has been made to explore the possibilities opened up by Sir Robert's remarks. Sir Robert Southwell was a scion of the Kinsale branch of the family. The Southwells were of ancient lineage who from the time of King Edward II had assumed the name of Southwell, having previously been known as de Suelle, which was an earlier form of the name Southwell, a town in Nottinghamshire. During the sixteenth and seventeenth centuries, the family had furnished the state with a number of distinguished men, great lawyers, naval and military leaders and, not least, the famous poet and martyr, Robert Southwell, the Jesuit who was executed in 1592. Our Sir Robert was born at Kinsale, County Cork; he enjoyed an immensely busy life, travelled widely through Europe as a British diplomat, and at one time served as Ambassador at Lisbon. He was one of the original Fellows of the Royal Society, being elected on 20 May 1663. On 1 December 1690, he became its President, a position he held till November 1695. Notwithstanding the important posts he held, his membership of the House of Commons and his wide scientific activities, his interests in his old home at Kinsale in Cork never tired. In 1679 he acquired a country seat at Kings Weston in Gloucester, but as if to compensate for this temporary desertion from Kinsale, he built and endowed in that town an almshouse to entertain eight needy parishioners. Southwell's relations with Ireland took, however, a more tangible form. In 1677 he became Vice-Admiral of the Province of

[1] Vol. I, p. 18.

Munster and on 25 July 1690 he was appointed Secretary of State for Ireland. He died in 1702 at the age of sixty-seven.

When Sir Robert made the statement referred to, he was fifty-eight years old, no great age as we reckon ages to-day, but one which in that period entitled him to be regarded as a man worthy of respect and credence. He makes four distinct statements: one that his grandfather was instrumental in introducing the potato to Ireland; the second that he got them from Raleigh; the third that Raleigh visited Virginia, and the fourth by implication, that Raleigh brought the potato back with him from Virginia.

The third and fourth of these statements need no prolonged discussion; we know that Raleigh never went to Virginia at any time, and that the potato was unknown in that settlement. It is not difficult to understand how Southwell, notwithstanding his wide education and experience, might be misled, knowing as he would, the intimate relations of Raleigh to the Virginian venture, and the legend to which Gerard had given currency.

The first two statements are on a different plane and one may well expect a high degree of accuracy on the part of Sir Robert in dealing with matters of family interest and, in particular, with incidents related to his old home in Ireland. The statement is clear: his grandfather introduced the potato, and he got his tubers from Raleigh.

Sir Robert's grandfather (see Pedigree, following p. 144), was Sir Anthony, who died in 1623, twelve years before Sir Robert was born. There was therefore no personal contact, and if it may be assumed that Robert would not have had any interest in the tradition till he was a grown lad, it might well be some twenty-five years after his grandfather's death, before he knew of it, or at any rate took an interest in such matters, quite long enough for it to have acquired, in the meantime, the Virginian accretion, more especially as at that time Virginia was much in the public eye.

But to return to Sir Robert's grandfather, Anthony: he and his brother Thomas were the sons of Richard Southwell of Spixworth in Norfolk and his wife Alice Cornwallis. He was born in 1579, his brother Thomas was presumably a few years older. Anthony died in 1623, when his son Robert, father of our Sir Robert, was but sixteen years of age. Sir Thomas, the brother and great-uncle to Sir Robert, died three years later. Without contesting the probability that Sir Robert's tale embodies a considerable element of truth, it is clear that its propagation as a family legend depended rather on tradition than direct communication. The importance of the tale, however, lies in the measure of support it gives to the widespread belief that Raleigh introduced the potato into Great Britain. To test the validity of that belief, it is necessary to explore the relations, if any, which may have existed between Raleigh and members of the Southwell family.

The brothers Anthony and Thomas were both country squires, born and brought up on the Norfolk estates, which their family had held for many generations. Some time early in James I's reign, the brothers migrated to Munster with James's encouragement and settled in County Cork; exactly when that happened, one cannot say, though it presumably took place before 1609, when the stream of adventurers and planters was directed to Ulster. A Thomas Southwell had already acquired land from Raleigh, as appears in a Deed 27 May 1597, which is recited in the transfer of the estates to Boyle.[1]

I am indebted to Miss Aher of Youghal, for the following:

In the *History of Youghal*, 1848, p. 21, the author of which is generally thought to be the Rev. Samuel Hayman, it is stated that 'Nathaniel Baxter, Warden of the College of Youghal who had been elected to the office five years before, and found the revenues of the house were threatened with the fate of most other monastic foundations. On the 25th August, 1597, he was obliged to pass his bond of 1,000 marks which was to be forfeited in case he did not, in 40 days after demand, resign his office into the Queen's hands, and did not suffer Thomas Southwell, Esq., of Brancaster, Norfolk, England, and John Fitzharris of Ballycroane, Co. Cork, to take possession of the same.'

This is the same Thomas Southwell mentioned in the conveyance of Raleigh's lands to Boyle, which reads: 'To Thomas Southwell, all his seignories, lands and tenements in Cork and Waterford Counties and elsewhere in Ireland, with other lands and things Dated 27th May, 40th Elizabeth, i.e. in 1598.'

Miss Aher is of opinion that the lands in Cork were situated at Kinsale, later to be the home of Anthony's son, and 'the lands elsewhere in Ireland', were in the City and County of Limerick.

Thomas Southwell is here described as of Brancaster in Norfolk. This is the first time I have met with this Norfolk town in relation to the family. Sir Thomas, the brother of Anthony, had a seat at Spixworth, but that would not rule out another at Brancaster, for the family had several extensive estates in the county. If this Thomas is the great-uncle of our Sir Robert, he would have been about twenty-one or twenty-two at the time he took over Sir Walter's lands. He would have won his first experience of plantation exploitation under the direct supervision of Sir Walter Raleigh or his agents. Thomas seems to have given up his residence in Ireland after the sale of the lands he occupied, to return once more with his younger brother Anthony some time in the early years of James I's reign. This time he settled at a spot called Polylong in Cork. In Archdall's 1789 edition of *Lodge's Peerage of Ireland*, it is said that Sir Thomas was 'sent into Ireland by James I to promote

[1] Hayman, Rev. Samuel (1852). *Annals of Youghal*, p. 18.

the plantation of Munster and was one of the Council to the President of that province'. Anthony seems not to have taken any prominent part in political life, but he settled in County Cork, and either he or his son acquired the estates at Kinsale which were held by successive generations of this branch of the family.

The identity of the Thomas Southwell, the tenant of Raleigh's lands, and Thomas the brother of Anthony, is much strengthened by an examination of the family pedigree. There is only one other Thomas Southwell of the same family who was alive in the period under discussion, the period of Raleigh's activity in Ireland, viz. from 1586–1602. He was a great-uncle of the Thomas under discussion, and he lived at Moulton near Norwich, and died in 1609. There is no reason to believe that he had any relations with Ireland, or was other than a local country squire.

If, therefore, this Thomas is, in fact, the brother and partner of Anthony, and Raleigh had the potato growing at Youghal, there is not the slightest reason to doubt Sir Robert's statement that his grandfather obtained the same from Raleigh, though it may have been through his brother Thomas, and that he cultivated them in Ireland.

Even were Sir Robert's memory to have deceived him as regards the part played by his grandfather, it is not difficult to establish a relation between Raleigh and two others of the Southwell family, into the hands of either of which the potato might have passed. At the time of the Armada, Richard Southwell commanded the *Elizabeth Jonas*,[1] and greatly distinguished himself, in consequence of which he was knighted on the deck of the *Ark Royal*. He lived at the chief Norfolk seat of the family, Woodrising, where Anthony was born and brought up, and quite close to the home of Thomas at Spixworth. In 1596 Sir Richard was a Rear-Admiral commanding the *Lion*, one of the six ships which formed the squadron under Raleigh which acted as the vanguard in the attack on Cadiz. The Admiral, who must have been intimate with Raleigh, was obviously in a position to obtain potatoes from Raleigh for his cousins and neighbours, Anthony and Thomas.

A third, but less likely, link with Raleigh is yet another Sir Richard Southwell: he was a scion of the junior line of the family, the one which later acquired the barony of Southwell. This Sir Richard was an intimate of the Earl of Cork who had acquired Raleigh's Youghal estates, and married, as his second wife in 1633, a lady attending on the Earl's daughter; he died in 1641. He would seem to have come too late

---

[1] Harrison, in his *Description of England*, 1577, gives the following explanation of the name given to this ship: 'The next hight, the *Elizabeth Jonas*, a name devised by hir grace in remembraunce of hir owne deliverance from the fury of hir enemies, from which in one respect she was no lesse myraculously preserved, then was the prophet Jonas from the belly of the whale.'

on the scene, to have had the necessary contact with Raleigh. By the time of his death, however, potatoes were certainly in full cultivation in that part of Ireland where he lived. It is doubtful, moreover, whether the potato would have competed successfully with Sir Richard's main interest, the monopoly to sell intoxicating liquors in no less than forty taverns in Limerick.

It would appear, therefore, that Sir Robert was not speaking lightly when he said that his grandfather had obtained potatoes from Sir Walter Raleigh. Certain it is that his grandfather was in the position to have done so, and that either he or his brother Thomas might well have been amongst the first to propagate them in Ireland. There can be no doubt that the claim proffered on behalf of Sir Walter Raleigh to have introduced the potato into Ireland gains additional support when carefully examined. To dismiss it summarily, as has been done by recent writers, is to abjure tradition, whilst neglecting contemporary evidence.

If, in fact, there was no one person who consciously introduced the potato, it may conceivably have reached Ireland by accident. When the Armada was dispersed, a number of ships sweeping round the east and north of Scotland, foundered on the west coast of Ireland. The Irish plundered the hulks, and the English and the peasants between them murdered most of the crews. These ships may well have carried potatoes as part of the cook's stores; if any survived, and the enforced prolongation of their voyage would militate against such, those falling into the hands of the Irish may have been planted in scattered spots along the coast of Kerry and Cork. Whether it came to Ireland in this way, or by the hand of Raleigh, the date of its entry would still be between 1586 and 1588.

If historical research has so far failed to identify, with certainty, any one person to whom may be ascribed the honour of its introduction either to the Continent or to Great Britain, in Germany public opinion has 'plumped' for Drake, and in Offenburg, in Baden, a statue has been erected to him (Pl. XXI, fig. 68).[1] The history of this monument is told by Safford,[2] and with greater detail by Reddick.[3] The sculptor, Andreas Friedrich, 1798–1877, carved it on the chance of selling it to a Strasburg magnate but, not succeeding in getting his price, he gave it to the City Fathers of Offenburg on condition that it should be erected with its back towards Strasburg, which was duly done in 1853. A silver goblet surmounted by a reproduction of the Drake statue was presented in return to the sculptor. The statue represented Drake holding a flowering potato plant, complete with tubers and haulm, in his left hand; the

[1] The Germans in 1918 struck a medal in honour of Drake and the potato (Salaman's manuscript notes). – Ed.
[2] Safford, W. E. Op. cit.
[3] Reddick, D. (1939). *J. Heredity*, vol. xx, p. 73.

plinth, which is decorated with a frieze of potato tubers, bears the following inscriptions on its four sides which, translated, read:

South: 'Sir Frances Drake, who spread the use of the potato in Europe, A.D. 1580.'[1]

East: 'Millions of people who cultivate the earth bless his immortal memory.'

West: 'As the help of the poor against need, [this] precious gift of God allays bitter want.'[2]

North: 'The gratitude of the town of Offenburg is due to the sculptor and giver of this statue, Andreas Friedrich, 1853.'

The chequered career of this equivocal monument is now at an end. It was removed by the Nazis during the recent war.[3]

[1] Reddick gives 1586; the date cut on the monument is 1580.

[2] The German original, *Bitterem Mangel steuert die Köstliche Gottesgabe als der Armen Hülfe gegen die Noth*, has been rendered by Reddick: 'This precious gift of God contributes to the stinging penury of the poor a help against misery', which would read rather more into the original than was intended.

[3] *The Times*, 20 December 1946.

CHAPTER X

Potato Varieties: Past, Present and Future

It is difficult to say when and where the first deliberate attempt to create new potato varieties occurred. In South America, its original home, a great variety of potatoes are cultivated to-day, and in the early days of the Spanish conquerors there were almost as many. But it would be rash to say that the native cultivators of the High Andean plateaux and valleys set out deliberately to create new and better varieties, whether by hybridization or self-pollination. How then did these many hundreds of native varieties come into existence? What probably happened was, that when each year the potato fruits, which form so readily on all the varieties and on most of the species cultivated in South America, fell to the ground,[1] and the seeds germinated in the next season, a large variety of seedlings would spring up, like weeds, in the potato plots. From time to time, one may suppose, one of these self-sown seedlings would attract a grower because of some visible character which appealed to him, and by propagating from its tubers he unconsciously created a new variety.

The vast majority of such seedlings would be the outcome of natural self-fertilization. This, in the potato, occurs through the pollen falling by gravity on to the pistil or, alternatively, by the action of insects, a method which obviously opens the door to cross-fertilization. There is reason to believe that such has occurred from the earliest times in Peru-Bolivia. The evidence lies in the existence of species, some of which have been taken into cultivation, which could only have come into being by the hybridization of two divergent species. Such hybrid types are themselves self-sterile.

Although rumours have been current for many years that native cultivators do occasionally raise new varieties intentionally from the seed of the berry, it is only now that more precise information has come to hand.[2] Certain Colombian natives collect berries from wild varieties in the Andes mountains in the Department of Nariño, the seed of which they sow in their plantations, selecting from the seedlings the better

---

[1] In Europe, fruit-bearing varieties are not very common. This is due to a dominant mutation which has occurred since its arrival, which inhibits the full development of the anthers. Salaman, R. N. (1910). Male Sterility in Potatoes. *J. Linn. Soc.* vol. XXIX, pp. 301–12.

[2] The substance of this information was communicated to me by Dr J. G. Hawkes, who had acquired the facts from a Colombian, Señor Garcia Barriga. Unconfirmed reports that this practice was pursued in some parts of Colombia reached me as early as 1920. (Now found to be a rumour, only. – Ed.)

types and the heavier yields. The interest of the practice lies in the fact that we have here a continuous selection and domestication of wild potatoes which may well be a century-old custom.

In the early days of the potato in Europe, fortuitous methods at first held sway, but it was not long before skilled cultivators purposely planted the seed from naturally formed berries, selecting from the resultant seedlings those plants possessing the characters they sought, early or late maturity, long or round, coloured or colourless tubers.

The original potatoes which reached Europe were themselves varietal hybrids, by which one means that they were not homozygous, i.e. pure for every single recognizable or unrecognizable character. It is unlikely that any potato variety in existence to-day is in that strict sense other than hybrid, though some may be less so than others. Many years ago, I raised a variety which was homozygous in all its recognizable characters, but there was no reason to think that it was any better on that account; indeed, the reverse is more likely. We know, however, that the selfed-seedlings of the original imports exhibited a range of variation, involving many different characters, thus affording to the selectionist a wide choice. As time went on, and hybridization came to be practised between the original varieties and their descendants, the opportunity for greater variation and a wider and richer field was provided from which to make selections. Indeed, it has been shown[1] that we can account for all the known characters of the thousand and one varieties raised in this country by the interplay of characters derived originally from the two varieties described by Clusius and Gerard respectively, at the end of the sixteenth century.

Throughout the seventeenth century there seems to have been, in general, but two varieties grown. John Tradescant, jun.[2] describes a white and a purple-flowered variety. Evelyn,[3] who had very little use for the new plant, records but one, and that a late variety. Mortimer,[4] says that the potato may be propagated by tuber as well as by seed. This latter method would imply the raising of new varieties, which accords with the fact that in the eighteenth century the number of recognized types in cultivation increased rapidly. The eminent agriculturist, William Marshall,[5] gives a full description of the methods employed in Yorkshire by farmers for raising new varieties. Marshall observed that many farmers grew in the same plot, a bizarre collection of what he calls sub-varieties, and pointed out how unwise it was to waste

[1] Salaman, R. N. (1926). *Potato Varieties*, p. 3. Cambridge University Press.
[2] Tradescant, John, junr. (1656). *Musaeum Tradescantium.*
[3] Evelyn, John (1664). *Sylva*, p. 209. 4th ed. 1745.
[4] Mortimer, John (1707). *The Whole Art of Husbandry*, p. 472.
[5] Marshall, William (1788). *The Rural Economy of the Midland Counties*, vol. I, p. 197, vol. II, p. 53.

time cultivating a scratch lot of sub-varieties when, by careful selection, one might procure one sort which would yield three or four times more than some of those in cultivation.

The breeding and selection referred to by Marshall, and all that followed after it till the middle of the next century, had but one object in view: to overcome the depressing effect of Curl in the varieties under cultivation. About 1775 the incidence of Curl, or what we should call to-day, 'virus disease', particularly Leaf Roll and 'Y' infection, was so serious that it threatened the continued cultivation of the potato. It had been found that curled potatoes never recovered, that tuber seed brought from the moorland near the sea, or from Scotland, grew much more vigorously than the curled or degenerate stocks. It was concluded that the disease was due to a failure of 'constitution', largely because of 'old age', and that the logical solution was to raise new varieties from seed, by which means, it was held, the parental stock was regenerated.

This was probably the first conscious effort to build new varieties of potatoes to meet a special need. Though it failed in its specific task, it was the means of providing the nation with a number of excellent varieties at the critical moment when, for economic reasons, it was beginning to take a serious interest in the potato.

It is, however, from the latter half of the eighteenth century that the creation of distinct varieties of outstanding merit may be said to date, though mention of some are to be found somewhat earlier.

George Rye[1] in his *Consideration on Agriculture*, 1730, mentions five sorts, of which three seem to have been popular. There was a white early to be set in January and harvested at the end of June, and a yellow fleshed variety which could be kept through the major part of the next summer. The pride of place, however, must be given to the Black potato, of which Rye says: 'But it is the black potato (not that the pulp is black, but that the skin is very dark), that is most valued by those who know it: the pulp affords a stronger invigorating Diet to the Labourer; it keeps till Potatoes come again....Since the people of this country found the peculiar goodness of this potatoe they will scarce cultivate any other. They will grow so large, as that some of them have measured four inches in diameter.' This variety was esteemed for its keeping qualities for over a century.

Miller,[2] in his *Gardener's Dictionary*, mentioned but two varieties, a red and a white. No further types are referred to until 1770, after which a great number of names purporting to represent new varieties are

---

[1] Rye, George (1730). Quoted from D. Davidson's *History of Potato Varieties*. *J. Dept. of Agric. Eire*, 1933, from whose painstaking work I have received much assistance in the writing of this chapter.

[2] Miller, Philip (1724). *The Gardener's Dictionary*, 2nd ed. 1733. 'Potatoes'.

to be found. Whilst it is probable that the majority may, in fact, refer to new varieties, it is certain that the practice of giving local names to the same variety was already in vogue, a practice which, in course of time, led to great confusion.

A number of the varieties which came into use during the last quarter of the eighteenth century and the early decades of the nineteenth century, had an outstanding effect on potato culture and deserve special mention, not only for their intrinsic merits, but because they exerted a distinct influence on the social economy of the day.[1]

The Howard or Cluster. This potato was introduced by the famous prison reformer in 1770. Parmentier[2] says that Howard obtained it from America, presumably the United States, in 1765—a statement confirmed by a contemporary writer.[3] It was grown extensively throughout the British Isles, in the main as a food for stock. It derived its name 'Cluster' from its habit of forming tubers on short stolons close to the stem. It enjoyed a variety of synonyms, and under that of 'The Turk', was much praised by Young as a potato which, on poor undunged land, still gave great crops.

The Irish Apple. This potato was in use as early as 1770 and was renowned for its dry and mealy consistency when boiled. It was a late variety and, owing to its exceptionally good keeping quality[4] was greatly prized in Ireland as it helped to bridge over the difficult months of July and August, when the old stocks were failing and the new not yet harvested. There seem to have been both red and white-tubered stocks grown under this name. It survived till 1846 but passed out of use after the coming of the Blight.

The Manly. This was one of the best known varieties. It was in common use in 1776 and survived to at least 1859. It was an early and said to be a heavy cropper.

The White Kidney. This was an exceptionally early potato and was much grown in Ireland before and after 1815, when it must have been of great service in supplying the people with fresh food in July and August.

Ox Noble. This was in use as early as 1787, a heavy yielder, with a large ugly tuber; it was said to be highly resistant to 'Curl'. Before long this variety came to be regarded as fit only for cattle feed and, as such, was used on an extensive scale for some fifty years. It is to this variety that belongs the credit of securing for the potato a place in the pageantry of our tavern signboards. The 'Oxnoble Inn' at Manchester acquired

---

[1] Further information on the history of varieties can be obtained from the author's book *Potato Varieties*, 1926. Cambridge University Press.

[2] Parmentier (1789). *Sur les Pommes de Terre*. Paris.

[3] Dossie, Robert (1771). *Memoirs of Agriculture*, vol. II.

[4] Townsend, Rev. Horatio (1815). *Survey of Cork*, vol. I, p. 217.

both its name and licence between 1804 and 1808. It occupies the original site within a few score yards of the Castlefield terminus of the Bridgewater Canal, where potatoes were landed on a sufficiently extensive scale as to cause the main wharf to be known for over a hundred years as the Potato Wharf. Assuming that the bulk of the potatoes were destined for the feeding of the milch cows stalled in the numerous dairies of the town, it would not be surprising that the Inn serving the needs of the men who dealt with the traffic, should have adopted the name of the product they handled.

The Yam. This was being grown about the same time as the above: it was a reddish-skinned variety with a reddish streak in the flesh. It was grown till recently in Arran Island off Galway Bay, as well as in the Hebrides, and was also known as the 'Surinam' and the 'Horse Potatoe'.

It is possible that the 'Yam' is of considerably earlier origin: Dossie[1] says that there is a legend, one with which readers by now will be familiar, that a potato was washed up on the shore of Northumberland and proved to be extraordinarily prolific. Some were planted at the Duke of Northumberland's London home at Sion Park: they were pinkish and the flesh often reddish marbled. Although he proceeds to say that they were the same kind as that raised by Howard, he nevertheless ascribes to the latter a quite different origin. It would seem more likely that the Northumberland potato was the original of the 'Yam', with which it agrees in the colour of skin and flesh.

The Lumper. This variety, as has been mentioned elsewhere, proved itself extremely susceptible to Blight, and played a sinister part in the famine years of 1845 and 1846; prior to that, it had been extensively grown by the poorer classes, especially in Ireland. Its outstanding merit was its great cropping capacity. Its quality was poor, but in the latter years of its career, this was said to have improved. It was in existence in 1808 and is still grown occasionally in Ireland and in the Hebrides.

The Cups. This was a very popular red-skinned variety and, like the 'Lumper', grown very extensively from 1808 onwards. It was regarded as the luxury potato and was a great favourite in both Ireland and England up till the famine. Its cultivation has persisted in scattered spots in Ireland till to-day. It was said of 'Cups' that they were more nutritive than were other varieties, but less digestible. In Ireland it was a common saying that 'they stay too long in the stomach'.

The Ashleaf. This was the outstanding 'early' of the major part of the nineteenth century, and was highly spoken of by Sir J. Sinclair in 1814. It was probably raised by a shoemaker of Retford, named Holberry, about 1804, from the seed of a 'mouse kidney'. Myatt's 'Ashleaf', which

---

[1] Dossie, Robert (1771). Op. cit.

was raised about 1853 and is still grown, must not be confused with the original 'Ashleaf', nor with the 'Immune Ashleaf' raised in 1891, whose correct name is 'Juli'.

The Lapstone Kidney. This was an outstanding second early variety which held its own during the second quarter of the nineteenth century. It was a long, well-shaped kidney tuber, a good cropper, which could be kept in excellent condition till the following May. It was raised by Major Hague at Thorner, near Leeds, in 1827.

It was not till early in the nineteenth century that any serious interest was shown by the scientific world in the cultivation of the potato or the creation of new varieties. The great herbalists of the early seventeenth century had been interested mainly in the botanical character of the potato; it was the speculative scientists of the latter part of that century and the next, who sensed its economic possibilities.

The eminent horticulturist, Andrew Knight[1] (1749–1838), who devoted much attention to the potato and himself made a serious attempt to breed early maturing varieties from early parents, prefaced his remarks as follows: 'The potato contributes to afford food to so large a portion of the inhabitants of this country, that every improvement in its culture becomes an object of national importance; and thence I am induced to hope that the following communication may not be unacceptable to the Horticultural Society.'

In Germany, Dr Carl Putsche,[2] equally impressed by the economic importance of the potato, has left us in a Monograph published in 1819, an invaluable description with abundant illustrations of the varieties current in his day.

These early incursions of the scientist cannot be said to have seriously influenced the production or the improvement of varieties at the time, but they did open the way to later and more fruitful contacts. It was not till a full century had elapsed that co-operation of the scientist with the professional plant-breeders and seedsmen materially affected the character of the varieties produced.

Throughout the nineteenth and twentieth centuries, it was the rapidly growing economic importance of the potato which led scientists to interest themselves in its physiological and pathological reactions as an horticultural crop.

To-day the problem is a wider one: the potato is much more than a cheap and useful food, vital to the nation in time of war; it is rapidly carving out for itself a niche as a raw material for industry and a basis for the exploitation of new and inhospitable territories. This development has received most encouragement in Russia, whose scientists are

[1] Knight, Thomas Andrew (1807). *Trans. Hort. Soc.* vol. I, pp. 57–9. Published 1815.
[2] Putsche, Carl (1819). Op. cit.

striving to create varieties adapted for every type of environment, as well as for a large range of diverse economic industrial needs, a task involving great technical knowledge and scientific acumen. It is because of this that in Russia, and to an increasing extent in England, the U.S.A., and Germany, variety raising is passing from the hands of the fancier to those of the trained scientist. We are, however, anticipating: the era of the skilled fancier had not yet reached its zenith.

Towards the middle of the nineteenth century, a few varieties of outstanding merit were introduced. The 'Prince Regent', which was being grown a few years prior to 1841, became extremely popular; it was known generally as the 'Regent'. It was much used by breeders towards the last quarter of the century, and in consequence is to be found in the pedigree of most of our present-day varieties. 'The Fluke', raised by a cottager, J. Turner of Middleton, near Manchester, in about 1841, was a long, flat oval, late variety of excellent quality. It dominated the markets in England till the coming of its rival, 'Paterson's Victoria'.

In Ireland at this time, 'The Rock', was the favourite maincrop variety, having replaced both the 'Lumper' and the 'Cup'; it held its own till its popularity was eclipsed by the 'Champion'.

No spectacular development took place in variety raising until after the crisis caused by the pandemic Blight (*Phytophthora infestans*) of 1845 and 1846. The failure of any of the existing varieties to exhibit the least resistance to this new and devastating disease gave both stimulus and directive force to a new era of plant-breeding.

The complacent confidence of the potato-growers had been rudely shaken. 'The time was', a correspondent writes in 1852, 'when we could hardly go wrong: no manure or any sort of manure, new soil or old soil, rich land or poor land, early planted or late planted, the tubers were all sound although of different qualities, according to the advantage each had. But how is it now? Every man has a scheme to recommend; but, do what you will, the potatoes, under every sort of management, are diseased.'[1]

All the known varieties in cultivation having proved equally susceptible, a search was made for new blood with which, it was hoped, the enfeebled stocks of the potato might be 'reinvigorated'. The Rev. Chauncey Goodrich of Utica, New York, in 1851, procured a small collection of tubers from South America: one which particularly pleased him, he called 'Rough Purple Chile'. The name was unfortunate because the potatoes, varieties of *Solanum andigenum*, were procured by the U.S. Consul in the market-place of Panamá, and had no connection with Chile.[2] From this variety Goodrich raised a number of selfed-seedlings, one of which,

[1] J. C. (1852). *Cottage Gardener* (30 Sept.), p. 408, quoted by Davidson, *J. Roy. Agric. Soc.* (1939), vol. C, pt. II.

[2] This point is questionable. See Hawkes (1967). Op. cit. – Ed.

'Garnet Chile', had a considerable vogue and was till recently grown in the States. Later breeders used Goodrich's stocks for hybridization with existing European stocks and in that way this new source of 'blood' entered into the composition of many varieties raised during the next fifty or more years.

Another South American *Solanum andigenum* type was introduced into Germany in or about 1830.[1] It was known as 'Daber', and its blood is to be found in many continental types, one of which, 'President', was grown extensively in England in the early decades of this century.

In England, Lord Portman (1846), who took a great interest in potatoes, grew in his garden varieties from Mexico and New Granada, but there is no evidence that they were made use of by breeders of that period.

I have already[2] given reasons for believing that the potatoes introduced into Europe in the sixteenth century, were varieties of what the Russians to-day call the compound species *S. andigenum*, as distinguished from *S. tuberosum*, the group of varieties common to Chile and Chiloé. If this view be accepted, then Goodrich's potato, being itself a variety of the *S. andigenum* group, there was no reason to expect that it would bring into the common pool of characters anything not already present in one or other of the existing varieties. The same holds true for many of the best economic varieties raised during the next half century, all of which can be traced back to 'Early Rose'[3] a daughter of 'Garnet Chile'. That not one of these varieties ever displayed any resistance to Blight, need cause no surprise, seeing that out of some 150 South American varieties tested in my laboratory, none evinced the smallest trace.

Amongst the new varieties there were some which made their mark, because of their outstanding economic merit; such were Paterson's 'Victoria' (1856), Nicoll's 'Champion' (1863), and Sutton's 'Magnum Bonum' (1876). These varieties, more particularly the 'Champion', were credited with the exhibition of some degree of resistance to *Phytophthora infestans*. In the case of the 'Champion', this was sufficient to save its crop in the season of 1879 when all other varieties failed. From that time till 1894, the 'Champion' occupied from 70–80% of the land under potatoes in Ireland. Eventually none of them proved any better than their predecessors, or, indeed their successors.

The Skerry Blue. A round, deep purple coloured tuber with very deep eyes, belongs to a rather different category from the above. It was an unattractive variety and no great cropper, but because of its alleged

[1] Rathlef, H. (1932). Die Stammtafeln des Weltsortiments der Kartoffel. *Kühn-Archiv*. Bd. xxxiii, pp. 297–431.

[2] See chapter v.

[3] 'Early Rose' was developed by Albert Breese of Hubbardstown, Vermont, USA (Salaman's manuscript note). – Ed.

relative immunity to Blight, was a favourite in Ireland and is still to be found there, growing in gardens.

A new era in variety production opened in the 1860's, when William Paterson of Dundee (1810–70), who had interested himself for many years in potato-breeding, began to plant out his newly raised and selected varieties on a large scale. Paterson's efforts were in the main directed towards the combating of 'degeneration', and to this end he obtained his breeding stocks from the Cape of Good Hope, America, Australia and England. There is no reason to suppose that these were other than the same varieties commonly grown at home but, as his own local stocks were 'degenerate', and had ceased to bear berries, he thought that fresh and healthier stocks might do so. In this he was not disappointed. Paterson produced a large number of distinct varieties and, in doing so, lost no less than £7,000, but by his example, whole-hearted devotion, and the large scale of his breeding and selection, he revolutionized the raising of potato varieties in Great Britain and the Continent. By the production of the famous Paterson's 'Victoria' in 1863, he definitely raised the standard of potato-growing in this country.

Paterson was the first of a succession of some half-dozen raisers who, in the fifty years following the appearance of the 'Victoria', achieved the highest possible success in variety raising based on selection rather than on that of purposeful hybridization. These men were not guided by any scientific doctrines as to heredity or immunity: they based their choice on the quantity of the crop and the quality and shape of the tubers. Much attention was paid to the character of the haulm. They avoided the tall, many stalked and stiffer types, and concentrated on full, rather soft and gracious types of foliage which, as the season progresses, fill out the rows. All of them relied on the natural selfed-berry rather than on hybridization.

Robert Fenn (1816–1912) was the next outstanding figure in the history of potato variety raising: he was a very careful worker and one of the first to realize that difference of name was no guarantee of difference of variety. Only one of his varieties, 'International Kidney', achieved lasting distinction, and that was rejected by Fenn himself, but introduced by R. Dean in 1879. This variety has proved the mainstay of the Jersey early potato trade ever since, in consequence of which it has acquired the local name of 'Jersey Royal'. Fenn was instrumental in the production of several varieties for Messrs Sutton & Sons, of which 'Reading Russet', 'Early Regent' and 'Ringleader' had considerable, if not long-lived success.

The next raiser of note was James Clarke (1825–90), a gardener living near Christchurch, Hampshire. Most of his new varieties were bought and produced by Messrs Sutton & Sons. Clarke may be said to have provided his own monument in the creation of 'Magnum Bonum' and 'Epicure', which Suttons put on the market in 1876 and 1897 respectively. The former, a late variety, enjoyed for a time the reputation of being a Blight resister and as such had a brilliant but relatively short-lived career; the latter is still the hardiest, most frost-resistant and heaviest cropping first early variety grown in this country. 'Epicure' was followed immediately by 'Ninetyfold', a most successful early, still very largely grown in Cheshire and Lancashire.

To Clarke also belongs the credit of having introduced the variety 'Maincrop', which has survived as the best eating quality maincrop potato of Western Europe, under the name of its russeted mutational form, 'Golden Wonder'.

John Nicoll (1830–90) will always be remembered as the man who bred the 'Champion': its origin is uncertain: he never knew which were the parents he used. Nicoll's own description of how he raised this variety is illuminating because it illustrates the haphazard methods of even the best of pre-Mendelian breeders of potatoes, and at the same time their marvellous flair for selecting the promising seedling. Nicoll, in answer to questions before a Select Committee[1] said: 'He planted in 1862 two white sorts and one red, one at least was one of Paterson's. He saved plums from these three sorts indiscriminately and saved seed, sowed in 1863 and selected the best.' Paterson's 'Victoria' was not introduced till 1864, so that this may be excluded as a possible parent.

Champion was introduced about 1876 and, as we have seen, proved its worth in Ireland in the year 1879, when there was a serious and widespread outbreak of Blight. It alone, it was said, yielded any harvest that year. Following on this outstanding success, 'Champion' was grown in ever greater quantities in Ireland till, towards the end of the century, it practically monopolized the area under 'late' potatoes. By 1921 it had lost all pretension to resistance and gradually passed out of cultivation.

Archibald Findlay (1841–1921), originally a potato merchant, began to interest himself in the raising of new varieties in 1877. His earliest productions have been subjected to severe criticism on the ground that they were mere selections from pre-existing sorts: the 'Bruce' from 'Magnum Bonum', and 'Abundance' from 'Jeanie Deans'. This matter is fully discussed by Davidson.[2] We have not to-day the material on which to form a final judgement, but the weight of evidence is in favour of their being selections and not original seedlings.

In 1891 Findlay introduced 'Up-to-date', one of the finest table varieties that has ever been grown. There is some doubt whether this, too, was not a selection from 'Scottish Triumph', a variety so similar,

---

[1] *Report Select Committee on Potato Crop* (1880). Q. 364.
[2] Davidson, W. (1939). Famous Potato Raisers. *J. Roy. Agric. Soc.* vol. c, part II.

that it ceased to be recognized, or grown as a distinct type. All that we know is that Findlay exhibited 'Up-to-date' to a gathering of farmers in October 1891, whilst the 'Scottish Triumph' was not introduced to the general public before being shown at the Kilmarnock Show in 1892. A large output of new varieties ensued, only two of which attained outstanding success: 'British Queen' in 1894, a splendid second early, and 'Majestic' in 1911, now the most widely grown late variety in Great Britain.[1]

Findlay was involved in the great potato boom of 1902–3, when a new variety of little merit, 'Northern Star', and an old one of still less, originally known as 'Evergood' but which was re-christened 'Eldorado', both launched by him, were sold at fantastic prices and acclaimed as the perfect potatoes, proof against every trouble.

The growing seasons of 1902 and 1903 had been very unfavourable, and sound potato seed was particularly scarce. Genuine potato-growers were in a state of anxiety: the majority of them were, like the public, generally ignorant of the progress of horticulture, and hence the more ready to believe in the 'wonders' of science. They both fell willing victims to the wiles of a small group of potato merchants, whose own credulity was at least as great as their greed. The wildest speculation ensued: people with no real interest in the potato paid fabulous sums for a few worthless tubers. In a lawsuit in 1904, evidence was given that, of a stone of one of the two varieties, three pounds had been sold in advance at £160 per lb. One of the merchants involved in the boom told me that he had bought a tuber for its weight in gold. In 1904 the weather was propitious, crops were good, and the boom collapsed. The matter has more than a passing interest; it, in fact, marks a turning point in the historic development of plant-breeding. It is unlikely that a similar ramp could be staged to-day, for the public are now accustomed to look to the scientific institutes and particularly the National Institute of Agricultural Botany, for guidance in such a crisis. It may be claimed that the 'Eldorado' boom marked the end of one epoch and the beginning of a new and better one.

As a tail-piece to the record of the old epoch, mention must be made of one of the most useful and popular varieties ever grown, and one still in great demand. The variety 'King Edward VII', whose parentage is unknown, was raised by a gardener in Northumberland who called his seedling 'Fellside Hero'. From Northumberland it passed into the possession of a grower in Snaith, Yorkshire, who brought it to the notice of a Manchester potato merchant. The latter could make no immediate use of it and gave his tubers to Mr J. Butler of Scotter, who eventually bought all the stocks that were in the hands of the Yorkshire grower. Mr Butler grew on, until he had 50 acres of the variety in hand. On the advice of a Mr Paxten, potato merchant of Manchester, he

[1] But see Introduction. – Ed.

rechristened the potato 'King Edward', and placed his stocks on the market in 1910 at £12. 10s. a ton. This variety is to-day the most popular in England, and commands the highest prices on account of its excellent cooking qualities.[1] This account, which I derived from Mr Butler himself, illustrates not only the spirit of the period then drawing to an end, but the fact that the producer of potato varieties is the last to reap any reward. Bred by an amateur, chance dictated its birth, a native flair its survival, and the juggling of names its successful debut.

The 'King Edward' variety confirmed one trend in fashion and introduced another. From the early years of the twentieth century onwards, the public has grown increasingly inclined to expect an oval or kidney-shaped tuber, white in the skin, and with a smooth surface. The old round, deep-eyed bulgy types, of which 'Epicure' is almost the only survivor, were looked on askance and have been discarded, with the result that we have lost some of the best cookers and most palatable sorts ever known.

The matter of skin colour, in the early days one of indifference, has assumed an importance out of all proportion to its worth, more especially when we remember that there is no evidence of any linkage between colour of skin, splashed or otherwise, and the cooking quality of the variety. White, pink, red, scarlet, light purple, and dark purple or black-skinned tubers, were at one time all welcomed; to-day, the purples, such as 'Arran Victory', are only countenanced in the north of Scotland and in Ireland. Wholly coloured red-skinned tubers are almost disqualified; it is only if the colour be splashed on a white background, that it is favoured. It is the appeal of the 'King Edward' to the housewife, which has caused her eclecticism to become the guiding star of the breeder. The 'King Edward' became a favourite in the kitchen because of its good shape, and the fact that it keeps its colour after boiling, better than most others; it was no more than a happy accident that its colour-splashed skin made it easy for the housewife to recognize it in the shop. Unfortunately, it is not immune to Wart Disease; hence breeders have struggled to produce new varieties which look like 'King Edward' but are immune, in the hope that they will receive the welcome hitherto reserved for their prototype.

Second growth, which used to be common in old varieties and leads to the formation of outgrowths and small accessory tubers, is rightly frowned upon to-day, both in field and kitchen. Other features have come into prominence because they fit into our more scientifically organized husbandry. The big farmer desires potatoes which bulk early, that is to say, his maincrop varieties should attain their maximum size and weight as early as possible, a feature common to 'King Edward' and

[1] Salaman, R. N. (1926). *Potato Varieties*, p. 275.

'Majestic'. The custom of waiting till November to raise a full crop, is long past; to-day we expect our 'lates' to attain their full weight by the end of September. Again, the producer much dislikes varieties which sprout in the pits—a fault which has cost one of the best of table varieties, 'Arran Chief', its life; whilst the absence of it has endowed 'Arran Consul' with a reputation which its behaviour in other respects denies.

The potato merchant shares in the likes and dislikes of both consumer and producer, and adds at least one of his own. The occurrence of Dry Rot, which usually develops whilst the potato is in transit, or immediately after delivery to his client, is the occasion of much trouble and loss to him. Although Dry Rot is, to a large extent, seasonal, yet certain varieties are more susceptible than others. It was for this reason that 'Doon Star' failed to maintain what seemed a leading position.

In every direction we are trying to mould the potato variety of the future to satisfy the requirements of a generation which is less concerned with exploiting the epicurean resources of the material than the saving of labour and the ensuring of profits.

With the launching of the variety, 'King Edward', the era of the mere raiser-selectionist may be said to have come to a close. Its methodology may have been empirical, its successes fortuitous, yet it had provided us with a wide range of varieties, exhibiting every shade of maturity and eating quality, combined with elegance of appearance and high yields. One after another, however, they ran their course and had their day; the great majority, sooner or later, fell victims to one of three fates. Either they failed to withstand the effects of virus infection; in other words, they succumbed to the 'Curl'; or they proved unduly susceptible to infection by *Phytophthora infestans*, i.e. they fell before the common Blight; or they collapsed in the face of the new enemy, *Synchytrium endobioticum*, viz. Wart Disease.

The three foes to potato-growing, may be regarded as 'limiting factors', that is to say, unless some means of circumventing, subduing, or holding in check their attacks, the potato crops of this country would be in danger of more or less complete destruction. From the moment that this was recognized, potato-breeding entered on a new phase.

The story of these combats against disease in the potato, were I but competent to do justice to the subject, would be not unworthy of taking its place amongst those epics of contemporary science which deal with man's struggle to free his fellows from the fear of want. A short sketch of the three campaigns[1] may suffice to show how fundamental are the issues involved.

[1] Large, E. C. (1940), in *The Advance of the Fungi* (Jonathan Cape), gives a fascinating picture of some of the aspects of the fight against Blight, and the important repercussions which ensued.

Wart Disease, the last of the three enemies to be encountered, will be considered first, because in this case, scientist and breeder, between them, achieved a complete and resounding victory. Wart Disease is produced by the invasion of the growing plants by a fungus, *Synchytrium endobioticum*, resident in the soil. Its attack produces wart-like outgrowths on the tuber and base of the stem which may, in susceptible varieties, grow to a great size, whilst at the same time destroying the tubers. Ultimately the whole tissue breaks down into a creamy, stinking mass, and the produce of the plant, and often of the entire crop, is lost.

The disease was probably present in isolated gardens in the northern Midlands of England, as far back as 1876, but it did not excite the attention of either the authorities or scientists till thirty years later. In 1896, an Hungarian, Schibersky, described both the disease and the causative fungus, but it was not till 1907 that its inroads gave any concern. It was in that year that the passage of the Destruction of Insect and Pests Act enabled the Board of Agriculture—as it then was— to appoint technical inspectors to report on the health of our crops. In 1908 one of the Inspectors, Mr George C. Gough,[1] was detailed to investigate this new trouble. He found that it was widespread in Lancashire, Cheshire and Staffordshire, and that it was causing much more serious loss to the growers than had so far been appreciated.

In the course of his visitation to the local farmers and growers, he chanced to inspect the farm of a Mr Swindell, who told him that although most of the potatoes he was accustomed to grow were destroyed from time to time, there was one variety, 'Snowdrop', he could always grow with safety. Armed with this clue, Gough soon discovered that some half-dozen other varieties had been found by one or another grower, to be equally immune. These observations had immediate repercussions, which have been of the greatest benefit to potato-growers and consumers the world over.

In order to determine which varieties were susceptible and which immune, it became necessary to set up Wart Testing Stations on highly infected soils, the first and most important of which was that at Ormskirk, which began work in 1915 under the supervision of John Snell, a man whose name should be remembered with gratitude and respect. It was Snell who first realized how entirely lacking in method and morale was the potato seed trade of the time. In testing a large number of named varieties for susceptibility to the disease, he found that one and the same variety might make its appearance in the trade under a score of different names. It was essential that this source of confusion should

---

[1] Gough, G. C. (1919). Wart Disease of Potatoes. *J. Roy. Hort. Soc.* vol. XLV, p. 301.

be cleared up, if the Ministry was ever to give any intelligent advice to the public as to what was and what was not, safe to grow. A Committee was set up under the Royal Horticultural Society, to assist in the work of sorting out and testing all named varieties, and this, as well as the whole of the testing for resistance to Wart Disease, was later taken over by the National Institute of Agricultural Botany in 1919, who appointed a Potato Synonym Committee to carry on the work. In 1920 John Snell died, and it fell to me to take over the Chairmanship of this Committee from that time till now. The Potato Synonym Committee's investigations extended over the entire range of old and new varieties of the potato and brought to light an almost incredible state of affairs. We found over 200 aliases or synonyms of the one variety 'Up-to-date', most of which were equipped in the catalogues of the different dealers with different characters: some might be described as new varieties only just put on the market, others as old and trusted friends; some as second-earlies, others as lates; some as rounds, others as kidneys; some as immune to Blight; and, to complete the confusion, they were offered at prices generally higher than the correctly named 'Up-to-date' stock itself. A similar state of affairs was discovered in relation to every variety, which had at one time or another, won popularity: 'Abundance' and 'British Queen', for example, had over seventy different pseudonyms apiece. The Committee, by dint of much work, and with the powerful assistance of some of the leading seed merchants, but against bitter opposition from the trade organizations, at length carried the day. Not only has the potato trade been rid of this mischievous custom, but other branches of the trade, notably that of the cereal seed dealers, have followed suit, greatly to the benefit of the grower, the seedsman and the public.[1]

All this has been accomplished with the minimum of bureaucratic control, except that no immune variety can be officially listed until it is certified as distinct by the Potato Synonym Committee of the National Institute of Agricultural Botany. There is no legal bar to the introduction of new susceptible varieties, but in practice, no new variety is launched to-day which has not passed successfully the test for immunity.

Gough's observation and the Ministry's well-directed campaign for combating this latest threat to the potato, supplied the impetus for a revival in potato-breeding. Donald McKelvie, the originator of all the 'Arran' varieties, had already produced several new and useful sorts,

---

[1] The use of synonyms and the like, was not quashed without a severe struggle. Those interested should refer to an article in *The Gardeners' Chronicle* (25 Nov. 1922), by R.N.S., and subsequent correspondence in that Journal, *The Nurseryman and Seedsman*, and other trade journals of that time. An annual report on synonyms is published by the N.I.A.B. in its Journal.

but from now on, his work was directed towards producing immune types to replace the susceptibles in the ranks of the early, second-early, maincrop and late groups.

Before long the authorities let it be known that no new variety, however outstanding its other qualities might be, would be allowed to reach the market unless it proved to be resistant to Wart Disease and had been certified by the Potato Synonym Committee as being distinct from all others. This policy helped to canalize the efforts of raisers in the production of none but immune varieties. Some ten years after the War of 1914–18, a new generation of potato-breeders sprang up; some of whom, trained as botanists, had imbibed the principles of the new science of Mendelism; such are John Watson of McGill & Smith, and William Black of the Scottish Society for Research in Plant Breeding.

In 1919, my colleague James W. Lesley, and I,[1] began our investigations of the genetics controlling the inheritance of resistance and susceptibility in the potato to the attacks of the fungus. Breeders had naturally turned to the proved immune sorts for the choice of the parents from which they sought to raise the seedling families, from which they hoped to select their new seedlings. Our work proved that it was not only possible, but might be a sound policy to secure seedlings fully immune to Wart Disease from certain classes of susceptible parents. This fact greatly extended the choice of parents available to the breeders.

Alongside these investigations, other workers, notably Dr E. Köhler in Dahlem, Mary Glynn, H. Bryan and Mrs McDermott in England, developed a technique for the rapid production of Wart on susceptible varieties. By this means a few tubers could be tested for susceptibility, under controlled conditions in the glasshouse, at any time. The glasshouse method, which ultimately replaced the earlier one of growing large numbers of tubers in the highly infected trial grounds at Ormskirk, has enabled the breeder to ascertain the reaction in its first year of a new seedling, within a few weeks.

In the last twenty years, potato-breeders have been increasingly ready to make use of the help which the scientist can put at his disposal: a lead was given by the veteran, McKelvie, and more recently his example has been emulated, amongst others, by John Clarke of Broughgammon, Ballycastle, County Antrim, the breeder of the 'Ulster' varieties, whose appreciation of the scientific approach is as outstanding, as is his flair for selecting the most promising seedlings.

If emphasis has been laid on the contribution of scientist and breeder in the fight against Wart, it would give but a very one-sided picture were

[1] Salaman, R. N. and Lesley, J. W. (1921). *Rept. Int. Potato Conf.* pp. 108–15.
Salaman and Lesley (1923). *J. Genetics*, vol. XIII, pp. 177–86.

no mention to be made of the part which the government authorities rendered. It is no less than the truth to say, that had not the Ministry of Agriculture and the kindred Departments in Scotland and Ireland adopted a determined and enlightened policy, the complete victory over a scourge which at one time threatened the entire industry, could never have been won. Indeed, the history of the campaign encourages one to believe that scientist, bureaucrat and statesman, can co-operate as successfully in defence of our crops against the ravages of a predatory fungus, as they have in these recent years in defence of our existence as a nation, against a foe no less pestilential.

The visitation in 1845 and 1846 of the Blight, *Phytophthora infestans*, the second 'limiting factor', caused, as we shall have other occasions to note,[1] a social upheaval, the like of which had probably never been experienced—at least locally—since the days of the Black Death in 1348. We have already learnt that no variety in 1846 was able to withstand the attack, and that although many, otherwise valuable, varieties were introduced between that day and our own, none proved to have any lasting resistance to the disease.

It is true that a few very late maturing varieties such as 'Champion', to which reference has already been made, 'Flourball' and its offsprings 'Shamrock' and 'Champion II', displayed a certain measure of resistance in their early days in the field, yet none of them can be regarded as immune to the disease. All these varieties and certain others, as 'Leinster Wonder', 'Skerry Blue' and 'Ben Cruachan', which in the early days of their career have shown some resistance to Blight, share one feature in common, their late maturity, and it is in this that their partial immunity from destruction lies.

That late maturing varieties display a moderate resistance to Blight, especially when weather conditions are not continuously favourable to the fungus and the attack not too prolonged, has long been recognized. Under such conditions, late varieties which commonly have not reached the height of their vigour by the time Blight appears, withstand the attack far better than do earlier ones whose seasonal career is at the time, physiologically speaking, on the downward path. Very late seedlings generally exhibit a remarkable freedom from Blight in the field in their first year, though they may readily succumb in their second, when they are planted from tubers and mature much earlier. The collapse of late maturing varieties, who in the early years of their career in the field showed some resistance, is almost certainly due to the fact that their stocks have, after a run of five to ten years, become infected with virus disease and, as a result, mature a week or two earlier. Such an advance in maturity, bringing them within the range of maximum physiological

[1] See chapters XVI and XVII.

susceptibility, lays them open to the full blast of the assault. This explanation, whilst fitting in with the experience in the field, gains indirect support from recent research in the laboratory. Miss O'Connor, and later Mr J. L. Petterson, working with me on the progeny raised from the selfing of our domestic varieties, examined some 10,000 seedlings in the first few weeks of their existence. The object was to discover whether any might exhibit resistance against attack by the two distinct and highly virulent strains of the *Phytophthora infestans* fungus. Amongst the varieties whose selfed-seedlings were thus tested, was 'Flourball', a variety which exhibited some resistance to Blight in the field in its early years, as did its own sibling, 'Champion II'. Not a single seedling of these or other domestic stocks was found to possess any resistance to either strain.

This explanation receives even stronger support from Dr Davidson's[1] work on the rejuvenation of the original 'Champion'. Following a painstaking examination of 'Champion' stocks growing both in Ireland and Scotland, he at length secured a few tubers of the variety which, after a searching examination in both field and laboratory, proved to be completely free from virus infection. Davidson multiplied this stock under isolation in the three years between 1925–27. In the latter year there was a sharp outbreak of Blight, and Davidson records: 'It was quite obvious that these Champion remained green longer and withstood the Blight better than any other of the varieties grown in the district, which included Up-to-date, King Edward, Arran Chief, Kerr's Pink, and Arran Victory.' Both the late maturity, and the relative resistance to Blight, were recovered when the crippling effect of virus infection was removed, and the variety once more regained its inherent lateness of maturity.

In the year 1906, desiring to know something of wild potato species, I asked the authorities at Kew to let me have a few tubers of *Solanum maglia*. A couple of white-skinned tubers arrived and were planted. The tubers of *S. maglia* should have purple skins: subsequent enquiry showed that Kew's stock of *S. maglia* had died out, and that another supposedly wild species had by accident acquired its label. I learned further, from my friend the late Mr Arthur Sutton, that he had acquired this very same wild species twenty years earlier from the Edinburgh Botanical Gardens, under the name of *Solanum etuberosum*—another misnomer. I mention these details, because it was owing to this confusion between the wild variety *S. maglia* and what has since been christened *S. edinense*, that I stumbled on to the unsuspected fact that a genuine resistance to Blight does, in fact, exist.

[1] Davidson, W. D. (1928). The Rejuvenation of the 'Champion'. *Proc. Dublin Roy. Soc.* vol. II, pp. 319–30.

The facts may be briefly epitomized as follows:[1] *S. edinense* itself at Barley proved almost, but not completely, resistant to the attacks of Blight, in the years 1906–10. I obtained self-fertilized seed from the parent *S. edinense* plants, which in 1909 gave rise to a family of forty plants. Blight was particularly bad that year and the next, and killed off all the neighbouring potato plants, whether established varieties or new seedlings derived from them. Thirty-three of the *S. edinense* seedlings were also killed, but seven were untouched. The seven resistant seedlings were grown on in subsequent years and retained their resistance. One which was allowed to remain in the kitchen garden at Barley for seventeen consecutive seasons, never showed the least sign of infection by Blight.

Extensive hybridization between the immune seedlings and domestic varieties, followed by selection of suitable types, was carried out, with a view to obtaining resistant seedlings endowed with good economic qualities.

The campaign against Blight had entered on a definitely new phase. It was carried on in Barley without intermission till 1926, when the stocks were transferred to the new station for Potato Virus Research, of which I became the Director.

Satisfied that true resistance could only be found outside the domestic varieties, I obtained several other wild species, including *S. demissum*, a wild potato from Mexico, which is almost devoid of tubers in our latitude. In 1910 I had a family of seedlings of this species in my trial grounds: they were unaffected by Blight. In the following year I commenced to hybridize it with our domestic stocks. By 1914 I had a series of such hybrid families, a number of the resistant individuals of which were crossed with the immune stocks previously obtained.[2]

By 1926 I was in possession of over a score of seedling varieties endowed with reasonably good economic characters which, no matter what their maturity, appeared to be immune to Blight. A few of these were sent to Ireland where they have been growing for over twenty years in the open and have retained a high degree of resistance to attack throughout.

Progress in research being so often dependent on technique, it may not be out of place to record how much the scope of the work was enlarged and accelerated by the use of a very simple device: At first, the method of testing for resistance to Blight was to plant in the open the seedling varieties together with susceptible stocks such as 'Majestic'

---

[1] Salaman, R. N. (1910). *J. Genetics*, vol. I, pp. 1–46.
[2] A short account of these researches will be found in *The Gardeners' Chronicle* (30 Oct. 1937), vol. CII, no. 2653, and in the *Indian J. Agric. Sci.* (Apr. 1938), vol. VIII, pp. 119–29.

and 'King Edward', and wait for the seasonal Blight, if there were any, to attack them. Later we used the method devised by Müller, of planting the seedlings in thumb-pots and exposing them when very young, to artificial infection in a glass chamber. This had the drawback of taking up much time and labour, as well as frequently ruining the few resistant plants on which our hopes were pinned, not by Blight, but by the adverse horticultural conditions of the chamber. The new method was to pick a few leaflets from the plant to be tested, place them, with the control leaflets on a layer of peat in a pie-dish, and spray them with a suspension of Blight spores, and cover the dish with a sheet of glass. The results can be read off, with ease and assurance, in under a week.[1]

In the autumn of 1932 our hopes were considerably dashed when certain of the immune seedlings, then growing in the open, showed signs of being attacked by Blight. In 1936 the attack was more serious, but it occurred a month later than that affecting the field crops in the neighbourhood.

It was thought probable that our 'immune' stocks were succumbing to some new form or biotype of *Phytophthora infestans*. My colleague, Miss O'Connor, set to work to isolate the same, studied the Blight fungus on the plants, and showed that our suspicions were correct. Later, another colleague Mr Petterson cultured the new biotype from a single spore. We then proceeded to find some other wild, or hybrid stock, which might be immune to the new biotype. O'Connor discovered it in a potato plant, sent me some years earlier, by Prof. Knappe from Poland, under the name of *Aya Papa* but which, in reality, was a hybrid of the domestic potato and our old friend, *Solanum demissum*. From this source during the next few years were raised several generations of hybrids, selections from which proved to be immune both to the common and the new form of Blight. On my retirement in 1939, the work was handed over to the Cambridge Plant Breeding Institute, who have continued and expanded the research.

Such, in outline, is the tale of the first decisive stage in the fight against a disease which, between 1845 and 1939, has cost the United Kingdom about five million pounds per annum.

Research on similar lines was commenced by Broili[2] at Dahlem in 1914, but was not seriously pursued till 1920, when it was taken over by K. O. Müller.[3] Russian workers have also recently entered the field. Had it not been for the appearance of the new biotypes of the fungus, of which at present at least three are known in this country, and many

---

[1] The insertion of a bed of moist peat, which much improved the procedure, was made at the suggestion of the senior laboratory assistant, Mr L. Selmes.

[2] Broili (1921). Mitteilungen der Biologisch. *Reichsanstalt. f. Land. u. Forstwirtscht.* Ht. xxi, pp. 154–8.

[3] Müller, K. O. (1930). *Angewandte Botanik*, Bd. xii, Ht. iv, pp. 299–324.

more claimed by the German workers, the great fight against Blight might have been regarded as won, as far back as 1926. As it is, it is not certain that fresh sources of resistance will be found with which to combat such new biotypes as may appear. But even if we fail to discover the appropriate resistant plant, the fact that the epidemic appears a week or two later would still give the new variety great economic value.[1]

Only patient and unflagging work on scientific lines, such as that being pursued by Black and Cockerham on the genetics of Blight and virus resistance, is likely to give us the answer we seek.

The third, but by no means the least of the 'limiting factors', is that induced by virus infections. In the second half of the eighteenth century, we first hear of a trouble in the potato crops which was spoken of as the 'Curl'.

The symptoms of the disease, though varying both with the nature of the virus and the variety attacked, may be summed up as consisting of a greater or lesser distortion and dwarfing of the green parts, combined with a quantitative reduction in the volume of the crop amounting to 75% and even more, of the normal. In some forms of the disease, the tubers may be so reduced in size and so disfigured as to render them unfit for human consumption.

Before 1775 the trouble had become so serious that in Lancashire and the north it was feared that the cultivation of the potato might have to be dropped. But it was only because the potato was more widely grown in the north, that complaints were mainly heard from that part of the country; similar trouble was experienced wherever the potato was grown. It became customary to speak of the 'Curl' and kindred defects as 'degeneration', a name which held the field till in recent years it had been shown that these troubles were in reality due to infection by a kind of germ called a virus.

Viruses, that is to say, agents capable of producing certain diseases in plants and animals, are so extremely minute that in respect to size they are, as compared with a bacillus of the *coli* type, as a mouse might be in comparison to an elephant. Nor is it at all certain that all viruses should be regarded as living organisms.

The study of the viruses affecting potatoes was initiated by Orton in the U.S.A. in 1913, who showed that there were several distinct kinds of 'degeneration', which he distinguished by the names of Leaf Roll, Mosaic, and Streak. Advances of great importance in our knowledge, were made by the Dutch scientist, Quanjer, who proved that Leaf Roll was infectious, and by his colleague Oortwin Botjes who, in 1920, showed that the disease was conveyed from plant to plant by a common species of green-fly or aphis. At the Cambridge Potato Virus Research Station,

---

[1] For a review of the more recent work on potato disease and pest resistance see: Howard, H. W. (1970), *Genetics of the Potato*. Logos Press, London; and Howard H. W. (1983), The production of new varieties. *In* Harris, P. M., *The Potato Crop*, Edition 2. Chapman and Hall, London. - Ed.

my colleague, Kenneth Smith, demonstrated the fact that some mosaics of the potato were due to a virus which he called 'X', which is conveyed from plant to plant by contact of the leaves, but not by any insect as far as we know, and that other forms including some types of Streak, are due to infection by a virus he called 'Y', which is conveyed, like Leaf Roll, by the green-fly. In Dublin, Murphy and McKay described a virus, conveyed by the green-fly, which they called 'A'. Virus 'A' when associated with 'X', was shown by them to be responsible for a form of 'curl' known as 'crinkle' which, though not very common, may at times severely cripple certain varieties. A notable sufferer in this respect is 'Golden Wonder', the potato possessing the highest table quality of any grown in Great Britain. Although other and valuable contributions bearing on the problem of virus infection of the potato, were rendered by all members of the Cambridge team, as well as by those of Dublin, we can here only deal with those which have a direct bearing on the causation of, and protection against, those virus diseases which, producing the symptoms of the 'Curl' or 'degeneration', may be said to act as 'limiting factors' to the cultivation of the potato.

It was said that the virus diseases as 'limiting factors' were of greater importance, or more correctly, a greater menace, than either of those previously considered. The reason for that statement can now be made clear: when a plant is affected by Wart Disease or by Blight, it is easy to cull from it one or more tubers which are entirely free from infection. That is to say, the infective agents act locally and not systemically, which means that the agent, in this case the virus, is to be found disseminated throughout all the tissues of the plant.[1] The consequences of this fact are all important in the case of the potato. When once a plant is infected by a virus, then with rare 'exceptions' every single tuber it bears becomes likewise infected. Inasmuch as the potato crop is propagated from tuber-seed, it follows that every tuber derived from a plant which has been infected in a previous season, will itself give rise to an infected plant. More than this, in the majority of cases, the degenerative symptoms which develop as a result of an infection are usually much more severe in subsequent seasons than they are in that in which the disease was first contracted. In a word, infected tuber-seeds give rise to 'degenerated' plants. Thus virus diseases of the potato are both continuing as regards infection, and cumulative as regards symptoms.

A further difference between the majority of virus symptoms and those occasioned by Blight or Wart, is that a seed-tuber infected, whether by Leaf Roll, the 'Y' virus, or the viruses 'A' and 'X', cannot usually be

---

[1] There is one major and a few minor exceptions to this rule: the former being that only very exceptionally is the flower seed of an infected plant itself infected, hence normal seedlings may be the offsprings of infected plants.

differentiated from healthy ones by the naked eye, and therefore one can rarely look for any assistance from the selection of harvested tubers, on the basis of their naked-eye appearance.

Of all the degenerative diseases to which the potato is subject, it is Leaf Roll and the infection induced by the 'Y' virus which are both the most common and the most crippling.

It will therefore be readily understood, that if we could control the development or the movements of the green-fly, we should have gone a long way towards controlling the incidence of 'Curl', using that term in its widest sense. If, in addition, we could at the start, eliminate all infected plants on which the fly might feed in the late spring, before it begins to migrate, we should be in a still stronger position. From the foregoing, it will be appreciated that the battle against 'degeneration' in the potato must, as it were, be fought on two fronts: one, directed against the carrier, or vector, of the infecting agent; the other, against the sources of infection upon which the vector feeds, and from which it transmits the virus. Till recent years, it was only against the second front that defences—at best empirical and often faulty—had been envisaged and, to some extent, practised.

It has been the subject of common observation for over a hundred years, that potato seed-tubers derived from highland moors, as a rule gave rise to healthier plants than did seed grown in sheltered enclosures anywhere in England. As more attention was given to this subject, it was realized that regions exposed to the sea air, and enjoying a high rainfall, were much more favourable seed-raising areas than sheltered inland regions where the rainfall was lower. In practice, this meant that seed-tubers grown in most parts of Scotland gave rise to stronger and healthier crops than those derived from tubers which had been raised in East Anglia, and in still greater degree than those from seed which had been grown in the south and west of England.

Since the early decades of this century, the best Scottish seed-growers have taken pains to eliminate as far as they can, any obviously infected and degenerate plants from their fields. But roguing out infected plants, is a much more difficult task than might be thought. There are plants which are carriers of virus and, as such, show so little sign of disease as to escape notice, yet they are a source of great danger to plants of other varieties. In this task of cleansing their stocks, the growers in Scotland have been greatly assisted by an elaborate system of official inspection.[1]

Notwithstanding, every few years the Scotch potato seed crop is liable to fall short of the high standards that are aimed at. The reason for such,

---

[1] All that has been said of Scotch seed, applies in equal measure to that raised in Ireland.

is an epidemic outbreak of virus disease, due to infection with Leaf Roll or the 'Y' virus, or both. That this should be, does not reflect on the skill of the grower, but is due to the fact that the climatic conditions of the eastern arable districts of Scotland permit, every now and again, both of the migration and rapid multiplication of the green-fly. Added to which, is the fact that however high the standard of husbandry, the frequency and extent of the potato crop make it impossible to completely eliminate such foci of infection as is afforded by 'ground-keepers'.

A further factor operating on this front, and perhaps the most important in this consideration, was discovered by a Welsh entomologist, W. Maldwyn Davies,[1] who unfortunately died as a young man. As a result of the most careful work, he discovered that the winged green-fly refuses to move from the plant on which it is feeding, if the wind is stronger than eight miles per hour, and that it is equally reluctant to move, if the humidity of the air is high; added to this, is the well-known fact that a heavy fall of rain will often destroy more or less completely, colonies of green-fly which may be established on the potato plants. Conversely, in hot dry climates with low winds, the flies travel from plant to plant, which they colonize in vast numbers and, if infected, they convey the infection to every new plant on which they feed.

We are now in a position to consider the bearing of these facts on the problem of raising healthy potato stocks. If the vector is absent, or, if present, is prevented by one means or another from migrating, there can be no spread of infection. If there is no infected plant, or other focus of disease, such as is afforded by ground-keepers from a previous crop or by the presence of the infected nightshade weed, *Solanum nigrum*, on which the vector can feed in the spring and early summer, then its migration, and the subsequent infestation of the plants, though undesirable in itself, is no longer a source of danger, in so far as the degenerative maladies are concerned.

From the above, two further deductions may be drawn: if we can start with a stock of potato seed which we know to be completely free of all virus infection, and plant it at such a distance from all possible sources of infection, then the chances are that no winged aphis reaching the crop, will behave as a vector of disease, and hence the crop will remain healthy. Again, if we can grow our virus-free seed in a district where the climatic conditions are such as to either eliminate or render static, such green-fly as may be present, then there is no reason to expect that the potato plants will ever be infected.

Realizing that the first and most vital step in the campaign was to gain

---

[1] Davies, W. M. (1935). *Annals of Appl. Biol.* vol. XXII, pp. 106–15.
—— (1935). Ibid. pp. 549–56.

the possession of small nuclear stocks of virus-free seed of the leading varieties, I set to work in 1925 to obtain the same. This was done by visiting growing crops in the western districts of Scotland and Ireland, and removing immature tubers from the healthiest plants I could find. These tubers were then planted, at first in insect-proof cages at Barley, and later in the insect-proof glasshouses at Cambridge, and tested periodically for virus infection. Those which proved to be absolutely free, were multiplied in pots in the glasshouses and maintained there from year to year.

In 1934, at the request of Mr, now Sir William Gavin, I laid before the Potato Marketing Board a scheme embodying the principles which I have outlined, for the production on a commercial scale of virus-free stock-seed in sufficient quantity to supply the normal seed- and ware-producing areas of Scotland. The main points were that the potato-growers of eastern Scotland should periodically import their virus-free seed stocks from those approved culture areas which enjoyed climatic conditions known to be adverse to the multiplication and spread of the aphis; and that these latter should, at the same time, be renewed by consignments from the virus-free tested stocks maintained in the glasshouses at Cambridge. For the next five years the scheme reposed undisturbed in the pigeon-holes of the Board. By dint of much importunity, at long last a Conference of leading members of the Trade, the Ministry, the National Institute of Agricultural Botany, and agricultural experts, was induced to meet in June 1939, to consider the possibility of putting the project into practice. The scheme was generally approved and considered worthy of a serious trial. The outbreak of war caused a further postponement.

Having made sure of healthy nuclear stocks, the next step was to find some place in the United Kingdom where tubers from these stocks could be multiplied in safety, i.e. where they would be safe from contamination by infected green-fly. It was well-known in scientific and official quarters, that potatoes growing on the western coastlands of Scotland were remarkably healthy, and that varieties which had long since passed into oblivion elsewhere, because they had succumbed to 'curl', might still be found growing luxuriantly in the gardens of crofters and others, on the west coast, or in the islands. A visit to the west coast and the Inner and Outer Hebrides convinced me that it was here, and more particularly in the islands, that one would find the ideal conditions, so far as the control of the aphid was concerned, for the safe propagation of the virus-free stocks.

On unenclosed land in the Hebrides, aphides are extremely rare, and the species which is most concerned in spreading virus disease, *Myzus persicae*, is practically absent.

This is not the place to consider in detail the various arguments for and against the growing of potatoes on a commercial scale in the Hebrides. On theoretical grounds, the case for the Hebrides or the west coast of Scotland, north of the Kyle of Loch Alsh, is overwhelming. On practical and economic grounds, there are objections and hindrances, the chief of which are the difficulty of communication and the expense of transport; a lesser one is the poverty of some of the soils, in essential minerals, such as calcium and potash, but the least of them is the inclement weather. Serious as most of these are, they are not decisive, in view of the fact that the crop to be raised is a valuable one, and can bear high costs of production.

In 1941 the National Institute of Agricultural Botany decided to adopt the scheme, and a start was made by multiplying the glasshouse stocks at Broughgammon, County Antrim, under the supervision of the potato-breeder, Mr John Clarke. It was still necessary, however, to seek some place where multiplication on a larger scale and under the best possible aphis-free conditions, could be carried out, and where potato-growing by others in the neighbourhood could be controlled.

Such a place I found in the Isle of Islay; here, by the courtesy and with the active assistance of Messrs Ramsden and Appleyard, who had recently taken over 10,000 acres of the island, we were able to secure almost ideal conditions. To-day there are close on 50 acres of reclaimed peat and other lands successfully growing these virus-free stocks.

It may appear that an undue amount of space has been devoted to the problem of the virus-free potato, but it is one which has far-reaching economic importance. Our potato crops up and down the country are, on the average, anything between 10–20% lower than they would be, were our potato fields planted with virus-free stocks only. In terms of money, that means a potential loss, on a pre-war basis, of probably not less that £5,000,000 per annum. A successful issue to the scheme would result not only in this loss being saved, but in the freeing of about 100,000 acres of the best arable land for cereal or other crops. Not least in its favour is the probability that its success would insure this country becoming the centre, from which healthy virus-free stocks would be distributed the world over.

In addition to the three limiting factors which have been referred to, two more relatively new to this country, now confront us. Both are the result of attacks on the potato by animals of very different families. First, by the Chrysomelid beetle, *Leptinotarsa decemlineata*, commonly called the Colorado Beetle; the second, by the eelworm *Heterodera rostochiensis*,[1] formerly *H. schactii*.

---

[1] Now classified as *Globodera rostochiensis* and *G. pallida*. – Ed.

The Colorado Beetle

The history of this engaging looking beetle is a commentary on the march of civilization. When it was first described in 1824, it was, as a native of the Wild West, enjoying a blameless life, feeding with apparent indifference on noxious weeds of the Deadly Nightshade type. Colorado was to all intent an uninhabited country, until the gold mines were discovered in 1858. Pioneers from the East poured into the virgin lands, bringing with them their accustomed foodstuffs, not least of which was the potato. The beetle who, throughout the ages, had been satisfied with the foliage of wild plants of the *Solanum* genus, soon discovered that the potato was in all respects the most succulent and desirable of this genus it had so far encountered. Whilst the white man trekked westward, the beetle, following his trail of potato plantations, steadily pursued its path in the opposite direction. By 1865 it had crossed the Mississippi into Illinois; by 1869 it had reached Ohio, and four years later was securely established on the Atlantic coast, where it rested before entering on its conquest of the Old World. Its spread to the north of America was slowed down by the severe winters, and in the far south by the hot summers, but in the intermediate zone it had, for a time, all its own way. Its depredations were severe, frequently destroying the entire potato crop over large areas. Meanwhile, it found new enemies amongst the birds of the field, no less than those devised by man; as early as 1869, American growers began to employ arsenical sprays which, when liberally used, kept the devastations of the insect under reasonable control.

In Europe the alarm was great, and the enactment of regulations against the importation of American potatoes became general about 1875; for a considerable time the enemy was kept at bay. In 1901 the beetle was found at Tilbury but prompt measures led to its extinction; in 1914 it was discovered in Stade on the Elbe, and again exterminated. During the War of 1914–18, a heavy infestation occurred at Bordeaux, near a camp which was occupied by American troops. Unfortunately, the French authorities never won the upper hand in the fight against its encroachments; efficient plans were prepared, but adequate manpower was never provided with which to carry them out. Between the wars the beetle spread steadily over practically the whole of France, passed into Belgium, and again invaded Germany.

In England a single beetle was found at Tilbury in 1933. This was the signal for an all-out search for further foci and the use of the most extensive precautionary disinfection. Again the danger was evaded. As far as England was concerned, it was almost certain that the beetle was not likely to make the journey across the Channel by its own flight, except under very exceptional circumstances, hence close scrutiny on cargoes from Brittany and America had been sufficient to secure its exclusion. Nevertheless, this country, with its enormous sea traffic, was recognized as very vulnerable to attack, and precautions were never relaxed. But with the advent of the aeroplane, the situation was altered, and the beetle had an alternative means of transit. In the course of the war, especially in 1942, two invasions occurred along two lines, one starting from the south coast, at Weymouth, and spreading into Dorset; and another from the west, spreading across Dartmoor.

Jersey, too, became heavily infected during the war, but the most vigorous measures against the beetle have been taken and it is confidently expected that its fields will once more be free from danger.

In 1945, several widespread foci of beetle infestation were discovered in England and more have been reported since then. With so great an area of contamination as now exists on the Continent, the country's potato crops are undoubtedly in a position of grave danger of attack. It is only by the use of extreme and unremitting vigilance that their defence can be assured.

The Ministry of Agriculture has, in the past, been successful in keeping the scourge at bay; it is to be hoped that the strenuous efforts it is now making, will succeed once more. To-day the tactics of our defence is an offensive, conducted with the weapons of chemical warfare. Should that fail, it may be necessary to construct a defensive strategy based on the unsuitability of the potato plant as a food for the invading beetle. There is evidence that such a potato plant could be bred by bringing in aid another wild species, such as S. chacoense, which is highly distasteful to the beetle and its larva. It might, however, take many years to bring it to perfection, by which time we should have to face the possibility that a new race of beetles would have learnt to regard it as a luxury.

Ever since 1917, a new scourge of the potato, due to attacks by eelworm, has created a problem of considerable difficulty and, by reason of its rapid spread, of great economic importance. The eelworm, or rather its cysts and eggs, can lie dormant in the soil for years; but when the land is cropped with potatoes, the plants as they grow, liberate into the soil a substance which has the effect of stimulating the egg to develop. The result is, that the newly hatched worms, in vast numbers, invade the root and stem of the very plant to whose influence they owe their opportunities in this life. After gaining access to the young potato plant, the female worm bores its way through the roots, leaving its swollen abdomen extruding; the male leaves the roots and fertilizes the female, whose abdomen develops into a cyst full of eggs, which adheres to the roots until it drops off as the haulm dies. These pearl-like bodies, the size of a pin's head, may be seen in their hundreds adhering to the fibrous roots.

The cysts are very easily transferred in soil adhering to the boots, the implements and, above all, to tuber-seed from infested soils. Another source which has operated extensively in Cornwall and Devon, is its conveyance in the soil attached to the young broccoli plants which are transplanted from fields previously down to potatoes. The infestation of the roots commonly causes the potato plant to wilt to a greater or lesser degree, with a corresponding reduction of its crop.

So far, no practical method has been found to destroy the pest in the soil; nor has any potato been bred which is resistant to its attack,[1] nor one which fails to excrete the substance referred to above. Of late, a hopeful line of research has been opened by impregnating the soil with very small quantities of mustard oil.[2] This substance has been found to neutralize the potato stimulant and thus prevent the hatching out of the worms and their subsequent infestation of the roots of the potato plants. So far, the only means of combating the trouble, that has proved of worth in practice, is by refraining from planting potatoes in the same field more than once—at most—in every four years. Such a course will allow of a reasonable crop, but it does nothing to eradicate the eelworm.

The domestication of a wild plant is but rarely a matter of simple association; man has ever attempted to mould the plant of his choice to suit his varied needs. But it is doubtful whether any other plant of economic importance, has shown such variety of behaviour, coupled with such ease of adaptation, as has the potato, when called on to meet man's ever-growing demands. Indeed, if the subject-matter of this chapter proves anything, it is that the pre-eminent position which the potato has won in the lives of the people, is due as much to the inherent plasticity of the species, as to man's ingenuity in making use of it.

Note added whilst in the Press

In 1747 a locally familiar type of potato was described as follows:[3] 'This differs completely from the foregoing [normal varieties] in regard to its haulm which is very soft (*milde*) and crinkled (*kraus*) resembling the brown Italian cauliflower. In this district of Gera the peasants call it a peruque-apple because the haulm suggests a wig.' References to 'curl' date from about 1773 and have been thought to indicate the presence of Leaf Roll infection. The symptoms of chronic infection by what came later to be known as the 'Y' virus were first described in 1921. It appears from the above that the disease was present in Germany early in the eighteenth century.

[1] There are now several resistant varieties on the market. – Ed.
[2] Ellenby, C. (1946). *J. Min. of Agric.* vol. LIII, pp. 219–23.
[3] Hoppe, T. B., 1747. *Kurzer Bericht von denem Knottlichten und essbaren Erdaepfeln.* Wolfenbüttel. Linnaeus' Library, The Linnaean Soc., London.

CHAPTER XI

The Potato in Ireland in the Sixteenth Century

The potato has, in the minds of more than half the world, an inalienable and time-honoured association with Ireland, comparable to the age-long dependence of many Asiatic peoples on rice. Examples of a rather different nature will readily occur to the mind, where some special food or dish has acquired a regional or national affinity, such as the eating of bouillabaisse in Provence or the importance of macaroni in the dietary of the Italian. The former is a regional custom and has no bearing, important or otherwise, on the economic life of the people; the latter has assumed the status of a national dish in Italy, and its sudden withdrawal would undoubtedly inconvenience and annoy the people, but would not necessarily have any serious economic repercussions. The hard wheat flour used for its manufacture would still be available for conversion into some other form of food. Very different is the case where a people has for some reason chosen to make a specific source of food, whether plant or animal, its sole or almost sole supply of nourishment. Nor is it material whether this has been brought about by economic factors over which the people have had no immediate control, or whether it has come about as the result of some specially developed gastronomic habit; in either case, the people have but one available lifeline which, if severed, must bring disaster in its train.

It was an experience of this kind that Ireland suffered in the middle of the last century: the result was catastrophic. Partial failure of the crop had given warnings of the possibility of the danger throughout the preceding centuries, but so completely had the potato woven itself into the web of the life and thought of the people, that no more attention was given to such warnings than would have been the case had they been told that the rains would cease to fall from heaven on their fields. It is in this latter sense that the potato has a special relation to Ireland, and rice a similar one to China. A measure of this interdependence can be seen in the fact that the potato is known to-day in the United States of America as the Irish Potato. The term, however, antedates the transference of the potato to North America by a group of Irish Presbyterians in 1719. It was used some years earlier by Salmon in his *Herbal*, whilst a still earlier reference occurs in the Manuscript Journal of the Royal Society under date 6 December 1693, when Dr Sloane discussed the origin of the 'Irish Potato', showing that, even at that date, the potato had become inseparably united in the public mind, with a single country, Ireland. For good or ill, Ireland has become the classical, though adopted, home of potato culture, and in no other country can its influence on the domestic and economic life of the people be studied to greater advantage. The uniqueness of Ireland's experience will be gauged by the fact that, within fifty years of its introduction, the potato had become the universal and staple article of the people's food in the greater part of the island, and this before it had obtained a foothold elsewhere in the British Isles. In the major part of England, 150 years had to elapse before it became acceptable at all to the masses, and even then it was only as an occasional dish that it was eaten. In certain parts of England, its adoption took place earlier but its progress, although more rapid, was still far short of that obtaining in Ireland. In fact, nowhere else in the Old World has the potato so dominated both the daily life and the economic outlook of a whole people as it had succeeded in doing in Ireland. In Spain and in the Netherlands, and in parts of Burgundy and Italy, the potato had been known for a dozen to thirty years before it reached the Irish shores, yet in none had it made any headway to speak of, amongst the people, nor did it do so for more than a hundred years.

It is obvious that there must have been a number of circumstances at once favourable to the potato, as a cultivated plant, and peculiar to Ireland which allowed it to play so important a part, in so short a time, in the economic life of the people.

The potato is a plant which delights in a moist, cool atmosphere and a deep, friable soil, both of which are to be found abundantly in Ireland. The rainfall in the western half of the island reaches 60 in., and in parts of the south-west coastal area as much as 80 in. per annum; it is only in a small area around Dublin that it falls so low as 30 in. per annum. In July the temperature averages 53° F. over the whole of the island, except in the south-eastern and part of the Midlands, where it is 60°, the same as that of the greater part of England.

The soils of Ireland are for the most part rich, deep and friable, whilst the bog-lands, once they are worked, have proved peculiarly suitable for potato-growing. Ireland is fortunate also in possessing just those climatic conditions which are so important in maintaining the potato free from the degenerative or virus diseases commonly referred to in the eighteenth century and onwards as the curl. These diseases, as is shown elsewhere, constitute a limiting factor on the continuous cultivation of any one variety. The moist atmosphere and the prevalent westerly winds from the Atlantic, check the spread of the aphis or green-fly which effects the transmission of these troubles through the crop. Had it been otherwise, with the primitive state of agriculture prevalent in Ireland up till the latter part of the nineteenth century, it is more than likely that the potato could never have played the role it actually did, during the preceding centuries. Young, who frequently refers to the damage caused by the curl in England, never mentions it in the account of his travels in Ireland. It is for the same reason that individual varieties have been able to hold their own for such long periods in Ireland. The 'Lumper', which was grown extensively in Clare in 1808 and spread thence all over Ireland, though superseded because of its poor quality and susceptibility to Blight, can still, 134 years later, be found growing vigorously in Ireland; whilst varieties like 'Skerry Blue', 'Garden Filler', 'Spry's Abundance', long since forgotten elsewhere, are quite common as garden, or small plot, crops in the west of Ireland.

If Ireland was especially favoured in this particular direction by its climate, it is well to remember that it was these very same conditions that were later to prove so disastrous to the potato and the whole Irish people when Europe was attacked by the Blight in 1845.

As far as the conditions for successful cultivation were concerned, Ireland offered all that could be desired. Even had nature not acted the part of a fairy godmother to this lonely immigrant, it is still possible that the potato would have played a major part in the historic development of Ireland, so extraordinary was the social setting in which its role was cast.

There are peoples, of which the Irish and the Jews are outstanding examples, the major part of whose long history is a record of suffering and tragedy. It is not unusual, that the simple joys of family life, the play of intimate human relations, of joys and sufferings shared in sympathy, go unchronicled. This notwithstanding, I doubt whether it would be possible to overstate the miseries and degradation of the peasantry of Ireland throughout the greater part of the sixteenth, seventeenth and eighteenth centuries. The whole country was haunted with 'the pestilence that walketh in darkness' and 'the destruction that wasteth at noonday', and from time to time was made bloody with the rivalries of two peoples whose differences of nationality and race were eclipsed by those still greater of social experience and religion. Ireland had become the stage on which the challenge of the insurgent dynamism of the English renaissance, to the sullen spirit of a medievalism bled white by centuries of strife, was to be fought to a finish. It is in such an atmosphere, over-charged with hatred and fear, that we must seek to evaluate the part played in the life and history of a people by an apparently harmless, and not very attractive, vegetable.

The potato came to Ireland some time during the last fifteen years of the sixteenth century, one of the stormiest periods in her troubled history. It came, as it were, silently and by stealth; there was neither government nor patron to urge its acceptance. One can only suppose that it won the confidence of the people because it fitted so readily into the economic structure of their life which had retained a certain basic and characteristic shape, to a large extent independent of the ceaseless internecine struggles of the Celtic chieftains and Norman-Irish palatine overlords.

Ireland was divided into baronies of various sizes, each constituting a more or less independent principality ruled over by a chieftain. The baronies, in their turn, were subdivided into townships; these varied in area according to the character of the land. Those comprising much moorland might be 1,000 acres in extent, but the average township contained 325 acres; there are 62,205 such in the country. A township does not imply the presence of a town or even of a village as we understand the term: it was essentially the communal holding of related family groups. Hence the occurrence of one or two surnames dominating a particular district and, as Estyn Evans[1] points out, the frequency of nicknames both in Ireland and Scotland, where a somewhat similar system of tenure prevailed.

Before proceeding further, we should halt for a moment to consider certain basic principles which were impressed on Celtic social life by the native Irish Brehon law. The chieftainship of a clan or tribal group was not strictly hereditary, though it was by custom vested within one family. The heir to the chief was chosen by the tribe: the eldest son if deemed capable, but if not, then some near relative would be selected. This custom, known as 'tanistry', gave rise to everlasting feuds and unrest, and was a premium on murder. The chief did not own the land, as did a feudal overlord: it belonged to the members of the clan. He could command the services of his people in war, and to a limited extent, their labour, to cultivate his demesne land. This latter was set aside by the clan for the maintenance of the chief in being, who thus had only a life interest in it. The demesne land was not held in common with that of his tenantry, as was general in feudal England. Perhaps the most important of the Brehon customs, and the one which had the most far-reaching influence on Irish life, and, in point of fact, on the spread of the potato, was that of Gavelkind. This law laid down that on the death of the father, the land was divided equally between all his sons. The daughters, at any rate, in the eighteenth century, were paid off in money, or the son-in-law admitted. The result of such a custom was, on the one hand, to lead to a minute subdivision of the land, and on the other, to ensure its communal occupation on a family basis, both of which, in fact, occurred. Brehon law and custom held throughout the country outside the English pale around Dublin, where, throughout the sixteenth century, little of law, whether Brehon or feudal, was current for long.

[1] Evans, E. Estyn (1942). *Irish Heritage*, p. 12. Dundalk: Dundalgan Press.

Notwithstanding special enactments, such as the Composition of Connaught (1585) in which Gavelkind and Common holding were expressly forbidden, we find Sir Morrogh O'Fflaherty,[1] who died in 1593, leaving his estates to be divided equally between his sons. The Composition of Connaught sought also to prevent the customary division of the common lands which in future were to be kept strictly common, as in England. Notwithstanding, the impress of these ancient customs on Irish peasant life was such, that centuries after their official decease had been enacted, they were still current usage, and to this day their memory and influence have not altogether faded away.

Medieval Irish life admitted of a very definite stratification of society. First came the lord, or chief, and his immediate family, whose demesne was cultivated by the botachs; then followed 'free' and 'base' tenants: the former performed military service, helped the chief in his government, and ransomed him in war; the latter were the fighting men of the clan. At the bottom came the botachs or cottiers who were the real cultivators of the soil, working on the farms of others, and having but a cottage and a small patch of land of their own; they were, in fact, serfs, except that they had an inalienable right of settlement in the township. Interjected into the clan group, were the Brehons, or judges, and one or more grades of bards. The influence of both was great, and was deeply resented by the English of the sixteenth century, who rightly recognized that they were largely instrumental in keeping alive the national spirit and fomenting opposition to themselves.

In the sixteenth century, apart from the chief and the leading members of the clan, there were but two classes who between them constituted the 'people': The kerns, or fighting men, and the churls who, as mere cultivators of the land, were looked down upon by the rest of the clan; yet the churl in many respects was better off than his social superiors. True, he was not, in Irish law, a free man, but was subject to the despotic will of the chief who exercised rights of life and death, even after the supremacy of English law was established; still, he owned a cottage of sorts, and had the use of certain lands to which he had a title recognized by custom, which was little short of ownership. His position was humble, yet its unobtrusiveness was his salvation. As Sigerson[2] says:

It must be borne in mind that in the wars the humble class of cultivators generally escaped the change and destruction that fell on their superiors in station. The honey was too welcome not to secure the toleration of the working bees. The English and Irish combatants looked down on them as hinds and churls, unfit for fighting, but apt to produce rent and cattle. Disinclined for

[1] Sigerson, G. (1871). *History of Land Tenure and Land Classes in Ireland*, p. 28.
[2] Ibid. p. 34.

war and revolts, if not pressed into them by intolerable oppression, they remained, even through Cromwell's transplantations, the one comparatively fixed element in Irish social history—a settled substratum.

This substratum could only be 'settled' if it enjoyed a measure of security in the soil itself. Security of tenure of the land and its continuity in the family, a principle derived from Brehon law, no matter how burdensome the services which the holder rendered, was a 'right' the importance of which grew through the centuries. It was to this the Irish peasant clung, and if necessary fought for, with the greatest tenacity. Its influence is seen to-day in the vast number of small-holdings to be found in all parts of Ireland outside the great central grazing country. The various Land Acts and Land Purchase Acts, operating during the last sixty odd years, have all been devised to ensure security of tenure and the maintenance of small, compact but adequate farms throughout the country, and incidentally, they have succeeded in their task.

Later the cottiers and kerns, in the guise of Tories and Rapparees, found their interests united in their struggle for the maintenance of such of the ancient customs and Brehon laws as had proved of value in their fight against oppression. In the course of the seventeenth century, the distinction between fighter and tiller vanished, and the peasant cottier class was, in fact, 'the people'.

An effort was made by the Tudor sovereigns to induce the chiefs to surrender their baronies to the Crown for regrant to them as its feudal dependents. By so doing, control of the chief by the Crown was, in law, though not in fact, secured by the threat that revolt would be countered by the legal confiscation of his revenues. By this transfer the clansman, instead of being part-owner, became a tenant. But, in truth, Henry VIII's policy brought no more advance towards the feudalization of the native leaders and occupiers, than had the efforts made by earlier monarchs. The Irish leaders were only induced to acknowledge his suzerainty whilst 'reserving yet their titles unto themselves, all their own former privileges and seigniares', says Spenser.[1]

In Elizabeth's reign, an alternative scheme was devised by which the chief and other leading personalities were regranted after surrender, freeholds of land varying proportionately to their respective rights within the clan.[2] By this means, numerous small freeholds were created, and the power of the chiefs reduced. This plan was not applied very extensively, but when it was, the chiefs generally had to be satisfied with the demesne lands, which, from of old, the clan had set aside for their support, although in some cases the more important lords acquired all

---

[1] Spenser, Edmund (1596). *View of the Present State of Ireland* (edit. 1934), p. 9.
[2] O'Brien, George (1919). *The Economic History of Ireland in the Seventeenth Century*, p. 16. Dublin.

the clan property. In either case, the bulk of the land still remained in the hands of the native Irish and the old Anglo-Irish throughout the Elizabethan period.

In James's plantations the greater part of the land was made over to the new English settlers and city companies. Natives who could claim more than 60 acres were given freeholds of the remainder. Those with less, were just deprived, and when they went to Dublin to lodge their complaints, they are said to have been shipped to Virginia as slaves.[1] The new Jacobean policy differed widely from the old: it had been introduced by the abolition of tanistry and gavelkind, and then by a legal quibble it was argued that the natives of confiscated lands could have no claim against the Crown which meant, in effect, that they were reduced to the status of squatters. It will be gathered that the object of post-Elizabethan policy was to prevent the establishment of a body of small freeholders. Experience in England had shown that they often exhibited an inconvenient spirit of independence.

In the end, labourers and cottiers retained their hold on the land because their services were far too valuable to be discarded, and in doing so, never surrendered their tacit claim to security of tenure but were willing to render 'duty service' even to the new masters, so long as they were allowed to cling to their cottage or holding, however small.

The rapid adoption of the potato in the seventeenth century, by endowing them with an adequate and reliable source of food, encouraged them in this attitude, and afforded some measure of protection even in Ulster, against the new settlers.[2]

We must now turn to the system of agriculture current in sixteenth-century Ireland, in order to learn whether it was favourable or otherwise to the root crop. The Irish system, known as rundale, which held throughout the island, was the Celtic counterpart of the Saxon open-field system which dominated the greater part of England for more than 1,500 years, and of which there were still examples to be found in almost every county in the Midlands and East Anglia in the first half of the nineteenth century. Even to-day there is an entire parish cultivated on the open-field system at Laxton in Nottinghamshire. The essence of all such systems is the communistic employment and control of the land, while still allowing the individual of the group or clan forming the township, the personal right of usure. In England, this had developed into ownership, subject to certain communally agreed conditions, of one or more unfenced plots situate in each of the large open fields contained within the township. These plots were known as strips and were usually 22 yards wide and 220 yards long, with an area of about an acre. In

---

[1] Butler, W. F. (1913). *Policy of Surrender*, p. 123.
[2] Evans, E. Estyn (1939). *Geography* (March), pp. 24–36.

Ireland they were of an irregular, more or less rectangular shape, and often smaller than a quarter of an acre. The safeguarding of the identity of such small plots was a matter of the utmost importance, and the failure to do so the cause of frequent dispute. Various devices were developed to protect them against encroaching neighbours. In Ireland it was usual to leave broad green baulks, as much as three yards wide, between contiguous plots, which served the double purpose of demarcating the boundary and affording grazing to the creel ponies.

The rundale open field was probably cropped continuously at the period we are considering, as was the corresponding infield of the runrig system prevalent in Scotland at this time. As far as I can ascertain, the Irish had no outfield, as had the Scotch; its place seems to have been taken by the practice of booleying. Estyn Evans describes a rundale farming township in Donegal to-day, where oats and potatoes are grown alternately for ten years, and in the last oat crop of the series, grass is sown and a period of grazing for some seven years follows, before the ley is broken up for oats once more. In the west of Ireland, 'rundale' was general all through the eighteenth century, but faded out in the nineteenth.

A rich cultivator might have the use of a score or more of such plots, or a communal group of twenty-nine persons might occupy as many as 422 plots in common, to quote an actual case. On the other hand, the system allowed of the reverse procedure: there are cases on record where as many as twenty-six people had shares in one single half-acre plot. A common, but not universal, feature of the plan as practised in Ireland, was the change-over of strips each year, when the system was known as 'changedale'. By this means, all shared the good and bad soil, but unfortunately it was to the interest of no one to improve a plot from which he would not reap the full benefit of his labour. The plots were employed at this time for spring-sown oats and barley. Wheat was not introduced till early in the seventeenth century; it had been grown in prehistoric times on the mountains of Wicklow, Antrim and Donegal, but the change of climate which set in about 500 B.C., resulting in colder and more rainy seasons, seems to have brought its cultivation to an end. All memory of this early culture must have been long lost, for wheat-growing was looked on askance by Irish patriots: 'Con O'Neil was so right Irish that he cursed all his posterity in case they either learned English or sowed wheat, or built them hooses.'[1] It may have been that wheat was not grown in Ulster or those parts remote from trading towns and ports, but according to Longfield[2] it was an important item of Ireland's export from Waterford during the earlier part of the sixteenth century, though later appearing as an import.

[1] Speed, John (1611). *Historie of Great Britaine.* 3rd ed., 1632. p. 1141.
[2] Longfield, Ada K. (1929). *Anglo-Irish Trade in the Sixteenth Century*, p. 32.

Apart from flax, which was more widely grown than to-day, barley and oats were the only other crops grown, the former was devoted to the manufacture of 'aqua vitae', the native *usquebagh*; the latter in the main to the horses, though some of it was eaten as oatmeal.

A difference of importance between this system and the English open-field, was that with the latter every strip-holder was originally obliged to sow the same kind of corn—spring corn in one field, wheat or rye in the other, and leave a fallow in the third. Some degree of diversity was allowed in regard to the spring corn, which included barley and oats, pease and beans, but the holders would, even so, be in practical accord as to their choice. In Ireland there seems to have been no such custom enforcing uniformity: this may well have been due to the absence of the open winter cornfield. In any case, such absence of customary law demanding uniformity, at least did not deter, if it did not actually incline the Irish peasant to try out a new crop such as the potato, which the more conservative, if more skilled, English farmer avoided as being a breach of the law of the manor.

A variant of the rundale system which was common in eighteenth-century Ireland, and probably existed much earlier, survived into the twentieth century. In this, areas of land, five to ten acres in extent, were held in common by a group which worked the whole communally without further subdivision. Arthur Young, who was so bitterly opposed to the common field and strip system in all its manifestations, nevertheless approved these partnerships, because they alone could compensate for the poverty and consequent impotence of the individual, who himself could not afford to acquire the bare essentials with which to cultivate the soil.

The rundale, open-field land, was manured with the cow and horse dung which had accumulated in the byre, which was, in reality, nothing but the lower end of the common living-room of the cottier's family. Liming the soil was not introduced till 1650 and did not become general till the eighteenth century.

The Irish relied to a great extent on a method of manuring which was also practised, though to a lesser extent, in parts of England and Wales; the skimming off and burning of the shallow layer of top soil and the spreading of the ash. This 'paring and burning', or, as it was called in Ireland, *denshiring*, was, according to Estyn Evans, a survival from ancient custom, and a peculiar tool, the 'flachter', designed for skimming, was probably developed for this purpose. Although some have deprecated the custom, there was much to be said for it, especially on peaty soils rich in unliberated sources of nitrogen. Just after the time of which we are writing, the method had been used with great effect, and was strongly advocated by Sir Richard Weston (1591–1652), the author of

Discourses of the Husbandrie used in Brabant and Flanders. It was he who first advocated the cultivation in England of flax, clover and turnips, which he himself grew on his estate in Surrey. He referred to the practice as 'Devonshiring', and in association with liming, used it for the recovery and cultivation of his heathlands prior to sowing with clover.

In Ireland, the old thatch of the cottage, soaked with the soot from the turf fire, was another valuable source of manure; mention may also be made of the special 'soot houses' built of turves and stones, which are still in use in Achill Island. They were designed to trap the smoke and soot of turves burnt for the purpose, both the ash and the soot being spread on the land in spring.

The standard of arable farming in Ireland lagged far behind that in the sister isle, notwithstanding that in England it had received a setback during the Tudor period, owing to the great increase in sheep walks, the debasement of the coinage, and an embargo on the export of corn. Apart, however, from these considerations, there had been little, if any, technical or horticultural advance since the thirteenth century, when English agriculture had already attained a high standard.[1]

The Irish plough was wooden and, as far as I can ascertain, it had an iron share and coulter, and was furnished with an upright mould-board which crumbled the soil but did not completely turn the sod over. This plough was derived from English models and was by no means general. A simpler plough, in use in Donegal but a hundred years ago, was no more than a 'crooked stick armed with a bit of iron, which only in the last particular varied from the plough of the Bronze Age'[2] and was in general use, whilst in many parts the old digging-stick was used, of which we shall have more to say later. The plough was drawn by two horses, by a rope attached to their tails.

Ploughing by the tail was a practice which aroused the most intense feeling of disgust amongst the English who, in their own dealings with the natives, were not often inclined to be squeamish. It may well be because of the Englishman's love of his horse, that he felt so strongly on this particular form of cruelty, at a time when baiting of bull and bear, fighting of cocks and the like, was the sport of kings and the delight of the town. This is supported by the fact that no protest was made against the Irish habit of picking the wool off the sheep by hand, and similar unpleasant treatment of domestic animals.

Notwithstanding the legislative effort of the English government and condemnation by public opinion,[3] from Tudor times onward, the

[1] Ernle, Lord (1936). *English Farming* (5th edit.), p. 91.
[2] Evans, E. Estyn (1942). Op. cit. p. 90.
[3] Fines inflicted on those convicted of this offence were not infrequently used in the sixteenth century for the maintenance of the local Anglican Church. Pinkerton, W. Ploughing by Tail. *Ulster Journ. Archaeol.* (O.S.), vol. VI, p. 212.

practice of ploughing by the tail survived in some places till as late as 1845.[1]

The harrow furnished with tines of cowhorn, was similarly attached. It seems probable that the reason this barbarous practice was so persistent was because of the small size both of the fields and of the plough: such a set-up allowed of easy turning within a small space. It would also have facilitated cross-ploughing which, according to Evans, was an old Irish custom, which again may have accounted for the rectangular shape of the Irish plots. In England, where the big-wheeled plough with its tandem teams of yoked oxen was in vogue, the long narrow strip was obviously the more suitable. It should be remembered that there is a growing volume of evidence to show that in England the rectangular plot preceded the strip system, but there does not seem any grounds for suggesting that the custom of cross-ploughing was carried over with the change; in fact it does not appear to have been practised at all in the English open field.

There appears to have been little or no attempt in Ireland to cultivate and weed the land between sowing and reaping; in fact the cottiers and their families would, during most of this time, be 'creaghting' on the mountains with their cattle. Another complaint against the method of Irish farming which is met with frequently in the sixteenth, seventeenth and eighteenth centuries, is that directed against the extraordinary habit of 'burning their corn in the straw'. The corn was cut and, unthrashed, set on fire, the grain being then winnowed from the ashes and milled.

The backward state of agriculture which these methods disclose, must have been largely responsible for the prevailing insecurity of food supplies. The advent of a new food-plant, such as the potato, which made so insignificant a demand on the time, the energy, and the skill of the peasant, would be assured of a warm and general welcome in the Ireland of the sixteenth and seventeenth centuries.

A word must be said about the dwellings of the people, who worked on the farms of their chiefs and tilled their own rundale lands. The township, it will be remembered, was a unit occupied by a small collection of families all more or less closely related. The dwellings were collected together in a cluster known as a *clachan*. But these groups of dwellings were not villages, as we understand the term; there was no regular arrangement of dwellings on either side of a high street. In fact, there was no street, only paths and narrow roadways linking up the various cottages, each of which might be set at a different angle. There was no church, no squire's hall, no school, around which the cottages radiated. These were to be found, if at all, in the towns.

[1] Jackson, R. W. (1941). *Irish Clerical Life*, p. 9. Limerick: Z. M. Ledger.

Later, when the rundale was replaced by individual small-holdings, the people's dwellings were scattered all over the township, and with every conceivable orientation. Each peasant owner or occupier built his shanty on his own field, and he placed it where he liked, or where chance dictated. It was said that in Donegal it was common for a man to throw his hat up in the air, and where it fell, he would build his house. In fact, the house was built with the help of his neighbours, who regarded it as a duty to co-operate in establishing each other's homesteads.

Roads, that is, main roads, in the sixteenth and seventeenth centuries were few indeed; local roads, as apart from tracks and ways, scarcely existed. This is not surprising, seeing that wheeled traffic was confined to the towns and service of the wealthy. Narrow horse-drawn slide cars and sledges were in use everywhere. However, heavy transport in the main was effected by horses carrying creel baskets suspended from the saddle on either side, but very much of the turf and the like was carried by men or, to be more exact, by women, in a creel suspended like a rucksack on the back, a practice which may be seen to-day in most parts. Corn and hay was tied in great bundles with straw ropes, and was carried by both men and women from the fields to the haggard. Wagons were not introduced till well into the seventeenth century; the few carts existing before that time were small, low, solid-wheeled concerns, which carried but a small load. The break up of the rundale system and the establishment of innumerable small-holdings, led to the creation of the complicated network of pathways and tracks leading to the separate holdings, which characterize so much of the Irish countryside to-day.

Of the houses—or should one say hovels?—in which, till recently, the Irish workers lived, it is not necessary to say much. They have been so often described and so frequently abused, during the last four centuries, that one might have thought there was nothing more to be said, still less, anything in their favour. But there is, and Estyn Evans has said it. In his book, *Irish Heritage*,[1] it will be seen that these very simple dwellings had much character and, when well built, made comfortable homes, well suited to the conditions which prevailed. Similar dwellings, it should be remembered, are to be found equally in the Western Highlands and the Hebrides. Behind them lies a tradition reaching back thousands of years and, like rundale and open field, they fulfilled the needs of those who occupied them and who led a life in which neither commercialism nor organized industry had as yet made any appreciable inroad.

There is another aspect to the question: many of the homes were in very deed hovels, and in the days of trouble and distress, of confiscation or eviction, one can well understand that there was neither time nor

[1] Evans, E. Estyn (1942). *Irish Heritage*, p. 57.

means to build much better. This style of cottage persisted into the beginning of the twentieth century. At the end of the eighteenth century, Fraser in his *Survey of County Wicklow*, says that the cost of building a better home with sawn timber was £5, but the ordinary ones might be valued at 30*s*. and were built in a few days.

Originally the cottages housed the milch cows, the calves, the pigs, and the poultry if any, as well as the family who grouped themselves around the central fire hearth. But there were better dwellings, some of which exist to-day, in which the byre and dwelling-room are separated, and in which the bed is built into a recess, and the hearth put at the gable end and supplied with a chimney and hood.

The Irish farmer and peasant, from time immemorial, has placed his turf fire on the floor, and cooked his food in a great iron cauldron, or crock, suspended above it. When the potato came into his home, the traditional methods were found to be ideal for its preparation. Of the crock, Bicheno writing in 1830,[1] says: 'it is essentially the potato boiler, but it is used for carrying and washing them, and all other washing too. It serves the pig... and [in it] the children collect the jetsam and flotsam of the cabin, and is alternately a vessel of honour and dishonour.' No adjustments were necessary, and very little change has occurred till recently in the domestic economy of the small peasant home (see Pl. XXIX, fig. 92).

The potato, instead of being a disturbing element, has actually been a stabilizer of the home front. Travellers, both before and after Young, have scornfully commented on the fact that the domestic animals and the children alike, are fed by their elders from the same pot of boiling potatoes. What better evidence could one find, that the potato was accepted without demur or delay, because it fitted so ideally into the domestic routine of the people?

Happy as this close adjustment of the food to the immediate circumstances of a people, economically and politically depressed, may originally have been, it nevertheless carried with it the seed of that which was to become a great danger to the stability of the state: a fact which was not recognized, even by critical observers, till some hundred years later. Those most concerned, the farmers and workers of the land, seemed to have looked on the association of an easily and cheaply produced food, and a home even more readily and inexpensively acquired, as a dispensation of Providence, rather than as a threat to their very existence.

This is not the place to discuss the relative merits of the various openfield systems and the small individually owned enclosed holdings which in most parts of Europe replaced them, or the large prairie type of farming which in recent years, under the influence of increasing mechanization,

[1] Bicheno, J. E. (1830). *Ireland and Its Economy*, p. 30.

is tending to absorb the latter. These matters, and much else which is inherent in the open-field and other systems of cultivation, are admirably dealt with by the Orwins.[1] What is of prime importance is, that the open-field and rundale systems were evolved and for centuries developed, on the tacit assumption of the principle of communal labour together with communal ownership, the common use of tools, equipment including horses and oxen, and, to some extent, other livestock.

In Ireland, where the feudal system had never made any headway, this communistic feature of the system never completely lost its hold on the people, not even when rundale itself had sunk finally into the limbo of the subconscious. This was partly the effect of political persecution, which forced people to help each other or perish together from starvation; when better times supervened, lack of cash encouraged the practice of local barter. This latter difficulty persisted in the more isolated rural districts into the second half of the nineteenth century, and was, we shall see, intimately bound up with the cultivation of the potato, and helped to stabilize agriculture on a subsistence level. In England, the communal character of the open-field was beginning to weaken before the thirteenth century. In the countryside of the sixteenth century, independent ownership, or tenancy on lease, and the payment of all dues in cash, had become the rule. Agriculture to a large extent was pursued as a trade, and could no longer be regarded as a subsistence culture, though local areas depended, in the first instance, on their own home-grown supplies.

The distinction between agriculture and social life in Ireland and England during the sixteenth and seventeenth centuries, was thus one of kind rather than degree: it was the difference between a people who looked on the land on which they lived and worked as the sole begetter of their means of subsistence, and others who regarded it, in the main, as a source of wealth to be measured in terms of cash, by means of which they could open the gate which gave admittance to an ever-widening and more adventurous world.

This is not to say that at this time there was no export of agricultural products from Ireland: there was, but it consisted notably of cattle. Cereal exports, which were in volume much below those exported from England, sufficed to pay for the heavy imports of wine from France and Spain.

One of the chief drawbacks to these early communal systems of agriculture was that there was little or no incentive to the individual farmer to improve the fertility of the soil.

In Ireland this was probably truer than elsewhere, partly because of the eternal unrest and violence, but also because certain customs of the country militated directly against such improvement. An outstanding

[1] Orwin, C. S. and C. S. (1938). *The Open Fields.*

deterrent was the right of all plot-holders after 31 October of each year, to turn their beasts, their sheep and their horses, their pigs and their poultry, out on to the stubbles, over which they were free to wander, regardless of individual ownership. This practice, like that of the redistribution of plots, acted as a check on any who might desire to improve his land by manuring, for there was nothing to ensure that he and not his neighbour would reap the benefit, which the improved scratch pasturage yielded. A similar custom in England and elsewhere, where common stubble-grazing commenced immediately after harvest, had not only a like effect, but was one of the chief causes which retarded the growing of any root crop, especially that of the potato.

In Ireland, the common grazing rights did not begin till 1 November, and in the early days of potato-growing they must have either lifted the crop before that time, or put up with the loss occasioned by its being trodden over. The result of this conflict of interests was that in England wherever the full open-field system continued to be practised, the potato and other root crops were excluded, whilst in Ireland it was the potato which won the day and hastened the decay and eventual disappearance of the rundale system.[1]

What, however, is particularly noteworthy is that the victory of the potato was an individual one, not one of principle; and hence it did not lead to an early or widespread cultivation of the other root crops such as the turnip. It was because of the unique appeal the potato made to the small cultivator that it was enabled to play so big a part in the reorganization of the agricultural system in Ireland.

So far, we have envisaged but half, and not the more important half, of the agricultural activity of the Irish cultivators. From earliest times they were cattle-raisers; tillage, though developed at a very early stage of their history, was always secondary to that of cattle-raising. The cattle, we have seen, were free from 1 November, to wander over the stubbles; at other times of the year their movements on baulks and untilled spots and hollows of the open field had to be strictly confined, lest they injured the spring corn, hence the habit in Ireland, by no means extinct, of tethering or hobbling horses, cattle, sheep, goats, and even poultry.

[1] Rundale existed throughout most of Ireland in the eighteenth century. Arthur Young (*A Tour in Ireland* (1780), vol. I, p. 161) describes one at Castle Caldwell, Fermanagh: 'The course of crops is: 1st year, Potatoes; 2nd, Potatoes; 3rd, Barley or Flax; 4th Oats; 5th, Oats; 6th, Oats; 7th, Layout for Grass. Wherever there are spots of meadow they are mown. Great numbers of farms taken in partnership in *Rundale*; indeed, the general course is so, upon a farm of 100 acres there will be 4, 5, or 6 families; but families will take such small plots as 5 or 6 acres. Farms in general rise from 5 acres to 300 or 400 acres; but the large ones are stock farms; in general none so high as twenty: all in Rundale, partnership or stock. Many of the latter part mountain, part arable, and these are the only farms of substance in the country.'

The season between St Patrick's Day, 17 March, and Halloween, 31 October, was devoted to the cattle who, half-starved from their wintering in the township, were driven up into the hills and remained there throughout the next six months, consuming the rough-grazing and wandering through the thick woodlands till the end of October. The peasants, their spring corn sown, spent no further time in cultivation in the field, but trekked with their families, cattle and flocks to the hills. Here the people lived in great content in crude huts, made of wicker-work covered with turves. This custom was universal and had been practised from the earliest times: it was called booleying[1] from booley, the milking place, which was identical with the family living-quarters. Booleying, or transhumance, as it is technically called, exists only in a few spots now, but it was an essential part of the same agricultural system as rundale; the one served the herds, the other the tillage. The progress of the potato gradually undermined both, though there was no conflict, agriculturally speaking, between its culture and booleying. The return of the cattle from the mountains to graze on the open field on 1 November, should have allowed the majority of small growers time enough to raise and remove their maincrop potatoes to a place of safety. It must, however, be remembered that the first potatoes grown in this country were invariably very late varieties and hence the tops would probably still have been green, the tubers not fully mature, and the crops unfit to lift for some time. Thus the ancient custom of communal grazing must have served as a direct incentive towards the development of earlier maturing varieties.

The preceding sketch of the agricultural conditions prevailing during the sixteenth century may now be summed up in terms of the advantage or otherwise they offered to the newcomer, the potato, which, unheralded, had crept into the land at the end of this period. The climate and soil, especially in the north, west and south of the island, were both extremely favourable. The cultivation of the land in small parcels was entirely to the advantage of a crop which was then and for a long time yet to come, worked by hand. Equally to the credit side, though doubtless not recognized till new and earlier maturing varieties were developed, was the late date on which the stubbles and fallows of the open field were thrown open to grazing. The treatment of the land by paring and burning went some way to give the potato the potash, necessary for its growth. The use of soot, referred to above, served the same purpose, as well as supplying an assimilable source of nitrogen.

Probably the feature of the environment most favourable to the potato as a new food plant, was the almost exclusive subsistence character of agriculture as practised towards the end of the sixteenth century in the greater part of Ireland. All surplus, especially corn, went to pay the rent. Food to store over winter, for themselves, their family and their live-stock, was their outstanding need; the potato filled these requirements as nothing else had done.

The stress which had hitherto been laid on cattle rearing received a severe check towards the end of the century by reason of the civil wars and the destruction of the woods, so that there was in the economic sphere of the domestic life of the people, a gap which would in any case have needed to be filled. The potato arrived at the auspicious moment.

No account of events in Ireland can, unfortunately, be complete with-out reference to civil disturbance, and to this aspect of the sixteenth-century stage, in which the potato was to make its debut, we must now turn.

It may seem a long cry from events such as the O'Neil rising, the Desmond revolt, and the like, to the adoption of the potato but, in fact, the relation between these so dissimilar events is not far to seek. The adoption of a radical change in the food habits of a people is never occasioned by the simple agricultural and horticultural relationship of plant and environment, however favourable they may be. There are always forces, economic, political, or both, which, given favourable en-vironmental factors, have a compelling effect on the character, direction and speed of development of social phenomena.

Such was to be found in the destruction of life, property and social values, which resulted from the bitter wars which the Irish and Anglo-Irish leaders waged both between themselves and against the suzerain power throughout the sixteenth century.

The previous century had, on the whole, been one in which Ireland had prospered. She had developed an important export trade carried in a large fleet of her own bottoms, of corn, wool, cloth, hides, and skins of the marten, the fox and the wolf; against which she imported all her iron and salt, and all the luxuries of Western European life, more particularly wine from France and Spain. That is not to say that she had not been subject to an abundance of legislative measures intended to direct her trade and her native wealth for the benefit of England. But the arm of the English government was in those days neither long nor strong. In the main, Irish economic and social life developed on their own lines. Parallel with this, there was a highly developed cultural life which was both broad in character and deep in its penetration amongst all classes of the people. According to Mrs Green, an eloquent and learned, if somewhat uncritical, not to say prejudiced advocate of the Irish nation, the Ireland of that date was culturally and socially far in advance of England, and the accusation of savagery and barbarous behaviour made in those days against Irishmen was not only absurd and unfounded, but, in truth, was the measure of the ignorance, the greed and the malevolence, of the English critics. As the sixteenth century proceeded, there can be no doubt whatever, that a widespread and increasing deterioration, cultural, social and economic, overtook the whole Irish nation. Here the responsibility must in the main be laid at the door of the English. Froude makes an illuminating suggestion in respect to the Irish policy of the Tudors: he thinks that the evil lesson which the Old World had learnt from observing the methods of Spain in America, had influenced the English in their behaviour towards a people whom they regarded as in some way subordinate.

A similar view is developed in an interesting manner by a recent writer, who sees a parallelism between the attitude of the Tudors in Ireland and that of the Spanish in Mexico.[1]

The peculiar ferocity of the struggle, and the bestial cruelty it evoked, was in large measure the result of the clash between two cultures, differing fundamentally both in content and development. In the district of the Pale, some sort of accommodation between the decaying medievalism of tribal Ireland and the insurgent arrogance of renaissance England had been reached. Outside the Pale lay a world which was culturally centuries behind, but which nevertheless was very conscious of having evolved a specific genius of its own. An Englishman of the thirteenth century would not have been at home in the Ireland of his day, and sixteenth-century Ireland had advanced not at all. It was inevitable that the English should have looked on and treated the Irish as little better than vermin. Even Shakespeare, who appreciated the fierce courage of the kern, could not free himself from a like attitude:

> Now for our Irish wars:
> We must supplant those rough rug-headed kerns,
> Which live like venom where no venom else
> But only they have privilege to live. (*Richard II*, II, i.)

Formerly the chief duty of the suzerain had been to introduce and maintain law and order. As time went on, the governing power admitted a considerable degree of local government under local chiefs, but commerce remained rather the business of the guilds than of government. Now the new commercialism led directly to monopolies in which the monarch not infrequently was a sleeping partner. The ideal was no longer trade as a means of supplying the wants of the people and a reasonable livelihood to the trader, but monopolistic control, with the concomitant wealth and power it was seen to command. The Spaniards had shown the way. They had captured vast quantities of gold in the

---

[1] O'Faolain, Sean (1942). *The Great O'Neil*. Longmans.

Americas, and they had acquired, by the crudest exploitation of the native races, unlimited supplies of silver. What they had done with such apparent success thousands of miles over the seas, why should not the English achieve here at their very door? History has pronounced its verdict on both in no uncertain measure; we are concerned only with the spirit and exploits of those times as they affected the progress of the potato, itself the direct outcome of the Spanish-American adventure. In this connection it is pertinent to recall the fact that the classic example of large-scale industrial exploitation which may well have fired the imagination of the English, was effected by means of the potato itself, the food on which the enslaved natives of Peru were maintained, and thereby the sole source of the energy by which the silver was wrested from the blind depths of the mines of Potosí.

During the reign of Henry VII, apart from local tribal quarrels and the active support of the pretenders, Perkin Warbeck and Lambert Simnal by the Geraldine Earl of Kildare, Ireland was relatively quiet. Henry's policy was to avoid open hostility at all costs, while his hands were fully occupied elsewhere; hence he prepared to leave the control of the country as far as possible in the hands of this Anglo-Norman family, with the result that the English of the Pale had little influence either on the political or the inner life of the Irish. In Henry VIII's reign, a report on Irish affairs made in 1515 shows how this policy of *laisser-faire* had affected the native population; it laments the entire lack of feeling for the general welfare amongst the old Irish nobility, and states that as a consequence 'there is no common folk in all this world so little set by, so greatly trodden under foot, as the King's poor common folk be of Ireland'. It then proceeds to state that 'there are sixty regions ruled over by chiefs calling themselves everything from kings to chiefs, all holding by the sword alone. And in addition innumerable petty captains each making war on the other without license of the chief captain and in addition thirty English nobles who followed the same style of living.'[1] Amongst the latter were the great houses of Kildare, Clanricard, Desmond, and Ormond, the latter two in a state of perpetual, or undeclared, hostility. Under such conditions, it is not to be wondered at that chaos reigned almost unchecked.

Henry VIII reversed his father's and his own earlier policy, by appointing as Deputy an Englishman: this had the effect of bringing the major issues into the open, though not before a short-lived rebellion had been suppressed. Henry was genuinely anxious to govern Ireland in the interests of the Irish, and although he attempted to feudalize the chiefs, he instructed his deputies to respect the customs of the people. The

[1] Froude, J. A. (1879). *History of England*, vol. II, pp. 131 and 141, quoting from *State Papers*, vol. II, pp. 17–18, and pp. 1–6.

manner in which Henry dealt with the revolt of 'Silkin Thomas', the son of the Earl of Kildare, in 1534, is typical. He commissioned the Earl of Ormond, to suppress, with the aid of English troops, Fitzgerald, his own rival, which he succeeded in doing, but not before he had ravaged the entire Kildare county, and lifted or killed all the cattle. The Kildare party, in their turn, conducted a guerrilla war, looting and murdering whenever opportunity offered. This particular campaign ended characteristically with the hanging of Thomas Fitzgerald and his five uncles at Tyburn in 1536.

About the same time, two events, very unlike in character but both of which were to have persistent repercussions through the following centuries, occurred. A body of four thousand Scotch kerns under McConnell of the Isles succeeded in establishing themselves in Ulster and were never dislodged. Their presence acted as a spearhead, for the penetration later, of further migrants from the Western Highlands, as an additional source of intrigue and disorder—and for the natives more poverty and suffering. The second event was the formal discovery by the English government of 'Absenteeism' as a major cause of chronic disorder. The disease was not only diagnosed but an attempt made to treat it appropriately. The 'Act of Absenteeism', passed in 1536, ordained that those who obstinately continued to absent themselves were liable to the confiscation of their estates.

In the latter years of Henry VIII, troubles of a different kind made their appearance. Henry had debased the coinage, and Ireland was supplied with that of the lowest intrinsic value. This occasioned great distress in the Pale, but less outside, as the chiefs withheld their corn from sale. With the reformation of the Church never far in the background in the minds of the suzerain power, the Governor adopted the facile process of seizing Church plate to replenish the treasury; but this did nothing to relieve the situation. The townspeople, merchants and particularly the people of the chief export towns such as Waterford, Cork and Youghal, continued to find their trade seriously handicapped by the debasement of the coinage, and their embarrassment was later passed on to the peasant cultivator.

The people on the land outside the Pale had little need of actual cash in their daily life, but inside the Pale, where the English ways of life prevailed, it was the coin of the realm which supplied the standard of values for commodities. If this, by debasement, was lower than the Dutch and Spanish coins which were current between the merchants, then the prices of native products and services were automatically increased. To such a degree did this prevail that it finally brought about widespread famine and disease. Edward VI attempted to restore the situation by sending over £3,000 worth of bullion and a gang of German miners to reopen and work the ancient silver mines of Wicklow, a project which unfortunately failed.

Related to this question of debased coinage, and much aggravated thereby, was the failure of the English authorities to pay the military regularly, or to clear up the ever-growing arrears due to the English garrison. As a result, sickness and inefficiency were more or less general, and open mutiny not infrequent. The reaction which concerns us is that this state of affairs led to an ever-growing abuse of what, even in its legalized form, was grossly unjust, namely, the right claimed by the Forces of the Crown to 'cess', i.e. to billet, soldiers on the people at absurdly unremunerative prices. As often as not, the soldiery just took what they could find, by force, so that the peasantry of the Pale suffered even more from these depradations than did their fellows outside who had for centuries been subject to the burden of 'Coshering', i.e. free entertainment of the clan chief when travelling, and in the case of the Ormonds, of a far more onerous exaction, viz. 'Coyne and Livery' throughout Kilkenny, or the right of free maintenance for himself and troops when on the march within his own territories, a right which even in those days was severely criticized, but which Elizabeth found it politic to confirm.

Henry had introduced the more predatory aspects of his reformation into Ireland, and the monasteries had been duly suppressed. The priests still functioned, but the loss of the Religious Houses had its influence on the economic life of the masses, for in Ireland the native church was essentially monastic in structure. The monks are held to be responsible for such agricultural progress as there was, a point in the circumstances hardly worth stressing; more important was the fact that they were the only body to whom the peasants could look for material relief in old age and sickness, in a country which had no Poor Law until 1836. In Mary's reign some of the monasteries were restored, and the Brehon law crept back and, with it, as Froude says: 'came anarchy as its inseparable attendant.' Be that as it may, during her reign, nothing worse occurred than the usual inter-clan raiding. With the advent of Elizabeth, the coinage trouble was intensified, for whilst she restored the value of the minted money in England, she shipped the surplus debased coins over to the sister Isle.

During the whole of Elizabeth's reign, the English forces and the Irish patriots were at grips. As the object of this sketch of the historic background is to depict as far as possible the conditions of the people, it may suffice to make mention of only the two most serious clashes, the rising of Sean O'Neil, the virtual king of the Ulster province, and that associated with the name of the Earl of Desmond, the ruler of Munster.

The O'Neil rising commenced in July 1566 and terminated characteristically with his murder, by one of his own allies, the Scots of Ulster, in June 1567. The English Deputy, Sir Henry Sidney, in his successful campaign against O'Neil accomplished two things: he selected the site for the camp which later became that of the City of Londonderry, and he ravaged the countryside. At Clogher, in the south of Tyrone, 'we stayed', said Sidney, 'to destroy the corn; we burned the country for twenty-four miles compass and we found by experience that now was the time of year [end of September] to do the rebel most hurt'. During October he marched through Mayo into Roscommon 'leaving behind them as fruitful a country as was in England or Ireland all utterly waste'.[1]

Following this campaign, peace reigned for a few years, and the country recovered in a manner which, if Cecil's correspondent may be trusted, seems miraculous, thus on 20 June 1567, George Wise writes:[2]

When before the poor people were so pitifully oppressed as they had no joy of their lives, now they fall to such plays and pastimes as the like was never seen in Ireland; so as if this government continue but three years more, they doubt not to live as merrily in Ireland as they do in the very heart of England. Lands that lay of long time waste, and of no profit to the owners, are now inhabited; and that which before was let for a groat now yields twelve pence. The honest husbandman, whom coyn and livery had so impoverished that he was fain to drive away his servants and family, as not able to sustain them, now calleth them home again, and retaineth more; the idle man that lived before upon coyn and spoil, now falleth to husbandry, and earneth his living by labour; and where before there was so little manurance and so much devouring by those raveners as that the country folk were not able to maintain themselves but by fetching their relief of grain from the good towns, now the country is so replenished that they come daily to the market to sell their superfluous store, so as the towns shall not need from henceforth to travel beyond the seas for their provisions as they have in times past been accustomed. To this time this poor country had in manner no feeling of good order, neither knew the poor fools God nor their prince, but as brute beasts lived under the miserable yoke of their ungodly Irish lords.

I do not believe one is justified in deducing more from Wise's letter than that Sidney, by good judgement and a strong hand, had suppressed disorder and imposed the restraint of government on the Anglo-Irish and native leaders.

The Spanish emissary sent by Philip II to report on the state of

---

[1] Quoted from Froude, op. cit. vol. VII, p. 565. Sidney to Elizabeth, 12 November. Irish MSS. Rolls House.
[2] Quoted from Froude, op. cit. vol. X, p. 218. George Wise to Cecil, 20 June 1567. MSS. Ireland.

Ireland, draws a picture which is more convincing. Speaking of Waterford, he says:

The trade of the port is with Gallicia, Portugal, Andalusia, and Biscay, where they send fish, hides, salt meat, and, at times, wheat and barley. The towns control the adjoining country, for the people depend on them to buy such things as they need, and to dispose of their flocks and wool. As a nation, the Irish are most improvident. They live almost wholly on meat, and use but little bread. The fault is not with the land; it is extremely fertile, and if properly cultivated would produce all that Spain produces, except olives and oranges; but the people are lazy, and do not like work. What four men sow, a hundred come to reap; and he who has most success in robbing his neighbours is counted most a man. There is little order among them beyond the jurisdiction of the towns. Every petty gentleman lives in a stone tower, where he gathers into his service all the rascals of the neighbourhood; and of these towers there is an infinite number.[1]

The Desmond rising came to a head as the result of the confiscation of the Desmond lands in 1568, on the grounds that the Earl, who had been summoned to London, had attempted to fly the country. On this occasion a group of adventurers, mainly from Devon, men with names either already famous, or soon to become so, Gilbert, Chichester, Carew, Grenville and Courtenay, were allowed to come to Munster and attempted to colonize it. This for the moment united all parties against the government. A campaign of slaughter and counter-slaughter was initiated in 1569, when Sidney commenced his punitive expedition. The struggle swayed alternately to either side, and the whole country, including Ulster, became involved. In 1572 the Earl of Essex was allowed to make his experiment in wishful thinking. No less was it, than that he should subdue the country at his own expense, in return for sovereign rights in the north; one need not follow the collapse of his dream, except to point out that it brought fresh disorder in the north which had enjoyed a short respite from anarchy. By 1574, Sidney, reinforced, recovered Ulster after raiding Antrim, and by the next year Munster was subdued. The destruction of life and property to date in this province had been terrible enough, but worse was still to come. In 1579 a small force with Irish and French auxiliaries landed in Smerwick, and the fighting became increasingly embittered, Mayo being almost the only part of Ireland that enjoyed some measure of peace. In September 1580, eight hundred Spaniards landed at Smerwick, were defeated, taken prisoner and ruthlessly massacred. This seemed to remove the last remnant of restraint.

The suppression of the rebellion from now on became a matter of the wholesale slaughter of leaders and people, with the destruction of houses and crops. In 1581 it was said 'that the lowing of a cow, or the voice of

---

[1] Quoted from Froude. Op. cit. vol. x, p. 220. Diego Ortiz.

the ploughman, was not to be heard that year from Dingle to the Rock of Cashel'.

To clear the country, Ormond with one force, and Sir William Pelham with another, started out from Kilkenny and Dublin respectively in March 1580, to meet at Limerick. 'We passed through the rebel countries', writes Pelham, 'in two companies, consuming with fire all habitations and executing the people wherever we found them.'[1]

When at last, in 1582, the final embers of revolt were stamped out, the condition of Munster, says Froude, 'was beyond imagination frightful', a verdict endorsed by Sir Warham St Leger himself. 'This country', wrote Sir Warham, from Cork in the spring of 1582, 'is so ruined, as it is well near unpeopled by the murders and spoils done by the traitors on the one side, and by the killing and spoil done by the soldiers on the other side, together with the great mortality in town and country, which is such as the like hath never been seen. There hath died by famine only, not so few as thirty thousand in this province in less than half a year, besides others that are hanged and killed.'[2]

It is with no desire to deepen the shadows in a picture of cruelty and devastation already so manifest, nor to show that the methods of Hitler are not unique, that I quote a passage from a soldier's weekly report dated May 1572, reproduced by Froude. I do so, but to demonstrate to what levels of misery and devastation the country had been brought, and how, inspired by fear of an enemy ready to knife them at any moment and at any place, men of noble character and high culture, as were Sidney, Pelham, Warham and Edmund Spenser, could be, and were induced to behave as, ravening monsters. The crudity of the account and the lack of any apologetic are, in themselves, evidence that it is a fairly representative sample of a system which was general in Ireland at the time. Its value in this respect is enhanced by the fact that it describes the activities of an ordinary patrol whose immediate duty was to deal with a party who had been marauding cattle in a relatively settled and peaceful part of the country, the Wicklow hills.

The first expedition against these people—for, as will be seen, there was a series—was of no particular moment. A party of soldiers made their way to the Barony of Shillelagh, where, the report says, 'they burned Garrald's house, with sixteen towns or hamlets, took a prisoner or two and forty-five head of cattle, and had other killing'.

The day following, their work lay in the beautiful valley of Imale, between Baltinglas and Blessington. There, reported the sergeant-major, 'they killed a foster-brother of James Eustace, Pat Tallon, and his brother David, whose

---

[1] Froude. Op. cit. vol. x, p. 569.
[2] Quoted from Froude. Op. cit. vol. x, p. 603. Sir Warham St Leger to Sir John Perrot, 22 April 1582. MSS. Ireland.

heads were sent (like a bag of game) to the Lord Keeper': another young fellow was run into and dispatched after a chase of three miles, and 'much spoil was taken'. After a few hours' rest, the soldiers swept round the base of Lugnaquilla to the upper waters of the Avanagh, and fell upon the MacHughs. Feagh MacHugh, of whom they were chiefly in search, was absent, but 'they slew two of his foster-brothers, four or five kerns, and as many others as were in five cabins'. This done they turned homewards. On their way they picked up a woman, whom Agard carried to the station, meaning, as he said, 'to execute her, unless she would serve his purpose'. Captain George, with a scouting party, encountered a party of Tallons, who had been abroad at mischief: one of them was killed; the rest, as the soldiers wanted amusement, were stripped naked, and 'put in the bog'.

The sergeant-major was moderately contented with these exploits, when spies brought him word that a further expedition might be made with advantage to a place called Glennes, now Glenmalure. The cattle there went down out of the gorge in the mornings to feed in the meadows, and the soldiers might 'have either kine or killing', so the report expressed it—either drive off the herds or catch the people in their beds and murder them. 'Whereupon', says Agard, 'I sent Captain Hungerford and the residue of the companies. On the 22nd of this month, being Thursday, they marched all night, and lay still most part of the day. On Friday, at night, they marched again; and on Saturday morning they were at the Glenne mouth, where the spy offered, if they would stay, to warrant them to have five hundred kine, or else to enter *to have some killing*, which Captain Hungerford and Lieutenant Parker rather chose. At the break of day they entered in and had the killing of diverse: what they were I know not. They brought away five swords with Gallowglasse axes. *They slew many churls, women, and children.* One of the soldiers was shot through the thigh, who with much ado was brought away. They brought with them thirty kine, sheep, and other pillage, and left while they were killing five hundred kine which they saw.'[1]

For nearly twenty years there was a lull, an unrestful and fitful peace, during which the Irish people nursed their wounds, the chiefs nursed their grievances, and the English tightened their hold on the country and avoided unnecessary provocation. The blood-red sunset over what once was prosperous Munster, was a sign and a warning, but only for the generation of that day.

The Armada had come, and gone to its destruction, and with it Philip's hopes and, one might have thought, the hope of the Irish for help from that quarter. But so deep was the dread of English rule in Irish hearts, so threatening, indeed so imminent the possibility of the suppression of the Catholic faith to the faithful everywhere, that Spain could not altogether refuse some show of help.

In 1595 the Irish chiefs were stung into yet another revolt: this time it started in Ulster under Hugh O'Neil, Earl of Tyrone, and spread to

[1] Froude. Op. cit. vol. x, pp. 255–7.

much of Connaught, all of Leinster and, finally, to Munster. At one period of the war, in 1600, all that was left under government control was the stretch of land between Dublin and Dundalk. The O'Neil and his friend and lieutenant, O'Donnell of Tyrconnel, conducted for close on eight years a guerrilla war against the English with great skill and until the final round, with amazing success. It was a campaign in which devastation of the countryside—the scorched earth policy of to-day— the ancient and accepted method of Irish clan warfare, was adopted by both sides, but improved on by the English under Mountjoy. As the struggle progressed, it developed on both sides into what was more and more a war of extermination. So seriously was English rule threatened, that in 1599 Elizabeth decided to send her own especial Paladin, Robert Devereux, Earl of Essex, to put down the revolt which, in truth, meant little short of reconquering the whole island. In so doing, the Queen sought to neutralize the ever-growing reputation and influence which O'Neil was winning in the Counter-Reformation countries of the Continent. How deeply this galled the Queen can be learnt from a letter of hers to Essex in which she says: 'Whereunto we will add one thing that doth more displease us than any charge or expense that happens, which is that it must be the Queen of England's fortune, who hath held down the greatest enemy she had, to make a base bush-kerne be accounted so famous a rebel as to be a person against whom so many thousand of foot and horse, beside the force of all the nobility of that kingdom, must be thought too little to be employed.'[1]

Essex's failure marked the zenith of O'Neil's success. The coming of Mountjoy heralded his downfall; in him, O'Neil was confronted by one who in his own person had outgrown the romanticism of the early renaissance. His patient and calculating methods belonged rather to the new era of commercialism which was taking form.

In 1601 Spain sent an army of 4,000 men under Don Juan de Aquila to Kinsale to support the rebels: this was defeated by Lord Mountjoy who sent him with his men back to Spain. By 1602 the rebels, exhausted, laid down their arms, but not before famine and its horrors had stalked the countryside.

Thus, within the ambit of a few years, there came to a close the most fateful century in Irish history, a century which had witnessed a hundred years of the tortuous rule of the Tudors, culminating in the slaughter of more than half the population, the destruction of the homes of great and small alike, as well as churches and monastic buildings. The countryside was ravaged, its once famous wealth of woods and cattle squandered. Great as was the material damage, the spiritual was no less; much that was fundamental and most of what was best in the social structure of

[1] O'Faolain, Sean (1942). *The Great O'Neil*, p. 215. Longmans.

Irish native life had been extinguished. A few years later, on 14 September 1607, what remained of a culture which, once long ago, had been the pride of Europe, sealed its own extinction with the flight of the Earls, O'Neil of Tyrone, and O'Donnell of Tyrconnel, never to return.

What, if anything, was there to record on the credit side? The observer of the times would, perhaps, have been buoyed up by the measure of peace and security which followed, and by the promise of a more understanding and intelligent governmental policy, both economic and political. The historian can indulge in no such fantasies: he will tell us that even these slender hopes were but partially fulfilled, and that but for a short forty years. What neither the Irishmen of the time knew, nor the historian has sufficiently realized, is, that as this fateful century drew to its close, a gift, humble and unobtrusive, had reached the hands of the peasantry, one which was to have the most far-reaching effect on the future of Ireland and, indeed, on Western civilization.

It may be asked, why should one have been at pains to describe a page of history, which neither English nor Irish can look back upon with other than shame and disgust? It is because it was the chaos which that struggle produced, which helped to open the way for the entry of the new food. The frayed out medievalism of Irish tribal life had finally collapsed. The attempt to force, at the point of the sword, a completely alien culture, religion, and system of government on the people, was met with the sullen obstinacy of men who had acquired no interest in the present and had lost such as they had in the past. The collapse of O'Neil and O'Donnell at Kinsale was much more than the end of two stalwart patriots, or rebels, as you will. It was the dying spasms of the old Irish life, which had long outlived its usefulness. From now on, a leaderless people were thrown back on their own meagre resources, as ignorant of what had been best in their own culture, as they were unwilling to accept that offered by their conquerors.

To the famine and misery, which followed thirty years of harrying and burning of homesteads, of crops and of cattle, and which had reached its apogee under Mountjoy's direct inspiration, must now be reckoned a spiritual famine no less destructive.

It may be thought that this sketch of Ireland in the latter end of the sixteenth century, has been painted in too sombre a hue. In answer, I would say: that the picture of Hitler's Europe is probably no more tragic than was that of Ireland in 1603.

The trade of sixteenth-century Ireland has recently been the subject of a fresh and close examination.[1] It reveals that in the fifteenth and the first half of the sixteenth century, Ireland enjoyed a strong position as a creditor country, whose exports were far in excess of her imports; the

[1] Longfield, Ada (1929). Op. cit.

greater part of the latter consisted of wine, luxury clothes and trappings. At the end of the sixteenth century the export of live cattle, meat, hides, sheep fells and linen yarns increased, but that of corn, furs, fish and manufactured clothes and linen had all fallen right away. Ports like Galway, which had earned £1,000 p.a. in 1584 by imports, collected but £100 in 1587, and none a little later.[1] Much of her heavier merchant tonnage Ireland had sold to Spain. She no longer manufactured her famous friezes and mantles, but was driven, by *force majeure*, to live on her capital.

The people were famished; to sow their usual crops, was but to invite their destruction. Every seed crop, be it oats or barley, rye or wheat, might be trampled over and ruined in a day; if it escaped that hazard, the garnered harvest might be raided or burnt overnight. The vegetable crops, cabbage and parsnip, were no less vulnerable, at best they were but auxiliary foods, and there was never much of either. It was under such conditions that the potato made its entry into Ireland. Its greedy acceptance by the people was no mere accident, for it satisfied their needs as efficiently as it symbolized their helpless degradation.

Already the resurgent wave of town to country, which, one hundred years later, was to grow so much stronger, had commenced. Inefficient and half-hearted as were the attempts of Elizabeth's parliament to check the manufacture of woollens in Ireland, it was enough to force many a burgher family back to the land.

In the potato, the weary and harassed cultivator had to his hand a food which was easier to prepare than any of which he had had experience; one which would feed him, his children and his livestock, out of the same cauldron, cooked on his open hearth of burning turves. There was, I believe, a still greater advantage which it offered: the potato could both be cultivated and stored in a manner which might outwit the spirit of destruction, and the malevolence of his enemy. Within a very few years, the Irish cultivator actually did develop such methods, and there is no reason to doubt that they went far to fulfil their purpose.

In addition to the social, agricultural, and political elements of the sixteenth century, which might reasonably be considered to have been capable of influencing the prospects of an entirely new and strange food, there is yet another factor in the pre-natal environment of the potato which demands consideration: that is the food of the people of Ireland prior to the seventeenth century.

The information I have been able to gather in respect to the dietary of the Irish people has not been very satisfactory. There are two reasons for this: Ireland, in the eyes of the Englishman of culture, was a wild and dangerous country, inhabited by a hostile people, whose habits were

[1] Green, Alice Stopford (1909). *The Making of Ireland*, p. 211.

as uncouth and incomprehensible, as the language they spoke. The few Irish noblemen, who came over to the English court, were Anglo-Normans who spoke English and, when in England, generally dressed as Englishmen, and of course whilst in this country conformed to our dietary. But the second cause of our relative ignorance of the details of this side of Irish life is that all our accounts come from the pen of English soldiers or statesmen, who spent a few arduous and harassed years in attempting to suppress revolts in one or other part of Ireland, a country 'in whose detestable service', said Sir William Pelham, 'was the grave of every Englishman's reputation'. Such men were prejudiced enough when they described the domestic life of some great Irish lord; but when, on the rare occasions, they speak of the way of life of the poor cottier who tilled the land, or the kern or gallowglass, who were perpetually on the look-out to strike at the English garrison, then it is rarely that the picture bears, on its face, the imprint of impartiality, much less that of objective knowledge.

In England, the dietary of the people prior to the seventeenth century, if not later, would need to be dealt with in two almost watertight compartments: the food of the upper classes, and that of the poor of town and country. In Ireland, it is true, the same distinction existed, if in the upper classes we include the great Anglo-Norman Barons, the Lords of the Pale, and the merchants of the chief ports. But if we confine ourselves to the native Irish, then it is probably true to say that there was no essential distinction, qualitative or quantitative, between the tables of the lesser chiefs and those of the kerns and churls who recognized their leadership. Still less was there, between the tables, and the way of living, of the farmer of twenty to a hundred acres and the small-holder or the cottier.

The difference in matters of domestic economy between England and Ireland was fundamental and must have been reflected in their respective dietaries. In the England of the sixteenth century, agriculture was in the main arable, with sheep-farming a close second; whilst cattle were kept primarily for draught, in the second place for milk, and only in the third for food. In Ireland, the order of precedence was reversed: cattle was the mainstay of Irish economy. The numbers kept must have been very great. In 1560 a writer,[1] speaking of the people of Connaught, says 'they are good and civil, and full of cattle always'. It was common to value articles of luxury in terms of cow-purchase, and that not only amongst the people: thus we hear that the Earl of Kildare bought a manuscript in 1482 for twenty cows.[2]

---

[1] Quoted from Green, Alice Stopford. Op. cit. Letter from Sir Henry Sidney, p. 91.
[2] Green, Alice Stopford. Op. cit. p. 256.

Patrick Joyce[1] draws a smiling picture of plenty in Ireland during the medieval period, in which meat, and especially pork, predominate; vegetables, cabbage, kale, parsnip and carrot were grown, but it would seem to no great extent. Milk foods were general: it is very uncertain whether the peasant on the land, as opposed to the immediate followers of the chief, shared in this abundance of his master's table. Certainly in times of famine he was driven to make use of boiled nettle-tops, as well as shamrock and watercress eaten raw, evidence that he had little or no reserves of food in garden or barn, whether cereal or vegetable, a fact which would suggest that he, too, was primarily a meat-eater.

Estyn Evans thinks that in the very early days of Irish history, the basic food of the people was oaten bread, baked as flat cakes over an open hearth. Cattle, it is thought, was of more importance in Irish agriculture during the Dark and Middle Ages, than in the sixteenth century, in which case it may be presumed that meat was never absent from the dietary of the people.

The Spanish emissary, Diego Ortiz, who, presumably, had not acquired any extensive first-hand knowledge of the Irish peasantry, says that 'as a nation the Irish are most improvident. They live almost wholly on meat and use but little bread.' Sir John Perrot[2] (1571) complained that the soldiers were dying in great numbers from the flux (dysentery), due to continuous eating of meat. This, though suggestive, cannot be accepted as conclusive evidence that the common people also ate large quantities.

In 1581, Andrew Trollope, writing to Walsingham, says: 'The common people ate flesh if they could steal it, if not, they lived on shamrock and carrion, with butter too loathsome to describe.'[3] The butter he condemns so forcibly is, of course, the famous sour butter, which was prepared by burying kegs of fresh butter in the peat, and leaving it there for years on end. Kegs of green butter are not infrequently dug now out of the peat, where they may have been buried for over a hundred years and their contents, as I have myself found, are, if edible, without attraction.

McManus[4] quotes Cuellar who in 1588, writing of the fate of the Spanish Armada, speaks of the Irish as follows: 'They do not eat oftener than once a day, and this at night; and that which they usually eat is butter with oaten bread. They drink sour milk for they have no other drink; they don't drink water, although it is the best in the world. On feast days they eat some flesh, half cooked, without bread or salt.'

In the field, the Irish kernes lived 'hard', and it is said that they rarely

[1] Joyce, Patrick Weston (1903). *A Social History of Ancient Ireland*. Longmans.
[2] Froude. Op. cit. vol. x, p. 220.
[3] Froude. Op. cit. vol. x, p. 600.
[4] McManus, M. J. (1939). *Irish Cavalcade, 1550–1850.*

ate meat when campaigning, but contented themselves with milk, curds and cheese.[1]

The English soldiery were, at times, as hungry and hard put to it to find any sort of food as the Irishry themselves. Lord Brough in 1597 complains: 'No bread, no beef, fish or flesh. We hear of great quantity of rye from England. The very report of it, makes our hungry jaws gape.'[2]

Mrs Green tells a similar tale; and adds that in the sixteenth century 'Irish whisky does not seem to have been much drunk by the poor country people or by the Irish soldiers out for war: water and buttermilk were the drinks of these hardy livers'. I find it somewhat difficult to accept this view, seeing that a little later it is admitted, on all sides, that whisky-drinking was both general and excessive, and that stills several hundred years old are frequently recovered from the bogs.

O'Brien[3] has only a passing reference to the food conditions of the Irish prior to the introduction of the potato, but he quotes the following: 'the common sort never kill any cattle for their own use being contented to feed all the year upon milk, butter and the like and do eat but little bread.'

Sir William Petty[4] explains this abstinence in the midst of plenty: 'As for flesh, they seldom eat it, notwithstanding the great plenty thereof, unless it be of the smaller animals, because it is inconvenient for one of their families to kill a Beef, which they have no convenience to save.'

The absence of villages and the scattered distribution of the cottiers' homes would explain this difficulty, especially when one remembers that all the salt required for preserving meat was imported and was not readily obtained in the countryside.

Fynes Moryson[5] who wrote at the beginning of the seventeenth century, had travelled widely throughout Europe and Asia before coming to Ireland in 1600, where he became chief secretary to Sir Charles Blount, and took part in the suppression of the revolt, during which he saw at first hand the devastation which had overtaken much of Ulster and the midland counties, bringing them almost into line with the ravished and stricken province of Munster. His picture of the Ireland of that day confirms all that has been said of the ruin and desolation which had resulted from the civil wars of the latter half of the sixteenth century.

The people [he says], live in caves and holes like wild beasts: the wild, and as I may say mere Irish, are barbarous and most filthy in their diet. They eat

[1] In a manuscript note Salaman later cast some doubt on the making and eating of cheese in Ireland. – Ed.

[2] O'Faolain, Sean (1942). Op. cit. p. 185.

[3] O'Brien, G. (1919). Op. cit. p. 36. Quoting Advertisements for Ireland, MS. T.C.D. London: Macmillan & Co.

[4] Petty, Sir Wm. (1691). Political Anatomy of Ireland.

[5] Moryson, Fynes (1617). Itinerary, edit. 1907.

meat unsalted, swine's flesh, more seldom mutton, but are particularly addicted to dead horse flesh. They never kill a cow till it is past milking and if they do kill one it is all devoured at one sitting. If they don't want to rear a calf it is turned out to be consumed by the wolves. They have no beer but drink much milk which they heat by placeing hot stones in the vessel. They eat all their corn by Xmas, they willingly eat the heart shamrock, being of a sharp taste which as they run and are chased they snatch like beasts out of the ditches.

Their chief foods, however, are the 'white meats', especially sour curds or 'Bonaclabbe'.

Moryson goes on to say that in time of war and shortness of food, they opened a vein of the neck of a cow or horse, and drank the blood. As a matter of fact, this custom was by no means confined to occasions of dire necessity. François Misson, who wrote an account of his travels throughout the British Isles in 1697, says:[1] 'Sometimes they bleed their cows and boil the blood with some of the milk and butter that came from the same beast; and this with a mixture of savoury herbs is one of their most delicious dishes.'

In Tyrone and Derry, the bleeding of the cows was done in summer 'in a smooth place, each layer of coagulating blood being strewn with salt until a little mound was formed, which was cut up in squares and laid by for use as food in the scarce time of the year'.

The bleeding of cattle was evidently an ancient, and deeply rooted, Celtic practice which was approved at least as late as 1780, when cows were still bled in Wicklow, and the blood mixed with meal for food.[2] It persisted in the Hebrides throughout the eighteenth century.

There is probably no one account of the dietary, which would be accurate, for the whole country. Thus, no mention has been made of fish, though in the next century the native Irish are said to have made much use of mussels and oysters. On the coast, fish was doubtless freely eaten in times of peace, but in 1600, fish was actually being imported from Newfoundland, and rye from Danzig, this latter as that imported in 1597 was doubtless intended for the use of the English troops.[3] Even at the best of times, the fishing industry was mainly in the hands of Spaniards, who exported their catches in salt to Spain.

Of vegetables, one hears but little: cabbage and parsnip were cultivated, though one suspects that in neither case was their cultivation general amongst the peasantry, but in times of trouble they are not likely to have been of much importance. In a diary of the early eighteenth century a parson of the Irish Presbyterian Church in County Down,

---

[1] Misson, François (1697). *Memoirs and Observations, etc.* Trans. W. Ozell 1719, p. 154. London.

[2] Evans, E. Estyn (1942). Op. cit. p. 78.

[3] O'Brien, G. (1919). Op. cit. p. 4. Quoting from *Calendar of State Papers (Ireland)*, 1600–1, p. 414.

recounting his activities, mentions 'sowing parsnips' as if it were rather a special effort.[1]

I think we are on safe ground in assuming that the people's food in the sixteenth century, outside the main ports, was derived entirely from what they themselves produced—meat, milk, and some oats; of the corn crops they might grow, it must not be assumed that they enjoyed any of the wheat nor much of the barley and oats. The best of these were, according to Longfield, exported, and inferior corn, such as rye, peas and beans, imported to replace them. The imported rye, however, could scarcely have found its way very far beyond the ports: lack of transport, to say nothing of continual disorder, would have prevented such an exchange taking place on an extensive scale.

If one cannot avoid the conclusion that the people's sufferings were, in the main, due to the policy of the intrusive English, it would be an error to imagine that all had been well within the Irish native, and virtually independent communities; still more, that the peasantry enjoyed a life of freedom, peace and plenty under their tribal chiefs. Such was far from being the case. Lecky thinks that the position of the humblest clansmen in the sixteenth and seventeenth centuries under the chiefs was 'miserable in the extreme'. Hickson says that all the social privileges had passed into the hands of chiefs, Brehons, bards and priests, and there was but little that remained for the clansman, his 'co-proprietorship with his fellows in barbarous poverty and semi-slavery was generally all that was left him'.[2]

By the end of the century the state of the peasantry must have been indeed terrible. The greater part of the countryside had been ravaged, especially in Munster; corn crops were either wanting or, if sown, more often than not destroyed, the cattle had been slaughtered in vast quantities, and no man knew if the few beasts sheltering in the homestead before he fled to the forest, would be there when the soldiers had passed. Such vegetables as were growing in their gardens would have perished when their homes went up in flames.

Thus the stage was set to the last detail, for a complete revolution in the dietary of the whole people, and the success of the newcomer, the potato, almost assured. The dietary of the people, never a generous one, had become so restricted, and its supply in the period of turmoil so precarious, that sheer necessity was sufficient to break down in a few years, the innate prejudices of a rural people which might otherwise have taken generations to overcome. The complete collapse of public security, with the disruption of the whole complex and routine of normal peasant

[1] Kennedy, Rev. Joh. (1724–30). Quoted by Jackson, R. W.

[2] Hickson, M. (1884). *Ireland in the Seventeenth Century and the Massacre of* 1641, p. 9. Longmans.

life, opened wide the door to a food which, though peculiar in its cultural requirements, strange in appearance and taste, offered the people a sporting chance of warding off the famine and pestilence which hammered at their doors. The fall of manna in the desert was not more opportune than the coming of the potato to Ireland. True, the Irish never suffered from physical repletion, as did the Israelites, but they, too, were to learn that seemingly beneficent gifts of Providence may conceal dangers to the body politic, which only the experience of centuries may reveal, and the fearless application of science and statesmanship avert.

CHAPTER XII

Ireland in the Seventeenth Century

O'Brien divides the economic history of Ireland in the seventeenth century into four periods: from 1603 to 1641 was a period of Construction. The next twenty years, 1641–61, were the years of Rebellion, and Destruction. The following thirty years which elapsed between the Restoration and the Revolution saw the resettlement of the land and the commencement of industrialization, and were a period of Reconstruction, whilst the fourth period, one of ten years, witnessed the foundation of the penal code through which the gradual ruin and degradation of Ireland was brought about by bloodless means. This is O'Brien's period of Redestruction.

There is no evidence to show exactly when the potato was introduced. Tradition[1] ascribes its first appearance in Ireland as the result of a shipwreck off the coast of Galway, a not unlikely sequence of the Armada (1588). If the Raleigh legend be correct, it was already in cultivation in the Cork district before the end of the sixteenth century. The first reference in which the potato is specifically mentioned, occurs in the Montgomery Manuscripts: 'Her ladyship (Sir Hugh Montgomery's wife) had also her farm at Grey Abbey and Coiner (= Comber, County Down), as well as at Newton, both to supply Newcomers and her house, and she easily got men for plough and barn, for many came over who had not stocks to plant and take leases of land, but had bought a cow or two and a few sheep for which she gave them grass and so much grain per annum, and a house and a garden plot to live on and some land for flax and potatoes, as they agreed on for doing their work.' This statement refers to the year 1606. The Rev. G. Hill, who edited the Montgomery MSS. in 1869, is troubled about this reference to the potato and comments thus: 'Popular belief that it was introduced about 1586 is probably erroneous. If only planted at that date by Sir Walter Raleigh in his garden near Youghal, it is not likely that during the war which desolated Ireland between 1586 and 1601 the potato should become so generally known and appreciated as this, to form an important article of food for the Scotch Settlers in the Ards so early as 1606.' This contention has been already answered and the directly opposite view maintained, viz. that the general devastation and misery, which dominated the closing years of the century, was just such as would lead to the breakdown of prejudice against, and the acceptance of, a new food. If such food filled

[1] Loudon, J. C. (1831). *Encyclopaedia of Agriculture*.

the belly and pleased the palate, was easy to grow and easy to hide, it fulfilled the essential requirements of rural life whether in peace or war. The writer of the manuscripts, it is pointed out by Davidson,[1] was born in 1633: he was a painstaking writer and would scarcely have recorded this note about potatoes, if he had not at least been familiar with them in his youth; he is therefore prepared to accept both his statement and the date. Davidson adds: 'If Montgomery's statement is correct, and there is no reason to doubt it, the potato must have been introduced early in the second half of the sixteenth century.' This is by no means a necessary corollary. Given suitable conditions, and I have shown that such existed in Ireland, we have evidence that a new food plant may reach a wide public in a matter of five to ten years, as the potato did in Seville, and the Jerusalem artichoke in Paris.[2]

Fynes Moryson (1602–3), to whom reference has already been made, does not refer to potatoes, but mentions artichokes when describing, in considerable detail, the food of the Anglo-Irish gentry, the English tenant-colonists, as well as that of the 'mere' Irish. The absence of any reference to the potato is of some significance and must be taken as evidence that at that early date its culture had not made a widespread advance. Davidson[3] appears to agree with an anonymous writer in the *Belfast Magazine* for 1825[4] that Moryson's artichoke was the potato, which he had mistaken for the Jerusalem artichoke. This view, which would put the Jerusalem artichoke on the map in the opening years of the seventeenth century, is untenable. The Jerusalem artichoke did not reach Europe at the very earliest till 1607, and although it had been received in court circles in France with much enthusiasm, it was not known in England till 1617.[5]

The actual passage in Moryson is of much interest; it runs thus: 'They desire no broth, nor have any use of a spoone. They can neither seeth artichokes nor eat them when they are soden.' The reference is undoubtedly to the Globe artichoke which had been grown in England since about 1548 and was much prized; it was usually boiled, but in France it was, and still is, occasionally eaten raw. The further remark that 'they do not eat this when soden', may refer to the very ancient custom of making a decoction from the roots sodden in water, which was used as an aperitif both because it encouraged a desire for alcoholic drink, and as possessing the virtue more often in demand, that of exciting

---

[1] Davidson, W. D. (1936). The History of the Potato and its Progress in Ireland. *J. Dept. Agric. Eire*, vol. XXXIV, no. 2, p. 7.
[2] Salaman, R. N. (1940). Why 'Jerusalem' Artichoke? *J. Roy. Hort. Soc.* vol. LXV, pts. 10 and 11.
[3] Davidson, W. D. (1936). Op. cit.
[4] Anonymous (1825). *Belfast Magazine*, vol. I, p. 159.
[5] Salaman, R. N. (1940). Op. cit.

lust. Salmon[1] finds yet another argument in its favour: 'for it sendeth forth plenty of stinking urine whereby the rank and rammish savour of not only the armpits, but of the whole body is much amended'. Moryson's remarks should be taken as intended to show how wholly uncultured and contemptible were the 'mere' Irish in the eyes of their overlords; they could not even appreciate an artichoke.

In the chapter on the 'Manners of the Irishry' in the 1610 edition of *Camden's Britannia* we find: 'As for their meals, they feed willingly upon herbs, and water cresses, especially upon mushrooms, shamroots (clover) and roots.'

The reference to 'roots' is puzzling: it is repeated throughout all the editions of Camden, and is even to be found unaltered in Gough's edition of 1789. It does not seem likely that it refers to potatoes, but rather to various kinds of weeds, for Camden's source of information on Irish affairs was a Jesuit, John Good, who was a schoolmaster in Limerick in 1564, and unlikely, therefore, to have been aware of the potato at the time Camden was making his first compilation, which was some time prior to 1586. It was also too early for it to have meant turnips, and although it could have meant parsnips, we have no reason to think that these were ever grown intensively: even had they been, one may be excused for doubting whether any people, not excluding the Irish, could have survived, for long, on a day-to-day diet of parsnips!

On the other hand, I am persuaded that the word 'root' in the following context, must mean the potato, for there is no other root which would have been grown at that time in sufficient quantity to merit the attention of the city council. The reference is of peculiar interest, coming, as it does, at this early date from Youghal. The council book of the corporation of the town, reports (p. 90) as follows: 'On May 26, 1623: Tolls and customs agreed upon by the Mayor, etc: For eggs, poultry, apples and such fruits, roots, herbs sold at once to the value of 2s. 6d., to pay ½d. and so upwards.'

If this contention be correct, then we may conclude that, even at that date, potatoes were being grown in the neighbourhood of Youghal in sufficiently large quantities, as to warrant the imposition of a special custom toll.

Another indirect reference is to be found in a Memoir whose probable date is 1623, ascribed to Sir H. Bourgchier.[2] He talks of the great productiveness of the people who, however, are idle and slovenly, which he attributes to their dietary—the poor 'do feed altogether on moist meals'. Had he meant milk or porridge, he would have referred

[1] Salmon, W. (1710). *The English Herbal.*
[2] Bourgchier, Sir H. (1623). Advertisements for Ireland. Reprinted *J. Roy. Soc. Antiq. Ireland*, 1923.

to it as white meats, the accepted term for such. It could not refer to any other vegetable, for none was eaten except very occasionally, and then only cabbage. The potato, always on the boil in the cauldron over the turves, was essentially a 'moist meal'. Whether it was the potato or not, he is convinced that no peasant in Europe lived so poorly and that his condition was vastly inferior to that of the English peasant.

Thus the forty years of reconstruction saw the potato quietly establishing itself throughout the length and breadth of the country, though it is not till towards the end of the period of destruction and after, that we begin to find specific documentary evidence of its ubiquity, and of the reliance which the people of the land had already learnt to place on it. The spread of its culture, and its acceptance as a food, must have taken place during those few decades of peace, wherein the vivid memories of the horrors and famine of the days of the Desmond and Tyrone wars may well have afforded no mean spur to action.

It is held by some, that whilst in the south its adoption may have been both general and rapid, this was not so in the north. That its progress was slower, may be true, but that it was not far behind, would follow from a passage in M'Skimsin's *History of Carrickfergus*, where, in 1676 it is stated 'Potatoes were sold at the high rate of 1s. 8d. per bushel', and that very old people told him that a few potatoes were used after harvest and as a treat for Halloween [1 Nov.] supper, with butter, but that they were already coming into general circulation.[1] This would suggest that they were a luxury in this part of Ulster about 1620.

The period of destruction commenced in October 1641, with the massacre of a number of the Protestant planters in Ulster and a general rising of the Irish people, which spread throughout the whole country. The suppression of the revolt was prolonged by reason of the concurrent and closely related struggle between Charles I and his parliament. But, that over, Cromwell himself took control of the army in Ireland and in less than two years (1649–50), the Irish Rebellion had been ruthlessly crushed everywhere.

The accounts of both victor and vanquished are at one in describing the havoc and misery which once more overtook Ireland. Slaughter by the sword and death by famine, vied with each other in the task of exterminating the greater part of the native Irish.

In a proclamation of Lord Broghill, issued in Youghal, 27 July 1644,[2] we catch a glimpse of the part the potato was to be called on to perform in an ever increasing degree. 'Whereas the gardens in and near this town and liberties are in great hope to be a good help to the inhabitants, if

---

[1] M'Skimin, Samuel (1676). *History of Carrickfergus*. Quoted from Croker, Crofton (1886), *Popular Songs of Ireland*, p. 54.
[2] Cauldfield, Richard (1878). *Ed. Council Book of the Corporation of Youghal*, p. 546.

care be taken that the roots [potatoes] and fruits growing in them be duly preserved from the violence of soldiers and other inhabitants who have of late most wrongfully entered and destroyed the same.'

Between 1641 and 1660, over and beyond the actual destruction of life and property, legislation had been devised to kill the shipping industry, whilst the woollen and linen industries were for the time brought to a standstill.

In 1652 so great was the distress, that cattle were actually imported from Wales into Ireland, previously the largest exporter of those times. The soldiery burnt the corn, and the rebels burnt the mills. Woods were levelled, and the iron-works destroyed. In 1641 the homes of Ireland were valued at two and a half million pounds; in 1652, at one-fifth that sum. The silver and lead mines of Dunally in County Tipperary were laid waste. The man-power of the country was either killed, deported, or had gone with their leaders overseas to Spain. A remnant remained to beg the streets of Dublin. The womenfolk and children, their homes destroyed, took to the ditches for shelter and there they died of starvation or plague, their bodies a prey to the wolves which once more roamed the countryside.

It is said that by 1653 as many as five-sixths of the people had perished;[1] so great was the local destruction of life and property that cases of cannibalism were reported, and there is no reason to doubt that many tales of the kind were well founded. It is now, in the latter half of the century, that we begin to hear of the root which saved the remnant of the people.

John Beale,[2] writing in 1672, tells how in the year 1629–30 there was a dearth in England, and that it had been suggested that turnip and meal might be employed for making bread to feed the people. 'Potatoes', he says, 'were a relief to Ireland, in their last famine; they yield meat and drink.' It may be that the Irish famine referred to, took place in the same year, a view held by Wilde.[3] Davidson[4] thinks that Beale probably refers to the famine which occurred during, and by reason of, the Cromwellian War, 1645–52, and as Beale was writing in 1672, so well known an event as the distress following the reconquest, might well be implied. A later communication to the Royal Society in July 1675 in which Beale says: 'The potatoes of Barbadoes [which he identifies with the Virginian potato, i.e. *S. tuberosum*] in our fresh memory relieved Ireland from two years famine, when the corn failed them'[5] confirms

[1] Prendergast, J. (1922). *The Cromwellian Settlement*, p. 307.
[2] Beale, John (1672). *Phil. Trans.* no. 90, p. 5172, 20 Jan. 1672/3.
[3] Wilde, Sir William R. (1856). Introduction and time of the general use of the Potato in Ireland. *Proc. Roy. Irish Academy*, vol. XI, ser. A, p. 356.
[4] Davidson, W. D. Op. cit.
[5] Beale, J. Op. cit. no. 116, p. 369, 26 July 1675.

this view. Beale was genuinely interested in the potato: in a letter to Robert Boyle dated 18 October 1659, which is to be found in the collection of the Boyle MSS. of the Royal Society, he outlines his plans for experiments to discover how far tubers may be cut for seed, and to what extent the taste of the crop may be improved by suitable composts.

Vincent Gookin, a member of a planter family long settled in Cork, has much to say about the problems of this period. He was one of the few Englishmen of that time who, having learnt to see through the miasma of racial and religious prejudice, and appreciate the good qualities of the Irish peasantry amongst whom he had been brought up, had the courage to testify to the fact in public. He was one of the six members for Ireland elected to the first Commonwealth Parliament in 1653, and sent a copy of an anonymous pamphlet[1] on the subject to all his fellow-members, as a result of which he was vigorously attacked by a certain Colonel Richard Laurence. Gookin wrote opposing the government policy: he argued that transplantation would injure the public revenue:

The Revenue or Contribution of Ireland is generally raised out of Corn and the Husbandmen of that Corn are generally Irish; the removal therefore of this necessity infers the failer of that, For, the Irish who raise this contribution out of Corn, live themselves on the roots [potatoes] and fruits of their gardens and on the milk of their Cows, Goats and Sheep, and by selling their Corn to the English, provide money for the contribution; if then the Irish should be thus transplanted, their corn would not be vendible, not to one another, for all would be sellers, not to the English: for to carry it 50–60, or 100 miles to the English Plantations, would make it so dear to the Buyer, and cheap to the Seller, that it cannot reasonably be thought practicable.

Sir W. Petty, writing some time about 1670,[2] in the course of his answer to the accusation so frequently levelled against the Irish by the English of his day, that they were lazy, gives us a measure of the extent to which the potato had succeeded in becoming the basic food of the people. 'Their food', he says, 'is bread and cakes, whereof a penny serves a week for each: potatoes from August till May.... As for flesh they seldom eat it.'[3]

Petty is inclined to regard the potato as responsible for certain peculiarities of Irish peasant behaviour. Thus, 'all the Irish live in a brutish nasty condition, as in Cabins with neither chimney, door, stairs nor window: feed chiefly upon milk and potatoes whereby their spirits are not disposed to war'.[4] The paucity of shipbuilding in Ireland

[1] Gookin, Vincent (1655). *The Great Case of Transplantation.*
[2] In *D.N.B.* 'Petty' gives 1672 as the date.
[3] Petty, Sir W. (1691). *Political Anatomy of Ireland*, p. 59.
[4] Ibid. p. 27.

he suggests is because 'the Irish had rather eat potatoes and milk on dry land than contest with wind and wave with better food'.[1]

Their lazeing seems to me to proceed rather from want of employment and encouragement to work, than from the natural abundance of Flegm in the Bowels and Blood; for what need they to work who can content themselves with Potatoes, whereof the labour of one man can feed forty; and with milk, whereof one cow will, in summer time, give meat and drink enough for three men; when they can everywhere gather cockles, mussels, crabs, etc., with Boats, Nets, Angles, or the art of Fishing; can build a House in three days.[2]

And then follows a passage which, coming from one who was a Protestant, an Englishman and, above all, an exceptionally shrewd speculator in confiscated land property, gives us an almost prophetic clue to the solution of our immediate problem. If destruction of property, fear of punitive raids and the like, encourage the widespread cultivation of the potato, why did not the return to peace constrain and reduce it, instead of driving the people with ever increasing momentum to look to this one food as their sole means of support? Here is Petty's answer:

And why should they desire to fare better, tho with more labour, when they are taught, that this way of living is more like the Patriarchs of old, and the Saints of later times, by whose Prayers and Merits they are to be reliev'd, and whose Examples they are therefore to follow? And why should they breed more Cattel, since 'tis Penal to import them into England? Why should they raise more commodities, since there are not Merchants sufficiently Stock'd to take them of them, nor provided with other more pleasing foreign Commodities, to give in Exchange for them? And how should Merchants have Stock, since Trade is prohibited and fetter'd by the Statutes of England?[3]

In the Council Papers of the Royal Society is a communication recording a discussion held on 20 March 1662 on potatoes, which will be considered in more detail in a later chapter. During the discussion, Robert Boyle, the great physicist, who was the owner of large properties in Cork and Waterford, said

that he knew that in a time of famine in Ireland, there were kept from starving, thousands of poor people by potatoes; and that this root would make good bread, mixed with wheaten meale; that it will yield good drink too, but of no long duration; that it feeds poultry and other animals well; that any refuse will keep them from frost; that the very stalks of them thrown into the ground, will produce good roots; that the planting of them doth not hinder poor people from other employment.[4]

---

[1] Petty, Sir W. (1691). *Political Anatomy of Ireland*, p. 16.
[2] Ibid. p. 68.
[3] Ibid. pp. 99–100.
[4] Royal Society, 1662. Miscellaneous Papers of Council, etc., 20 March.

Boyle's remarks foreshadow the sinister part which the potato was to be forced to play in the stabilization of the lowest practical standard of social well-being amongst the workers.

About this time occurs the first reference to the potato in Erse literature. It is a comic rhyme introduced between the stanzas of an epithalamium dedicated to Oliver Stephenson and his bride Eleana Burke in 1674 by O'Bruadair.[1] In English it runs:

For he [one Monegan] is a rustic who wields a cudgel and strikes his wife under her eyebrow with his fist, though before they were married he used to salute her with kisses, affected primness and potatoes.

Dineley, antiquarian and traveller, seemed to regard the Irishman's diet, habits and vices, as interdependent.

They have certain concomitants, nastiness and laziness, wherefore having enough beforehand to furnish them with potatoes, milk and tobacco, which they toss from one another in a short pipe with this word 'shaugh', sitting upon their hams, like greyhounds in the sun, near their cabins, they'll work not one jot, but steal, which is such an inseparable vice to them that a gentleman in the County of Clare complained to me that they stole his box of pills because gilded.[2]

From now on, every writer, and there are many, who touches on the home life of the Irish people, has much the same tale to tell: the food of the people is the potato, and milk. As time goes on, and we pass into the next century, the milk grows scarcer, and the quota of the potato more voluminous. Whilst there is a certain monotony in these descriptions, a monotony, which must have been far more real to those directly concerned, one recognizes, in an ever increasing degree, that the establishment of the monophagous diet is linked in ever closer union with the social degradation of its devotees.

A vivid picture of the cottier's home is drawn by Stevens,[3] one which is relatively cheerful compared with that which Arthur Young depicts a hundred years later; for by then the potato had usurped, on most days of the year, the position of all other articles of food: writing in 1690 he said:

The meaner people content themselves with little bread but instead thereof eat potatoes, which with sour milk is the chief part of their diet, their drink for the most part water, sometimes coloured with milk; beer or ale they seldom taste, unless they sell something considerable in a market town. They all

[1] O'Bruadair (1674). *Cuippead Cluany ap & pobony.* [I owe both the reference and the translation to the kindness of Ed. MacLysaght, author of *Irish Life in the Seventeenth Century*, p. 258 n. Longmans, 1939.]

[2] Dineley (Dingley) Thos. Observations made on his Tours in Ireland and France 1675–80. *J. Roy. Soc. Antiq. Ireland*, 1870, pp. 17–18.

[3] Stevens, John. *Journal*, 1689–91 (ed. R. Murray). Oxford, 1912.

smoke, women as well as men, and a pipe an inch long serves the whole family several years, and though never so black or fowl is never suffered to be burnt. Seven or eight will gather to the smoking of a pipe, and each taking two or three whiffs gives it to his neighbour, commonly holding his mouth full of smoke till the pipe comes back to him again. They are also much given to taking of snuff. Very little clothing serves them, and as for shoes and stockings much less. They wear brogues being quite plain without so much as one lift of a heel, and are all sowed with thongs, and the leather not curried, so that in wearing it grows hard as a board, and therefore many always keep them wet, but the wiser that can afford it grease them often, and that makes them supple. In the better sort of cabins there is commonly one flock bed, seldom more, feathers being too costly; this serves the man and his wife, the rest all lie on straw, some with one sheet and blanket, others only their clothes and blanket to cover them. The cabins have seldom any floor but the earth, or rarely so much as a loft, some have windows, others none. They say it is of late years that chimneys are used, yet the house is never free from smoke. That they have no locks to their door is not because they are not thieves but because there is nothing to steal. Poverty with neatness seems somewhat the more tolerable, but here nastiness is in perfection, if perfection can be in vice, and the great cause of it, laziness, is most predominant. It is a great happiness that the country produces no venomous creature, but it were much happier in my opinion did it produce no vermin.

Their food is mostly milk and potatoes, their clothing coarse bandrel cloth and linen, both of their own make; a pot of gruel, a griddle whereon to bake their bread, a little salt, snuff, and iron for their ploughs being almost all they trouble their shopkeeper or merchant for. A little hut or cabin to live in is all that the poverty of this sort hope or have ambition for....

Their dwellings or cabins—an English cow-house hath more architecture far; the Lord Mayor's dogs kennel is a palace compared to them; the walls are made of mere mud mixed with a little wet straw. For beds instead of feathers and flocks they use rushes and straw....Such of them as live in the plain and fertile parts of the country are generally slaves to the English or to their Irish landlords, and live by their daily labour, working for threepence or fourpence a day and their dinner, their stock is generally a cow or two, some goats, and perhaps six or eight small Irish sheep which they clip twice a year and convert their wool into coarse frieze to cover their nakedness; when the lambs of their few sheep do fall they preserve some part of them to keep up their number and those they half starve for lucre of the milk, the rest they sell in the markets for sixpence or eightpence a piece.

Some forty years later, it is evident that the impermanence of their dwellings is associated with the insecurity of their tenure on the land.

Their house or cabins made of earth or dry stone, there is little difference in the expense of time employed in erecting or demolishing them; and this is done just as gentlemen [landlords] incline to break up their lands and improve things by lettage, or as they lay them down under grass and enlarge their sheep-walks and grazing farm; and by this means the poor, who remove with little trouble, are turned adrift and must remove to some other place where they can get employment.[1]

It is not to be wondered at that, under such conditions, the cottier contented himself with a crop like the potato, which secured him more food to the acre, demanded less cultivation, and was more easily conserved than any other. How firm was the hold the potato had acquired on the economic life of the people, can be appreciated when it is remembered that this was the time when Ireland was exporting the major part of her wheat and other cereals to England and the Continent.

The impression which Irish cottage economy made on Englishmen at the end of the century, may be gauged from the following: 'Some Historians do speak of them to be very tender and careful of their Young ones; but wherein that tenderness consists, is not readily to be found out. For their Food is not in the least degree better than they allow their Pigs, Bonny-rowre for the Summer, and Potato roots in the Winter are their choicest Dainties:'[2]

John Dunton writes from Ballymony to a lady in England, in a similar vein:[3]

Behind one of these cabins lyes the garden, a piece of ground sometimes of half an acre, and in this is the turf-stack, their corn, perhaps two or three hundred sheaves of oats, and as much pease; the rest of the ground is full of those dearly beloved potatoes, and a few cabbages, which the solitary calf of the family, that is here pent from the Down, never suffers to come to perfection, Madam, I should more exactly have described their dwellings or cabins, if I durst have adventured oftener into 'em; or cou'd have staid in 'em (for lice and smoak) when I was there.

Just as there is neither record of how, nor when, nor where, the potato reached Ireland, so are we equally ignorant of how they learned to cultivate it. It must be remembered that the potato differed from any edible plant the Irish of that day had hitherto cultivated, by the fact that it was propagated not by true seed, as were their corn and their parsnips, but by the setts in the earth of similar tubers to those which they had but recently consumed. It might have been thought that they would have employed a plan of cultivation closely akin to that which they made use of for growing corn: that having ploughed the field, they would have inserted or dibbled the tubers beneath the overturned turves, and left the potato to make the best of it. But that was not what happened.

[1] Anon. (about 1728). From Alex Thom's *Tracts on Ireland*, 1860, p. 411.
[2] Ward, Edward (1699). *A Trip to Ireland*, p. 9 (attributed to Ward), ed. Thoyer, H. *Facs. Text. Soc.* 1933.
[3] Dunton, John (1699). Some Account of my Conversation in Ireland in a letter to an Honourable Lady. Reproduced in Appendix B, Letter 4, of MacLysaght's *Irish Life in the Seventeenth Century*, 1939.

The Irish developed a system of their own, which has been, rather unjustly, dubbed with the name of 'the lazy-bed system'. One says, 'of their own', but whether it was really a development *in situ* by the Irish, is a question I am unable to answer.[1]

The potatoes were grown at first, and for a long time, in the gardens or haggards, which were attached to the cottages, or on small pieces of land not available to the plough. Later the potato was grown on the rundale in-field, where the rigid restrictions, prevalent in our own common fields, did not hold sway.

When potatoes were grown in the in-field it would seem that all who owned strips, employed some at least for this purpose at the same time. Coles,[2] writing about the middle of the century, says: 'but the soil of Ireland doth so well agree with them, that they grow so plentifully that there be whole fields over run with them, as I have herein found by divers soldiers which came from thence'. It is unfortunate that Coles was under the impression that these were the Spanish or sweet-potato which, in fact, never grew in Ireland; but that does not invalidate the evidence of the soldiers that 'whole fields' were under potatoes.

The cultivation in all cases was by hand, and the instrument used was a spade; but that, even in Ireland to-day, is a loose generic term for a veritable host of different tools. A modern spade factory in Galway turns out 150 shapes of blades.[3] One species of spade of which there are several varieties, is known as a 'loy', or 'fack': it has only one 'ear' to the blade, and not two, as has the common spade of this country. The blade is about 10 in. long and 4 in. wide; at its upper end, it expands upwards into a socket 6 in. long and 3 in. wide, which is bent at an angle of about 160° with the plane of the blade, and is open behind; into the socket is fixed the staff, a stout ash-pole, 4 ft. long, with no terminal handle. It is held in position by a wooden wedge, which is expanded at its upper end into an 'ear' or foot-rest. The use of a wooden rest for the foot, rather than an iron one, was dictated by the fact that the Irish native worker of this period went bare-footed to his work. The tool is more or less identical with the Highland-Scotch *lascrom*, and very similar to the Peruvian *taclla*. The shape and structure of the loy suggests that at some time it was made entirely of wood. Estyn Evans is of opinion that, from very early times, the digging-stick, to which the loy is related, rather than the plough, was in general use in Ireland. The influence of the digging-stick may still be seen in the common use of the dibbler for planting potatoes.

---

[1] It is by no means excluded, that the method of cultivation on raised beds was known long before the introduction of the potato.
[2] Coles, William (1657). *Adam in Eden.*
[3] Evans, E. Estyn (1942). Op. cit. p. 113.

The preparation of the land to be used, which, in the early days was probably rough grassland or moss covered turf, was concurrent with the actual spring planting.

The lazy-bed is in use to-day, in an up-to-date guise as well as in its primitive simplicity: it is the latter which is here described. The first stage consisted in spreading such manure as was available, over a strip of land about 4 ft. wide and 20 yds. long; when the land is very wet, the strip may be as narrow as 2 ft. The length depended on the requirements of the household and the lay of the land.

The Irish peasant always had the manure of the milch cows which shared his cottage and, in many parts, of his pig also; whilst on the coastlands he made use then, as he does to-day, of the wrack or sea-weed.[1] In the latter part of the eighteenth century, and for long after, his store of dung was often denied him; the farmer from whom he hired his conacre land, frequently demanded this, which was credited against the rent, but used on the farmer's fields, and not on the peasant's potato patch.

The potato sets, in the old days, were placed on the manured turf; to-day the ridge is ploughed and the sets laid on the new upturned soil after it has been smoothed over. On either side of the strip, a ditch or furrow is opened, and the first spit is laid on the manure, face down, and thus covers the tuber sets. The ditch is from 2 to 3 ft. wide; and the turves removed from it are used as a further cover to the sets. As the young potato plants appear above ground, they are loosely covered with further turves removed from the trench.

Usually, this completed the cultivation, but to-day, where a higher standard of farming prevails, there is generally a further earthing up.

The lazy-bed culture, as opposed to the modern 'drill' method, has often been spoken of with contempt, especially by Young, but such is unmerited, where the cultivation is well done. That it is very open to neglect and abuse is certainly true. A complaint made by Young is illuminating: he says that in order to cultivate the potato in lazy-beds, nineteen-twentieths of all the manure of the country is employed to that end, and that much of the best ley-land is broken up for their formation. All of which shows that the potato dictated the arable policy of the countryside.

The advantages of the lazy-bed on wet, badly drained ground,

---

[1] An interesting development of this usage is to be found in the south of Co. Down. The potatoes are grown with sea-weed as manure, and well salted before being gathered. The salt is said to swell the tubers and so render them easily peeled by machinery, whilst their high humidity prevents them absorbing as much oil as do others, when fried. For these reasons, a large trade has sprung up between this part of Ireland and the mining districts of Wales where these potatoes are sold in the fish and chip shops. Evans, Estyn E. (1942). Op. cit. p. 151.

especially peat bogs, is not to be denied, though the relief afforded was limited to the bed itself, and did not lead to any thorough schemes of drainage and reclamation. By laying the seed on the manure and close to the two opposed grass surfaces of the bed, viz. that of the untouched bed and that of the first upturned turve derived from the trench, the manurial value of the herbage is retained and put at the disposal of the growing plant, whose roots attain a full run in the loosely packed soil. The trenches, which may be a couple of feet deep, provide excellent drainage. When the potatoes are removed, the bed, if it is on wet-lying land, may be used for next year's crop, whether potatoes or oats.

I have not been able to discover whether the lazy-bed was in existence in pre-potato days, or whether it was especially devised for the potato. If the latter is the case, then the similarity, amounting almost to identity, of the Irish method, and that which has been in use for untold ages in the great uplands of Peru and Bolivia, suggests an intriguing problem. Nor, as we have seen, is the similarity confined to the 'bed'; it is equally apparent in the tools used, the *taclla* and the *loy*; and in the social background, for both in Ireland and Peru the whole of the cultivation is, or, in the case of Ireland we must say 'was', a communal undertaking. I am not prepared to deny the possibility that we have here evidence of a transfer of culture, though I think it as unlikely in this case, as in that of the terracing of the mountain slopes in the Old World and in the Andes in the New; in the former, vines and corn were grown, in the latter, potatoes. I would rather suggest that these widely separated peoples were confronted with like problems and in so far as soil conditions and the tools at their disposal were concerned, with similar environments. Both peoples found identical solution to their problems, for both experienced the most insistent urge known to mankind, the necessity to produce essential food supplies, by the safest, easiest, and quickest means available.

The lazy-bed had other advantages: once the seed was planted and covered, it was immune to frost and, to a considerable extent, to the attack of man. If the household were raided, it was easy to trample down, or turn the cattle loose into the corn; but the narrow, raised lazy-bed, with its two protecting ditches, was a hindrance to man, and a substantial obstacle to cattle, who, moreover, have no particular liking for potato-tops. But, assuming that the farm was overrun by soldiers, or the hostile kerns of another clan, the young potato haulms, it is true, might be damaged; but if the raid took place early in the season, the seed tubers, still secure between the overlying turves, would throw up new haulms, or, if the raid was too late for that, the new crop, so far as it had grown, would remain hidden out of sight, after all trace of the tops had died away. By cultivating the potato in this manner, the peasant was assured both of his food and of his seed for the next year. Indeed, it is evident that Boyle's gardener overwintered both his ware and his seed in the potato-bed itself. It is probable that in disturbed times, the lazy-bed was left more or less untouched at harvest time, so that after removing such tubers as were required for the immediate food of the family, the bed was recovered with fresh mould from the trenches and, with the tubers left in it, was ready, without further cultivation, for the next season.[1] Several writers, without, unfortunately, any supporting references, have declared that by these means the native Irish may occasionally have succeeded in outwitting the soldiery during the Cromwellian wars of suppression.

Houghton[2] evidently was of this opinion, for in 1699 he writes how the potato was introduced to Ireland by Raleigh 'where it thrived well and to good purpose, for in three succeeding wars, when all the corn above ground was destroyed, this supported them; for the soldiers, unless they had dug up all the ground where they grew, and almost sifted it, could not extirpate them'. The three wars would presumably be those of the O'Neil rising, the Cromwellian campaign, and the campaign of William III. The following, written as late as 1789, probably refers to this practice: 'When all the corn above ground was destroyed, potatoes became the chief support of the people.'[3]

Even without the urge of secreting his potatoes from an enemy, the system, especially when carelessly handled, automatically assures the cultivator continuity of a crop of sorts, by means of the ground-keepers, and in such parts of the country where degenerative disease is at a minimum, no difficulty or harm to the seed stocks need occur by such haphazard cultivation. In any case, the potato lends itself to concealment far more readily than does a cereal crop; whilst corn needs to be stored in a dry place and in no great bulk, the potato will keep well under far less exacting conditions. It will survive burial for a year in a pit if reasonably dry, and adequate ventilation is ensured.

Harvesting was done by hand; the earth removed from the surface and thrown into the lateral trenches, the crop picked up, and the remaining soil returned to the trench. On suitable soils the whole procedure may to-day be carried out with a plough. The system in essence remains the same, although various adjustments and modifications are to be met with.

The normal procedure for storing the potato crop is by 'clamping'. The tubers are heaped in as dry a place as possible in the field, covered

---

[1] See the remarks of John Beale, chapter XII, p. 226.
[2] Houghton, J. (1699). *Collection of Letters*, 15 December (Bradley's edit. 1727), vol. II, p. 468.
[3] Adam, James (1789). *Practical Essays on Agriculture*, vol. II, p. 2.

with straw or fern, which, in turn, is covered with turves cut from around the base of the heap, a procedure which tends to keep the clamp drained.

Defence of the lazy-bed system does not mean that the tillage of the seventeenth century was satisfactory—indeed such was far from being the case; the people had for years been driven from their lands, the greater part of which remained as grass-land, and even when peace returned, the habit of 'creaghting', or retiring to the mountains with the stock for six months, must have discouraged any cultivation of the growing crops, so that Sir W. Brereton's[1] observation in 1635 that 'the soil was overtilled and wronged...slothfully and improvidently ordered, much impaired and yielding much less than if well husbanded', must be taken as a serious criticism. There is, however, reason to believe that the peaceful settlement which lasted till 1641 did, in some places, induce better and more successful agriculture. It was not the system which was to blame for bad tillage, but the social and economic consequences of a long drawn-out political and religious strife, which crippled agriculture and forced a people to accept the least common denominator, the potato, as the standard, both as regards the crops grown, and their cultivation.

It must be remembered that as a result of the wholesale confiscations, plantations, and other restrictive measures, the Irish farmers were driven out of all the best lands, and accommodated on the poorer hill-lands and bogs. The lazy-bed system seems, if not to have been developed to meet this particular political and economic development, to have been peculiarly well adapted to overcome the difficulties of cultivation on the bog-lands. Indeed, apart from extensive draining and reclamation, it is difficult to see how bog-cultivation could otherwise have been undertaken.

Although we have evidence that later in the seventeenth century the well-to-do English planters were growing the potato, it was the poorer Irish churls who, in an amazingly short time, adopted it, learnt to cultivate it on the lazy-bed system, and made it their staple food. This fact may account for its rapid spread, as well as the uniformity of method employed in its cultivation throughout the whole island.

The steady recovery of Ireland, both politically and economically, after the Cromwellian campaign, gathered momentum and showed itself in devious ways as the century progressed.

The Irish peasantry, painfully supported by the potato, still held their own on the land. An English land-owner in Wexford writes: 'But ye great support of the poor sorts of people is their Potatoes which are much used all over the country.'[2]

[1] Hore, Herbert Francis (1858). *Ulster J. Archaeology*, vol. VI, p. 109.
[2] Leigh, Robert (1684). An Account of Ye Towne of New Rosse. *J. Roy. Soc Antiq. Ireland*, 1858, vol. V, p. 466.

The woollen and linen industries supported a relatively large number of workers. In domestic service, in the homes of the English, the Irish native was once more ousting the English soldier workers, by reason of his persuasive manners and, above all, his modest requirements. In an anonymous play of 1675 the position is made abundantly clear:[1]

> Who unto Doggs do throw the children's bread
> And will use means to save an oxe or cow
> Of their owne, but their poor countreyman now
> They would have no need of, for he looks for cates
> They say: is too fine mouthed, and at the rates
> The Irish do can't live. Give them potatoes
> They'l boyle and roast; and stroke up their Mustachoes.
> This makes them Teige employ, 'cause he will serve
> For lesser than English can, so they must starve.
> Thus Irish fare, must serve the man that labours
> Which hath destroy'd many poor English Neighbours.

In the end, Teige, the Irish servant, succeeds in installing all his relatives into his master's household at the expense of the former English servants.

A recent historian[2] of the late seventeenth-century Irish life thinks that it was only by the poorest of the people that the potato had at that period been accepted as the chief article of their diet. I do not think that such a view is justified. In Ireland, the social distinctions within the non-gentry class, were neither so many nor so marked, as they were in England. The labourers, cottiers, small and larger farmers, formed the basis of, and accounted numerically for, about nine-tenths of Irish society; it was with them that the potato largely displaced the old dietary of meat, milk and oatmeal. Amongst the Anglo-Irish landlord class, and the richer townsmen, it may well have been, as our author suggests, only an extra in a dietary, which included an abundance of meat and poultry. 'None', says Stevens, 'but best sort of the inhabitants of great towns eat wheat or bread baked in an oven or ground in a mill; the meaner people content themselves with little bread but instead thereof eat potatoes which with sour milk is the chief article of diet.'[3]

The evidence is conflicting as to its use amongst the upper classes. 'The Irish gentlemen', says Le Gouz, writing in 1644, 'eat a great deal of meat and butter, but little bread, they drink milk and beer into which they put laurel leaves and eat bread baked in the English manner.'[4] Gouz is probably referring to the Anglo-Irish of the Pale. Out in the country we know of at least one estate, that of Robert Boyle,

---

[1] Mercer, William. Attributed to 1675. *The Moderate Cavalier.*
[2] MacLysaght (1939) ed. Op. cit. p. 180.
[3] Stevens, John. Op. cit. p. 159.
[4] Le Gouz, de la Boullaye (1644). Quoted from the Introduction to the *Journal of John Stevens*, p. lvii. Oxford, 1912.

where potatoes were being grown, and we have a letter written to him by his gardener, accompanying a bag of tubers for distribution amongst Boyle's friends of the Royal Society. The letter is dated 8 April 1663:[1]

I have according to your desire sent a box of Potato rootes; my care hath been to make choice of such, that are fit to set without cutting; for many, that have not small ones enough, are constrained to cut the great ones; but I doe not approve of that husbandry, neither do I make use of it, because when they are cut, the wormes doe feed on them, and so devouring the substance, the branch groweth the weaker, and the roote small: the ground which they thrive best in is a light sandy soyle, where ferns or briars do naturally grow. Their nature is not to grow fruitful in a rich soyle because they will spring forth many branches, and so encumber the ground, that they will have but small roots. You may cause them to be set a foot apart or something better, whole as they are, and there will be great encrease, and the branch will bring forth fruit which we call the Potato-apple, they are very good to pickle for winter and sallets, and also to preserve; I have tasted of many sorts of fruit, and have not eaten the like of that, they are to be gathered in September, before the first frost doth take them. If you are minded to have great store of small rootes which are fittest to set, you may cause them to lay down the branches; in the month before named, and cover them with earth three or four inches thick, and the branch of every joint will bring forth small rootes in so great number that the increase of one yard of ground will set twenty the next season, and it must be the care of the gardner to cover the ground where the rootes are with fearns or straw, halfe a foote thick and better at the beginning of the winter, otherwise the frost will destroy the rootes; and as they have occasion to dig out the great rootes, they may uncover the ground, and leave the small ones in the earth, and cover them as before and preserve the seed.

Now the season to dig the ground is April or May, but I hold it best the latter end of April, and when they dig the ground let them pick out as many as they can find small and great, and yet there will be enough for the next crop left; let the covering which they are covered withall be burried in the ground, and that is all the improvement that I doe bestow. I could speak in praise of the roote, what a good and profitable thing it is, and might be to a commonwealth, could it be generally experienced; as the inhabitants of your towne can manifest the truth of it, but I will be silent in speaking in the praise of them, knowing you are not ignorant of it.

The experiments which Boyle's highly intelligent gardener carried out, in order to increase his supply of seed potatoes, are the first of this kind recorded. His remark that it [the potato] might be of value to the commonwealth as it has proved in 'your towne' is of no less interest. Davidson thinks that by 'your towne' Lismore is meant, but Wilde argues in favour of its being Youghal, which, if true, would suggest that the potato was, at least generally, accepted in that neighbourhood, and

[1] Boyle, Robert (1663). *Royal Society Letter Book*, vol. I, p. 83.

adds weight to the evidence already adduced as to the place of its introduction. For neither of these towns can a very good case be made out. In 1636 the old Earl of Cork executed a septpartite indenture, under which Robert Boyle was given a residence in Mallow, and lands in Tipperary and Kildare. After the Great Earl's death in 1643, Robert inherited many scattered properties all over Ireland, but there is no mention amongst them of Youghal or Lismore. The gardener's reference to the use of the green potato fruits as a salad, so similar to that made by Evelyn, is surely the natural reaction of the wealthy cultivator who is looking for fresh dietetic luxuries, rather than for further sources of food in a newly introduced plant.

Another interesting record of the potato in the houses of the great, again, comes from the south. Two cavalier soldiers visited the home of the High Sheriff of Wexford, Mr Poer, sometime prior to Cromwell's descent on Ireland, and there supper is described:[1]

> And now for supper, the round board being spread:
> The van a dish of coddled Onions led;
> I' th' Body was a salted tail of sammon
> And in the Rear some rank Potatoes came in.

The meaning ascribed to the word 'rank', is doubtful: it could mean 'plentiful', or, not unlikely, 'lustful', thus recalling the supposed association of aphrodisiac qualities accredited originally to the sweet-potato, its literary and folklorist progenitor.

A shipwrecked Englishman has left us a charming picture of the household of a poor parson of the Church of Ireland in the year 1673:[2]

> What meat they had they did set before us—oat-cakes baked on a hot stove, and home brewed beer. On the following day the parson expressed his kindness in a more liberal way, and desir'd us to dine with him: we had but one dish for entertainment, and that so crammed with such varieties of God's creatures that this dish seem'd to me to be the first chapter of Genesis; there was such beef, mutton, goat's and kid's flesh, bacon, roots, etc., and all so confounded, that the best palate could not read what he did eat...this hodge-podge proceeded from custom more than from curiosity, and this was one point of their husbandry, to boyle all together to save charges.

In other words, our traveller was given a dish of the original Irish stew!

The use of the term 'roots' for what was obviously potatoes, is of interest, because it is evidence of the ignorance of the average Englishman concerning the new food, which later became as firmly established in the homes of the well-to-do as in those of the poor.

[1] Weaver, Thomas (1654). *Songs and Poems of Love and Drollery.*
[2] Jackson, R. Wyse (1941). *Scenes from Irish Clerical Life.* Limerick: Z. M. Ledger.

One dish, known as 'Colcannon', or 'Calecannon', was much favoured, and found its way to the tables of the upper classes in England. It was composed of a mash of potatoes and brussels sprouts, highly flavoured with ginger and the like, and then cooked with milk and an abundance of butter.[1]

But prosperity was not for long. Ireland as a result of the Revolution of 1688, suffered another set-back, almost as severe as that of 1649. The familiar scenes of a harassed countryside, and a hunted, half-starved peasantry, were re-enacted; agricultural prosperity was everywhere destroyed; famine once more stalked the land. The marvellous recuperative power of the Irish, based as it is on the fertility of the soil, might once more have restored her, at least to her former condition, had there not set in a new, and direful, political reorientation which, for the next hundred years, made all hope of recovery impossible.

A weapon appeared, forged in the fires of religious intolerance, tempered by fear and whetted by avarice, which was permanently to divide Irish and English, Catholic and Protestant, to hamstring every effort to develop the resources of the country and to degrade the masses of the people to a state comparable to that of the serfs in Russia.

The Penal Laws were introduced in 1690: their object was twofold: social and economic or, in the language of the apologists, spiritual and judicial. The former was to be attained by outlawing the Church, denying the Catholic Irish any part in the control of their own country, and excluding them as landed gentry, scholars, or teachers, from any opportunity of exercising influence, social or political, on the conduct of affairs, or the welfare of their people. By such means it was hoped to bring the mass of the people into the fold of the Anglican Church, and to break the spirit of the native Irish, once and for all. The latter object was to be obtained by the simple, and deliberate, policy of killing Irish industries. The first in large measure, failed, the second succeeded only too well. But, it may be asked, were not the two goals but one in reality, the desire for dominance?

> State Policy and Church Policy are conjoint
> But Janus faces looking diverse ways.[2]

The policy had not the excuse of being untried. In 1666, to please the English landlord interest, it will be remembered, an embargo on the importation of live cattle was created, and not finally abolished till 1758. The result in Ireland was to switch the cattle industry from the live market to that of provisions—a trade which prospered exceedingly,

---

[1] The *Oxford Dictionary* suggests that cole=cabbage, and cannon refers to the pounding of the mixture with a cannon-ball.
[2] Tennyson. *Queen Mary*, Act III, Sc. ii.

and led to the conversion of much of the south and west to an exclusive grazing industry. This, in turn, induced the landlords, in these parts, to insert a clause in their leases prohibiting tillage and confining the cottier to the smallest possible patch of land for his potatoes. Continual protest in and out of parliament was raised against these clauses. Swift's most pungent criticisms of the English misgovernment of Ireland were directed against their refusal to pass the Tillage Acts. But all was without effect. The people grew daily poorer, and their reliance on the potato ever greater. It was not till people lay dead in hundreds from starvation, as a result of the famine following the failure of the potato crop in 1728 that these clauses were declared nugatory. This was the first victory of the potato in the political field, the harbinger of greater ones to come.

It is difficult to understand how regulations, economically so retrograde, so wantonly cruel, and so inimical to the best interests, political and commercial, of England itself, could have won the unquestioning support of her statesmen and merchants. The reason may well be found in the fact that in the beginning of the eighteenth century there was little difference in the size of population of the two islands. A prosperous Ireland might, had she had the necessary coherence and organization, have put in the field armies numerically equal to, or even superior to, those which England at short notice could herself mobilize. Fear, has ever been the begetter of persecution.

However, the economic attack upon the people of Ireland was directed with skill and thoroughness. All ancient Irish land customs, especially those giving security of tenure to the cultivator, were swept away, except in Ulster, where they were replaced by a more rigid system, known as *Ulster right*, by which a tenant enjoyed, not only a reasonable security, but a right, sanctioned by popular convention, though not by law, to the monetary value of any improvements he may have introduced.

Other restrictive measures included a provision by which, should the eldest son of a Catholic landowner embrace the Protestant faith, he *ipso facto* became the owner of the estate, and his father the tenant. No Catholic was permitted to buy land, nor to rent land on a lease exceeding thirty-one years; nor must his rent be less than at least two-thirds of the improved yearly value, and whosoever should discover the same, could take the benefit of the lease. This latter measure prevented any Catholic from improving his holding. No Catholic could inherit land from a Protestant; nor could he accept any annuity arising from landed property. Perhaps the most ingenious measure was that which re-established gavelkind, against which the English authorities had waged war since Tudor times. From now on, a Catholic landowner must leave his property to be divided equally amongst all his sons, which effectually prevented any one becoming too powerful. These measures were intended, and indeed largely succeeded, in debasing the landowning class to the position of tenants and labourers.

Other laws were framed to prevent Catholics serving in the army or civil service, practising the law even as clerks, teaching in schools, trading in arms, or employing more than two apprentices, except it be in the hempen or flaxen manufactures.

The most formidable weapon in the armoury of the dominant power, however, was the new right, assumed by the English parliament, to by-pass the Dublin parliament, and to legislate on Irish affairs as affecting Ireland's trade, and not merely, as in the previous century, England's own attitude to Irish exports. A few of these measures may be mentioned. In 1695 laws were passed which led to the practical exclusion of West Indian exports to all Irish ports, unless they were first unloaded in England and consigned in English bottoms. This excluded such essential products as sugar, cotton, indigo, Jamaica wood and dyes and, last but not least, tobacco. The Irish peasant, as well as the town worker, had succumbed to tobacco, with as much zest as they had to the potato: it was consumed, as we have seen, communally from a short clay pipe passed from mouth to mouth as the family sat on the ground around the open hearth.

The immediate reaction to these measures was to kill most of Ireland's flourishing industries. More serious was the prohibition of all exports of woollens from Ireland (1698) to any country, for this was essentially a home industry, bringing in a weekly cash return. This matter of cash wages assumed a great importance in Ireland because the uncritical and hazardous reliance on the potato as the main food supply had, as will be shown later, the effect of neutralizing cash as the economic medium of social life amongst the cottiers and small farmers. Its further repercussions were to drive some 20,000 to 30,000 workers overseas, to foster and enlarge the smuggling trade, and to drive still more back to the countryside, to eke out a miserable living from over-rented patches of potato-land.

The trade in woollens was, however, by no means scotched. The home market remained largely in Irish hands, and the use of the home manufactured cloths was regarded as a patriotic duty. Smuggling of wool, both raw and spun, from the western coast, grew into an organized industry, officially connived at, and not seldom abetted by those in power. France welcomed this valuable source of raw material, which she manufactured into the finished article, and thereby fiercely competed with the woollens from England. Payments for the raw materials were made in hard cash at Brest and Rochelle, the ports of arrival. Later, when the drain on French bullion became serious, the goods were exchanged for French wines, brandy and silks,[1] a substitution which scarcely benefited the common folk.

As a sop for this forced gift to the British trade, Ireland's linen industry was to be given every encouragement. In truth it needed none, for it had already attained high standards in both quality and quantity, more especially since the Duke of Ormond had brought over 500 Huguenot families from the continent in 1668 to introduce new methods.

And so we draw at length to the end of the seventeenth century, which opened under the shadow of revolt and closed under a cloud of destitution and despair. The shackles which had been so securely fastened on the industries of the country during the last decade had so far checked, but not completely halted, progress. The workers displaced from industry had begun to trek back to the countryside to swell the growing army of the new poor. Many, who formerly had been large landowners, cultivators or graziers, had now, by reason of the confiscations, and the penal laws of the last half of the century, returned to the land to take their place alongside the peasantry they had in former times contemned. Already the poverty-ridden cottier class, driven by economic and political forces over which it had not the slightest control, had adopted the potato as its main source of food. From now on, this same prolific root was called on to maintain the greater part of the entire Irish nation. In the beginning of the century under review, the potato, a new type of food plant, a complete stranger to Europe, had reached the Irish people at a critical moment, without credentials or réclame, with no accredited representative to blaze its path, or acclaim its merits. Its arrival coincided with that moment in Irish history when destruction of the material basis of existence had reached its climax, and the amenities of life their nadir. The people, rich and poor alike, were in dire need of a foodstuff which would withstand the vagaries of nature and the malignity of man.

It took but a few years for the potato to prove that it was indeed capable of fulfilling both these functions. Arrived as a foundling, adopted as a favoured child, we see it slowly, but inevitably, dominating the shape of the economic life, first of the peasantry, then of the former landowning aristocracy, and later of the industrial workers. In this, its success was due at least as much to the economic blunders of the English government, as to its own intrinsic merits.

In the nineteenth century the subtle danger of this dominance to the common weal, was to be revealed in all its nakedness by a national calamity, unsurpassed even in Irish history.

The confiscations and repressive measures to which reference has been made were directed against the Catholic landed and middle classes,

---

[1] Froude, J. A. (edit. 1881). *The English in Ireland*, vol. I, p. 502.

and not against the churls or landworkers who remained where they had always lived. The Acts of Transplantation had expressly exempted from their provisions, ploughmen, husbandmen, labourers, artificers and others, whose property did not exceed £10—a sum which to-day might be estimated at £60—so long as they were not of those exempted from pardon by reason of their previous military record.

These cottiers who were left on the land had, at the best of times, neither enjoyed the sweets of liberty, nor the responsibilities of possessions. Little, if at all, removed from serfs, and having nothing to choose by a change of masters, they readily engaged themselves to the incoming English and Scottish settlers.

Thus the new dietary and the methods of its cultivation spread from the vanquished to the victors.

The incoming planters were generally in great need of labour to till their newly gotten estates, and it was from their Irish labourers that they learnt the value of the new food plant. It is true that both James I's and Cromwell's planters were supposed to bring labourers with them, but that part of the scheme, because of the difficulties of its execution, was in large measure evaded. This suggestion receives indirect support from the fact that in some parts of Ulster, where Scottish Presbyterians were in great force, they were not so dependent on native labour, and here the potato was not accepted so generally. Those sturdy fundamentalists objected that the potato was not mentioned in the Bible, and hence it was impious to grow it. A similar prejudice delayed its cultivation in the Western Highlands of Scotland.

CHAPTER XIII

The Potato in Ireland in the Eighteenth Century

The Penal Laws and trade restrictions were, as we have seen, introduced towards the end of the seventeenth century. The early decades of the eighteenth century saw their range extended and their disastrous influence disclosed. Three-quarters of a century had yet to elapse before this was patent to all those engaged in this incredible drama of spite and imbecility.

The first industry to be attacked, after the crippling of the woollen, was the flourishing brewing trade: this was easily shackled by the simple device of prohibiting imports of foreign hops (1731), and arranging that those brought over from England were not allowed the rebate, which they received when exported to foreign countries (1720). Imports of beer to England were hampered by high duties amounting to prohibition, whilst English beers were admitted to Ireland on payment of a tax of only 10 %. A similar prohibitive tariff on Irish imports to England was raised against woollen cloth, stuffs, tallow, candles and soap. The export of glass, a growing Irish industry, was prohibited absolutely (1746), and this was accompanied by another clause permitting imports of glass to Ireland only from England. The direct import of tobacco from the West Indies was forbidden, though it was permissible to bring it in from English ports. Indeed, the same rule had applied to all other exports from the West Indies since 1697. On the other hand, the cultivation of home-grown tobacco was encouraged.

For a time the linen trade was favoured, but in 1750 this, too, was attacked, and sail cloths and canvas were so taxed as no longer to be worth importing into England. In 1767 the finer linen industry was destroyed by the prohibition of imports of cambric and lawn to England. Irish traders were excluded from the Indian markets, all of which were under the control of the East India Company.

The English Parliament was not satisfied by the mere destruction of the export and external trade of Ireland: it also insisted on the lowest possible duties being imposed on English imports of consumption goods to Ireland, with the result, that the home markets were flooded with English goods. The Irish manufacturers, whose output was limited because of their exclusion from foreign markets, were unable to produce at prices which could compete with the English and so they, in their turn, were driven to the wall.

The above is but an outline sketch of a large and connected series of measures devised, and carried out, for the express purpose of crippling Irish industry, a task which succeeded only too well.

Trade restriction was not alone in bringing about the collapse of Irish economic life in the eighteenth century; as an auxiliary, there was that all too familiar social background, the insecurity of land tenure, the rack-renting by middlemen of farm-lands, which they took no steps to conserve, much less improve; the absenteeism of the landlord class; the payment from the Irish exchequer of large sums as pensions to political hangers-on, and annuities to royal mistresses, and the enforced maintenance of an alien Church which served barely a tenth of the population. All these played their part in inducing a nation-wide state of poverty and discontent. The more immediate result of all these forces was, as O'Brien has shown, to throw the burden of the support of the nation on to the cultivation of the soil. As a consequence, the major part of its products, and particularly the potato and lower grades of corn, were consumed at home, and the best quality corn sold to England.

Although there was no open rebellion to disrupt the social life of the country till the very end of the century, the political atmosphere, especially in its latter half, was anything but peaceful, on account of the more or less continuous agrarian unrest. This took the form of isolated attacks by young men of the cottier class on persons who, for one reason or another, were distasteful to the local Catholic nationalists. Secret groups pledged to maintain native rights, grew up all over the country, and were commonly known as Whiteboys. The houghing and slaughtering of cattle in the field, and the abduction of Protestant young women, and their forced marriage, according to Catholic rites, whether prior or subsequent to their violation, were characteristic features of their activity. Lawlessness had become endemic in a country where religious intolerance and economic repression, together with the vast smuggling trade which resulted therefrom, were the outstanding features of everyday life. Irishmen lived in a perverted social atmosphere, maintained at an economic level, probably lower, than that ever before attained in Western Europe. This level was like one of those rope bridges which spanned the narrow Andean canyons in the original home of the potato. Should its single strand give way, there was nothing to intervene between the unwary passenger and certain death. So with the potato: if that failed, the agrarian population were faced with no less a disaster—famine and death.

All the evidence goes to show that adverse social factors, such as excessive rents, the absence of cash wages, even the disturbance and eviction of the peasant cultivator, as a consequence of the spread of grazing, so far from checking, rather increased the dependence of the people on the potato. In 1703 it is reported of the people of Cork that they live 'mostly on sour milk and potatoes'.[1] Only when, much later, social conditions were improved by the introduction of home industries, and a small weekly cash return reached the family, did the dominance of the potato in the life of the people tend somewhat to recede, and some mitigation of the squalor which had characterized its supremacy, supervene.

Ireland was not then, or now, the only country to have drawn its economic strength almost entirely from the soil. It was only unique by reason of the fact, that neither the disposal of its products, nor the control of its imports, were in its own hands, and that its people had, to an ever increasing degree, become dependent on a single crop for their food.

The cultivation of the potato was itself not free from economic difficulties. The rents of potato patches, even on the bog, were invariably high, not to say exorbitant, a state of affairs which, as it could not impede the growing of what had now become an absolute necessity, merely succeeded in reducing the grower to the verge of bankruptcy.

One element in this process of bankrupting a nation, was the growth of the custom of 'conacre' letting. Just as there grew up amongst the Irish a distinctive method of cultivating the new food plant, so there emerged a special system of tenure designed to meet its requirements, dictated by the unique social conditions current in, and peculiar to, Ireland till the latter quarter of the nineteenth century. The potato being essentially a subsistence crop, each family needed a definite area, roughly an Irish acre[2] for six persons, on which to grow its supply of tubers. The majority of the people being of the cottier class, held little or no land of their own, saving, perhaps, a small patch of land around the hutment, and the grazing right for a cow. To grow sufficient potatoes, more land was needed, and the cottier must needs hire it. Hence the custom of 'conacre'.

Conacre was defined by the Devon Commission as meaning 'a contract by which the use of a small portion of land is sold for one or more crops but without creating the relation of landlord and tenant between the vendor and vendee, it being rather a licence to occupy than a demise'. The system was known under different names in different parts of Ireland: 'muck ground' in Clare, 'dairyland' in the south-east, 'stang' in Wexford, and 'quarter land' and 'root land' in other districts. Conacre letting, according to O'Brien,[3] was more frequent in Munster and Connaught than in the other two provinces. In Ulster it was only employed for potato culture, in the other provinces flax, oats and potatoes might be raised and the land retained for successive years. I have not succeeded

---

[1] *The Journal of Francis Rogers* (1703), p. 197 (Bruce Ingram, edit.). Constable, 1936.
[2] An Irish acre is equivalent to 1·6 statute acre.
[3] O'Brien, G. (1921). *Econ. Hist. of Ireland, from the Union to the Famine*, p. 11. Longmans.

in discovering when the system of conacre was first introduced, but it was certainly in full use in the eighteenth and nineteenth centuries, and was general up till, and for some time after, the Great Famine. In 1846, of the 1,237,441 statute acres under potatoes, 132,444 acres were grown as conacre.[1] To-day conacre is still in use in some parts of Ireland, especially in the west. The spread of tenant proprietorship has to a great extent met the demand for potato land, which conacre lettings previously satisfied.

In general, the cottier entered into a contract with his nearest farmer neighbour, himself a tenant of some great landowner, on the following terms. The farmer provided the land, tilled it, and left it ready for sowing; the cottier accepted it for a period of eleven months only, thus disavowing any claim for further continuity in the usure of the land. The cottier sowed, raised and removed his crop within the agreed period. If the cottier supplied the manure, then he might pay nothing for the use of the land, or he might arrange to take it a further year on payment; if, however, he found nothing but his own potato seed, he agreed to pay a rent which, in the nineteenth century, ranged from about £7 to £10 per annum per Irish acre, though on rich leys it might be as much as £14. He further agreed to discharge that debt by his personal labour: this was valued invariably at the lowest market price. The farmer made sure of his rent by insisting on payment before the potatoes were removed. The conacre system lent itself to abuse, partly because of the custom of discharging the rent by cheap labour, but also because the rentals were artificially raised by middlemen, who speculated in conacre. The cottier gambled even more desperately over the deal: in his case the stakes were the lives of himself and his family and they were heavily weighted. If he won, he secured his food requirements for the year, but had no cash reserve other than that which resulted from the sale of the pig which shared the potatoes; if he lost, it was not only a shortage of essential food that he suffered, but all such cash resources as he might have commanded and, not seldom, his home itself. Whether it was the hiring of conacre, the tenancy of a small-holding or a few bare acres, the small man, commanding neither capital nor liquid cash, generally had a rough deal.

An anonymous writer, probably Judge Robert Hellen, has given us a picture of the relation of landlord and tenant which is worthy of a pre-exilic Hebrew prophet:[2]

There is indeed no legal, but there is real Vassalage: the Lord is a poor Tyrant and the Peasant a poorer Slave. Hear me Ali, the Lord seldom parcels

[1] Anon. (1847). The Yield of Irish Tillage Crops. *J. Dept. of Agric. and Tech. Inst., Ireland*, vol. XXI (reprinted 1921).
[2] Anon. (1757). Letters from an Armenian in Ireland to his friends at Tresibond. Lond. B.M. 8145.66.6.

out his land among the cultivaters of it; his ample estate is divided into a few parts, and hired by a few who are puny lords and servile imitators of him; each of these subdivides his part, and sets it to as many more; all these have a profit from it, proportionable to their degrees of subordination and quantities of land; at last it is broken into small portions among the poor peasants, whose sweat is to support the idleness, perhaps, of twenty superiors; while all the poor remains of their labour hardly yield bread for themselves. Their food is barely sufficient to support the day's fatigue, and their habitations will not defend from rain the straw on which they repose; while their unkind lords are wasting life in riot and luxury regardless of the hand that supplies them with the means. Such is the condition of more than two third parts of the immediate land-holders in this Kingdom.

It was common knowledge that there was nothing between the cottier and famine, than the potato he grew on his grossly over-rented allotment.

What galled the peasantry most was the imposition of tithe on the potato; it was resented for a variety of reasons. Because the potato was a new crop, its legality was in question. Because its proceeds went to support an alien Church and, being collected by a proctor, who took a commission of as much as 2s. in the pound from the cottier, it was oppressive. By inducing them to render payment on oath by bonds, and thus submit themselves as debtors, it held them at the mercy of those they had little reason to trust. A common trick was to value the crop on the basis of a famine year, and the yield on one of plenty: a case was quoted in the Houses of Parliament in 1783 where, by this device, as much as £2. 18s. 6d. was levied as tithe, on an acre of potatoes. Grattan remarks: 'the clergyman who in rating his parishioners takes advantage of a famine and brings up as it were the rear of divine vengeance, becomes in his own person the last scourge of the countryman.'[1]

Young[2] speaking of proctors, 'who are civil to gentlemen, but exceedingly cruel to the poor', describes them in another passage as 'vultures ready to strip and skin the peasant'. Those who could take a wider view, hated the tithe, because much of it left the country to support absentee clergymen, and not least because in many livings the tithes were canted, i.e. put up for auction to the highest bidder. But possibly most resentment was felt because tithe was not collected from grass-lands, owing to the opposition of the wealthy graziers and powerful landowners, yet grass-lands were unquestionably liable to tithe and were not freed by Act of Parliament until 1800.

An official report published in 1831[3] was devoted to the question of tithes, from which it appears that the potato was not tithed uniformly.

[1] *Grattan's Speeches* (1822), vol. II, p. 39.
[2] Young, A. (1780). *Tour in Ireland*, vol. I, p. 181.
[3] Report of Select Committee of the House of Lords on the Collection and Payment of Tithes in Ireland, 1831–2.

Throughout the counties of Clare, Limerick, Tipperary, Kerry, Cork, Waterford, Wexford, Carlow, Kilkenny and Queen's County, the southern half of Wicklow, the southern sixth of King's County, that is, the whole of the south, the potato was liable to tithe. The whole of Connaught was exempt, and all Ulster except the entire county of Londonderry and the northern half of Donegal. In general, plots of a statute acre or less, and garden plots, were exempted, but this was not always so. In the worst days of the tithe farmer, the highest limit suffered to go free was a quarter of an Irish acre. The average tithe, collected in the seven years prior to 1821, was 6s. 8d. per statute acre, which the church authorities argued was less than half of that to which they were strictly entitled. Other authorities have pointed out that they were, in exceptional cases, as high as 32s. per acre.[1] The Commutation Act, which went far to remedy some of the abuses, still left the burden to be borne by the tenant. The manner of the payment by the cottiers was peculiar. As the Archdeacon of Armagh remarked, giving evidence before the Commission, both the farmer, from whom the cottier hires his conacre, and the cottier himself, compete to pay the tithe direct to the incumbent. The cottier because he thinks that by pleading poverty he can make the better bargain, and moreover get a year's credit; and the farmer because he can recover the tithe, and something in addition, from his tenant, when he parcels out the total sum paid on his holding, amongst the small areas he sublets. He further never allowed the potatoes to be removed from the land till the cottier had paid both his rent and his tithe. In practice, the Church generally dealt with the farmer, because it not only saved the incumbent trouble, but because the conacre plots were so often closely packed together with little or nothing to distinguish one from another. The question of the legality of the tithe on the potato was discussed, and it was stated on behalf of the Church that the potato crop was legally subject to tithe, and its exemption was alone due to the forbearance and indulgence of the clergy.

In 1838 the tithe was converted to a rent charge, adjusted every seven years, payable by the owners but recoverable in the rent. With the disestablishment of the Church in 1871, the tithe was finally liquidated.

Grattan[2] made the position absolutely clear in regard to the potato and its effects on the workers, in a speech in the Dublin House of Commons, delivered on 28 October 1783:

As to potatoes, the clergyman ought not to proceed with reference to the produce, but the price of labour; in the parts of which I have been speaking,

[1] O'Brien, G. (1918) *Economic History of Ireland in the Eighteenth Century*, p. 148.
[2] *Grattan's Speeches*, vol. I, p. 181.

the price of labour is not more than 5*d*. a day the year round; that is, £6. 4*s*. 0*d*. the year, supposing the labourer to work every day but Sunday; making an allowance for sickness, broken weather, and holidays, you should strike off more than a sixth; he has not, in fact, then more than £5 a year by his labour; his family average about five persons, nearer six, of whom the wife may make something by spinning (in these parts of the country there are considerable manufactories). Five Pounds a year, with the wife's small earnings, is the capital to support such a family, and pay rent and hearth-money, and, in some cases of illegal exaction, smoke-money to the parson.[1] When a gentleman of the Church of Ireland comes to a peasant so circumstanced, and demands 12*s*. or 16*s*. an acre for tithe of potatoes, he demanded a child's provision; he exacts contribution from a pauper, he gleans from wretchedness, he leases from penury; he fattens on hunger, raggedness, and destitution.

In less rhetorical terms, a similar indictment of tithe, more particularly that on the potato plots of the peasants, was made by Thomas Reid,[2] one of the most reliable writers of the early nineteenth century on the problems of Ireland.

It is of interest to note that it was not the confiscation by enclosure, of the relatively few small commons remaining, which gave rise to the Whiteboy movement in 1760, but the harshness and chicanery employed in the collection of the tithe on the potato, and the resentment felt in Munster at the conversion of tillage, which included the potato patches of the poor, to grazings. It was not the first time in history in which the potato, as such, made its entry on the political stage but, as in 1728, its role was essentially a social-economic one.

The degree to which the potato had come to dominate Irish life may be gauged from the writings of contemporary authorities both political and agricultural.

Swift[3] writes in 1727:

My heart is too heavy to continue this journey longer, for it is manifest that whatever stranger took such a journey would be apt to think himself travelling in Lapland or Iceland rather than in a country so favoured by nature as ours. The miserable dress and diet and dwelling of the people, the families of farmers who pay great rents living in filth and nastiness upon buttermilk and potatoes, not a shoe or stocking to their feet, or a house so convenient as an English hog-sty to receive them.

The great danger to the people which their dependence on a single food entailed, is illustrated by the disaster which followed on the failure

---

[1] Smoke-money was the colloquial term for a tithe on turves, which was entirely illegal, but was quite commonly demanded by the collectors.

[2] Reid, Thomas (1823). *Travels in Ireland*, p. 335.

[3] Swift, J. (1727–8). *Short View of the State of Ireland* (Temple Scott edit.), vol. VII, p. 89.

of the oat crop in 1727. Thus, Archbishop Boulter of Armagh,[1] in a letter supporting the Tillage Bill, says:

Last year the dearness of corn was such that thousands of families quitted their habitations to seek bread elsewhere, and many hundreds perished; this year the poor had consumed their potatoes, which is their winter subsistence, near two months sooner than ordinary, and are already, through dearness of corn, in that want, that in some places they begin already to quit their habitations.

This famine, which was the occasion of Swift's 'Modest proposal' (1729), a satirical essay, in which he suggests that Irish children should be fatted and eaten, thus relieving the burden to their parents and their country, has a special interest inasmuch as it was not the potato which failed, but it was for want of potatoes that the people starved. It was the custom to tide over the 'blue' months between the exhaustion of the previous year's store of potatoes, and the raising of the new potato crop, by using greater quantities of oatmeal. Although oats were of far less importance than the potato in the dietary of the masses, yet some were eaten throughout the whole year in all but the poorest homes. If the oat crop failed the people naturally fell back on their store of potatoes. On this occasion, these latter were consumed two or three months too early, thus leaving a gap of something like five months entirely unprovided for.

Swift tells how mothers with three to four children at their skirts, are to be seen wandering about the roads in town and country, ragged and starving. The essay, with its bizarre suggestion elaborated with vitriolic humour, is almost too painful to be read, but when the bitterness of his sarcasm has been discounted, it is only too obvious that he bases his fantasy on solid fact, and rational speculation. He estimates that the population is one and a half millions; that of them, 200,000 are women of child-bearing age, and that only 30,000 of them are in any proper sense self-supporting. He also makes the interesting statement that amongst the tenantry 'money is a thing unknown'. This, as we shall see later, was a sequel of the dominance of the potato in the economy of the people, and persisted till some time after the Great Famine.

November of 1739 witnessed one of the severest frosts that Ireland has ever experienced. It destroyed the potatoes, both in field and clamp, and produced widespread famine, and fever in the following year, a record of which remains to this day, in the obelisk surmounting Killiney Hill, which bears the following inscription:

Last year being hard with the poor, the wall around these hills and this were erected by John Mapas, Esq., January 1742.[2]

---

[1] Boulter, Hugh, Abp. Armagh (1770). *Letters*, vol. I, p. 226.
[2] Ball, F. E. (1902). *History County Dublin*, p. 1.

It is said that on this occasion one-fifth of the population perished;[1] a more conservative estimate was 300,000.[2]

The peculiar relation between oats and potatoes in the life of the people is commented on by Varley:[3]

Oats being so general a crop in Ireland, one might expect them to be very cheap; but, however, though a great many are grown, there is also a great consumption as all the poor in general eat no sort of bread except that made of oats; and the time of the year when potatoes are out of season [May, June and July] their whole living is oat bread and buttermilk, but so long as potatoes are good they supply the place of bread: therefore oats bear a better price than could be expected, being so general a crop.

The three months of the year referred to, is the maximum period of time which might elapse between the exhaustion of the last year's crop, and the raising of the season's early varieties where such were grown. In Ulster the name given to July was the 'blue month', for the same reason.[4]

Bishop Berkeley, when he asks[5] 'Whether it is possible the country should be well improved, while one half is exported and our labourers live on potatoes', and 'whether the bulk of our Irish natives are not kept from thriving by that cynical content in dirt and beggary which they possess to a degree beyond any other people in Christendom', tends to discount the importance of the oat, whilst clearly envisaging the dangers that lay ahead.

Of all the writers on eighteenth-century Ireland, none can compare with the famous agriculturist, Arthur Young, in the extent of his technical knowledge, his width of vision, his sense of statesmanship, or the honesty of his convictions. Of the man himself, more will be said in a later chapter; here we are concerned with his tour through Ireland, which he made in the years 1776–9.[6]

As he toured the country, Young was not content merely to chronicle where the intelligent use of new methods had induced progress, nor where the old slovenly habits were impeding it. In Ireland, as in his tours both in England, and France, Young always had his finger on the pulse of the people's welfare. If he rejoiced in the company of the great, and described, in detail, their stately mansions and collections of art, he was equally at pains to depict the life of the poor and to voice their grievances. To-day, reflecting on the condition of the 'poor', as he

[1] O'Rourke, J. (1875). *The History of the Great Famine*, p. 24.
[2] Wilde, W. R. (1858). *Proc. Roy. Ir. Acad.* vol. VI, pp. 356–69.
[3] Varley, C. (1770). *A New System of Husbandry*, vol. III, p. 73.
[4] Evans, E. Estyn (1942). Op. cit. p. 77.
[5] *The Querist* (1753), Nos. 19 and 169. 1735.
[6] Young, A. (1780). *A Tour in Ireland*. London.

describes it, one might be inclined to regard his condemnations as lacking in vigour, but when one remembers that Young was himself a country squire, writing in the last quarter of the eighteenth century, at a time when the privileges of the nobility and landed gentry of England were at their zenith, it must be conceded that his protests on behalf of the labourer, and the criticisms of his own class, display an exceptionally high standard of integrity and courage.

As to the prevalence of the potato as the food of the people, a few examples from different parts of the country will suffice, if one keeps in mind that similar descriptions are recorded by Young at practically every spot he visits.

Ballynogh, County Cavan. 'The poor live on potatoes and milk, it is their regular diet, very little oat bread being used, and no flesh meat at all except on Easter Sunday and Xmas Day. Their Potatoes last them through the year; all winter long, only potatoes and salt.'

Furness, County Leitrim. 'In respect of labour, every farmer has as many cottiers as ploughs, whom they pay with a cabin and one acre of potatoes, reckoned at 30s.; and a cow keep through the year, 30s. more. Every cabin has one or more cows, a pig and some poultry. Their circumstances just the same as 20 years ago. Their food, potatoes and milk for nine months of the year: the other times wheaten bread and as much butter as the cow gives. They like the potato fare best. Some have herrings; and others 6s. to 10s. worth of beef at Xmas. Sell their poultry, but many eat their pig. The sale of the fowls brings a few pounds of flax for spinning, most of them having some of that employment.'

Gloster, King's County. 'Their food is potatoes and milk for ten months, and potatoes and salt the remaining two; they have however a little butter.' In this district Young records that a barrel of potatoes containing 280 lb. will last a family of five persons a week, or 8 lb. per individual per day; as three of the family would have been children, the quantity eaten by an adult man must have been in the neighbourhood of 12 lb. a day.

Armagh, Ulster. 'Their food principally potatoes and oatmeal, very little meat...many of them live very poorly, sometimes having for three months only potato, salt and water.'

Shaens Castle, Antrim. 'They [the weavers] are by no means in grand circumstances but much distressed by every demand in respect to living: their diet is milk, potatoes, and oat bread; very little butter as they sell what they make. A family consisting of a man, his wife and four children, will eat 3 bushels of potatoes, and 20 lb. weight of oatmeal a week.'

Farnham, County Cavan. 'Potatoes and milk and butter are his food, and oaten bread when the potatoes are not in season; scarce any flesh meat among the poor.'

Wexford. Where the economic conditions were, as here, more favour-able, the dietary was mixed and more generous. 'The poor have all barley bread and pork and herrings etc. and potatoes.'

Needen on the Kenmare, County Kerry. 'Their food in summer potatoes and milk; but in spring they have only potatoes and water, sometimes they have herrings and sprats. They never eat salmon.'

Newry, County Down. Young observes that the 'manufacturers', i.e.the weavers and their families as opposed to the labourers, live on a more varied and better diet. 'They do not live entirely on them [potatoes], but have oatmeal, oaten bread and sometimes flesh meat, once or twice a week.' The 'manufacturers' could earn 9s., his wife about 1s. 2d., and his daughter another 9d. per week; the labourer but 3s. 6d. in winter, and 4s. in summer. Here, at least, it was not the potato which reduced the standard of living, but grinding poverty which tied them to the potato standard.

These examples will suffice to show how universal was the dominance of the potato in the people's dietary, in all parts of the island. Where there is variation, it is due to the proximity of sea or river, which allowed of a certain amount of fish. In general, the whole countryside, whether it be the farmers, both large and small, or the working cottiers, they were all alike poor. In the few cases where farmers were prosperous, the labourers were neither better off nor better fed; in fact, the reverse was often the case, especially in the grazing districts.

In the *Complete Farmer* (3rd ed. 1777), a Mr Irwin is quoted as saying, that in time back the peasants were better off, and potatoes not so much used. Now, with labour at 4d.–5d. per day, and rents increased, it had become their staple support, a tendency which reached its climax in the next century.

Young was greatly impressed by the rich grazing lands of Limerick, and gives us the following picture of the district around Castle Oliver:

Great quantities of flax sown by all the poor and little farmers, which is spun in the country, and a good deal of bandle cloth made of it. This and pigs are the great articles of profit here; they keep great numbers, yet the poor in this rich tract of the country are very badly off. Land is so valuable, that all along as I came from Bruff, their cabins are generally in the road ditch, and numbers of them without the least garden; the potatoe land being assigned them upon the farm where it suits the farmer best. The price they pay is very great, from £4 to £5 an acre with a cabin; and for the grass of a cow, 40s. to 45s. They are if anything worse off than they were twenty years ago. A cabin, an acre of land, at 40s., and the grass of two cows, the recompense of the year's labour: but are paid in different places by an acre of grass for potatoes at £5. Those who do not get milk to their potatoes, eat mustard with them, raising the seed for the purpose. The population of the country increases exceedingly, but most in the higher lands; new cabins are building everywhere.

A contemporary writer,[1] commenting on much the same theme, dilates on the importance of attempting to improve the potato itself, if the poor are to be fed:

For a poor labourer in that ill-fated country is driven to seek his sole refuge for subsistence in this root, for the inexorable imposition of a hard-hearted landlord (sorry I am to have it to say, too many of them grind the poor; but hope it will not be long the case) who thinks he cannot get too much out of the persons, or purses, of his dependents, and who hath so inverted the old custom, that a hewer of wood and a drawer of water (and many of these perhaps descendants of former proprietors) can afford himself but a miserable scanty platter of potatoes, seasoned with a palatable grain of salt, and watered down with a draught from the rivulet to support the fatigue of thirteen hours (statute quantity) of unceasing labour, whilst in his ancient mansion-house, or in his elegant gardens, are well laid out closes, or refreshing bog-holes.[2]

Some light on the relation between the use of the potato, and the economic life of the peasant, may be gleaned from the information Young gathered on his tours concerning the home-life of the poor, in fifty-one different localities distributed throughout the four provinces. In all, he records that the potato was the mainstay, and often the sole food, of the family, except for a modicum of oatmeal and milk. Fortunately, he rarely failed to note whether the conditions of the poor were better, or worse, than they had been twenty years prior to his visit. Without exception, the conditions under which the small farmers, cottiers, and labourers lived, were deplorable; indeed, judged by the standards of to-day, they were impossible. To Young it was a question of degree. In a few places, the rural population were contented and relatively happy, however poor and unhygienic their homes; in others, they were living on a starvation basis. Of the fifty-one places visited, in eleven there had been no improvement in the living conditions during the last twenty years, which implies that they were at that time at a very low level; in fourteen there had been a deterioration, and in twenty-six an improvement during the same period. Improvements were noted in 45% of cases in the north, 44% in Munster, 64% in Leinster, and 75% in Connaught. This, of course, does not tell one much, unless one knew what the previous conditions were like. The distribution of the localities which had deteriorated is, perhaps, more instructive, because for a cottier's condition to have been worse than it was in the 1750's, suggests some fresh factor at work. Deterioration occurred in 20% of the places visited in the north, 33% of those in Munster, 21% of those in Leinster, and 25% of those in Connaught. In view of the small numbers involved,

---

[1] *The Complete Farmer or Dictionary of Husbandry* (1st edit. 1766; 3rd edit. 1777), article 'Potato'.

[2] I have been unable to discover what the author means by '*refreshing* bog-holes'.

one cannot say more than that the extent of the deterioration in the standard of living was greater in Munster than elsewhere. The decline in the well-being of the agricultural folk of that province coincides with the extension of grazing which had occurred in the first half of the century.

Improvements in the condition of peasant life were recorded in 45 % of the localities recorded in the north, 39 % of Munster, 57 % of Leinster, and 75% of Connaught. Again, we must not try to deduce too much from these figures, because often the improvement is trivial, and in any case the numbers involved are too few. That Munster should be lowest in the list may again be attributed to the ill effects of the grazing industry. That Connaught should be highest may be due to several factors: the woollen industry was beginning to infiltrate into the province, the people were making use of their own fisheries, and there was much less interference from the government, and less opportunity for Catholic-Protestant feuds here than elsewhere in Ireland.

Taking the country as a whole, out of the twenty-six localities where improvements are recorded, twelve, or 46 %, can be directly correlated with the introduction of the linen or woollen industries into the home; two only, were due to improved agricultural methods. Significant also, is the fact that wherever an improving landlord is resident and active, a marked improvement in the social condition of the peasantry follows: such accounts for four, or 15 %, of the improved localities observed. In general, the improvement in social conditions expresses itself by the use of a rather more varied diet, and especially by the introduction of meat, and occasionally by that of poultry. Neither wheaten bread, nor manufactured commodity articles, had as yet made their way into the cottier's home. Better clothing followed in the wake of better food. In a couple of cases only, was the housing materially improved.

On the social repercussions of a potato diet Young[1] has no misgivings:

Is it, or is it not a matter of consequence, for the great body of the people of a country, to subsist upon that species of food which is produced in the greatest quantity by the smallest space of land? One need only to state, in order to answer the question. It certainly is an object of the highest consequence, what in this respect is the comparison between wheat or cheese, or meat and potatoes?

Young's experience in Ireland did much to modify his views on the value of the potato. In 1771, five years before this visit, he did not regard it seriously as a food for men, but advised the farmers of Yorkshire that the potato should be grown as a field crop of an acre or more in extent, for consumption on the farm by the cows and pigs. In his

[1] Young, A. (1780). *A Tour in Ireland,* vol. II, p. 24.

writings subsequent to the Irish visit, he constantly preached its value as a staple food for men, and particularly for 'the labouring poor'.

During the eighteenth century, the political stage was occupied, in the main, with the old problems: the prerogative of the English, and the claims of the Irish parliaments, both inseparably bound up with the jealousies of Catholic and Protestant, and the not unreasonable fear of Irish participation in the Jacobite adventures. To these there was now added another and even more bitter source of conflict: that between the Presbyterian Scots and the Established Church of Ireland. These matters are relevant here, only so far as they affected the general welfare of the people, and are reflected in their dietary. That they were so related, is obvious. Anti-Catholic discrimination in the matter of ownership of land, and the raising of mortgages, led cultivators to adopt grazing; this, in due course, brought about the displacement of the cottier class, who were driven to the mountains where perforce they lived almost exclusively on potatoes. The Presbyterian-Anglican jealousies drove vast numbers of Ulster's most energetic sons to emigrate to America, leaving the homeland the poorer, spiritually as well as industrially and agriculturally. The loss of numbers was of little moment in those days of rapid increase of population; the loss of men of vigour and enterprise was of far greater importance.

But to the international relations between England and Ireland, rather than to the pseudo-religious jealousies, must be assigned the greater portion of the blame for the economic distress of the period. It was the economic weapon forged by the English manufacturers against Irish industry, which forced ever increasing numbers out of the crafts back to the land. There, without capital, or knowledge of improved methods, they went to swell the army of the poor, already dependent for their barest livelihood on what they could wrench from their patch of potato-land. But, it may be asked, why should they have been obliged to stake the chances of their very existence on the potato? There were several reasons, but the most important were that the tenant was responsible for the erection and maintenance of buildings, fences, and the payment of tithe, in addition to the payment of an exorbitant rent. Under such conditions, it was essential that he should grow a crop which could be cultivated cheaply, would give him the greatest return per acre, and make no demand on barns and the like, for storage. The potato was the obvious solution to his problem.

The problem, so far as it concerned the relations of landlord and tenant and the national welfare, was examined dispassionately by Young; his comments, like those on the economic conditions of the Irish cottier are invaluable, derived as they are from first-hand knowledge and personal observation. He had convinced himself that at bottom, the misery of the peasantry and the ruin of many great landlords, had resulted from a land policy which had admitted of the interjection of a middleman, or a series of them, between landowner and tenant, a view confirmed recently.[1] This system had resulted in the ultimate tenant, the cottier, having neither security of tenure nor fixity of rent, being but a tenant at will, and in his paying often as much in petty, and degrading services, valued at much below cost, to his middleman landlord, as he did in rent. A further consequence was that intermediate tenant-landlords made no improvements to land or buildings, leaving the same to their tenants, who had neither the capital, nor the inducement of security, to attempt them. Young's opinion of the average middleman-landlord is expressed in picturesque language. He had no sympathy for these hard-drinking squireens, with their wretched packs of foxhounds: 'surrounded by their little under-tenants, they prove the most oppressive species of tyrant that ever lent assistance to the destruction of a country.' Some of the improving landlords having taken over control of their own estates, let direct to the cottier tenants, a policy which, he maintained, should be followed throughout Ireland. 'If such a landlord finds himself obliged to distrain for his rent' his tenant's stock, says Young, he 'finds abundantly more valuable than the laced hat, hounds and pistol of the gentleman jobber, from whom he is more likely in such case to receive a *message* than a remittance.'[2]

As the small tenant-farmer had practically no capital by which to finance his farm, Young explains that he can only provide for his labour by letting off some of his land to cottiers for potato-land [conacre], in return for their labour, whilst he grazes their cows at so much a head. Meanwhile, he and his family live at the lowest possible level, converting his poultry, eggs and pigs into cash. Young then proceeds to give some sound advice to the landlord, insisting on absolute honesty and justice in his dealings with the cottier, to whom he advises a maximum of 4 acres [= 6 statute acres].

Young next discusses the conditions of the 'labouring poor', i.e. the cottiers. He accepts as axiomatic that they live almost exclusively on potatoes, and their 'garden' is just a potato patch. The size of such a tenement, he tells us, varies from ½ to 1½ acres, and on it the cottier either finds or builds himself a cabin. For this accommodation the average rent is £1. 13s.; he further arranges for the 'keep' of a cow, for which he pays his immediate landlord—usually a small farmer—about £1. 12s. per annum. These two basic sums the cottier pays for in labour at about 6d. per day, and master and man keep record of such by the ancient method of tally and notch. In many cases the patch of ground

---

[1] Maxwell, Constantia (1940). *Country and Town in Ireland under the Georges*, p. 116. Harrap.   [2] Young, A. (1780). Op. cit. vol. II, p. 15.

around the cabin was not large enough for the family requirements. In the case of cabin-dwellers in the towns, and squatters by the roadside, the occupiers had no land at all; all such persons hired further potato-land as conacre. Young studied the conditions under which hiring of conacre-land was carried on, and found the rents varied from £4. 5s. to £8 throughout the land, per Irish acre, with an average of £5. 10s. 2d. or £3. 8s. 6d. per statute acre and a crop estimated at 6½ tons per statute acre. 'I think', says Young, '£5. 10s. 2d. for liberty to plant a crop so beneficial to the land as potatoes, a very extravagant rent, and by no means upon a fair level with the other circumstances of the poor.' When one remembers that the rent demanded is equivalent, in to-day's money, to a least £12 per statute acre, one cannot but agree with Young, though he seems to have overlooked the fact that such exorbitant rents are the natural sequence of a system in which nearly every individual in the kingdom demands the same thing, at the same time, for the same purpose, namely the production of their major source of nourishment and their only defence against famine.

Next, Young turns to the problem of the people's dietary, that is, to the consideration of the use and value of the potato. It is reproduced here in full, not merely because of its intrinsic interest, or as a contemporary picture of Irish rural life in the last quarter of the eighteenth century, but because Young examines the problem from a philosophic angle, reaching conclusions which appeared adequate for his time, but which, from the vantage point of to-day, 160 years later, can be seen to be superficial and misleading.

The food of the common Irish, potatoes and milk, have been produced more than once as an instance of extreme poverty of the country, but this I believe is an opinion embraced with more alacrity than reflection. I have heard it stigmatized as being unhealthy, and not sufficiently nourishing for the support of hard labour, but this opinion is very amazing in a country, many of whose poor people are as athletic in their form, as robust, and as capable of enduring labour as any upon earth. The idleness seen among many when working for those who oppress them is a very contrast to the vigour and activity with which the same people work when themselves alone reap the benefits of their labour. To what country must we have recourse for a stronger instance than lime carried by little miserable mountaineers thirty miles on horses back to the foot of their hills, and up the steeps on their own. When I see the people of a country in spite of political oppression with well formed vigorous bodies, and their cottages swarming with children; when I see their men athletic, and their women beautiful, I know not how to believe them subsisting on an unwholesome food.

At the same time, however, that both reason and observation convince me of the justice of these remarks, I will candidly allow that I have seen such an excess in the laziness of great numbers, even when working for themselves, and such an apparent weakness in their exertions when encouraged to work, that I have had my doubts of the heartiness of their food. But here arise fresh difficulties, were their food ever so nourishing I can easily conceive an habitual inactivity of exertion would give them an air of debility compared with a more industrious people. Though my residence in Ireland was not long enough to become a perfect master of the question, yet I have employed from twenty to fifty men for several months, and found their habitual laziness or weakness so great, whether working by measure or by day, that I am absolutely convinced 1s. 6d. and even 2s. a day in Suffolk or Hertfordshire much cheaper than sixpence halfpenny at Mitchelstown: It would not be fair to consider this as a representation of the kingdom, that place being remarkably backward in every species of industry and improvement; but I am afraid this observation would hold true in a less degree for the whole. But is this owing to habit or food? Granting their food to be the cause, it decides very little against potatoes, unless they were tried with good nourishing beer instead of their vile potations of whisky. When they are encouraged, or animate themselves to hard work, it is all by whisky, which though it has a notable effect in giving a perpetual motion to their tongues, can have but little of that invigorating substance which is found in strong beer or porter, probably it has an effect as pernicious, as the other is beneficial. One circumstance I should mention, which seems to confirm this, I have known the Irish reapers in Hertfordshire work as laboriously as any of our own men, and living upon potatoes which they procured from London, but drinking nothing but ale. If their bodies are weak I attribute it to whisky not potatoes; but it is still a question with me whether their miserable working arises from any such weakness, or from an habitual laziness. A friend of mine always refused Irishmen work in Surrey, saying his bailiff could do nothing but settle their quarrels.

But of this food there is one circumstance which must ever recommend it, they have a bellyfull, and that let me add is more than the superfluities of an Englishman leaves to his family: let any person examine minutely into the receipt and expenditure of an English cottage, and he will find that tea, sugar and strong liquors, can come only from pinched bellies. I will not assert that potatoes are a better food than bread and cheese; but I have no doubt of a bellyfull of the one being much better than half a bellyfull of the other; still less have I that the milk of the Irishman is incomparably better than the small beer, gin, or tea of the Englishman; and this even for the father, how much better must it be for the poor infants; milk to them is nourishment, is health, is life.

If anyone doubts the comparative plenty, which attends the board of a poor native of England and Ireland, let him attend to their meals; the sparingness with which our labourer eats his bread and cheese is well known; mark the Irishman's potatoe bowl placed on the floor, the whole family upon their hams around it, devouring a quantity almost incredible, the beggar seating himself to it with a hearty welcome, the pig taking his share as readily as the wife, the cocks, hens, turkies, geese, the cur, the cat, and perhaps the cow—and all partaking of the same dish. No man can often have been a witness of it without being convinced of the plenty, and I will add the chearfulness, that attends it.

Young proceeds to consider the houses of the Irish and their equipment:

The furniture of the cabbins is as bad as the architecture; in very many consisting only of a pot for boiling their potatoes, a bit of a table, and one or two broken stools; beds are not found universally, the family lying on straw, equally partook of by cows, calves and pigs, though the luxury of sties is coming in in Ireland, which excludes the poor pigs from the warmth of the bodies of their master and mistress;...I have been in a multitude of cabbins that had much useful furniture, and some even superfluous; chairs, tables, boxes, chests of drawers, earthern ware, and in short most of the articles found in a middling English cottage; but upon enquiry, I very generally found that these acquisitions were all made within the last ten years, a sure sign of a rising national prosperity. I think the bad cabbins and furniture the greatest instances of Irish poverty, and this must show from the mode of payment for labour, which makes cattle so valuable to the peasant, that every farthing they can spare is saved for their purchase; from hence also results another observation, which is, that the apparent poverty of it is greater than the real; for the house of a man that is master of four or five cows, will have scarce anything but deficiencies; nay, I was in the cabbins of dairymen and farmers, not small ones, whose cabbins were not at all better, or better furnished than those of the poorest labourer: before, therefore, we can attribute it to absolute poverty, we must take into the account the customs and inclinations of the people.[1]

The last sentence discloses the same line of thought as that above, where he compares diets of potato and meat, to the advantage of the former. Saturated in religious thought as he was, Young seems to have forgotten that 'man cannot live by bread alone', and far less so on potatoes. It is not enough to merely fill the belly, in a house little better than a pig-sty. The amenities of life count, the old Wykehamite motto 'manners maketh the man' embodies a valuable truth. In Ireland the potato had reduced the art of living to that of the beast in the field. At that level it is superfluous to talk of the customs and inclinations of the people, for their customs had been determined and their inclinations limited by an enforced subservience to a single source of food, the cultivation of which dictated the whole economy of their lives. At that level, they were but helpless victims of the social and political forces of their environment.

[1] Young, Arthur (1780). *A Tour in Ireland*, pt. II, pp. 23–6.

CHAPTER XIV

The Period of Irish Self-Government

The latter quarter of the eighteenth century was one of the most eventful periods in Irish history: it witnessed the relaxation of many of the penal laws, amongst them the most irksome socially, and the most detrimental economically. Catholics from now on could take leases and raise mortgages on land which, together with the great demands made by the French wars for provisions, stimulated the production of corn. Events moved rapidly: by April 1778, a large measure of Free Trade with England was won by a combination of propaganda and threat of force. In 1780 Ireland was in control at last of its own industrial life. The American War affected Irish industry adversely, in so far as her export of linen necessarily ceased, but it more than made up for this by inducing in England a more chastened state of mind, which allowed of the repeal of the laws restraining industry.

In 1782 England relinquished her overriding power on Irish parliamentary procedure. For the remainder of the century, Ireland was governed by an Irish parliament, led by the Irish statesman, Grattan. Under this government in 1784 'Foster's Corn Law' was passed, an Act which had a profound effect both on the agriculture of Ireland and on the social structure of her people. The Act was designed to encourage the production of cereals and pulses, more especially the former, by means of bounties on exports, and duties on imports when the prices were low, and prohibition of exports when they rose too high. In Ulster, where shortage of cereals amongst the weaving population was chronic, the export of oats could at any time be prohibited altogether. The Act made it possible to clear the surplus stocks of the country when plentiful, retain them when short, and use them first and last for the benefit of the people. The result of this measure went far beyond increasing the output of cereals. It naturally led to a demand for arable land, but as evicted farmers, no less than displaced cottiers, were as numerous as they were pitiably short of capital, few were able to take over large acreages. The consequence was, that the land became subdivided to an extent, the like of which had not been known before, and which was only rendered possible, because new cabins could be built almost overnight, and both farmer and labourer were accustomed to live on the potato and very little else.

The first twelve years of Grattan's Parliament have been credited by some with having done great things to restore Irish prosperity, whilst others would deny it any spectacular success. O'Brien[1] devotes much attention to this problem and comes to the conclusion that this period 'was marked by all the generally accepted criteria of economic progress, namely, (a) a rapid growth of population, (b) a rise of rents, and (c) a great increase in the volume of industry'.

So much may be granted, but what, in truth, is the measure of a nation's prosperity? Surely the well-being, physical and spiritual, of the mass of the people. It is difficult to determine what are the competent yard-sticks with which to measure these states. I will not attempt to assay either the quality or measure the depth of the spiritual progress made, if any, but it is relevant to point out that it is in this period that the accusations of drunkenness and laziness reached their climax.

Drunkenness at the beginning of the century was a vice of the upper classes; at the end of the same, it was the working classes who were involved, and that to a degree which even their most devoted friends have admitted to have been a real danger to their well-being, and a gross impediment to their efficiency. As one might expect, the trouble was seen at its worst in the cities, not that it lagged so far behind in the countryside, for it was here that it received a special stimulus due to the Act of 1758 which prohibited the distillation of spirit. As happened in America, under incomparably better economic conditions some 160 years later, illicit whisky stills were set up in great number, on lone bog and mountain-side, throughout the country. The habit of manufacturing 'poteen', as it is called, which then grew up, became both general and persistent. It is not for me to say whether such exists to-day, but it certainly did a score of years back.

The subject of 'poteen' whisky has more than a passing interest for, contrary to the general belief that it is manufactured from barley and malt, some at least in recent times is, and doubtless in the eighteenth century also was, distilled from potatoes. One may assume that in the poverty-stricken countryside of that period, the potato would have been used in preference to corn.[2] Thus did the potato complete the conquest of the Irishman's dietary.

The accusation of laziness, preferred against the Irish worker of the period, must also be conceded; but its cause lies deeper. The potato demanded and received, at least in the eighteenth century, the minimum of cultivation; the actual time spent by the cottier in the preparation of

---

[1] O'Brien, G. (1918). *Econ. Hist. of Ireland in the Eighteenth Century*, chapter XXXII.

[2] The procedure is to expose medium-sized tubers to frost over several nights, then cut them into slices, soak in water indoors for ten days with occasional stirring, strain the liquor off and add some treacle and yeast. The 'wash', as it is now termed, is allowed to ferment: after an adequate time, it is carefully distilled without being allowed to boil. I owe this authentic recipe to a late very distinguished Irish friend, who obtained it direct from an exponent of the art.

his ground, the sowing, earthing up, harvesting of the crop—of weeding it got none—would probably not amount, if put together, to as much as three months. The remainder of his time was left without any urgent task other than the feeding of his pig and cow, and the cutting of his turf. Such a regime called neither for haste nor energy, whilst the virtual impossibility of rising in the social scale, excluded the possibility of either entering his mind. If inertia in human affairs ranks as laziness, then the Irishman was lazy, and with good reason.

There is another feature of Irish rural life which developed to such an extent during the eighteenth and nineteenth centuries that it came to be looked on as almost a national habit. I refer to begging. Swift,[1] complaining of the enormous number of beggars, declared it was due to the laziness of the natives, the excessive rents, the ruin of agriculture, and the early improvident marriages. Leaving aside those malingerers, who pretended ailments and the like, in order to defraud the public, there remained a large body of men, and particularly women, who made begging a feature of the yearly routine. Travelling round town and country, with their children at their side, they begged during the mid-summer months at the time when their own potatoes were exhausted, appealing for money and for old potatoes on which to live. An interesting account of the custom is to be found in an Essay written in 1728:[2]

Native Irish in the mountains, that have homes and small farms where they have sown their corn and planted their potatoes, and cut the turf for firing, do either turn out their cows or send them to the mountains, then shut up their doors and go abegging.... Thus they pick up enough to pay their rent, and by the help of their cattle, corn and potatoes, live idle the whole winter.

Begging continued to form an integral part of peasant life in Ireland right through the nineteenth century, but it must not be taken, in any sense, as a measure of depravity, nor necessarily as evidence of complete penury, but rather as a practice which, basing itself on the age-old custom of 'creaghting' during the summer months, took a new direction, as the result of the economic helplessness which the political structure of Irish life had created, and the adoption of the potato which the unbridged interval between the old and the new crops had confirmed.

Drunkenness and begging are social habits which in all countries exhibit a pronounced time-lag in relation to the environment which created them or encouraged their continuance, and hence they are not fair evidence of lack of progress over so short a period as that covered by the Grattan movement. If political and economic disabilities had

---

[1] Swift, Jonathan (1765). *Considerations about Maintaining the Poor*, vol. VII, p. 339. Temple Scott's edit.

[2] Thom, Alex (1729). *Tracts on Ireland.* Dublin 1860: *An Essay upon the Trade of Ireland*, 1728.

been the sole or the main cause of the people's desperation, one would have expected their removal to be followed within a relatively short time by a recognizable improvement in the social welfare of the people. But when we consider the physical well-being of the people, we are confronted by a paradoxical state of affairs. Ireland, in a large measure, had recovered her liberties, and for the last eighteen years of the century had conducted her own affairs in her own interests. During that time undoubted, though limited, industrial progress took place. Following that, after a brief period of disturbance, the Union of Ireland and England was effected in 1801; a few years later, most of the material disabilities to which the Irish had been subjected, had been removed for ever. Yet, when we turn to examine those criteria of social betterment which really count, the food, housing, hygiene and education of the vast majority of the population, that is to say, of the small farmers, cottiers, and agricultural labourers, no improvement whatever can be registered. Throughout the whole century, and indeed well into the next, we find the same evidence on every side, of poverty and degradation, only to be illumined every few years by the lurid glow of famine and disease.

Cairnes[1] goes so far as to compare the Irish cottier with the European serf, the difference being to the advantage of the latter. The serf 'is bound to the soil by law and custom: the Irish are bound by necessity only. He can leave of his own free will or be turned out by that of his landlord. The serf is safe. The rent of the Irish is determined by competition and paid by labour at rates determined by competition.'

A similar comparison with the serfs of Russia has been made in regard to the English peasant of the eighteenth and nineteenth centuries, but with far less justice; for he lived on a cash basis, and enjoyed a mixed dietary. The Irish cottier lived on, and by, and, one might almost say for, his potato, thus binding himself hand and foot to the fortunes of this enigmatical root. As Cairnes shows, he was not a serf—he was much nearer akin to a slave.

Ireland had never known a time when political differences were not punctuated, at intervals of a decade or two, by organized violence, and the eighteenth century was no exception to the rule. Compared with the tempo of the preceding century, there had been up till 1778, apart from the activities of the Whiteboys, relative peace, and the tillers of the soil had not been disturbed.

In 1771 the Marquis of Donegal and a Mr Upton, on finding that the leases on their Ulster estates were falling in, and much higher rents might be obtained, demanded of their tenants, all of whom happened to be Protestants, heavy renewal fines: these they were unable to pay, although they offered to pay an annual interest on the amount demanded.

[1] Cairnes (1873). *Political Essay*. O'Brien, G. (1921). Op. cit. p. 97.

Donegal was not satisfied with the offer and proceeded to negotiate with a Belfast capitalist, who paid the renewal fines, and ejected between six and seven thousand tenant families. The land was then let to the highest bidders, who, in many cases, were Catholics. The Presbyterians of Ulster, both enraged and alarmed, reacted by creating marauding bodies, the chief of which was known as Peep-of-Day-Boys, and another as Hearts-of-Steel; both adopted the methods of the Whiteboys and harassed the Catholic tenants, large and small. The latter, in their turn, formed a counter organization known as Catholic Defenders, and the two opposing parties maintained an atmosphere of continuous tension. Lord Gosford, the Governor of Armagh, told the magistrates of that county in December 1795, that Catholic tenants, innocent and guilty alike, were being made to suffer 'confiscation of all property and immediate banishment'. At the hands of Protestant bands, 'more than half the inhabitants of a populous country', he said, 'were deprived at one blow of the means as well as the fruits of their industry, and driven out in the midst of an inclement season.'[1] Those who could, escaped to Connaught.

These troubles were at first confined to Ulster but, eventually, brought about a degree of disorder in the countryside reminiscent of that which had resulted from the politico-religious jealousies of previous centuries. Like the latter, the new disorders tended to widen still more the gap between native Irish and English, Catholic and Protestant. This progressive dissociation between the great majority of the people of the land and a small but powerful minority, naturally increased the social stagnation of the masses. In this process the potato played an important part. Its extraordinary competence to serve wellnigh as the sole source of the people's food, facilitated such stagnation, whilst the 'ascendancy' of a small minority, in its turn, sterilized any effort to dislodge it from the unique place it had acquired in the social system of the nation.

At long last, a new force which, though the offspring of fratricidal war, was integrating rather than disrupting, brought a certain measure of peace and understanding to all classes of the people, the effect of which has survived even to this day.

The war with America had produced so serious a drain on the British forces, that the garrison in Ireland was seriously denuded. In 1778 the Government sanctioned the creation of a volunteer movement which, beginning in Belfast, spread rapidly throughout the whole country, till it numbered 50,000 men. Officered by the aristocracy, manned by the peasant both Catholic and Protestant, and armed by the government, it grew rapidly under the leadership of the Duke of Leinster and Lord Charlmont, becoming in the process, progressively more conscious of

[1] Quoted from Bryce (1888). *Two Centuries of Irish History*, p. 146.

its ability to unite all parties, and exercise its power in the realm of current politics. The movement grew daily in strength, by means which were constitutional in the letter, but insufficiently so in the spirit, to do more than camouflage the obvious determination of the people to secure by force of arms what they might fail to obtain by persuasion.

The spirit of the French Revolution ran like wine in the veins of the leaders of the Irish Nationalists who, fired with hope, were now ready to emulate the success achieved by the colonists in the American War, so many of whom were but recently their neighbours in Ireland. It was not long before their example inspired the majority of the Irish people, uniting for the time, Protestant Whigs and Catholic Nationalists, in one common endeavour. The movement found its leader in Theobald Wolf Tone, and its expression in the 'United Irishmen' (1791). This organization rapidly acquired strength throughout the whole country, and though in the main recruited from Catholics, it succeeded in including a strong leaven of Protestants, notably amongst its leaders. Its programme was simple, to obtain under the British Crown, complete independence and equality of citizenship.

Agrarian disorder, however, was still rampant, especially in Ulster, where it reached its climax in a bloody fray in September 1795, between strong bodies of the Peep-of-Day and the Defender's respective fraternities, which ended in the defeat of the latter. The Protestants in Ulster, inspired by fears for their safety, no less than by determination to maintain their ascendancy, took this occasion to knit themselves together in a still closer union, by the creation of Orange Lodges, which embodied the Presbyterian elements throughout all Ulster. The policy of the lodges was more anti-Catholic than Protestant, more pro-Ulster than pro-British. For a long time to come, the Orange Association was one of the most potent factors in maintaining the spirit of Protestant ascendancy, a policy which involved as an inevitable corollary the suppression and pauperization of the Catholic rural population. A familiar phenomenon, the monotony of whose occurrence was rendered possible by the fact that maintenance of life was assured, no matter how devoid it was of amenities so long as there were enough potatoes in the cottier's crock to keep body and soul together.

Even the great demand for corn, which lasted throughout the Napoleonic wars, and the high price it commanded, failed to arouse the cottier and rescue him from the morass of poverty and squalor within which, trusting all too confidently in the potato for his subsistence, he was so firmly entrenched. Though the cottier was prepared to commit almost any deed of violence, in order to retain his hold on his cabin, and his potato patch, he was not easily roused to fight for fundamental political or religious rights. It was different with the Irish middle classes and intellectuals: they felt keenly the weight and the shame of the penal laws. It was they who, now that the worst of the disabilities had been removed, were determined at any cost to complete their abolition. Hence it was that the next upheaval was political in origin and only took on an agrarian aspect when the military attacked the cabin and the croft.

Repeated failure to obtain the abolition of the remaining Penal Laws, and particularly that which deprived Catholics of their right to sit in the legislature, led the United Irishmen in 1796 to arm themselves and seek French aid. The latter materialized in two abortive attempts at invasion, one in 1796 and the other in 1797. In the spring of the following year, the authorities proceeded with success to disarm the malcontents, North and South, by means of the yeomanry, whose lawless violence exacerbated the feelings of Protestant and Catholic alike. The unrest which had been growing for seven years, and which affected the well-being of all classes, and the very existence of British ascendancy, burst into the active flame of rebellion on 24 May 1798. Within a month all was over, and the leaders dead or in exile. The scene of most of the fighting was in Leinster, and in particular at Wexford. 'The greater part of Ulster stood aloof. Connaught and Munster remained tranquil and the priests with some notable exceptions, took no share in the rebellion.'[1]

If Ulster was relatively quiet, she was evidently not unprepared. It was here that a great number of peasants were accustomed to foregather, it was said under the pretext of digging potatoes. In one case as many as 6,000 men had come together, as they averred, to dig some poor woman's potato-patch for her, a ruse which apparently did not deceive Sir G. Hill, who writes: 'The main object of the potato digging is probably to enable the leaders to ascertain how their men will act at the word of command.'[2] Hill may have been correct in his interpretation but, in fact, it was a well-established custom for neighbours to join in planting and harvesting the potatoes of those they held in high esteem, or of some poor widow who could not do it herself.

Whilst the 1798 Rebellion was more carefully prepared, and politically more dangerous than any of the risings of the preceding century, it disturbed to a far less degree the current of life and husbandry in the countryside. The suppression of the actual rebellion, the subsequent unlicensed pillage and massacre by the soldiery, and the savage reprisals of the peasantry, however, cost many thousands of lives. The ease with which the rebellion was quelled, and the lack of cohesion it displayed, together afforded a measure of the people's inherent lack of discipline and education, in the conduct of affairs and, more particularly, of their own government. The social life of the great majority of the people, to

---

[1] Gooch, G. P. (1907). *Camb. Mod. Hist.* vol. IX, p. 702.
[2] Lecky, W. (1892). *History of Ireland*, vol. III, pp. 475-6.

all of whom the Penal Laws had denied the most elementary education, had been such as to encourage a degree of inertia, and an incapacity for sustained political effort, commensurate with their poverty, and a barbarity in keeping with the crudity of their homes and the elemental simplicity of their dietary.

Cornewall Lewis,[1] nearly a hundred years ago, observed the same thing:

It may be remarked [he writes] that some active interference, either actual or apprehended, with the ordinary state of the peasantry, is required in order to arouse them to aggressive measures; some positive ill-usage, or infliction of evil, such as ejectment from land, driving for rent, etc., to the mere passive state of suffering produced by scantiness of food or the failure of the potato crop, the Irish peasant, a class remarkable for their patient endurance, are willing to submit, and hence we find that at times when a large part of the population are hanging over the verge of starvation, the country is nevertheless for the most part tranquil.

A recent writer[2] arrives at a similar conclusion. After a survey of Irish history during the last 200 years, he is convinced that neither the racial differences as between Celt and Saxon, nor the religious as between Catholic and Protestant, had any basic importance. 'Throughout the whole period, the Irish cause was frequently championed by men of Saxon origin and the Protestant faith, the trouble throughout was economic.' He continues:

The cause of the troubles in the eighteenth century were—poverty, misery, oppression—a peasantry ground down by extortionate rents, broken by years of unremitting toil, clothed in rags, living in filthy hovels, always on the verge of starvation, deprived of the necessaries of life, with no comfort in the present, or hope for the future—from such causes sprang the disturbances and outrages that marked the eighteenth century. We have it on the authority of Fitzgibbon, the Attorney-General, who stated in 1787, that of 'the commotions which for the last sixty years have tormented and desolated Ireland, they all sprang immediately from local oppressions'.

How seriously the conditions of the peasantry had deteriorated by the end of the eighteenth century, may be gauged from the remarks of a competent authority, speaking of the food of the agricultural workers in County Kilkenny:

Potatoes with milk as often as can be procured, forms almost the whole food of the poorer classes in these parts; before the introduction of the kind called 'Apple Potato', a great portion of the sustenance of the poor consisted of oaten bread and milk; from April to August barley bread was sometimes used, and in the hilly parts of the parish, rye bread; but since the cultivation of the

[1] Lewis, Sir George Cornewall, Bart. (1836). *Local Disturbances*, p. 91.
[2] Lloyd-Dodd, F. T. (1942). Land Tenure. MSS. lent to R.N.S.

'Apple Potato' has become general, the poor continue to eat them until new potatoes come in. Before their introduction, the cottagers frequently sowed beans and other esculent vegetables and had little plots somewhat like a small kitchen garden at the rear of their cabins, but the 'Apple Potato' suppressed everything of the sort. They do not grow onions, only use salt with their potatoes, a herring is a luxury.[1]

No better example could be found of how blind a bystander may be to events taking place under his own eyes. The 'Irish Apple' was indeed an excellent variety which had been in popular use for thirty years, but it would need a force more potent than even its charms, to lead a people to discard all other sources of food. Those forces were poverty and political oppression.

If amongst the common people, the intellectual and cultural streams had become silted up and stagnant, so that little else but the crude realities of the struggle for existence was manifest in their waters, conditions at the other end of the social scale were no healthier. Amongst the gentry replete though it was with the external trappings of cultured London and the exotic experiences of the European tours, we see a moral irresponsibility, not to say dishonesty, which was far more sinister than the boorish simplicity of the peasant. In the one, the spirit of enterprise and the hope of betterment had spent themselves in a featureless existence, dominated by the potato and its culture; in the other, the same causes which had led to this unique dominance, had allowed the landowner to regard his estate, and those whose lives depended on its cultivation, as so many tools, designed by Providence, for the production on his behalf, of an assured income.

It was not surprising that the readiness of the Irish gentry and aristocracy at the close of the century, to agree to the extinction of their own legislature, to the loss of independence of their own countrymen, and to the Union of their country on equal terms with Great Britain in exchange for ready cash and coronets, greatly shocked contemporary opinion, even in those days of political corruption. To the student of to-day who has learnt that the ruling classes are ever less nationalistic than the peasantry, it only confirms the truth of the complaint so often made, that there was no bond of interest, understanding or sympathy, between the common people of Ireland and the landlord class. Even where the latter were residents, their mode of life was so fundamentally different from that of the potato-controlled cottier, that at their best, the relations between landlord and the peasant remind one much more of that which Tolstoy described in Russia of the nineteenth century, and Murasaki in the Genji novels of Japan in the eleventh, than such as existed in contemporary England. The Irish aristocracy were not, as at

[1] Tighe, W. (1802). *Statistical Observations relative to the County of Kilkenny*, p. 479.

home, an upper stratum of a relatively homogeneous people, they were divided from the people who cultivated the land from which they derived their fortunes and their titles, as it were, by an unsurmountable wall. If any should doubt this, I would recommend to them a recent book[1] in which the life of an 'ascendant' upper middle-class family history in the south, is very frankly, and naïvely recounted. The period is the 1880's, and the vertical barrier, which obviously shut out any real knowledge of the people's life, was built of Protestantism resting on a basis of extreme political conservatism, the two cemented together with an impenetrable assurance of superiority; in short, by the drawing-room version of the authentic spirit of ascendancy.

[1] Robinson, Lennox (1932). *Three Homes.* Michael Joseph.

CHAPTER XV

Ireland in the Nineteenth Century

In 1801, the Union of Ireland and Great Britain was finally consummated; dictated by England, sullenly accepted by the Irish people, it was at best a *mariage de convenance* in which absence of affection, disparity of age, and inequality of fortune, were for the time overshadowed by the fear that if England did not secure her as a bride, her coquetry might end in bringing her paramour, France, unpleasantly near to his gate. A Protestant clergyman who had advocated the union, on being disillusioned fifteen years later, wrote: 'I cannot avoid comparing the attachment of England to her sister island as the hug of the harlot who clasped her satiated wooer in her muscular embrace until he had thrown into her widely distended lap his last solitary shilling.'[1] A harsh if partial picture, but not without a considerable element of truth.

That the marriage should have been unhappy in view of the past history of the two partners, was not to be wondered at, but that union with the wealthy and powerful Britain, should have further impoverished the already stricken land of Ireland, is one of the most extraordinary facts of modern history. It must not be supposed that the failure was due to deliberate ill-will, or neglect, on either side. Had statesmen but sat down and considered impassionately the not very complicated factors, determining the existing relations between the two countries, they could hardly have failed to see that a union based on the assumption that the partners stood on an equality, economic and social, was so demonstrably at variance with the facts, as to render a miscarriage inevitable. Had they even remembered their own so recent failure to retain the American colonies, they might have avoided some of the worst mistakes.

There was much that might be said in excuse. The recent rebellion in Ireland, with the insurgent growth of Irish Nationalism, as a political force, no less than the French wars, demanded a consolidation of the home front. Of equal moment was the demand for ever wider markets to satisfy the rapid growth of British industry and the dictates of an increasingly powerful mercantile middle-class. A class completely ignorant of Irish history and traditions, whose acquaintance with Irishmen was confined to the ragged bands of quarrelsome labourers they employed at harvest, men who were content to sleep in any old outhouse, live on little but potatoes, and work for lower wages than the English.

[1] Major, Henry (1815). *Observations Demonstrative of the Necessity of Ireland's Welfare, etc.* From O'Brien (1918), p. 570.

How powerful was the urge to settle the Irish problem, as it was hoped once and for all, is shown by the fact that responsible statesmen in Whitehall ignored, or at least discounted, the truth that the two countries were economically poles apart. At the time of the Union, about nine-tenths of the Irish population was subsisting almost entirely on a single source of food, the potato, whilst at home in England the working classes were a meat-eating people who insisted on wheaten bread and beer. The English masses had been in receipt of cash wages for centuries, whilst the Irish in the countryside, practically speaking, never handled the coin of the realm at all. Neither Irish farmer nor peasant had any security of tenure, a benefit which the unwritten custom of centuries had secured for the English. The landlord in Ireland was merely a receiver of rack-rents, much of which he spent outside Ireland, whilst in England he was the friend, adviser, and banker of his tenant, considerations which Drummond[1] must have had in mind when he launched his famous aphorism: 'Property has its duties as well as its rights.' Yet so it was; and there seems to have been no suspicion amongst statesmen of the danger of neglect to bring the agrarian and social problems of the two countries into harmony, before effecting the union. The disastrous failure of the potato crop in 1845 and 1846 demonstrated beyond cavil, the false premises which underlay the economy of Ireland and, as a corollary, that of the Union.

There can be little doubt that the motive uppermost in the minds of England's responsible statesmen was fear. England was at deadly grips with Napoleon, on uneasy terms with America, had but just put down a rising in Ireland, which had been supported by an invasive force from France, and hence was not in the mood to consider finer issues. Moreover, one must not forget that at the opening of the century, the population of England was no more than twice that of Ireland; to-day it is ten times as great.

To consider in any detail the grossly unequal development of industry in the two countries, or the absence of an industrial revolution in Ireland, comparable to that which was in full spate in England, would take us too far from the immediate object of our study. Under Grattan's parliament, certain protective duties had been established which led to a considerable development of Irish industries whose market was, in the main, the home one. The Act of Union contained provisions designed to maintain these duties for a period of ten years, and to reduce them gradually till complete free-trade between the two countries should be established as, in fact, it was, in 1824. The result was that every single Irish industry other than Belfast's linen trade, steadily declined, and such as had not

---

[1] Bridges, J. H. (1888). Quoted from *Two Centuries of Irish History*, p. 373. Thomas Drummond in a public letter to Lord Donoughmore, 1837.

expired by 1830, or thereabouts, did so soon after, when exposed to the bleak winds of the free-trade and *laisser faire* policies, which were to dominate British trade for the next hundred years. In all this, the good intentions of Great Britain are less in question than her failure to understand Irish conditions.

As industry declined, the number of those who were destitute increased. As there was no Poor Law Relief in Ireland till 1838, the displaced workers had no alternative between returning to the land, begging in the streets, or starving. Return to the land had only one meaning—the use of a plot of land, however small, and the raising on it of potatoes on which to live.

Several tendencies had been at work between 1780 and 1815, which encouraged subdivision of the land. The influence of Foster's Corn Act has already been mentioned: the concession to Catholics in 1793 of the parliamentary vote, and the establishment of the franchise at the 40s. freehold level which, in fact, was interpreted as meaning a lease for life of land estimated to be of this value, or more, had led the larger landlords to take quite a different view as to the presence of large numbers of cottiers on their estates. So far from being regarded, as hitherto, a nuisance, they now became a political asset; their votes insured the owners, or their nominees, political influence in Dublin, which not infrequently took the form of lucrative positions within the Irish State, and in any case assured the presence of an overwhelming majority of the landed and Protestant gentry in the parliament, both when it sat in Dublin, and later when it sent its members to Westminster. Indeed, the great houses appointed special men, not inappropriately known as 'drivers', to control the votes of their cottiers. It was their job to troop them off to the booths, there to record their votes for their landlord, which they could scarce avoid doing, in those days of the open ballot.

The Napoleonic wars were a further and potent factor working for the conversion of pasture to tillage; the demand for corn for use in England and in the army, was great, and prices soared. The conversion of pasture to tillage necessitated a great increase of labour and this, in turn, led to closer settlement. Quick changes from pasture to tillage, and vice versa, were possible in Ireland, where, at all times, there were to be found large sections of the rural population living on the very verge of starvation, dependent for their subsistence on a small patch of potatoes on the mountainside, and for their shelter on a hut built of wattle and covered with turf. Such people, when the call came, descended to the better lands, and either secured some conacre land for individual cultivation, or entered into agreements with each other or the sitting farmer, to till, as a family group, a few acres, rarely more than fifteen, between them. Each married couple, and each man of marriageable age, built for himself a cabin, a matter of less than a week's work, and if not already married he, basing his family life on the proceeds of the potato patch, promptly became so. An authority on Irish life writing in 1815 says:

In other countries, to make provision for a family is so serious an undertaking that marriage is seldom ventured on at an early age, until a man has acquired a competence for its support. Here marriage is delayed by no want, except sometimes want of money to purchase a licence—to Providence and their potatoe garden they commit the rest. Children abundantly follow, for barrenness is almost unknown among the lower class. The prevailing causes of increasing population are further promoted by their love of home, and the universal custom of inoculating children for the smallpox, a disorder which was little less injurious in its ravages than the plague.[1]

The poorer, it was observed, married at a much younger age than the better off: 'their inclination to early marriages increases in proportion to their wretchedness, and decreases in proportion to their knowledge of comforts'. As the Catholic Bishop, Dr McGilligan said, in answer to the question: Why do they marry so young? 'They cannot be worse off than they are, and that they may help each other.'[2]

In 1841 there were about 700,000 holdings under 15 acres, as against less than 130,000 over 15 acres in extent.[3] The intensive subdivision of the land, with the close settlement it involved, resulted in a rapid rise in the population. Prior to 1821, we have to rely on estimates for the population figures, and that of five million is generally accepted as being valid for the year 1800. There is, however, good reason to think that this is an underestimate, in view of the fact that in the year 1821 the census return was 6,803,000. Such a large increase is very improbable, seeing that in the interval there had been no improvement in hygiene or medical services, nor was it characterized by any commensurate expansion of industry, or by any increase in the rate of wages, and, still less, by any betterment of the amenities of life. Nevertheless, the population was certainly rising, and this, as Clapham suggests, was probably due to the fact that there had been no serious famine or potato failure since 1739–41.[4]

Close settlement, when accompanied by a sharp demand for cereals, should itself lead to an increase of population, because it demands the creation of many new married homes, which otherwise would never have been established, or would at least have been delayed till opportunity afforded a favourable occasion to the more adventurous. By reason

[1] Townshend, Rev. Horatio (1815). *General and Statistical Survey of the County of Cork*, vol. I, p. 94.
[2] *Irish Poor Inquiry* (1835). Selection from Evidence, p. 274.
[3] Mansergh, Nicholas (1942). *Britain and Ireland*. Longmans.
[4] Clapham, J. (1926). *Econ. Hist. Mod. Brit.* vol. I, p. 56.

of their origin and their character, the majority of these people would, in any country which enjoyed a self-determined economic life, have contributed a powerful stimulus to the development of its rural life, and the remainder would have been absorbed in its growing industries. Not so in Ireland, where no serious attempt was made, either by private enterprise or government action, to absorb this excess of potential workers in the extension of Ireland's agricultural or industrial life.[1]

The Devon Commission, reporting in 1845, pointed out that there was as much as 1,425,000 acres fit for tillage, and 2,330,000 acres fit for pasture, which awaited recovery from the waste lands alone. Some of this only needed liming, the majority required drainage to make it, what much of it has since become, valuable agricultural property. Nothing was done. Industrial development might have helped towards a solution, had it not been strangled during the eighteenth century, and its revival in the nineteenth in the face of English competition become a forlorn hope.

It was typical of the state of Anglo-Irish relations that the attitude adopted by statesmen as well as by public spirited generous-hearted men and women of affairs, and, above all, by the people themselves, was one of resignation to the inevitable. If the cup could not be enlarged to hold more wine, then there was no alternative but to pour the excess down the drain; in other words, to send these hungry, unwanted peasants to the American colonies. And that is exactly what they did, often at the expense of the landlord. Nor was the policy wholly selfish. It was dignified by a new philosophy and Malthus was its prophet. All economic evils were due to excess of population, and were not all authorities in agreement that Ireland was over-populated?

Emigration was no new palliative. Of an earlier wave, Primate Boulter speaks in his correspondence to Sir Robert Walpole and the Duke of Newcastle, describing with alarm the emigration of Ulster Presbyterians to the West Indies and the American Colonies. In the summer of 1727 alone, three thousand had left their homes. The Primate complains that the passion to leave Ulster has become a veritable madness and is due to the action of the landlords who, finding it to their advantage to convert their holding back to pasture, had cleared many farms as their leases expired, and rack-rented the remainder, whilst the whole burden of tithe was borne by those tenant-farmers who tilled the soil.[2]

A century later, exactly the same ideas swayed the people and obsessed the landlords. The *émigrés* of this later period were also of the best elements in the country, but now they included Catholics as well as Presbyterians. The latter, incensed by the hostility of the Anglican Church, and their exclusion by the Test Act from all offices of trust

[1] Sadler, Michael Th. (1828). *Ireland, its evils and their remedies*. London.
[2] Godkin, James (1870). *Land War in Ireland*. Macmillan and Co.

in the state, had formed, with those who had preceded them to the colonies on the mainland, the backbone of the colonial forces which fought against the mother country. The American War, in its turn, delayed for several years the flow of emigration, and so intensified the pressure of the people on the resources of the land.

By the beginning of the nineteenth century, there must have been nearly two million Irish natives who contributed little, if anything, to the national wealth, and who were regarded as being surplus to the economic requirements of the country. These people, without security of home, work, or sustenance, maintained an exiguous existence based almost entirely on the potato.

In Clare, the cottier had come to live the whole year round on nothing but the potato; formerly he had enjoyed a certain amount of milk, but now such had become a rarity. The 'blue months' were no longer served by a supply of oatmeal, for varieties were now used which kept throughout the year.[1] The rents had increased, land 'for burning', i.e. plots on which the cottier was expected to burn the top turf, fetched as much as £8 per acre, and was often but poor land at that. The average consumption for a family of six, with its pig and poultry, was 22 barrels, an amount which could be easily harvested from 1 acre of land. The average wage for work on the farm was 6½d. per day, with food, but only 5d. per day when credited against rent for cottage and potato patch.

The home conditions of the poor were, as we have seen, utterly mean and nasty, and those of the well-to-do farmer in Clare were, at least in the kitchen quarter, but little better.

Conditions in the County of Armagh at this time were decidedly better than elsewhere.

The dwellings of the poor are far better built and equipped than are to be found elsewhere in Ireland. This is not solely due to the prosperity of the linen trade, for in Cavan and Moneghan, which have similar trade advantages, the amenities are far behind, and there is no such evidence of wealth and civilization.... To build a superior type of cottage costs £7. 19s. 3d., but a cheaper could be built for £3. 4s. 0d.; a rood of ground is allowed for each cottage.

It is on record that four neighbours erected a home for a newly married couple, which was built and occupied within thirteen hours.[2]

'The food of the lower ranks are potatoes, stirrabout, oaten bread, garden vegetables, bacon in summer and beef in winter; there is no part of Ireland where the people consume so much fresh meat.'[3] That a relation exists here between the dietary and the social and economic status of the people, can scarcely be denied.

[1] Dutton, Hely (1808). *Stat. Surv. of the County of Clare*, p. 43. Dublin.
[2] Reid, Thomas (1823). Op. cit. p. 202.
[3] Coote, Sir Chas. (1809). *Stat. Survey of County Armagh*, p. 249.

If necessity made the potato the food of the masses, the habit it created was certainly not confined to them. The middle-class, though free to choose a more varied diet, became confirmed potato addicts and consumed what we to-day should consider preposterous quantities. A vignette from one of Griffin's novels gives one an intimate glimpse into a comfortable Munster farmhouse in the first quarter of the nineteenth century: 'Minny O'Lone was quietly seated by the breakfast-table making a rapid progress through the reeking mountain of steak-coated potatoes and virgin-white milk that covered the board.'[1]

By the year 1841, the population of Ireland was approaching its zenith. The census return for that year was 8,175,124, an increase of nearly $1\frac{1}{2}$ millions in twenty years. In 1846, the year of the potato famine, it is estimated that the population had reached close on 9 millions. Against this, there was no corresponding growth of industry. Indeed, by 1821, all, excepting the linen and brewing industries, were entering on that decline which terminated in their virtual extinction before the middle of the century.

The continuous and rapid increase of population, especially during the first half of the nineteenth century, has naturally excited much speculation. A favourite explanation has been to ascribe it to the influence of the potato. Whilst there is a large measure of truth in this view, it is obviously not the whole tale. The failure of industry to hold its own in competition with that of England, the resulting exodus from the towns, Foster's Corn Law, and the 40s. franchise, were all agents which encouraged the establishment of young married couples in new homes. It was the potato alone which made such unions possible, and allowed them to be fruitful. During this period of population expansion, no advance took place in agricultural methods, no attempt to improve the injustices of land tenure, and no approach to the problem of the payment of compensation for improvements, other than that already in practice in Ulster. The only reaction of the countryside was that the landlords, whenever possible, freed themselves from the middlemen, to whom they had granted long leases at low rents, and then proceeded to rack-rent their small tenants themselves.

An anonymous author[2] addressing Lord Wellesley in the first decade of the nineteenth century writes:

The cultivator of the land seldom holds from the inheritor; between them stand a series of sub-landlords and tenants, each receiving a profit from his lessee, but having no further interest or connection with the soil. The last in the series must provide for the profits of all—he therefore parcels out, at

---

[1] Griffin, Gerald (1827?). *The Half Sir*, p. 123.
[2] *A Sketch of the State of Ireland, Past and Present*, p. 34, 2nd edit. London: John Murray, 1822.

rack-rents, the land to his miserable tenantry. Here is no yeomanry, no agricultural capitalist; no degree between the landlord and labourer; and the words 'peasantry' and 'poor' are synonymous.

Where the middlemen still held sway, it was they who screwed up the rents of their farmer-tenants who, in their turn, raised the price of potato-patch and conacre to the cottier. For whether the rent could be eventually paid or not, the cottier had perforce to obtain his spot of land or die of starvation; not infrequently he did both for, as we shall see, the potato as he cultivated it, might fail.

The period of the American and French wars was thus one in which there had been a return to tillage and close settlements, a period of high prices and higher rents, of increasing population, unaccompanied by any betterment of the social condition of the vast majority of the people. A vivid picture of the time is given by Baron Fletcher's address to the grand jury of Wexford in 1814: He ascribes the cause of unrest to high rents, following high prices, till they reached a figure far beyond that which the cultivation of the land could yield. To meet this, the peasantry took to illicit distillation of spirits, in which they were abetted by the landlords, anxious for an outlet for their grain, and an insurance against their rent. He is particularly severe in his condemnation of the agrarian disorder, brought about by the rivalry of Orange Lodges and Ribbonmen. The former, in his opinion, are the more to blame, and are the more pernicious, inasmuch as the justices of the bench are either members of, or in sympathy with, the Lodges.

These associations poison the very foundations of justice, and even magistrates under their influence have in too many cases violated their duty and their oathes. He protested against the peculiarities of grand juries—the harassing of the poor by the tithe proctors, who oppressed most those who best cultivated their land, the absentee landlord who extracted the last penny out of the tenant with no consideration of past services, eviction of the whole countryside. What could the peasant do? Chased from his birth-place, left without means of existence, he rushes into crime and violence and ends on the gibbet. Nothing, as they imagine, remains for them, thus harassed and thus destitute, but with strong hand to deter the stranger from intruding on their farms, and to extort from the weakness and terror of their landlords, from whose gratitude or good feeling they have failed to win it, a preference for their ancient tenantry.[1]

The learned judge, at the end of his address, introduced us to one of the features of Irish rural life which, though by no means new, was from now on to become the subject of the most bitter dispute, both political and physical, in the life of the people, and one which was bound up inseparably with the cultivation of the potato.

[1] Bridges, J. H. (1888). *Two Centuries of Irish History*, p. 262.

Eviction from his holding and his cabin, was a measure over which the small man had no control whatever, and against which he had no redress. In Ireland the landlord exercised the fullest possible authority over his property. He could turn off every tenant on the land, if he so liked, and let it go to waste; if the tenant were a tenant at will, and the vast majority were, his rent could be raised at any time, and he must either pay it, or go. If his rent was in arrears, he could be sold up without further ado, and, except in Ulster, lose the value of any building or improvement to the land he might have effected. If the farmer or cottier were a sub-tenant, and the intermediate landlord had failed to pay the overlord his rent, then the latter could come down on the under-tenant and demand the rent from him. Should the latter have already paid his immediate landlord, that made no difference: he must, and not infrequently did, pay his rent twice over. Eviction was a weapon in the hands of the landlords which was capable of the grossest abuse, and was extensively and grossly abused. It must not be supposed that there were no good landlords in the eighteenth- and nineteenth-century Ireland, who would refrain from misusing their rights; there were, but they were exceptional. The power of eviction might be used for punitive, political, or financial purposes. It is with the latter that we are mainly concerned.

It has already been remarked how relatively easy it was in Ireland, so far as law and custom were concerned, to switch the agricultural system over from one of pasture to one of tillage, or vice versa. It is true that the switch-over was paid for in terms of human suffering, and with the very lives of the cottiers. But were there not demonstrably too many? In England such a change was a slow and difficult business, brought about in post-Tudor times, more often by the action of a new type of capitalist tenant than by the landlord. Over at least half the English countryside, the small arable farmer was still firmly established in the open fields of the village, and nothing less than specific Acts of Parliament could move him.

Economically, it would seem to be highly desirable to be able to switch over quickly from pasture to tillage or, if needs be, reverse the process. Such a change, under our modern system of mechanized agriculture, can, as we have seen in this war period, be brought about with great rapidity, and with no violent interference with personnel.

Had Ireland in the nineteenth century only used its capacity for agricultural change, in response to economic demands, with due consideration of the rights and welfare of the people, it might have been as great a blessing as it was, in fact, a curse. The Irish landlord, generally an absentee, was only interested in his estate from the point of view of its rent roll. If arable cultivation paid best, then he would let it out in as many small parcels and at as high a rent, as the market would pay. If the trade in live beasts, or provisions, was on the upward trend, then it was equally easy to evict his small tenant, and let great parcels of the estate off to graziers who were ready to pay a higher rent. Lack of right of tenure, and the power of eviction, were his weapons, but they would have been powerless, if the potato had not been there to bridge over that narrow gap between living and starvation, with which the Irish peasant was all too familiar. A peasant cultivator of Navan in Meath, whose family consisted of a wife and seven children, said to his interrogator, who had noticed that the only food in the cabin was a great bowl of potatoes: 'Our fare is well enough, satisfies us all; my only concern is that I cannot earn sufficient to cover the nakedness of these poor children; could I clothe them, I should be happy.' This same man was paying £5 per acre for his land, and, when the landlord provided the manure, double that amount.[1]

The very insecurity we have been depicting was a means of attaching the peasant the more securely to his potato patch and conacre. In the parish of Thurlee 43% of the land of nine small farmers was under potatoes in 1833.[2]

When the farmer was evicted, then the conacre land went also, hence the cottier and farmer, if he were a small one, generally found themselves in the same boat. When the farmer was bigger, then the fate of the two in face of distress diverged, especially if scarcity was due to a shortage of potatoes. The farmer had his corn fo fall back on, and in the nineteenth century not seldom a substantial sum in his bank. The cottier had neither corn nor cash.

If eviction took place in normal times, that is, not in times of famine, then the ejected people wandered off in search of new lands, and if they had cash, which they rarely had, were relatively safe. Those who were mere tillers of some five acres, or cottiers with only a potato-patch and conacre land, had little to live on bar the potatoes they had harvested. Many would go begging and would be given potatoes enough for the day's food. Others would engage to cultivate some small plot on a farmer's land, at almost any rent, whilst others would squat on the roadside, build a shelter, and by any means secure a scrap of land on which once more to grow their potatoes.

It was the belief in the mind of the landlord, or his agent, that ultimately the evicted would get hold somehow of enough potatoes to keep them alive, which salved their consciences. Their sensibility may not have been high, but even the most callous would not have liked to

---

[1] Curwen, J. C. (1818). *State of Ireland*, p. 162.
[2] Simington, Rbt. (1942). Eire. Tithe Applotment Books of 1834. *J. Dept. Agric., Eire*, 1942, vol. XXXVIII, pp. 239–343.

think that his orders were, in truth, mass executions. The Irish, unfortunately, had not learned the Japanese technique of performing hari-kari on the landlord's doorstep.

The victory of Waterloo was followed by a great slump which very seriously affected the working classes both at home and in Ireland. In the former they suffered from lack of employment to a greater or lesser extent; in the latter they found themselves evicted on the roadside. Fortune's wheel had suddenly gone full circle. The demand for corn fell, a return to pasture was indicated; this meant the consolidation of holdings and the abolition of the small ones. A wave of eviction, second only to that following the famine of 1846–7, set in. It started gradually, and as it grew, acquired for itself recognition as a definite policy to be known as 'Clearance'. This policy reached its maximum about 1830, when it was halted by the Whiteboy opposition. Poulett Scrope wrote:[1] 'But for the salutary dread of the Whiteboy Association, ejectment would desolate Ireland and decimate her population....Yes, the Whiteboy system is the only check on the ejectment system, and weighing one against the other, horror against horror, and crime against crime, it is perhaps the lesser evil of the two.'

By Acts of Parliament, passed between 1816 and 1820, eviction was not only rendered easier, but power was given to the landlord to distrain on the tenant's growing crops; keep them till ripe, and sell them when harvested. This meant, in fact, that his staff of life, his potatoes, whether they were off his conacre land, or from the patch of land near his cabin, could be seized, and he and his family left literally without food. It may be observed that the Irish landlord, so often a mere collector of rents, thus came to enjoy a power over his tenant, which the English landlord, in comparison a father to his tenant, never even dreamt of expecting. By a further Act of 1826, the landlords could withhold the right of subletting, which meant that the evicted, homeless poor could be prevented from regaining a foothold on the land.

It is not surprising that many sought occasion by which they might find themselves lodged in prison, where at least they would be spared the pangs of hunger. Reid, who was deeply interested in prison reform, visited the chief prisons of the country. He found little to say in favour of the accommodation but was fully satisfied as to the dietary. In general, the allowance of potatoes was 7 lb., of oatmeal 1 lb., and of milk 1 quart per day; if the oatmeal was omitted, the potato ration might be as high as 14 lb. per day. In most prisons on two days of the week, the diet was varied: instead of potatoes and oatmeal, 2 lb. of best white or light brown bread and a quart of milk was substituted. It was not because of lack

---

[1] Scrope, G. Poulett (1834). *Letters to Lord Melbourne.* O'Brien, G. (1921). *Econ. History of Ireland from the Union to the Famine*, p. 55.

of food in the country that the people starved, but for the wherewithal
to procure it.[1]

The abolition of the 40s. franchise in 1829 acted as a further stimulus
to the clearance policy, for the cottier who lived on his acre of potatoes
was no longer a political asset to the landlord. How insecurity of tenure,
parliamentary encouragement of eviction, and the vital problem of
finding some spot on which to grow their potatoes, combined to harass
the peasantry, may be learnt from the evidence submitted to the Commission of Inquiry on the Irish Poor by cottiers and labourers.[2] A man,
Jennings, living in the village of Cong, Co. Mayo, relates how 'he was
married to an industrious woman, a dressmaker who could earn a
shilling a day'. When she died, he was reduced to depend, like the rest
of his class, on his labour and his conacre; being unable to pay the rent
of his last conacre, the crop was seized and auctioned to satisfy the
demand: he says:

I was left without provisions, if my children dropped dead, I would not
get a potato for them, as I had not the rent; I was left to depend altogether
on my chance savings. If I had three or four days work one week, I might
not have a day the next. I should make some shift to keep alive. Often I had
a meal one day and had not a bit the next, and many of my sort had my story
to tell. I never asked anything of my neighbour, but they were kind to me
of themselves. My next-door neighbour on my right or left, would guess
and know of my distress and make it known to others; and the Lord would
inspire them to help me. If they thought within themselves that I was going
to bed fasting, they would come in and give me a plate of potatoes, they would
leave it with myself or my children, discreetly, and say nothing about it.
I have done it in my turn for others; though I am a shabby, poor fellow to-day,
when my wife lived I was decent and fit to appear before a congregation.
I had plenty of potatoes, often a bit of meat, and was able and willing to help
a neighbour.

A further aspect of the social conditions prevailing is illustrated by
another witness, Malowney:

Some of my neighbours, who cannot buy a pig to rear for the rent, fly off
to Leinster to earn it, the moment they have planted their potatoes; some take
their families with them. They must beg; and I have seen four or six in family
leave home, and have but one fold of a blanket to take with them to cover
them all. . . .Of the families that are left at home, some have early potatoes
to support them, others must beg. I know that these labourers beg their way
to Leinster, and their way home; if they did not, they would have but little
of their wages. Some of my neighbours have been out since August; if they
do not bring home the rent, they have no other means of support but to follow

---

[1] Reid, Thomas (1823). Op. cit. pp. 158–321.
[2] The Irish Poor Commission (1835). Selection from the Evidence, p. 203.

on the begging at home for the winter, and the person they will ask relief from is the neighbour that holds a little land, and is almost as poor as themselves.

Malowney goes on to tell that he 'has known labourers who were unable to redeem their conacre, and were thus left without a stock [of potatoes] for the succeeding year, to work the ensuing spring with farmers for potatoes and to eat one part of them while they planted the other'. He says: 'They fast all the summer—by fasting', he explains, 'I count it equal to fasting when a man and his wife and four children had to live on a quart of meal or a stone of potatoes for 24 hours, and I have known them to live on that.'

As a measure of the poverty of the Irish cottier at this time, it would be difficult to find evidence more eloquent than that embodied in the colloquialism that they preferred their 'praties with a bone in them'. Here is the account of a visitor to a cabin near Ballygawley, Tyrone:[1]

The family were at dinner: the repast consisted of dry potatoes only, which were contained in a basket[2] set upon the pot in which they had been boiled; this was placed on the floor in the middle of the cabin. The father was sitting on a stool and the mother on a kreel of turf; one of the children had a straw box, the youngest even sprawling on the floor, and five others were standing round the potato basket. [The potatoes were only half boiled.] We always have our praties hard, they stick to our ribs and we can fast longer that way.

These conditions were not peculiar to the south or west. In the more prosperous province of Ulster, the picture is very much the same. Attention is also called to the incredible usury, prevalent in Ulster, and practised by the shop people and hucksters who, in this relation, were known as Gombeen men.

In Derry, employment on the land averaged only two days in the week throughout the year: during the summer many go to England for the harvest; the remainder of the year they fill in their spare time by weaving. In winter they have more food than in summer, generally their own potatoes, with a salt herring or some leeks, but no milk. They usually have a little patch of land or the use of it for manure. If thrown on the market [i.e. if they had to pay a competitive rent for it] they could not live at all. In summer they have but little potatoes, but some milk; they then get meal and give their labour for it afterwards; the highest intermediate price between the time of getting credit and the time of paying, being the usual bargain...when potatoes were 1s. 6d. a bushel, they would have been glad to have got two meals a day of them....In July the potatoes are generally 10d. a bushel, three bushels a week, which is a small allowance for a family [usually regarded as six souls] would be 2s. 6d. a week; there is no fund that offers them any assistance. When heads

[1] Reid, T. (1823). *Travels in Ireland*, p. 203. London: Longmans, Hunt.
[2] See chapter xxxiv, and Pl. XXIX, fig. 93.

of families are out of work, it is very common for the wives and children to beg, not however in the immediate neighbourhood.[1]

All the relevant evidence taken by the Devon Commission from every part of Ireland, is at one on the dependence of the entire cottier class on their potato crop. Nor was it limited to them; the farmers of 5 to 20 acres of land were rarely in better case. In Carrickmacross, County Monaghan, the Rev. James Mulligan[2] says: 'they [i.e. small farmers] live on potatoes and milk. It is considered that he is a very fortunate man if he has milk for his family. He sells his butter and never uses oatmeal in his house.' It is not often that one finds oatmeal excluded, though throughout the vast volume of evidence collected by the Commission, it is obvious that it played a quite secondary role in the household economy of the poorer classes.

The position in the households of the better-off class of cottiers and small farmers had not, in fact, altered very much. Sir George Nicholls the famous authority on the Poor Law in 1841 says their diet 'will consist chiefly of milk, oatmeal, potatoes and vegetables, he then goes into details of the household cookery in which the potato is the all-important food, oatmeal a quite secondary one, and bacon a rare luxury.[3]

A similar view had been expressed in 1818: 'The first and most important object in the rural economics of Ireland is the crop of potatoes, for on these exclusively depends the existence of all the lower orders not resident in towns', and then, a little later:

The potato, which in some points of view, may justly be regarded as one of the greatest blessings to our species, is capable of operating the greatest calamities, when it exclusively furnishes the food on which a community is content to exist, for as the cultivation of a single statute acre may successfully and easily be attended by one individual and as its produce on an average would give food for at least ten persons the year round, at 7 lb. each day, which may be considered as an abundant allowance, what chance is there for manual exertion in such a society among whom a patrimonial aversion to labour and an habitual attachment to idleness are paramount to every other consideration.[4]

Ireland remained a perpetual source of anxiety and embarrassment to the British Government. In Westminster, whilst O'Connell led a losing fight for Repeal, two measures of importance reached the Statute Book, and gave some relief to the native Irish. Tithes were commuted in 1838; and the Act demanding the offensive oaths, which

[1] See chapter XIV, p. 265.
[2] Devon Commission (1845). Q. 21, vol. I, p. 894.
[3] Nicholls, Sir George (1841). *The Farmer's Guide*, p. 165.
[4] Curwen, J. C. (1818). Op. cit. pp. 107 and 121.

prevented Catholics from sitting in the House, was annulled. Against this, Coercion Acts were passed or re-enacted every few years, itself a measure of the agrarian unrest. The political aspect of the problem was summed up by Disraeli: 'A starving population, an absentee aristocracy, an alien church, and the weakest executive in the world.'[1]

The social aspect received the fullest attention from the Devon Commission, whose *Report* was published in the fatal year 1845:

The potato enabled a large family to live on food produced in great quantities at a trifling cost, and, as the result, the increase of the people has been gigantic. There had, however, been no corresponding improvement in their material and social condition, but the opposite. The Census Commissioners of 1841[2] divided the house-accommodation of the country into four classes. The lowest or fourth class comprised all mud cabins having only one room. This class admittedly consisted of buildings unfit for human habitation, according to the ideas of civilized society; yet it appeared that in Down, the best-circumstanced county in this respect, twenty-four per cent of the population lived in houses of this class, whilst in Kerry the proportion was sixty-six per cent. The average of the whole population of Ireland, as given by the Census Commissioners, showed that in the rural districts above forty-three per cent of the families, and in the urban districts above thirty-six per cent, inhabited houses of the fourth class. They were the houses of the cottier and the labourer —the class which depended for a precarious existence on the cultivation of a mere patch of land, and on the receipt of uncertain wages, mostly obtained by harvest work in England. Their sufferings, borne with exemplary patience, were, in the opinion of the Devon Commissioners, greater than the people of any other country in Europe had to sustain.[3]

The Devon Commission advocated recovery of wastes and more production, but the public in England and the great majority of the propertied classes in Ireland, adhered to the view that the whole trouble was due to over-population, itself based on the use of the potato as the food of the poor.

A few there were who felt uneasy as to the reliability of the potato, in all seasons, to sustain the people. It was thought that the potato was losing its vigour, that the methods of cultivation were both deleterious and inadequate. There had been failures of the crop in 1822, 1831, 1835, 1836 and 1837 in various parts of the country, and occasionally such had involved whole provinces. The distress had been great, but generally local; especially serious was the famine of 1822, which followed the rotting of the 1821 potato crop, when it was said that many thousands of people died of starvation and fever. On this occasion, there had been a good harvest of corn; what was needed was cash wherewith to purchase

---

[1] Disraeli, Benjamin. Speech in H. of C. 16 Feb. 1844; *The Times*, 17 Feb. 1844.
[2] *Report of the Census Commissioners*, 1841, p. 14; vol. I, p. 126; vol. II, p. 1116.
[3] *Devon Commission* (1845), p. 1116.

it. This, under the potato system, was never to hand. The Government advanced £300,000 and charitable funds another £334,000, most of which was spent on relief works.

Attention had been drawn to the threatened danger often enough. Was there not a monument on the hill overlooking Kingstown, Dublin, recording the unhappy experiences of just a century ago?

As we draw near to 1845, we find nothing to relieve the sombre picture of poverty and misery, starvation and evictions, which enshrouded the lives of so great a majority of the people of Ireland. The area under potatoes had reached its maximum: close on two million acres, and by far the greater part of it in plots less than one acre, most of which was cultivated by the spade.

The Union, it was obvious, had brought neither prosperity to Ireland, nor peace of mind to England. George O'Brien points out that in the first thirty-one years of the century, parliament had appointed no less than one hundred and fourteen commissions and sixty-one committees to report on Irish affairs. But, reports notwithstanding, the political tension between the two countries increased as the masses in Ireland grew, each year, more numerous and ever poorer.

All responsible people recognized that something in the whole make-up of Ireland and its relations to this country, was radically wrong. Much disappointment was felt that the removal of disabilities and the friendly advances which England had made during the last fifty years, had been so sterile of results. People talked of a vicious circle, and that it must be cut. But which were the elements which went to make up that circle, what their sequence in time and importance, and where the circuit should or could be cut, were questions which were then, and indeed still are, largely unsettled.

The events which followed the visitation of the Potato Blight in 1845 and 1846 did much to clarify the problem, and to those we must now turn.

CHAPTER XVI

The Potato Famine: its Causes and Consequences

On several occasions prior to 1845, the potato crop had failed, but such failures had been more or less local.[1] In 1845 and 1846 Ireland was confronted with a failure which was universal. Warnings of the serious consequence which might be expected to result from such a failure had been frequently given. So recently as 1835, the Select Committee on the Advances for Public Works in Ireland, with all the weight of its authority, reported: 'If the potato crop be a failure, its produce is consumed long before the peasantry can acquire new means of subsistence and then a famine ensues.... Thus the present system not only creates poverty and rapidly augments the population, but also entails on the country all the horrors of famine.'[2]

In 1839, Captain Chad, R.N., who administered famine relief following a potato failure in the west and midland counties, touched on the essential differences between dependence on a sole source of food such as the potato, as against an equally exclusive reliance on a cereal food-stuff. He reported that periodic famines were inevitable so long as the people 'subsist on that species of food which in a year of plenty cannot be stored up for the next, which may be one of scarcity'.[3]

The loss of the 1845 crop, however, was a new experience in every way. The disease attacked without warning the growing plants, destroying, in a few days, fields of potatoes which till then had been proudly re-splendent in all their pomp of dark green leaf and purple bloom, leaving nothing but black and withered stalks. Nor were its ravages halted by the death of the tops: before the peasants had time to harvest the crop, the tubers were found to be stained and were beginning to rot. Those who had gathered their crop and placed them in the clamps, found them rotten and useless within a few weeks. Prior to this, failures of the potato crop had been local, scattered, and discontinuous. This time it was general, no large area anywhere entirely escaped, though Ulster was less severely affected in 1845 than the rest of the country. Farmers on higher land, and those in drier districts, suffered rather less than others, but very few escaped the visitation altogether, nor was any one variety immune. A feature which may not have interested the Irish cottier, who

[1] See Appendix No. 1.
[2] Quoted from O'Brien (1921). *Econ. Hist. of Ireland, from the Union to the Famine*, p. 260.
[3] Quoted from Trevelyan, Sir Charles. Irish Crisis. *Edinburgh Review*, no. CLXXV, p. 170, January 1848.

had lost his all, but which did the biologists the world over, was that a similar disease had made its appearance at the same time in Great Britain and indeed throughout the whole continent of Europe.[1] It was its universality which caused many to recognize the outbreak as an economic problem of the first importance.

Another character of the new pestilence which impressed all in those dark days, was the universal, infiltrating stench of the rotting plants. This smell of the charnel house went far to induce many of the peasantry, and still more of their social superiors, to believe that they were confronted by no ordinary trouble, but that this was a visitation from on High, a scourge to punish the sins of the people. Many regarded it as a form of cholera which had spread to the potato, and recalled with alarm how, on previous occasions, failure of the potato crop had coincided with an outbreak of that plague.

As examples of the approach to problems of the kind, made by the middle-class generation of early Victorians, the following are of interest. A writer, having given it as his opinion that the trouble was due to volcanic action within the earth, says:

The ways of Providence are dark and inscrutable. It may please Him for wise purposes, no doubt, to pour forth the vials of His chastizement upon that ill-fated land for a longer period; or He may have ordained this signal visitation, as sent only for a time to redeem the past, to cause government to improve the conditions of the lower classes, which ought to have been done long ago, and to elevate a long-suffering race to a higher grade in civilized society.[2]

Another is convinced that it is the potato alone which has been the cause of all Ireland's troubles, not excluding her excessive fecundity; whilst the association with the pig created by a common food has reduced man to the level of his companion. Notwithstanding that all this has been going on for over 200 years, a fact overlooked by our author, he is prompted to the pious conviction that this final catastrophe may be the means by which a wise and merciful God is preparing to raise the Irishman to a higher social rank![3]

The views of one of the leading surgeons of his day, Alfred Smee, a Fellow of the Royal Society, are equally characteristic of this age of incredible complacency. With much show of authority, he will have nothing of Berkeley's fungus which was, in fact, the true cause of blight, but regards the infestation of the crop by aphids as responsible for the 'gangrene'. His mistakes are his own, but his attitude to the social

[1] Vrolik, G. (1846). *Observations et Expériences relative à la Maladie des Pommes de Terre.* Amsterdam.
[2] Parkins, J. (1846). *Gardeners' Chronicle*, p. 773.
[3] Elly, Samuel (1848). *Potatoes, Pigs and Politics.* London: Kent and Richards.

problem, revealed in all its nakedness by the famine, was characteristic of his time and his class: 'This effect of depending too exclusively on the culture of the Potato is fearfully exhibited in the Irish people where the potato has begotten millions of paupers who live but are not clothed, who marry but do not work, caring for nothing but their dish of potatoes.' Then he advances his solution of the Irish problem, which seems to have been as acceptable to the cultured society of the time, as it was indicative of the policy of *laisser faire*. 'If left to itself', says Smee, 'this fearful state of things would have remedied itself: for had the people the control of their own community, and had the potato crop failed to the extent to which it has this year, these people having no relation with any other, would have been left to their own resources, which being destroyed would have left them without food.'[1] In short, it was only the interference of an all too beneficent government, which prevented the Irish problem from being settled once and for all by Providence.

The scientific aspects of the new disease have been dealt with in a most illuminating manner by Large.[2] Suffice it here to say, that the cause, after much controversy, was found to be a fungus, known to-day as *Phytophthora infestans*, and that it came from America, where it had been recognized as early as 1843. The disease came to be known as Late Blight, and is with us to this day.

On 16 August 1845, the *Gardeners' Chronicle* contained a report from Dr Bell Slater of a new disease which had appeared in the Isle of Wight.[3] The next week, the famous editor, Dr Lindley, reported that 'a fatal malady had broken out amongst the potato crop. On all sides we hear of the destruction. In Belgium the fields are said to have been completely desolated. There is hardly a sound sample in Covent Garden'. And he followed this up with a remarkably accurate account of the various stages of the disease, from the early spot on the leaf, which turns black, to the spread of the 'gangrene' down the stem and into the tubers.[4] Before the end of September, news from the Continent showed that the potato fields of Poland, Germany, Belgium and France were all involved.

The season, up till the beginning of July, had been most favourable, and the potatoes everywhere were looking their best. A change then set in: the weather was overcast, with a minimum of sunshine, cold rain and fogs followed each other alternately, and the average temperature was seven degrees below the normal. On 12 September the *Gardeners'*

[1] Smee, Alfred (1846). *The Potato Plant*. London: Longmans.
[2] Large, E. C. (1940). *The Advance of the Fungi*. Jonathan Cape.
[3] In the account that follows, I am indebted for much of that which deals with the immediate scientific and economic consequences of the Blight itself to Mr E. C. Large's valuable and delightful book.
[4] Actually the fungus does not reach the tuber via the stem and stolon, but directly from the soil.

Chronicle gave prominence in the most dramatic manner to the news that Blight had appeared in Ireland. 'We stop the Press, with very great regret, to announce that the Potato Murrain has unequivocally declared itself in Ireland. The crops about Dublin are suddenly perishing. The conversion of potatoes into flour, by the process described by Mr Bodlington in this issue, becomes of the first national importance.' 'For where', asks Dr Lindley, knowing only too well how bound to the root the Irish people were, 'will Ireland be, in the event of a universal potato rot?'

Where, indeed! Now at last the truth was to be made manifest, that the domestic economy, nay the very existence of the major part of an entire nation of over eight million people, had been allowed to grow up, to balance itself, as it were, on the goodwill of a single food, the potato, and in a large measure on a single variety of the same, the 'Lumper'. Now, too, it was to become clear that the miserable cottier, from whom such extortionate rents had been wrung that he might grow his 'Lumpers', was, after all, the goose who laid the golden egg. For, the famine not only killed or crippled the peasantry but, as it proceeded, the middle classes joined the ranks of the starved and ruined, and before all was over, many of the large estate-owners were ruined too. But we are anticipating.

In the 1845 attack, the early varieties had been lifted, and so escaped. This availed Ireland but little, as the cottiers' crops were almost entirely late varieties, so late, indeed, that they were generally left in the ground till cut down by frost.[1] The 'lates' had suffered severely. When the peasants found that the tubers were rotting in the ground at the time of digging, many left them on the surface to take their chance. Those who stored them in the usual clamps fared worse, for in these the rot was found to spread with alarming rapidity, whilst many of those left on the ground had only the frost to contend with. The damage in 1845, in Ireland alone, was estimated to be about half the crop, and to represent a loss in money of £3,500,000,[2] and in Great Britain as a whole, £5,000,000.

The small farmers and cottiers, who together accounted for about 4½ million persons, consumed what was fit for food of their harvest, and when that was gone, they found themselves without food, and generally without cash. The pig, to which they looked to pay the rent, with no potatoes on which to feed, was only a liability. Distress was general, but far more severe in the south and west, where the peasants lived almost exclusively on the potato. In Ulster, oatmeal generally found a place in every home; though a minor source of food, yet it helped to stave off famine for a while.

---

[1] Knight, Thomas Andrew (1810). On Potatoes. *Trans. Hort. Soc.* (2nd edit.), vol. I, p. 190.

[2] Pethybridge, G. (1940). The Potato Blight. *R. Cornwall Polytechnic Soc.* vol. IX, pp. 48–61.

At first, the people could not believe that their winter supplies were rotting away before their eyes: they were numbed, not knowing where to look for help. It was only when landlords pressed for their rent and proceeded to evict, that agrarian trouble occurred. Some landlords generously forgave their tenants the current year's rent: Lord Kildare was one of these, and so delighted were his tenants, that bonfires were lit on the hills of Donegal in his honour.[1] Others might have wished to have done the same, but their estates were encumbered, and themselves in debt. The majority of the landlords followed their old policy of squeezing the last penny out of their tenantry, quite regardless of the catastrophe which had overtaken them.

Peel's government at once sent out a commission to Ireland to investigate. It consisted of one very distinguished botanist, Dr Lindley; Dr Lyon Playfair (later Sir Lyon), Professor of Chemistry, a man much in the public eye; and Sir Robert Kane, a Professor of Chemistry in Dublin. They reported faithfully on the alarming extent of the epidemic, and suggested methods for preserving the tubers as far as possible, but these were not such as the Irish peasant was likely to adopt, nor, in fact, would they have been of any value. Their report had the merit of demonstrating to the government the alarming social, economic, and political possibilities of the situation.

In Ireland there was plenty of corn, but following the usual routine, it was being shipped to England at the rate of 16,000 quarters weekly. But had it remained in the country, the starving peasantry would not have benefited from it, except the government had intervened, for they had no cash wherewith to purchase it. This extraordinary situation had existed for generations, but its danger had never been exposed on a large scale till now. The cottier had long been in the habit of paying for his conacre on which he grew his potatoes, by his own personal labour, at a specified rate per hour—a rate often not much more than half the current cash value for casual labour. The proceeds of the plot, he, his family and his pig consumed. When cow or pig was sold, the proceeds went to pay his rent. If there was anything over, it was needed for the payment of tithe, fees to the Catholic priest, and for the few domestic articles, including tobacco, which he or his wife did not make with their own hands. Cash was so rare a commodity, that there are abundant examples in the literature of Irish cottiers actually pawning pound notes for a few shillings.

In the spate of pamphlets which the famine called forth, there was one devoted to what the author calls 'the potato truck system'.[2] He describes the normal relation of cottier and farmer:

[1] Large, E. C. (1941). Op. cit. p. 34.
[2] Rogers, Jasper W. (1847). The Potato Truck System of Ireland; ....

The farmer engages his labourers from year to year, giving them land to produce their potato crop and seed when necessary, charging in almost every instance, a rent much beyond his own; and if a cottage be included, frequently in a similar ratio. Against this, he credits the labourers' work, keeping strict account of *days* and *half-days*, as the weather permits labour, and once a year— perhaps in some instances twice, the account is settled and the balance either way struck. Thus the 'truck system' in its worst form exists in Ireland and has so existed for ages.

When the potato fails, it is not only that the cottier has no cash, but his 'potato coin' fails him at the same time. The author points out that this abuse of the 'truck system' has prevented about £13,000,000 of coin from circulating but, still more serious, is the habit it has engendered in men of the farming classes to take farms without capital, engage to pay exorbitant rents, and then borrow at rates up to 300 % in the hope of paying off their debts in the first year or two. In this the farmer invariably fails, because his men, working on truck, do not put their energy into the job. This last is borne out by the fact that the man-power per acre employed for cultivation in Ireland was just about double that needed in England.

As the autumn of 1845 proceeded, the position became more alarming. The home government were alive to the dangers, but there were great ramparts of traditionalism and vested interests to be scaled, before any programme could be sketched out, much less put into practice.

Contemporary Irish journals, such as the *Limerick Chronicle*, sounded the alarm on 17 September; by the end of October it predicted famine and advised everybody to save three times the usual quantity of seed, and to plant early varieties, such as 'Early Farmer', which had escaped destruction.[1]

Ireland spoke with two voices, the hungry cottiers, and the new politically conscious intelligentsia with O'Connell at their head. The former saw their food for the winter gone, their seed for the coming season imperilled, and their pig, on which they relied to pay the rent, killed and eaten because there were no potatoes on which to feed it. Their minds were obsessed by the dread of eviction from their homes, and coloured by the conviction that no help could ever be expected from England. The latter lost no time in formulating a programme: meetings were held at the Mansion House, Dublin, and addresses sent to the Queen and the government. Their plan was, that the ports should be closed immediately against export of corn, that public granaries be erected throughout the country, and the corn sold direct to the people at moderate prices, that the use of grain for whisky distilleries should be forbidden, and that public works should be undertaken. Both the

[1] *Limerick Chronicle* (1845). 17 September, 31 October and 22 November. [According to Dr Bourke (1985) *pers. comm.*, the *Limerick Chronicle* did not actually 'sound the alarm' until 1 November 1845. – Ed.]

first and the last of their proposals had, in fact, been enacted in the famine period of 1765.

On 22 November 1845, Lord John Russell published his famous letter in *The Times*, in which he declared himself at one with the Anti-Corn Laws League, and in favour of the complete and immediate repeal of laws, which he described as 'the blight of commerce, the bane of agriculture, the source of bitter division amongst classes, the cause of penury, fever, mortality and crime amongst the people'. On 2 December, Peel presented the outline of his Bill to the House, by which great reductions in the Corn Duties were to be made at once, and be followed by their abolition in the near future. So sudden a break with the traditional policy of the landowners who formed the majority of his cabinet, and the backbone of his party in the country, was too much for most of his supporters. It is doubtful if any of the latter shared in Peel's conversion to the belief that, contrary to his former expectation, high prices did not lead automatically to higher wages, and that, in consequence, food taxes were an unfair burden on labour. On 4 December, *The Times*, having learnt of Peel's intended proposals through the indiscretion of Lord Aberdeen,[1] published the statement that at the opening of parliament on 6 January, Peel would announce an amendment of the Corn Laws leading to their total repeal. Notwithstanding officially inspired denials, *The Times* repeated the statement, saying that: 'We adhere to our original announcement that Parliament will meet early in January, and that a repeal of the Corn Laws will be proposed in one house by Sir Robert Peel, and in the other by the Duke of Wellington.' By this time, Peel realized that he had not got his cabinet with him. The action of the Duke of Wellington was typical: he was ready to sacrifice his own political conviction that the Corn Laws should be maintained, in favour of the still stronger one, that the Queen must be supported by the best possible administration, and such, in his perfectly honest opinion, was one controlled by Peel. Peel resigned on 5 December, and on 10 December the Queen called on Russell to form a government; in this he failed, and resigned. Peel was once more called to take over the government. On 2 January 1846, the speech from the throne mentioned the government's intention to deal drastically with the Corn Laws. Peel explained that he had become a convert to the Manchester School of Free Trade, and that he hoped to introduce its principles into all the departments of our trade. On 27 January, Peel presented his Corn Bill which, though it fell somewhat short of complete abolition,

[1] The incident is referred to by George Trevelyan in his *British History in the Nineteenth Century*, 1782–1901, p. 272 n. He writes: 'It was Peel's colleague, Aberdeen, who told *The Times* this secret that proved half untrue, not Mrs Norton, as Meredith supposed when he wrote *Diana of the Crossways*.'

afforded a great relief to the poor. On 25 January 1846, the Bill passed both houses, but at the moment of doing so, Peel's government was defeated in the Commons. Six months had elapsed since the potato blight had appeared, and by now, what originally was but a shortage of food, was taking on the dimensions of a famine. Relief works, of which we shall speak directly, had done little to alleviate the general distress, and agrarian trouble was prevalent wherever the landlords had shown an unsympathetic attitude. The government had felt it necessary to place a Coercion Bill before the house: this, O'Connell and his followers naturally opposed. On this occasion, however, they were joined by the Whigs, whose policy in regard to coercion in Ireland, when exercised by others, was that it must be accompanied by some legislative relief of grievances. Such a situation would have been dangerous, though not fatal, had it not been taken advantage of by Disraeli who, for the ten years he had been in the House, had not hitherto found an appropriate opportunity of showing his metal. His hour had struck, and he lost no time in taking advantage of it. He placed himself at the head, or rather, acted as the inspirer and spokesman, of a band of Tories who now felt convinced that Peel had betrayed them, and were determined to be revenged. The Coercion Bill, which normally they would have supported, was their opportunity; Disraeli led his followers into the lobby against it, and it was lost. Peel resigned. In the speech announcing his resignation, he said:

But it may be that I shall leave a name sometimes remembered with expressions of good will in those places which are the abode of men whose lot it is to labour and to earn their daily bread by the sweat of their brow—a name remembered with expressions of good will when they shall recreate their exhausted strength with abundant and untaxed food, the sweeter because it is no longer leavened with a sense of injustice.[1]

To what extent the failure of the potato was responsible for the conversion of Peel to the doctrine of Free Trade, has been much discussed. A semi-official view was that his change of mind was entirely due to the collapse of the potato.[2] The more correct interpretation seems to be that the potato, in bringing about Peel's conversion to the doctrine of Free Trade, determined the time, rather than the character, of that event. His biographer writes:

That question [Protection] was being fast brought to a crisis by public opinion and the Anti-Corn-Law League. Peel had been recognized in 1841 by Cobden as a Free Trader, and after experience in office, he had become in principle more and more so. Since his accession to power, he had lowered the duties of the sliding scale. He had alarmed the farmers by admitting

---

[1] McCarthy, Justin (1880). *A History of our Own Times*, vol. I, p. 412.
[2] Carr, F. C. *Handbook of Administrations*, 1801–69 (edit. 1901).

foreign cattle and meat under his new tariff, and by admitting Canadian corn. He had done his best, in his speeches, to put the maintenance of the Corn Laws on 'low ground', and to wean the landed interest from their reliance on Protection. The approach of the Irish Famine in 1845 turned decisively the wavering balance.[1]

Whilst accepting these views, it would be a mistake to minimize the credit due to Peel, and shared by his colleague the Home Secretary, Sir James Graham, of having immediately grasped the full implication of the threat to Ireland's chief source of food, the urgency of prompt remedial measures, and the securing of an adequate supply of seed for the coming year. One fact emerges beyond dispute: Peel had made up his mind that repeal was the only remedy. Letters written on 13 October 1846, which crossed, leave us in no doubt as to their respective views. Peel writes: 'I have no confidence in such remedies as the prohibition of exports, or the stoppage of distilleries.' Graham, who seems to have had a far more intimate understanding of the problem as a whole, explains his attitude: 'A great national risk is always incurred when a population so dense as that of Ireland subsists on the potato; for it is the cheapest and the lowest food, and if it fail, no substitute can be found for starving multitudes.'[2]

The parliamentary struggle we have so briefly sketched, was not only historic on its own merits, seeing that it ushered in the great era of Free Trade, but it is the outstanding instance of a political event of the first magnitude, being precipitated by the behaviour of a simple vegetable. That such was possible, was due to the unholy monopoly acquired by the potato in the agricultural system of Ireland. To-day we can see the action as a whole; contemporary observers realized only the part which the potato had played in the penultimate act of the political drama whose final phase shook Great Britain to its foundations. We will quote only two: Disraeli:[3] 'As for their command over Nature'; said Tancred, 'let us see how it will operate in a second deluge. Command over Nature! Why the humblest root that serves for the food of man has mysteriously withered throughout Europe, and they are already pale at the possible consequences'. He also tells us how the Great Duke summed up the situation in characteristic manner: 'Rotten potatoes have done it all— they put Peel in his damned fright, and his country gentlemen looked on aghast.'[4]

The Duke had had a long experience of potato failures. Eight years

[1] Parker, Charles Stuart (1929). *Encyclopaedia Britannica* (14th edit.), vol. XVII, p. 435.

[2] Lever, Tresham (1942). *The Life and Times of Sir Robert Peel*. Allen and Unwin.

[3] Disraeli, Benjamin (1926). *Tancred* (Bradenham edit.), vol. X, p. 319. London: Peter Davies.

[4] Guedalla, P. (1926). In Notes to *Tancred*.

earlier he had declared: 'I am firmly convinced that from the year 1806, down to the present time, a year has not passed in which the government have not been called on to give assistance to relieve the poverty and distress which prevailed in Ireland.'[1] But this time it was not the old enemies, rain or frost, which had brought it about, but a new and devastating disease.

The Irish famine, consequent on the destruction of the potato crop in 1846, precipitated not only a major political crisis, but a financial one of no less magnitude, the most severe the country had experienced since 1816.

During the 1840's, the tempo of railway construction in England had greatly increased, and both English capital and enterprise were engaged on similar tasks on the Continent. With so keen a demand for capital, the 'city' was in a very sensitive mood, and ill prepared to withstand the crisis, which it was soon to be called on to face. At the close of 1845, the outlook was already threatening, but the extent of the potato failure in Ireland had not been so great as had been feared, and there was as yet no call on the gold reserves to pay for the import of foreign corn. In the autumn of 1846 the position was very different; the potato failed, and this time completely. The demand for corn was both immediate and imperative. 'Wheat prices rocketted up from a minimum of 45s. 1d. in August 1846, to an average of 80s. 6d. for the three months ending 29 May 1847, and to 94s. 10d. for the six weeks ending 26 June. During May there were sales in Mark Lane at 115s.' And, as Clapham continues: 'The world's corn-bins were scraped for wheat, oats, rice and maize—any food grain that the starving Irish would or might eat.' The corn market became a theatre for the wildest speculation. When, however, the potato crop of 1847 was found to have escaped disease, and that the grain harvest at home was particularly promising, the market broke. Prices fell all through July and August and reached an average price of 49s. 6d. in September. The final crash was staggering: bankruptcies mounted in number and value. The first and the majority of the heaviest casualties, were amongst the corn trade and included that of the firm of Robinson, whose senior partner was the then Governor of the Bank of England.[2]

The crisis spread as the end of the year approached, and overwhelmed many country banks, including three of the biggest in Liverpool; the London banks held, but the wave of bankruptcy swept on over the Stock Exchange and involved many of the overseas trades, reaching its climax in the spring of 1848.

[1] Wellington, Duke of (21 May 1838). Speech in the House of Lords, on the introduction of the Irish Poor Law. From Trevelyan, Charles (1848). Op. cit. p. 12.

[2] Clapham, John (1944). The Bank of England, vol. II, pp. 197 seq. Cambridge Univ. Press.

The truth was, 'there had been every kind of reckless business and doubtful business in the wake of cheap money and the railway mania, all of which the crisis now brought into the open'.[1]

A contemporary writer estimates that 33 million pounds were spent on corn to meet the Irish needs, that the consequent drain on the gold reserves led to a refusal of discounts, which precipitated bankruptcies to the value of 22 million pounds in all, whilst industry everywhere was checked by the rise in loan interest, which leapt from 3% to 9%, whilst national revenue dropped.[2]

It was not only the capitalist interests which were threatened by the failure of the potato crop. Labour, too, received a severe check—strikes gave place to lock-outs and to reduction of wages, against which the Trades Unions were powerless.[3]

As the year progressed, though thrones on the Continent were tumbling on all sides, the financial crisis at home passed away, but not before the suspension of Peel's 1844 Bank Act controlling the relation of gold and supply of credit, had restored confidence though, in point of fact, no notes beyond the normal limit were issued.

While the political struggle was proceeding and the financial crisis maturing, efforts were being made to deal with the acute distress in Ireland. Peel had on his own authority induced the banker, Baring, to buy secretly £100,000 worth of maize, and this was distributed for sale in March 1846 through the local tradesmen, to those who could be induced to buy the 'yellow dust', or 'Peel's brimstone'.

Peasantry, the world over, are proverbially conservative in their domestic habits: the Irish cottier, by reason of his complete dependence on the potato, excelled all others in this respect. 'His wife's knowledge of cookery, it has been said, did not extend beyond the boiling of a potato.'[4] Hence it was not till their stocks of potatoes were exhausted, that they would make use of any strange foreign foodstuffs.

As the year advanced, and the 'meal months' of July and August came along, the distress increased. Public relief works had been established, and new roads and harbours were being built all over the country, but not always with a view to their ultimate economic utility. By August, 97,000 men were being so employed.

In 1846, the people, renewing their courage and hopes with the spring, planted a still bigger acreage of potatoes than usual. O'Rourke[5] quotes estimates of the acreage under potatoes in four provinces, as follows:

[1] Ibid. p. 199.
[2] Elly, Samuel (1848). *Potatoes, Pigs and Politics*. London: Kent and Richards.
[3] Cole, G. D. H. and Postgate, Raymond (1938). *The Common People*, p. 311. Methuen.
[4] Trevelyan, Charles (1848). Op. cit. p. 6.
[5] O'Rourke (1875). *History of the Great Irish Famine*, p. 153.

Ulster 352,665 acres, Munster 460,630 acres, Leinster 217,854 acres, and Connaught 206,292 acres. The whole crop was valued at 16 million pounds; all of it was lost.

Blight in 1846 was first observed in the neighbourhood of Cork, on 3 June, but did not make serious headway till the latter part of July, when it spread rapidly. Whereas the attack had been variable in the previous year, and some fields, and even considerable areas, had escaped destruction, this year scarcely a plant in the whole four provinces was spared— the destruction of the crop was all but complete; the terror and desolation it brought in its train, no less.

One might fill another volume with the descriptions, only too truthful, of the ghastly conditions which resulted from a second year's failure of the potato crop. A careful perusal of the accounts, given by different authors of the state of Ireland in the winter of 1846–7, has convinced me that it would be impossible to exaggerate the horrors of these days, or to compare them with anything which has occurred in Europe since the Black Death of 1348. Some even include references to the eating of flesh from human corpses. Considered as a whole, the annals of the Irish famine constitute one of the most tragic memorials of which we have record, in man's long chronicle of suffering. We will confine ourselves to just a few witnesses, who may be regarded as reliable and not inclined to exaggerate.[1]

Father Mathew, a Catholic priest, possibly the most beloved and respected man in all Ireland at the time, and the only one who, unaided, contrived to wean the Irish peasantry from their beloved whisky for eight years, including three of the famine, wrote:

On the 27th of last month [July 1846] I passed from Cork to Dublin, and this doomed plant bloomed in all luxuriance of an abundant harvest. Returning on the 3rd instant [August] I beheld with sorrow one wide waste of putrefying vegetation. In many places the wretched people were seated on the fences of their decaying gardens, wringing their hands, and wailing bitterly the destruction that had left them foodless.[2]

In these few lines, Father Mathew conveys to us, not only the fact that the people had rested their entire economic existence on the potato, but the psychological effect born of such a slavish dependence; for when the potato was suddenly denied them, having no alternative source of food, they could do nothing but bemoan their fate and wring their hands. For them the issue was simple—the potato or starvation.

---

[1] Of the classical works on the Famine Years, the chief are: O'Rourke's *History of the Great Irish Famine*, Dublin; Trevelyan's 'Irish Crisis', to which frequent references are made in the text, and *The Transactions of the Central Relief Committee of the Society of Friends*.

[2] Mathew, Father (27 July 1846). Letter published in *Parliamentary Papers*. Quoted from O'Brien, op. cit. vol. III, p. 236.

The reactions which were to follow the destruction of a people's food supplies for the year, did not take on their catastrophic character till the turn of the year (1846). Then, with startling rapidity, shortage passed to famine, famine to starvation, and starvation to death which, if it brought peace to its elect, augmented the suffering of those it spared.

The government, thinking that the 1846 crop would be adequate, had brought its relief works to an end by 15 August. When, shortly afterwards, the people began to lift their potatoes, the tops of which had been transformed into a black, evil-smelling slime, such optimistic views collapsed. The large tubers were either already rotten, or succumbed to attack soon after their removal, and all that was left was a handful of minute tubers, of which one witness remarks: 'it took twelve to weigh four-and-a-half ounces, the weight of an average edible tuber'. But even these poor remnants were of little value, being miniature and watery.

In June of 1847, Lord Dufferin and the Hon. G. F. Boyle[1] made a journey to Skibbereen in Cork, which they heard was the district in which the most acute distress had been experienced. As a matter of fact, they had no sooner left Dublin than they were met by sights which dismayed them. Dead bodies lay on the roadside; in some towns they could not be buried because of their number. Everywhere typhus was raging and, wherever they stopped, they were besieged by starving, almost naked beggars. They found deserted cabins, often containing unburied corpses, and everywhere a spirit of hopelessness. In the small towns they learnt that the tradesmen were ruined, and many in no better case than the cottiers.

It is remarkable that the most disastrous effects of the potato failure occurred in the west. It is true that the potato had, in those parts, won its most complete victory, yet easy access to the fisheries in coastal areas such as Dingle and Skibbereen would, one might have thought, have gone far to make good the loss of the people's food. Such was not the case. O'Brien[2] writes: 'The Commissioners of Public Works reported that no industry had suffered so severely through the famine as the fishery, partly because there was a prejudice among the country people against the use of fish, unless they could obtain potatoes to use with it, and partly because the fishermen had been compelled to pawn or sell their tackle to meet their immediate needs.'[3]

Famine, continuous and severe such as this, which commenced in the autumn of 1845, and gathered increasing momentum as spring followed winter, was only to be endured if the approaching harvest brought a

---

[1] Dufferin, Lord, and Boyle Hon. G. F. (1847). *Narrative of a Journey from Oxford to Skibbereen.*
[2] O'Brien, G. (1921). Op. cit. p. 293.
[3] *Facts from Fisheries* (1848). Waterford.

message of hope, food and succour. But alas! Just as the people were looking with anxious eyes on their potato fields pregnant with the promise of plenty, the fell disease smote the land once more, and the whole fabric of their dream vanished. This final calamity broke what spirit was left in the people. They had but little more fight in them, and this was to be dissipated by the inadequacy of the relief works. These, even where efficiently administered, had proved, if not a failure, at least a very poor substitute for a normal livelihood.

The famous clause of the 1847 Poor Relief (Ireland) Act, by which no man who possessed more than a quarter of an English acre, i.e. about one-sixth of an Irish acre, was eligible for poor-law relief, was, perhaps, the last straw which, added to their spiritual and material burdens, finally broke the heart of the people. It has passed down to history under the name of its proposer, William Henry Gregory, who was M.P. for Dublin. It is fitting that it should be recorded here in full because, although there is no mention of the potato, its inevitable effect was to rob the poorest of the people of their potato plots:

And be it further enacted, that no person who shall be in the occupation, whether under lease or agreement, or as tenant at will, or from year to year, or in any other manner whatever, of any land of greater extent than the quarter of a statute acre, shall be deemed and taken to be a destitute poor person under the provisions of this Act, or of any former Act of Parliament. Nor shall it be lawful for any Board of Guardians to grant any relief whatever, in or out of the workhouse, to any such occupier, his wife or children. And if any person, having been occupier as aforesaid, shall apply to any Board of Guardians for relief as a destitute poor person, it shall not be lawful for such Guardians to grant such relief, until they shall be satisfied that such person has, *bona fide*, and without collusion, absolutely parted with and surrendered any right or title which he may have had to the occupation of any land over and above such extent as aforesaid, of one occupation.

Interpreted in plain language, it meant that the starving cottier must vacate his home, and his scrap of potato land, before he and his starving children could be given a crust of bread. The effect of the clause can be gauged from the Report of the Officers of the 'Friends', dated 31 January 1848:

Persons holding over a quarter of an acre of ground, with several other denominations of poor, whom the stringency of the law excludes from relief are those by whom distress is now most severely felt.

Another of their correspondents shows how this same clause led to gross abuse:

I have heard that many clearances are effected by the landlords refusing, as *ex officio* Poor Law Guardians, to recommend their starving tenantry to out-door relief, unless they consented to give up their holdings. The people in many instances clung to their bit of land with the energy of drowning men.

The Gregory Clause acted both as a justification and a cloak for such sharp practices.

The Act became law on 16 April 1847. On 6 October of the same year there appeared in *The Times* a letter from the Chief Famine Administrator from which it is clear that the man on the spot had a far sounder understanding of the basic economy of the cottier system than had the member for Dublin:

A family in the West of Ireland, once located on from one to three or four acres of land, was provided for; a cabin could be raised in a few days without the expense of a sixpence; the potatoes, at the cost of a very little labour, supplied them with a sufficiency of food, with which from habit, they were perfectly content; and a pig, or, with some, a cow or donkey, or pony, and occasional labour at a very low rate of wages, gave them what was necessary to pay a rent, and for such clothing and other articles as were absolutely necessary, and which, with a great proportion, were on the lowest scale of human existence. The foundation of the whole, however, was the possession of the bit of land; it was the one and the only thing absolutely necessary; the rent consequently was high, and generally well paid, being the first demand on all money received, in order to secure that essential tenure; and only what remained became applicable to other objects. Although of the lowest grade, it was an easy mode of subsistence, and led to the encouragement of early marriages, large families, and a rapidly-increasing population, and at the same time afforded the proprietor very good return of profit for his land.[1]

Sir Charles Trevelyan's comments on the above, completed the picture of an Irish peasant's life, and show how narrow was the frame in which it was confined:

The relations of employer and employed, which knit together the framework of society, and establish a mutual dependence and good-will, have no existence in the potato system. The Irish small-holder lives in a state of isolation, the type of which is to be sought for in the islands of the South Sea, rather than in the great civilized communities of the ancient world. A fortnight for planting, a week or ten days for digging, and another fortnight for turf-cutting, suffice for his subsistence; and during the rest of the year he is at leisure to follow his own inclinations, without even the safeguard of the intellectual tastes and legitimate objects of ambition which only imperfectly obviate the evils of leisure in the higher ranks of society.[2]

The cost of the potato famine in terms of life and health of the people is very difficult to estimate. We have certain fixed points. The population of Ireland in 1841 was 8,175,124. In 1851 it was 6,552,385, a diminution

[1] Burgoyne, Sir John (1847). *The Times* (6 October).
[2] Trevelyan, Sir Charles (1848). Op. cit. p. 4.

of 1,622,739, but this cannot be accepted as the number of people lost to Ireland by starvation, disease and emigration, for it takes no account of what the natural increase of population would have been by the census year of 1851 had there been no potato blight and consequent famine. The Census Commission devoted the most careful consideration to this problem, and came to the conclusion that the population in 1851 would have been 9,010,798, so that Ireland was the poorer by about $2\frac{1}{2}$ million persons. They then proceeded to estimate how many may be assumed to have lost their lives by the famine and its consequences, and find it amounts to a million. O'Rourke's[1] independent estimate is about a quarter of a million higher.

It has already been mentioned that famine was followed by disease, the character of which was very largely determined by the peculiar conditions of the people's habits of life. A people who had lived, in the main, on the potato, was well furnished with vitamin C, and, with its loss, scurvy was inevitable, unless fresh vegetables were to hand. But the Irish peasantry were not vegetable growers; after a time, only nettles and herbs were available, and scurvy was not only common but appeared, in a large number of cases, in its acute and fatal form, purpura. The Commissioners of Health were very much concerned; they rightly attributed it to the absence of the potato, but they also thought it was induced by the use of so-called potato flour, made from blighted tubers. It is interesting that they were of opinion that half-cooked food was responsible, and therefore strongly recommended that the relief ration should be given in a cooked form, and by so doing, they reduced the available vitamin.

Dysentery, so common a sequel of famine, accounted for 25,446 recorded deaths in 1847, and the number was maintained for several years to come. In 1848 cholera broke out in the debilitated masses, and accounted for over 30,000 deaths.

But of all the immediate consequences of the famine, the most devastating was that caused by typhus fever; a disease which, conveyed by body lice, was endemic, as might be expected amongst a population, the mass of which lived under such unhygienic conditions, as did the peasant classes of Ireland. The pre-famine death-rate was 7,249; it rose in 1846 to 17,145, and in 1847 to 57,095. In 1848 conditions began to take a turn for the better, and the death-rate from typhus fell to 45,948; in 1849, after the successful potato harvest of 1848, there was a substantial drop to 39,316. In 1850 the incidence was 23,545, though still very high, it was definitely on the decrease.[2]

---

[1] O'Rourke, John (1875). *The Great Irish Famine*, p. 499. O'Brien, G. (1921). Op. cit. p. 246.

[2] Census of Ireland, 1851, pt. v, p. 247. O'Brien, G. (1921). Op. cit. p. 244.

Deaths can be numbered, and their causes roughly catalogued, but our knowledge of the physical and mental suffering induced in a peasant society, catastrophically disrupted by famine must needs be fragmentary. Two troubles were said to have increased enormously: ophthalmia, leading to blindness, and insanity. The former resulted from the deficiency of vitamin A, owing to the absence of fresh vegetables, and the failure of supplies of fat and milk, both of which followed the cottier's loss of his pig and his cow which he had fed to a very large extent on the potatoes he raised. That insanity should have increased as the result of misery and exposure, is not to be wondered at; but it is possible that nervous debility, and even dementia, may have been increased owing to the absence of vitamin B_7, which in normal times was supplied in ample quantities by the potato and the milk, of the peasants' dietary.

A situation of the kind such as developed in Ireland, had not been experienced in Europe since the Black Death. The Great Plague of 1665 killed off something between 60,000 and 100,000 people in London, and possibly as many more in the great and small towns of England. But it was neither accompanied by famine, nor preceded by an all-embracing poverty; moreover, the Plague was no regarder of persons: the stroke fell on rich and poor alike. In Ireland, whilst some of the rich may have become poorer, the entire poor of the country were left completely destitute. One historian says of the famine: 'In importance it holds a place beside the Rebellion of 1641–52, and the war of the revolution.'[1] Certainly the bitterness it evoked in the minds of the Irish, was scarcely second to that aroused by the memory of Cromwell.

An event so unique, so all-embracing, and devastating, as the potato famine of Ireland, naturally evoked a corresponding response from the administration, and the general public of Great Britain. Although it was not the first time that the Central Government had been called on to help distressed areas, such occasions had seldom met with any commensurate response in money or kind from the government. One such followed the potato failure of 1756 and 1757, when the first official act of the Lord Lieutenant, the Duke of Bedford, was to provide a sum of £20,000 from government funds to relieve the poor.[2] I am inclined to believe that the famine of 1846 and 1847 was the first occasion in English history, on which the government deliberately planned and financed relief measures on a large and comprehensive scale.

In estimating the spirit in which the relief was conceived, its nature, its scope, and the ability with which it was administered, the lack of experience of all concerned must not be lost sight of. To judge either

[1] Dunlop, R. (1910). *Camb. Mod. Hist.* vol. XII, p. 67.
[2] Lecky, W. (1892). *A History of Ireland*, vol. I, p. 468. Longmans.

their intentions or their results, on the basis of the standards acquired to-day, by public and private organizations, after long and varied experience at home and abroad of large-scale problems of hygiene and epidemic diseases, would be very unfair. Sir John Burgoyne, Chairman of the Second Relief Commission appointed under Lord John Russell's government, was, in fact, perfectly justified when he wrote that the relief work was 'the grandest attempt ever made to grapple with famine over a whole country'.[1] Much of the bitterness, which exists to this day in the minds of Irishmen, who have learnt by local tradition as well as in school, of the horrors and the blunders of those famine days, is due to lack of perspective, and is not really justified. On the other hand, it is impossible to defend such measures as the Gregory Clause, and the callous cruelty of the evictions, both during and after the famine period, whether judged by the standards of the nineteenth or the twentieth century.

Two departments of government were responsible for Famine Relief: the Board of Works drew up development schemes and organized the work to be done in their execution; the Commissioners' Relief Office provided food at convenient places throughout the country, regulated prices, but did not sell direct to the people, except in those parts of the country where the customary channels of distribution had not been developed. In their work they were assisted by voluntary relief bodies, notably that organized and conducted by the Society of Friends.

The public collections in Great Britain reached about 1½ million pounds,[2] whilst government advanced £7,132,268, of which £3,754,739 was to be repaid within ten years, but the greater part of which was actually remitted. In addition, the people of the United States of America and Canada sent large consignments of maize and other provisions, as well as of clothing. Much of this was sent on American men-of-war, from which the guns had been removed.[3] 'The freight and charges on the supplies of food and clothing sent to Ireland by charitable societies and individuals, as well from the United States and Canada on the one side, as from England on the other, were paid by the government, to an amount exceeding £50,000; all customs dues were remitted'.[4]

At first, relief works were instituted, and men employed at a daily wage. These works were mainly concerned with road, canal and harbour construction. It was unfortunately laid down—in all good faith—that the relief works must not benefit private individuals. But inasmuch as huge areas of land were owned by single landowners, it was, more often

---

[1] Quoted from Trevelyan, Sir Charles (1880). *The Irish Crisis*, p. 65. London: Macmillan.

[2] The Society of Friends. Relief Committee of. *Trans.* 1846–7.

[3] Godkin, J. (1870). *The Land War*, p. 300. Macmillan.

[4] O'Brien, G. (1921). *Op. cit.* p. 247.

than not, impossible to direct the work so as to make it of value to anybody, if a few individuals were to be denied special advantages. It is true that in October 1846, the Prime Minister, through Labouchere, the Irish Secretary, issued a Proclamation, known as the 'Labouchere Letter', which allowed certain work to be done to the advantage of private proprietors, but the restrictions were so hampering that little use was made of this concession.

The relief works were, in the main, confined to the construction of roads, many of which, being left unfinished, soon degenerated into level tracks, which led from nowhere in particular, to nowhere at all. Much criticism was levelled at the system, both at the time and later. The two views chiefly urged were, one, Ireland being over-populated, what was most needed was the recovery of waste lands and the opening up of the same to the people; the other, that the potato, having failed two years running, and having been destroyed, not by such recognized causes as frost or excessive rain, but by a mysterious disease which clearly indicated that something had collapsed in the construction of the plant itself, it should be realized that the day of the potato had passed. One able exponent of this belief was Sir Randolph Routh, Chief of the Commissariat Office in Dublin during 1846. His view was that

the transition from potatoes to grain requires a tillage in the comparison of three to one between grain and potatoes. All this requires a corresponding increase of labour; and wages so paid are a mere investment of money, bringing a certain and large profit....It is useless to talk of emigration when so much extra labour is becoming indispensable to supply the extra food.... If industrious habits can be established, and the waste lands taken into cultivation, it is very doubtful whether there would be any surplus population or even whether it would be equal to the demand.[1]

Such a criticism was eminently reasonable but, in the event, the government's policy, if not far-sighted, was not far wrong. The potato had not succumbed; its failure, costly as it had been in human suffering, had neither destroyed the people's confidence, nor inclined them to accept a more concentrated cereal diet. In nothing is man more conservative than in his food.

Up till 15 August 1846, relief works had been financed as to one-half by the government, and the other by the rates; if further relief was required, it was decided that public relief works should be paid entirely out of rates 'which made the landlords liable for the whole amount on tenements under £4 yearly value and a proportion, generally amounting to half, on tenements above that value'.[2] Meanwhile, the government advanced the necessary sums to the local authorities, at 5% interest.

---

[1] Memorandum to Commissionary-General Hewetson, Commissariat Series, p. 452. Quoted from O'Rourke, J., op. cit. p. 181.   [2] O'Brien (1921). Op. cit. p. 250.

In the late autumn of 1846, the authorities introduced a system of task-, or piece-work to replace day-work. It was an innovation, and therefore disliked. Owing to the feeble condition of the majority of the poor, its working could not be other than unjust. Resentment was general, and led to many acts of violence. A delay or breakdown in the paymaster's department might, and indeed did, result in deaths. Such was inherent in a system of relief, in which experience had not had time to mellow the dictates of the new economists, a view endorsed by Lord Stanley in his speech on the address in 1847.

At Clare Abbey a steward had been fired at, and the Board of Works retaliated by shutting down the relief works. The local inspector, Captain Wynne, writing to the authorities on Christmas Eve 1846, said:[1]

I must again call your attention to the appalling state in which Clare Abbey is at present. I ventured through that parish this day, to ascertain the condition of the inhabitants, and although a man not easily moved, I confess myself unmanned by the extent and intensity of suffering I witnessed, more especially among the women and little children, crowds of whom were to be seen scattered over the turnip fields, like a flock of famishing crows, devouring the raw turnips, and mostly half-naked, shivering in the snow and sleet, uttering exclamations of despair, whilst their children were screaming with hunger. I am a match for anything else I may meet with here, but this I cannot stand. When may we expect to resume the works?

O'Rourke reproduces some of the headings from the newspaper files of these days: their reading is a sad business 'Starvation and death in Dingle'; 'Deaths at Castlehaven'; 'Death of a labourer on his way to the Workhouse'; 'Coroner's Inquests in Mayo'; 'Four more deaths on the roads at Skibbereen'.[2] Such was the daily fare of news, in those black years. It came as a relief when, with a touch of sardonic humour, a coroner's court, as at Skull or Bantry in the west, sitting on one of the hundreds of cases of deaths by starvation, brought in a verdict of 'wilful murder' against Lord John Russell.

The distribution of food was left as far as possible in the hands of local traders, and the necessary administration was expected to be run by the local gentry but, in fact, it generally was left in the hands of the civil servants of the Board of Trade, with the result that the organization became increasingly centralized, and correspondingly inefficient. Discontent amongst the poor was rife, and frequently resulted in assaults on, and even murders of, officials. In October 1846, 114,000 men were employed on relief works, and by January of 1847 the number had grown to 570,000.

1 Quoted from O'Rourke, J. (1875). Op. cit. p. 207.
2 Ibid. p. 262.

Throughout this crucial period, the general criticism, that much of the relief work was economically valueless, was strengthened by the fact that the distress in England in 1841–2 was relieved by a great development of railway reconstruction. In England and Scotland, 2,600 miles of railroad had already been completed by 1846; in Ireland, but 65 miles. The delay in Irish development was due to the poverty of the country, and the absence of industrialism; both causes closely associated with the low level of the social and economic life of the agrarian population which itself was, in part at least, due to its being grounded on the use of so all-sufficient a food as the potato. When the potato was in the ascendancy, it may be said indirectly to have kept the railway builders at arm's length. Now that it had failed, its very failure only missed by an ace bringing about what might have been the biggest programme of railway construction in the British Isles.

The project found its leader in Lord George Bentinck, who adopted the recommendations made by an *ad hoc* commission in 1836, that railway development in Ireland should be undertaken without delay. O'Rourke remarks[1] that had these recommendations been adopted, the consequences of the Blight might have been quite different, for a large mass of the people would have been in receipt of cash wages, and their thraldom to the potato brought to an end. Bentinck's proposals, which he laid before parliament in February 1847, contemplated the laying of 1,500 miles of track and the employment of 108,000 men under conditions which, on paper at least, were far better than the majority of them enjoyed at home. Bentinck urged that no time should be lost. Speaking of the disastrous state of affairs which the failure of the potato crop had induced, he said:

I can only express my great surprise that, with the people starving by thousands—with such accounts as we have read during the last two days, of ten dead bodies out of eleven found lying unburied in one cabin; of seven putrid corpses in another; of dogs and swine quarrelling over, and fighting for, the dead carcasses of Christians; of the poor, consigned coffinless to their graves, and denied the decencies of Christian burial, that the price of the coffin saved might prolong for a few days the sufferings of the dying, I, Sir, for one, look with amazement at the patience of the Irish people.[2]

Russell treated the motion as one of confidence and rallied all his party's strength to defeat it. We need not follow the tortuous methods by which its defeat was accomplished; it is enough to say that once more Ireland evaded her good angel.

The principle of paying the relief workers slightly less per day than the current agricultural wage which, without the family potato-patch,

[1] O'Rourke, J. (1875). Op. cit. p. 337.
[2] Ibid. p. 344.

had never been adequate to maintain the man and his family, tended to increase rather than alleviate the general distress. The numbers on relief grew ever greater, so that by March 1847, 734,000 men were so employed, which, taking their families into consideration, represented at least 3,000,000, or nearly half of the population. One of the reasons which led to their ever growing number, was the habit of landowners and employers of planting their labourers on to the relief works, rather than employing them on their own undertakings.

The extent of the relief and its distribution throughout the four provinces in the years 1846–7 was as follows:

At the beginning of December, they were thus distributed in the four provinces: Ulster, 30,748; Leinster, 50,135; Connaught, 106,680; and Munster, 134,103. At the close of the month the same proportion was pretty fairly maintained, the numbers being: for Ulster, 45,487; for Leinster, 69,585; for Connaught, 119,946; and for Munster, 163,213. According to the Census of 1841, there were in Ulster 439,805 families; in Leinster, 362,134; in Connaught, 255,694; and in Munster, 415,154. From these data, the proportion between the number of persons employed on the relief works in each Province, and the population of that Province, stood thus at the close of the year 1846: in Ulster there was one labourer out of every nine and two-thirds families so employed; in Leinster there was one out of about every five and a quarter families; in Munster, one out of every two and a half families; in Connaught, one out of every two and about one-seventh families.[1]

At the opening of parliament in January 1847, the debate on the address turned on the subject of the famine in Ireland. Criticism was directed in the main to two points; the unproductive nature of the relief works, and their inadequacy, seeing that thousands were still dying of starvation. It was felt that the people were being sacrificed on the altar of the new economic faith. It was common agreement that in normal times it should be left to the unfettered action of private enterprise to cater for the wants of society; that people should compete in the labour market for their livelihood, that charity was degrading; and idleness in the poor, a sin. Yet all realized that this was no normal time, and that to insist on task-work, for those who grew feebler every day, and consequently earned less and less, was both stupid and brutal. Government must fill the gaps which private enterprise had failed to close. This point of view was represented very ably by Lord George Bentinck:

With respect to the supply of food to the people he, for one, cannot agree altogether in those principles of political economy which had been advanced by the Right Hon. gentleman, the Irish Secretary. This political economy of non-interference with the import and retail trade may be good in ordinary times, but in times such as the present, when a calamity unexampled in the

---

[1] O'Rourke, J. Op. cit. pp. 218–19.

history of the world has suddenly fallen upon Ireland—when there are no merchants or retailers in the whole of the West—when a country of which the population has been accustomed to live upon potatoes of their own growth, produced within a few yards of their own doors, is suddenly deprived of this, the only food of the people, it was not reasonable to suppose that, suddenly merchants and retailers would spring up to supply the extraordinary demands of the people for food. Therefore, I should say that this was a time when her Majesty's Ministers should have broken through these, the severe rules of political economy, and should, themselves, have found the means of providing the people of Ireland with food. The Right Hon. gentleman has said, that ministers have done wisely in adhering to this decision, but I think differently from them. When, every day, we hear of persons being starved to death, and when the Right Hon. gentleman himself admits that in many parts of the country the population has been decimated, I cannot say, that I think ministers have done all they might have done to avert the fatal consequences of this famine.[1]

Lord John Russell, answering for his government, assured the House that from now on, they would set up local committees which would be provided with funds from the rates, private sources, and the government; their duty, it would be, to establish soup kitchens throughout the country, which would distribute food without any task labour. Such relief was to be given 'free' to those who had no obvious means.' The recipients were to be encouraged to work on their potato plots for the next harvest. As regards relief works, no new ones were to be begun, but roads already under construction were to be finished.

In the course of the debate, Smith O'Brien, the advocate of Repeal, estimated that the monetary value of the loss to date of the potatoes destroyed, and the pigs which would have been otherwise raised, and the rise in prices, was between 20 and 30 million pounds—a conservative estimate.

On 16 April 1847, the new Act came into operation, and soup kitchens, which seem to have been first employed by the Friends in relieving the potato famine of 1740, were established, and by the beginning of July 1847, there were 3,504 kitchens in full operation. Cooked food was given to 3,000,000 people each day. 'The ration consisted of one or other of the following: one and a half pounds of bread, one pound of biscuits, meal or flour; or one quart of soup thickened with meal, with a quarter ration of bread, biscuit or meal.'

A good deal of controversy raged around the 'soup' ration. The government had induced the head chef of the Reform Club, M. Soyer, to concoct suitable recipes and to initiate the kitchens in Dublin. He devised soups with meat, and soups without; the recipe for the former was leg of beef 4 oz., dripping fat 2 oz., flour 8 oz., brown sugar $\frac{1}{2}$ oz.;

[1] Ibid. p. 302.

water 2 gallons. To this was to be added some onions, turnip parings and celery tops. The cost would work out at ¾d. per quart. A rival chef, M. Jaquet, of Johnson's Tavern, in Clare Court, questioned whether this soup had any intrinsic value to speak of, and, if experiments must be made, thought that the 'destitute poor' were not the best subjects. *The Lancet* wrote with considerable vehemence, pointing out that whilst there was nothing wrong with the soup as such, it had no claim whatever to be considered an adequate dish to maintain man or child for 24 hours. The Queen's physician, Sir Henry Marsh, now entered the lists, pointing out that working-men needed a solid diet which contained sufficient real food to replace the energy consumed in a day's work. This settled the issue; it was not long before soups were replaced by a hot, thick porridge, and Soyer's soup took rank with the curry powder devised by the Duke of Norfolk of the day, which he claimed would charm away the people's hunger pangs.

A quart of Soyer's soup may have done little to nourish the starving; but it was at least tasty, and with the accompanying biscuit and bread greatly appreciated, even though the spoons were chained and the basins fixed to the long tables of his Model Kitchen. Before leaving Dublin, Soyer[1] published a sixpenny Cookery Book designed for Irish Famine conditions. He speaks of the desolation that had overtaken the people, and the necessity for the use of the utmost skill in conserving available supplies. 'It requires more science to produce a good dish at trifling expense, than a superior one with unlimited means.'[2]

It was found 'by experience that the best form in which cooked food could be given was stirabout, made of Indian meal and rice steamed, which was sufficiently solid to be easily carried away by the recipients. The pound ration thus prepared, swelled by the absorption of water to three or four pounds.'[3]

The relief service, regulated by strong local committees, functioned till October 1847, when the abundant corn harvests of that year, and the good crop of potatoes, although from a much reduced area, rendered further relief in kind unnecessary. The Blight had abated, prices had receded, but distress amongst the people was still severe. The highest peak in the campaign was reached on 5 July 1847, when 3,020,712 rations of food were distributed in one day, of which all but 99,920 were paid for by the recipients. When the issue of cooked rations came to an end on 11 September, there were still 442,739 receiving them.

If the failure of the potato brought almost untold suffering to millions,

---

[1] Mrs Helen Morris has produced a fascinating book on Soyer, *The Portrait of a Chef*. Cambridge Univ. Press, 1938.
[2] Soyer, Alexis (1847). *Charitable Cooking* or *The Poor Man's Regenerator*.
[3] Trevelyan, Sir Charles (1848). Op. cit.

it also occasioned an abundance of honest, disinterested and devoted work from both the official and lay workers, who were responsible for dealing with the vast mass of human wreckage it induced. The following is one of the innumerable examples which might be given, illustrating the spirit which animated the majority of the workers. A member of the Board of Works wrote: 'It appears to me not a succession of weeks and days, but one long, continuous day with occasional intervals of nightmare sleep. Rest one could never have, when one felt that in every minute lost a score of men might die.'[1]

The great work undertaken by the Society of Friends, in which they were ably seconded by their colleagues in America, was beyond praise. It was based on the determination to go further than to relieve distress, however urgent that might be. They saw, because they were not fogged by political or religious bias, that if no radical change was effected in the social and economic system of Ireland, there was nothing to prevent a recurrence of a like catastrophe. Two main ideas underlay their policy: the one, that Irish society could never be other than beggarly, and unstable, so long as the land-tenure system remained in its existing state; the other, that the potato had failed for good, and a new source of food must be found. In pursuance of this latter, they introduced the cultivation of carrots, turnips, parsnips and the like, on the small holdings and cottiers' plots. They also encouraged green crops, for field use, on the larger farms. Both projects were carried out on a large scale. In 1847 they distributed 40,000 lb. of turnip seed alone. In order to give a permanent direction to their policy of agricultural reorientation, they established in 1849 a Model Farm of 900 acres at Colmanstown, County Mayo, where, in 1852, we find they vindicated their principles by putting down to potatoes less than 3 acres, out of the 220 acres then under the plough. Apart from inspiring agricultural enterprise, they also made great efforts to re-establish and improve the fisheries of the west coast, which were still being conducted in a manner reminiscent of the stone age.

It is on record that the loan of £100 by the Friends to the fishermen of Galway, enabled them to make a profit of £800 in three months.[2]

An anonymous writer of the time suggests that potato-growing should be dropped, and tobacco and sugar-beet grown in its place.[3]

The relief which had been started by the Quakers, was supported by all denominations, and from all parts of the Empire, but it is to the Friends that must be given the credit of introducing new and constructive ideas.

---

[1] Godkin, J. (1870). Op. cit. p. 298.
[2] Scrope, G. Poulett (1847). *Reply to Archbishop of Dublin*. London: Ridgway.
[3] Anon. (1847). *Letter to Lord John Russell by Anglo Hibernicus*. London: Cleaver.

When Queen Victoria, because of the famine, proclaimed Wednesday, 24 March 1847, as a day of prayer and intercession, Church, Chapel and Synagogue all took part. Special services were prepared, and prayers written for the occasion. In the Church service, the special prayer contains two paragraphs of interest. The first reads: 'For the removal of those heavenly judgements which our manifold sins and provocations have most justly deserved, and with which Almighty God is pleased to visit the iniquities of the land by a grievous scarcity and dearth of divers articles of sustenance and necessaries of life.' The second occurs in another part of the service, in which prayer is said for those 'who in many parts of the United Kingdom are suffering extreme famine and sickness'.

The first represents an attitude of mind towards natural phenomena happily no longer common. In the mid-nineteenth century, it formed the text of a shoal of pamphlets, written both about the Blight, as such, and of the famine which it entailed. What was more important, it was this same attitude, which was the subject of the great struggle, between authoritarian Christianity and Science, towards the end of the century, which ended in a victory for rationalism, and the re-establishment of the position, which Job had won for humanity nearly 3,000 years earlier.

Science has not only justified its opposition, but has shown that similar disasters can be avoided.[1]

The second paragraph is the nearest approach any of the services make towards declaring the reason which occasioned the appeal for Divine help. The word 'potato' does not occur anywhere.

The Synagogue services were even more discreet: 'Deliver them', they prayed, 'from distress and fear, so that to no creature his bread shall fail, nor shall he fear destruction or famine, but that the earth may again yield her fruits in abundance, and furnish food to all flesh.' The Chief Rabbi, convinced that the scourge was the result of sin, said 'We have failed in our duties; the failure of the crop must ensue.' In a long discourse the word 'Ireland' appears but once; that of the potato not at all.[2]

In another direction we find evidence at this time of direct relations between organized religious bodies and the potato. The attitude of the ministers of the Irish Church to the sufferers of the potato famine, was not always as disinterested as it might have been. The opportunity to impress the tenets of their religion on the stunned, starving, Catholic peasantry, whose dire needs they were relieving, was too great a temptation for some. 'One meets the remains', says O'Faolain,[3] 'of these

[1] See chapter x.
[2] Adler, Nathan: Chief Rabbi. Sermon, 24 March 1847.
[3] O'Faolain, Sean (1940). *An Irish Journey*, p. 138. Longmans.

colonies of converted Papists, in many such isolated regions. Along the wildest part of the Clare coast. Up in Connemara, behind Carna. In Achil... Catholics who were won over in the bad century of evangelizers are generally called "soupers", because in the Famine times they took soup from the tempters.'

Doubtless the famine provided an exceptionally favourable opportunity for the employment of such methods, but they were by no means new. Asenath Nicholson,[1] whose travels on foot in 1844 in Ireland present an illuminating picture of the sordid potato-ridden society of both country-side and town, tells of 'soupers' she encountered in Dingle.

No accountancy of the losses sustained by Ireland by reason of the famine would be complete which omitted mention of the wave of emigration it evoked. The Census of 1851 reports that:

The annual emigration to the end of 1845 was 61,242 persons. Such however was the effect of the potato blight and the warning voice of the pestilence, that the number rose to 105,953 in 1846, after which the emigration seemed to partake of the nature of an epidemic and in 1847 the numbers who left the country more than doubled those who departed in the previous year. Owing to a slight mitigation of the potato blight, and a consequent improvement in the harvest of 1847, there was an arrest of the exodus at the beginning of 1848, when the numbers who emigrated only amounted to 178,159; but in the following year they again rose to 214,425. In 1850 the amount of emigration was 209,054. Emigration reached its highest point in 1851, when the numbers amounted to 249,721.[2]

O'Brien calls attention to the fact that the greater part of the emigrants proceeded to the United States and not to the British Colonies, and that most of them sent home money in order to hasten the departure of their friends and relatives.

Larger numbers of the Irish peasantry left at this time for England, where they joined their compatriots in the great cities of the North, especially Liverpool and Manchester, living there, as they had done in the homeland, mainly on potatoes.

At the time, the wholesale depopulation by means of emigration, loss of life by disease and starvation, which had reduced the population of Ireland by half in a single generation, was, from both the economic and the political points of view, regarded with favour by most of the landed interest and, there is good reason to believe, by the government also. In those days the economic value of a half-starved, illiterate Irish worker was possibly even less than the sentimental one, and that was not very high. This is well shown by the fact that the public authorities in

[1] Nicholson, Asenath. *Ireland's Welcome to the Stranger*, p. 233 (edit. 1844). London.
[2] *Census of Ireland* (1851), pt. v, p. 243. From O'Brien, G. (1921). Op. cit. p. 241.

Ireland already had powers to aid emigration, and these powers were extended in 1847 and widely acted on in the years following the famine.[1] Nevertheless, there were not wanting some, who were alive to the fallacy of such views, who 'wept to see emigrants leaving, when so much waste land is there to be tilled and turned to gold'.[2]

It must not be forgotten that by far the greater part of the emigration was in no sense voluntary. The Gregory Clause provided a tool by which some landlords could and did evict their tenants, both large and small, after they had spent all their cash, realized their farm stock, and been obliged to go on to the poor law relief. Before they took this last step they were, by reason of this clause, forced to vacate their farm-holdings or their half acre of potato land. The choice was simple: hold on to the land and starve, or give it up and emigrate. Those who still had strength and energy accepted the latter alternative and left Ireland for ever.

One of the most outstanding repercussions of the failure of the potato in 1845 and 1846, was this vastly increased flow of emigration to the United States, which has been maintained, though not at the same level, up to our own times. The emigrants of the famine period were, as the Devon Commission had pointed out was the case before the famine, the most able of the cottier class. Unfortunately they carried with them into their new life overseas an inverted love of their old home, in the form of a deep anger and a bitter hatred of England, to whom they ascribed not only the old historic grievances, but the cruel misfortunes which had overtaken them in consequence of the potato famine. The good and sincere work which was put into relief by the government and English public bodies was discounted, and the few blunders and stupidities which marred it, magnified.

Most of the hostility, and much of the lack of understanding since then, which has from time to time dogged the mutual relations of England and America, can be traced to this feeling of bitterness, which has been passed, like an heirloom, from the ragged, starving immigrants of the middle of the last century, to their descendants, now influential and prosperous lawyers, politicians and party managers, who play so potent a part in moulding American public opinion. It may truly be said that it was the potato, which determined the atmosphere in which the subsequent relations between Americans, Irish and English, were to develop in the next hundred years. It is only too true that even to-day we have not altogether rid ourselves of this *hereditas damnosa*.

---

[1] O'Brien, G. (1921). Op. cit. p. 278.
[2] Niven, N. (1846). Letter to the Duke of Leinster. *The Potato Epidemic.* Dublin: J. McGlashan.

CHAPTER XVII

The Potato in Post-Famine Ireland

It is impossible to exaggerate the significance of the famine of 1846–7: it combined in the minds of the people the terror of a plague, and that sense of human fallibility and awe, which an earthquake inspires. It literally shook Ireland to the very roots of her economic, social and political being. Its immediate effect was to reduce the population: within a span of three years, it had fallen by some two million persons, and it continued so to sink, till it reached a relatively stable equilibrium round about four millions, rather less than half that attained before the coming of the potato blight. The immediate disaster did not in fact cease with the good potato harvest of 1847. Encouraged by its success, farmers and peasants realized every available asset in order to purchase an increased supply of seed for the next year. When in August 1848 the Blight reappeared and spread with alarming rapidity, they discovered they had lost everything including the opportunity of emigration for that year.[1]

As we have seen, the decline was initiated by about one million deaths due to actual starvation and disease, directly consequent on the potato failure. The ruin of the small farmers and cottiers, and the beggary of the labourers, led to a very large number of tenants defaulting on their rents: this in turn encouraged the landlords, as a class, to carry out evictions on a scale never before dreamt of. The victims, with their families, swelled the now ceaseless stream of emigrants to the New World. In the years 1847, 1848 and 1849, 32,531 applications for evictions were presented to the courts, and 25,739 were granted; between the years 1849 and 1853, 58,423 families were likewise evicted; that is, within six years, 84,162 families, or close on half a million people, were turned roofless and penniless on to the roads.[2] The landlords' policy was dictated by the new economic conditions resulting from the catastrophic failure of the potato. The famine had been the occasion for the abolition of the Corn Laws, and as soon as protection was withdrawn, corn growing in Ireland for export, ceased to be profitable. The home consumption of wheat by a people, the great majority of whom had been brought up on potatoes and oats, was confined to the Irish gentry and the better-off townsfolk; hence its volume was negligible, compared with the quantities

[1] Hansen, Marcus (1940). *The Atlantic Migration*, p. 269.
[2] Macdonell, G. P. (1888). Part author of *Two Centuries of Irish History* (ed. by James Bryce), p. 425.

which, in recent years, had been exported to England. By eviction, the landlord recovered possession of the land, and through the economic collapse of the small farmers, the way was opened for its immediate and profitable use. The creation of large grazing farms was the inevitable consequence of the attack on the potato by the microscopic spores of an hitherto unknown fungus.

Between 1850 and 1914 the land under the plough throughout all Ireland declined by 50%, whilst that in Meath, West Meath, Limerick and Roscommon, fell by 72%. In 1841, of all holdings over 1 acre in extent, 45% were less than 5 acres, and 7% were of 30 acres or more. In 1860, farms of 30 acres and over, had increased over threefold, and farms of 15 acres and less had, between 1841 and 1851, declined from 697,549 to 307,615, i.e. more than half had been converted into grazings. This change over brought about the extinction of some 25% of the total dwellings in Ireland. The loss, however, fell exclusively on the poorest, the occupants of one-roomed cabins, of which 355,689 were deserted or destroyed between the famine and 1851. The former inhabitants of these cabins, and the farmers who tilled the small farms and provided conacre land for the labourers and cottiers, had all of them, till then, depended almost exclusively on the potato for their food.

The economic lessons to be learnt from the potato famine may appear obvious enough to us, but it was not till thirty years later, that the majority of the people began seriously to realize the danger of building their social structure on so narrow and precarious a basis.

The change in the land system had its inevitable influence—the withdrawal of man power from the cultivation of the soil. In 1841 the number of men employed per 1,000 acres reached 523; by 1851 it had dropped to 370, and in 1861 to 301. This loss of man power on the land, it must be remembered, took place before agricultural machinery had exerted any appreciable influence on Irish husbandry. The fall was consequent, not on improved methods of cultivation, but on the suppression of a large proportion of the small-holdings, the occupants of which had not the same opportunity as their fellows in England, of being absorbed into industry. For them it was the old choice—starvation or emigration. Extensive as was the turnover from tillage to pasture, there was still a large residue of small farmers cultivating plots of 5–15 acres of land, with rights of pasturage for a cow or two on the hillside; nor was the much harassed conacre cottier eliminated, though his numbers were greatly reduced.

The two tragic years of famine led inevitably to a hardening in the formulation of the people's demand for a solution of the eternal land problem, security of tenure, freedom of sale, and tenant right. It might have been thought that the natural and immediate reaction of responsible persons of all classes, shaken out of their complacency by so over-whelming a disaster, would have been a reorganization of an agricultural and land system which had so signally failed. Not so in Ireland, where the obvious course seems always the last to be put into execution.

The following letter from the Duke of Wellington to Lord Mahon, later fifth Earl Stanhope, illustrates the difficulty which the best English-men of the time experienced when considering the Irish problem, especially when it took on so specific a guise as the Famine. It was not till Gladstone attacked the Irish problem, that English legislators began to realize that the degradation of the people was due primarily to an inequitable land system allied to an aggressive Protestant policy of Ascendancy. Nor is it yet realized that the universal dependence of the people on the potato was the economic consequence of such a policy. It was a dependence which inevitably reduced the social standards of the people to one commensurate with the cheapness of its culture, the abundance of its crop, and the ease of its storage.

The circumstances in which Ireland is placed are calculated to puzzle even wiser and more experienced men than ——. The failure of the produce of potatoes in two consecutive years, and the probability that the future culture of this root will be abandoned, or that, at all events, even if the culture should be persevered in, the produce will not be sufficient for the consumption of the people—have rendered it necessary for the Government to consider seriously of the anomalous state of social life in Ireland.

The whole of the labouring population, to the amount of some millions of people, living exclusively upon the very lowest description of the produce of the earth; the most precarious; that least capable of being preserved in stores of any kind.[1] That root, not commonly purchased in the market as food for the consumers thereof, but raised almost by each individual labouring con-sumer for himself, at all events for his family, upon a certain quantity of land, for the rent of which he engages or mortgages the remainder of his unemployed time for the year, to be employed in labour for the advantage of him who lets the land.

Supposing the quantity of potatoes not to be sufficient for the consumption of the labourer and his family, from the period at which he commences to consume one crop till that at which the next is reaped, which is not uncommon, and is rendered more frequent by the uncertainty of the climate and the various evils to which that root in particular and its preservation are liable, the labourer and his family must starve for a certain number of days, weeks, months, unless some extraordinary means should be discovered of employing his time if he should have any leisure after fulfilling his engagement to him to whom his labour had been mortgaged, in order to pay the rent of the field in which the potatoes for the food of the labourer and his family for the year had been planted.

---

[1] The Duke who displays an intimate knowledge of the cottiers' economy is in error as regards the matter of 'storage', see *ante*, p. 234.

This state of things is the cause of the constantly recurring distress of the labouring population of Ireland, of its aggravated state in 1845, and still more aggravated state in 1846 on account of the increased failure of the potato crop.

There is no doubt that this state of social life requires the earnest and steady attention of Government.

There was possibly no remedy for it of easy attainment excepting the gradual improvement of the state of the people by the growth of time, and their becoming by degrees accustomed to better things than the lowest description of food, clothing, and lodging, and their self-exertion to improve their own condition.

In the meantime some apprehended famine and fever in 1845, and real famine, fever and death in 1846.

The Government has imposed upon it the task of giving instant relief to the most pressing evil—hunger and its consequences; to provide the means to defray the expense of the performance of this duty, and next to discover the road to a remedy to the real cause of all the evil—the state of social life in Ireland. This remedy might under any circumstances require the perseverance of a series of years to carry it into execution.

But the circumstances of the times render some early attempt imperative; while on the other hand such attempt has been rendered more difficult and less likely to be successful by the demoralized state of the labouring classes themselves: their disinclination to work for hire; their expectation that they should be supported *gratis*, giving no work in return; and their growing disposition to riot and to acquire subsistence by plunder.

On the other hand, it is melancholy to see the accounts of the want of capital in the possession of the proprietors of land in Ireland in general, excepting in that of very few of the largest proprietors.

I am not astonished that — does not see his way to a solution of all these difficulties.

I don't know who does.... [1]

A bitter and prolonged political warfare had yet to be waged, in the course of which new political weapons, the Land League, the Plan of Campaign and Boycotting, were improvised by the tenant classes and met by alternate concession and coercion by the government. Nor was assassination and senseless outrage wanting in the struggle against a generally well-intentioned, if unimaginative, government still allied to an impoverished body of absentee landlords, the majority of whom were wedded to a policy of land exploitation, founded on eviction and consolidation. It is not my task to trace the sequence of events during the following sixty years, a period which culminated in the creation of the Irish Free State, and the self-governing Dominion of Northern Ireland. It is only necessary to point out that the potato famine gave this century-old conflict between Ireland and England an increased tempo and a new

---

[1] Stanhope, Philip H., Earl (1888). *Notes of Communications with the Duke of Wellington*, 1831–1856 (World's Classics, 1938), p. 319.

character. Its new character was derived by the grafting of the lessons of the American War on to those previously acquired from the French Revolution, both of which were learnt by the famine emigrants, and transmitted to their children. Its tempo was perpetually renewed by the outraged feelings of the people themselves. A sense of bitterness, almost religious in its uncritical fervour, developed in the minds and hearts of the Irish peasantry, and to an even greater degree in those of the emigrants who had found a haven in the United States of America. Whilst the resident Irish tenantry nursed and fomented their hatred against the landlords, the *émigrés* sublimated theirs into a fanatical hostility to England. Such bitterness, however unreasonable and cruel it may seem to-day, can only be rightly assessed against the background in which it was engendered. What that background was, I have attempted to show.

A starving people does not stay to consider the difficulties, still less to discount the blunders, not even the innocent ones, of the governing power. Torn from his home, the emigrant does not lightly forget the scenes of his youth, nor the memory of parents and brethren he left, homeless and starving, in the land of his birth.

Whatever excuses may be made for the partial failure of the authorities to whom it fell to relieve the famine, the fact remains that tens of thousands died from sheer want of food; that whole villages were literally wiped out by starvation and disease before relief reached them. And of those who remained, peasants and small-traders, both were ruined throughout the length and breadth of the country. Facts such as these might afford sufficient ground for dissatisfaction in a country less given to suspect the intentions of their rulers than the Irish; but it was the evictions which were in progress before famine conditions had passed away, which turned suspicion into hatred, and love of country into a passion for revenge.

After such a collapse, it might have been expected that the position of the potato in the domestic economy of the people could never be quite the same. Many thought that after such a lesson agricultural reform would be the order of the day, and that green crops might win victories even greater in Ireland than they had achieved seventy years earlier in East Anglia. One writer, convinced that the potato, with its ready accomplice, the pig, were the source of all Irish troubles, demanded that the chief reforms must be large fields, good dwellings, the feeding of cattle in yards and, above all, the cultivation of the turnip.[1]

In point of fact, the supremacy of the potato was scarcely shaken for another thirty years. The acreage under potatoes in 1846 was 1,237,441 acres. Prior to that date it has been held to have been in the neighbourhood of 2,000,000 acres. In 1847 it fell to little more than one-eighth

[1] Elly, Samuel (1848). *Potatoes, Pigs and Politics*. Kent and Richards.

of this amount, viz. 284,116 acres; this was but temporary, and due to the fact that there was little or no seed from the 1846 crop in the country. The 1847 crop was dependent on fresh seed from Scotland, much of which was imported by the Friends.

The 1847 harvest was exceptionally heavy, and must have gone a long way towards reassuring the people that the potato had not forsaken them. In 1848 the acreage jumped up to 742,899 acres and from then on it increased gradually till in 1859 it reached its new maximum of 1,200,247 acres, a figure only a little below that of 1846,[1] though it served a population which had decreased at least 25 %.

Unfortunately, the 1848 crop was again attacked severely by blight, which led to the great increase of emigration, already recorded for that and the succeeding year. The Catholic clergy, who had done their best to urge their people to remain at home, now advocated their departure. But the strongest incentive to emigration came from their relatives in America, whose letters home told of a land of plenty, and advised their relatives to 'follow us'.[2]

Before leaving the subject of the Great Famine, a word must be said on the repercussions on the great English centres of industry, induced by the sudden inrush of a poverty-stricken, potato-eating, mass of Irish labourers. These emigrants must not be confused with those who, following the tradition of a century, made the yearly summer migration to England for harvest work. The majority of the latter were employed in the Home Counties, and in particular in Hertfordshire. They were for the most part sojourners who kept entirely to themselves and, living in farms and barns in the countryside, away from towns, had little or no influence on the life and habits of the general population. Seasonal migrants from Ireland continued their visits to England during the hay and corn harvests till recent years. The mechanization of English farm lands has seriously checked such movements of labour, except for that from Donegal which reaches Scotland to raise the potato crop by hand. Very different was it, with those who settled permanently in the cities of England and Scotland, more especially in Liverpool, Manchester and Glasgow. This movement was by no means new; there had been a small but fairly steady infiltration all through the eighteenth century, and indeed earlier. In London it was these Irish immigrants who initiated potato-growing in the market gardens on the outskirts of the town.[3] In the 1820's this immigration[4] gathered momentum, but it was as nothing compared with the tidal wave which followed on the famine.

---

[1] Fisher, Joseph (1862). *How Ireland may be Saved*. London: Ridgway.
[2] O'Brien, George (1940). *New Light on Emigration*. Harvard Univ. Press.
[3] Clapham, J. (1939). *Econ. Hist. Mod. Britain*, vol. I, p. 57.
[4] Marshall, W. (1811). *Rev. Reports, Board of Agric.* vol. V, p. 179.

The Irish immigrants, and more particularly those from the famine period, maintained their own way of life, thereby exciting a certain amount of xenophobia. Not all those who reached the English shores settled permanently; many became vagrants and were returned by the local authorities to Ireland. Of those who did leave Ireland for good, it was complained, and with good cause, that they settled in, and before long, monopolized the poorest quarters of the town, and that they lived, as they had done in their old homes, almost exclusively on potatoes. Following their home custom, they even kept the potato-fed pig in their living-room and having no standards to speak of, in the matter of clothing, cleanliness, or household equipment, they remained for at least a couple of generations, segregated from their fellow citizens, whose standard of living was in every respect a higher one. Although conditions have vastly improved, and differences in social habits have largely disappeared, the fact that the great majority of the Irish are Roman Catholics, has perpetuated a division in the great cities, which originated in a distinctive social structure consequent on the almost exclusive use of the potato.

The most serious cause of complaint was that the low standard of living of the Irish enabled them to work at lower wages, and thus drag down those of their fellows. 'Beyond question', says Clapham,[1] 'J. R. McCulloch, the Economist, was right, if harshly right, when he spoke before a Parliamentary Committee in 1825, of the infinite harm done during the ten or fifteen years last passed by the Irish immigration, in lowering wages and, what was worse, their standard of life. I do not know that any such serious mischief was ever inflicted on the west of Scotland.' Engels[2] describes the loathsome conditions and miserable dwellings of the hand-weavers in the Manchester cotton industry in 1844, who were being squeezed out by the factories. He adds, 'their food consists almost exclusively of potatoes with perhaps oatmeal porridge, rarely milk and scarcely ever meat. Great numbers of them are Irish or of Irish descent.' Much the same had been noted earlier by Carlyle.[3] Writing sixteen years before the full tide of emigration had set in, he describes in periods, aflame with the fire born of a hatred of all that was mean and cruel, the condition of Ireland, and the degradation of her people, for which he held the British Government primarily responsible. Carlyle was fully convinced of the fundamental soundness and sanity of character of the common people of England, but he realized that the progress of industrialism under the competition of the cheap

---

[1] Clapham, J. (1939). Op. cit. vol. I, p. 62.
[2] Engels, Frederick (1892). *The Condition of the Working Class in England in 1844* p. 140.
[3] Carlyle, Thomas (1858). *Past and Present* (2nd edit.), pp. 19–20.

labour of half-starved Irish emigrants, was a peril to the welfare, moral even more than economic, of the great mass of the working classes.

Carlyle insists that one must realize that one-third of the Irish population 'has not for thirty weeks each year enough potatoes as will suffice him', and that 'Sanspotatoe', as he calls him, must be recognized as a real danger to the moral and economic health of his neighbours.

He is the sorest evil this country has to strive with. In his rags and laughing savagery, he is there to undertake all work that can be done by mere strength of hand and back; for wages that will purchase him potatoes. He needs only salt for condiments; he lodges to his mind in any pighutch or doghutch, roosts in outhouses; and wears a suit of tatters, the getting off and on of which is said to be a difficult operation, transacted only on festivals and the hightides of the calendar. The Saxon man if he cannot work on these terms, finds no work. He too may be ignorant; but he has not sunk from decent manhood to squalid apehood: he cannot continue there. American forests lie untilled across the ocean; the uncivilized Irishman, not by his strength but by the opposite of strength, drives out the Saxon native, takes possession in his room. There abides he, in his squalor and unreason, in his falsity and drunken violence, as the ready-made nucleus of degradation and disorder....

This soil of Britain, these Saxon men have cleared it, made it arable, fertile and a home for them; they and their fathers have done that. Under the sky there exists no force of men who with arms in their hands could drive them out of it; all force of men with arms these Saxons would seize, in their grim way, and fling (Heaven's justice and their own Saxon humour aiding them) swiftly into the sea. But behold, a force of men armed only with rags, ignorance and nakedness; and the Saxon owners, paralysed by invisible magic of paper formula, have to fly far, and hide themselves in Transatlantic forests. 'Irish repeal?' 'Would to God,' as Dutch William said, '*You* were King of Ireland, and could take yourself and it three thousand miles off,— there to repeal it!'...

With this strong silent people have the noisy vehement Irish now at length got common cause made. Ireland, now for the first time, in such strange circuitous way, does find itself embarked in the same boat with England, to sail together, or to sink together; the wretchedness of Ireland, slowly but inevitably, has crept over to us, and become our own wretchedness.[1]

Carlyle credits the cheap potato-fed Irish with having been the means by which British manufacture expanded so rapidly, and Clapham[2] thinks that the Lancashire men would have agreed that the expansion of the cotton trade could not have been effected without these potato-eaters. The price of labour in some occupations tended to approximate to their standards; bricklayers' wages were prevented from rising between 1831 and 1850, because of the Irish immigrants, whilst those of the hand-loom weavers, itself a dying industry, were further reduced for the same reason.

[1] Carlyle, Thomas (1858). Op. cit. pp. 19–20.
[2] Clapham, J. (1939). Op. cit. pp. 61, 548, 552.

Nassau Senior[1] writing in 1868, refers to those parts of Manchester which had been inundated by the Irish.

As I passed through the dwellings of the mill hands in Irish Town, Ancoats, and Little Ireland, I was only amazed that it is possible to maintain a reasonable state of health in such homes. These towns, for in extent and number of inhabitants they are towns, have been created with the utmost disregard of everything except the immediate advantage of the speculating builder. A carpenter and builder unite to buy a series of building sites (i.e. they lease them for a number of years) and cover them with so-called houses. In one place we found a whole street following the course of a ditch, because in this way deeper cellars could be secured without the cost of digging, cellars not for storing wares or rubbish, but for dwellings of human beings. Not one house of this street escaped cholera. In general, the streets of these suburbs are unpaved, with a dungheap or ditch in the middle; the houses are built back to back, without ventilation or drainage, and whole families are limited to a corner of a cellar or a garret.

It would be unfair to hold the immigrant Irish responsible for the barrack-like slums, which sprang up at this time as outskirts of our aforetime beautiful provincial towns. But the low standards with which they were content, went far to neutralize criticism which would otherwise have condemned these abominations for, bad as they were, they were at least better than their own homes in Ireland.

It was not only the poor Irish Catholic who carried the potato 'complex' to his new home. The Brontë father, a Northern Irelander, when at the Haworth Parsonage, objected to his young children eating meat, insisting on their midday meal being confined to potatoes, with which they are said to have been perfectly satisfied. Emily's biographer remarks: 'The Rev. Patric Brontë had grown to gigantic proportions on potatoes; he knew no reason why his children should fare differently.'[2]

Where competition was not so intense, the Irishman held his own without debasing the existing standard of living of the population by his reliance on a potato diet.

The great programme of English railway construction offered abundant opportunity to Irish navvies, who seemed to have been freely employed, generally through the medium of the middle-men, who invariably exploited their countrymen's labour. In the reclamation of Exmoor in 1820, two hundred Irish were imported by Sir John Knight, the owner of the forest: from these he formed a guard to check the stealing of sheep and deer. 'But I find these potato-eaters must all come from the same part of Ireland, or they will do nothing but fight.' In fact, Knight's

[1] Senior, Nassau (1867). *Journals of Ireland*. Quoted from Engels' *Condition of the Working Class in England in* 1844, p. 63. Also Hammond, J. L. and B. (1917). *The Town Labourer*, 1760–1832 (ed. 1936), pp. 43–4.

[2] Gaskell, E. C. (1857). *The Life of Charlotte Brontë* (edit. 1924), p. 38 and n.

Irish were drawn from the estate of his brother-in-law, Lord Hedley, in Kerry.[1]

In 1848 a French Railway advertised for Irish labourers, offering them one-third higher wages than their own workers.[2]

It is no mere coincidence, that information on the changes in the social status of the Irish countryside reaches us, because of further failures of the potato crop. It will be evident from the figures which have been given, that, notwithstanding the heavy loss in population, and the abolition of a large proportion of the smallest holdings, the relation of the area under potatoes to the population living on them, had not materially altered by 1861, nor, indeed, did it do so till much later. The potato remained the food of the people, which accounts for the serious alarm aroused and the distress occasioned, by later failures of the crop. In 1859 the potato blight reappeared, and was followed by famine conditions in some districts, with which the Government seems to have dealt successfully. This particular failure would have been forgotten, had it not been the occasion for a fresh spurt of evictions, notwithstanding the suspension of the Gregory Clause (see p. 302), so far as indoor relief was concerned. A more critical situation arose in 1879. Following an abnormally wet year, the potato crop failed in many parts of Ireland, and in several localities in the west country famine conditions supervened. The Duchess of Marlborough, wife of the Viceroy, at once started a relief fund, and the Friends again sent their experienced and trusted administrators to the danger points.

James Tuke[3] who, with Forster, had been in command of the Friends Relief in the old famine days, returned to Ireland in 1879, to investigate and relieve the famine of that year. Of the famine itself, little need be said. Relief was prompt and sufficient. A special Act[4] was passed to facilitate the introduction of sound potato seed; no lives were lost, though here and there much privation was experienced. The authorities at least, had learnt their lesson. Tuke visited much of the same country which he had worked over in 1846 and 1847. It may be said that in the west generally, Donegal, Mayo, Galway and Kerry, the social conditions of the small farmer and cottier were still very bad. The evictions which

---

[1] Orwin, C. S. (1929). *Reclamation of Exmoor Forest*, pp. 32 and 154. Oxford.

[2] O'Rourke, J. (1875). Op. cit. p. 323.

[3] Tuke, J. H. (1880). *Journal.* Irish Distress and its Remedies. A Visit to Donegal and Connaught. London: Ridgway.

[4] This Act was known as the Seed Supply Act of 1880. By it, Local Guardians could apply to the Local Government Board for a loan for the purchase of seed potatoes and oats, repayable without interest in two annual instalments. The Guardians, in their turn, provided the growers with the seed, charging them the cost price in addition to transit charges and the like, the loan to be repaid in two annual instalments together with the Poor Rate and recoverable in the same manner. The Guardians had a right to inspect the crops raised from such seed and insist on adequate cultivation of the same.

followed the last famine had infuriated the people, especially those of Galway and Mayo, and created a most difficult atmosphere. The peasantry and small farmers were still dependent on the potato to a dangerous degree. In these parts, moreover, the old custom was still general, of paying rent in labour and labour in kind, based on the long-established custom by which the potato crop replaced the coin of the realm as a means of exchange.

Elsewhere in Ireland, Tuke found that social conditions had much improved—not, it is true, generally, but at many, if scattered, points. Wherever there was a subsidiary industry, such as stocking-making, or weaving, whether conducted in home or factory, the home conditions improved at once, and the food tended to become more varied.

Other authorities speak with less confidence. Sir James Caird[1] revisited Ireland in 1869 and was unable to observe any improvement in the agriculture of the country, though he admits the people were better housed and clothed. Another author points out that by 1870, agricultural wages were double those current before the famine, and that there had been a marked decrease in the number of the wretched one-roomed cabins, except in the west, where the potato still held the chief place in the people's dietary.[2]

Tuke had the satisfaction of seeing the policy of introducing alternative crops, which he initiated in 1847, especially turnips, carrots and clover, making headway, and the 'Champion' potato, seed of which he had imported from Scotland, rapidly establish itself as the most widely grown maincrop variety. Another change which he records is the spread of poultry farming which, competing with the pig for *lebensraum* in the peasant's cabin, developed, like the latter, into a species of cash crop.

An attempt to displace the potato in the affections of the poorest, was made by the Poor Law Unions, but I am not sure whether this extended to the west country. In 1852 an observer records that no potatoes are being served in any workhouse, 'in the hope it will have the effect of rendering the people of Ireland less dependent on this treacherous root and more attached to cereal food'.[3] Nature also seems to have taken a hand in the same enterprise, for in that year at least one-third of the crop of tubers was diseased and rotten throughout the land.

One foodstuff which had been introduced to combat the famine, maize meal, remained to stay, and had established itself in many parts of the country. Ten years later, an Englishman made a tour of the country, recording not only what he saw, but particularly what he heard in the

[1] Macdonell, G. P. (1888). Part author of *Two Centuries of Irish History*. Quoted on p. 506. London: Kegan Paul.
[2] Macdonell, G. P. Op. cit. p. 505.
[3] Forbes, John (1852). *Memorandum made in Ireland*, vol. II, p. 236 and vol. I, p. 37. Smith Elder and Co.

cabins, the public-houses, the clubs and the homes of the great. He notes the increasing popularity of the turnip, and the improved manuring and cultivation to be found almost everywhere, except in the west, where he finds much poverty and little, if any, progress. At Spiddal in Connaught, he writes: 'There is nothing between the people and a famine but these little bulbs.' At Clifden, near by, he puts up in a cottier's cabin, which he describes as follows:

In the evening I found myself still far away from Clifden in a heavy rain, so I asked at a little cabin by the roadside for hospitality, and was welcomed cordially. There was only a kitchen and one room. In the kitchen were a cow, a calf, a dog, three or four hens and a cock fluttering noisily about, and in a corner a coop full of chickens. Here I slept on the ground near the ashes of the glowing peat fire; and in the other room slept the family—father and mother, two girls and a boy. The silence of the night was broken from time to time by the thud and splash of dung on the mud floor, and the crowing and clatter of the fowls woke me early. There was one chair, one bench, and several boxes to sit on, but no table; and some rude harness hanging from pegs on the wall was the only ornament. 'Michael, rise up!' shouted a man's voice, about seven o'clock, and a boot, as it seemed, struck violently against the wooden partition. Michael lounged in, and rekindled the peat fire from the dying embers. In a few minutes in came his mother, and milked the cow in front of the fire into a series of dirty-looking little tin pots, that reminded me of old tomato cans. She then fed the calf on some milk and raw potatoes, and in a little time gave me a cup of excellent tea and a piece of potato bread.[1]

In Ulster the recession of the potato was more evident than in any of the other provinces, and had proceeded further as one passed eastwards from the coastal districts of Donegal. In these latter there was but little, if any, change in social conditions.

Stir-about and potatoes are what the people live on. All they buy from the shopkeepers is tea and drapery. The blue cloth cloaks are, indeed, of West of England manufacture, but the friezes they wear about Gweedore are home-made.[2]

At Letterkenny, his informant says:

The people raise potatoes, flax and oats. Very few use oatmeal; they usually get Indian meal, and often feed the pigs on it....There is not much suffering here, if you think people who live on dry potatoes don't suffer, for few eat butter except in winter, and meat or fowl only once or twice a year.[3]

At Dungannon, the breakaway from the old potato-ridden life was in full swing:

Near me there are a lot of small farms of ten or twenty acres on the slopes of the mountains. Formerly, with the help of his sons and with cheap labor,

---

[1] Pellew, George (1888). *In Castle and Cabin*, p. 174. New York: Putnam's Sons.
[2] Ibid. p. 234.   [3] Ibid. p. 238.

the farmer reared cows and pigs, made butter, and raised oats and potatoes, and so paid his rent. Now labor is dear, and the young men, after getting a national school education, go into the constabulary or emigrate; the farmers cease to grow potatoes and oats, and the money from the calves and the butter goes to buy Indian meal, etc., for family use. So things got worse and worse. The style of living has changed for the better, perhaps, but the farmers are very incompetent.[1]

In the Belfast district, the agricultural problem is seen through the eyes of a politically conscious merchant, who, when he refers to serfdom, has undoubtedly in his mind the hand-to-mouth days of the cottier, selling his labour in return for a patch of potatoes:

Till within the last 15 years the peasants were in a condition of serfdom, afraid of their landlords, whom they always approached as a debtor would his creditor, making a poor mouth. Their votes were their landlords, until the Ballot Act. Since then they have obtained secrecy of voting, and an independent interest in their holdings; but as yet not half a generation has been born under the new conditions, and the people are now led blindly either by the priests or the agitators....

Agriculture must be on a big scale, 'till we get our population down to 3 millions we shall never come to any good'.[2]

In truth, Ireland had begun to free herself from the economic thraldom of the potato after the passing of the Land Act in 1870, which gave the tenant compensation for improvements. Much of the arable land had returned to pasture, but what remained was better cultivated and much more generously manured. Till 1850, potato cultivation had been by hand, and for the most part on very small holdings; now the plough had largely taken the place of the spade, and the number of farms of over 30 acres in extent, rose from 30,000 in 1841 to 160,000 in 1860.

By 1870 agricultural wages had doubled,[3] and the number of one-roomed huts greatly diminished. It was only in the west, more particularly in Galway and Mayo, in districts such as Clifden, isolated from both town and railway, that even as late as 1883 conditions had deteriorated. There the potato was still the dominating, indeed the controlling factor, in the lives of the people. But whereas, prior to the famine, they cultivated their meagre lands in the belief that they would reap the harvest of their labours, now they had lost interest in both home and holding, and looked, with yearning, across the ocean for an escape from their toils and disappointments. So broken in spirit were the peasantry of those parts, that if they had but the least reason to expect a passage, they would often neglect to till their plots in winter, or to plant their

[1] Ibid. p. 249.
[2] Ibid. pp. 254 and 260.
[3] Macdonell, G. P. (1888). *Two Centuries of Irish History* (edit. J. Bryce) p. 505.

seed in spring. Faith in the sufficiency of a civilization, based on the potato, had seemed natural and bearable when all alike were poor, but now that conditions in the greater part of Ireland had improved, the abject nakedness of a social order, in which the distinction between the amenities of human life and those of the beasts of the field had become blurred, was too humiliating to be endured. At long last the peasantry realized that in fact, they had been but puppets occupying the lowest grade of a culture, whose only claim to fame was that it was based on the cheapest food man had as yet discovered. 'Send us anywhere, your Honour, to get us out of our misery. What will we do then in our poverty?' was the cry which greeted James Tuke and Sydney Buxton wherever they went whilst engaged in organizing the emigration of those years from the west to the United States.[1] The tragedy of the famine years had not been suffered in vain; the economic reign of the potato was slowly drawing to its inglorious end.

In 1890 Ireland was once more visited by a heavy attack of the Blight. On the lighter lands it was not serious, but on the heavier ones, and especially on the west boglands, it was very grave. A Ministry Report[2] states that on the west coast 'where chronic poverty prevails', the disease was worse; the crop fell to less than half the normal, and the people sold their pigs, as they had not the wherewithal to feed them. Very disappointing was the failure of the 'Champion' variety, which hitherto had stood up well to the disease, and on which the hopes of the agricultural world had been placed for the last twelve years. To replace it, 'Magnum Bonum' was introduced, a variety which proved peculiarly susceptible to the disease.

The Report gives one a good idea of the position of the potato in the economy of the people. 'The time when the people were entirely dependent on the potato has long gone by and in every part of the west, bread, tea, stirabout, milk and sometimes salt fish and eggs form items of daily consumption.' Even so, the writer assesses the loss due to this epidemic as 'the loss of a midday meal and a part of a supper for part of the year.... There are still congested areas where the potato is the mainstay of the population and the loss means a very serious deprivation.'

The Commissioners were, perhaps, too optimistic, for in 1894 the potato crop failed once more, and in some parts of the country famine conditions supervened, although this time the normal value of the potato crop was but 5 % of all the agricultural produce of Ireland. In England

---

[1] James Tuke Fund (1883). Emigration from Ireland. Second Report Nat. Press Agency.
[2] Report on the Failure of the Potato Crop and the Condition of the Poorer Classes in the West of Ireland (16 February 1891). Dublin.

the potato also failed, but there was no distress. The difference between the experience of the two countries, it is suggested, lay in the fact that in Ireland 45 % of the whole value of the produce went to the landlord and in tax, as opposed to about 10 % in England.[1]

It was only when the land was progressively freed from these heavy burdens by successive Acts passed between 1870 and 1903, that any substantial change in the economic and social welfare of the small growers and cottiers took place. With that betterment came the final release of the grip by which, for close on three centuries, the potato had controlled the standard of living of the people.

Before we leave the Irish scene, a word must be said as to the part played by the potato, to-day, in the life of the people. This may be described under two heads: its use as a foodstuff, and its use as an article of commerce. As regards the former, the loosening of its hold on the social structure of the great mass of the people which, as we have seen, set in in the seventies of the last century, has made continued headway. To-day, throughout most of the country, the potato is eaten because it is liked, not because it is necessary. Its consumption, though much reduced in comparison with the generous measure of last century, is still on a far more liberal scale than that in England, doubtless due to the traditional place it had won for itself in the social structure of Irish life. The potato is happily, no longer the arbiter between a bare sufficiency and starvation. In the west, it still plays a more important role than else-where, though the sharp demarcation between east and west, which existed at the end of the last century, tends to disappear. Wholemeal bread, a luxury in many parts till recent years, and stirabout of maize or oatmeal, have been co-opted as articles of daily diet, by the people on the west coast. Nevertheless, so strongly entrenched is the potato, that though only served twice a day, the average consumption is said to be about 3 lb. per head, trifling, no doubt, compared with the 14 lb. per diem eaten in the pre-famine days, but nearly four times the average pre-war consumption in England. In the Island of Achill the people, as late as 1879, were entirely dependent on their own produce, and at least half of their arable land was down to potatoes. To-day, potatoes are said to be used but once a day.

Whilst the potato plays a more important part in Ireland than it does in England, it is true to assert, that even a complete failure of the crop would not, to-day, bring about anything more than inconvenience and domestic difficulty. The old-time fear of privation and famine, or, indeed, anything approaching a repetition of the famine and misery of 1846 and 1847, would be impossible in times of peace, in any country

[1] Lough, E. (1896). *England's Wealth and Ireland's Poverty*, p. 118. Fisher and Unwin.

equipped with modern means of transportation and controlled by an honest government.

For many years Ireland maintained an export trade of 'ware' potatoes to England. In the north, Counties Donegal, Monaghan and Louth have regarded this as their chief cash crop. In the south, the export is relatively less, averaging about 30,000 tons per annum before the war. During hostilities Eire consumed all her potatoes other than those raised for seed.

Ireland entered on a new economic path when, in the second decade of this century, she began to develop a high quality potato-seed trade. Whilst the seed raised in north and south alike has attained a remarkably high standard of excellence, that of Eire is of particular interest, because the trade has been built up on strictly scientific lines from very small beginnings. It has now developed into an important industry, and in this development the control of quality by trained scientists has been maintained. The late Prof. Paul Murphy, one of the foremost and earliest of Plant Virus Research workers, realized the necessity of obtaining virus-free potatoes for scientific investigation, and after much patient search, secured healthy stocks of two varieties. I have since added about a score more, many of which are being grown on a large scale to-day in Great Britain. The late Dr W. D. Davidson, Chief Inspector of Potatoes in Eire, working in the closest co-operation with Prof. Murphy, built up a large and growing trade which dealt only in the highest quality seed. Though, unhappily, Prof. Murphy died a relatively young man, soon to be followed by Dr Davidson, both these scientists lived to see the research they conducted in the laboratory and experimental plot develop into a well-organized scientifically supervised and successful industry in the hands of the small farmers of Western Ireland. In my visits to these parts, in company with my late friends, I have found it difficult to recognize in these knowledgeable, intelligent and efficient growers, the direct descendants of those who, less than fifty years ago, had been degraded and exploited by the same potato. A contrast which recalls the old couplet:

> A man without knowledge, an' I have read,
> May well be compared to one that is dead.[1]

[1] Ingelend, Thos. C. (*c.* 1560). *The Disobedient Child.*

CHAPTER XVIII

The Potato's Part in the Tragedy of Ireland

In the foregoing chapters an attempt has been made to describe the part played by the potato in the social and economic development of the Irish people during the last 300 years. To have endeavoured to tell the story *in vacuo*, would have been in vain, for in no country, and least of all in Great Britain, can one afford to disregard the political forces which, in so large a measure, mould the environment within which social development takes place. It was necessary, therefore, that contemporary political and socio-economic sequences should be studied in close relation to each other, before attempting to determine in what manner, and to what extent, the potato has been responsible for the peculiar character which Irish society assumed.

During the period under review, and indeed for long before it, Ireland has, in the eyes of the English, and of the Western World, occupied a peculiar position which has never been exactly defined. It is possibly for this reason that the affairs of Ireland have been regarded as constituting a special problem without parallel elsewhere. Between the two countries there have always existed dissensions, seemingly incapable of solution, though not necessarily because of their inherent difficulty. To the English, the problem presented itself as a political one; to the Irish, what originally was a struggle to retain a specific national and religious structure, later merged into one to maintain an economic and social existence independent of that of England. With the merits of the political issues, as such, we are in no way concerned, and we may therefore confine our attention to the Irish scene.

Differences of race and religion, the Protestant ascendancy, land tenure, over-population, poverty and, last but not least, the potato, have all been cited, either singly or in various combinations, as being the source of Ireland's distress. However, if we seek for the predominant symptom of the disease, rather than its cause, there is no difficulty in recognizing a distinctive pattern imprinted on the web of Irish social history, during the last 400 years. I refer to the appalling poverty of the Irish people—a poverty involving at least four-fifths of the population, and which had no parallel in any so-called civilized country. The continuous and clamant poverty of the Irish people throughout the entire period, till the middle of the nineteenth century, helped to keep alive, and indeed fomented, political and religious passions which otherwise might have found their legitimate satisfaction.

We have, therefore, to ask ourselves what was the prime cause of this all-pervading poverty? Such eminent authorities as Mill in the last century, and O'Brien in this, are in agreement that the basic cause was the cottier system. Such a conclusion is doubtless correct; but it must be remembered that the system, as it existed up to the time of the famine, was itself due to lack of social equilibrium. The lack of balance originated with the grafting of the Tudor conception of feudalism on the basic clan system of the native Irish. As a result, the tribal chieftain had been expropriated, and the landworker, formerly a serf, from the seventeenth century onwards, though nominally free, had lost those traditional rights in the land, with which the clan system had endowed him.

Mill's analysis of the Irish situation is of the utmost value:

The produce, on the cottier system, being divided into two portions, rent, and the remuneration of the labourer, the one is evidently determined by the other. The labourer has whatever the landlord does not take; the condition of the labourer depends on the amount of rent. But rent, being regulated by competition, depends upon the relation between the demand for land and the supply of it. The demand for land depends on the number of competitors, and the competitors are the whole rural population. The effect, therefore, of this tenure, is to bring the principle of population to act directly on the land, and not, as in England, on capital. Rent, in this state of things, depends on the proportion between population and land, as the land is a fixed quantity, while population has an unlimited power of increase; unless something checks that increase, the competition for land soon forces up rent to the highest point consistent with keeping the population alive. The effects, therefore, of cottier tenure depend on the extent to which the capacity of population to increase is controlled, either by custom, by individual prudence, or by starvation and disease.... But it is not where a high standard of comfort has rooted itself in the habits of the labouring classes that we are ever called upon to consider the effects of a cottier system. That system is found only where the habitual requirements of the rural labourers are the lowest possible; where, as long as they are not actually starving, they will multiply; and population is only checked by the diseases, and the shortness of life, consequent on insufficiency of merely physical necessaries. This was the state of the largest proportion of the Irish peasantry. When a people have sunk into this state, and still more, when they have been in it from time immemorial, the cottier system is an almost insuperable obstacle to their emerging from it. When the habits of the people are such that their increase is never checked but by the impossibility of obtaining a bare support, and when this support can only be obtained from land, all stipulations and agreements respecting amount of rent are merely nominal; the competition for land makes the tenants undertake to pay more than it is possible they should pay, and when they have paid all they can, more almost always remains due.[1]

---

[1] Mill, J. S. (1821). *The elements of Political Economy*, book II, chapter 9.

As O'Brien[1] points out, this implied that under the cottier system, when the population was rapidly increasing, the cost of living would rise out of proportion to the increase of wages, which is what happened in the early decades of the nineteenth century.

In short, says Mill, the cottier system and the lowest possible level in the standard of life, go necessarily hand in hand.

The cottier system as it developed in Ireland, was, in fact, dependent on the combination of a peculiar political autocracy and the potato, an easily raised, nutritionally adequate[2] and abundant food.

If it be true that the cottier system was the cause of Ireland's poverty, then the potato, which rendered its continuance possible, must share in that responsibility. What that share was, and how the potato came to exert it, has been studied in the foregoing chapters; here, we need only outline the conclusions which were reached.

When one compares the structure of English and Irish society up till the middle of the nineteenth century, a basic difference between the two becomes manifest. In England society was, and still is, constructed on a horizontal system of stratification, with the classes ranging from duke to dustman. That the differences between them are largely unreal, and for the most part based on false values, is their saving grace; for thus is ensured the permeability of the strata, the more or less easy passage of individuals from below upwards and, what is no less important, from above downwards. Such convection currents in society, are most noticeable in the middle classes, the most fluid portion of the whole social structure. At their lower level they are perpetually infiltrated by members of the working classes, and at their upper by the younger sons of the aristocracy, seeking professional or financial careers, as well as by those who by moral or intellectual weakness fail to retain their position, even in the sheltered environment of their birth.

That such a society may be riddled with snobbery and flunkeyism is unpleasant, but unimportant in comparison with the evils of a society such as that of the Russia of Alexander II, or the similarly conditioned society depicted in Murasaki's novels of eleventh-century Japan. Both were stratified horizontally, but in neither was there any appreciable movement between the strata. Such a society, where social stasis has become permanent, must either break its barriers, or die of inanition.

In Ireland, the social structure was not, as in England, achieved by a series of horizontal strata, separated by semi-permeable layers of hardened custom and make-believe, but rather by an impermeable, vertical wall, which cut the entire people into two unequal groups,

---

[1] O'Brien, G. (1918). Op. cit. p. 407.

[2] As explained in chapter VII. The potato with milk in addition constitutes a complete if monotonous diet.

between which there was little or no communication. On the one side stood the vast majority of the people, Celtic in blood, Erse in tradition and speech, Roman Catholic in faith; on the other, the English and Scottish settlers, with a wholly different tradition, speaking what to the majority of the Irish was a foreign tongue, and professing variants of the Protestant faith, which served the double purpose of estranging each other, whilst forming a common platform on which they might, when necessary, exhibit their united hostility to their Celtic neighbours. In fact, the Anglo-Saxon minority was, as we have seen, sustained by a species of political philosophy which was summed up in the one word 'Ascendancy'.

The implications of this philosophy, and they were fully realized, was the maintenance in the hands of a small minority of all political power, central as well as local, legislative as well as administrative; of a monopoly of the property in the land, and as much as possible of the trade of the country. Until the end of the eighteenth century, nine-tenths of the people of Ireland had few, if any, of the basic rights and privileges enjoyed by the commonalty of England. As we are not concerned with the social conditions of the Ascendancy minority, we can confine our attention to those of the majority.

The metaphor of a vertical social cleavage in Irish society, as opposed to the horizontal layering of English society, is, I think, fully justified; for, when we examine the majority section, we find that it is wellnigh devoid of horizontal stratification. It is true that there was still a remnant of the old Celtic clan aristocracy, but it was for the most part abjectly poor and degenerate, and exercised only a romantic influence over its former henchmen. There were, in some parts of the country, wealthy graziers, and in others an occasional, fairly substantial, arable farmer, but one and all, the very few rich and the very numerous poor, held their land at the pleasure of some great landlord who, in the vast majority of cases, was a Protestant Englishman and, more often than not, an absentee. Such a society was essentially static.

A people who had neither opportunity for improving their status, nor for the exercise of their administrative capacity, had no occasion to develop a stratified society.

Whilst it is true that there were a few big farmers, the majority occupied between 5 and 20 acres of land, and not one had any security of tenure. Alongside, rather than beneath them in the social scale, were the cottiers, holding an acre or so on lease and hiring annually a plot of conacre land; and in a similar relationship came the agricultural labourers, who cultivated the patch of land around their cabin, if there was such, and some conacre if they could get it, and for the rest, worked for others. In Ireland, the landlord-squire, the resident clergy, the local doctor, the village school-master, and others of the professional and mercantile middle class, were either wanting, or belonged to the Ascendancy. The usual signs of social demarcation between the various types of occupiers of the land, were also generally lacking.

In the English countryside of the nineteenth century, the landlord lived in the great house, a handsome, capacious mansion; the big tenant-farmer occupied a large well-built manor-house, or a specially designed, roomy and comfortable farmhouse; the small-holder, himself generally a tenant, had a lesser but substantial homestead, and the married labourer his cottage, which rarely had less than three rooms, some out-house or barn, and at least one fire-place with a chimney. The unmarried labourers either lived in their parents' cottages or had accommodation, rough enough, but dry and warm, in the barns or, in the northern counties, in special bothies, of their employers.

What of the Irish? All these graduations vanish. The Irish chief, where he still existed, may have in rare cases, occupied a brick or stone-built house, where such had survived the civil wars, but more usually he had migrated to the town, there to fulfil his own declension. The farmers whether big or small, lived, as did the cottiers and the labourers, with but slight variation, in the same type of dwelling, the mud cabin. We have spoken of these dwellings and it is not necessary to enlarge on their nakedness. Some were better, some a little bigger than others; in some the cattle and pigs were separated by a thin wall from the dwelling-room, but one roof covered both. Differences there undoubtedly were, in the amenities of the households, but they were small and quantitative, and hence did not lend themselves to social differentiation.

When we look at the furnishing of the homes, the differences between the English and the Irish loom even larger. It is unnecessary to enlarge on the beauty of the Tudor and Jacobean furniture of the English homes, both large and small. In the nineteenth century the farmers invariably had well-furnished homes and, not rarely, a well-stocked wine-cellar. The labourer's cottage, it is true, was but poorly furnished, yet he would have at least a kitchen-dresser, table, chairs and beds. In Ireland, chairs in the cabin were practically unknown, and tables, if anything, rarer; in all but the poorest there might be found a rough dresser, but that only after the recovery from the famine period. A bed was a rare luxury, reserved to the man and his wife, the children were disposed on the floor, whilst coverings were poor and scanty in the extreme. From all accounts, there was very little to choose between the home surroundings of the larger farmer, and those of the cottier. Even when a farmer was relatively well off, he took great care to hide the fact by avoiding any appearance of extravagance in food or clothing, fearing that any show of prosperity would be the occasion for the demand for a higher rent. Again, we get the impression of a society which is completely static, and wellnigh moribund. If we turn to the personal clothing of the people, we get a similar, but even more convincing picture. What people who had anything to hope for from life, would have been content with such rags as the Irish peasant wore? Reliable writers such as Arthur Young, describe the children of the countryside as running about practically naked, and their elder sisters and mothers as being in but little better case.

We have already considered the respective dietaries of the working classes in England and Ireland, more especially in the latter half of the seventeenth, the eighteenth, and the first half of the nineteenth centuries. The difference between them is fundamental. The English labourer's food may not have been a subject for self-congratulation, but it was in general, varied in character, reasonably concentrated, and adequate in quantity, and up till the latter end of the eighteenth century, nutritious. The Irishman's potato diet, eked out by a little oatmeal, was uniformly monotonous, entirely unconcentrated, only adequate in quality when consumed in enormous quantities, and only fully nutritious when accompanied by a supply of fresh milk.

The monotony of the potato diet was depressing enough, but the ease of its preparation and, above all, the knowledge that in a normal season the crop of an Irish acre was enough to maintain a man, his wife and six children, for at least three-quarters of the year, could scarcely fail to reduce the art of living to its lowest functional value. The fact that the potato demanded no other help to its ingestion than some salt, nor to its service but bare fingers, was not inducive of refinement, personal or otherwise. What pride could be taken in the home, or what call was there for ceremony however elementary, to welcome a meal that was about to be shared with the pigs and the poultry, and from the same cauldron?

Feuerbach, pursuing a philosophical rather than a physiological line of argument, concluded that man's social reactions were determined by the character of his diet, and embodied this view in the well-known aphorism 'Der Mensch ist was er isst' (Man is what he eats).[1] He applied his theory to Ireland: 'You [Irish] cannot conquer, for your sustenance can only arouse a paralysing despair not a fiery enthusiasm. And only enthusiasm will be able to fight off the giant [the English] in whose veins flow the rich, powerful, deed-producing blood [roast beef].'[2]

Others following Feuerbach, have condemned the potato as the *fons et origo* of Ireland's misfortune, regardless of the fact that this view has neither the support of physiology nor of history. The Irish had lost their freedom long before the introduction of the potato; it was a century or

---

[1] Feuerbach, Ludwig (1862). *Sämmtliche Werke* (ed. 1911), vol. x, pp. 41–67.
[2] Hook, Sidney (1936). *From Hegel to Marx*, p. 270.

more before the latter achieved the stabilization of their political and social degradation.

The extent to which the abundance of the potato undermined parental responsibility, doubtless varied considerably, but that it was one of the chief, though indirect, factors, in bringing about the enormous increase of the rural population in the eighteenth and first half of the nineteenth centuries, is, I think, certain. For what call was there on the young people, either to delay marriage or restrict childbirth, seeing that a £3 hut and an acre of land, sufficed to maintain a family? The old gibe that Ireland only emerged from the stone age after the great potato famine, was not without its basis of truth.

It may be said that the political and civil backgrounds of the two peoples on either side of the Irish Sea were so different that one is not justified in making any deductions of importance from such outstanding differences in their respective dietary as undoubtedly existed. It would be pertinent to our argument, could we compare the condition of the Irish peasantry with other groups or peoples, in which the major difference between their social systems consisted in the use of a dietary not dominated by the potato.

One cannot expect to find in the field of human relations, a state of affairs such as an experimentalist might devise, in which, between the communities, all is common except for one variant, and that the one whose influence is to be determined. History has been, however, not altogether ungenerous in this respect.

The Palatinate Settlements in Ireland afford an instance which more or less closely conforms to a scientific experiment. In the course of the Allied War against Louis XIV a large body of Moravians from Heidelberg, Mannheim, Spires and Worms, who had been subjected to religious persecutions, passed over into Marlborough's lines. The English Government took 10,000 of them under its care and arranged for their passage via Rotterdam to London. On arrival, 2,000 were found to be Catholics and were duly returned, many others went to America, but finally, 3,073 persons were sent to Dublin. In England, £300,000 was subscribed and a grant of £25,000 was made by the Irish Government for the purpose of settling them on the land, where it was hoped they would add strength to the Protestant ascendancy. Most of the immigrants settled in Limerick, on the estate of Sir Thomas Southwell; another settlement, known still as Palatine Town, was set up in Carlow, Colonel Blennerhasset settled others at Castle Island, whilst some settled at Adare, where they are still to be found.

The newcomers were all arable agriculturists and practised a rotation of potatoes; wheat or barley; wheat; oats, besides raising crops of flax and hemp. Everywhere they were noted for the high quality of their cultivation and the excellence of their crops. They retained their faith and lived and for several generations married, only within their own fold. All accounts are at one in dilating on their well-built homes, and their ample and tasteful furniture. John Wesley made two visits to their settlements and remarked on one occasion: 'They retain much of the temper and manner of their own country, having no resemblance to those among whom they live', and goes on to note how they turn all their land into a garden. Arthur Young visited them and he, too, notes how superior are their methods of culture. In particular they used a wheeled plough, drilled in and ploughed out their potatoes and although they had done the like for thirty years, not one of their neighbours had adopted the method. Wheeled carts were used by them whilst the Irish were still employing slide cars.

They fed on sour kraut [says Young], but by degrees left it off, and took to the potato, but now subsist on these and butter and milk, but with a great deal of oat bread and some of wheat, some meat and fowls, of which they raise many.... They are remarkable for their goodness and cleanliness of their houses. The women are very industrious, reap the corn and plough the ground sometimes. They also spin and make the children do the same.[1]

The colonists were certainly specially favoured both as regards the tenure of their holdings and their rents, but although these advantages were all cancelled in 1760, that did not appear to have occasioned any economic setback.

The French traveller, Latocnaye, in 1796, visited their colonies and is amazed at the superiority of their farms and the neatness of their homes, 'palaces in comparison to those of the native Irish'.[2] In the middle of the next century, just before the potato failure of 1845, another visitor, Samuel Hale, comments on their beautifully kept and furnished homes and the abundance of their food, their great stores of home-cured bacon. Twenty years after the famine, they are included as one of the 'seven distinct nations in Ireland' in these words: 'In Central Ireland, the Germans of the Palatinate have founded a colony whose influence extends over a large proportion of Queens and Kings County.'[3] At the end of the nineteenth century they are still noted for the excellence of their gardens and orchards.[4]

From information kindly supplied me by correspondents, I think there is no reason to doubt that the Palatine small-holders still residing in County Limerick, held their own successfully during the famine period; for in contrast to their neighbours they have preserved no

[1] Young, A. (1780). *A Tour in Ireland*, p. 311.
[2] Latocnaye, de (1796). *A Frenchman's Walk through Ireland*, p. 118.
[3] Adair, R. A. Col. (1886). *Ireland and her Servile War*. London: W. Ridgway.
[4] Hayes, Richard (1937). The German Colony in County Limerick. *North Munster Antiq. J.* vol. I, p. 45.

memories of communal distress. Indeed, such evidence as one has been able to collect points in the reverse direction, thus, one learns that in the Adare district the colonists employed in their homes many of the young native girls who might otherwise have perished, paying them 2s. 6d. per month. At Castle Hewson the colony was strong and active in 1850 and capable of sending some sixty men out to help a neighbour get in his harvest.

It has been mentioned earlier that nowhere in Ireland did the famine produce more havoc than in Kerry, where starvation and disease more than decimated the native population. It is therefore of peculiar interest to learn how the Palatine colonists in that province fared when faced by the loss of their potato crops. The small farmer and cottier class of Kerry, who had based their entire social and economic structure on the potato, collapsed under the strain as surely as did the temple of Dagon when Samson tore down its pillars. The Palatines who had been living in their midst just on a hundred years, may in the past have enjoyed considerable advantages over the native Irish, as auxiliaries of the Ascendancy. But, in a part of the country in which transport was notoriously bad, and in which political and religious distinctions had already lost much of their acerbity, this relationship ceased to possess any material value in the naked struggle for existence, which reigned during those fateful years.

The majority of the Palatine groups in Kerry were settled about 1750 by Colonel Blennerhasset of Ballyseedy, Tralee, on his Kerry estate in the Ballymacelligot district. From there, about ninety years ago, a few families wandered to Annascaul and Ventry. Another group reached Tarbert in Kerry from Rathkeale, Limerick. Up till the year 1800 the Kerry Palatines retained, more or less intact, their German traditions, language, customs, Moravian religion and, above all, their methods of cultivation. Since that time, although there has been some intermarriage and occasional change of faith, the Palatines retained their identity. Notwithstanding the good relations between themselves and their neighbours, both Catholic and Protestant, the Palatines are still regarded as distinct from the native Irish.

As regards their worldly position, the Palatine community are all in comfortable circumstances, whilst some are reputed to be wealthy. The majority of the Kerry Palatines still retain those high standards of arable cultivation which they were the first to introduce into Ireland. As of old, their own houses are invariably well appointed and beautifully clean, and nothing is allowed to take precedence whether in the field or the city, over the claim of house and family. In contrast with the native Irish Catholic peasantry, but few memories or traditions reaching back to the famine period have been handed down to the present generation of Palatines, but from the information I have been able to gather, one may conclude that they also were not seriously affected, economically or physically, by the potato failure of 1845 and 1846. By reason of the wider range of their cropping, they were able to fall back on turnips for the feeding of their pigs and other live-stock, and thus maintain the continuity of their farming, and enjoy, to some measure, the mixed dietary to which they were accustomed. Nor is there any record of post-famine trouble amongst the Kerry Palatines, who in contrast to their neighbours, sent no emigrants to the United States of America until the eighties of last century.

Whilst allowance must be made for the difference of tradition and customs of the Palatine and native Irish, those of the Irish had been, to a great extent, moulded by their dependence on the potato which influenced them both directly and indirectly. The Palatines were under no such constraint. When the crisis came and the potato failed the Irish cultivator, it was more than the loss of food, it was the basis of his whole social system which had been withdrawn; his collapse was inevitable. To the Palatine, with his mixed farming, the failure of the potato meant little more than a serious inconvenience. One tale from Kerry which has come down to the present generation, illustrates the point. One of the Fitzelles, a well-known Palatine family of Tarbert, used to tell her son, now in Annascaul, how her family in the famine period were in comfortable circumstances and maintained a large number of pigs; owing to the potato failure, her father had to feed them on turnips. One day, as the pigs were being fed, three emaciated men appeared and started devouring the turnips when, to the horror of her father, one of them fell down dead before he had swallowed the first mouthful. It would seem that the chief factor differentiating the economic position of the Palatine farmer and these starving men, was the diversity of their attitude to the potato: the former had made the potato his servant, the latter his master.[1]

In England, as in most other countries, the potato made no progress as a food of the people, until industrialists discovered that the easiest way to produce cheap goods, in order to capture the foreign market, was to pay the lowest living wage, and that workers could only be induced to give of their labour under such a system if the cost of living was kept at the lowest possible level. The potato came as a heaven-sent gift to the leaders of industry; its use was urged not only by the employers, but by many well-intentioned persons who failed to appreciate its implications.

In Ireland, the case was essentially different; so far from the potato

[1] I have received much assistance, from many sources, in my efforts to discover how the Palatines fared in the 1845–7 crisis. In particular I should like to record my thanks to Miss Lucy Gwynn of Parteenalax, Limerick, and to Mr Jerome Murphy of Cloonalour, Tralee, for that concerning those in Limerick and Kerry respectively.

being forced on the people from above, it spread through the entire social organism from below. It had no sponsors. It needed none; arriving at a critical moment in the people's history, it had filled the yawning gap which the wars of the sixteenth century had torn in the tenor of their lives. As soon as the potato was established, the standard of living automatically became fixed at a level commensurate with the energy its production demanded. The more the potato fulfilled the requirements of the household, the sooner was endeavour damped down, and sloth and slovenliness exalted. As time went on, the sequence— poverty, potatoes; larger families, more potatoes, and greater poverty, became ever more firmly established, till nothing but revolution or catastrophe could break it.

It is not too much to say that for close on 300 years the potato both stabilized and perpetuated the misery of the Irish masses. It was, as it were, the least common denominator of Irish life, for by reducing the cost of living to the lowest possible limit, it caused the value of labour to fall to a corresponding level, whilst it permitted, if not encouraged, an ever-growing population.

Malthus may well have had the condition of Ireland in his mind when he wrote:

If every person were satisfied with the simplest food, the poorest clothing and the meanest houses, it is certain that no other sort of food, clothing, and lodging, would be in existence, and as there would be no adequate motive to the proprietors of land to cultivate well, not only the wealth derived from convenience and luxuries would be quite at an end, but if the same divisions of land continued, the production of food would be prematurely checked and population would come to a stand long before the soil had been well cultivated.[1]

His words were indeed prophetic. The low standard of living which, following the acceptance of a potato diet, had overtaken the common people, led students of the economic problem in Ireland, whilst they deplored the lack of enterprise of the landowners, the backwardness of the cultivator, the neglect of the so-called waste lands, to advocate but one remedy, a reduction by any means, of the population.

As the pressure of numbers told on the available means of support, that is to say, the area of land made available for potato cultivation, which in Ireland by 1845 was already some five or six times that attained in England per unit of population, a crisis became inevitable. The only choice for the people lay between emigration and death. It will be recalled that those, in fact, were the two alternatives considered by the authorities during the whole of the eighteenth and nineteenth centuries.

[1] Malthus, T. R. (1820). *Principles of Political Economy*, p. 8.

CHAPTER XIX

The Potato in Scotland

Notwithstanding the economic importance of the Scotch ware and seed-potato trade, no study, serious or otherwise, seems to have been made of its history. A few of the commonly known facts are set out in a recent book on the Potato by a Scottish writer,[1] but the characteristic reactions of the different parts of Scotland to the new food have escaped attention.

The earliest mention of the potato in Scotland so far recorded, is to be found in James Sutherland's[2] *Catalogue of the Plants in the Physical Gardens of Edinburgh*, published in 1683. The entry is as follows: 'Solanum tuberosum esculentum Matth. ed. Bauh: Battatas Virginiana *Ger., Park.*; Pappas Americanum I. B.; *Virginian Potato's.*'[3] Sutherland, who died in 1719, was appointed in 1675 the first Keeper to the Physical Gardens, recently founded by Sir Andrew Balfour and Dr Robert Skibald. The garden was established in the grounds of Holyrood Palace, but subsequently removed to Trinity Hospital. Sutherland maintained intimate relations with the leading botanists in England and on the Continent,[4] and it is probable that he received his tubers from Prof. Morison of Oxford, who had taken a deep personal interest in Balfour's project, and who writes of the potato as growing freely in 'our gardens' at Oxford.

John Reid[5] includes the potato amongst the plants to be grown in the kitchen garden. He recommends only five rows and that one should 'spend them with parsnips' which presumably means they should be used with or treated as parsnips. That he only envisaged quite small quantities follows from his injunction as to storage that 'in housing spread only through a broad floor'. He recommends planting in March and their use as a table dish during the months of December, January and February. In the 1766 edition there are slight differences in the text. Potatoes are a dish for November as well as for December and

---

[1] McIntosh, T. P. (1927). *The Potato*. Edinburgh: Oliver and Boyd.

[2] Sutherland, James (1683). *Hortus Medicus Edinburgensis*.

[3] The contractions may be read as follows:

Matth. ed. Bauh: = Matthiolus's Commentary on Dioscorides (ed. by Gaspard Bauhin, 1598).

Ger. = Gerard's *Herball*, corrected by Johnson, 1633.

Park. = *The Theater of Plants*, by John Parkinson, 1640.

I.B. = John Bauhin's *Historia plantarum Universalis*, 1651.

[4] Cowan, John Macqueen (1938). *The History of the Royal Botanic Garden, Edinburgh*. Notes from the Roy. Bot. Gardens, Edinburgh, vol. XIX, Nos. xci–xcv.

[5] Reid, John (1683). *Scots Gardener*, p. 107.

January, the month of February is omitted. On the other hand, it is during this month that planting is advised. On storing he is more explicit: 'Spread them only through a broad floor.' It would seem that in this edition he regarded the potato only as a minor feature in the private kitchen garden. In *Husbandry Anatomized*[1] which appeared in 1697, elaborate instructions are given as to the preparation for the table, from which it would appear that they were more widely known than is suggested above. Thus: 'Some make bread of them by mixing them with oats and barley meal', others eat them 'among broth and broken with kale'. Against this, in *The Lady's Recreation*, 1717,[2] there is a portion devoted to the kitchen garden, in which the potato is hastily dismissed with a quotation from John Evelyn's *Kalendarium*, which merely directs you to dig your potatoes in November, and store them with the carrots and parsnips in the cellar. Clearly, only the latest maturing varieties were known at this time. How little headway the potato had made by the beginning of the eighteenth century in Scotland, is shown by the fact that the Duchess of Buccleuch in 1701 paid as much as 2s. 6d. for a peck of potatoes; equivalent to about 9d. a pound at present-day prices.[3]

When the second of the Preston brothers who succeeded Sutherland, published a new Catalogue of the Edinburgh Collection in 1716,[4] he described the potato as *Battata Virginiana*, a latinization of Gerard's potato of Virginia,[5] which suggests that his botanical acquaintance with the plant was neither intimate nor accurate. So far the potato in Scotland was little more than a museum specimen: its destiny had not, as yet, been influenced by the peculiar social and political circumstances of the country into which it had made so modest an entry.

So late as the close of the eighteenth century, Scotland was far less uniform in national feeling and social development, than England. Parts of the Lowlands might have been culturally more or less on a par with the English Home Counties, but they were poles apart from the Highlands, not to speak of the Hebrides. The Lowlander, Boswell, regarded his and Johnson's visit to the Isles as a great adventure, as indeed it was, for to Johnson the manners and language of the people were not less strange than would have been those of the peasantry of the Balkans. In truth, there were at least two distinct Scotlands, and we must need trace the progress of the potato in each.

[1] Reid, James (1697). *Husbandry Anatomized*, p. 129.
[2] Evelyn, Charles (1717). *The Lady's Recreation*, p. 192.
[3] Quoted from Sanders, T. W. (1905). *The Book of the Potato*, p. 8. London.
[4] Preston, George (1716). *Catalogue of Plants*. Edinburgh: Moncur.
[5] Cowan, misled by the change of name, has stated that the potato was omitted from Preston's Catalogue. I am indebted to Dr A. D. Cotton, of the Royal Botanic Gardens, Kew, for allowing me to examine this very rare book.

CHAPTER XX

The Potato in the Highlands of Scotland

Much as the Highland differ from the Lowland districts in their physico-geographical characters, a glance at the map of Scotland, on which the so-called Highland Line[1] is drawn, will convince one that something more than the presence or absence of mountain and glen went to make that wide gulf which once severed the people of Scotland into two more or less distinct nations, a distinction which two centuries of peace have not succeeded in effacing.

The Highland Line which 200 years ago meant much more than it does to-day, can be defined as starting on the north side of the Clyde and passing east in a straight line through Dumbarton to Dunkeld, and on through Clova in Angus, to near the juncture of this county with Kincardine; from thence, the line turns to the north-east across Aberdeen to the west of Aboyne, and passes in a westerly direction to Inveraven on the Spey, and through Dunphail in Moray to Nairn. Continuing on the northern side of the Moray Firth, the line passes up the eastern border of Sutherland and, cutting Caithness completely away, ends at Port Skerra on the Atlantic.

All to the north and west of the line is regarded as Highland, and that to the south and east as Lowland. It will be obvious that if there is relatively little low-lying and level land in the Highlands as compared with the Lowlands, there is much true mountain country on the lowland side of the line, especially in the counties of Perth, Banff and Elgin. Nor is mountainous country wanting to the south of the line of the Clyde and Forth, where the heights of the Hartfell rival in grandeur much of that to be found in the Highlands themselves. The outstanding physical difference between the two divisions of Scotland is the dissection, often minute, of the Highland mainland, by innumerable fiords, lochs, rivers and mountain massifs, a process repeated in the numerous islands lying out in the Atlantic, which moreover are frequently cut off from each other and the mainland by tempestuous seas. Intercommunication, always difficult and often impossible, has induced a state of local isolation both in space and spirit, the like of which is not to be found in the Lowlands, nor elsewhere in the British Isles. This difficulty has only been recently overcome, steamship and motor car not withstanding, by the use of the aeroplane and that, of course, only on a few selected routes. What it meant two hundred, or even one hundred years ago, can be readily imagined. Even Queen Victoria was imprisoned

[1] See Introduction for comments. – Ed.

by an unusually heavy snowfall for several weeks in one of the shooting-boxes on the Balmoral Estate. It was this isolation of districts, with the consequent localization of interests and restriction of social impacts, which gave the clan organization its opportunity for intensive development and allowed of its survival in a world which had long outgrown that form of social economy.

It is held by some, that the essential difference between the social development of Highlander and Lowlander can be ultimately ascribed to the poverty of the highland soils in essential mineral constituents. Such is supposed to have led to the early exhaustion of both arable and pasture. Although it is true that in several parts of the Highlands there is a deficiency of minerals, it is doubtful whether the lowlands are in much better case. Parts of Lowland Aberdeen are as deficient as those in the Highland districts of the county. Calcium deficiency, which is outstanding for so much of Scotland, is as much felt in Kirkcudbright-shire as in Ross-shire, and the trace element, cobalt, is equally wanting in both.[1] In coastal regions of the Highlands and the Hebrides, there are unlimited quantities of shell-sand available; all that is wanting is the necessary enterprise to take it inland and spread it.

In Banff and Inverness, as well as in Shetland, there are extensive limestone deposits which are now being developed. Whilst there are many large tracks of land which have almost ceased to have any value, because lack of mineral in the soil and water-logging of the raw humus has led to peat formation, yet there are still more where the fertility of the soil only waits on drainage, to manifest itself.

The excessive rainfall and high winds make cereal growing, other than oats, impossible, whilst the harvesting of the latter is a prolonged and wearisome gamble. If there were but one ultimate cause responsible for the difference of social development in Highland and Lowland, then the difficulty of communication must be the first to be indicted. It is this which, now as in the past, determines the cost of the fertilizers of which the poorer highland soils are most in need.

The Highlanders are for the most part Gaels, who had been driven into the inland mountain fastnesses by invading Scandinavians and Saxons who retained for themselves the richer Lowland districts of the country. Differences of speech, tradition and race, all helped to intensify the cultural distinction, which geographical factors imposed between the peoples of the Highlands and Lowlands of Scotland, respectively.

The requirements of the Highlander were few, and money as such, played but a very small part in his economy. His home was never more than a miserable one-roomed 'black' hut, similar to those which have

[1] Communicated to R.N.S. by Dr A. B. Stewart of the Macaulay Institute, Aberdeen.

been already described as common to the peasantry of Ireland. His clothes were made from the wool of his own sheep, spun and woven into cloth by his womenfolk. His agricultural implements were of the simplest and made locally; his crops were limited to oats, barley, and an occasional plot of peas or beans. His food consisted almost entirely of oatmeal, and bread made from barley or oats. The cattle were bled from time to time and the blood mixed with oatmeal made into cakes, but this was probably his only luxury as far as food was concerned. Meat was a great rarity,[1] though sheep and cattle were there, but they were held for sale through the chief or his agent the tacksman, to the nearest town, or taken in droves to the Lowlands. Whale and seal meat were fully enjoyed in the Orkneys and Shetlands and were not unknown in some of the Outer Hebrides. Sea-birds and their eggs were, in the more remote islands, a staple article of diet. Milk was drunk in considerable quantity by all. Of the few sheep which were kept, some of the ewes were housed in the peasants' huts and from their milk and that of goats, cheese was made.

In settlements along the coast or within reach of loch or river, and there were few that were not, fish was always available. The herring fishery, in particular, flourished in the west, especially after 1745, and some of the catch was consumed by the local population, but Johnson was probably not far wrong when, in this connection, he wrote: 'I believe man never lives long on fish, but by constraint, he will rather feed on roots and berries.' Of vegetables prior to 1845, the Highlanders knew only kale, which it is said, was introduced by Cromwell,[2] but few seem to have taken the trouble to cultivate even that; it was, however, a constant ingredient of barley-broth, a dish much in favour in the south.

A visitor to the Highlands and Western Isles in the early part of the nineteenth century, says that the Highlander never makes a garden, and that you might as well ask for bananas as a cabbage, a leek or an onion. Only in the Shetlands and Orkneys did he find the need for green vegetables recognized and met.[3] Even the Laird of Corrichatachin (Skye) so late as 1773 'has literally no garden; not even a turnip, a carrot or a cabbage'.[4] Pigs were not kept by the Highlander, who at this time seems to have entertained an age-old prejudice against swine-flesh.

---

[1] Evidence on this point is conflicting, but the probability is that the Highlander only rarely enjoyed a flesh meal. The repeated tales that he cooked his meat in the paunch of the beast [Anonymous; Scotland in 1745, by an Officer of Cumberland's army quoted in The Contrast (publ. 1825), London] would seem to refer to the opportunities afforded by raids on cattle and the occasional poaching of deer.

[2] Johnson, Samuel (1775). Journey to the Western Islands of Scotland (Oxford edition, 1924), pp. 24 and 92.

[3] Macculloch, John (1824). Highlands and Western Isles. Letter to Sir W. Scott, 1811. London: Longmans.

[4] Boswell, J. (1785). Journal of a Tour to the Hebrides (6th edit.), p. 266.

Of all his possessions, the proudest was his arms. Education prior to 1745, apart from a knowledge of the Bible, scarcely existed.

The system by which the land was cultivated in the Highlands—and we are speaking of the period prior to 1745—was twofold: where the land lent itself to farming on a reasonably large scale, as in the fertile glens, individual farms might extend over as much as 150 acres, though they were generally very much smaller. In any case they were divided into two parts, the 'infield' and the 'outfield': the former was always the better land and near the homestead. All the manure went to the infield, which enabled it to be cropped continuously in oats and bere (barley) alternately. The outfield was only manured by the folding on it of the cattle overnight; the folds made of earth surrounds, were shifted every eight or ten days. It was cropped in oats, year in, year out, till the return was no more than the seed employed, when it was allowed to fall down to grass for some five or six years, after which it was ploughed and the cycle renewed. There were no fences other than an occasional dyke between the outfield and the 'hill' or mountainside, on which each tenant and cottar had certain definite rights of grazing. The farm was not held by one tenant but by several, each of whom had a number of strips of land interspersed in both the infield and outfield, and these strips were redistributed by lot in some districts every third year, in others, annually. The strips were generally divided by balks of grass, which occasionally were broad enough to be used as pasture for a tethered ox or horse.

Occasionally the farm was held in common by a small group living in a cluster of huts, jointly responsible for the rent. This system was commented on by Samuel Johnson in 1773 and was still current twenty years later.

The laird's Mains or demesne land, might be held as a continuous whole or, as often as not, consisted of strips distributed amongst those of his tenants in the runrig fields.[1]

The moment the harvest was gathered, all the land was thrown open to pasture for every kind of beast and fowl that laird and tenant possessed. This system of 'runrig' was, prior to 1745, general throughout most of Scotland; it was similar to that which still held in a few places in Ireland and in its general character was akin to the open-field system still current in much of England at that date.

Besides the tenants of the runrig farms, there were small holders of two to five acres occupied by a poorer class of clansmen known as crofters: these worked their own land, kept their cattle on the hills, but in addition assisted the larger farmers and rendered their service to the laird in the busy seasons of the year. Still lower in the scale were those

[1] Grant, I. F. (1924). *Everyday Life on an old Highland Farm.*

who had a hut and a patch of land and worked for others: they were known as cottars.

In general, the standard of arable cultivation was extremely poor: except for the preparation of the land for broadcasting in the spring, and the intake of the crop at harvest, very little work was done on the land at any time, and none at all during the summer months. It was then that the whole community moved up into the hills with their cattle, goats and sheep, and encamped in sheilings or temporary huts on the mountains.

The system which neither encouraged individual industry nor called for prolonged and sustained labour, has been held responsible for the indifference to hard work which is so frequently alleged against the Highlander. One who knew him well, writes: 'Towards the beginning of the present century (eighteenth), the people of the country were averse to industry. The spirit of clanship which prevailed was very unfavourable to it. The different clans spent a great part of their time in avenging themselves of each other. The man who could best handle his sword and his gun was deemed the prettiest fellow, and the attentive and industrious man was a character held in a degree of contempt.'[1] It is not necessary to defend him, for his outlook was ever different from that current around him. He was a soldier, not a tradesman; so long as there was food enough to eat, and money enough to equip himself with tartan and weapons, he was satisfied. Moreover, what little work he did do in the field required much more energy than would the same to-day. His tools were so clumsy that it needed up to twelve oxen to draw the plough, and so inefficient that it required four to five men to keep it at work,[2] 'and if the whole party managed to overturn one ridge at a yoking, the husbandmen's hopes were realized'. Hence, though output was low, the demand for seasonal labour might be high. In any case Highland agriculture, even when in the hands of the bigger farmer, was conducted on an almost purely subsistence basis. The black cattle were of far greater importance to the Highlander than his sheep, they represented his movable property and his potential cash reserve. If they were liable to extinction in the turmoil of inter-clan warfare, they were as frequently renewed by raids on the Lowlanders' preserves. Indeed, the whole set-out of the farm in infield, outfield and on the hill, probably owes its origin and long-continued existence to the necessity of keeping the cattle under the close supervision of the owner. One writer in the last decade of the eighteenth century records how he 'remembers when the people of this county (Perth), kept each a watch

---

[1] Stuart, Rev. Patrick (1796). *The Statistical Account of Scotland*, vol. XVII, p. 383.
[2] Grant, I. F. (1924). *Every-day Life on an old Highland Farm*, 1769–1782, p. 45. Longmans.

in the summer months for protecting their cattle, and their watch kept up a daily round of duty at certain periods'.[1]

A correspondence which took place in about 1660 between Alan Cameron of Lochiel and the Laird Grant of Moynes, offers a rather delightful picture of the 'tragical-comical' Highland wars. Cameron and his men raided Grant's lands in Nairn, when many persons on both sides were injured. Grant wrote to Lochiel objecting that they were really 'friends'; Cameron replied that he was very sorry; it was all a mistake; they had quite forgotten that Moynes belonged to Grant. They had merely intended to carry out a 'spreath' on cattle in Moray, where, as Grant would agree, 'all men take their prey'.[2]

Childish as these forages may seem, we must remember that the constant threat of such was a real and potent factor in the life of the Highlander. Progress can have no meaning in a society chronically mobilized for war. Such amenities, not to speak of refinements, as the English peasant might enjoy, were denied the Highlander. The utmost simplicity in food, dress and housing, were the inevitable consequence of the social system in force.

Some lay much stress on racial difference as explaining the peculiarities in the social structure of the Highlands compared with that of the Lowlands. It is doubtful whether such has any validity when compared with that induced by the reactions, traditional and cultural, which have resulted from the different environments of the two people.

The Highlands lay outside the influences of the Roman occupation: they were neither conquered by the Normans nor ever effectively brought within the feudal structure of the later Middle Ages, in force elsewhere. Not that they were left untouched by feudalism; it was rather that the latter was forced to accommodate itself to an existing and distinct clan system which the peculiar isolation and localization of the Highland country rendered immune to outside influence. Towards the end of the fifteenth century, James IV of Scotland attempted to establish feudalism in the Highlands, but it resulted in a serious uprising in 1503. Under the clan system, the chieftain and clansmen constituted one great family, united, at least theoretically, by blood and their common rights in the land, and consolidated into self-contained units by devotion to their chief, love of their homeland, hatred of their neighbours, and, above all, by pride in their personal and communal prowess in war.

It was natural that such a system found its chief expression in inter-clan warfare, much of which bore the character of primitive tribal vendetta. Within the clan, there was a very large measure of social equality, subject always to the overriding devotion to a chief who

[1] Grant, Rev. John (1794). *The Statistical Account of Scotland*, vol. XIII, p. 149.
[2] Ibid.

possessed unlimited powers, including those of 'Pit and Gallows', over the individual clansmen. The clansmen had an immemorial right to live within the clan area, to till enough land to raise the necessary oats and barley for their sustenance, and to rear black cattle and a few sheep on the hillside. What exactly these rights amounted to, was probably never clearly defined. A recent author says that the tenant had an absolute right in the land and the chief was in reality a trustee.[1] An earlier authority takes the view that the position of the chief was absolute, and the peasant had no rights.[2] Subsequent events would seem to support this latter interpretation. The clansman, so far as he regarded riches as such, reckoned them in cattle, the chieftain in the number of men he could summon to arms, either to war against a neighbour or to rob the Lowlander and raid his cattle.

The clansman's duties to his chief or his representative the tacksman, were not, however, discharged merely by following him to battle; he owed and paid many 'services': he tilled the lord's land, dug and lead his peat, a most onerous duty, and harvested his crops; all this in addition to paying a rent in kind, often with the addition of 'kain' fowls. In the more isolated parts, the people ground their home-grown oats and barley by means of a hand quern; elsewhere, the chieftain owned the mill and the people were 'tied' to it by a system known as 'thirlage', whereby they surrendered anything from one-sixteenth to one-eleventh of their corn as a 'multure'. Even death did not close the account: not infrequently a 'heriot'—the best beast on the holding—was exacted.

Against this, it must be said, the debt was not all on one side. Chieftains, doubtless, varied widely in the seriousness with which they discharged their duty to their tenants, but they were never ignorant of the fact that such existed. No man would be allowed to starve, just as no man was allowed to marry till he had prepared or acquired a home.[3] In evil days, the chief made himself responsible for the maintenance and safety, so far as he could, of the clan. It was a self-contained and self-supporting system.

It would be a mistake to assume that the clansman, whose relations to his chief were so circumscribed, was himself conscious of, much less outraged by their servility. Rather did he feel himself to be a member of one great family, to the chief of which, reverence and honourable service were natural tributes. The society in which he lived, was far more equalitarian than that of eighteenth-century England. The Chieftain and his immediate family, or the tacksman, who on the larger

---

[1] Cameron, John (1912). *The Old and the New Hebrides*. Cameron: Kirkcaldy.

[2] Anderson, John (1827). *The State of Society and Knowledge in the Highlands of Scotland*. Edinburgh: W. Tait.

[3] Stewart, David, Col. (1822). *Sketches of the Character etc. of the Highlanders of Scotland*.

estates, acted as both steward and middleman, were his social superiors and leaders; they were neither foreigners nor alien conquerors, but united with him in blood, language, tradition, religion and, above all, in the necessity for association in the never absent danger of attack. To the Englishman, the Highlander appeared uncouth and ridiculous as a civilian, and little better than a savage on the field of battle.

Defoe[1] has left us a vivid picture of a Highlander in the streets of Edinburgh as seen through the spectacles of a cultured Londoner in 1706. If it exhibits a certain xenophobia on his part, it leaves one in no doubt as to the Highlanders' over self-assurance:

They are formidable fellows and I only wish Her Majesty had 25,000 of them in Spain, as a nation equally proud and barbarous like themselves. They are all gentlemen, will take affront from no man, and insolent to the last degree. But certainly the absurdity is ridiculous to see a man in his mountain habit, armed with a broadsword, target, pistol, at his girdle a dagger, and staff, walking down the High Street as upright and haughty as if he were a lord, and withal driving a cow! bless us—are these the gentlemen! said I.

It is not surprising that in the eyes of the Lowlander, the Highlander was incurably lazy; the term 'aboriginal indolence' so frequently used, was intended to convey both the fact and its explanation. It cannot be denied that the clan system seriously hindered continuous constructive labour, but when later the easily cultivated potato came to be adopted, the stigma which had attached to the Highlander's race was transferred to his diet.

Such, in general, was the condition, social and agricultural, of the Highlands and Hebrides for some six centuries prior to 1745. Within that area it is probable that there was not a single potato plant grown, either at that time or indeed, with minor exceptions, for a score of years later.

'Probable' but may be, not certain! It will be remembered that Johnson fell in with Boswell's suggestion to visit the Hebrides because he still cherished the feeling of adventure which he experienced when, as a boy, his father had given him Martin's 'Account' to read. Martin[2] visited the Western Islands in 1695; speaking of Skye, he says:

The diet generally used by the natives consists of fresh food, for they seldom taste any that is salted, except butter. The generality eat but little flesh, and only persons of distinction eat it every day and make three meals, for all the rest eat only two, and they eat more boiled than roasted. Their ordinary diet is butter, cheese, milk, potatoes, colworts, brochan, i.e. oatmeal and water

---

[1] Defoe (1706). *Letter to Harley*, Nor. Hist. MSS. Comm. Portland Papers, vol. IV, p. 349.
[2] Martin, Martin (1703). *A Description of the Western Islands of Scotland*, p. 201. London: Andrew Bell.

boiled. The latter taken with some bread is the constant food of several thousands of both sexes in this and other isles, during the winter and spring; yet they undergo many fatigues both by sea and land, and are very healthful.... There is no place so well stored with such great quantities of good beef and mutton where so little of both is consumed by eating. They generally use no fine sauce to entice a false appetite, nor brandy or tea for digestion, the purest water serves them in such cases.

This is repeated verbatim in the 1716 edition published three years before Martin's death. Donald Macleod,[1] the editor of the 1934 edition, is confident that these are not only Martin's own words, but is of opinion that they represent the facts as Martin observed them. But if we accept Martin's statement, then we must concede that the people of Skye were, so far as the potato is concerned, dietetically in advance of any part of Great Britain except Ireland. As such is highly improbable, it is desirable to seek corroboration elsewhere. Martin himself contributed a paper to the Royal Society[2] in 1697 on his Tour, and discusses the habits and beliefs of the natives, but unfortunately makes no mention either of dietary or potato; as regards their drinking habits, he alleges that in Ferintosh in Ross, children drink Aquavitae from infancy, and in his book he refers frequently to the abuse of whisky in the Western Isles. All of which it is hard to reconcile with the exemplary habits of the men of Skye, a people wedded to the 'purest water'. Johnson[3] may have criticized Martin's style somewhat ungraciously, but one feels more inclined to be sympathetic when he observes that 'it is a very imperfect performance and he is erroneous as to many particulars even some concerning his own island, Skye'.

In support of Martin is the fact that in Macdonald's *Gaelic Dictionary* of 1741, under Edible Roots, the word 'buntata' is given for the potato,[4] which may be no more than a literary essay to create a word for an 'edible root' which might have been either the sweet or the common potato, and one not necessarily known to the Gaelic-speaking people.

In a collection of *Essays*, two distinguished authors refer to the date of the introduction. The one[5] says 'the potato was introduced to the Highlands at the end of the seventeenth century'; the other[6] that 'the potato did not come into general use until the second half of the eighteenth century, though they were known in some parts as early as the seventeenth

[1] Macleod, Donald (1945). Letter to R.N.S. 27 February.
[2] Martin, Martin (1697). *Roy. Soc. Trans.* vol. XIX, p. 727.
[3] Johnson, Samuel (1775). *Journey to the Western Islands of Scotland.*
[4] Macdonald, Alexander (1741). *Gaelic Dictionary,* p. 59.
[5] Mackay, W. (1911). *Industrial Life in the Highlands. Leabhar a'Chlachain.* Glasgow: Robert Maclehose and Co.
[6] Mackenzie, W. C. (1911). *The Social Life of the Community. Leabhar a'Chlachain.* Glasgow: Robert Maclehose and Co.

century'. Unfortunately, neither gives details nor their authorities. Nor does the *Statistical Account* help us, as it gives no dates for its introduction into Skye. In view of the fact that we have quite an impressive volume of data placing the introduction of the potato at about the beginning of the second half of the eighteenth century, it seems impossible to accept Martin's word that it was a common article of the people's diet in 1695.[1] How he came to make that statement can only be a matter of conjecture, but it is worth recalling that in discussing the Western Isles he frequently refers to Ireland and appears to have been well informed as to conditions there; indeed, he invariably refers to the language of the Highlanders as 'Irish'. This in itself may have no great weight because the Gaelic language was indifferently referred to as Erse or Irish: thus in a letter to Johnson, Boswell[2] discussing the Macpherson-Ossian controversy, says: 'it is affirmed that the Gaelic (call it Erse or call it Irish) has been written in the Highlands and Hebrides for many centuries'. It is suggested therefore, that Martin's ascription to the natives of Skye of a food which he knew to be universal in the sister isle, was possibly a *lapsus calami*.

The late arrival of the potato in the Highlands presents a problem the solution of which throws some light on the part it has played in modern civilization. Various explanations present themselves. Was it that the potato never came within their purview; that they were, in fact, ignorant of its existence, or at least of its uses? Could it be that the people were so liberally supplied with foodstuffs that they were never conscious of any shortage, and thus had no reason to try out a new food? Was the Highlander so prejudiced against innovation of any kind, or so at ease within his environment, as to have achieved an equilibrium which left him unmoved by periodic distress, and deaf to that call, which incited the workers in the Lowlands and in England, to improve their social condition?

The Highlander, a Gaelic-speaking Celt, was by race, language, and above all the traditional structure of his life, closely akin to the majority of the Irish natives. From 1400 onwards, groups of Hebridean Scotsmen, mostly under the leadership of the McDonnells, had crossed over to County Antrim, and this infiltration increased steadily in volume during the sixteenth century. Prior to the settlement in 1609 in Ulster under James I, colonies of Scotch folk had been established under Sir Hugh Montgomery and Sir James Hamilton in the Aards of Down and the neighbourhood of Belfast. During the seventeenth century Scotch and especially Highland Scotch emigrants, poured into Northern Ireland, so that by about 1660 the ascendancy of the Scotch Presbyterians in Ulster was firmly established. The Scotch settlers maintained throughout

---

[1] Gunn, A. and MacKay, J. (1897). *Southerland and McReay County*. They quote a description in about 1645 of a covenanting fugitive who was hidden by a girl in the trench of a lazybed of potatoes (Salaman's manuscript note). – Ed.

[2] *Life of Dr Johnson*. Boswell to Johnson, 18 February 1775.

a sympathetic relationship with their folk at home, and it is wellnigh unthinkable that they should not, on their journeys to their relatives in the Highlands and the Western Isles, have brought with them from Ireland not only the knowledge of the potato but samples of its tubers, as we know that some in fact did, on their visits to the Lowlands. It is difficult therefore to contend that the Highlander of the seventeenth century knew nothing of the potato, though one may readily allow that its existence failed to interest him.

The latter consideration suggests the possibility that the Highlanders were normally sufficiently supplied with foodstuffs, as to be able to disregard new sources, and that a bulky vegetable such as the potato, made no appeal to them. That they were not generally undernourished is certain, for all accounts agree that the Highlanders of the seventeenth and eighteenth centuries were an outstandingly sturdy folk; the endurance of their fighting men on long marches over trackless hill and dale, constantly excited the admiration and envy of the officers and men of regular English troops. Both women and children seem also to have enjoyed good health, and families were notoriously large. Rickets, so prevalent elsewhere, is not complained of in the Highlands, where indeed the fishermen of the Western Isles considered fish liver a remedy for that trouble as well as other bone affections.[1] Scurvy, however, was common in all great towns, including those of Scotland. In some parts of the Highlands it had been rampant, as at St Fergus in north-east Aberdeenshire, but disappeared after the potato had been introduced.[2] In Arngask, Perthshire, scurvy was still common as late as 1792, but here potatoes are not recorded amongst the crops raised.[3]

It must not be assumed that food supplies were both assured and ample. Indeed, the contrary was the fact. The extreme isolation of many districts and the difficulty of intercommunication already referred to, necessitated the raising of enough food locally for current use, a duty which was communal as well as individual. The custom of discharging tenant dues in the form of services and the provision of kain fowls and the like, had its counterpart in the maintenance of unmarried 'hinds' in the farmer's household, in the payment of wages to the married men in 'bolls' of oat and barley meal, a custom, memorialized in the term 'boll-man' applied to a cottar in the Orkneys. In this way laird, tacksman, and clansman, were mutually concerned in the provision of adequate food supplies for the community. So long as seasons were favourable, all went well, but in the event of a shortage due to late frosts, or very wet harvest weather, neither of which were uncommon, it rested

---

[1] *Encyclopaedia Britannica* (3rd edit. 1797). Article: Rickets.
[2] *The Statistical Account of Scotland*, 1795, vol. xv.
[3] Ibid. 1791, vol. i, p. 414.

with the chief to attempt to feed his peoples by the import of meal from other districts. This, even with the best of good will, was no easy task, seeing that everything had to be carried on the backs of the small native horses, and that the mountain streams were rarely bridged. The truth is that local food shortages, sometimes amounting to famine conditions, were all too frequent, and many such disasters have been recorded in the course of the seventeenth and eighteenth centuries. One such occurred at Kirkhill in Inverness during the latter part of the eighteenth century, when the people are said to have lived on herbs and wild mustard.

The last four years of the seventeenth century and the first three of the next, long remembered as the 'seven ill years', were disastrous: wet weather destroyed the crops each year. Although the Privy Council took strong measures to check profiteering, and allowed imports of corn free of tax, the loss of life was so great that it left a lasting mark on Scotch economic life.[1] In 1709 severe famine was again experienced, and many emigrated to Ireland, but no one throughout Scotland called in the Irish potato to their help. Shortages sometimes amounting to famine were indeed inevitable with an economic system so inelastic as that of runrig, especially as practised in the Highlands. It may be said, therefore, that whilst in normal years the food supply was adequate, the local agricultural methods were so primitive, and communications so restricted, that the people were quite unable to deal with the failure of any one of the two or three crops that they grew.

Why then, it may be asked, did the Highlander not adopt the potato till well after the beginning of the second half of the century? The answer is really implicit in what has been said of the system under which he lived, and the peculiar tenour of his life, neither of which for at least 600 years had experienced any real change. Had Providence permitted an elderly Highlander of the pre-1745 period to have sat down at the same table with an ancestor of the thirteenth century and his own grown-up grandchild, he would have been thoroughly at home with the former and hardly have had anything in common with the latter. He was completely conditioned to the demands of the older age; and if occasionally made painfully aware of its shortcomings and its dangers, the more did he appreciate its dignified leisure, the glamour of his clan's prowess, and the security obtained through the efforts of his chief and his fellows. Why then should he worry about a root, that some interfering innovator said might replace the oatmeal which had fed his people since the beginning of time? That this was the attitude adopted is illustrated by the few accounts which have come down to us of the

[1] Graham, H. G. (1906). *The Social Life of Scotland*, p. 150. Edinburgh: A. and C. Black.

earlier attempts made to induce the Highlander to grow and eat the potato.

Nor can the prejudice entertained against a food on the ground that it is not mentioned in the Bible be lightly dismissed.[1] Even if it were but a cloak to that attitude of conservatism and suspicion so common to a people, cut off from the main stream of culture, it might still have been a very real obstacle to change.

After the potato had become an established food of the Highlanders, it was by no means uncommon for some passing epidemic to be attributed even by men of education to a surfeit of its tubers. In the disastrous year 1782, the all too frequent occurrence of dropsy—actually the result of famine—was frequently ascribed to the excessive consumption of potatoes which, that year, had been seriously affected by the abnormally late frosts.

'In the spring of 1743 Old Clanronald was in Ireland upon a visit to his relatives the MacDonalds of Antrim; he saw with surprise and approbation, the economic practices of the country and having a vessel of his own brought home a large cargo of potatoes.'[2] The tubers were distributed to his tenants in south Uist and probably those in Benbecula also. The tale goes that it was only after he had thrown some of them into prison that they consented even to plant them.[3] In Benbecula, he is said to have insisted that his people should plant the potato tubers he had acquired for them; they did, but when harvest time came round, they deposited the crop in sacks at his front door, saying that they had neither the desire nor intention of eating them themselves.[4]

Similar difficulties were experienced in Lewis when in 1757 an attempt was made to induce the people to grow potatoes.[5] Col. Stewart's father first planted potatoes on his estate at Garth, Perthshire, in 1770: 'It required', he says, 'much time and persuasion to induce his servants to eat them. It was thought they could not support a man at work.'[6]

The runrig system itself might be thought to have put a ban on a late root crop, because, pursuant to the common right of pasturage after harvest, the cattle would trample and destroy the crop. In the Lowland south, this did prove a hindrance, but in the Highlands, where the corn harvest was so late, the potato crop could be brought in before the corn crop was harvested. Later, when potatoes came to be an accepted crop,

---

[1] Wilson, John (1849). *Rural Cyclopaedia*, p. 899. Pink, James (1879). *Potatoes and How to Grow Them.*

[2] Walker, John (1808). *Economic History of the Hebrides*, vol. I, p. 251.

[3] *Report of Departmental Committee on Deer Forests.* Scotland, 1919.

[4] These two tales are in some accounts mixed: in others, transposed. Clanronald was the overlord in both Isles.

[5] Sinclair, Sir John (1797). *The Statistical Account of Scotland*, 1797, vol. XIX, p. 249.

[6] Stewart, David (1822). *Sketches of the Character, etc., of the Highlanders of Scotland*, p. 136.

they were raised on the runrig plots as well as in the crofters' small-holdings and the cottars' plots.

Up till 1825 a 400-acre farm in eastern Ross was occupied in runrig, and the old system of cropping rigorously observed, with the exception that one of the two small portions of the infield which were manured in the spring was planted with potatoes each year.[1]

The defeat of the Pretender at Culloden in 1746, marked not only the climax of a dynastic and political schism in Great Britain, but the beginning of an entirely new chapter in the life of the people of the Highlands. The Government's policy was simple, its methods effective; its aim to destroy once and for all the power for mischief, actual and potential, of the clan chieftains. To effect this, it proceeded to disarm the clans, both physically and spiritually. By the Act of 1747, the judicial rights of the chieftain were abolished, the carrying of arms, wearing of the tartan, and playing of the pipes, prohibited, and the speaking of Gaelic discouraged as far as possible. About forty great estates were escheated and their rent-roll used for agricultural improve-ments, but far more important was the conversion of the chiefs into proprietors, or heritors as they were termed, of the clan-lands, which had as its corollary the final disavowal of any claim entertained by the ordinary clansman to any right of tenure or usure of the land by virtue of his agelong relation to the local chieftain. Thus at one stroke the whole traditional nexus between chief and clansman was destroyed, its ghost alone surviving in that peculiar cloud of romance which has illuminated our literature to the same measure wherewith it has obscured our judgement.

Like Othello, the chieftain found his occupation gone; his strength, his influence and his power, which he had been wont to measure by the number of men he could summon to his banner, were dissipated. From now on, his status, like that of other great proprietors, ultimately depended on his command of convertible wealth.

Almost at once, there began a scramble to make this conversion a reality. In the Highlands, as industrial development was not a practical issue, two methods only were open to the large heritor, one, to improve the methods of agriculture and raise larger and more valuable crops, a project which required abundant capital; the other, to cut down outlay to a minimum by the conversion of his estate into a sheep-walk. It was this latter policy which was adopted by the great majority of heritors.

Before the invasion of the sheep in the Highlands had attained serious dimensions, the chief tacksmen had already enjoyed a brief flush of prosperity, which reached its maximum between 1766 and 1769. Following on the greatly increased demand for black cattle at an

[1] Report on Select Farms. *British Husbandry* (1840), vol. III.

enhanced price, the larger tacksmen squeezed their under-tenants to the utmost, who, in their turn, demanded more and more grazing ground; between them the small men and the cottar went under. At this point the landlords seized the opportunity to improve their position.[1]

The temptation to use the great tracts of hill country for enormous flocks of sheep was irresistible, at least very few tried to resist it, seeing that the cost of their keep on the hillside involved but one or two shepherds and a few dogs. The movement began in 1762 when Annandale sheep-farmers moved into Argyll and it rapidly gained momentum. The wintering of the flocks, however, presented a serious problem; although the successful experience of John Campbell, an inn-keeper of Tyndrum, who had allowed his small flock to overwinter on the hills in Breadalbane, appears to have been seized on as a temporary solution, its application to the great numbers of the more delicate Cheviot breed which were being put on the hills throughout the Highlands, was not found to be economically practical.[2] There remained but one alternative, the utilization of the glens, with their better grass-lands and greater protection against the weather. It was unfortunate that they were already devoted to arable cultivation, and that in them, farmers, crofters and cottars had not only lived and laboured from time immemorial, but had fondly imagined that they had a right so to do. Those rights, real or imaginary, faded away in a night. The first move was to withdraw the privilege of summer pasturage in the sheilings; the second, to remove the people bodily from the glens. The former is said not to have materially injured the people though it is difficult to believe it; the latter undoubtedly did so, and was deeply resented.[3]

The mechanism by which the change was effected was simple. Rents were raised, sometimes as much as fourfold. The old tenant-farmers, unable to pay and powerless to protest, quitted, thus making room for a new class of capitalist undertakers who, adding farm to farm, converted large tracts of the countryside into sheep-ranches. The crofters and cottars having no leases, were required to vacate their holdings and where they refused to do so, were evicted and their dwellings destroyed.[4] In this manner the age-long sympathetic relationship which had existed between chief and tenantry, and had done so much to condition the Highlander to a life of hardship and poverty, was broken for ever.

Engrossment became general; but instead of leading to the creation

[1] Ramsay, John (1888). *Scotland and Scotsmen*, vol. II, p. 507.
[2] Ibid. p. 512.
[3] Skeene, William F. (1880). *Celtic Scotland*, vol. III, p. 373.
[4] For a full, if somewhat partisan, account of the evictions in Scotland, reference should be made to Thomas Johnston's *History of the Working Classes in Scotland*, 1923. Glasgow: Forward Publishing Co.

of great arable farms, as the same movement was doing in most of the Lowlands and in England, it reproduced the social and economic revolution of Tudor England against which More and Latimer had so eloquently protested.

We have lately seen 31 families, containing 115 persons, dispossessed of their lands, which were given to a neighbouring stock grazier, to whom these people's possessions lay contiguous. Thus, as a matter of convenience, to a man who had already a farm of nine miles in length, 115 persons, who had never been a farthing in arrear of rent, were deprived of house and shelter, and sent pennyless on the world.[1]

This policy began to take shape shortly after Culloden and proceeded steadily for the next twenty years, then, gaining momentum, it reached its climax with the Sutherland evictions 1811–20 'when 15,000 people were cleared from the one county of Sutherland, with all conceivable brutality'.[2]

Less than a generation back, such a policy would have been unthinkable. The relation between clansman and chief, however feudal, had never lacked a cloak of sentiment to disguise its crude servility. The Act of 1747 abolished the former; the callous greed of the majority of the chieftains rent the latter beyond repair. In this final act, the potato was to play no small part.

The immediate effect of the domination of the Highlands by sheep, was a wholesale displacement of the population. Various avenues of escape were seized upon. Some of the younger and more enterprising, followed the footsteps of the pioneers of the 1720's, and went to America; others trekked to the Lowland industrial towns, or made their way into England; many thousands of the younger men joined the elder Pitt's 'fencibles' and later greatly distinguished themselves in the Napoleonic wars. The great majority, however, removed to the coastal borders, where they were supplied with, or acquired, small plots of land. Those who had been independent farmers on the runrig lands, now became crofters; those who had been crofters were lucky if they could re-establish themselves in their new home as cottars, and most of those who had been cottars left the Highlands for good. Between 1760 and 1783 it is said that 30,000 individuals left Scotland for the Colonies,[3] and between then and 1808, 12,000 more left for America alone.[4]

In general, the new settlements were agriculturally of less value than had been the old holdings in the glens, but the rents demanded were

[1] Stewart, Col. David (1882). *Sketches of the Character, etc., of the Highlanders of Scotland*, p. 200 n. Edinburgh: Constable.

[2] Mackenzie, Agnes Mure (1940). *The Kingdom of Scotland*, p. 315. Edinburgh: W. Chambers.

[3] Ibid. p. 301.

[4] *Scottish Economic Committee on the Highlands* (1938).

far higher. High winds, excessive moisture, and a boulder-strewn soil, characteristic of so much of the coastal land in the western Highlands, was a serious deterrent to the raising of cereal crops, which in any case was handicapped by the loss of power and capital, previously represented by the stock of cattle and horses, which had ranged the hillsides in the old homes. If anything, more serious was the great reduction in milch cows, which previously had enabled all to enjoy an abundance of milk. The following contemporary account makes it clear that a social revolution of the first magnitude had taken place. That it excited relatively little public attention then or later, was due to the absence of bloodshed and a certain gradualness in its development. But what, in fact, occurred was little short of a miracle: a quarter of a million people made the economic journey from the thirteenth to the eighteenth century, not in 600 years, but in less than sixty. A miracle not wrought by magic carpet or time machine, but by the use of a new foodstuff which, once scorned and rejected, was to become the cornerstone of their social structure. Neither State, nor Church, nor public opinion, intervened to help or protect the Highlanders, though they were not ignorant of the distress of the people. The Law Lord Kames, so admired by Boswell, writing from Blair Drummond in 1776, urges the planting of the potato 'as potatoes are a comfortable food for the low people, it is of importance to have them all the year round...of late years they have been found to answer even till April;[1] which has proved a great support to many a poor family as they are easily cooked and require neither kiln nor milk'.[2] Twenty-five years back, would any one have suggested that the Highlander was short of milk?

The philanthropist, Thomas Garnett,[3] thought that the rich ought to encourage the poor to grow potatoes as a prevention against the famine they so often experienced, and closed his remarks with 'How little does mankind really want.' Not inappropriately, he dedicated his work to Count Rumford, the deviser of Famine Soups.

It was the potato alone which prevented this unique pilgrimage from developing into a catastrophe.

When the valleys and higher grounds were let to the shepherds, the whole population was drawn down to the seashore, where they were crowded on small lots of land, to earn their subsistence by labour (*where all are labourers and few employers*) and by sea-fishing, the latter so little congenial to their former habits. This cutting down farms into lots was found so profitable, that over the whole of this district, the sea-coast, where the shore is accessible,

---

[1] It is obvious that the storing of the potato was at fault. Eden complains that the Scotch generally had not learnt how to store their potatoes and that they were generally exhausted by March. Eden, Sir Frederick (1797). *The State of the Poor*, vol. I, p. 502.

[2] Kames, Lord (1776). *The Gentleman Farmer*.

[3] Garnett, Thomas (1800). *Observations on a Tour through the Highlands*, vol. I, p. 72.

is thickly studded with wretched cottages, crowded with starving inhabitants. Ancient respectable tenants, who passed the greater part of life in hospitality and charity, possessing stocks of 10, 20, and 30 breeding cows, with the usual proportion of other stock, are now pining on one or two acres of bad land, with one or two starved cows, and, for this accommodation, a calculation is made, that they must support their families and pay the rent of their lots, not from the produce, but from the sea; thus drawing a rent which the land cannot afford.... There are still a few small tenants on the old system, occupying the same farm jointly, but they are falling fast into decay, and sinking into the new class of cottars.[1]

As in Ireland, so here, the uprooting of the masses from their homes, the break up of their traditional life, and the introduction of a strange new food, involved fundamental problems of social and ethical behaviour which it would be outside the scope of this work to discuss. If at the time they excited very little condemnation by Church or State, it is well to note the verdict on them which the highest court of the nation has passed in our own age. 'When their [the landlords] action is viewed now in the cold light of History, it is clear that the power of wholesale evictions by private persons was one, which ought never to have been permitted, and one which, was rendered doubly odious by contrast with the patriarchal relations, which existed between chief and clansmen down to the rising of 1745.'[2]

Not infrequently it was the parish minister who was the first to grow the new root in his garden or on his glebe. Such was the case at Assynt in Sutherland. After trying it out in 1765, he obtained a half-boll for his parishioners in 1766, and showed them how to use it. At first, 'the Natives were indifferent but later their scruples were overcome and it became increasingly popular, so that in 1794 they frequently take in new land from the moor and plant them with potatoes'.[3]

Pennant[4] ascribes to an Irish Scot, Alexander Christie, the merit of being 'the first person who introduced the right culture of potatoes into this country'. This took place at Tulloch in Inverness-shire about the year 1722. Assuming that the facts are correct, one can only conclude that Christie failed to find any support, for there is no reliable evidence that potatoes were grown anywhere in the Highlands before the middle of the eighteenth century. This is borne out by a manuscript in the possession of the British Museum written in 1750 by a Secret Service man named Bruce, who describes his tour of the Highlands and the food and resources of the people; nowhere does he encounter the potato,

[1] Stewart, D. Op. cit. p. 148.

[2] The Act on Deer Forest, 1919. Quoted from *Scottish Economic Committee on the Highlands*, 1938.

[3] MacKenzie, Rev. Will. (1795). *The Statistical Account of Scotland*, vol. XVI, p. 163.

[4] Pennant, Thomas (1772). *Tour in Scotland, and voyage to the Hebrides*, pt. 2, note p. III of 1776 edit.

though he thinks it might prove to be of great value both to the people and the land.[1]

Information as to the exact date of introduction of the potato into the different Highland parishes is hard to come by, but the following are culled from *The Statistical Account* and may be taken as giving a reasonably accurate estimate of the rapidity of its acclimatization. With but one or two exceptions it had spread by 1775 throughout the Highlands to every crofter's and cottar's plot. Prior to 1774, 'if I have not been greatly misinformed, the very freitage of potatoes coming from Cantyre has amounted in some years to several hundred pounds',[2] a vague statement, but evidence of the rapid expansion of its cultivation in this part of the Highlands. By 1790 it had won its place in the field of nearly half the farms, whether the land lay in open runrig, as much still did, or was held in severalty and enclosed.

The immemorial custom of the commune was somewhat crudely adjusted to meet the new situation: thus, in the central Highlands, Marshall[3] found the usual infield and outfield general, with commons and pasture in the hills. Everybody had their 'patch' in each 'field', from which the straying sheep and cattle were continually harried. 'Potatoes', he says, 'are the principal food of the common people and are considered the greatest blessing that modern times have bestowed on the country: in having it, it is probable, more than once, saved it from the miseries of famine.'

Below are the recorded dates of the introduction of the potato into various parts of Highland Scotland.

Highland parish	County	Date of introduction
Tulloch	Inverness	1722*
South Uist	Inverness	1743
Benbecula	Inverness	1743
Lochalsh	Ross	1750
Fortingal	Perth	1754
Clyne	Sutherland	1756
Lewis	Ross	1756
Edderachylis	Sutherland	1760
Urray	Ross	1764
Kilmalie	Inverness	1764
Boleskine and Abertarff	Inverness	1764
Assynt	Sutherland	1766
Garth	Perth	1770

* This date is doubtful.

By the year 1790 there was but one parish in the mainland of Scotland in which it is recorded that the potato was not grown, viz. Ardersier in Inverness, whose people are described in 1792 as being very hostile

[1] Lang, Andrew (1898). *The Highlands of Scotland*, p. 144.
[2] Campbell, John (1774). *A Political Survey of England*, vol. I, p. 429.
[3] Marshall, W. (1794). *General View of the Agriculture of the Central Highlands*.

to all improvements. It is noteworthy that in the disastrous season of 1782 when the corn crop failed, this parish which had no potatoes, was reduced to starvation. Elsewhere, all classes grew it, farmers, crofters and cottars; the latter devoting their small plots of land to it often in preference to oats. For at least five and more often nine months of the year, the potato assumed the leading place in the people's dietary. Where they were not grown in sufficient quantities, such as at Tobermory and Kilfinichen in Mull, they were imported from outside. In some districts, as Strachur and Stratbehar, the area under potato culture rivalled that devoted to oats, in the more remote parts it was the more important foodstuff.[1] In Glenorchy we are told that before its introduction 'people pined away of hunger' and now (1790) *mirabile dictu*, 'even the rich occasionally eat it'.[2] Sometimes, the adoption of the potato came about, because of a local economic collapse; it was so at Nigg in Ross-shire, where the people's main industry was fishing, agriculture being carried on by the runrig system, with wages paid in kind. There had been no agricultural improvements of any kind, when suddenly the herring forsook the local waters. The result was an immediate and urgent demand for potatoes which, after fetching very high prices, developed into one of the chief crops of the district.[3]

At Tarbet in Ross-shire, the potato had gained its ascendance owing to successive failures of the oat and pease crops, and soon became the established food of the people for nine months of the year. In varying degrees the same was true for most places in the Highlands both on the Mainland and in the Isles, which would appear to show that the wholesale adoption of the potato was an economic necessity, a victory of force rather than persuasion. In the words of an Agricultural *Report*, on the County of Perth, 'the potato has done more to prevent emigration than any device whatever'.[4] It may be that the parish of Kilmorack in Inverness-shire was an exception to the rule: here the tenants of Strathglass were sufficiently well off to import annually oatmeal to the value of £500, but from 1780 onwards they had reduced these imports to nil, replacing them by home-grown potatoes. In general, the proprietors seem to have encouraged the cultivation of the potato by the working classes, but from Banff it was reported that 'the great Landholders were alarmed lest it should be the means of depreciating the value of grain and this be it noted in 1795, when wheat had risen from forty to fifty shillings in the decade 1760–70, to seventy-eight shillings'.[5]

[1] Sinclair, Sir John (1814). *General Report of the Agricultural State and Political Circumstances of Scotland*, vol. III, p. 253.

[2] MacIntyre, Rev. Joseph (1793). *The Statistical Account of Scotland*, vol. VIII, p. 335.

[3] Macadam, Alex. (1794). *The Statistical Account of Scotland*, vol. XIII, p. 13.

[4] Robertson, James (1794). *General View of the County of Perth*, p. 39.

[5] Gordon, Abercromby. *The Statistical Account of Scotland*, vol. XX, p. 326.

From a distance the dominance of the potato appeared as an unmixed blessing, even to so astute an observer as Eden:[1] 'In the Central Highlands of Scotland potatoes are become the principal food of the people and are considered as the greatest blessing that modern times have bestowed on the country—before the introduction of this inestimable root, famines were frequent in the Highlands.' They were to prove, if less frequent, far more serious after its introduction.

It is important to stress the fact that the potato did not make its conquests of the Highlands by reason of its intrinsic merits, however great they may be, but rather that it came about as the inevitable solution to the economic crisis resulting from the politico-social upheaval consequent on the defeat at Culloden. The disruption of a social system, inspired by the communism of the early Middle Ages, when suddenly brought in contact with an alien capitalistic civilization, might have found a different solution had it not been that the bridge by which the chieftain spanned the gulf between the pre- and post-1745 days, viz. the sheep-run, proved effective and permanent, whilst that of the clansman, emigration to America, broke down first during the war with America (1776–83) and again after a fleeting revival of their hopes, by the Napoleonic wars (1793–1815).

Although evicted from their homes, their cattle gone, and faced with actual want, it is to the Highlanders' credit that they so rarely resorted to violence. That they did not do so, is probably to be explained by the fact that they had 'discovered' the potato, and with its help could just hold their own in the land of their birth.

As a matter of fact, in the western Highlands and the Isles, the population, notwithstanding the sheep-run policy, maintained its numbers. This, without doubt, was due to the adoption of the potato. The Earl of Selkirk, than whom there was no more understanding critic of the economic condition of the Highlands, referring to the potato, wrote: 'If the effects of the grazing system had not been modified by such a cause of increase, the depopulation of the Highlands must have proceeded with much more rapidity.'[2]

The movement to the coast was originally directed by two motives, one to exploit the fishing, the other to manufacture kelp.

Kelp, an alkaline ash, rich in potash, derived from the burning of seaweed, was used extensively in the manufacture of glass long before it was recognized as a source of iodine. Its manufacture was strictly seasonal: in Harris it was confined to the period between 10 June and 10 August; elsewhere the season might be rather longer but was always

---

[1] Eden, Sir Frederick (1797). *The State of the Poor*, vol. I, p. 305.
[2] Selkirk, Earl of (1805). *On Emigration and the State of the Highlands* (2nd edit. 1806), p. lviii.

brought to a close early in September. As much as 1,200 tons p.a. was exported in the 1790's from North Uist alone; as it required rather more than about 20 tons of wrack to make 1 ton of ash, it called for abundant labour over a short period. The kelp trade was brought from Ireland into the Highlands in 1730. Up till 1750 the product was sold at from £2 to £5 per ton, but during the last decade of the eighteenth century, the price averaged about £6 per ton, and for a time fetched as much as £20 per ton. Though the major part of the proceeds of the kelp manufacture went to tacksman and landlord, Clanranald alone deriving as much as £30,000 p.a. from it,[1] by its means the crofter at least enjoyed the privilege of a cash income. At the height of the kelp boom in 1812 a family might earn as much as £7 in the year; the average, however, was nearer £3. It is probable that this helped to damp down what little ardour the crofter had ever had for cereal tillage; in any case, from now on, he devoted most of his land and energy to the growing of potatoes. Indeed, it was said to be the only crop which he weeded or tended.[2]

Over a period of about sixty years a kind of working partnership grew up between the 'cash crop' kelp and the purely subsistence crop, the potato. When, however, Napoleon's embargo on imports to Britain collapsed, a cheaper source of alkali was found in barilla from Spain.[3] With its return, for it had been employed by the glass-workers as early as 1702, the Highlander's source of ready money rapidly decreased; with the removal of the Import Tax in 1823 it disappeared, the potato alone remained. Strengthened now in its hold on the impoverished crofter, it had free play to establish and maintain during the next fifty years in the Highlands, the lowest standard of living which the nature of the environment permitted.

Although at this time the potato was suffering in many parts of Great Britain from a virus infection known as the 'Curl', which brings about a heavy reduction in its crop, yet confidence in it, though severely shaken in the north of England, here remained firm. This was because in the coastal area the crops were very rarely infected, a fact which promises to have important repercussions to-day. (See chapter x, p. 179.)

Even when the unhappy coincidence of shortage of crop and depression of the kelp trade after 1812 had hit the crofters so hard that they were obliged to seek charitable support from the chieftains, they still regarded the potato as the sheet-anchor of their existence.[4] Sinclair at the time wrote: 'It is difficult to conceive how the people of this country could

---

[1] *County Histories of Scotland* (1897), vol. IV, *Inverness*, p. 275.

[2] Macculloch, John (1824). *The Highlands and Western Isles of Scotland*, p. 217.

[3] Barilla, *Salicornia herbacea* (the Glass-wort), is a member of the Chenopodiaceae and common to the seashore.

[4] Garnier, Russell M. (1895). *Annals of the British Peasantry*, p. 354. London: Sonnenscheim.

have subsisted, had it not been for the fortunate introduction and extensive cultivation of this most valuable plant.'[1]

Although the majority of the crofters and most of the farmers were, by our standards, extremely badly off, there were degrees of poverty between one district and another, and to some extent we can gauge them by noting the extent to which the potato had become a field crop. But here we should remember that a field crop in the Highlands had at this time a different connotation from one in the Lowlands. In the latter, the inclusion of a new crop such as the potato, implied an improved system of husbandry, with drill sowing, drainage, enclosures, and the like. In the Highlands, it generally meant no more than that the potato occupied part of a rig in the open field, which was possible so long as the old rules controlling the cropping of runrig farms were not strictly enforced. These rules which included penalties for their infraction, were laid down long before potatoes were introduced into Europe, and would have excluded them from the common field. Fortunately they had of late been disregarded, so that the potato had no difficulty in securing its place in the various strips. Thus on a 400-acre farm in East Ross which was in runrig prior to 1825, the practice had been to grow oats for five to six successive years without dung, then manure and sow part with barley and the remainder with potatoes.[2]

The data from *The Statistical Account* for the years 1790–97 allows the following comparison to be made:

	Highland districts			Lowland districts	
County	Field crop	Home plots	County	Field crop	Home plots
Aberdeen	19	54	Berwick	15	17
Argyle	19	35	Dumfries	27	30
Inverness	12	20	Fife	36	45
Ross and Cromarty	12	26	Lothian	21	29
	62	135		99	121

Of the 135 Highland parishes, in 46% the potato was grown in the home plot as well as in the field, even when the latter was in runrig, as the majority were, whilst of 121 Lowland parishes it was being grown both in the home plot and in 82% of cases in the field, very often as a rotation crop.

In a few cases only, was the Highland field crop treated as a cash crop, whereas in the Lowlands, especially in the neighbourhood of the towns, a far higher proportion had acquired this character.

There is another factor which operated throughout all Scotland in establishing the potato as the diet of the poorer classes, independently

[1] Sinclair, Sir John (1812). *An Account of the System of Husbandry in Scotland*, p. 269.
[2] Report on Select Farms. *British Husbandry* (1840), vol. III, p. 88.

of purely agricultural or industrial reasons, and that was the absence of any Poor Law in Scotland before 1845. In some country parishes and all the more important towns, there were small if totally inadequate charitable endowments, but elsewhere the relief funds were derived from the hirings of the Church mort-cloth, i.e. funeral pall, where such did not go by custom to the magistrates; to these must be added small gifts from the heritors. No pains were spared to make the needy poor feel that, only in the last extremity, would help from the parish be forth-coming, and even then, they were often obliged to sign away their personal belongings to be sold at their death for the benefit of the public, before receiving it. In other parishes they might have to consent to wear a badge proclaiming they were paupers. There can scarcely be any literature so depressing and cynical as that to be found in the accounts contributed by the parish clergy on this head throughout *The Statistical Account*. Every possible effort was made to ensure that the poor should live on what they could raise themselves or be bought at the cheapest rate, and what was cheaper or easier to raise than the potato? An excuse for what some of the authors admit was harsh treatment was, curiously enough, the fact that the Lowland parishes were so often invaded by roving bands of Highlanders, admittedly driven from their homes by the sheep run and engrossment policy of the great landlords. It was considera-tions of this nature which made so many leading public men advocate the extended use of the potato, rather than attack the problem at its source.

The use of the potato as food for animals was very little developed in the Highlands prior to the nineteenth century, which is not surprising seeing how they had enjoyed the immemorial right of grazing their cattle on the hills, added to which was the prejudice generally enter-tained, against the keeping of pigs. The old grazing rights were in large measure lost by the policy of engrossment, and prejudices tended to disappear as contact with the Lowlanders became freer and more friendly. Whenever in *The Statistical Account* the practice is mentioned, it is always associated with the growing of the 'yam', which is often referred to as if it were a distinct plant. The 'yam' was a potato variety the more correct name of which was the 'Surinam': it was a heavy cropper but coarse in shape, soapy in texture, and of indifferent taste. Its use in England and the more agriculturally advanced parts of the Lowlands was confined to cattle feeding.

The final disappearance of the Highland prejudice against pig-rearing may be attributed in no small degree to the cultivation of the 'yam', for experience showed that swine throve on it remarkably well. At Killin in Perth the swine population definitely rose with the increasing cultivation of the potato.[1]

[1] Rev. Pat. Stuart. *The Statistical Account of Scotland*, 1796, vol. XVII, p. 383.

The progress of the potato in the Hebrides followed much the same line as that in the Highlands on the mainland. Its cultivation, however, began rather later, but once the initial prejudice was overcome, its popularity was no less.

Pennant, who visited the islands in 1771, describes the people's food in some detail, from which it appears that the potato had already assumed a dominating position. In Skye it is 'the saviour of the people'; in Jura, Rum, Colonsay and Islay, it is the mainstay of the people, their barley being no longer consumed by the people, now went to the distilleries; 'their competence of bread is very small'. In Gigha the potato crops are particularly good.[1] A couple of years later, another visitor[2] states that the potato flourishes in Lewes, Mull and Skye, but does not record its presence elsewhere in the Hebrides.

In the Islands, the people were more dependent on homegrown food-stuffs than were those on the mainland, but their capacity to produce them was controlled by the current system of land tenure and the method of farming, both of which were still medieval at the end of the eighteenth century, having suffered but little change even fifty years after Culloden. It was because of the inertia born of the economic stasis, which had ruled so long in the Islands, that the potato was able to entrench itself firmly in their midst, so that within a generation it had gained control of the domestic economy of the great majority of the Highlanders and Hebrideans in a manner which differed only in degree from that which it had obtained over the working classes of Ireland.

In contrast to its economic importance the potato's influence on Highland agricultural methods was almost nil. One can get some measure of this by comparing it with that exerted by the turnip. The introduction early in the eighteenth century of the turnip in East Anglia, soon brought about a drastic change in husbandry, which found its chief expression in the four-course rotation of crops and the feeding of the livestock over winter. The revolution spread throughout most of England and penetrated at an early date into the Lowlands of Scotland. If we examine *The Statistical Account of Scotland*, published between 1791 and 1798, it will be seen that in the Lowlands turnips are almost everywhere grown as a field crop raised by the drill method, and that their cultivation is invariably correlated with the spread of enclosures, land drainage, the use of up-to-date farm implements, the redistribution of land, the recovery of wastes, and the granting of long leases. Where the turnip was grown as a field crop, it was not long before the potato joined it.

---

[1] Pennant, T. (1772). *A Tour in Scotland and Voyage to the Hebrides.*

[2] Campbell, John (1774). 'Of the Production of Great Britain arising out of the Soil.' *Political Survey*, vol. II, chapter III.

In the Highlands, even at the end of the eighteenth century, the turnip had scarcely penetrated to the gardens where the potato had long since firmly established itself. Even where the potato had achieved the status of a field crop, rarely did it open the door to the turnip. Not only this, it failed to achieve what the turnip invariably accomplished in its forward stride, an improvement in the current methods of husbandry. In this respect, the major part of the Highlands' arable land and practically all that of the Western Isles, remained unimproved for another fifty years, where it had not sunk back into pasture.

The explanation of this divergent reaction on agricultural practice would seem to follow from the fact that the potato was imposed on the people by their rulers, and only out of sheer necessity was it subsequently accepted as a food.

The new food fell, perhaps inevitably, a victim to the devices of so intensely a class-ridden society as that of eighteenth-century Scotland. A contemporary writes: 'The potato is the true root of scarcity which promises to set Famine at defiance. The poorer sort of people dine and sup chiefly on potatoes, in the season of them. But those that are in a state of servitude [i.e. those who are fed in their employer's house] are commonly above eating potatoes.'[1]

Under such conditions, its cultivation tended to supplant, rather than improve, the raising of other food crops. With the turnip it was otherwise: it was grown to feed cattle, not men, and therefore it required from the first, large areas and adequate mechanization, which necessitated drastic changes in the existing agricultural method. As one of the ablest observers of the time said: 'Necessity, or self-preservation, the most powerful of all motives, dictated the cultivation of the latter [the potato], whereas convenience in a great measure suggested the utility of the former [the turnip].'[2]

And what when the final dividend came to be paid? In the case of the turnip, it took the form of hard cash; in that of the potato, more children to be fed.

Thus the turnip may be regarded as the symbol of economic progress in husbandry, inducing the betterment, social and material, of the farmer and those of the middle class who handle the products of his improved industry, but having little, if any, effect on the well-being of the labourer. The potato in the Highlands, as in so many other lands, was both harbinger and agent of a social and economic retrogression which affected exclusively the working classes whether on the land or in the factory. The seed of expediency was sown in the middle of the eighteenth century; the harvest of retribution was to be reaped just a century later.

---

[1] Playfair, James. *The Statistical Account of Scotland*, 1797, vol. XIX, p. 334.
[2] Robertson, James (1808). *General View. Inverness*, p. 156.

In the Highland districts of Scotland it is neither difficult to follow the sequence of events, nor to recognize the main forces at work. Nor is the validity of either confined to this particular area. A similar social pattern, it will be found, tends to appear wherever the potato assumes a dominating role in the dietary of a people.

The turn of the century saw the Highland stage set for inevitable disaster. First political and then purely economic forces had uprooted a people who for centuries had enjoyed a balanced and logical, if primitive, form of society, and presented them with another which could lay no claim to either attribute.

In the process, they had lost home, property, and traditional rights; in compensation they had been offered the option of resettlement as crofters on the barren marginal coastlands of their old homelands, with the strange new vegetable as their sheet-anchor. They had but the two alternatives: either to accept these terms, or to leave their native country for ever. A considerable number, generally estimated at 30,000 persons, accepted the latter course, the great majority the former.

Much of the emigration was undirected; an exception was that which took place under the aegis of Thomas, fifth Earl of Selkirk,[1] who convinced himself that modern arable agriculture was impossible in the Highlands and at his own expense organized emigration to previously selected places in Canada. The settlement in Prince Edward Island in 1802 was an immediate success; that in the Red River Valley of Manitoba in 1811 after many years of tribulation eventually made good and its memory is perpetuated to-day by the town of Selkirk. The Highland settlers of Prince Edward Island developed the potato as their chief crop. To-day the Island is famous for the high quality of its seed.

In their new Highland settlements, the people built themselves hutments on their small crofts, maintained a few beasts and horses on the hillsides, developed the kelp trade, and, where possible, engaged in deep-sea fishing, whilst they maintained themselves on the potato with the addition of a little oatmeal, and as much fish as fortune's favours allowed. On the surface, not an unpleasing picture of what should have been a simple and happy existence. Indeed, so it might have been, had peasant, kelp, and potato not been the mere tools of an entirely alien social mechanism represented by capitalist heritors whose chief concern was to exploit the opportunities which uncontrolled power over the land and the fruits of the sea had put into their hands.

The situation which had developed as a result of the Act of 1747 began to take definite shape in the sixties and seventies of the eighteenth century; by the beginning of the nineteenth century, it had the dimen-

[1] Selkirk, Earl of (1805). *Observations on the Present State of the Highlands* (edit. 1806), p. 214.

sions of a social problem, whose implication was beginning to be recognized by all. The course of events was simple: the removal of the clansmen allowed the fertile glens to be let at greatly enhanced rents; their resettlement on the coast cost nothing, for the land and the adjacent hill pastures had been practically valueless. Nevertheless, these new crofts were rented at a high figure and brought in a handsome return. The rent was paid in kind, mainly in the form of kelp and fish. As the price of kelp rose, and it was the landlords who enjoyed the lion's share of the profits, they bound their crofters to devote themselves to their work. In fact, the kelp industry developed into a kind of slavery not very different from that which had obtained in the Scotch coal and salt mines, where real slavery or, more correctly, indentured labour for life, was in force till 1775.

As a result, the peasants neglected their cereal crops and their vegetable plots, but concentrated on the potato which, by the ease of its culture, the health of its stocks, and its generous harvests, won an easy dominance over the entire economy of their lives.

The food problem thus solved, and the old clan regulations as to marriage having gone, there was nothing to hinder young couples setting up new homes, except the erection of a new hut and a piece of ground on which to grow the necessary potatoes. These simple essentials were met by the subdivision of plots, whether on croft or runrig. 'It was the policy of the landlords in the county [Orkney] to subdivide the land and encourage the increase of the population as much as possible for the purpose of obtaining a sufficient number of labourers to manufacture his kelp; and now when they would fain adopt an opposite policy, and enlarge the size of their farms, the excess of the population meets them with an insuperable difficulty.'[1]

Malthus records that the same policy was common in many parts of the Highlands, and particularly in the Western Isles. In Delting in Shetland, it was the avowed policy of the landlords to encourage marriage in order to ensure cheap labour for the Ling fishing.[2]

For more than half a century the economic and social life of the western Highlands and the Isles followed the pattern which has been outlined. It provided all the desiderata for an increase of births. The potato ensured them maintenance, and the now widely accepted practice of vaccination, their survival. Thus was there converted a potential, into a real increase of population.

When the kelp trade failed, almost every minister of a Highland parish

---

[1] Ritchie, The Rev. George (1840). On Cross and Burness. *New Statistical Account of Scotland*, vol. xv, p. 85.

[2] Malthus, T. R. (1806). *An Essay on the Principle of Population*, 3rd. edit. vol. I, p. 488.

who contributed in the 1840's to the *New Statistical Account*, complained
of the over-population of his district, and the minute subdivision of the
peasant holdings, or, if he were a Lowlander, of the sturdy Highland
beggars who invaded his parish. Many Highlanders left to work in the
factories of the south, and not a few emigrated. The great majority
stayed where they were. The landlords attempted to forbid further subdivision, but it was too late; they had set the example, the peasantry had
bettered it. Young people determined to make homes, built their huts
on any waste land and shared the potato plots of their elders. In North
Uist in 1840 there were no less than 390 such families living in this
manner and paying no rent.[1]

The extent to which the potato dominated the husbandry of the Highlands can be gauged from the annual values ascribed to the crops in and
around 1840. Taking the data as one finds them in the *New Statistical
Account*, the following may be regarded as a fair sample. Under 'grain'
are grouped oats, barley and wheat; of these, the last is negligible in
quantity, whilst oats usually outvalue barley by about three to one:

County	Parish	Value of grain raised £	Value of potatoes raised £
Argyll	Glenurchy	2,350	2,000
	Strachur	1,800	854
	Kilmartin	2,200	1,700
	Knapdale	4,800	4,500
	Kilchoman	10,000	6,000
Inverness	Boleskine	2,262	1,324
	Glenelg	1,000	650
	South Uist	7,719	8,276
	Harris	2,500	3,000
Ross-shire	Stornoway	4,870	2,000
Sutherland	Durness	800	400
		£40,301	£30,704

The figures show that the value of the potato crop, some seventy years
after its adoption by the people in the Highland districts, was about 75%
of that of the total grain raised. So far as the Highlands and Western
Isles are concerned it is probable that these figures are an understatement,
seeing that the Famine Relief Committee of 1846 found that on the
average, potatoes constituted between three-quarters and seven-eighths
of the food of the Highland families.[2] In the Lowlands outside those
districts which specialized in the production of potatoes for the great
towns, the corresponding ratio is under 25%.

In 1835 the potato crop in the Highlands failed more or less com-

---

[1] On north Uist. *New Statistical Account of Scotland*, vol. XIV, p. 181.
[2] *Destitution in the Highlands* (1848). Statement issued by the Committee of the
Free Church.

pletely, owing to an exceptionally cold wet season; everywhere the people went short, and in some places, as in Skye, they literally starved, yet confidence was nowhere shaken, and dependence on the root grew ever greater. In Kilcalmonell in Argyll, the minister reports that the cottars pay £2. 5s. a year for their hut and plot, and are content if they can command a daily meal or two of potatoes. He adds, however, that they are mostly engaged in illicit distilling.

Whisky distilling, whether licit or illicit, was to some extent correlated with the dominance of the potato over the lives of the peasantry. The distillery trade in the Highlands had grown by 1840 to great proportions and by absorbing the greater part of the locally raised barley, made it less accessible as a foodstuff in the home. In Islay, this had assumed serious proportions prior to 1794. Here the distilleries, being exempt from excise duty, pre-empted the entire barley crop by making advances to the growers. The place of barley was filled by the potato; the same process, though for different reasons, was taking place in regard to oats. Notwithstanding that oatmeal had been the people's mainstay for centuries, the combination of poverty and indolence gave the potato an advantage, which is sufficiently illustrated in the figures quoted above. The more the potato was eaten, the less essential was the oat.

The Census of 1841 registered the highest point to which the population of the Highlands ever attained, but had there been a valuation of the real income of the people, it would have undoubtedly registered the lowest since Culloden, notwithstanding that in this brief interval of time, the people had acquired one of the most valuable foodstuffs man has ever discovered.

The years 1845–7 were years of crisis. The Blight smote the potato crop of Scotland, as it had done in all the lands of Western Europe. From the social economic point of view, the blow which fell on the Highlands was very similar to that which overwhelmed Ireland; the main food supply of the people was threatened. Fortunately the disaster involved less than a twentieth of the number affected in Ireland, which made the work of rescue far easier, and prevented the development of a tragedy, on the purely physical side, comparable to that which the Irish sustained.

The potato blight attacked Scotland both in 1845 and 1846. Indeed, the evidence is fairly convincing that the same disease appeared in various parts of Scotland in 1844, and possibly at a few spots in 1843.[1] The 1845 epidemic spread with varying intensity over Scotland. Much of the north, including the Orkneys, Caithness, Sutherland, Ross, and most of Inverness, seem to have escaped any serious damage, though in Argyll

---

[1] Johnston, James (1845 and 1846). *The Potato Disease in Scotland*, pts. I, II and VI.

and the isle of Islay at least one-third of the crop was lost. By 15 December 1845, the more remote Highlands, which presumably included the Outer Hebrides, were in the main said to have escaped damage. The Lowland crops, on the other hand, suffered severely, especially in the Lothians. In 1846 Blight reappeared, but this time with a virulence which swept the entire land, destroying the growing crops everywhere, and leaving but few sound tubers to be collected at harvest-time, and most of those rotted during the winter.

In the Highlands the shock to the people was almost as great as it had been to the Irish. Owing to the poor communication, it was not easy to bring relief to bear, and there is no doubt that in the more remote districts, more especially in the Outer Hebrides where, in contrast to the Argyll estates in Cantyre the old runrig farming in its most primitive condition still obtained,[1] the loss of the potato precipitated real famine. If only a few persons actually died of starvation, as in Brocadale and Barra, hunger and suffering were widespread throughout the whole of the Highland area.

As in the case of Ireland, there were never wanting those who comforted themselves that the calamity which had overtaken the masses elsewhere, was a punishment from Above for 'our' sins. So in the Lowlands a Clackmannan farm bailiff says: 'They may crack as they like about it, but its just a punishment on us for our sins, for we've never been half thankful for our mercies', to which his master adds 'and this is one of the truest and most sensible remarks that I have yet fallen in with about the matter'.[2] Such views notwithstanding, the Lowland urban committees responded vigorously to the call for help, though they had their own troubles to attend to, especially in Glasgow, where 10,000 persons were in receipt of relief and many thousands of Irish immigrants, who were not eligible, suffered severely.

Voluntary committees in Edinburgh and Glasgow were promptly set up; they collected £100,000, sent out oatmeal to the affected districts, and started relief works on drainage, bridge-building, roads and railways. Some of the former chieftains and great landlords, such as Sir James Riddell of Strontian, Fort William, and Matheson of Lewis, played an honourable part in this campaign of relief and reclamation. When the trouble was at its height in Skye, the people of Dunvegan begged that the so-called 'fairy banner' of the MacLeods might be unfurled.[3] It was decided, however, that this was not an occasion to put to the test for the third and last time those magical powers that were claimed for

---

[1] Fyfe, J. G. (1942). *Scottish Diaries and Memoirs, 1746–1843*, p. 570.
[2] Johnston, James (1845). *The Potato Disease in Scotland*, pt. 1. Edinburgh: W. Blackwood.
[3] Campbell, John (1902). *Superstitions of the Scotch Highlands*. Glasgow.

it by both lord and peasant.[1] Whatever may have been the view of the MacLeod of MacLeod as to the efficacy of the banner, it is greatly to his credit that he made such vigorous efforts to feed his tenantry that he wellnigh ruined himself, and was obliged to let Dunvegan Castle for the next fifteen years and seek his livelihood in London.[2]

It is true to say that the crisis evoked an unprecedented response. Henry Cockburn writes in his diary for 14 January 1847: 'the Free Church collects over £11,000 at Church doors to relieve poor Highlanders. Such a sum has never before been raised in Scotland for charity.'[3]

Alison,[4] an ardent disciple of Malthus, devoted much study to the famine conditions in the Highlands. He quotes the Relief Committee as saying that the population had risen to 448,500 souls, and that in 1847, three-quarters of the food supplies had been lost. By March 1847, 86,000 out of 115,000, i.e. 75% of the people of the Hebrides, were absolutely destitute, and that in 106 parishes in which there was no assessment for the poor, immediate food relief was needed.

His study of the whole situation he felt afforded ample proof of his two main theses. The first, which supports the views of Malthus, he states as follows: 'When we find a population, therefore, living chiefly on potatoes and reduced to absolute destitution, unable to purchase other food when the potato crop fails, we have at once disclosed to us the undesirable fact that the population is redundant.' The second contradicts Malthus's postulate, that legally enforced poor relief necessarily destroyed that moral restraint on reproduction which he, Malthus, regarded as the only real check to over-population. Alison was persuaded that the repercussions of the potato failure in England and Scotland afforded ample evidence to prove that it is rather 'when the legal provision against destitution is absent, not when it is present, that a redundancy of population is really to be apprehended'. Although the first proposition as it stands is not much more than a truism, Alison reverts later in his brochure to it, with an argument which brings us considerably nearer a correct appreciation of the problem.

The Commission on the Occupation of Lands in Ireland 1847 had just reported 'that the potato may perhaps be regarded as the main cause of that inertia of the Irish character which prevents the development of the resources of the country'. To this Alison remarks:

I would observe that in this case as in the Highlands, the fundamental evil appears to be, the existence of a population, such as nothing but the potato

---

[1] MacLeod, of MacLeod, Flora (23 March 1944). Letter to R.N.S.
[2] The 'fairy banner' is thought to be a flag of the Knights Templar, and to have been brought to Scotland after one of the Crusades.
[3] Fyfe, J. G. (1942). Op. cit. p. 408.
[4] Alison, William Pulteney (1847). *Observations of the Famine of 1846–47*. Edinburgh: Blackwood.

can support, who 'cannot find employment', as these Commissioners themselves state, 'during several months of the year', and therefore cannot afford
to purchase any other food and whose only recourse when they cannot find
employment, is beggary; and that it is the absence of skill and capital to give
them work rather than the presence of the potato to keep them alive, which
ought chiefly to fix the attention of those who wish to see the resources of the
country developed.

Alison's diagnosis of the Irish solution, correct no doubt as far as it
goes, is inadequate to explain the cause of the economic breakdown in
the Highlands, where the social and political background was different.
It would be nearer the truth to say that in the Highlands, all unconsciously,
the potato had been used to serve as a mediator between the interest of
a peasantry, accustomed to an ancient semi-communistic system demanding little more than a subsistence economy, and a heritor class who
had suddenly become capitalists and found themselves in a position to
assume the personal advantages, without either bearing the burdens, or
fulfilling the duties of feudal landlords. When the bridge collapsed, it
was only to be expected that the casualties amongst the peasantry far
outweighed those of the landlords. Moreover, the landlords had a
remedy to hand, of which they made full use. The crofters had never
been given leases, hence any default in rent could be followed with
eviction, by force if necessary, and such indeed was the policy widely
pursued. To make doubly sure that the people should not remain to be
a burden on the landlord, the old hutments and cottages were destroyed
on a scale as extensive, says Poulett Scrope, as ever occurred in Ireland.
Indeed, he himself witnessed the eviction of 700 families involving
3,000 persons, from the Macdonald estates of North Uist.[1]

If many landlords experienced, at least for a time, a loss of income,
the more galling because of the fact that they now had to meet the cost
of the maintenance of the poor, it was the peasants who lost all, and for
them the only escape was emigration.

The emigration following on the potato famine did, in fact, assume
great proportions, for it was actuated by the desire of the peasants to
reach new lands where they would no longer be subject to the arbitrary
treatment of their landlords, and by the propulsive force of the latter
anxious to clear their lands, of what for some twenty years they had come
to regard as hungry, useless mouths.

The sombre character of the Highland scene in those days of economic
collapse was not without occasional relief. Such, for example, was to
be found on the great estates of Gairloch in Ross-shire. Here improvements had been introduced, inspired by an intelligent and sympathetic

[1] Scrope, George Poulett (1849). *Some Notes on a Tour in England, Scotland, etc.*,
p. 10. London: John Ridgway.

regard for the traditional and sentimental claims of the indigenous peasantry. The first step had been to replace the runrig farms by adequate crofts of an average size of five acres.

The result of the system which was begun on the Gairloch estate early in 1846 and the benefits of which have been extended to nearly 500 crofter tenants, is, that a population of between 4,000 and 5,000 souls, which the failure of the potato would, under other circumstances, have reduced to absolute destitution, have been enabled, with comparatively little extraneous aid, not merely to maintain themselves during these last four disastrous years, but greatly to improve their original position, and many of them are now in a fair way of obtaining one of positive comfort and prosperity. The improved crofts which I went over exhibited flourishing crops of turnips, carrots, mangel, beet, cabbage and clover, as well as of potatoes and oats and this in a district which never till the last few years grew anything beyond the last.

These lines were written by an eminent scientist and politician who set out to find the solution to the problem 'whether our labouring population be really redundant',[1] which has never been fully solved, without it be, as it is sometimes claimed, in Soviet Russia.

The rest of the tale can be told briefly: till the end of the century, poverty became chronic throughout the greater part of the countryside; those who had salt to their potatoes in some of the Hebrides were considered lucky. From time to time the monotony was broken by further failures of the potato, as in 1851 and 1856, when hunger intervened. The tale of evictions mounted ever higher. After the middle of the century, a new force came into play: the wild deer of the mountains were recognized as a realizable asset, resulting in vast tracts of the countryside being let for the purpose of sport to wealthy Englishmen. The movement began in the 1860's and gradually acquired sufficient momentum to drive out the sheep and their shepherds, as well as the few remaining inland crofters, from great areas of the Highlands and Hebrides. Deer-stalking, however, required the services of a number of gillies and other gentlemen's gentlemen who, being well paid, were no longer dependent on the potato. The tourist trade which developed on the mainland at the same time, also created a certain amount of seasonal employment but did nothing towards making the native Highlander a better cultivator. To this day, when there is no real problem of destitution, the supply of vegetables remains as meagre as its choice is limited, whilst the potato, though no longer the mainstay of the people, is still of great importance, and because of the ease of its preparation and its value as a foodstuff, it seems to have largely prevented the Highlander from attempting further culinary exploits.

[1] Scrope, G. Poulett (1849). Letter to the *Morning Chronicle*. Published as pamphlet, *Some Notes on a Tour in England, Scotland and Ireland*. London: John Ridgway.

Many of the crofters who had settled on the coast, and whose livelihood was dependent on the fishing, and their maintenance on the potato, emigrated towards the latter part of the century to New Zealand and other parts of the Empire. Still later, emigration was assisted by the state under the 1897 Congested Districts Act. More recent legislation (1919) has brought about local improvements, security of tenure, and larger and better crofts at fairer rents; all measures which have happily tended to dethrone the potato from its former dominance. The Highland population, notwithstanding, has steadily declined, though its economic status has somewhat improved.

Earlier in this chapter, reference was made to the consequences of clan warfare prior to 1747 (p. 350). It was observed that a state of chronic mobilization necessitated the sacrifice of many of life's amenities. In the Highlands, when preparedness for war ceased to have any meaning, economic upheaval robbed the people of the chance of acquiring those amenities which were becoming available to their neighbours in the Lowlands.

The home conditions of the Highlander prior to the 1747 Act might be characterized by their primitiveness and simplicity; a hundred years later by their hopelessness and stagnation. Enforced dependence on the most bountiful and cheapest of foods must be held responsible for having permitted the depression of a free people to this, the lowest economic level.

The Orkneys and Shetlands

Of the two groups, the Orkneys are the more favoured; rather less than half their total area is arable and consists of a deep friable and very fertile soil, which has always been put to good use. Although the methods which were in use in the eighteenth and early nineteenth centuries were as primitive as those employed in the Hebrides, the greater diversity of their crops, and their heavier yields, allowed of a richer social life than was common in the Highlands. The holdings were, and still are, very small; they were arranged in runrig, the system prevalent through-out both Island-groups. To-day the Orkney farmers are small-holders and crofters, who live in good stone-built houses. In the Shetlands the land is poor, and only one-fourteenth of it under cultivation; the remainder is grazed. The occupiers are crofters holding a few acres each, who combine a primitive agriculture with fishing.

In both groups the medieval pattern of life persisted into the nineteenth century: it was feudal in type, but remnants of the ancient 'Udal' tenure prevailed, by which the ownership of small lots was absolute, and independent of any documentary basis. Such land, unlike the remainder, was not subject to the various 'services and favours' of which

Sinclair[1] writes 'Everything now belongs to one man Lord Dundas and his exactions in kind are scandalous.' The outstanding distinction between life in the Orkneys and Shetlands, and that in the Hebrides and Highlands, was the absence in the former of clan rule, with its inevitable strife and disorder. To the same cause may be ascribed the greater spirit of enterprise exhibited in the Orkneys, especially, where although the instruments of cultivation were primitive, yet a much greater variety of crops was cultivated than in the Highlands of the Mainland or in the Hebrides. For the same reasons, these distant Islands were spared the repercussions consequent on the upheaval of 1745, and equally, the economic blizzard to which they gave rise.

The fishing industry, herring, cod and ling, had for centuries been the mainstay of the islanders. Until the salt tax destroyed the trade in 1712, it had been almost entirely in the hands of the Dutch; a revival took place towards the end of the century, when the fish was sold through the heritors, who took part in payment of rent. In the meantime, the kelp trade, which had been introduced by James Fea in 1722, developed apace throughout the islands, to the great benefit of the islanders, employing 3,000 hands who earned on an average £2 each in cash during June and July of each year.

Cattle and sheep, horses and much swine, were raised throughout both groups. The crops grown in the Orkneys prior to the introduction of the potato, apart from oats and barley, differed widely from those raised in the Hebrides. Large quantities of the various broccoli, as well as carrots, artichokes, onions, garlic and turnips were raised, all of which were practically unknown in the Highlands. When in the latter half of the eighteenth century the potato was brought to their notice, there were neither prejudices to be allayed nor active resistance to be overcome, it was just one more crop to try out, and, if approved, adopt.

At Flota, in Orkney, where in 1790 the potato was not grown, a group of seventy-one Highlanders from Sutherland settled about 1794. They had arrived with practically no possessions at all, having left because of the conversion of their home land into a sheep-run. It is highly probable that they grew potatoes on their plots in the new home, for there was little else for their maintenance.

The impression gained is that in these islands the potato, though extensively grown, never won that dominating position in the economy of the home that it had secured in the Highlands. It was accepted as a useful article of food, but at no time were the islanders so dependent on it that its failure could spell disaster. The people were poor enough, measured by present-day standards, especially if wealth be measured by money, yet they were neither harassed by economic forces, nor

[1] Sinclair, Sir John (1795). *General View. Northern Counties.*

tyrannized by political ones, prerequisites, as we have seen in the case of Ireland, if a community is to be enslaved by the simplicity of its own dietary.

In the last decade of the eighteenth century, the cultivation of the potato in the various parishes of the Orkneys and Shetlands seems to have been as follows:[1]

The Orkneys

Parish	Date of introduction	Extent of cultivation
Holme	?	Unknown
Firth and Stenness	?	,,
S. Ronaldshay and Burray	?	,,
Stronsay and Eday	c. 1780	,,
Sandwich and Stromness	c. 1750	,,
Shapinshay	?	,,
Rendall	c. 1769	,,
Evie	1784	,,
Cross and Burnes	—	A little
Hoy and Graemsay	c. 1780	,,
Westray	c. 1790	,,
Orphir*	?	A few on all farms
St Andrews and Deerness	?	A little
Birsay and Harray	?	A little
Walls and Flota	—	None

The Shetlands

Delting	?	Abundant
Aithsting or Sansting	?	Unknown
Northmaven	c. 1750	,,
Unst	?	Abundant
Tingwall	?	,,
Walls and Sandness	?	,,

* Of this island the narrator in *The Statistical Account*, vol. XIX, says: 'The advantages of this parish are fire, water, and fine women. Notwithstanding which, most of the heritors reside at a distance.'

Before leaving the subject of the Highlands and Western Isles, the outstanding difference between the trend of the population curves there and in the Lowlands, and their relation, if any, to the vogue of the potato, needs some consideration.

In Fig. 69, p. 383, the two curves are shown. The figures prior to 1801 are estimates, that of 1755 being made by Webster. The Lowland curve shows a steady increase from a million and a quarter in 1755, to 4½ millions in 1931, with a slight check between 1850 and 1870, brought about by the emigration which followed the distress of the 1840's. The curve is very similar in character to that for the population of England and Wales. The curve for the Highlands is altogether different. After a steady increase up till 1801, it rises sharply,

[1] The data have been abstracted from *The Statistical Account of Scotland*. In a few parishes no mention is made of the potato, which must not be assumed to imply that it was not cultivated there.

reaching a maximum in 1841; from then on, it falls steadily away, till the population in 1936 is but one-seventh greater than it was 150 years earlier.

In the Highlands, excluding the sheep- and cattle-walks which gave employment to but few, the only industries of any importance which engaged the people as a whole were that of kelp and fishing. Both of

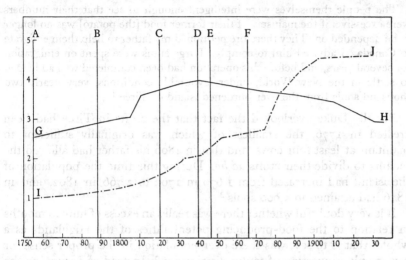

Fig. 69. I–J, represents in millions, the population of Scotland, less that of the High-lands and Western Isles, between 1755 and 1931. G–H, represents in hundreds of thousands, the population of the Highlands and the Western Isles, over the same period. A, indicates the introduction of the potato into the Highlands, and the beginning of the sheep-walk policy and creation of coastal crofts. B, indicates the time when the kelp industry sprang into great activity and the majority of the people had been removed from the fertile glens. C, indicates the time when the kelp industry of the Highlands, having reached its highest point in 1812, was definitely on the down grade. D, indicates the time when the potato in the High-lands reached its greatest development. E, indicates the famine following the onset of Blight. F, indicates the beginning of the policy of converting the sheep-walks of the Highlands into Deer Forests.

these were carried on by crofters who, for reasons already discussed, depended very largely on the potato for their bare existence during nine months of the year. Fishing alone was not, in those days, able to main-tain the population; this is shown by the steady fall which followed the cessation of the trade in kelp, and the failure of the potato in 1846–7. Between 1760 and 1840, the population curve rises rather more steeply than it does in the Lowlands; it will be remembered that a great many families left the Highlands during this period; had they remained, the rise would have been relatively greater. It is in this same period that the potato gradually won its dominant position as the food of the people, and by so doing allowed the kelp industry to be conducted with the cheapest possible labour.

By the middle of the nineteenth century, one repeatedly meets with the complaint that the Highlands were grossly over-populated. This view, which was held by many of the great landlords, is well represented by the 8th Duke of Argyll:

> The people themselves were intelligent enough to see that their numbers were excessive, if the mainstay of their former food [the potato] was no longer to be depended on. They therefore petitioned my father to help them emigrate to Canada. I advised him to comply. Large sums were spent on emigration for several years, and before this operation had been completed we had helped to settle in the New World, under favourable conditions, very nearly two thousand souls from the over burdened island of Tiree.[1]

But the Duke overlooked the fact that the crofts in Tiree had been created in 1776, the smallest of which was originally sufficient to maintain at least four cows, and that in 1806 his father had allowed the tenants to divide their crofts *ad lib*. During this time the population of the island had increased from 1,670 in 1769 to 2,766 in 1802, and in 1846 had attained to 5,000 souls.[2]

It is very doubtful whether there was really an excess of human mouths in relation to the food-producing potentialities of the Highlands as a whole; that is to say, was there over-population in the proper sense, or was it only a question of faulty distribution? Instead of occupying the more fertile glens, as they had done prior to 1760, the people were forcibly huddled together on the coast, a policy only rendered possible because they were able to maintain themselves there on the potato. When the kelp trade faded out, the potato failed and return to the fertile glens was barred by sheep: the people, having neither adequate employment nor sustenance, left the country for good.

One is tempted to speculate as to what would have been the course of events had there been no potato. It is more than probable that the sheep-walk policy would still have been attempted and the people driven out of the glens, but its full development might have been delayed till after the kelp industry had failed, because without the potato the people could not possibly have maintained themselves on their small coastal crofts. Labour, however, was so essential for the landlords' exploitation of the kelp, and the results so profitable, that they would have been obliged either to enlarge their crofts into economically self-supporting units which would have drawn off more man-hours than could be spared from the kelp, or to have suffered a return of a large proportion of the

---

[1] Campbell, George Douglas (later 8th Duke of Argyll), 1942. From J. G. Fyfe's *Scottish Diaries and Memoirs*, p. 576.

[2] Argyll, Duke of (1883). *Crofts and Farms in the Hebrides*. Edinburgh: Douglas.

people to their old homes in the glens, which would again have reduced the volume of labour.

The other alternative would have been either to cut down the volume of the trade in kelp, or bring in outside labour from Ireland, as was being done to some extent for the industries in the Lowlands. This latter policy would have involved a larger supply of food, which was not available and therefore can be dismissed, even supposing the Irish would have come in the absence of an adequate supply of potatoes.

We are left, therefore, with the conviction that it was only by promoting the use of the potato, that the kelp industry could be fully developed and the landlords enabled to make enormous incomes without any corresponding outlay of capital; and that it was by this same means that the workers were ultimately so impoverished as to be forced to leave their homes.

In the Lowlands, the cultivation of the potato led to greatly improved methods of husbandry. In the Highlands, notwithstanding the vital part the potato played in the economic life of the people from the middle of the eighteenth century onwards, it cannot be credited with having effected any serious change in their agricultural methods, which remained unaltered till after the middle of the nineteenth century. On the other hand the potato certainly did much to retard the cultural development of a people who in happier surroundings played a foremost role in the great social evolution of the last century.

CHAPTER XXI

The Potato in the Lowlands of Scotland

The Lowlands comprise all that part of Scotland south of the Firth of Forth and Clyde, all Fife, Stirling, Kinross, Clackmannan, Forfar, Kincardine, the low-lying south-east corner of Perth, the eastern and northern portion of Aberdeen, the northern parts of Nairn, Moray and Banff, and all Caithness.

The differences, geographical, ethnological, social and political, which existed between the Lowlands and the Highlands, in the eighteenth and early nineteenth centuries, have already been referred to (p. 346). It remains now, briefly, to consider those economic and social features, which affected the progress of the potato in the Lowlands.

The Union of England and Scotland called a halt to the growing divergence in political outlook and economic practice, which had resulted from the subordination of Scotland under the Dual Monarchy. Prior to 1707, intercourse between the citizens of the two countries had been very restricted and in the main confined to the border counties, which on the Scotch side could not be said to represent the highest culture of that country, whilst on the English it illustrated what was perhaps the most primitive. Communications, hampered by tariffs and the appalling state of the North Road, acted as a deterrent to any social interchange between the Scots and the English; the journey between the two capitals took almost a week to accomplish, and was by no means free from risk.[1]

Scotland in the beginning of the eighteenth century was a very poor, England, in comparison, a very rich country; in the latter, industry had long since spread its tentacles throughout most of the land, and agriculture, if still awaiting the full tide of that renaissance which was to overtake it within the next forty years, was immeasurably more advanced than that common to Scotland. In England, about one-third of the land was already enclosed, and that which was still in 'open field' was generally well cultivated, produced sufficient cereal and other food not only to feed its own rapidly growing population on a higher scale than in Scotland, but to export larger quantities abroad.

In Scotland the runrig system, already described (p. 349), was universal. Wheat, except in East Lothian, was unknown; in the border counties, man-power being no longer at a premium as moss-troopers, the countryside had been converted into a great sheep-walk, a forerunner of the fate which was to overtake the Highlands. At the time of the Union, there

---

[1] Trevelyan, G. Macaulay (1944). *English Social History*, p. 418. Longmans.

was probably not much to choose between farming as practised in the Lowlands, and that in the Highlands, except that the former enjoyed more favourable soil conditions. In both, the instruments were primitive; as late as 1716 a wheeled vehicle was practically unknown in Aberdeen, nor were things much better thirty years later. In the Lowlands there was no sign of change till the after-effects of the Jacobite rising of 1715, in which some of the great landlords were deeply involved, had passed away, nor indeed much more till after the 1745 rising, in which the Lowland population were onlookers rather than participants. It was, however, in the two preceding decades that the early stirrings of a veritable tornado of reforming zeal began to be felt; a movement which put the Lowlands ultimately in the van of agricultural practice.

The prerequisites for a radical change in agricultural policy were to hand. In the main, the land was possessed by a few aristocratic owners, who enjoyed a completely free hand over their property, and in the treatment of their tenants, who had neither leases nor customary security. Enclosure required no Act of Parliament, as in England, but was a purely personal matter, determined by the landlord. It was he also, who dictated the rotation of crops, which began to hinge itself on to the growing of the turnip for winter feeding.

The existing system of infield and outfield, combined with runrig tenancy, allowed of changes being effected in easy stages. The first was to get rid of the runrig ridges and let large blocks of land to one tenant-farmer instead of to a group. The second was to enclose the infield, always the best land, and let it at a greatly improved rental. Finally, the outfield could be let at an easy rent, subject to improvement by the tenant. After 1745 the Lowland aristocracy were tending to look increasingly towards England for advancement both material and intellectual, and it was there that they found the most advanced large-scale agriculture in the world. If the driving force was a desire for higher rents, yet there were not wanting men of vision amongst the landlords. As early as 1736 John Dalrymple, the second Lord Stair, to whom Scotland is indebted for the turnip and cabbage as field crops, and John Cockburn of Ormiston, founded a society for the advancement of agriculture. Amongst the new class of substantial farmers which was growing up, there were many who shared the same enthusiasm, and after the middle of the century there was scarcely a parish in which one could not find the counterpart of Galt's 'Mr Coulter'.[1]

In some ways, the new type of Lowland farmer was better off than his opposite number in England: his tenancy was now secured by a nineteen years' lease, his choice of crops was unfettered, and he was neither hampered by a fluctuating tithe, nor irritated by its collection

[1] Galt, J. (1821). *The Annals of the Parish*. Edinburgh: Blackwood.

in kind. In Scotland, the basis of the teinds, as they were called, had been fixed once and for all, in 1633.

Substantial agricultural reform prior to 1750 was, however, small in volume, and mainly to be found in the neighbourhood of Edinburgh, Glasgow and Dundee. At the time of the first *Statistical Account*, viz. *c.* 1790, Lowland agriculture, in comparison with that in the High-lands, was greatly advanced, yet in fact not half the parishes were fully enclosed, and many were still in runrig. The difference between the two Scotlands was, however, fundamental: in the Highlands the clock of progress was deliberately set back; in the Lowlands, forward.

Doubtless several reasons could be suggested for so fundamental a difference in policy carried on by much the same type of landlord. The temperamental reaction of the two peoples was not the least important. Two centuries of religious feud had not been entirely misspent. The Lowlander of the eighteenth century had thereby already acquired a taste for philosophic thought and logical argumentation which had facilitated the exchange of the pen for the claymore; he had indeed been transformed 'from a fierce feudal vassal, ignorant of all save sword and plough, into the most educated peasant in Europe'.[1]

The existence of the seat of government and of the universities in the one section might also be credited with a share of the responsibilities for a difference both in outlook and in tempo, but hardly for one of direction. The latter would seem to find its explanation in the fact that in the Lowlands, coal and iron were to hand, and had for long been exploited; these had encouraged other industries, especially woollens, carpets and linen to spring up early in the century. Later, towards the end of the century, the cotton industry was introduced. With this industrial development, the ports of Glasgow and Leith assumed in-creasing importance. Industry demanded workers, and their needs stimulated the production of essential foodstuffs which, owing to poor communications, were of necessity produced locally. The response of both landlord and tenant led to greatly increased output both of cereals and fat cattle and was reflected in the rise of rents which was often fourfold.

The part that the potato played in this campaign must now be traced.

In the greater part of the Lowlands, as in England, the potato gained its entrance through the main portals of the houses of the great at a time when the servants' hall refused to receive it. In Ireland and in the High-lands of Scotland the potato had crept in at the back-door, and became the chosen mainstay of the worker and his family before it ever reached the table of his master. Such different lines of approach do something

[1] Trevelyan, George Macaulay (1926). *History of England*, p. 335.

more than illustrate the specific reaction of divergent social systems to one and the same intruding element: they offer us a clue to the solution of the problem of how so simple a foodstuff could become an economic weapon profoundly influencing the structure of society. Ireland has afforded us the classical example, but the contrasting societies of the Lowlands and the Highlands of Scotland offer an even better field in which to study the mechanism of its action.

The potato was not destined to remain for long a museum specimen: early in the eighteenth century it began to find its way into the kitchen gardens of some of the great houses of the Lowlands. In the Lochore Papers there is an entry to the effect that one of Robert's ancestors purchased potatoes from a 'cadger' who called in the year 1717 at the house in Strathaven, Lanarkshire, with a pony carrying two creels of tubers, these being the first seen in the district. He ate some, and planted others with good results in his garden.[1] John Cockburn of Ormiston, near Edinburgh, the first in Scotland to sow turnips in the field, grew potatoes in his garden in 1724.[2] In the following year it is said to have been brought from Ireland to Galloway, where it was treated as a delicacy; indeed, the tenant-farmer who raised it, used to carry the produce on his saddle into Edinburgh and sell it there by the pound, and even the ounce.[3] Lord Hepburn says that his father first saw the potato, which he said was brought to Leith from Ireland, in 1740. He believed that they were growing at a somewhat earlier date in Argyll.[4] From his diary it appears that in the year 1748, the Lord Advocate, Dundas of Armiston,[5] frequently enjoyed a broth of gravy-potatoes for his supper: but he must have been somewhat exceptional in this respect, for Wesley records that 'when I was in Scotland first [1762], even at a nobleman's table, we had only fish, meat of one kind, and no vegetable of any kind'.[6] Amongst the middle classes, even in the capital, the potato was by no means common so late as the middle of the eighteenth century: thus Wilkie (1721–72), commonly known as the 'Scotch Homer', achieved the further nicknames of 'Potato Poet' and 'Potato Wilkie' because he was so keenly interested in its cultivation on his farm near Edinburgh, which he did not leave till 1753.[7]

Away from the great towns, its spread during the early decades of the eighteenth century, from the laird's dining-room to the cottar's hut, must have been as slow as it was silent. In 1740 the needs of Paisley's

---

[1] Communicated to R.N.S. by Prof. J. D. Mackie of Glasgow.
[2] Brown, Hume (1911), in his *History of Scotland*, vol. VII, p. 353, gives the date as 1726.
[3] Fyfe, J. G. (1942). *Scottish Diaries*, p. 285 n. Stirling: Mackay.
[4] Hepburn, Lord (1808). Communication to the Board of Agriculture, p. 254.
[5] Ormond, Edward (1887). Editor, *Armiston Memoirs*, p. 108.
[6] Wesley, J. *Journal*, vol. IV, p. 418.
[7] Page, Frederick (1943). *Notes and Queries* (10 April), vol. CLXXX, no. 8, p. 224.

5,000 inhabitants were satisfied by a couple of sacks:[1] it was the failure of the corn crops of that year, however, which gave the necessary spur to its cultivation. It was thus that it came to Elgin, where, grown at first in odd corners, it soon invaded the fields.[2]

In the Lowlands, the truly critical phase of its culture may be said to have been reached when it came to be grown in the fields as a farm crop, for it was from that moment that it began to exert an influence on the food of the industrial workers. The earliest records of such culture relate to the village of Kilsyth in Stirling: Robert Graham, who was born in the parish and was the factor to the Kilsyth Estates, had, like others in the neighbourhood, long grown the potato in his garden; in 1739 he planted half an acre in the croft at Nielstone. This was a bold innovation, for it was popularly supposed that it would not flourish except in small plots; finding that his field crop was a success, he invited all the leading agriculturists of Scotland, amongst whom was the 'unfortunate Earl of Perth', to see his experiment. With prophetic zeal he rented fields for purposes of demonstration in Renfrew, Perth, Dundee and Edinburgh, obtaining in each case premiums for their cultivation.[3] Dr William Wright of Edinburgh, the eminent Scotch botanist[4] of the late eighteenth century, credited the Kilsyth experiments to Thomas Prentice, a day-labourer, who succeeded so well that all his neighbours copied him; he gives 1728 as the date. That such a man was interested in the potato is not in dispute, for Wright says that he died, at the age of eighty-six, in the year 1792 in Edinburgh, and that he saved £200 as a result of his potato experiments, which he invested in an annuity; but the scene of his activities is not clear. It is possible that some confusion may have arisen between Thomas Prentice and Henry of that name who is said to have introduced the potato into the Lothians in 1746. This latter individual, however, is described as 'a wandering Jew type of body who picked up the knowledge of the practice either in Ireland or Lancashire'.[5] which would seem to differentiate him from his more provident namesake.

By the beginning of the second half of the eighteenth century, the potato was well on its way to becoming an established field crop in many parts of the Lowlands. Chirnside in Berwickshire affords an example of the type of reception it received in the more prosperous Lowland districts. It was introduced shortly after 1740 and was grown on the

---

[1] Graham, Henry Grey (1906). *The Social Life of Scotland*, p. 172. London: Black.
[2] Donaldson, James (1794). *General Views of Agriculture, County Elgin.*
[3] Rennie, Robert (1796). *The Statistical Account of Scotland*, vol. XVIII, p. 214. Also *The New Statistical Account*, 1845, vol. VIII, pp. 147–8.
[4] *Report to Board of Agriculture, 1795, on the Curl.* Appendix, p. 75.
[5] Robertson, George (1763–1832). Diarist. See Fyfe, J. G. (1942). *Scottish Diaries.* Stirling: Mackay.

runrig farms. A foodstuff so easily grown, and one 'which might replace bread, was a great alleviation to the people', and its cultivation was pushed until in 1760 its market value fell so low, that further large-scale production ceased. By this time both farmer and cottar had learnt to depend on it and tradesmen and artisans, here spoken of as 'acre-men', had established the custom of hiring plots of land on which to grow their own crop.[1] Forty years later, this parish, now one of the best cultivated in Scotland, grew only enough potatoes to serve as an auxiliary diet, but instead raised large crops of turnip for feeding to stock.[2]

In 1753, Mr Hay of Aberlady, East Lothian, grew potatoes in the field;[3] about the same time, John Symes of Annandale in Dumfries, by demonstrating that potatoes if properly cultivated were an excellent preparation for flax and wheat, overcame the prejudice against them which had existed up till then. Sir Archibald Grant took a rather similar line: they might serve well enough as an 'ameliorating crop' between 'the scourging or white crops', but as for feeding, they were only fit for swine and 'those they won't fatten'.[4] This, however, was not Sir Archibald's first reaction: on his own farm in 1746 he had planted them between his trees in the orchard, and in 1754 he advised his lesser tenants to enclose an acre or two and put a quarter of the same to potatoes for their own use.[5] In Ayr the Earl of Eglington, with the assistance of a farmer from East Lothian, carried out in 1753 extensive improvements on his estates, and took the opportunity of introducing the potato, till then almost unknown in the county, a policy 'which enabled the lower class to live better'.[6] In the important town of Peterhead, Aberdeenshire, as late as 1755, no potatoes were grown, but a few were imported from Ireland and Norway; by 1794 the traffic was reversed and large quantities were exported from Peterhead to Norway and England. At Yarrow, near Peebles, the potato was known in gardens as early as 1745, but it was everywhere regarded as a mere curiosity. Five years later, attempts were made to introduce the turnip, but it was not till 1759 that W. Dawson of Frogden succeeded in growing 100 acres of the new crop. This success caused it to be widely grown, which, in turn, induced M. Scott of Woll in 1769 to adopt similar methods for the cultivation of potatoes, which soon led to the potato becoming a staple food in both cottage and hall.[7] Kames of Blair Drummond also strongly advocated its use as a field crop, but his

[1] *The Statistical Account of Scotland*, 1795, vol. XIV, p. 15 n.
[2] *New Statistical Account of Scotland*, 1845, vol. II, p. 124.
[3] Buchan-Hepburn, G. (1794). *General View of Agriculture, East Lothian*.
[4] Grant, Sir Archibald (1756). *The Practical Farmers' Pocket Companion*, pp. 8–11.
[5] Hamilton, H. (1945). *Monymusk Papers*, pp. 159 and 170. Edinburgh University Press.
[6] Fullarton, Col. (1793). *General View of Agriculture, County Ayr*, vol. v.
[7] Russell, James. *Diary*. See Fyfe, J. G. (1942). *Scottish Diaries*, p. 581.

mind was swayed by social and economic rather than agricultural considerations:

John Ramsay[1] (1736–1814) of Ochtertyre, Menteith, tells how rare were kitchen gardens before 1745 and how they were devoted to herbs with which to make the staple foods, including potatoes, more palatable. In 1757 the effect of high prices for corn "had been alleviated by the plenty of potatoes, a root which twenty years before had been confined to gentlemens gardens". The major changes consequent on the inflow of English money and methods was felt about 1760; Lime came into use but the turnip still lagged behind the potato because of runrig.

From *The Statistical Account of Scotland*, compiled during the last decade of the eighteenth century, it appears that whilst the potato had, with but few exceptions, become firmly established in the gardens and crofts of the peasantry throughout the length and breadth of the country, its progress as a field crop varied widely in different districts, and was closely correlated with the progress of enclosures and engrossment of the arable land. In Dunkeld, Perthshire, the potato reached the fields in 1772 when they were still in runrig. In Grange, Banffshire, enclosures and the raising of potatoes as a field crop were both delayed till the year 1780. In the country south of Clyde and Forth, this dual policy, though by no means universal, had generally attained an earlier and greater development than elsewhere, with the result that in the best arable districts the potato had already taken its place as a rotation crop, with an ever-increasing acreage to its credit. What proportion it bore to that occupied by the cereal and pulse crops combined, it is difficult, except in a few isolated cases, to say, but forty years later we know that in this same district it reached a fifth or more (see p. 400). If in 1790 it were but half that amount, and it was almost certainly no less, it would imply that an economic and social readjustment of much importance had taken place in the previous forty years, when the potato had been confined to the privacy of the kitchen garden of a few great houses.

The reactions which the increasing use of the potato induced on the structure of society at the close of the eighteenth century, took definite shape at three distinct social levels, the agricultural, the industrial, and the middle class. Although the potato had for a generation reached the infields of the runrig farms in many Lowland parishes, it was necessary to harvest both it and the turnip directly after the cereal harvest, lest they be destroyed by the customary invasion of the cattle. Husbandry had therefore to undergo considerable readjustments before any sizeable field crop of potatoes could be raised. Foremost amongst these were the abolition of the common rights of grazing the stubble, followed by the

[1] Ramsay, John (1888). *Scotland and Scotsmen in the Eighteenth Century* (edit. Alex. Allardyce), vol. II, p. 246. Blackwood.

abolition of runrig, its replacement by enclosures, and the granting of nineteen-year leases. Secondary technical effects followed in due course, such as the employment of all available manure on the land destined for the potato crop; the planting of the seed in plough-drawn drills; the use of the potato as a cleaning crop, either alone or with the turnip, as an alternative to a bare fallow. In Callander, Perthshire, on the Highland Line, this process had advanced so far, that before 1793 the potato had completely replaced the turnip as a fallow crop. In the best arable districts, however, expansion of the potato took place at the expense of the cereal crops. How far this latter might proceed is seen in the case of the parish of Fintry in Forfar, where we have the data for the two years 1760 and 1790 respectively:[1] at the latter date, three-fifths of the arable land was devoted to potatoes which at the earlier were entirely absent. Many similar examples are to be found in the first *Statistical Account*, though exact figures are generally wanting.

The agricultural renaissance of the Lowlands which began in the early decades of the eighteenth century, was closely associated with the cultivation of the turnip which, contrary to the sequence of events in the Highlands, preceded the potato in the attainment of field rank. Nevertheless, towards the end of the century the potato attained an importance equal to that of the turnip in the production and the maintenance of Lowland agricultural pre-eminence. Alongside the reorganization of the existing infields and outfields, the landlords pursued, or it would be more correct to say encouraged, the policy of reclamation of adjacent moorlands. To this end it was found that as a cleaning crop, none could compare with the potato, especially on the poorly drained and rather acid soils. For similar reasons, the potato was frequently planted on those less workable parts of the estate which were given over to afforestation with conifers, where it acted as a nursery crop to the young seedlings.

In the Lowlands the potato was adopted primarily as a food for humans, but within a couple of decades it had come to be fed to stock of all sorts. Horses in particular were held to thrive on them, and the 'yam' variety was grown for their especial benefit. The turnips on the farm were given to the cattle and sheep but these, too, were frequently fed on potatoes, the variety 'Tartar' as well as the 'yam' being those mainly used. We have seen how in the Highlands the introduction of the potato led to an increase in the raising of pigs; exactly the same occurred in the Lowlands. The contributor of the article on Avendale,[2] in Lanark, voices the opinion of many others of his contemporaries when he wrote prior to 1793: 'This cleanly sort of feeding has reconciled the people here to the use of swine flesh which was once held in abomination.'

[1] *The Statistical Account of Scotland*, 1793, vol. v, p. 226.
[2] Ibid. 1793, vol. ix.

What appears to be a typical attitude towards the potato by the leading authorities in the wealthier parts of the Lowlands is exemplified by the author of the *General View* of Fife.[1] Writing in 1800 he says 'in this country about 60 years ago, it was to be seen chiefly in gardens; few were planted in the fields. It is only within the last 20 or 30 years that its value has been understood, and the cultivation of it has become general.' He considers it 'cleanses and ameliorates the soil'.

It is found to be a wholesome, nourishing and palatable food for both man and beast. The abundance of the produce is likewise a powerful recommendation of this plant....In short, since this root came into such general repute, the nation has never been exposed to such scarcity, as was experienced before that time, and which sometimes bordered upon famine....On every farm a considerable quantity is planted for the tenant and his cottagers. And on the lands in the immediate vicinity of the towns and villages, which are very numerous in Fife, a still greater quantity, in proportion, is raised.

The major part of the crop was fed to horses and cattle. It constituted, he thought, one-third of the food of the common people for eight months of the year. About 6,000 acres (Scotch) were devoted annually in this county to the crop.

The history of the origin, development and influence of the cultivation of the potato in the Lowlands and Highlands respectively, demonstrates how, within the compass of one small state, the same agent, when set in distinctive social environments, may bring about very different results.

In the Highlands, the potato was introduced by the chieftains, in order to give means of subsistence to a people whose economic life had been disrupted, at a time when none thought of providing them with an alternative industry. The consequences of a one-sided policy, which to-day seem so obvious, were at the time obscured by the conflicting impulses of sentiment and greed which inspired the chiefs' action. The people, freed from the dread of famine, sank economically into a bondage far more insidious than any they had experienced in the former days of clan rule, and this time at the hands of the very agent which had almost miraculously protected them from want. More important, however, was the influence of the potato on the life of the landworkers. This was exerted in two main directions: directly as a foodstuff, and indirectly as a controlling factor in the return of wages.

In the Lowlands the potato only occasionally dominated the labourer's dietary, though when such happened it seemed always to have been associated with a reduced standard of living. Thus, in the prosperous district of Kirkcaldy, Fifeshire, meat was eaten freely, both oat and wheaten meal were common, and the potato remained a mere accessory food. In Kilconquhar, a fertile district in the same county, between

[1] Thomson, J. (1800). *General View of the Agriculture of the County of Fife*, p. 181.

1753 and 1793 the potato supplied half the food of the poor, was freely used by the better-off, and not a little found its way into the whisky distilleries. At Loggie, in Forfar, it was beginning in 1790 to be one of the principal foods of the poor, but still lagged behind oat and bear meal. Convenience, rather than necessity, may, in a few instances, have dictated its wholesale use, e.g. in Bathgate, Linlithgow, a coal-mining centre, the potato is stated to have constituted two-thirds of the workers' diet for nine months of the year, whilst at the same time 'there is much more wheaten bread eaten in one month than in a year forty years ago', i.e. in 1750.

Generally, contributors to the first *Statistical Account* make it abundantly clear that a greater use of the potato in the homes of the workers is due to the high price of meat and cereals, and to the fact that the price of potatoes remained steady owing to the large amount grown at home. At Sprouston in Roxburghshire, notwithstanding the prevalence of 'high wages', one shilling a day, in summer, and eight to ten pence in winter, it is stated that the people could not possibly hold out, without the potato, so dear were corn, butter and cheese. In Dunkeld, Perthshire, it is complained that the poor devote too much attention to the potatoes, though it is admitted that 'it has saved the tenants from the ruinous necessity of purchasing meat for their families to a prodigious extent', and that it is 'an excellent succedaneum for meal and a standing dish on the tables of the rich and poor'. In Kinglassie, Fife, the lower classes, it is stated, have given up meat and live on meal, potatoes, milk, small beer and kail. Finally, in Kirkpatrick, Dumfries, a district almost entirely given over to pasture, the dependence of the workers on the potato was all but complete.

But the use of the potato was by no means confined to the working classes: it had, by the beginning of the nineteenth century, become almost equally firmly established in the households of the middle class. A passage from the *Ayrshire Legatees* illustrates the point: one of the characters, speaking of a potato betel, a kitchen utensil to which reference will be made later,[1] says: 'but a potato beetle is not to be had within the four walls of London, which is a great want in a house; Mrs Argent never heard of sic a thing';[2] evidence also of the position attained by the potato itself in the domestic economy of the well-to-do London household; here it was but incidental, in the Ayrshire Rectory, all important.

The adoption of the potato did not necessarily cause a fall in standards. Where the district was particularly fertile and accessible, happier results might follow. In Kilwinning in Ayrshire there were no potatoes in 1742, the land was unimproved, and both farmer and worker lived on oatmeal,

[1] See chapter xxxiv, p. 594.   [2] Galt, J. (1821). *The Ayrshire Legatees*, p. 223.

milk and butter, only tasting meat, and then but little, during harvests. In 1790 all classes enjoyed tea twice a day, and lived largely on meat and potatoes.

In its second capacity its influence was both hastened and extended by the custom prevalent in some of the agriculturally more advanced districts, by which the farmer gave a working cottar family land free of rent for the cultivation of his potatoes, on condition that the cottar would devote all his manure to the crop. At Dyke and Moy, in Elgin, this procedure, it is specifically stated, 'has greatly lessened the consumption of grain, and potatoes are now the chief food'. A more direct effect on the daily life of the landworkers was induced by an extension of the truck system, so as to include the provision of potatoes as such, or, alternatively, the land on which to grow them, as a substantial part of the wage. Even seasonal workers like shearers, as at Carnworth, Ayrshire, prior to 1794, might be paid 21s. to 25s. for the harvest and be allowed to sow two to four pecks of potatoes on the farmer's land free of cost. This practice, which in the Lowlands is referred to only occasionally in the first *Statistical Account*, became general in the next century, when it acquired a distinctive form. The contract between labourer and farmer would include a small money wage, a cottage, pasturage for a cow, some bolls of oatmeal, and anything from 1,000 to 1,600 yards of potatoes, i.e. the produce of drills up to that length situated in the farmer's potato field, became the property of the labourer. It was clearly to the master's advantage to encourage a system that tended to strengthen the 'fixation' between the worker and potato, which, whilst embarrassing neither party, discouraged the latter from seeking his fortune in the towns.

Sir John Sinclair points out how general had become the custom of giving the landworkers facilities for growing potatoes as part payment of wages and adds: 'The importance of this privilege is too obvious to be insisted on. This mild and wholesome root is a prime article of food to the industrious peasant and to his children in particular.'[1]

Landowners and farmers frequently helped the individual poor by a similar method: the Minister of Colmonell in Ayrshire writes in 1794: 'It is the chief means of subsistence to the poorer classes of the people, for at least three-quarters of the year. No one who has land in his possession refuses a potato rigg to a poor person; and very often they have the land and dung for nothing.' It was not till the potato failed, that the disadvantages of this and like arrangements became manifest.

The industrial revolution started later in the Lowlands than in England, but it made rapid strides during the last decades of the eighteenth

---

[1] Sinclair, Sir John (1812). *An Account of the System of Husbandry adopted in the more improved Districts of Scotland*, pt. II, p. 132.

century. Unlike its counterpart in England, with the exception of the
Carron Iron Works, founded in 1760, it lacked the long semi-capitalistic
preparatory stage in the villages of the countryside, but instead took
immediate shape as a factory system in the towns, some of which, like
Glasgow, Greenock and Dundee, developed rapidly into great industrial
centres. Later, cotton-mills were established in small villages in Renfrew,
Lanark and Ayr, but it was not till much later that agricultural districts
anywhere in Scotland were seriously invaded by industry. Hence it is
we find that all except the largest urban settlements were in the
main supplied with their daily food from the immediate neighbourhood.

Industrial development necessarily led to the settlement of artisans,
the majority of whom were derived from the cottar families of the
district, who had been displaced by the change in the agricultural
system; in addition, and in ever-increasing numbers, they were joined
by Highlanders and Irishmen,[1] both potato addicts, and its potential
missionaries. The demand for increased food supplies stimulated the
neighbouring agricultural districts to greater efforts, and it is most
noticeable how, in the vicinity of the new industries, potato culture
developed rapidly and extensively. Although, in the main, the crop was
dealt with on a wholesale basis, yet before 1793 the industrial workers
of Glasgow and Greenock cultivated plots of potatoes in the outskirts
of the towns, a practice which became increasingly popular.[2] The
second *Statistical Account* mentions several other parishes where factory
hands hired land from the neighbouring farmers on which to grow their
own potatoes on a basis identical with that of the conacre system
prevailing in Ireland.

Statistical evidence as to the measure of the progress and use of the
potato in the Lowlands before 1795, is scanty and not very reliable, but
a comparison of the two great *Accounts of the State of Scotland* compiled
around the years 1795 and 1840 respectively, to which reference has
been so frequently made, allows of an approach to the subject from a
more factual point of view.

Cultivation of the turnip was the hall-mark of the new system of
husbandry borrowed from England which, introduced into the Lothians,
spread throughout the Lowlands. The abolition of runrig, and a wholesale policy of enclosure, were carried out, in order that the new root crop
might be grown and the winter feeding of the ubiquitous black cattle

---

[1] A judicial decision in 1824 gave Irishmen the same immunity from removal under
the Poor Law in Scotland as was enjoyed by natives, a fact of much importance at the
time in Clydesdale, and later throughout the country, in the days of the Railway
development. [Fay, C. R. (1932). *Great Britain from Adam Smith to the Present Day*,
p. 348. Longmans.]

[2] *The Statistical Account of Scotland* (1794), vol. XII (Glasgow); (1793), vol. V,
(Greenock).

made possible. It should be remembered that the mainstay of Scottish agriculture hitherto had been the raising of black cattle and that the export of stores to England was an important branch of the industry. The cultivation of the turnip brought about a veritable revolution, allowing for the maintenance of a much greater number of cattle of a far higher standard than had hitherto been possible. In so doing, the turnip enriched the farmer and middleman, but only indirectly affected the welfare of the Scottish agricultural worker, and scarcely at all that of the Scottish industrialist worker.

The authors of the 1795 *Reports* generally provide a sketch of the agricultural condition of the individual parishes during the period under review, which allows one to examine the relative importance of the potato and turnip crop during the latter part of the eighteenth century. From this it appears that so late as 1795, there were practically no turnips grown in the Highland counties of Argyll, Inverness, Sutherland, Ross and Cromarty, or in the Hebrides, the Orkneys, or the Shetlands, though in a few Highland parishes of Perth and Aberdeen near to the Lowland portion of those counties, the turnip had won a foothold. Nor were conditions much different in far-away Caithness where, except in the Thurso district, the turnip had not yet penetrated. It was, however, just in those turnip-less areas that the potato had become the staple food of the people and its cultivation general, whether the land was enclosed or not. Here, then, we find confirmation of the view that the potato in the Highlands was not the working tool of an improving husbandry, but solely an expedient for feeding the masses.

In the Lowlands the position was not so simple; the new husbandry, contrary to the view commonly held, did not sweep across the country in one great wave; its development varied immensely in degree, even in neighbouring parishes, as well as from one county to another. In some districts it had almost reached its zenith by 1795; in others, it had scarcely obtained a footing. Nor did it always follow the same pattern. Generally the first step was to get rid of multiple ownership and the individual runrig ridge; this would frequently be associated with the engrossment of smaller farms. The next step was often to replace oxen by horses and make use of the English plough and drill. After this, progress might be halted for several years, to be followed later by the removal of the distinction between infield and outfield. Generally the last stage of the transformation in this period, because the most expensive, was the enclosure of the fields.

It was this last feature which in very many cases controlled the issue as to whether field crops of potatoes or turnips were to be grown. If the land lay in a district where sheep or cattle abounded and were not separated from the arable lands by natural obstacles, root culture in the unenclosed field was all but excluded. The exceptions but prove the rule; thus, there is an interesting record of a man in Logie, Forfar, who circumvented this difficulty as early as 1746 before any enclosures had been made, by obtaining a public proclamation forbidding people to allow their cattle or sheep to stray on to a field of clover, which he was the first to introduce.[1]

In consequence, the turnip had no serious effect on the rotation of crops in the fields till about 1770, but even in 1795 one frequently meets with cases where, notwithstanding extensive improvements, turnips, it is complained, cannot be grown because of the ravages of the cattle.

Where development had proceeded unhindered, as in many parts of the Lothians and Dumfries, we find both turnip and potato grown prior to 1795 as rotation crops. In most of them, however, it is the potato which is the field crop, though on a small scale, whilst the turnip is wanting. This is to be explained by the fact that farmers very frequently let off separate acres of their field to labourers and tradesmen, who manured the land, and thus the farmer obtained all the advantages of a field root crop with a much higher cash return than that which the turnip would have given him. Although it was generally the potato which was the first to attain field rank, exceptions are to be found, as in Peterhead and Channelkirk in Aberdeen; elsewhere their advent was almost simultaneous, as in Monifieth, Fife, where the turnip was introduced in 1753, and the potato in the following year. Indeed, for many years the potato preceded the turnip as a fodder crop for cattle and pigs and poultry.

In the 1795 *Account*, figures of the acreage under potatoes and turnip are given for seventeen Lowland parishes. That for potatoes as compared with the total area under grain is for Dumfries 0·07%; for Fife, 0·06%; and for the Lothians, 0·04%. The corresponding figures for the turnip acreages are 0·03%, 0·05% and 0·02% respectively. These latter disclose the total area involved, as the turnip was very rarely grown in the cottage gardens. It was otherwise with the potato: every working-class home which could boast of a garden plot at all, devoted the major part of it to the potato, so that the field crop may be looked on rather as a measure of the growing needs of the new industrial workers than those of the peasant classes.

Between the compilation of the two *Accounts*, i.e. roughly between 1790 and 1840, great changes took place: in the Lowlands, 'improvement' had spread throughout, and very high standards of husbandry reigned almost everywhere. By 1840, Scottish Lowland agriculture had adapted itself to the new industrial developments at home, and was becoming increasingly interested in the demand for potatoes as ware in the rapidly growing cities of northern and western England. Fortunately

[1] Peter, Alex. Rev. (1793). *The Statistical Account of Scotland*, vol. IX, p. 33.

the 1840 *Account* is far richer in statistical data than the earlier one,[1] and we are able to gather an accurate idea of the extent of the land occupied by both the potato and turnip throughout the country, as well as of the relative monetary value attached to them.

Data as to the acreages and values of the different crops are given for 401 parishes. Fig. 70 represents the relations in area and monetary value of the two crops, potato and turnip, expressed in each case as a percentage of the combined value or acreage, respectively, of the cereal and pulse crops grown in the same parish. In actual fact, although it was thought best to include the pulse crops, as giving a more just picture of the relative position of the potato, they are relatively unimportant. For practical purposes the figures may be accepted as showing, in bold relief, the relation between the cereals and the root crops.

In Fig. 70 two scales are shown: one relates to the potato, the other to the turnip crop; on the left-hand side of each is the average relative values in sterling of the crop in each county, and on the right, the relative area occupied; both expressed as percentages of the value and acreage respectively of the combined grain and pulse crops.

In the forty-odd years which elapsed between the two *Accounts*, the maximum area in the Lowlands under potatoes rose from under 1 to 40%, and the minimum from 0·3 to 4·0%. In general terms, more than a twentyfold relative increase had taken place in little more than a generation. The development of the area under turnips is equally striking and of much the same magnitude.

The question naturally arises as to whether the increase has been effected by the reclamation of new land or by the use of areas previously under cereal cultivation and if the latter, has it been compensated by heavier yields of the cereals and pulses? There is no doubt that all these processes have been at work either singly or in combination.

Throughout the purely Highland districts, the potato tended to replace the cereals, more especially the oat crop, a fact which is reflected in the high monetary value of the crop which in Argyll is actually greater than that of the cereals. These high monetary values are further inflated in the Highland counties because wheat, which was highly priced, was not grown, and the yields per acre of oats and bear were relatively low.

In the Lowlands, increased acreages were attained by a more economic

---

[1] Although figures are plentiful, no consistent and uniform method has been adopted in their presentation. Many of the authors fail to state whether the acreages given are imperial or Scotch; nor do they always use the same 'acre' for each crop. Much care has been taken to overcome these deficiencies. Details of acreages and values, more or less complete, are given for 401 parishes out of the 942 described in the fifteen volumes of the *Account*. Figures for Highland parishes are generally unsatisfactory; acreages of any kind are rarely given, and the valuations of the crops are less reliable than those tendered for the Lowlands.

use of the land, particularly that following on the abolition of the distinction between infield and outfield, but still more by the reclamation of new land, in which both potato and turnip played a notable role. In the neighbourhood of the larger towns the potato seems to have increased literally at the expense of the cereal crop, but to that point we will return directly.

Turning now to the scale of acreages and values of the turnip crop, Fig. 70, it will be observed that the range of the figures is more restricted than in the case of the potato, and that the position of any one county on either side of the scale does not differ by more than a few points. In general, the ratio between the turnip and the cereal crop in sterling is a few points lower than that of their respective acreages, this because the average cash value of the turnip crop was less than that of the average cereal crop, even when the more valuable grain, wheat, was not grown in the district. When, exceptionally, the reverse occurs, as in the case of Ayrshire and Stirlingshire, it is probably to be explained by their prosperous dairy industry, which created a high demand for the turnip and hence increased its value. Thus whilst turnips were generally worth about £6 per acre, in Ayrshire they rose to £7. 4s., and in Stirlingshire to £11.

Examination of the scale of potato values discloses two facts: the far greater range of the monetary value ratios, and the often very wide differences between the position on the scale of certain counties in respect to their acreage and sterling ratios, as compared with that attained by the turnip. Paucity of data as regards acreage ratios in the Highlands makes it difficult to explain adequately the position of Argyll, Inverness, Bute, Ross and Cromarty, and Sutherland; but we know that the value of the cereal crop per acre in those parts was necessarily low because of the absence of wheat and the poor and uncertain returns of oats and barley, in consequence the relative value of the potato crop would be somewhat higher than elsewhere. Both the earlier and later *Accounts*, however, make it clear that the cultivation of the potato in the Highlands was in many places carried out on land which would otherwise have been devoted to the cereal crops. The extraordinarily high sterling potato-cereal ratio certainly supports this view.

In the Lowlands, information as to values and acreages for such typical counties as Ayrshire, Dumfriesshire, Fifeshire, Lanarkshire, Renfrewshire and Perthshire about the year 1840 is abundant and accurate; hence we must regard the outstanding disparities in these counties between the figures on the scale for area and value as significant. In all six counties potato-growing was by this time a well-established industry: in Renfrew and Lanark, the relatively high value of the potato crop was due to the ever-expanding demand in the busy town of Glasgow; in

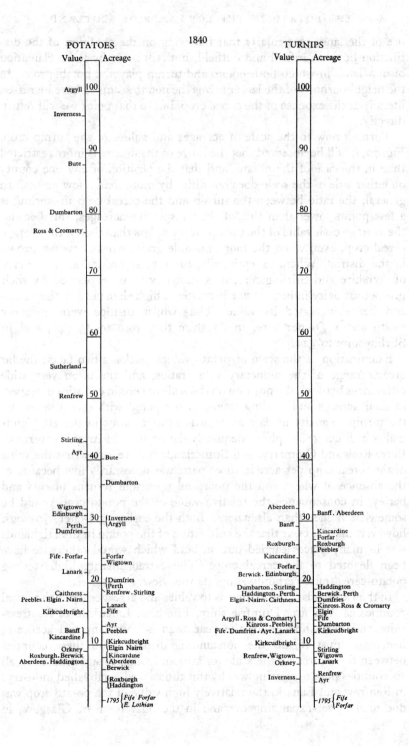

Ayrshire growers may have begun to specialize on the raising of earlies in addition to the maincrop varieties, with which they had developed a trade in the rapidly growing industrial centres of the county, so that here, too, favourable local markets ensured high prices. Fifeshire exported its potatoes mainly to Dundee and Glasgow, as well as shipping some to the London market. In Dumfries, one of the best cultivated counties in Scotland, the explanation of the high value of the potato crop is probably to be found in its very heavy yield, part of which was fed to pigs, whilst the remainder seems to have been absorbed locally. In the lowland areas of Perth, the large export trade in potatoes which had already grown up with London, must have kept prices at a high level, for in many districts in the county the potato crop in the field is valued at £10 per acre, as compared with the common rate of £7 per acre. In all these counties, the potato flourished to some extent at the expense of the cereal crops.

The study of the figures for the area of land devoted to the potato crop in the two *Accounts* provides the key to the solution of the problem as to the provenance of the extra food required to support the growing population which, between 1780 and 1840, by reason of immigration from the countryside and by natural increase, had accumulated within the larger urban centres. Better husbandry doubtless enlarged the supply of grain, as did turnip cultivation and the winter feeding of the cattle that of meat, but neither in sufficient degree to meet the needs of a rapidly growing population. It was the potato, raised in the Lowlands, which provided the bulk of the extra food required during this period.

Scotland had, in this respect, an advantage over most of England, other than the north-western counties, inasmuch as the potato had firmly established itself as an essential article of the people's diet both in town and countryside before the shortage and mounting prices of wheat, which occurred during the Napoleonic wars, became acute. The people were thus better able to weather the economic tempest of the post-Waterloo years, than were the industrial and agricultural communities of England.

Some forty years later, the soundness or otherwise, of the economic relation between the subsistence of the workers and the use of the potato, was subject to a further test.

Fig. 70. The column on the left refers to the potato crop; that on the right, to the turnip crop; they record data derived from *The New Statistical Account of Scotland* for the year 1840. On the left of each column is shown the value of the respective crop as a percentage of the total value in pounds sterling of the combined cereal and pulse crops of each county. On the right of each column is shown the acreage of the potato and turnip crop respectively, as a percentage of the total acreage occupied by the combined cereal and pulse crops of each county. The counties in italics with date 1795, refer to data recorded in that year in the first *Statistical Account of Scotland*.

Although the Blight of 1846 and 1847 affected the Lowland potato crop as badly as elsewhere, distress, except amongst the poorest in the great towns as in Glasgow, was not acute. The Lowland population as a whole, long since accustomed to a mixed and fairly generous diet, unlike the Highlanders, readily adjusted their home economy to meet the new emergency.

Before 1795 potato cultivation was showing signs of developing into an organized industry: large crops were raised, especially for sale in the markets of the nearby large towns such as Glasgow, Paisley and Dundee, there to be consumed by the artificers. Indeed, the local supplies must have been before long inadequate, as large quantities were imported into the Glasgow district from Ireland. The trend of events is shown by the entry in 1790 in the account of Greenock: 'Potatoes are sold at 6d. a peck [about 14 lbs.], and good fresh herrings at 7 or 8 a penny. What a blessing to the poor families!' Between 1795 and 1840 the industry grew greatly both in volume and importance. By the latter date we find the Lowlands pouring potatoes into the north of England, and Perth sending many thousands of tons a year to London. It will be observed that it was not in the Highlands, where the potato dominated the whole life of the people, that industry developed and prospered, but rather in those parts where the people, enjoying higher economic standards and better social amenities, were content to employ the potato as an accessory, albeit an important object of diet. This geographical disposition has remained unchallenged till to-day, notwithstanding the very good reasons which can be adduced for developing a special section of the potato industry in the Western Highlands and Hebrides.

The subsequent development of the potato industry followed certain well-defined lines: in Ayrshire the warm coastlands between Largs and Ballantrae offered favourable opportunities for the raising of early varieties which, from 1857 onwards, were grown there in ever-increasing volume, so that before long it became the most remunerative husbandry in the county. Prior to that date there seems to have been no organized attempt to supply early varieties in bulk to the market, and but little to grow them for domestic use. Here, too, according to McIntosh,[1] arose the custom of buying the standing crop, the farmer's responsibility ending with the delivery of the tubers to the nearest railway station. The custom, however, was already well established in the Lothians by 1841.[2] A somewhat later development was the auctioneering of the growing crop in the field.

---

[1] McIntosh, T. P. (1943). The Potato Industry in Scotland. *Scot. J. Agric.* vol. XXIV, p. 137.

[2] Greg, Robert Hyde (1842). Scotch Farming in the Lothians. *Manchester Guardian*, 9 September 1842.

The varieties which were tried out in the Ayrshire district were many, but a few stand out because of their quality and the length of time they dominated the market, viz. 'Regent', 'Puritan' and 'Epicure'; the last has held its own for over fifty years and is still popular with growers, especially in the Girvan district. From Ayrshire the raising of early potatoes spread to the Lothians, Renfrew, Wigtown, and Bute. Most of the crop went to Edinburgh and Glasgow but some, from about 1894, found its way to London, Manchester and Newcastle. Up till 1939 the early ware crop from the Western Lowlands was marketed in northern England.

The beginning of the second half of the nineteenth century coincided with the discovery of gold in Australia and California, and resulted in a sharp rise in the prices of all commodities, including wheat and meat. As a result, the farmers shared in the new wave of prosperity which overtook producers of all kinds, though it failed to reach the agricultural workers of England in a like degree. This boom in agriculture induced an emigration to southern England of many capable and well-equipped farmers from the Lothians and the south of Scotland. According to Campbell[1] the newcomers brought with them their own seed potatoes, and discovered that they yielded far better than the average seed produced in England. This may well have been the determining factor which converted an existing trade tendency into a definite industry. Such a 'tendency' did exist, as is shown by the export of immature seed potatoes from Berwick to Hull and parts of Yorkshire at the end of the eighteenth century.[2] The superiority of Scotch and moorland raised seed was referred to by Tuke[3] in 1794, and Kirschoffer[4] some twelve years later.

The observation was in fact in line with that which growers in Lancashire and Yorkshire had discovered as a result of the great increase of virus disease in the last quarter of the eighteenth century, that seed derived from the high moorlands was much less likely to suffer from Curl than that raised on the clay-lands lower down. The demonstration of the superiority of Scotch over home-grown seed, was rapidly followed by economic action, viz. the creation of an important and for many years unique seed-potato trade, an enterprise which has had its repercussions the world over.

For some sixty years the Scotch seed trade enjoyed an unchallenged monopoly in Great Britain. It was conducted on the usual commercial basis of that time, maximum profits being both its goal and its

[1] Campbell, W. J. (1928). The Scottish Seed Potato Trade. *Scot. J. Agric.* vol. XI, pp. 1–8.

[2] Hepburn, Baron (1808). *Communication to the Board of Agriculture*, p. 254.

[3] Tuke, J. junr. (1794). *General Views of the Agriculture of Yorkshire*, p. 43.

[4] Kirschoffer, G. (1806). *Communication to the Board of Agriculture*, vol. III, pp. 181–5. For a further discussion of this problem, the reader is referred to chapter x, p. 179.

justification. Sheltered by its monopoly, the trade was more often threatened from within than from without; from time to time it would be thrown into a state of frenzy when, for example, some interested persons would place on the market, seed of a variety with a high-sounding name, and boom it till it reached fantastic prices.[1]

Of late years, the Department of Agriculture for Scotland, the English Ministry of Agriculture, and the growers themselves, have acquired a much more responsible attitude to this important industry. This has come about, partly because of the growing education in the matter of good seed, engendered by the National Institute of Agricultural Botany, but more particularly as a result of the volume of new knowledge concerning potato seed which we owe to the scientific work carried out between the two great wars in Cambridge, Dublin and Edinburgh. Nor must the growing competition of other seed areas be lost sight of; notably those in Northern Ireland and Eire, both of which produce seed of the highest quality.

It was the introduction in 1893 of the variety 'Up-to-date' and its subsequent popularity which gave rise to the Scotch seed trade outside Great Britain. This outstanding variety became a great favourite abroad, especially in South Africa, where the demand for fresh and healthy stocks led to the export of large quantities of seed from Scotland. Between the two great wars, most of the potato-growing areas on either side of the Mediterranean which supplied the early market in Great Britain, adopted a like policy, whilst distant parts of the Empire also renewed their stocks every few years by the import of Scotch seed. Prior to 1839 the greater part of the demand outside Great Britain was confined to but a few varieties. 'King Edward' for Spain and North Africa; 'Champion' for Malta; 'Up-to-date' and 'Majestic' for South Africa and Australia, and 'Royal Kidney' for the Canaries, Portugal, Italy, Algeria and South America. Small quantities of the varieties 'Epicure', 'Arran Banner', 'Great Scot', and 'Kerr's Pink' were also exported.

Whilst the Scotch seed potato industry is, in the main, one of export, the ware crop is largely consumed at home. The production of ware has been dictated in the main by soil conditions and by local demand. The best potato soils, and the finest land generally, are to be found to the west of the country lying south of the Clyde and the Forth, and to the east of that north of the Forth, and it is there that its cultivation flourishes. Some localities have achieved a special place in the public estimation for the excellence of their potatoes. Such is the case with the Dunbar region where the tubers are generally large and well shaped and acquire from the adherent fine red soil a characteristic and pleasing appearance,

[1] See chapter X, p. 173.

which may proclaim their origin but which cannot without further proof be accepted as evidence of high quality.[1] Nevertheless, public opinion has for one hundred years and more sanctioned a superior price for the Dunbar potato in the English market. The ware from the large potato areas in the Lothians, Lanarkshire and Dumfriesshire, serves Edinburgh and Glasgow and the industrial centres of the Clyde. Dumfriesshire seed potatoes mainly go to the south. The value of the crop in the eastern potato-growing districts accounts for from 20% to 30% of the total production of the farms, whilst on the cattle-feeding farms it is but 5%. In the Border area it is still lower.

Prior to 1939 the area under potatoes in Scotland was declining. It had reached its maximum of 189,161 acres in 1881,[2] and by 1939 had fallen to 134,334 acres, although the population had stepped up from $3\frac{1}{2}$ to 5 millions. The average output between 1884 and 1931 was 882,000 tons. McIntosh[3] estimates that the gross production per head of the population in Scotland has declined from 5·8 cwt. in 1867 to 4·1 cwt. in 1939. If we take into consideration how large a proportion of the Scotch crop now leaves Scotland as seed, the decline in home consumption will be much greater than that indicated by the figures of production. Indeed, if the whole crop had been devoted to human food, it would imply a daily consumption of 1·8 lb. in 1867 and 1·2 lb. in 1939.

Prof. Cathcart[4] gives the following estimates for the year 1933:

Rural workers in Angus and Perthshire consume 0·67 lb. per day.

Skilled workers in Glasgow consume 0·60 lb. per day.

All classes of workers in St Andrews consume 0·55 lb. per day.

These figures, as well as the gross uncorrected ones, demonstrate a remarkable falling off in consumption during the course of the century.

The Scottish Lowland husbandry has, since the early part of the nineteenth century, been famous for its high standards of cultivation and land management. The impulse which induced the change-over from a peculiarly retrograde form of open-field husbandry, had its origin in the political and economic reactions following on the Union, which were sharply reinforced by the social and political reactions consequent on 1745. The immediate character of the change, however, was derived from the revolutionary Norfolk system of rotation, and the adoption of root crops. In East Anglia, the turnip was the root which was grown almost exclusively for the first eighty years of the new era. In Scotland, the turnip and the potato were introduced nearly simultaneously into

[1] Parker, W. H., Salaman, R. N. and Brandreth, B. *J. Nat. Inst. Agric. Bot.* vol. III, p. 408. Brandreth, B. Ibid. vol. IV, p. 192.

[2] The production during the war-years 1940–5 is excluded, for which see chapter XXXII.

[3] McIntosh, T. P. (1943). Op. cit.

[4] Cathcart, E. P. Quoted from unpublished material by T. P. McIntosh, *Report on the Marketing of Potatoes in Scotland*, p. 24. Dept. of Agric. for Scotland, 1933.

the new rotation, the potato being the earlier, and at first the more widely adopted, and in some localities the one to which most land was devoted. We may therefore say that the Lowland agricultural methods owe their high reputation in no small measure to the introduction in the middle of the eighteenth century of the potato as a field crop.

The story of the potato in Scotland illustrates the argument which has, in fact, been presented earlier in the case of Ireland. Given a backward economic situation, associated with a repressive social system, such as held sway in the Highlands and Western Isles during the eighteenth and first half of the nineteenth centuries, then the potato will act as a depressant of the moral, and ultimately the economic and social status of the entire people. On the other hand, given a *milieu*, such as that which held in the major part of the Lowlands in the latter quarter of the eighteenth century, in which there is opportunity for free and dynamic movement in economic and social spheres, then the potato plays only a small part in the moulding of the structure of that society but, fulfilling its true mission, serves as a valuable dietetic asset in the life of all classes of the people.

In the Lowlands, the potato was not imposed from above, but established itself partly because it was admirably suited to a peasantry, rapidly passing from the stage of small communal holders into landless labourers, and also because, as a crop, it fitted into and helped to fortify the new system of husbandry which, during the latter part of the first half of the eighteenth century, had overtaken that part of the country. The steady progress the potato made before the close of the eighteenth century was undoubtedly due to its increasing use as a family food, which followed after its worth as a cleaning and forage crop had first been established. The more dramatic increase which took place between the years 1795 and 1840, was a response to the industrialization of the south, and the consequent growing demands of an urban factory population for larger supplies of food.

CHAPTER XXII

The Potato in Wales

In Wales the history of the potato begins with the usual legend of the shipwreck of a barque from Ireland on the coast, but on this occasion both time and place are uncertain. That it reached this part of the United Kingdom during the seventeenth century is certain; the evidence though scanty, is reliable, and suggests that it gained more than a solitary local lodgement.

The first reference is to be found in Merrett's *Pinax*,[1] the original edition of which was destroyed in the Great Fire of London, so that the earliest extant copies are reprints put out in the following year. In this work occurs the passage: 'Potatoes with white and ash coloured flowers planted in many fields of Wales.' As Merrett was a native of Winchcombe, Gloucestershire, it is not unlikely that he may have visited the nearby lowlands of Monmouthshire and seen them growing there for himself. The same considerations apply to the reference by Worlidge[2] who in his first edition speaks of potatoes 'as in many small Welsh territories adjoining to the highways'. In subsequent editions, the reference to Wales is omitted, which may only mean that they were becoming more common in England itself. Beale[3] in a letter of 1 April 1664 refers to the growing popularity of the potato in Wales and Forster[4] in 1664, remarks that they 'prosper and increase exceedingly in Wales, to which they were brought from Ireland'.

It would be hazardous to deduce from these four references, that the use of the potato was at all general, in seventeenth-century Wales, since it was by no means universal a hundred years later, though most of the conditions which have prompted its adoption elsewhere were to hand. Taylor, the water poet, writing in 1650, and 'W.R.' in *Wallography or the Briton Described*, 1682, make no mention of the potato, though both refer to the people's dietary in some detail: the latter makes amends by dilating on the devotion of the Welsh to toasted cheese, the Welsh rarebit of to-day. The paucity of references to its cultivation in the seventeenth century will surprise no one who has searched the literature for information concerning the domestic life of the Welsh people, whether at that period or later. Up till a hundred years ago, most English writers and

---

[1] Merrett, Christopher (1667). *Pinax Rerum Naturalium Britannicarum.*
[2] Worlidge, J. (1688). *Systema Horticulturae*, p. 163.
[3] Beale, John (1664). MSS. v. Bi. Fol. 39: Royal Society.
[4] Forster, John (1664). *England's Happiness Increased*, p. 14.

travellers knew little or nothing of Wales outside the main ports and towns. Those eighteenth-century travellers, who penetrated farther inland, devoted much of their space to expressions of wonder at the wild beauty of mountain and stream, and surprise at the splendour of the few great houses of the nobility; but about the lives and customs of the 'mere' people, they are reticent; nor has modern research, as yet, done much to fill the gap. There is, however, some indirect evidence which suggests that at least in some parts of Celtic-speaking Wales, the potato was well known at the opening of the eighteenth century. In an English-Welsh Dictionary by John Roderick of Shrewsbury published in 1725[1] the word 'Pyttatws' occurs, which shows that the word 'Potato' had by that time acquired the characteristic Welsh plural form and was a colloquial term. Dr E. G. Bowen of Aberystwyth informs me that the earliest use of this word in Welsh literature is in a poem of 1763, describing household life, but it offers no clue as to whether it was grown in field or garden.

How little known it was in the early eighteenth century in Caernarvonshire, appears from the following tale: 'A person in 1805 heard an old man, who, had he been living would have been 104 years old, say that when a boy he had seen a couple of potatoes brought to his father's house in Llanbedrog and that the man who brought them told the people present that they were eatable. Some present bit them and finding them nauseous threw them away. This was the first root of that kind seen in Lleyn,'[2] and the date would be about 1710.

Prior to the nineteenth century, Welsh agriculture was almost entirely pastoral; mountain sheep and black cattle were and, except that the latter have been largely replaced by Herefords, still are raised in great numbers in the hill-country and exported to England. Even in Anglesey only one-eleventh of the cultivated land was under cereals, very little wheat was grown, and only such oats and barley as was needed for home consumption.[3] In most of the Principality, especially in the hill-country, the arable land, of which there was never very much, was enclosed, following the policy initiated as a result of Henry VIII's Act of Union in 1536. However, Norden's *Survey of Wrexham* made in 1620 shows that the open field with its multiple owners and occupiers of quillets was still functioning.[4] In districts lying in the south, east and north-eastern parts of Wales below the 600 ft. level, where the Norman manorial system had made itself felt, a few open arable fields persisted for nearly 200 years longer and were not all enclosed until the end of the eighteenth century.

[1] I am indebted to Prof. G. J. Williams of Cardiff for this information.
[2] Fenton, Richard (1804–13). *Tours in Wales*, p. 331. Bedford Press.
[3] Davies, Walter (1810). *General View of Agriculture in North Wales*, p. 140.
[4] Palmer, Alfred Neobard (1883). *The Town, Fields and Folk of Wrexham*. Manchester: Henry Gray.

In Wales it has been stated that, neither the right of common pasturage over the autumn stubbles, nor the necessity of limiting any given field to one type of spring or autumn crop existed;[1] in consequence there should have been nothing to hinder the planting of the potato in the open field if such were desired. We have, however, no direct evidence that this occurred. It would seem that this rule cannot have been in force throughout the country, for in Caernarvonshire the unprotected state of the arable fields is given as an excuse for the absence of turnips and green crops.[2]

On the other hand, an interesting custom reminiscent of the old open-field days survives, or did till lately, in many parts of Wales. Labourers, and even strangers, were allowed to plant two or three rows of potatoes in a farmer's field, in return for help during harvest. Dr Peate[3] tells how his father had a few rows in each of three farms; the farmer did the planting and the latter the lifting, and that in return both he and his father would help in the harvest, together with a number of men and women who had otherwise no connection with the farm.

The majority of the eighteenth-century enclosures were contemporaneous with the great movement proceeding in England, but in Wales it was almost entirely concerned with the commons and uncultivated waste lands, the loss of which was deeply resented by the peasantry. The commons had served the people in good stead for the pasture of their stock throughout the last 300 years and, what was not less important, large numbers of peasants had become 'squatters' and had established themselves permanently on these common lands. Towards the end of the century, it had been quite usual for peasants to filch small pieces from the commons, for use as potato patches. So well recognized was this type of encroachment, that in 1800 an Act of Parliament was presented, which proposed to relegate portions of the commons to the cottagers for this purpose. It was supported by Wilberforce but hotly opposed by Sir Watkin William Wynn as 'a violation of property big with the greatest mischiefs'.[4] The commons duly passed into the hands of the big landlords.

The customary system of gavelkind which had been in force prior to Henry's intervention, had led to a subdivision of the land into small parcels, which was one, and not the least important, factor in preserving Wales as a land of peasants, as opposed to the system which developed across the border, where great estates and large farms were served by

---

[1] Gray, Howard Levi (1915). *English Field System*, p. 202. Harvard University Press.

[2] Evans, J. (1812). *The Beauties of England and Wales*, vol. XVII, p. 325.

[3] Peate, Ionerth (1941). Keeper of Department of Folk Culture, Cardiff, in a letter communicated by Principal J. Rees, Cardiff University, to R.N.S.

[4] Dodd, A. H. (1933). *The Industrial Revolution in North Wales*, p. 80.

a class of workers, for the most part landless. The Welsh peasantry from the seventeenth century onwards, were not freeholders but tenants, between whom and their landlords there was very little in common. An estrangement between the classes which grew up as a legacy of the spoliation of the monasteries,[1] developed into an increasingly wide economic and cultural barrier, which was fostered by that spirit of independence which the spread of Nonconformity did so much to strengthen. In the eighteenth century and probably earlier, in addition to the smallholders, there existed a class of 'free workers' who often passed with the farm almost like heirlooms; they were paid very largely in kind, in which the potato patch on the farmers' holding played an important part.[2]

The standard of living throughout Wales, as is usual in a pastoral peasant community, had for centuries been stabilized at a low level and remained the same, till the coming of the railways. The black huts built of mud and clay, generally devoid of chimney and with no glass to the windows, served both master and man. In fact the housing of the working-class community in Wales was nearly as bad as that obtaining in Ireland and certainly far behind that ruling in England, at the end of the eighteenth century; and how bad that was, is not generally appreciated. Everything they wore, as well as all about the house, was either the work of their own hands or that of the village tradesmen.

If one is to believe the accounts which have come down to us,[3] the sixteenth-century Welsh peasantry enjoyed an abundance of everything, including meats of all kinds. In the next century there was either a serious falling off, or our authorities are more accurate, but even so, the Welsh workers were probably better fed than their fellows in England or Scotland. Evidence for this may be found in the fact that till the eighteenth century the old Poor Law remained a dead letter. As Davies says, 'there was poverty but little pauperism'.[4]

In the eighteenth century, if the housing was lamentable, the food was still generally abundant, with plenty of milk, cheese and eggs, barley bread and bacon broth, and in the small neatly cultivated gardens, potatoes were generally to be found.[5] Such, at least, we are assured, was the condition in 1775 of the peasantry in the vale of Glamorgan and

[1] Lloyd, Sir J. E. (1935). *A History of Carmarthenshire*, p. 268. Quotes in full W. Vaughan's *Golden Grove* (1608).
[2] Jones, Evan J. (1928). *Some Contribution to the Economic History of Wales*, p. 22. London.
[3] Owen, George (1552–1613). Quoted by Davies, D. J. (1933), *The Economic History of South Wales*, p. 83.
[4] Davies, D. J. (1933). *The Economic History of South Wales*, pp. 79 et seq.
[5] Warner, Rev. Richard (1798). *A Second Walk through Wales*. 2nd edit. 1800, pp. 60 and 187.

the Merionethshire mountains of Dinas Mawdwy.[1] From the accounts of Walter Davies in 1810, it would appear to have been much the same throughout North Wales. It was even true for South Wales before 1790, where the Welsh labourers' money wage was lower than that current in England, owing to the custom of payment in kind, in which the potato played a foremost part. The available cash for purchase of goods was always very low. We hear of labourers in Pembrokeshire receiving three good meals a day in the farm-house, in which doubtless potatoes were a part, and, in addition, a money wage of 3*d*. per day in winter and 4*d*. in summer.[2] It is not long since, when 'potatoes with butter milk', and 'potatoes with butter' were household dishes in all Welsh peasant farmers' homes.

The Welsh social and economic background was in certain respects peculiar. It was essentially a community of peasants and smallholders, the tenants of landlords with whom their relations were rarely sympathetic or intimate; as a result there grew up a radically self-conscious form of nationalism. The best lands were enclosed, but up to the nineteenth century the large areas of common and waste afforded free pasturage for their cattle. The landless labourer was the exception, and even he had generally the use of a garden. The mountainous character of most of the country and the very poor communications, induced a high degree of communal isolation. Agriculture, apart from the export of cattle and sheep, was on a subsistence basis; the standard of its husbandry was of the lowest, embodying the sins of the runrig system without its virtues, thus allowing the small-holder to neglect the land as much as he pleased. Towards the end of the eighteenth century there were signs of a new spirit stirring in favoured districts, but it did not make much headway till the end of the first quarter of the nineteenth century.

In such an environment, it was to be expected that the potato would have every chance of being grown in the home plot for immediate use of the family, and scarcely any of being raised in the field. This indeed proved to be the case, and so firmly was this distinction entrenched, that it gave a specific and lasting character to the cultivation of the potato in Wales, the reflection of which was to be observed in the reaction of Wales to the demand for more potatoes in the recent war.

Apart from work on the land, the peasant family was helped out by the produce of spinning-wheel and loom, and the knitting of stockings. A cottage industry in woollens which had not varied in character since Tudor times, was common throughout Wales during the eighteenth

[1] Cullum, Sir Thomas Gery (*c.* 1775). A recently found Diary. Communicated to me by Dr E. G. Bowen, Aberystwyth.
[2] Warner, Rev. Richard (1798). Op. cit. pp. 187 and 300.

century: it was not large in volume, nor was it so well organized on a capitalistic basis, as the industry had long since been across the border. All the cloth of North Wales was sent to Shrewsbury to be finished; its value in the middle of the eighteenth century was about £100,000, as compared with £2,000,000, the value of the Yorkshire woollens.

The progress of the potato, in the eighteenth and early nineteenth centuries, illustrates how nearly balanced were the forces engaged. It is not surprising, that in a description of Wales published in 1724, the potato is not even mentioned.[1] In Anglesey, possibly owing to the level ground and the rich soil, the potato became established earlier and more firmly than elsewhere.

The Diary of Edward Wynne, an Anglesey squire (1681–1757) who lived at Boderwyd, where he was known as a notable pioneer in agricultural matters, records how he grew a variety of crops in the field, including hops, potatoes and turnips; the latter he had grown since the year 1714. Wynne bought his potato seed from Ireland via Liverpool and in 1730 it is recorded that he had three 'Potato gardens'.[2]

In the household accounts of the Henblas Estate in the same county,[3] potatoes are mentioned twice about the year 1732, but in each case they were received as presents. This does not necessarily imply that they were scarce or even luxuries at the time, for there existed a custom, which persons living in 1814 recalled, of sending potatoes from house to house on All Saints' Eve as presents for a national repast.[4] At Henblas in 1749 they were probably confined to the gardens, for neither potatoes nor turnips are recorded on the estate as field crops. Nevertheless they must have been gradually growing in public favour, for one of the Henblas correspondents writes from London complaining, amongst much else, that he misses the potatoes and milk he enjoyed in his Welsh home. Without doubt both Wynne and the Squire of Henblas were, agriculturally, in advance of their small farmer neighbours. In 1740 potatoes were sold retail in Anglesey usually for 4½d. to 5d. but occasionally for as much as 7d. per peck, which was considered a very high price. We may usefully compare these prices with those in Yorkshire, where in 1734 they fetched 2d. per peck,[5] which would suggest that in Wales the potato had not by then attained the popularity it achieved in the north of England. Moreover, those bought in the market were destined for the tables of the upper classes.

[1] Moll, Herman (1724). *New Description of England and Wales.*
[2] Jones, Francis (1940). A Squire of Anglesey. *Trans. Anglesey Antiq. Soc.* p. 76.
[3] Evans, Nesta G. (1936). *Social Life in Mid-Eighteenth Century Anglesey.* Cardiff.
[4] Davies, Walter (1814). *A General View of the Agriculture, etc., of South Wales,* p. 504.
[5] Evans, Nesta G. (1936). Op. cit. p. 151.

It is obvious that in Anglesey by about 1730 the potato had established itself firmly in the households of the well-to-do. Owing to bad seasons, potatoes were in 'great asking' in 1735, and for the next few years people were prepared to pay from 9*d*. to 1*s*. 4*d*. for a 'cibbin', or half bushel, which was regarded as an 'extraordinary price'. It was probably some decades later before they became, as they were in 1800, the food of the poor, a development which the absence of any organized Poor Relief tended to accelerate.[1]

Caernarvonshire was not far behind Anglesey in the matter of potato cultivation: the story is told in *The Beauties of England and Wales*:[2]

The raising of that useful root, the potatoe, is coming into fashion; and several parts of the county grow considerable quantities. Previous to the year 1758, Mr Pennant remarks, all the district of Nant Conwy was obliged to import this necessary article; and subsequent to that period, as appears by the Custom books, it has been able to spare a large surplus for exportation. This has been the case in the district adjacent to Caernarvon; which a few years since was necessitated to derive its supply from Lancashire; and such has been the extension of this kind of culture, that it is now enabled partially to furnish Liverpool, where Welsh potatoes obtain a preference in the market, for their superior flavour.

In Brecknockshire, certain of the gentry founded a Society for the improvement of agriculture in 1755: its foremost policy was the introduction of turnips, as a result of which they 'succeeded in promoting the more extensive growth of clover and potatoes'.[3]

In the six weeks' tour undertaken in 1767, Arthur Young[4] visited the south of Glamorgan: he observed that the country folk had excellent beds of potatoes in their gardens and advised that they should extend its cultivation to the fields which it had not then reached.

In the north, at Hawarden, it would appear that the people were not so well provided with potatoes. A mill-stone with the following inscription was lately unearthed there, which tells its own tale. 'This Mill was built in A.D. 1767 by Sir John Glynne, Bart., Lord of the Manor.... Wheat was in this year at 9*s*. and Barley at 5*s*. 6*d*. a bushel. Luxury was at a great height and Charity extensive, But the poor were Starving, Riotous and Hanged.'[5]

It is of interest that some short time prior to Young's visit to Glamorganshire, an English farmer had been ridiculed by his neighbours for planting a couple of acres of turnips[6]—which looks as if the usual order

[1] In 1745 they reached 1*s*. per peck, probably as a result of the Jacobite disturbances.
[2] Evans, Rev. J. (1812). *The Beauties of England and Wales*, vol. XVII, p. 325.
[3] Rees, Thomas (1815). *The Beauties of England and Wales*, vol. XVIII, p. 58.
[4] Young, Arthur (1768). *A Six Weeks' Tour.*
[5] Dodd, A. H. (1933). *Industrial Revolution in North Wales*, p. 379.
[6] Russell, P. (1769). *England Displayed*, p. 288.

of precedence had been reversed, and it was the potato which opened
the way for the turnip.

Sir Thomas Gery Cullum notes, in the Dinas Mawdwy district of
Merionethshire, 'the neat little well packed gardens. Potatoes much
cultivated in them'.[1]

In Montgomery potatoes are said to have gained a foothold in the
early part of the eighteenth century: in 1769 they were being sold at
2s. 4d. per bushel, or £4. 13s. 3d. per ton, a high price for those times.

Young visited Wales again in 1776.[2] Landing at Milford Haven, he
made his way eastward via Carmarthen, Brecon and Monmouth to
Mitchels Dean. He found that potato cultivation had of late greatly
increased. The poor lived on them and every garden had its plot of
potatoes, usually planted on the lazy-bed system. In the towns they
were on sale at prices varying from 1s. 4d. to 2s. 6d. a bushel.

In Glamorgan potatoes, which were widely grown in the latter part
of the eighteenth century, were commonly held responsible for the decay
of the orchards, which had occurred a couple of generations earlier in
that county. Edward Williams, better known by his bardic name, Iolo
Morganwg, used to tell how, years back, an Irish vessel was wrecked on
the coast, and the beach strewn with potatoes. The people were so
pleased with these novel roots that they dug up their orchard ground
and planted potatoes between the trees. As time went on, they neglected
the trees in favour of the potatoes, which were supposed to have exhausted the land to such a degree, as to bring about the decay of the
trees.[3] The tale may seem fanciful, but a very similar process actually
took place in Jersey in the early sixties of last century. In any case, it
shows how impressed the peasant folk were by the sudden arrival in
their midst, of an entirely new type of food.

In some parts of the Principality it was not grown at all, and elsewhere
it remained essentially a garden crop,[4] helping to furnish out, but in no
way dominate, the dietary of the family. Towards the end of the century,
a change in economic conditions set in: modern methods of husbandry
were introduced; especially in the south, turnip, rape and cole seed now
began to be grown in the field.[5]

The county of Anglesey illustrates the first phase of the change:

They were first cultivated on a large scale in the last quarter of the eighteenth
century, when the herring fisheries fell off; and during the same period con-

[1] Cullum, Sir T. Gery (1775). MSS. Diary, Nat. Lib., Aberystwyth. Communicated
by Dr E. G. Bowen to R.N.S.
[2] Young, A. (1776). Tour in Wales. London School Econ. Reprints, No. 14.
[3] Waring, Elijah (1850). Recollections and Anecdotes of Edward Williams, p. 12.
London.
[4] Henry, David (1771). The Practical Farmer, p. 275.
[5] Davies, D. J. (1933). The Economic History of South Wales, p. 89. Cardiff.

siderable quantities were shipped from Conway. Landlords and farmers gradually acquired the habit of planting them as a regular field crop not merely to supply their own tables. Labourers who were lucky enough to own a garden, or could get permission for a trifling payment, to plant in the farmers' fallows, found in the potato crop a useful supplement to wages and a standby in time of unemployment.[1]

That there was no acute economic pressure as yet, urging their use, is shown by an unpublished note prepared for the Board of Agriculture in 1800 by Iolo Morganwg who, in private life, was a land surveyor:

Potato crops, however plausible in theory, can never be generally cultivated, for there would be no consumption for them, they are a very perishable produce and Bristol, Swansea and other places can always be more cheaply supplied with [them] from Ireland, Scotland, Lancashire, etc., than from any part of Wales. In Glamorgan the markets are sufficiently supplied from the gardens of cottages only. What hopes then for a potato farmer? In Cardiganshire, where they are necessary as a wheat fallow, they are so cheap that cottagers no longer cultivate them.[2]

In Brecknockshire, both potatoes and turnips were well established as field crops in the south and south-eastern part of the county, early in the nineteenth century.[3] In Snowdonia the peasantry lived simply, wisely, and extremely well—milk, cheese, barley or oat-bread, goats' flesh, with potatoes as a constant dish,[4] and in the Laugharne district of Carmarthen, bread was made of barley, and potatoes and butter-milk were looked on merely as additional foodstuffs.[5] Here, at the end of the eighteenth century, bread and potatoes were regarded as the natural food of the poor.[6]

It would seem that the life of the people as a whole was in no serious danger of being moulded on a dietetic regime standardized by the potato, although the destitute poor of the country at this time depended almost entirely on barley bread and potatoes.[7]

Thirty years later, this was still true for much of Wales; the counties of Caernarvon, Merioneth and Cardigan were, between the years of 1821 and 1853, not inquired into by the Parliamentary Commission, because 'they were self-sufficient; barley bread, leek broth, cheese, pork, potatoes, cabbage and herrings were their food', and the vicissitudes of wheat

---

[1] Dodd, A. H. (1933). *The Industrial Revolution in North Wales*, p. 49.
[2] Edward Williams (Morganwg, Iola) (1800). MS. note discovered by G. J. Williams, Cardiff University, and communicated by him to R.N.S.
[3] Rees, Thomas (1815). *The Beauties of England and Wales*, vol. XVIII, p. 52.
[4] Williams, E. (1816). *Cambria Depicted*, p. 131.
[5] Donovan, Edward (1805). *Excursions through South Wales*, p. 237.
[6] Board of Agriculture (1795). *Report Committee on Culture and Use of Potatoes*.
[7] Eden, Sir Frederick (1797). *The State of the Poor*, abridged edition, 1928, p. 103.

farming did not affect their slow emergence from very primitive agrarian conditions.[1]

The Industrial Era

The mountains of Wales, pasture ground from the dawn of history for the flocks and herds of her people, in large measure dictated the national way of life until the end of the eighteenth century. Nor were the rich treasures below the surface long denied her, for many hundreds of years, coal, copper, lead, silver, and even gold, had been won from the northern hills. It was not until the early part of the eighteenth century, that the mining and allied industries seriously affected the tenor of life in the Principality. Then it was that the iron industry, which had migrated from southern England, took on its main development in South Wales; later with the advent of machinery, the copper mines of the north were exploited, on a large scale, and coal was recovered in ever greater quantities and exported to Lancashire. But even this had but little effect on the Welsh people as a whole, for except in the slate quarries, the majority of the miners were imported from England. Moreover, these enterprises in North Wales never attained large dimensions and were financially very unstable.

In the south, the latter half of the century witnessed an economic industrial development, based on the great coal and iron fields of northern Glamorganshire and Monmouthshire. Nevertheless throughout the greater part of the eighteenth century Wales remained pre-eminently an agricultural country whose internal economy was closely adapted to peasant needs. An industrial proletariat, however, was in the making, though not yet big enough to determine either the tempo or character of the social development of the whole.

The Industrial Revolution which had overtaken England nearly half a century earlier, was only now preparing to gather Wales into her embrace. As yet villages had not swollen into towns, nor had the Rhonda Valley been converted into a continuous alley of sordid dwellings. The demand for more extensive supplies of food was beginning to make itself heard, the day of the potato was imminent.

If the material side of life in Wales had stagnated, that of the spirit and intellect had progressed and acquired a distinctive character. The translation in the second half of the seventeenth century into Welsh of the Litany and the New Testament brought a new light into the sombre homes, from which religious enthusiasm has never departed. On this foundation just a hundred years later was modelled a system of public education which was so eagerly accepted that by 1761 one-third of the

[1] Clapham, J. H. (1926). *Econ. Hist. Railway Age*, p. 136, quoting S.C. on Agric. 1833, Q. 175.

population could read the Scriptures in Cymric. From that time the cause of Welsh education never looked back.

Those who have read the chapters on Ireland and the Highlands will recognize that the picture of the Welsh countryside in the eighteenth century contained many of the elements which in those countries favoured a potato-controlled economy. An impoverished small-holding peasantry, enclosed lands, mean homes, poor communications, and an almost complete lack of monetary resources, all were present. Against its domination there were powerful defences, both material and spiritual; of the former, the most potent was a supply of good, if simple food, adequate for the agricultural and industrial population of the day; of the latter, an awakened interest in religion, accompanied by an educational renaissance. Still more important was the absence of political domination by an alien upper class, such as had bedevilled Ireland, or of an highly developed hereditary and feudal control, such as had dominated the Scottish Highlands. Indeed, in this latter respect the Welsh were possibly better off than the English.

In Ireland, as in the Highlands, each of these political systems had created an unbridgeable gulf between the dominant class and the people of the soil. Materially and spiritually starved, their people fell easy victims to an economy controlled by the cheapest available food, the potato.

Wales had escaped both these political dangers, so that when in mid-nineteenth century, she embarked in the south, on a vast industrial development, the standard of life was, at least, not jeopardized from the start. However, its immunity was not for long: the fluctuation of trade during and after the Napoleonic wars, together with the high prices and general shortage of food during them, reduced the industrial workers, especially in the south, to hunger and misery. These found expression for their discontents in strikes and riots which abated with the passage of the Reform Bill in 1832, only to be renewed and intensified throughout the next ten years when Chartism in its most violent form inspired the hungry workers.

There is no doubt that at the beginning of the nineteenth century Wales was a very long way behind England in respect to her agriculture. There were vast areas of unenclosed 'wastes' in the hill-country, and it was here that squatters had established themselves, with the aid of the potato. The wholesale enclosures which took place between 1790 and 1815 led to the eviction of the more recent of this class, who could not afford to buy their plots. The change seriously affected the poor, who had maintained themselves very largely on their potato-patch and were now left to be supported in public institutions.

Wales was thus far less prepared to deal with an industrial revolution than was England, fifty years earlier; she had developed no large-scale arable farming capable of producing the food required for her growing towns. But when large-scale industry did get under way, it was the potato crop which showed the greatest capacity to expand in relation to the call for abundant and cheap food.

By the middle of the nineteenth century, changes in the agricultural methods occurred: the county of Caernarvon went over almost completely to sheep, so that it is reported 'scarcely a grain of corn or a potato patch were to be seen'. On the other hand, in the district of Ruthin potatoes were replacing turnips in the field rotation, and at Cador Idris they had become the most important crop and were often grown three times in succession.[1]

In Wales generally, potato-raising was a matter for the home: every household had its garden plot or a potato-patch for use in the kitchen and the yard, a practice which persists amongst all farms, however small, the produce being rarely sold abroad. Allotments were not popular because they were not needed.[2] The result was a low standard of living, but little hunger. The miners, quarrymen and industrial workers of Denbighshire and Flintshire generally had their own potato-patch, but their margin of safety was a narrow one. The Poor Law Commission of 1834 reported that although work was then plentiful, labourers could only just maintain a family by living on potatoes, oatmeal, milk and little else.[3]

Although the potato has never completely dominated the economy of the Welsh home, it won for itself in the minds of the people a unique position second only to that of bread, in the composition of which, it was not to be denied, for the Welsh housewife still adds a portion of potatoes to her dough. The Welsh Department of Agriculture, in its 'Dig for Victory' campaign, tried hard to bring about a modification of the Welsh view that the potato is first amongst the vegetables, with cabbages and onions coming second, and the rest nowhere. How far it will succeed, remains to be seen.

Since the beginning of this century, a change has taken place in regard to potato-growing in Wales; indeed it began to be noticeable during the last decades of the eighteenth century. The official Ministry of Agriculture's returns, which do not concern themselves with holdings of under one acre in area, show a steady decline in the acreage under potatoes, except in the war years: In 1866 the acreage in thousands was 47·5; in 1900 it had fallen to 34·7; in 1905 to 30·5; in 1914 to 26·0; in

[1] Rowlandson, Thomas (1846). The Agriculture of North Wales. *J. Roy. Agric. Soc.* vol. VII, p. 533.
[2] Clapham, J. H. (1932). *Econ. Hist. Modern Britain*, vol. II, p. 288.
[3] Dodd, A. H. (1933). *The Industrial Revolution in North Wales*, p. 368.

1925 to 23·6; in 1930 to 20·6; in 1935 to 18·2; and in 1939 to 16·6. After seventy-five years, only a third of the original acreage under potatoes remained.

Thus, whilst the population of Wales was increasing, the area under potatoes was no less rapidly falling, so that as compared with some seventy-five years ago, there is to-day but about one-sixth the area per individual devoted to the potato.

Except for parts of Glamorgan, Carmarthen, Denbigh and Flint, Wales, neither by its soil nor the economic outlay of its farms, offers favourable conditions for large-scale cultivation of the crop. The farms are small, and with the change over to grass at the latter end of the nineteenth century, have lost much of their labour—without which, potatoes cannot be raised as a field crop. The great industrial centres of Wales are now dependent for their supply of potatoes on imports in part from Ireland and Scotland, but in the main from the Eastern Counties of England.

In the war period, the potato acreage shot up to 67,000 acres in 1944, i.e. four times that of the pre-war years. In this great effort, all the counties took an honourable part. Although the largest acreages were supplied by the counties of Pembroke, Carmarthen, Cardigan and Glamorgan, they are amongst those in which the relative increase over pre-war cultivation was the least. It is in the mountainous counties of Brecon, Montgomery and Radnor that the highest relative increases occurred. Monmouthshire is an exception: here, the increase in the potato acreage, greater than elsewhere, was sevenfold, as against sixfold in Brecon and fivefold in Radnor and Montgomery.

These war figures are instructive, for they throw light on what had been taking place when the Welsh potato acreage began to fall. War, with its demand for home-grown food, brought into cultivation once more the marginal hillside lands which, before the days of peace and cheap imported food, had been just worth cultivating for potatoes. In Monmouthshire a reverse process took place: a county of rich valley lands, it had specialized in dairy farming, sheep grazing and orchards; to meet the demands of war, the wholesale conversion of pasture land to arable occurred, which allowed of an increase in potato acreage from 885 acres in 1939 to 6,589 acres in 1944.

The cause of the fall by 50% in the potato acreage of Wales since the beginning of this century still remains somewhat of a puzzle. A change of agricultural policy was inevitable when it was clear that potato prices did not share in the financial recovery which followed the revival of agriculture after the depression of the nineties. The reduction in the farm population has doubtless been an important factor, and access to cheap imported food still more so. Possibly outweighing both, is the decrease in arable, following the practice of leaving the grasslands down instead of ploughing them every three to five years, and taking one or two crops of potatoes off them.[1]

A comparison of the disposition of the area under potatoes in Wales and England, brings to light a characteristic difference between the two countries.

In England, the annual area under potato cultivation as estimated by the Ministry of Agriculture differs from that of the Potato Marketing Board in that it always exceeds the latter by about 10%. This difference is due to the fact that the Board takes cognizance only of potato areas of one acre and over, whilst the Ministry includes all potato areas over quarter of an acre, gardens and allotments excluded, so long as they are included in holdings of an acre or over. Hence the difference of about 40,000 acres in England represents the total of small field plots under one acre in area. The corresponding figures for Wales are entirely different. The Ministry Reports for 1939 account for 16,671 acres; that of the Board for only 5,324 acres. That is to say, the small field plots of under an acre in Wales, exclusive of gardens, forms two-thirds of the total potato acreage of the principality. This peculiar distribution is of course linked up with the character of Welsh land tenure and social economy. It expresses in a striking manner the essential difference between the two countries; England, the country of the capitalist farmer, served by landless labourers, and Wales a country of peasant proprietors carrying on in the main a system of subsistence farming. The Welsh distinction long antedates the coming of the potato, though the latter lent itself readily to its perpetuation.

Seed Production

Between the two wars, a small but well-designed potato seed industry has been developed in Wales which owes its origin to the untiring efforts of Prof. T. Whitehead, Agricultural Botanist of Bangor. Having by careful and scientifically controlled surveys of suitable districts, selected such as were freest from green-fly infestation, he proceeded to induce the farmers in each chosen district to combine and form local seed-raising associations, whose task is to grow very carefully, high-grade seed relatively free from virus infection, derived originally from Scotland, and to maintain the subsequent generations in a state of health. The work began in the neighbourhood of Bangor with a couple of varieties, 'Kerr's Pink' and 'Great Scot': since then, the range of varieties has been extended, and the number of stations increased.

---

[1] I am indebted to Prof. T. Whitehead of Bangor for many of the facts relating to present-day affairs.

Inspection of the growing crops is rigorously maintained. The latest returns show a remarkable advance during the war period:

Seed Association	1939 acreage	1945 acreage
North Wales	110	424
Crymmych (Pembrokeshire)	200	294
Brecon and Radnor	nil	199
Powysland (Montgomery and Merioneth)	nil	204
	310	1,121

Hitherto the seed has been sold for local use; the further expansion of the scheme cannot fail to raise the ware crop returns per acre, as well as to bring economic benefit to the farming community of the Principality.

CHAPTER XXIII

The Potato of Shakespeare and the Jacobeans

The fact that it is necessary to devote a chapter to the references made by the Elizabethan and Jacobean dramatists to the potato, demands a few words of explanation.

Long before our potato (*Solanum tuberosum*) reached these shores, the sweet-potato had been imported from Spain and sold in London, mainly as a candied sucket, but also as a fresh vegetable. It was a luxury only to be enjoyed by the wealthy who, regarding it as a potent aphrodisiac, were ready to pay exorbitant prices for it. This embarrassing reputation which incidentally had no basis in fact, was firmly established in the public mind and shared by men of learning, as well as physicians, before the end of the sixteenth century. Though fully exploited by the dramatists of the period, it was not they who were responsible for its creation.

Harrison, as early as 1577, speaks of 'the potato and such venerous roots as are brought out of Spaine, Portingale and the Indies to furnish up our bankets'.[1]

In a book of 1596 devoted to housewifely recipes for kitchen and sick room we find:[2]

To make a tart that is a courage to a man or woman.
Take two Quinces and two or three Byrre roots and a Potaton, pare your potaton and scrape your roots and put them in a pint of wine and let them boyle till they bee tender and put in an ounce of Dates, and when they be boiled tender draw them through a strainer, wine and all and then put in the yolks of eight eggs and the braynes of three or four cocke-sparrows, and strain them into the other and a little rose-water and seeth them all with sugar cinamons and gynger and cloves and mace and put in a little sweet butter and set it upon a chaffing dish of coles between two platters and so let it boyle till it is something bigge.

Venner, a physician deeply interested in hygiene and dietetics, in 1620 ascribed nutritive and strengthening qualities of the highest order to the potato.[3] In the 1650 edition of the same work, it is not only clear that he has the common potato in mind, but he takes occasion to add to its other virtues 'and incite to venus', which had previously been the attribute of the Spanish sweet-potato.

---

[1] Harrison, William (1577). *Description of England*, bk. II (Furnivall edit.), New Shakespeare Soc. 1877, p. 149.
[2] Dawson, Thomas (1596). *The Good Huswife's Jewell*, p. 20.
[3] Venner, Tobias (1620). *Via Recta ad Vitam Longam*, p. 20.

The sweet-potato of Spain was not the only, nor perhaps the chief aphrodisiac known at this period, but it was rarely omitted from a dish intended to 'excite venus'.

It is by no means clear why nor where the sweet-potato acquired this character. Its shape, which is often of a somewhat elongated ovoid character, might possibly suggest the likeness of a phallus, seeing that such fantasies are never difficult to conjure up, if the desire so to do is present, but it is doubtful if that is the real basis of the myth. If the shape of a vegetable were the determining factor, then the carrot should have earned a like reputation centuries earlier, but it has escaped that distinction. The idea would seem more likely to have arisen from the fact that the employment of aphrodisiacs and the circumstances in which they were indulged, were only available to the wealthy; such agents were expensive. A rare and costly luxury, especially when imported from abroad, would for these reasons, if no other, tend to acquire exotic attributes. Such conceits were not unknown in our own generation, as witness the oysters and champagne of pre-war *Jeunesse-dorée*.

Shakespeare refers twice to the potato. Thus Falstaff exclaims: 'my doe with the black scut! Let the sky rain potatoes; let it thunder to the tune of "Green Sleeves", hail kissing-comfits, and snow eringoes; let there come a tempest of provocation, I will shelter me here.'[1] When Shakespeare speaks of the sky raining potatoes, it may well be that he had in mind the dried sliced and sugared potato suckets pouring down on their heads, rather than fresh tubers the size of a man's fist. On the other hand, Thersites uses the coarser and possibly phallic metaphor, in which the whole tuber is evoked: 'How the devil luxury, with his fat rump and potato-finger, tickles these together! Fry lechery, fry!'[2] In both cases the potato is regarded not as a food but solely as an aphrodisiac.

The date of composition of the plays, viz. 1599 and 1602, excludes the idea that it could be other than the sweet-potato (*Ipomoea batatas*) which is intended. In fact there is no reason to suppose that Shakespeare knew of the existence of our potato (*Solanum tuberosum*), for Gerard's description of the latter did not appear until 1597.

In his introduction to *Measure for Measure*,[3] Dr Dover Wilson has an interesting discussion on 'bawdry' in Shakespeare who, he points out, if he envisaged love at its highest, was not blind to its fun or its dangers—with 'a saving grace of coarseness' he could laugh honestly and heartily at its reflection from the lower planes of human nature. But Shakespeare, compared to his contemporaries, is an innocent in this respect, and it is in their writings that we find more frequent and direct references to the licentious connotation of the potato.

---

[1] *The Merry Wives of Windsor*, Act. v, sc. v.   [2] *Troilus and Cressida*, Act v, sc. ii.
[3] Wilson, Dover (1922). Introduction to *Measure for Measure*, p. xviii.

In a 1592 pamphlet describing a dispute between a 'Hee Conycatcher' and a 'Shee Conycatcher', occurs the passage: 'If it were not for whores, potato roots [would] lye deade on their hands.'[1]

Dekker, borrowing from Marston, illustrates the merely lecherous character in the lines:

> Potatoes ike, if you shall lack
> To corroborate the back.[2]

In a translation of Plautus's *Menaechmi* made in the year 1595, on the basis of which Shakespeare is said to have founded his *Comedy of Errors*, a dinner is described which had been ordered by the hero for his mistress: it included oysters, a mary-sole or two, some artichokes and potato roots.

Another allusion to the supposed 'venerous' power of the root, and to its epicurean rank, occurs in one of John Marston's 'Satyres', 1598:

> Valladolid, our Athens, gins to taste
> Of thy rank filth. Camphire and lettuce chaste
> Are clean cashierd, now Sophie ringoes eate
> Candid potatos are Athenians meate.[3]

Athenian meat implies that the potato was the dish of the cultured, not to say pampered epicure, and therefore, caviare to the general. Its use in this connection throws light on a rather obscure passage to be found in *Histrio-Mastix*. This play, the authorship of which in its present form is ascribed to Marston,[4] is supposed to have been a recension made in 1599 of one written by G. Peele (1558–97).[5] In a scene in which 'Plenty' sits enthroned amidst a heap of gold and riches with Bacchus, Plutus and Ceres paying homage, there is discovered a market-stall with a city wife making her purchases:

Wife. Ha' y' any Potatoes?
Seller. The abundance will not quite cost the bringing.
Wife. What's your Cock-sparrows?
Seller. Ther's for a dozen; hold.

The meaning would appear to be—so abundant now are the riches at the disposal of all, that such well-known aphrodisiacs as cock-sparrows and imported sweet-potatoes could be had for a song, implying that in real life they were costly articles of luxury.

In this same comedy, *Histrio-Mastix*, there occurs a play within the play, namely a sketch of Troilus and Cressida. The author returns again

---

[1] Greene, Robert (1592). *A Disputation betweene a Hee Conycatcher and a Shee Conycatcher, whether a thiefe or a whore, is most hurtful in cousanage to the Commonwealth.*

[2] Dekker, Thomas (1612). *If it be not God, the Devil is in it* (ed. John Pearson, Covent Garden, 1873), vol. III, p. 285.

[3] Marston, John (1599). *The Scourge of Villanie*, Satyre III (ed. Halliwell, J. O. 1856), vol. III, p. 257.

[4] Marston, J. (*c.* 1630). *Histrio-Mastix*, Act II, sc. i, ll. 74–9.

[5] Chambers, E. K. (1923). *Elizabethan Stage*, vol. IV, pp. 17–18.

to the old theme—the lust inspiring root. On the stage enters a Roaring Devil with Vice on his back, Iniquity in one hand, and Juventas in the other. They sing:

> Give your scholars degrees, and your lawyer his fees
> And some dice for Sir Petronell Flash;
> Give your courtier grace, and your knight a new case
> And empty their purses of cash.
> Give your play-gull a stool, and my lady her fool,
> And her usher potatoes and marrow;
> But your poet were he dead, set a pot to his head
> And he rises as peart as a sparrow.[1]

The suggestion would seem to be, let each have his normal and expected reward, but for what, if not his folly? The gentleman-usher, a superior flunkey, would welcome the 'venerous' root, and the most dainty of dishes, marrow.

Later writers, in the main, continued to use the potato as a symbol of lechery which took rank in the menu as a costly hors-d'œuvre. But one can observe a gradual change: the physical character of the potato in these allusions assumes a more substantial form; still a luxury, it appears with other more or less exotic articles in the form of a pie, a substantial dish to be served at a banquet. However, it is not till we reach the middle of the seventeenth century that the potato, i.e. the common potato, *Solanum tuberosum*, began to take its place as a normal though expensive article of food in some of the great houses of the rich.

This development is illustrated by the following quotation from Ben Jonson:

Why, I'll make you an instance: your city wives, but observe 'hem, you ha' not more perfect true fools i' the world bred thin they are generally, and yet you see, by the finenesse and delicacie of their Diet diving into the fat capons, drinking your rich wines, feeding on larks, sparrows, potato pies and such good unctious meats how their wits are refined and rarefied.[2]

And again:

I could eate water-gruel with thee a month, for this jest my dear rogue. O by Hercules, 'tis your only dish; above all your potato or oyster pies in the world.[3]

The potato thus invoked by Elizabethan authors, was commonly associated with other reputed aphrodisiacs, particularly eringoes, i.e. candied sea-holly (*Eryngium maritimum*). George Chapman[4] describes

---

[1] Marston, J. Op. cit. Act II, ll. 304–12.
[2] Jonson, Ben (1598). *Every man out of his Humour*, Act II, sc. iii, ll. 51–5.
[3] Jonson, Ben (1601). *Cynthia's Revels*, Act II, sc. ii, ll. 51–5.
[4] Chapman, George (1611). *May Day*, Act II, sc. i, ll. 511–13.

a scene where a lover about to meet his mistress, is provided amongst other things with 'a banquet of oyster-pies, potatoes, skirret[1] roots, eringoes, and divers other whetstones of venery'.

In *The Loyal Subject*, for which Fletcher is considered to be responsible, soldiers disguised as pedlars sing bawdy songs:

> I have fine potatoes,
> Ripe potatoes!
> Will your Lordship please to taste a fine potato?
> 'Twill advance your wither'd state.
> Fill your Honour full of noble itches.[2]

The association of lechery with the potato retained its lodgement in the minds of the dramatists for some decades longer, notwithstanding that both they and their audience were beginning to acquire some knowledge of the common potato and, one would have thought, of its blameless character. The myth still held, and even found its most outspoken expression between 1630 and 1640.

In Fletcher's play *The Elder Brother*, which was probably revised and finished after his death by Massinger in 1637, there occurs the following:

> A Banquet!—Well! potatoes and eringoes
> And, as I take it, cantharides! Excellent!
> A priapism follows; and as I'll handle it
> It shall, old lecherous goat in authority.[3]

The same idea is found in a play of Markham and Machin:

Truly master, I think a marrow-bone pye, candid eringoes, preserved dates, marmalade of Cantharides were much better harbingers; cock sparrows stewed, doves brains or swans pizzles, are very provocative; roasted potatoes or boil'd skerrets are your only lofty dishes, methinks these should fit you better than I can do.[4]

Our authors did not always confine themselves to the theme of the potato as an agent of lechery. It and kindred bodies could give courage in other ways, more particularly by stimulating endeavour and encouraging fortitude. A striking example is to be found in a play of Massinger's, when a special potion is devised for a youth about to undertake an exhausting journey:

> Here, drink it off; the ingredients are cordial,
> And this the true elixir; it hath boil'd
> Since midnight for you. 'tis the quintessence

---

[1] Skirrets or Skerrets: Water parsnip (*Sium sisarum*), cultivated once in Europe, or possibly still, to a very small extent. – Ed.

[2] Fletcher, John (1617). *The Loyal Subject*, Act. III, sc. v.

[3] Fletcher, John (1637). *The Elder Brother*, Act IV, sc. iv.

[4] Markham, Gervase and Machin, Lewis (1608). *The Dumbe Knight*, Act I, sc. i. *Dodsley's Old Plays* (1825), vol. IV, p. 388.

Of five cocks of the game, ten dozen of sparrows,
Knuckles of veal, potatoe-roots, and marrow,
Coral and ambergris: were you two years older,
And I had a wife, or gamesome mistress,
I durst trust you with neither: you need not bait
After this, I warrant you, though your journey's long;
You may ride on the strength of this till to-morrow morning.[1]

In view of the date of the composition, Markham's use of the potato referred to above, might be taken as heralding the transference of the venerous quality from the sweet to the common potato. It is as if the author were saying: 'True all these costly luxuries will excite desire, but for you the common home-grown skirret and potato will suffice.' We find a similar juxtaposition of the potato with a common home-grown vegetable some twelve years later in Burton's *Anatomy of Melancholy*. When inveighing against the use of all vegetables as predisposing to melancholia, Burton admits that some approve of potatoes and parsnips, but all must be corrected for their windiness.[2] The association of the potato with the parsnip, a root growing at that time in every man's garden, might be held as evidence that Burton had in mind the common potato, *Solanum tuberosum*. Against such an assumption is the fact that at that time the home-grown potato cost at least 1s. a pound, equivalent to about 10s. of our money. This, however, cannot be held to exclude its possibility, seeing that the Spanish sweet-potato at the same time cost nearly 3s. a pound.

Should this be the correct interpretation, then Burton is possibly only second to Venner[3] in making the earliest mention in English literature, outside the Herbals, of the common potato.

Hindley[4] thinks it is to our potato that Fletcher referred in the *Loyal Subject*, but that would appear improbable, for at that date it is unlikely that the *S. tuberosum* would have been common enough to be cried in the streets by hawkers, whereas sweet-potatoes certainly were hawked in those days in the neighbourhood of the Royal Exchange, and 'purchased when scarce at no inconsiderable cost, by those who had faith in their alleged properties'.[5] They were probably sold also at the vegetable stalls which were set up in the neighbourhood of St Paul's, and which encroached on the Churchyard until, in 1673, they were ejected, by which time Covent Garden Market had come into existence.

What the hawkers of the Royal Exchange were offering for the most

---

[1] Massinger, Philip (1632). *A New Way to Pay Off Old Debts*, Act II, sc. ii.
[2] Burton, Robert (1621). *Anatomy of Melancholy* (ed. A. R. Shilleto, 1893), vol. I, p. 252.
[3] Venner, T. Op. cit. See above, p. 424.
[4] Hindley, Charles (1881). *History of the Cries of London*.
[5] Banks, Joseph Sir (1805). *Trans. Hort. Soc.* vol. I, p. 8.

part, were 'suckets', or Spanish sugar-plums and slices of candied sweet-potatoes. Fresh tubers of the latter were also imported and offered for sale; indeed Clusius records that he bought some in London in 1581, intending to take them to Vienna, but they rotted before he could plant them.[1] A similar fate befell those purchased by Gerard[2] and planted in his garden.

It is not always easy to distinguish between the lure exerted by the supposedly aphrodisiacal effect of a plant such as the sweet-potato and the desire to enjoy the same because of its rarity. The point is delightfully put by the 'Water Poet':[3]

> So Blackberryes that grow on every bryer,
> Because th' are plenty few men doe desire.
> Spanish potatoes are accounted dainty,
> And English Parsneps are coarse meete, though plenty.
> But if these Berryes or those Rootes were scant,
> They would be thought as rare, through little want,
> That we should eate them, and a price allow,
> As much as Strawberryes, and Potatoes now.
> Why Bread is common, having still our fill:
> We think not on, because we have it still:
> But if we want Bread, then we doe remember
> We want the groundworke of our belly timber.

Whether the sweet-potato was considered at the time a particularly costly luxury, naturally depended on the position of the intending purchaser. Moffett,[4] who had travelled widely in Italy, where he would have encountered the sweet-potato, compiled a book on *Health* in 1595; in it he speaks of potatoes, and from the context it is obvious that he has the sweet-potato in mind. Of these he says: 'Potato Roots are now so common amongst us, that even the husbandman buys them to please his wife. They nourish mightily...engendering much flesh, blood and seed, but withal encreasing wind and lust.' That in itself does not necessarily mean that they were to be bought cheaply, for a class of wealthy farmers living in handsome manor-houses was a feature of the social panorama of the late Tudor period. Moffett's work was corrected and enlarged in 1655, but obviously with no great care on the part of the editor. Whilst it would not have been unreasonable at that date to state that potatoes, implying tubers of *S. tuberosum* 'are now so common amongst us', the same cannot be said of the further comment that

---

[1] Clusius (1601). *Rariorum Plantarum Historia*, p. lxxvii.
[2] Gerard, John (1597). *The Herball*, chapter 334, p. 780.
[3] Taylor, John (c. 1621). *Collected Works*, 1630. The Spenser Society, 1868. The Goose Fair at Stratford, Bow. The Thursday after Whitsuntide.
[4] Moffett, Thomas (?1595). *Health Improvement*. Corrected and enlarged by Christopher Bennet, 1665.

'even the husbandman buys them', for assuredly the farmer, if he attached any value to them, would have grown them in his own garden.

Whatever may have been the case in 1655, there can be little doubt that in 1630 it was still the expensive imported sweet-potato which the contemporary dramatists had in mind. Its association with all that is extravagant and bizarre, is illustrated in the following lines of Massinger,[1] though here, as in previous examples, it is well to remember that our authors were merely making professional use of a hackneyed cliché. The niceties of physiology, and still less those of botany, did not concern them.

> The elder Madam,
> Is drinking by himself to your ladyship's health
> In muskadine and eggs; and, for a rasher
> To draw his liquor down, he hath got a pie
> Of marrow-bones, potatoes and eringoes,
> With many such ingredients; and it is said
> He hath sent his man in post to the next town
> For a pound of ambergris and half a pound
> Of fishes call'd cantharides.[2]

which is met by the retort that he is pruning himself up as if he had to act a bridegroom's part.

In a play of Heywood's, a young man orders a dinner and after enumerating a long series of delicacies, concludes with:

> Caviare, sturgeon, anchovies, pickle-oysters; yes,
> And a potato pie; besides all these
> What thou thinkest rare and costly.[3]

After a time, acquaintance with the potato began to reach the public by other paths though, even so, the divorce from its earlier and less reputable associations is generally incomplete. We find it both as a lenten dish for the hypocrite, and a tasty morsel for the epicure.

In a letter written in 1634 on Ash Wednesday, Howell is inspired to discourse in verse on the mockery of fasting, when the act is unaccompanied by an inward fast of the spirit. He proceeds to chasten those who in Lent avoid the grosser meats, only to feast on the most exquisite luxuries they can procure:

> Or to forbear from Flesh, Fowl, Fish
> And eat Potatoes in a dish
> Done o'er with Amber, or a mess
> Of Ringo's in a Spanish dress.[4]

---

[1] Massinger, Philip (1629). *The Picture*, Act IV, sc. ii.
[2] Ibid.
[3] Heywood, Thomas (1633). *The English Traveller*, Act I, sc. ii (Mermaid Series, 1888), p. 167.
[4] Howell, James (1654). *Familiar Letters* (ed. Joseph Jacobs, 1890), bk. IV, p. 564.

En revanche Fletcher calls in the potato-pie as a restorative following the exhaustion of Lent: 'Will your Ladyship have a potato pie? 'Tis a good stirring dish for an old lady after a long Lent.'[1]

The association of eringos and potatoes, if it does not necessarily imply the sweet-potato, at least assures us that it was the tarnished reputation of the latter that Howell had in mind.

In time the venerous character of the potato became sublimated into the 'do you good', 'strengthen you' qualification commonly attributed to costly rubbish as the tonic wine, once so dear to the women of the country-side. An example may be found in the writings of no less an authority than Francis Bacon, who prescribes a broth made of chicken boiled in beer, and proceeds to advise that 'Triall should be made of the like Brew, with Potato Roots or Burre roots (pears) or the Pith of Artichokes which are nourishing meals'.[2] The alternatives offered are readily understood in view of the price which potatoes commanded about this time.

From this attitude it is an easy step to the 'Olepotrige', or, as it is sometimes spelt, *Olla podrida*, a favourite Spanish dish which was, to all intents, equivalent to our Irish stew. Markham, in the first edition of his *Huswife*, describes it as a Spanish dish, and gives a recipe which contains the words 'put in Potato roots, Turnips and Skirrits'.[3] For an English housewife in 1615 to pour sweet-potatoes at 3s. equivalent to about 30s. a pound to-day, into a stew, is unthinkable, but we are not on that account at liberty to assume that he was referring to the recently introduced *Solanum tuberosum* which, if obtainable at all, would have cost not less that 1s. per pound.

Markham was, above all, a copyist, and probably had never seen an 'Olepotrige', which is reproduced in almost identical words, in both the 1631 and 1660 editions. This last was issued twenty-four years after Markham's death, so that it might be assumed that the new editor intended to refer to *S. tuberosum* which, by that time, though very far from being in general use was, in comparison with the sweet-potato, a cheap food for the well-to-do, though still beyond the means of the working classes. Incidentally, as neither Markham nor his collaborator Lawson, mention the potato as a growing plant in their descriptions of gardens, it would be rash to attach any value to their evidence as to the progress made by the common potato in the first half of the seventeenth century.

We get a truer idea of the symbolism evoked by the *Olla podrida* from a letter of Howell addressed to Lady Cornwallis, in which it may well

---

[1] Fletcher, John (?1623). *Love's Cure or the Martial Maid*, Act I, sc. iii (ed. Alex. Dyce, London 1846), vol. IX, p. 119.

[2] Bacon, Francis (c. 1626). *Sylva Sylvarum*, par. 46.

[3] Markham, Gervase (1615). *The English Huswife*, ditto 1631 and 1660.

be that he had our common potato in mind; though seeing that he was recommending a cook 'who has seen the world' and whose speciality was a Spanish dish, he may have made no conscious effort to differentiate the two potatoes.

You ask for a cook here is one....He is passing good for an Ollia, he will tell your Ladyship that the Reverend Matron Olla potrida hath intellectuals and senses. Mutton, Beef and Bacon are to her as the will, understanding and memory are to the soul. Cabbage, turnip, Artichoks, Potatoes and water are her five senses and pepper the common sense. She must have marrow to keep life in her, and some birds to make her light; by all means she must go adorned with a chain of sausages.[1]

Towards the close of the seventeenth century, our potato had almost freed itself in the eyes of the public from its material relation, though less completely from its spiritual bondage, to the sweet-potato. This was due to the fact that its price, which had been a shilling a pound in the second decade, had dropped to a penny or two by the end of the century. The potato was no longer the prerogative of the wealthy; it was in process of becoming democratic and in so doing, had lost its earlier special appeal; in Beale's own words 'The Virginian Potado is become *plebeian* in Shropshire'.[2] The transition is exemplified in the 1678 edition of Phillips:[3] 'a sort of fruit, coming originally from the West Indies [the home of the sweet and not the common potato], but now common in English gardens, whose Root is of great vertue, to comfort and strengthen the body.' From now on, our potato advanced slowly but steadily in the public favour; its fame as a saviour of the people, in times of scarcity, eclipsed its earlier, less reputable and entirely apocryphal association. The potato ceased to interest the dramatist so soon as it became the plaything of the social philosopher and economist. At the close of the century, even the hawkers in the Strand, carrying their open baskets of fresh vegetables on their heads, could find no more to say about it than 'Fyn Potatoes, fyn'.

[1] Howell, James (1654). *Familiar Letters* (ed. Joseph Jacobs), vol. 1, xxxvi, p. 286.
[2] Beale, John (1662). MSS. v. Bi. fol. 17: Royal Society.
[3] Phillips, Edward (4th edit. 1678). *A New World in Words, or a General Dictionary*.

CHAPTER XXIV

The Seventeenth Century: the First Hundred Years of the Potato's Progress in Great Britain

The Potato a Luxury Food

When the potato reached this country at the end of the sixteenth century, the farmers of England grew no root crops of any kind in the open field. It cannot be said that they were ignorant of 'roots', for the carrot and parsnip had long been familiar garden stocks; skerrets also were grown at this time, and turnips had been introduced some hundred years. In the fifteenth century, according to Lord Ernle, rape, carrots, parsnips, turnips, cabbages, leeks, garlic, as well as numerous 'herbes for potage' and 'herbes for salads' are mentioned in books on gardens and in the recipes of cookery books. This, however, is no evidence that they were at all extensively grown. Katherine of Aragon imported a Flemish gardener to raise her salads[1] and Catherine Parr, the last surviving Queen of Henry VIII, was obliged to send regularly to Flanders in order to get her's because none were available at home.[2]

It would appear that the Tudor period marked the lowest ebb of vegetable-growing, and that in medieval days cauliflowers, carrots, parsnips, turnips, beets and innumerable herbs were certainly grown in the gardens of the castles and the great monasteries, even if they were neglected in those of the people. How rich such gardens were, can be learnt from a poem on Gardening, dating from the middle of the fifteenth century.[3] William Harrison[4] writing in 1577, is more definite, and asserts that such herbs, fruits, and roots were raised from seed, and were very plentiful in the reign of Edward I, but in the time of Henry IV the decline had so far advanced, that in the reigns of Henry VII and VIII, 'there was little or no use of them in England, but they remained either unknown, or supposed as food more meet for hogs and savage beasts to feed upon, than mankind'. Whether Harrison is correct about their use in the earlier period may be doubtful, but there is no reason to think

[1] Curran, J. O. Observations on Scurvy. *Dublin Quart. J. Med. Sci.* August 1847 quotes Anderson, Adam, *Hist. of Commerce*, 1764.

[2] Johnson, G. W. (1829). *A History of English Gardening.* Quoted from Drummond and Wilbraham.

[3] Tyssen-Amherst, The Hon. Alicia (1894). *The Feate of Gardening*, by Master Ion Gardener, *c.* 1445 A.D. Reprinted in *Archaeologia*, vol. XIV.

[4] Harrison, William (1577). *Description of Bretaine and England* (ed. Frederick Furnival, New Shakespeare Soc.), pt. I, 2nd bk., p. 324.

that he would be ignorant of the conditions reigning in the lifetime of his own father, not to say of his own youth.

The shortage of fresh vegetables in the dietary of the people, might be expected to have shown itself by the occurrence of scurvy and such, indeed, seems to have been the case. Drummond and Wilbraham[1] in their fascinating book, *The Englishman's Food*, are of opinion that throughout the Middle Ages and well into the seventeenth century, the working classes were, for the most part, in a more or less chronic scorbutic condition. They point out that the disease was not fully recognized in England till the later part of the sixteenth century, when the following very accurate description of it is given by Gerard in his *Herball*:

The gums are loosed, swolne and exculcerate; the mouth greeuously stinking; the thighes and legs are withall verie often full of blewe spots, not vnlike those that come of bruses: the face and the rest of the bodie is often-times of a pale colour; and the feete are swolne, as in the dropsie.

It is probable that amongst the rich the trouble was less common, as they seem at least to have eaten freely of fresh salads. Two hundred years later it was the potato which was mainly responsible for remedying this condition amongst the working classes of the country.

In the latter part of the Elizabethan period an interest in gardening for its own sake, derived probably from Flanders and Italy, manifested itself; its influence did not extend beyond the gardens of the great houses, which were then springing up on all sides, often the residences of the new rich industrial class, which had infiltrated into the old landed aristocracy. The recent dissolution of the monasteries and the acquisition of much of their lands by a *nouveau riche* aristocracy doubtless quickened the interest in gardens.

It is true that the flower garden, which long since had been a feature of the Italian 'palazzos', now took the place of honour in the new Elizabethan homes, but the kitchen garden, which had been borrowed from Flanders and brought to this country by refugees from Alba's terror 1568–72, though relegated to less conspicuous parts of the demesne, was none the less regarded as an essential feature in a domestic economy which, in the privileged class, had passed from the stage of subsistence to that of artistry and luxury. The gourmand of the Middle Ages had become the gourmet of the Renaissance.

Vegetables which had in the late Middle Ages formed so small a part in the dietary of the people, rich or poor, now began gradually to win their way into the houses of the great. Here, their forward march was, as it were, halted, and a century or more elapsed before they were admitted freely into the houses of the people. This is demonstrated by

---

[1] Drummond and Wilbraham (1939). *The Englishman's Food.* Jonathan Cape.

Robert Child, who says in Hartlib's *Legacie*, 1651, that in Surrey some old men remembered 'the first gardiners that came into these parts to plant cabages, collerflours and to sowe turneps, carrets and parsnips and to sow Raith pease, all of which at that time were great rarities, we having few or non in England, but what came from Holland and Flanders'. Whilst in the great houses, other than in the north and west, a growing interest in the kitchen garden was a feature of the late sixteenth and seventeenth centuries, the people as a whole relied almost entirely on bread and meat for their sustenance. A yeoman's welcome is thus forcibly expressed: 'To-day or to-morrow, when he comes he shall be welcome to bread, beer and beef, yeomans fare; we have no Kickshaws; full dishes, whole belly fulls.'[1]

Roots in particular were far less popular than cabbage, and the turnip, which had not yet reached the stage of field culture, was obviously not very familiar to the middle classes even in 1598, as witness Anne Page's remark:[2]

> Alas, I had rather be set quick i' th' earth,
> And bowled to death with turnips.

In the sixteenth century vegetable produce was made available to the citizens of London by means of the market-gardens in the north-east of London. This new industry had been inspired by the Dutch, the produce was sold near St Paul's and later in the courtyard of the Cathedral, but in 1673 the market was relegated to Aldermanbury and Broad Street. An extension of the industry, coincident with the rapid growth of London westwards, led to the creation of the Covent Garden Market by the 5th Earl of Bedford about 1670. It is with the produce of this market that the salesmen perambulated the streets of London, making them re-echo with their 'cries', a few of which were still to be heard in the lifetime of some of us.

It must, however, be remembered that all these vegetables, including such root crops as were raised, were annuals grown each year from seed. The sixteenth-century English gardener knew nothing of the vegetative propagation of vegetables. It is true, that the sweet-potato (*Ipomoea batatas*) was cultivated in this manner by the planting of slips from the growing plant and that it had been introduced to the tables of the rich during the latter part of the sixteenth century, but there is no evidence that it was ever grown in this country; indeed, it is more than doubtful whether it could be raised in the open in our climate, even in the most favoured situation.

The Jerusalem artichoke, introduced into England about 1620, re-

---

[1] Dekker and others (1621). *The Witch of Edmonton*, Act I, sc. ii.
[2] Shakespeare, W. (1598). *The Merry Wives of Windsor*, Act III, sc. iv.

quires a similar method of cultivation to our potato, but it failed to win favour and seemed never to have reached the gardens of the middle still less those of the working class.

The potato raised from tubers was, therefore, not only a strange new vegetable, but demanded a kind of cultivation hitherto unpractised in England. In Horsted Keynes, Sussex, even so late as 1765, no one knew how to plant it, and an old man from another county used to come over on Old Ladyday especially to plant the villagers' tubers.[1] It is possible that reasons such as this played some part in retarding its adoption but, as will be shown, other and more far-reaching influences delayed its spread in the more populous parts of England. We have, however, no reason to be astonished at the delay in accepting a novelty, however desirable. Even in our days of rapid communication and mechanization, a first-class discovery rarely takes less than twenty-five years to reach the consciousness of the outer world. Prior to the latter half of the eighteenth century, a lag of a hundred years generally separated the genesis of a great idea from its practical realization. The history of the potato in England is no exception to the general rule.[2]

We have seen (chapter VI) that the potato made its first recorded appearance in England in Gerard's garden in Holborn and from thence it doubtless spread to other large gardens, such as that of Lord Burghley in the Strand, of which Gerard was the superintendent, though specific references to it are scanty during the next few decades. Fuess[3] states that in 1620 Prof. Matthaus of Herborn obtained tubers of the potato from a professor in Oxford. Though unable to confirm this, it is not improbable; in any case it was growing in the Physic Gardens at Lambeth, belonging to the younger Tradescant, who mentions it in the catalogue of his garden, published in 1656.[4] As father and son were Court gardeners to Charles I, it may be assumed that all the leading horticulturists of the day would have had access to their collection.

There is an intriguing reference to the potato ascribed to Thomas Overbury and said to occur in his *Characters*: 'The man who has not anything to boast of but his illustrious ancestors is like a potato, the only good belonging to him is underground.' Actually, it has not been possible to verify the reference: it would appear not to belong to the original series and therefore must have been current after 1613 and before 1673, the last of the twenty editions. It suggests that the growing plant was a familiar object and that readers would appreciate the humour of the comparison. In any case it must be the common potato which is referred

[1] Moore, Giles, Rev. (1848). *Sussex Archaeological Collection*, vol. I, p. 97.

[2] The delay was certainly due to the adverse photoperiodic reaction, bred out by the late eighteenth century (see Introduction). – Ed.

[3] Fuess, W. (1935). Die Urheimat der Kartoffel, ihre Einführung u. Ausbreitung in Europa. *Die Ernährung der Pflanze*, Bd. XXXI, Heft 17.

[4] Tradescant, J. (1656). *Catalogus Plantarum*, p. 89.

to, as few would have travelled to the south of France, or Spain, and seen the sweet-potato growing.

Parkinson[1] places the potato amongst the kitchen garden plants, and compares it unfavourably as regards both size and taste with the sweet-potato. It is very doubtful whether at this date it was to be found in more than a few gardens, for even in 1664 it was still a luxury in the kitchen of Oliver Cromwell's wife, Joan.[2]

At this time Sir Richard Weston, an improving squire of Surrey, having been an active supporter of Charles, fled to Holland. Impressed by the new crops and cultivations he saw there, he described the same in a manuscript which he designed as a legacy to his sons. Samuel Hartlib secured an imperfect copy of this and published it under his own name in 1650. Happening on a more perfect copy in the following year, he wrote to Weston asking him to enlarge and correct the *Discours*. Receiving no answer, he republished the *Discours* in 1651, again under his own name.[3] Here the cultivation of potatoes in foreign countries is described and farmers urged not to be frightened of adopting new crops 'seeing that many such as cherries, hops, liquorice and potatoes, have been brought to perfection even in our days'.[4]

To this appeal there was no noticeable response, though doubtless a slowly increasing number of farmers grew it in their gardens. More than a hundred years were to pass before the potato invaded the fields of England in any considerable strength.[5]

The few available references to the potato as a growing plant to be found in the literature during the first half of the century, go to show that the writers had little first-hand knowledge of the subject: it is questionable whether any of them had ever eaten the tubers, for it was, as we shall see, a costly dish.

When we proceed to trace its history during the same period as an article of food, we are confronted with the fact that in the early seventeenth century the name 'potato' was commonly applied to the Spanish or sweet-potato; hence we need to be careful to avoid interpreting references intended to apply to the sweet-potato, *Ipomoea batatas* as if they referred to our common species, *Solanum tuberosum*.

The confusion which reigned between the sweet-potato and our potato in the minds of so many of the writers of the early decades of the

[1] Parkinson, J. (1629). *Paradisi in Sole.*
[2] Eden, Sir Frederick (1797). *The State of the Poor*, p. 509.
[3] Hartlib's action, severely condemned by Lord Ernle (*English Farming*, ed. 1936, p. 477) is defended by G. E. Fussell (*Old English Farming Books*, p. 21, 1947).
[4] Hartlib, S. (1651). *Legacy of Husbandry.*
[5] The original edition of Sir Hugh Platt's *The Jewell . . .* appeared in 1594; that of *The Floraes Paradisi . . .* in 1608: neither contain any reference to the potato. It is, however, surprising that the enlarged editions of 1653 and 1675 respectively, are equally silent on the subject, although there is abundant reference to common vegetables.

seventeenth century, has been referred to in the preceding chapter. The best criterion by which to decide as to which root a seventeenth-century writer refers, is to be found in the price which was paid. Indeed, the lure of the Spanish (sweet-) potato lay not a little in the high price it commanded. We know from a reliable source[1] that in 1660 the price of sweet-potatoes was 2s. to 3s. per lb., that even as late as 1720 to 1760 it never fell below 1s. The few examples of the price of the common potato in the seventeenth century are as follows: in 1632 4d. per lb.,[2] in 1636 6d. per lb.,[3] and in 1701 2d. per lb.[4] With these figures in mind, we may be satisfied that a purchase of 'potato roots' in 1607 at 10d. per lb. must refer to the common, and not the sweet variety. When the price is not mentioned, the season of the year during which the potatoes were put on the table is of moment. For at this early date, the common potato was a very late variety, and could not be served till October at the earliest, whilst the Spanish potato was available as a fresh imported vegetable in the late summer, and as a candied 'sucket' at all seasons.

In Rogers's[5] list of prices for 1590 occur the following entries for the Queen's table: two pounds of potatoes at 2s. 6d. per lb., two more at 1s. 4d. per lb., and a further pound at 1s. The first entry, it may be assumed, refers to sweet-potatoes which, as Rogers states, were probably of foreign origin, and the latter two may well have been for the purchase of the common potato, which he thinks were of Dutch origin.

What is possibly the earliest reliable record of the use in England of the potato as a dish for the table, has till now been overlooked. Sir Joseph Banks[6] communicated to the Society of Antiquaries a transcript of a manuscript, which he had purchased, from the sale of the Library of the Marquis of Donegal. It describes in great detail the officers and appointments of a nobleman's household in the year 1605. In addition there is set out for each month of the year a list of available viands, and an amazing collection it is, from which selections are made for my lord's dinners and suppers in each month. There is a further list of foodstuffs, in which the potato is included, which appear to be regarded as stores ready for use at least during one or other season of the year. These, described as the 'necessary provisions for the whole year', contain meats of all kinds, some 'dried', some 'soused', whilst still others are described as 'green', i.e. fresh. Condiments such as 'verjous', the juice of unripe

---

[1] Beveridge, W. and others (1939). *Prices and Wages in England.*

[2] Rogers, J. E. T. (1866–87). *Hist. Agric. Prices*, vol. VI, pp. 230 and 234.

[3] Simpkinson, John Nassau (1860). *The Washingtons*, App. A (2).

[4] Sanders, T. W. (1905). *The Book of the Potato*. London: (no reference given).

[5] Rogers, J. E. T. Op. cit. vol. VI, pp. 230 and 234.

[6] Banks, Joseph, Sir (1800). Copy of an original manuscript entitled 'A Breviary touching the order and governments of a Nobleman's House'. *Archaeologia*, vol. XIII, p. 315.

grapes, vinegar and mustard are well to the fore and were essential for preserving. Next we find salted articles like anchovies and caviare, or partially preserved ones, as olives; followed by artichokes which were probably dried and eringoes which were candied. There is also included a group of fruits and vegetables, many of which would keep a considerable time, apples, wardens,[1] oranges, lemons, melons, and turnips, onions, skirrets, carrots and potatoes. Perishable vegetables such as cauliflowers and lettuce are also mentioned. The inclusion of any particular article in this list of provisions for the year cannot therefore be held to imply that it was available throughout the year, still less that it was artificially preserved.

Returning to the menus we find potatoes, in all cases baked, are recommended in October for supper, in November for both dinner and supper, and in December for dinner only, but at no other time of the year. Inasmuch as the potato is also included in the list of necessary provisions, the question arises, as to whether the potato was preserved in any way, or merely kept in store for as long as was convenient and safe. The fact that the use of the potato was restricted to the three late autumn months would appear to be both evidence against their being artificially preserved and in favour of their being raised in the kitchen garden of the great house and put in store at the end of September. The same argument justifies us in concluding that we are dealing with the common and not the sweet-potato, for this latter was not growing here but was imported from Spain and would have been served during the summer months. William Goodyear notwithstanding, authorities are agreed that there are but few spots on the west coasts of the British Isles, and then only in exceptionally warm seasons, where the sweet-potato could be raised.[2] Beale,[3] writing to Oldenberg on 21 December 1682, notes that they are not grown in England and considers whether they might not be raised in the sandy soils of Shropshire.

It might be objected that the sweet-potato was often candied like the eringo and that it might, after all, be that to which reference is made. But our nobleman ate his potato 'baked', which is a further argument that we are concerned with the common *Solanum tuberosum*, and not the *Ipomoea batatas*.

The mention of potatoes, without any introductory note, would suggest that they were not quite newcomers to the household larder and must have been known for at least a few years. It would not be unreasonable to assume that they were being grown in the kitchen gardens

---

[1] 'Wardens' may refer to a long-keeping pear of that name or to a variety of pea which was used as a conserve in the sixteenth century. Parker, Mathew (1504–75), *A proper Newsbook of Cookery* (ed. Frances Frere).

[2] See supra, p. 105.

[3] Beale, John (1662). Op. cit.

of some of the great houses at the very beginning of the seventeenth century, if not earlier.

The next reference to what would appear an unequivocal account of a purchase of 'potatoes' is to be found in a detailed and priced list of all the food and appointments of a great feast costing £1,000 given by the Merchant Taylors' Company to James I, on 16 July 1607: on this occasion sixty pounds of potatoes were purchased at 10d. per lb., presumably from the market gardeners, who were beginning to establish themselves in the nearby suburbs.[1]

Here reference may be made to the oft quoted statement that Queen Anne, wife of James I, paid 2s. per lb. for potatoes for her household— a sum which would be equivalent to something approaching £1 of present-day money, and that these were the common variety. Another version of the tale which puts the price at 1s. per lb., is referred to by Eden,[2] the only author to quote his source. Phillips,[3] following Eden as regards price, gives 1619 as the date, but not his authority. McIntosh,[4] who adopts the 2s. per lb. version, bases his statement on Krichauff[5] who mentions that 'in a written' book for housekeeping kept by Queen Anne the wife of James I, it is stated 'that a small quantity of potatoes was purchased at 2s. a lb.' Beckmann[6] improves on all other commentators of the tale by stating that 'in the year 1619 the common market price of the potato was 1s. per lb.'

The document is to be found in the Harleian MSS.:[7] it consists of thirty-five beautifully written sheets, bound at a later date in a thin quarto volume. The subject dealt with is the requirements, in respect of food and drink, of the royal household of Anne, wife of James I of England. The MSS. cannot be later than 1619, the year of the Queen's death; pasted on the cover is a paper which reads 'A Booke made Anno dom. 1613...'.

Each item of importance is set out separately and the quantities and cost of the same recorded in detail. The basis of the estimates is the quantity of any article required for a 'mess'. The number of persons constituting a mess is not stated, though in accordance with tradition it may be presumed to be four.

Potatoes are given a separate column in each estimate, from which it appears that though only served to a few of the many messes catered

---

[1] Clode, Charles (1875). *Memorials of the Guild of Merchant Taylors, London*, p. 170.
[2] Eden (1797). *The State of the Poor*, p. 510, refers to Harleian MS. no. 157, 1613.
[3] Phillips, Henry (1822). *History of Cultivated Vegetables*.
[4] McIntosh, T. (1927). *The Potato*, p. 12. Edinburgh.
[5] Krichauff, Hon. T. E. (1896). The Tercentenary of the Introduction of Potatoes in England. *J. Roy. Hort. Soc.* vol. XIX, p. 224.
[6] Beckmann, John (1780–1805). *A History of Invention* (Bohn's 4th edit. 1846), vol. II, p. 354.
[7] Brit. Mus. Harl. MSS. No. 157.

for, they were available both on 'ordinary' and on 'fish' days; the quantity served per 'mess' on the former was 4 lb., on the latter 2 lb., but the portion on those occasions when 'double fares' were served was 3 lb. In every case the price is constant, viz. 1s. per lb.

As usual, we are confronted with the problem: Is it the sweet-potato from Spain, or our own potato, *Solanum tuberosum*, to which the MSS. refers? In favour of the former it might be argued, that as there is no indication of a cessation of supplies in the summer and early autumn, it could not have been the common potato which, at that period, was not stored in bulk.

We are in no less a difficulty if we assume that it is the sweet-potato which is referred to, for that was regarded specifically as an aphrodisiac and it would be strange indeed, if it were consumed on each of the 220 meat and 125 fish days throughout the year, which are covered by the estimate.

In view, however, of the small quantity actually consumed by the whole household, it might very well be that it was, in fact, only served during a limited period of the year. Against the possibility of it being the sweet-potato is the fact that the price paid by the 'cofferer' of the household was 1s. per lb., as against 3s. per lb., the price usually paid for sweet-potatoes in the early seventeenth century.

The absence of any concomitant purchase of eringoes or cantharides with which the sweet-potato was commonly associated, together with the indication that the potatoes were baked and not candied, materially strengthens the view that the potatoes referred to were, in fact, the tubers of *Solanum tuberosum*. Most of the entries are followed by the letters 'ba: or al', which presumably means 'baked or otherwise'.

That the new vegetable was regarded with much favour, would appear from the fact that the 'cofferer' was prepared to spend £60 per annum, equivalent in our currency to at least £600, for a supply totalling only half a ton.

Below are reproduced in facsimile the general statement prefacing the summary of purchases, and the particular statement referring to those of the potato for the whole year.

Transliterated they read: 'Here followeth a general, declaration, what, and how much of every kind of provision, for all occasions of service, will furnish for one year, as well the ordinary diets daily served, as feasts, extraordinary diets and double fares; as also; Incidents, of all kinds whatsoever allowed, with wages and all other charges, for so much as is usually paid for by Mr Cofferer; which is cast up and summed, according the market as if the same were an account made up for one years expences in her Majesty's house.' (Fig. 71.)

'Potatoes:—spent for ordinary diets to ba: [bake]: 4 pounds a day is in 220 days 880 pounds: and 2 pounds a day is in 145 days 290 pounds: for feasts and entertainments—30 together—1200 at 12*d*.—£60.' (Fig. 72.)

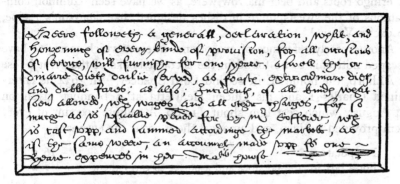

Fig. 71. Introductory note to the estimates of the Household Expenses of Queen Anne, the Consort of James I, *c.* 1613.

How little progress our potato had made as a food by 1626, even amongst the landed classes, may be gathered from Francis Bacon's recipe, to which reference has already been made.[1] This was probably due to the high prices reigning at the time, hence the alternative ingredients suggested. In an unpublished MSS. volume[2] of recipes ascribed to the years 1645 and 1658, although various dishes of stewed meats with vegetables are described, no mention is made of the potato.

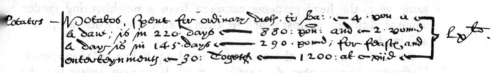

Fig. 72. The entry in the Queen's household estimates referring to the provision of potatoes.

Bacon's recipe awakens the suspicion, that even in the philosopher's mind, the old association between the sweet-potato and its supposed aphrodisiacal property may have been unconsciously transferred to its vulgar rival. Forty years later there occurs in a cookery book a recipe, the only one dealing with the common potato, in which such a transfer is obvious.[3] The tubers are to be cooked in water already brought to the boil, then bleached and seasoned with nutmeg, pepper, cinnamon, butter and salt. They are then transferred to a slab of pastry and to them

[1] Bacon, Francis (*c.* 1626). See supra, p. 432.
[2] University Library, Cambridge. Add. 3071.
[3] May, Robert (1665). *The Accomplisht Cook*, p. 261.

are added eringo roots, beef marrow, large mace, sliced lemon and butter, the whole is then covered with another slab of pastry and treated with butter and sugar and iced with rose water and sugar. The presence of eringo roots and beef marrow were, as we have seen, common companions of the sweet-potato in dishes designed, like Dawson's recipe, to excite Venus.[1]

Another early reference of exceptional interest which seems to have escaped notice, is to be found in the account books of the great house at Althorp, the home of the second Lord Spencer.[2] In 1634 he entertained Charles I and his Queen Henrietta at a banquet given on 14 August, which cost him about £1,300. A minute account of every item provided is given, and amongst them occur the entries:

For potatoes   – 16 0
For a box for the potatoes and a porter to carry them   – 1   2

The date on which they were eaten, at once excludes our potato. That it was the sweet-potato may be inferred by the further fact that it was specially sent to Althorp from London and was sufficiently precious as to need a special box for its carriage. Unfortunately we do not know how many pounds the box contained. In contrast to the above an entry on 7 January 1635 in the Althorp accounts shows that six pounds of potatoes were purchased for 3s. From a comparison of the cost, there can be no doubt that they were our common variety. Although an expensive dish, worth in to-day's money between 4s. and 5s. per lb., they evidently met with favour, for in November of the same year, the head gardener acquired from a neighbouring garden some seed tubers, against which he enters, what is evidently a tip, one shilling.[3]

An earlier entry in the accounts, dated 15 February 1623, reads: 'Jerusalem hartichoakes, di; a strike 0–5–0.' If we may assume that the bushel was half a hundredweight, then 60d. were paid for some 56 lb. of tubers, that is to say, Jerusalem artichoke tubers were not worth more than about 1d. per lb.

The Jerusalem artichoke reached England about thirty years later than did the potato, but it gained an initial start, which the respective prices of the two tubers makes sufficiently clear. As the century proceeded, the tables were reversed, a striking encomium to the sound if unaided judgement of the public.

Coles,[4] the herbalist, in 1657 describes the 'Virginian potato' which

---

[1] Dawson, Thomas (1596). Loc. cit. p. 20.
[2] Simpkinson, John Nassau (1860). The Washingtons, App. A (2).
[3] Simpkinson. Ibid.
[4] Coles, William (1657). Adam in Eden.

is our common potato, the Canadian potato which is the Jerusalem artichoke, and the Spanish or sweet-potato. The latter, however, he confuses with the 'Virginian' for of them he says: 'the soil of Ireland doth so well agree with them that they grow there so plentifully that there be whole fields overrun with them as I have herein found by divers soldiers which came thence'. These, of course, were the common potato. He, however, goes on to say that in our gardens 'they decay rather than increase', which would be true of the Spanish or sweet-potato, which needs a subtropical climate.[1]

The truth is, the potato at this time was almost unknown in England except to a few botanical and horticultural experts. Blyth,[2] who was an enthusiastic advocate of new crops, recommends the cultivation of clover, sanfoin, turnip, hops, liquorice, saffron, madder and woad, but never even mentions the potato.

The Potato, a possible Food for the Masses

The potato still remained a luxury food till after the middle of the century, when we begin to hear a new note in regard to its use. It is no longer as a strange and costly food that it finds favour, but rather because of the hope it holds out of being a veritable manna for the poor. Evelyn,[3] who never thought much of the new root which he says tasted 'like an old bean or roasted chest-nut', thought it might be of 'excellent use for relief of poor, yea and one's own household when there are many servants, in a dear year'.

Speed[4] advises its use for human food, as it can be grown everywhere, and that the Jerusalem artichoke, whose sway was drawing to a close, should be relegated to the pigs.

If the immediate progress of the potato was not sensational, its penetration into the home life of an ever increasing circle of the people, was now becoming assured. Robert Morison,[5] Professor of Botany in Oxford, writes in 1680 that the potato was a familiar plant in most gardens: it had, in fact, been recorded in the University Botanical Garden's *Catalogue* as early as 1658. This may probably mean no more than that it had spread from the gardens of the great houses to those of the smaller, but yet substantial homes, of the larger farmer and the professional classes.

---

[1] *Ipomoea batatas* is grown occasionally in the French Midi; it is, however, a regular crop in Algeria, where it reaches the market in October. Really hot weather and where possible, irrigation, is desirable for its cultivation.

[2] Blyth, Walter (1652). *The English Improver Improved.*

[3] Evelyn, John. *Diary* (ed. Wheatley, 1879), vol. IV, p. 441. London.

[4] Speed, Adolph (1659). *Adam out of Eden.*

[5] Morison, Robert (1680). *Plantarum Historia Universalis*, vol. II, p. 522 (1658), *Catalogus Horti. Botan. Oxon.*

To have surmounted this social barrier was no mean triumph, even if the cottager, the landworker and the small artificer of the towns, constitutionally averse to innovations, still held the new vegetable at arm's length. Indeed, it has often happened in the history of the potato that not even famine conditions were sufficient to overcome the inertia, or allay the prejudice, of peasant or artisan. Such was the case in Naples; about the year 1770 a cargo of potatoes was sent there to relieve a famine, but the people refused to touch them.[1]

Evelyn[2] had recommended the berries as a salad, and proceeds: 'the root being roasted under the ecula or otherwise, opened with a knife, the pulp is buttered in the skin, of which it will take up a good quantity, and is seasoned with a little salt and pepper. Some eat this with sugar together in the skin, which has a pleasant crispness; they are also stewed and baked in pies'.[3] This note apparently records Evelyn's first and more favourable impression of the new vegetable, which he evidently regarded and treated as a luxury. In the adjoined 'Gardeners Calendar' he appears to have changed his mind: 'Plant potatoes in your worst ground', and gives emphasis to this slighting view by his advice for November: 'Take up your potatoes for winter spending: there will be enough remain for stock, though never so exactly gathered.'

Evelyn notwithstanding, the potato made its way into the kitchen gardens of an increasing number of rich houses. A health authority of the day regarded the potato as a valuable hygienic agent, due to the fact that, like turnips, they 'grow almost on the top and surface of the earth, are better than other roots and more familiar to our natures... because they participate more of the influences both of the air and sun than the others'.[4] A few years later the same author inveighs, with justice, against the appalling amount of food the rich consume and says they must always have different kinds of meat and are not content unless they are followed by a variety of dishes of fish, vegetables and puddings. In this indict-ment potatoes are noted as one of those unnecessary additions to an overburdened table.[5]

It is significant that the suggestion, that the new vegetable might have a far-reaching economic and social value, received both its expression and its earliest stimulus from the recently organized body of English scientific and literary men whose interests and habits of thought were beginning to be freed from the old religious and philosophical back-ground.

[1] Green, Thomas (1816). *Universal Herbal.*
[2] Evelyn, John (1664). *Sylva. Tena. Pomona acetaria and Kalendarium Hortense.*
[3] 'Under the Ecula' presumably means in a small dish (*écuelle*) with a cover.
[4] Tryon, Thomas (1683). *The Way to Health*, p. 213.
[5] Tryon, Thomas (Phylotheus Physiologus) (1688). *Monthly Observations for the Preserving of Health.*

The possibility of the potato having economic importance was discussed as early as 1662 by the Royal Society. A Somersetshire gentleman, Mr Buckland, had written to Oldenburg, the Secretary, suggesting that the cultivation of the potato would be a protection against famine. A committee was appointed to consider the proposition and reported on 20 March as follows:

The Committee appointed by ye Society March 18, to consider of Mr Bucklands proposition to plant Potatoes through all ye parts of England, did meet at Mr Howards lodgings in Arundell house: where were present My Lord Brounker, Mr Howard, Mr Boyle, Sir Robt. Moray, Dr Goddard, Dr Whistler, Mr Ball, Mr Oldenburg.

Mr Bucklands letter containing the said proposition, together with ye whole way of planting, and ordering potato's, and the benefit thereof in time of scarcity of food was read; and ye substance thereof considered and approved, with the result, 1. that all those members of ye Society, as have land, should be desired, to begin ye planting of this root, and to persuade their friends to doe ye same. 2. that in order thereunto Mr Buckland should be desired to send up what quantity he could of ye smaller potato's to furnish those, yt have conveniency to plant them in order to which, Mr Boyle offered to provide as many of them, as he could: as also, to communicate such notes of his, concerning this root and their diffusiveness as he could recover. 3. yt Mr Evelyn should be desired to insert this proposition and ye approbation thereof, together with ye management of planting and spreading ym, into ye Treatise which he is now publishing by order of ye Society concerning ye planting of Trees. 5. yt provision being made of these roots, ye way and usefulness or planting ym, should be published and recommended to ye Nation, in ye Diurnalls, without further naming the Society in it, and yt therein direction should be given to certain places, where they may be had for those, yt have a mind to plant ym.

It was on this occasion that Boyle told of his experiences of the potato in Ireland (see chapter XII, p. 238).

That the Royal Society had taken Buckland's suggestion seriously, appears from the fact that when specialist committees were set up to deal with the different groups of subjects, such as Astronomy, Chemistry and the like, that concerned with Agriculture, known as the Georgical, a body of thirty-two persons, sixteen of whom had already served on the Buckland inquiry, now took over the problem of investigating the uses of the potato.[1] Boyle's promise to make a further communication on the subject, does not appear to have materialized, but in the Boyle manuscripts kindly put at my disposal by the President and Council of the Society, there was found an undated note which seems to have been written in preparation for the promised communication. As the note has

[1] Lyons, Sir Henry (1944). *The Royal Society*, p. 62. Cambridge.

not been published hitherto, and has some interesting observations casting doubt on spontaneous generation, it is given below in full:[1]

That ye seminall principles of some, I say not of all or most plants may reside in their sap seems probable from hence, that if you take a branch of willow and cut it slanting yt ye raine may not lye upon ye tops into several short peices each of those peices being stuck in a moist and convenient soyle will take root and grow into a tree sometimes with such celerity that I have not considered it without some wonder. And not to repeat what has been formerly delivered concerning the propagation of Potatoes by their stalkes which elsewhere and partly in this very Discourse mention to you other plants which may, without root or seed be propagated after such a manner, Soe that it appeareing possible that the juice of a vegetable should containe its seiminall principle and also yt a vegetable juice may likewise sometimes retaine its very odour or colour in spight of ye alterations it passes thorow in an Animall body it seemith not impossible but yt many of ye creatures that are supposed to be produced by ye putrefaction of ye body juices or excrements of Animalls may properly enough be referred to a seminal origination.

In 1663 Beale,[2] writing to Robert Boyle, advocated the use of the potato as a defence against famine, and states that he has known the time when 'the better sort of yeomanry and tradesmen have been relieved from real famine by these vulgar potadoes'. He is probably referring to the West Country.

In 1664 another voice was raised, whose avowed object seems to have been similar to that of the curiosos of the Royal Society, though its more immediate one was to create a monopoly of value for the king. John Forster dedicated his book *England's Happiness Increased*, to Charles II, describing it as a great national boon for the poor, and as an alternative title called it *A Sure and Easie Remedy against all succeeding Dear Years*. Following on this, the title-page continues with:

A plantation of the Roots called Potatoes, whereof, with the addition of wheat flower, excellent, good and wholesome Bread may be made, every year, eight or nine months together, for half the charge formerly.

Also—By Planting of the Roots ten thousand men in England and Wales, who knew not how to live, or what to do to get a maintenance for their families, may of any one acre of ground make thirty pounds a year.

Invented and published for the good of the Poorer Sort by John Forster Gent.

He then elaborates his plan.

Potato tubers are to be imported from Ireland as seed: one bushel cut, he says, will serve for sowing four poles, equivalent to a seeding of one ton per acre. The right to plant potatoes is to be strictly regulated; the King should retain the monopoly for himself and grant licences, the number of which should be limited, to one man for every hundred

---

[1] Boyle, Robert. *MSS.* vol. xxvi. *Science,* VII, p. 129 verso. Royal Society.
[2] Beale, John (1663). *Boyle, MSS.* v. Miscellaneous. Royal Society.

families. Each licensee was to pay £5 to the Crown for the privilege of being the sole person in his district empowered to grow or sell potatoes. The King would reap further indirect advantages. The people by the use of potatoes both as a vegetable food and as an important constituent of their daily bread—a point Forster is very insistent on—will necessarily consume less wheat; in consequence, more will be freed for export abroad, which will in turn encourage a corresponding amount of imports. Such a traffic will foster friendly relations with the Continent, which will enable the King to rely on the service of mercenaries maintained abroad, ready to defeat invasions or suppress domestic trouble at home. When the foreign troops are in England, they will be easily maintained, presumably on potatoes, without raising the home prices of any kind of grain whatsoever.

This, probably the potato's first entrance into the realm of high politics, is of peculiar interest. The creation of a monopoly was only legal if the product was a new one or, in the case of the potato, if the manner of its raising was new. In any event the monopoly would have only been valid for seven years, hence the advantages it offered, were scarcely sufficient to attract even a monarch, so chronically short of money as Charles. The suggestion that such a monopoly would react favourably on our foreign trade, is in harmony with the very active, not to say aggressive, spirit which then inspired the leading merchants of London and Bristol.

In the rest of England the progress of the potato, though slow and halting, was not to be denied. John Beale, greatly impressed by the part that potatoes were playing in Ireland, tried them out on different types of soil, and recommended them both as a food and as a basis for fermented drink. 'Every way they are strong and wholesome nourishment for labourers.' In Bristol and Wells they were being sold at 4s. a bushel (i.e. £8 a ton), and he significantly adds 'dear enough in respect of their use', and notes that the children of the poor eat them raw without harm. The price in to-day's currency would not be less than £50 a ton, evidence enough that it was still a rarity and surely beyond the reach of the working man. Beale further records that he saw them growing in a variety of different soils from the north of Shropshire to the Dorset coast,[1] presumably in gardens.[2]

Beale's enthusiasm notwithstanding, the Georgical Committee set up by the Royal Society of which he was one of the secretaries, when reporting on the crops and cultivations current throughout England failed to make any mention of either potato or turnip.[3]

[1] Beale, J. (1675). *Phil. Trans.* (26 July), No. 116, p. 359.
[2] R. Blume (1686) (*Gentleman's Recreation*) had no doubt that the potato would grow in England as it did in Ireland and America (Salaman's manuscript notes). – Ed.
[3] Lennard, Reginald (1932). English Agriculture under Charles II. *Econ. Hist. Rev.* vol. IV, p. 23.

We get further evidence of the potato's progress in England proper, before the close of the century, if we examine the different references made to the potato by John Worlidge in his *Systema Agriculturae*. In the first edition, 1669, he says:

These are very usual in foreign parts, and are planted in several places of this country to a very good advantage, they are easily increased, by cutting the roots in several pieces, each piece growing as well as the whole Root; they require a good fat garden mould, but will grow indifferently well in any, they are commonly eaten either buttered or in milk. I do not hear that it hath been as yet assayed whether they may not be propagated in great quantities for food for swine or other cattle.

In 1681 appeared the third edition, in which the above is repeated. In the 1688 edition, we read:

Potatoes are much used in Ireland, as in America, as Bread, and are themselves also an unusual food. They grow in mellow ground and are increased by cutting the roots in pieces and planting them as *scorsonera*. These and the Jerusalem Artichoke, which are by much the meaner food, although somewhat like them, may be propagated with advantage to poor people, a little ground yielding a very great quantity, as the many small Welsh territories adjoining to the Highways in those parts, planted with them plainly demonstrate.

Scorzonera, a native of Spain, has a black-skinned root and is prepared for the table in the same way as the nearly related salsify; it is, however, not propagated by root-cuttings but by true seed. This mistake, and the reference to America, which presumably refers to North America, in which, at that time, England was very active, and to which the potato had not yet been introduced, is evidence that Worlidge had no close personal knowledge of either plant, the cultivation of which must still have been very restricted. However, what is of great significance is the fact that the most distinguished agriculturist of the day, whose influence extended well into the next century, gave his support to the suggestion that the potato would be a particularly suitable food for the poor. Little did he realize how two-edged a weapon the harmless-looking tuber would prove in the hands of the rising generations of capitalists. In the 1699 edition and in subsequent ones published after his death, the work now known as the *Compleat System of Husbandry*, the reference to its value as a food for the poor is omitted.

Nevertheless, it is doubtful whether, south of the Trent, the middle classes, much less the poor, had anywhere accepted the new 'root' as a normal household article of food.

Rapid Progress in Lancashire and the North

In much of the west of England, the history of the potato runs on somewhat different lines from that pursued elsewhere. In Lancashire a tradition exists, that early in the seventeenth century, an Irish ship was wrecked off the coast, and amongst the stores washed ashore, were potatoes. The scene of the disaster is variously stated to have been North Meols, the Southport of to-day, the mouth of the Ribble, and Formby Point, a few miles to the south of Birkdale. In the *Penny Encyclopaedia* (1833–43) and in the *Rural Cyclopaedia* for 1850, the date of the shipwreck is given as 1565, at least forty years in advance of the potato's arrival in England.

Tradition claims, and not without reason, the district of Formby as the first seat of the cultivation of the potato in Lancashire.[1] We reach more solid ground in this matter in the year 1680 when, at the Michaelmas Leet of Wigan, it was ordained 'that the potato markett and other rootes be made according to the order (at the last Leet) and to begin at 9 o'clock in the morning and toll to be paid on every load'. That such tolls were paid, we know from the records of St Luke's Fair at Wigan, when for the year 1700, entries occur of the tolls gathered by the bailiff on the eve of the Fair for 'Potatoes and other things'.[2] Similar entries occur regularly in subsequent years. The potatoes which were disposed of at Wigan came from Ormskirk.

A special market for the potato in a county town, besides indicating that considerable quantities were being raised in the fields of the district, is evidence that the town-dwellers were demanding them on a scale sufficient to justify specific arrangements for their marketing, and that for several years prior to its establishment, the potato must have won a place in the dietary of the native inhabitants. How many years one cannot say, but we have further indications of the trend of events which inclines one to put the date of the first cultivation not further back than some fifteen to twenty years. The earliest record concerns Dame Sarah Fell of Swarthmore Hall, Lancs, who purchased seed 'pottaties' for her garden in the years 1673 and 1674.[3] She paid 8*d.* for '1 p', and 3½*d.* for '1 hoo'. I am indebted to Mr John Nickalls, Librarian to the Society of Friends, for the identification of these measures; 1 'p' in the context refers to a wooden hooped container equal to quarter-of-a-peck. 1 'hoo' is the volume of fluid between two consecutive bands of the

---

[1] Baines, Edward (1836). History of the County Palatine and Duchy of Lancashire (quoted from March *Notes and Queries*, 28 May 1887).

[2] Hawkes, Arthur J. (1940). Early Cultivation of the Potato in Lancashire. *Notes and Queries*, 7 December.

[3] Penney, Norman (1920). *The Household Account of Sarah Fell*, 1673–8, pp. 5, 141 and 155. Cambridge University Press.

measure and would here seem to correspond to one-eighth of a peck. It would thus appear that Mrs Fell paid about 2*d*. per lb., or more than 1*s*. in to-day's money. In 1684 the potato was said to have been planted in small patches as a field crop,[1] and to have been extensively cultivated throughout the county.[2] This may be somewhat of an exaggeration, but it had at least become sufficiently widespread as to bring the question of its tithing to the fore.

In 1686 Charles Layfield, the Rector of Croston, Lancs, successfully sued thirteen of his parishioners, cultivators of Mawdesley, for a tithe on the potatoes they had grown in 1683 and 1684; the whole amount was £8, which gives one some idea of the value of the crop in those years in that particular parish. The suit was regarded as a test case, and costs were to be remitted if the defendants undertook to pay regularly in the future. Mawdesley is a small village some seven miles north of Ormskirk, which seems to have been in the past, as it is to-day, one of the most important potato-raising centres in the county. From what is known of the Church's sporadic efforts to claim tithe on potatoes, it is unlikely that the claim would have been postponed for many years after the new crop had become established as a feature in the farming economy of the neighbourhood, for had many years elapsed between such cultivation and the making of the claim, the courts would have been disinclined to allow it.

The infiltration of the potato into Lancashire was rapid and widespread. On 13 March 1700, we find a reference to a potato bed at Garstang, and on 14 April of the same year, the author's manservant sold three pecks of potatoes for 2*s*. 11*d*., a little less than £8 per ton retail.[3] About the same time, one hears of 'Lobscouse', a highly flavoured dish of potato, meat and onions, which was particularly associated with the seamen of the Lancashire ports,[4] so popular was it that Ned Ward declares that 'the ship's cook has sent the fellow a thousand times to the Devil that first invented Lobscouse'.[5] In time 'lobscouser' came to be a nickname for a sailor.

Houghton, at the end of the century, refers to the potatoes of Lancashire as derived from Ireland and 'very numerous'. The author of a standard work on Agriculture which appeared in the latter part of the next century, states that it was in Lancashire that the first field crop was grown, and that potatoes were more common there than in Ireland.[6] The first statement is probably correct; the second is certainly not. It

[1] Eden, Sir Frederick (1797). *The State of the Poor*, p. 501.
[2] Rawstoyne, L. (1848). *The New Husbandry*, vol. VI, p. 533. Preston.
[3] Brockbank, Rev. Thomas. *Diary and Letter Book*, Chetham Society (n.s. 1930).
[4] A Lancashire Man (1795). *Ann. Bot.* vol. XXIV, p. 573.
[5] Ward, E. (1707). *Wooden World Dissected* (4th edit. 1749), p. 59.
[6] Henry, David (1771). *The Complete Farmer*, p. 275.

may, however, be truthfully said that in Lancashire the cultivation of the potato was as far advanced in 1680 as it was a hundred years later anywhere else in England, and infinitely more so than it was in the Eastern Counties at this later date.

Towards the end of the eighteenth century, Liverpool, not content with the larger supplies it drew from Ormskirk, imported some 100,000 bushels of 90 lb. each from Cheshire.[1]

By the middle of the eighteenth century, Lancashire had built up a considerable export trade in potatoes, the first of its kind in England. Consignments reached Gibraltar and other unspecified ports, but the most remarkable outlet for their surplus was Dublin, to which some twenty shiploads were dispatched annually from Liverpool alone.[2] It was probably this trade which led to the conversion of the site of the old Castle ditch into a potato market, some time prior to 1769.[3]

The potato market of Manchester, probably in use at a still earlier date,[4] was situated on the present site of the Exchange.

Important as these tendencies may be, they would not have brought about this early adoption of the new food had not the existing conditions of land tenure and husbandry allowed of its cultivation.

Lancashire's priority in this matter of the potato, compared with the rest of England other than Wales, is too outstanding to be merely accidental. Even if we accept the tale of its early arrival, it does little to account for her lead, for an even earlier introduction can be confidently claimed for London and the Home Counties. It is not so much the date, or the manner of its arrival, which determines the future success of a new food crop, as the character of the social and agricultural environment it encounters.

In Lancashire the open fields, together with the fixed cropping and the common right of post-harvest grazing, so inimical to late root crops, had long since disappeared, and been replaced by small-holdings with their diminutive enclosed and protected fields. But it was not only the lay-out of the land, which favoured potato cultivation: the deep moss soils and moist mild climate likewise played their parts in making the north-west counties not only the first, but amongst the foremost potato-raising districts in England. Notwithstanding these advantages, the potato never won such a position that it dominated the dietary, still less the lives, of the people. The potato flourished in Lancashire, not because of the poverty of the people or of their political subjection, for there was less of either than elsewhere. It was because the worker, relatively the

---

[1] Wedge, Thomas (1794). *General View, etc. Chester*, p. 18.
[2] Grant, Archibald, Sir (1756). *The Practical Farmers' Pocket Companion*, p. 16.
[3] Picton, J. A. (1903). *Memorials of Liverpool*, vol. II, p. 126.
[4] Harland, J. (1866). *Collecteana relating to Manchester*, vol. II, p. 108. Chetham Society.

best paid and best fed in England, had both the opportunity and the leisure to cultivate his own land in such a manner as to lend itself best to the support of himself and his family. The potato used in this manner allowed the worker greater freedom to purchase more expensive foods.

An interesting parallel is reported a hundred years later from York-shire. In the Rochdale district in 1773 there was an extraordinarily heavy crop of potatoes: this induced such a fall in the local price of wheat as allowed 'the poor an opportunity of buying bread'.[1] It was not often that things worked out that way.

The Potato in Relation to Wheaten and Oaten Dietaries

Wheat in Lancashire has always played a secondary role to oats as a cereal crop; thus in 1881 there were 39,373 acres under the latter, to 26,492 of the former,[2] whilst the potato area was 42,809 acres. In earlier days the bias in favour of oats was probably much greater. Certainly in the eighteenth century the people were essentially oatmeal and rye eaters, and in the seventeenth century it is unlikely that they were less so. People who have come to rely in the main on oatmeal for their bread, because the climatic environment denies them the opportunity of replacing it by wheat, the aristocrat of the cereals, would be more ready to welcome a new, palatable, readily grown and easily prepared food such as the potato, than those living in districts where wheat, barley and oats all flourish. The bias of these latter has been constantly directed towards the white wheaten bread, favoured and adopted by the wealthy upper classes, and they were only debarred from its attain-ment by economic considerations which they eventually overcame.

It will be seen that there is a high degree of correlation, between the position of oatmeal or barley and the potato in a people's dietary; in the sense that when either of the former is the chief cereal used, then the potato is a far more important article of diet than in those districts where wheat is the principal cereal consumed. One has but to review the relative quantities of oatmeal and potatoes eaten to-day by the generality of people in the Highlands, the Lowlands, the Isle of Man, the northern counties and the Home and Southern counties, respectively, to realize that this relation still exists. But not even in the Highlands, where the quantity of potatoes consumed is highest, does this preference amount to a domination of the dietary, such as occurred in the eighteenth century. The reason for this difference of reaction is doubtless complex, but the lessons to be learnt from Ireland, the Highlands of the eighteenth century and Poland in the twentieth century, all indicate that the determining

---

[1] Hunter, A. (1777). *Georgical Essays*, p. 301.
[2] *History of Lancashire* (1881). Historica Publishing Co.

factor which converts such a preference into a domination, is some form of political or social oppression rather than simple economic pressure.

In Lancashire, neither the earliness of its introduction nor the extension and volume of its culture, led to its domination of the people's food. Even in the 'hungry forties', though its importance was great, we learn that milk and bacon still maintained their position in the workers' dietary.[1]

We may conclude this sketch of the first hundred years of the potato in England with a reference to views published in a weekly newsletter on 15 December 1699. This publication, the earliest newspaper devoted in the main to agriculture and industry, was edited and published by John Houghton, a Fellow of the Royal Society, and appeared regularly from 1681 to 1683, and again from 1692 to 1703. It was characteristic of the awakened interest in natural philosophy that from the first it adopted a sound scientific attitude towards agricultural problems. On the date mentioned, Houghton devoted his leading article to the potato and its culture, and ends by saying: 'In some places it may be worth while to plant abundance if it were only to feed cattle and poultry. I believe the more husbandries we have, the better.' He was right. Before the potato could play the part of fodder for the poor, it was necessary that it should prove its worth as food for swine.[2]

[1] Curtler, W. H. R. (1908). *Victoria County Histories, etc. Lancaster*, vol. II, p. 419.
[2] Houghton's article is to be found in the edition of his *News-letters* published in book form and edited by Richard Bradley, Professor of Botany in Cambridge in 1727. The writer has searched for the original sheet issued on 15 December 1699, in the British Museum; the University Library, Cambridge; the Bodleian, Oxford; the National Libraries of both Wales and Scotland; the Library of Trinity College, Dublin; and that of Rothamsted, without success.

CHAPTER XXV

The Eighteenth Century

It was during the latter quarter of the eighteenth century that the potato began to assume a place of importance in the dietary of the working classes of England; that this was not due to its merits as a palatable and wholesome food, may be gathered from the very slow progress it had made so far. Rather should it be regarded as the outward sign of an economic change, so far-reaching as to influence the innermost citadel of the people's home.

In order to estimate the strength and character of the forces which induced the change, we must needs study them in relation to the political, social and economic atmosphere of the time. To that end it is desirable to sketch in outline, however briefly, the major influences which were at work in the formation of the eighteenth-century environment as experienced by the great majority of the people; that is to say, by the working folk of this country.

One is apt to approach the eighteenth century in a spirit of disappointment. Not only are the giants of the Elizabethan era no more, but the peculiar glamour which illumined such names as Drake, Raleigh and Boyle, cannot be dragooned to do a like service for Marlborough, Captain Cook, or even Newton. A different, not necessarily a less worthy spirit, would seem to have inspired both the leaders and the common people of this later period.

The effervescent spirit of adventure which inspired the Elizabethans, at the same time covered their naked lust for power and gold with a garb of seeming romance. In the England of Cromwell and William III, this spirit had developed into a commercialism whose piratical intentions were but inadequately shrouded by the cloak of Puritanism.

Many of the major social and political hazards which had so often destroyed the peace and endangered life, in the Elizabethan and Stuart periods, were no more. An air of security had begun to be felt rather than fought for. If there was less assertiveness and flamboyance, there was a greater self-assurance about the leaders, and more confidence amongst the people of this later generation.

Although it is true that much that was regrettable took shape in this period, yet it was now that the country as a whole, took a bolder step forward on the path to liberty than had ever been contemplated before.

The 'glorious revolution' of 1688 had cleared the political stage of much archaic lumber besides the doctrine of Divine Right; the ascendancy of Parliament, though threatened by George III, was never seriously challenged by the Crown again. The victory of the Common Law over the Prerogative Courts had established the supremacy of law throughout the land, though it needed another 150 years to bring its practice in alignment with the dictates of humanity. So great a weight had been lifted from men's minds with the disappearance of Star Chamber, Ecclesiastical Commission, and the Councils of Wales and the North, that Englishmen began to foster actively the idea that all men were equal in the eyes of the Law. This assurance, though far outstripping reality, gave to the common man a certain fortitude and independence which never quite forsook him even in the darkest days that were to follow.

Gone, too, in England and Wales, were all but the last traces of feudalism, though the social void was filled by an intensified form of class distinction, whose basis changed as the century proceeded, from one founded on territorial power, to one which might indirectly be reared on money and capitalistic control. In Scotland where, as we have seen, tenants continued to pay irksome and indeed heavy feudal levies in labour, food and money, the social relation between hind and laird was far easier and more pleasant than that which grew up between master and labourer in the latter part of eighteenth-century England. To this subject we shall return later.

Eighteenth-century class distinction, however, must not be confused with the idle snobbery of to-day, for it at least rested on the basis of a genuine aristocratic control of both executive and legislature. The large landowners, themselves often peers, as part of a definite policy, acquired by purchase of the land as many parliamentary boroughs as possible. With a similar object they enlarged their estates, buying out the smaller freeholders and extinguishing their votes, whilst at the same time increasing their roll of tenants, who thus came more closely under their influence and control. In this manner the great aristocratic families obtained control of both houses. In the scramble, the independent member was all but extinguished.

In the reign of Queen Anne, the Tories were in power for the greater part of the time; throughout that of the first two George's, it was the turn of their opponents, who established the famous 'Whig Oligarchy' which ruled the country from 1714 till 1760.

But it mattered little, or nothing, to the common man whether Whig or Tory was in power, for he had no say in their election, nor more interest in their politics than they had in him. So long as the common man was ready to work and abstained from poaching their game, all was well.

The English labourer did not feel an outcast because he knew himself to be the freest of his class in Europe.[1] He had, moreover, faith in the

---

[1] Trevelyan, G. M. (1926). *History of England*, p. 512.

power of the Law, a faith which was not misplaced, for the Judicature was ever jealous. But in truth Parliament and Whitehall meant but little to the common man, in whose eyes all authority was invested in the local Justices of the Peace who, recruited from the squirearchy, were for the most part Tories. It was through them that the country was actually ruled. It was they who administered local government and, what was more important, controlled wages, and to some extent food prices. If tyranny there was, it was social, not political. The economic policy of the squirearchy was to maintain the price of wheat at a high, and wages at a low level, to keep the working man off the rates or, failing that, to see that he should cost the community as little as possible and get back to work without unnecessary delay. It was their sincere opinion that only by so doing, could the strength and prestige of the country be maintained in a Europe jealous and hostile.

This type of aristocratic government worked admirably so long as the old system of village self-sufficiency held good, but when during the latter quarter of the century the factory system became increasingly firmly established and the urban workers had begun to compare in numbers with those of the countryside, then its deficiencies became manifest. Aristocratic government knew little of the actual lives of the people and understood less. That the demand of industry for man-power was growing faster than the country's means to provide adequate food, homes, or education for the workers, was never seriously considered. It was not until towards the close of the century, when the scarcity of corn became acute and the potato had been called in to make good the shortage, that the masses awoke to the anomaly of their political and economic situation. Even so, it took another thirty years before the accumulated sufferings of the workers reached a climax, and the ruling classes of the country were confronted with the alternative of revolution or reform.

It would not have been surprising had the wars against France, that of the League of Augsburg, 1689–97, and that of the Spanish Succession, 1701–13, proved a heavy drain on the country in both men and money, and by so doing had depressed the standard of living and hastened the adoption of the potato. But the wars had rather the contrary effect: the number of Englishmen engaged was never great: Trevelyan observes that Marlborough had only 9,000 British troops at Blenheim and that an engagement of that magnitude was fought only once in every two years.[1] The cost of maintaining our troops and those of our allies was of course great, but was more than offset by the acquisition of new markets and the great stimulus it gave to industry at home. Except for those who were wounded or fell, the mass of the people seems to have

[1] Trevelyan, G. M. (1926). *History of England*, p. 487 n.

benefited rather than otherwise by the Continental wars of Queen Anne's time. It was the landed interest who paid the land tax, and it was they, more especially the Tories, who resented its continuance and the heavy cost of the maintenance of Army and Navy.

Even the change of dynasty and the existence of the Jacobite Court of St Germain were not disquieting elements in the economic and social life of the people. In Scotland it was otherwise, but in England Jacobitism was the plaything of a relatively few aristocratic families; it did not disturb the tenor of life of the middle or lower classes. It was only military ineptitude which allowed the Young Pretender to reach Derby in 1745; the people of England were completely passive.[1]

In the religious sphere, the eighteenth century was in some respects fortunate. The old conflict between the Established and the Independent Churches had, at the time of the Restoration, shed whatever little spiritual content it ever possessed, and had taken on an almost purely political and social guise, with the result that what it gained in intellectual acerbity, it lost in its potential for violence and cruelty. As far as the ordinary citizen was concerned, the change was all to the good, for it brought him not only a measure of intellectual freedom, but the opportunity to seek for religious inspiration outside the Established Church from those who spoke his own language, shared his own thoughts, and were content, like him, to find their spiritual guidance in the Scriptures themselves. Against these immediate benefits must be placed the decay of higher learning, except in the topmost layers of society, and the degradation and sterilization of the Universities of Oxford and Cambridge, both of which had become little more than appanages of the Established Church.

The long drawn-out fight between the Anglican and Roman Church, so far as it was expressed in plot and counter-plot, had ended before the century began, in the complete political supremacy of the former, the social implications of which were not allowed to pass unheeded. The disabilities borne by Catholic subjects were many and galling, but not physically oppressive, and in practice they affected only the political fortunes of a certain small but distinguished layer of the aristocracy. The masses in England and Wales, being overwhelmingly Protestant, were spiritually and economically unaffected. If during the first three-quarters of the century the Church had but little influence on the lives of the masses, this cannot be said to hold for the last quarter.

As we shall see, the potato was only adopted by the working classes

---

[1] 'It was not till Prestonpans had been fought that Claydon knew anything of the 1745 rising. The men went on with their hedging and ditching, their reaping and thatching, unaware of the astonishing victories that "Bonnie Prince Charlie" was winning in Scotland.' *Verney Letters* (1930), p. 198.

in the greater part of England, as a result of actual want, which overtook them towards the end of the century. This critical condition, though precipitated by war conditions, had been gradually developing during the previous twenty years as a consequence of the struggle between labour, which had neither weapons nor leaders, and employers who were convinced that labour was but a commodity to be bought in the cheapest market, and towards which, other than by the payment of wages, they had no obligations. In this movement, the clergy with but few exceptions, of which the poet Crabbe in this century and Gradlestone in the next, were examples, identified themselves socially and economically with the squirearchy and farmers, and were amongst the foremost in recommending the potato because of its cheapness, as a substitute to a people whose wages they knew were insufficient to buy bread.

Remarkable developments had meanwhile taken place in the realms of industry and foreign trade. The dauntless individualism of the Elizabethan and Stuart adventurer, part merchant, part pirate and wholly egoist, had blazed the path to new worlds. But, now, it was realized that the continued exploitation of the wealth of the Indies could only be secured by a much greater degree of organization, material and political. The principle which originated in Elizabeth's reign of creating monopoly trading companies, took on a greater development as Joint Stock Chartered Companies were formed, owning fleets of armed trading vessels. These secured their right of entry into American, Indian and Far Eastern ports by means which were appropriate to their day, and in so doing employed a large number of the younger sons of the squirearchy, which helped to break down the insularity and widen the outlook of our ruling classes. The Chartered Companies, no less than the Bank of England, the creation of National Debts, the General Post Office and the Penny Post for London, were the outcome of these new currents of thought.

In the first half of the eighteenth century, these same currents gathering strength, expressed themselves in ever bigger and wilder ventures, some of which were but poorly controlled. The South Sea Company of 1710, in which most of the moneyed classes in the country had taken shares, brought widespread ruin with its collapse in 1720; this for a time checked foreign investment but left the working classes untouched.

A few decades later, it was the turn of the home country to experience the full blast of mercantile adventure; in the wake of the hurricane, the entire system of both our agricultural and industrial life ultimately underwent a radical change. Together the Industrial Revolution and the great Enclosure campaign launched this country on the broad highway, towards a new orientation of society. In this development the potato, occasionally in the open, but more often camouflaged as a philanthropic *Deus ex machina*, played an important part.

Thanks to the enterprise of trader and middleman, a class which was growing in numbers and prominence, fresh markets sprang up throughout the country for the products of the village craftsmen. At this time the more wealthy merchants of the towns, desirous of becoming identified with the old squirearchy, acquired landed estates and generally spent large sums on their improvement. This reciprocal relation between town and country did something to soften the antagonism between the interests of the two, the inevitable consequence of the Industrial Revolution. How intensive was the development of home-manufacture as organized through the agency of the merchant-middlemen, in the first quarter of the century, may be gathered from contemporary descriptions of Stourbridge Fair, the looms of Taunton, the great clothing towns of the western Midlands and particularly that of Leeds, already the emporium for the cloth trade with the Colonies and Europe.[1] It has been well said: 'This interplay of the activity of town and country, not yet subversive of the old social order, gave to Queen Anne's England a fundamental harmony and strength, below the surface of the fierce distracting antagonisms of sect and fashion.'[2]

The Housing of the Labourer

The housing of the English labourer throughout the eighteenth century reflects, with remarkable accuracy, the degree of class distinction current both in time and place. Our climate doubtless has played its part in inspiring the rich to demand a high degree of permanence in the construction of their own dwellings, and in the provision of homes for their workers they have assumed a similar permanence notwithstanding their failure to supply the necessary material with which to attain it. Hence it is that there is a prolonged time-lag between any amelioration in the social conscience, and its translation into bricks and mortar. Here, too, may be the reason why humanitarianism, the outstanding ethical contribution of the nineteenth century, only began to register a nascent influence on the housing of the poor, after a lapse of seventy or more years. Other factors, it is true, played in the past, a more deterrent role than they do to-day, such as the nature of the local building material, the degree of industrialization of the district, and the means of transport. Yet, however adverse these influences may have been, had the social conscience been sincerely awakened, the demand for better housing for

---

[1] Defoe, Daniel (1727). *A Tour through the Whole Island of Great Britain* (ed. G. D. M. Cole).

[2] Trevelyan, G. M. (1930). *England under Queen Anne*, p. 4.

the workers would have been general, and there is not the slightest doubt that it could have been satisfied. Ethics apart, good housing is also good business, an asset whose dividends are paid in terms of less disease, lower mortality, greater industrial efficiency, and higher intellectual standards. The conviction that labour was but a commodity and self-interest the major motive in industry, blinded the employers to a policy which would have ultimately been to their own advantage.

In England, cottages were best south of the Thames, where they were often substantially built of brick or half-timbered, but as one proceeded northwards and westwards the standard deteriorated till the dry stone huts of the north and the mud homes of Dorset became the common types. Towards the end of the century and in the early part of the next, a few of the great landlords built rows of well-constructed roomy cottages on their domains: such may be seen on the Penrhyn, Bedford, and Milton Abbas Estates. In not a few cases these cottages were so designed as to make a distinctive architectural feature in the village, and thus create a picturesque effect in harmony with the Great House and its surroundings. The cottages on the Bedford and some other estates were kept under the direct control of the owner rather than be allowed to pass under that of the farmer, a policy which afforded a considerable measure of protection to the labourer.

Nathaniel Kent, an eminent agriculturist, at the beginning of the last quarter of the eighteenth century, complained that half the population live in 'shattered hovels', and recommended the erection of well-constructed homes with an half acre of arable land adjoining, for potatoes and carrots, and three acres of pasture for a cow. His powerful advocacy led to a few of the larger landlords in Rutland and Lincolnshire erecting a number of these on their estates.[1] Kent also refers to the growing scarcity of homes for the poor and the tendency of the farmer, occupying the new engrossed farms, to destroy cottages. When the poor rates rose to unimagined heights during the Napoleonic wars and after, a greater number of cottages were deliberately destroyed in order to evade the poor rates.[2]

Nowhere in the eighteenth century could the housing of the poor be regarded as other than unsatisfactory. According to Young[3] who was not given to exaggeration, 'cottages are perhaps one of the greatest disgraces to this country that remains to be found in it', and he proceeds to prove his case without much trouble. Even in counties such as Hampshire,

---

[1] Kent, Nathaniel (1777). *Hints to Gentlemen* (ed. 1793), pp. 207, 211 and 216.

[2] Within a couple of miles of the writer's home, there is a village, Little Chishill, Cambs, in which all the cottages were for this reason deliberately burned down by the landlord.

[3] Young, Arthur (1804). *Annals of Agric.* vol. XLII, p. 284.

Sussex and Kent, where there were some relatively good cottages, mud hovels were still in common use till well into the next century. Cottages as opposed to the mud hovels, often contained but one sitting-room and one bedroom; although two-bedroomed cottages were perhaps more numerous, those with three were very scarce. Neither individual water supply nor drainage were ever considered, and are absent to-day in most country districts. One thing may be said of the generality of cottages in England: they always had one bricked fireplace and chimney, which was duly taxed, and the windows were at least glazed, even if they did not always open.

Throughout the greater part of the century the labourer's home, besides sheltering himself and family, had other functions to fulfil. As the family workshop, it served the wife and children for the spinning and carding of wool, and the husband for the working of his loom. Of no less importance was the use of a piece of land either attached to, or let with the cottage. The area and character of such plots or gardens varied widely; only rarely was the Elizabethan minimum of four acres to be found. But whether wholly arable or partly meadow, the possession of such, in adequate amount, was of greater importance to the welfare of the rural workers than any advance in wage which reached them during the eighteenth or nineteenth centuries.

Poor as the eighteenth-century cottages were, there seems no reason to doubt that during the first half of the century there were at least enough of them to provide shelter for all the rural workers. By the end of the century this was no longer the case. The enclosures had rendered many of the smaller steadings useless, whilst as a result of engrossment and rearrangement of farms, many cottages and buildings were no longer required: these either fell into decay, or were pulled down. Another group of cottage homes, those roughly built shacks which squatters had erected on the commons, fell easy victims to the same movement, and were swept away by the 'improvers'. The net result was that the housing problem, which to the workers in the early part of the century had been a question of the choice of a home, with greater or lesser amenities, towards its close resolved itself into the acceptance of whatever was available however poor, or having no home at all.

Fuel and Clothing

Fuel was cheap and plentiful in the neighbourhood of woods, but elsewhere, or where the commoners had no rights of 'lop and top', its acquisition often became a serious problem, especially as sea-coal rarely reached as far as the villages and, when it did, was too expensive. On moorlands the common people frequently had the right of turbary, or cutting of peat. In general, the enclosures deprived the people of most of its sources of cheap or free fuel.[1]

In many parts of the country the shortage of fuel was a serious problem for the cottager's wife who, in the warm weather, would not want to keep a fire burning all and every day. Where such conditions held, it acted as a definite deterrent to the use of the potato as a daily article of food.

The clothing of the agricultural workers was, it may be assumed, adequate; much of the cloth was woven at home, and the village tailor and bootmaker did the rest; later in the century, broadcloth from the large village factories replaced the homespun, and the Northampton and Staffordshire shoemakers the local botcher. Commodities of all kinds were finding their way into the homes of the better paid artisan—not least welcome of which were the much improved candles.[2] From the accounts of Arthur Young and others, it seems unlikely that the agricultural labourer shared in these benefits.

The Food of the People

The dietary of the lower middle classes at the beginning of the century appears to have been generous. Baxter[3] enumerates the different food-stuffs commonly consumed by the smallholder at the end of the seventeenth century, viz. milk, butter, cheese, whey and buttermilk; cabbage, turnips, parsnips, carrots, onions and potatoes; apple-pies, pease-pies, puddings, and pancakes; gruel, flummery and frumenty. It will be observed that there is no mention of meat or fish; the former had become very expensive, viz. 5d. per lb.; it was to be but half this price thirty years later; and the latter very rarely reached the inland villages. So poor were the means of communication that even salted herrings, which had recently been introduced, were rarely available. Doubtless recalling his experience in the West Country, Baxter recommends that they should plant a quarter of an acre with potatoes, or better still, with Jerusalem artichokes, which he assures them 'will find you a half year's wholesome food'. The landless labourer could not have enjoyed so wide a range, nor so ample a supply of food.

[1] For an interesting dispute on the rights of Lop and Top, see Gilbert White's *History of Selborne*. Cobbett in his *Rural Rides*, frequently refers to the great advantage enjoyed by labourers who lived in wooded districts, because of their ancient right or privilege to gather fuel.

[2] Cobbett (1821, *Cottage Economy*, p. 144; Peter Davies, 1926) suggests that it was the potato which reduced the quantity of meat in the workers' homes, hence the absence of grease with which hitherto they had made their rush lights. In truth, the cause of both was simply low wages and high prices.

[3] Baxter, Richard (1611). *The Poor Husbandman's Advocate*. John Ryland's Lib. Bull. vol. x, no. 1, pp. 22 and 58, 1926.

A reference from a more official source a decade later, bears this out. Here, although the potato is reported to be growing 'in several parts of our country and to very good advantage', and to be more wholesome than Jerusalem artichokes, which had now definitely fallen from favour, it is obvious that it was by no means an established source of human food, or even well known to the writer, as would appear from his final sentence which runs: 'These same are planted either of the roots or of the seed and may probably be propagated in great quantities and prove good for swine.'[1]

In East Anglia, neither as food for man nor beast, had the potato at this date gained a foothold. In the Harvest records and accounts extending from 1682 to 1692 of a large farm at Fowlmere, Cambridge,[2] no mention of the potato occurs. This is not surprising, seeing that in a Suffolk squire's home in 1709, 6½d. was paid for a pound of potatoes, as against 3d. for a chicken, 4d. for a rabbit and 4½d. for a pound of butter.[3]

Between the reigns of Queen Anne and George III, food prices were abnormally low: wheat was 33s. per quarter, the price of meat averaged 2½d., butter 5½d., and cheese 2d. per lb. Vegetables were not greatly favoured although kale, carrots, turnips and onions were commonly raised in the cottage gardens. Many homes brewed and drank their own beer. The use of the commons afforded the workers an opportunity to keep a few head of poultry and even one or two cows; few labourers were without a pig.

As an example of the fare of the poorest stratum of society, the dietaries of the representative workhouses are instructive. In 1714 the Bristol Workhouse fed their inmates three times a day on the highest quality food—meat, green vegetables, turnips and potatoes, and the best beer obtainable: the average cost was only 16d. per week for each girl of the one hundred in the house.[4] Another account, from a Bedfordshire Workhouse[5] in the early part of the century included meat six times a week, wheaten bread and cheese for supper each day, to which should be added the milk from cows fed on the common, and the bacon from pigs which were fed on the 'wash and dregs' from the house.

It will be seen that during the first half of the eighteenth century the food of the people was mixed, nutritious and in general adequate. There was only one serious fault with the dietary of this period, and that was

[1] *Dictionarium Rusticum, Urbanicum et Botanicum* (1704). London.
[2] Baker, W. F. (1941). A Seventeenth-Century Harvest Account Book. Lecture to Cambridge Antiquarian Society, 13 October 1941.
[3] Halliwell, J. O. (1852). *Some Accounts of a Collection of Several Thousand Bills, etc. of the Archer family.*
[4] Eden, Sir Frederick (1797). *The State of the Poor*, vol. 1, p. 278.
[5] Ibid.

the excessive consumption of cheap gin which, mainly confined to the towns, took place between 1720 and 1750. It is generally held that it was this which was responsible for the high mortality rate in London. The racket was controlled by taxation in 1751.

The Open Fields

In most parts of England, in addition to their gardens, the labourers enjoyed specific rights on the village commons which served them for the maintenance of their poultry, their cow and their pony and, not seldom, provided them with their fuel.

A few village commons up and down the country, and the famous parishes of Axholme in Lincolnshire and Laxton in Nottinghamshire, are all that remain of a system of land management which, current in most of England for over a thousand years, was brought to an end during the latter part of the eighteenth and the first half of the nineteenth century. The greater part of England in the period we are discussing, was under the open-field system. It is not possible here to go into the history and development of the open-field system, nor into the many attempts throughout the ages to convert it from one of common tenure into one of severalty; such attempts were local and scattered, so that by the eighteenth century, in a district which was mainly 'open', there might be a variable amount of the land already enclosed, and in the hands of individual farmers. It was not uncommon for enclosed land to lie within the confines of the open field itself.

In the Tudor and Stuart periods a great deal of waste land and ex-forest, or assart land, throughout the country was cleared by the Lords of the Manor and enclosed forthwith; such land had never been open arable, but had been subject to certain common rights of pannage and fuel which were lost on their enclosure. The enclosures which followed after 1760 were on a much larger scale and involved whole parishes. They were carried out by special Acts of Parliament and intentionally altered the entire economic system of the countryside.

The essence of the open field was that the arable land of a parish was divided into three distinct areas or fields and that each year each field was either sown wholly with wheat, spring corn including pease or beans, or was left fallow. In that way the land was only in bearing twice in three years. Each of the three fields was divided into a large number, running often into hundreds, of strips known as lands or ridges; each cultivator might possess few or many such 'lands', but, whether few or many, they were always scattered both over the three fields and within each of the three.

Another essential feature of the system was the right vested in every strip-holder, directly the harvest was carried, of turning his cattle and other stock out on the stubble to wander over his own and his neighbours' lands. This right had a definite and adverse influence on the cultivation of any new crop, and more especially on roots such as the turnip and potato.

To work the system it was essential to formulate a common policy and this in turn led to the creation of special *ad hoc* parish councils or courts-leets, at which the strip-owners met to determine the cropping and cognate matters for the coming year. A considerable degree of co-operation and forbearance as between occupiers was necessary from the start, which centuries back had led to the close grouping of the individual cultivators, and so to the formation of villages.

It would be misleading to suppose that the open-field system, because of its inelasticity and its inherently conservative character, constituted a permanent and insuperable barrier to the introduction of new methods of husbandry, and particularly to such autumn crops as the turnip and potato. It is true that changes were long delayed, difficult to come by, and frequently engendered bitter quarrels between the strip-owners, but throughout the centuries adjustments had occurred, and towards the end of the eighteenth century they were by no means infrequent.[1]

In the earlier efforts to meet changed conditions, it was the spring-sown field which was chosen for innovations;[2] thus it was not uncommon to divide it into two, making a four-field system, one half being sown with spring corn, the other undersown with clover, vetches, or rye grass, the right of 'shack' or stubbling being foregone on this portion. A similar division of the fallow in Bedfordshire to allow of turnip growing was in practice prior to 1794, by which time most of the old open-field regulations had lapsed in that county.[3]

In Berkshire portions of the open field might be 'hitched', i.e. the common grazing rights suspended so as to allow the cultivation of clover, turnips or potatoes.[4]

Although an Act was passed in 1773 to facilitate the growing of turnips in the open field, it had no immediate success. In the seventeenth and early eighteenth centuries, turnips, where grown at all, had generally been confined to those small enclosures protected from 'shack' which, as we have seen, were often to be found lying in the midst of the great open fields. It was not until towards the end of the century that the

[1] There is an unconfirmed statement by a Mr Sterling of Menmure, that the potato was grown in the open field in both England and Scotland as early as 1684. *Gardeners' Chronicle*, 1844, 31 August, p. 596.
[2] Gonner, E. C. K. (1912). *Common Land and Enclosure*, p. 32.
[3] Stone, Thomas (1794). *General View of the Agriculture of the County of Bedford*, p. 18.
[4] Ernle, Lord (1912). *English Farming* (edit. 1936), p. 248, quoting from *General View, Berkshire*.

turnip invaded the fallow field, when its presence, it may be said, 'sounded the death knell of the three course system'.[1] Such invasions had occurred in isolated cases earlier, for example, at Alverton near Stratford-on-Avon, where turnips had been admitted to the open field in the first decades of the eighteenth century.[2] An example of the same procedure later in the century may be seen in the case of Hooten Pagnell where in 1781 the Court-Leet agreed 'that any owner or tenant in the open arable field shall be at liberty to sow such land or ground with turnip the year that such open field or any of them shall be summer fallowed, but not at any other time'. The potato followed in the wake of the turnip but though, under the open-field system, neither were looked on with much favour, the potato soon became the more popular of the two, chiefly because farmers frequently allowed their men to grow them on the fallows.

Young records that he had never seen the potato in the open field prior to 1764;[3] his first encounter would appear to have been on the Northern Tour in 1768.

The two extant examples of the open field, viz. Laxton, Notts, and the Isle of Axholme, Lincs, illustrate the two extremes of policy. At Laxton a rigid adherence to the three-course system was maintained until 1904 when arrangements were made to grow crops such as potatoes in certain fields.[4]

At Axholme, the right of 'shack' having been relinquished, potatoes displaced turnips more or less completely, and became established as a definite crop after 1750. By 1794 the commoners were sending large quantities of potatoes to London via the Trent.[5]

From all sides the desirability of introducing the potato into the open field was urged. Official support was given by the Board of Agriculture, which in 1801 advised that a Bill be presented to Parliament to allow the fallows in the open fields to be planted with potatoes and the cottagers be recompensed for their grazing rights.

The custom of giving potato land to the agricultural labourer, in exchange for manure and cultivation, became common throughout the country and helped, no doubt, to popularize the use of the potato during the last phases of the open-field era. An example is to be seen at Deddington, Oxfordshire, where potatoes had been grown by the poor on the open-field fallows for some years prior to 1809.[6]

Nor was it only the poor who used the open fields in this way: we hear

---

[1] Ruston, A. G. Witney Denis (1934). *Hooten Pagnell*.
[2] Styles, Philip (1945). Communicated to R.N.S.
[3] Young, A. (1771). *A Course of Experimental Agriculture*, vol. III, p. 209.
[4] Orwin, C. S. and C. S. (1938). *The Open Fields*, p. 191.
[5] Orwin, C. S. Communicated personally to R.N.S.
[6] Young, A. (1809). *General View of the Agriculture of Oxfordshire*, p. 185.

of a farmer at Barkway, Hertfordshire, who grew 36 acres of potatoes in 1804.[1] Elsewhere in Hertfordshire, Young records considerable acreages of potatoes, though it is not clear that they were all in the open field.

An interesting account of the introduction of the potato into Bluntisham-cum-Erith in Huntingdonshire has recently been published.[2] On 18 November 1800, the Court-Leet met at the 'Black Bull' and decided that certain portions of the open field, which are described in great detail, shall be sown with turnips and that 'no cattle shall be allowed to go upon the aforesaid part of the field more than ten days after the first tares are sown'. The way was thus opened in the village for the potato, and on 31 January 1805 the Court, meeting this time at the 'Royal Oak', agreed that 'Causeway Side Furlong...be planted with potatoes in the spring of 1806 and that the hogs be kept off after harvest.' This 'furlong' contained 45¾ acres and consisted of 105 separate lands occupied by 79 different persons, a good example of the old system both at its worst and its best.

These examples are sufficient to show that the open-field system when capably administered, could go a long way towards meeting the urgent call for increased food supplies which the nation, at war, demanded. That it could be no less obstructive, when badly handled, may be seen from the behaviour of the strip-holders of Eversden, Cambridgeshire, who blocked up the opening into the main drain of the hollow drain system, which an enterprising fellow-holder had laid down in his holding, in order to improve the land and ensure better cropping. Not content with this, the Court-Leet 'served him with a notice to refrain at his peril from the cultivation of turnips in the open field'.[3] How common such active opposition to progress was, it is difficult to determine; that it was not general, even within the same district, appears from the fact that at the same date, in the neighbouring village of Arrington, turnips were being grown in the open field. There can be little doubt, judging from the frequent adverse comments of Young and Cobbett, that it was bigoted opposition of this kind, which hastened the movement for enclosures throughout the country.

From the point of view of husbandry, the open field failed because it did nothing to prevent the gradual exhaustion of the soil, which began to make itself felt even before the Black Death. When therefore a vastly increased population had to be fed, the whole system failed to meet the needs of the time.

This is not the place to discuss in detail the relative merits of the open-

[1] Young, A. (1804). *General View of the Agriculture of Hertfordshire*, p. 102.
[2] Tebbutt, C. F. (1941). *Bluntisham cum Erith, St Neots*, pp. lix and lxi.
[3] Vancouver, Charles (1794). *General View of Agriculture of the County of Cambridge*, pp. 92 and 97.

and enclosed-field system.[1] The latter was certainly of great advantage to the rapidly expanding economic life of the kingdom as a whole, and as a measure for feeding the people during the prosecution of the twenty years' war against Napoleon, was probably essential. The old system, in its turn, had conferred invaluable advantages on the small man and agricultural labourer. By owning, or renting, a few strips in the common field and making use of his rights on the common, he had the opportunity of planting his feet on the lower rungs of a ladder, by which he could attain to the position of an independent farmer, a development which often occurred.[2] It is alleged that the strip system led to much petty quarrelling between neighbours and there is undoubtedly some truth in the statement, but this was more than compensated by the encouragement it gave to the development of a communal consciousness and a sense of mutual responsibility amongst the labourers and their masters which, in the latter part of the century, was almost entirely lost. This final stage in the change over from the open- to the enclosed-field system, completed the transition of the English peasant into a landless worker, and indirectly exerted a profound influence on his attitude towards the potato as the century proceeded.

Although agricultural wages were lower than they were later in the century, yet as they provided more of the essential necessities of the home, the workers were better off. Even at the danger of appearing a *Laudator temporis acti*, one would be blind if, in a survey of the social conditions of the working classes during the eighteenth and nineteenth centuries, where so much is sombre and depressing, one failed to realize that for at least fifty years prior to 1770 the workers in this country were free from anxiety as to their immediate needs in respect to food and shelter, to an extent unknown to later generations.

Malthus[3] pointed out that between the last forty years of the seventeenth and the first twenty years of the eighteenth centuries, the average price of corn was such that the labourer was able to purchase two-thirds of a peck of wheat with a day's wage; from 1720 to 1750 the price of wheat fell, whilst wages rose, so that he could then purchase a whole peck. Ernle[4] estimates both the fall in price and the rise in wages to have been about 16%, and is of opinion that real wages had never been so high since the reign of Henry VI. Indeed, like several others, he thinks that 'the reign of George II was the nearest approach to a Golden Age of the labouring classes', a view which seems to be well founded so far as the workers on the land were concerned.

---

[1] An excellent discussion of the question will be found in Lord Ernle's *The Land and its People*, Hutchinson, 1923.

[2] Orwin, C. S. and C. S. (1938). *The Open Fields*, p. 195.

[3] Malthus, T. R. (1820). *Principles of Political Economy*, p. 253.

[4] Ernle, Lord (1936). *English Farming*, pp. 148 and 262.

Adam Smith[1] considered that the average wage, i.e. prior to 1775, still left a small surplus over for hard times, but in doing so he invoked the aid of the potato.

The Spirit of the Times

We have left to the last the consideration of the non-material, or if the use of the term be allowed, the philosophic relationship, which was in process of evolution between the employer and his workers. The result of this evolution began to show itself in the latter half of the eighteenth century. Prior to this, the rural 'labouring poor' were influenced by the aristocracy, or their representatives, the farmers, to both of whom the guiding principle 'the unqualified rights of private property was tempered by a sense of communal responsibility'.[2] To an increasing degree urban workers, and to some extent rural ones also, began to find themselves under a new type of master; men who, having had a very different upbringing, had acquired a distinctive outlook, which expressed itself politically in their support of the Whigs and philosophically in their adherence to Radicalism. To these men the guiding principle was 'the unqualified value of free competition'.[2]

These men, free from many of the more obvious failings of the aristocracy, acquired, exaggerated and misinterpreted their class consciousness, giving it a peculiar character which made it far more dangerous to the working classes. The attitude of the older privileged class towards those they felt to be below them, was based on tradition and blessed by the Church. It was a kind of glorified selfishness, whose nakedness had been draped and whose features adorned, by the refinements of what was probably the most cultured age in our history. The radical industrialist came with a different outfit. In him, selfishness, sublimated as a spirit of enterprise, reappeared on the social stage as a virtue, the possession of which was envied by the Established, sanctified by the Dissenting Churches, and measured by both in terms commensurate with the bank balances of the virtuous. The corollary, that failure and poverty were evidence of darkness and sin, was inevitable.

Selfishness having suffered this spiritual transformation, obviously needed spiritual protection; such was ready to hand. Indeed, in the writings of the famous economists and philosophers of the latter part of the eighteenth century there was to be found a whole armoury. Careful selection from the masters, provided the employers with a theory which settled for them the one question always uppermost in their minds: how to keep the worker in a suitable condition of subservience, and at the same time obtain his services at the lowest possible price.

[1] Smith, Adam (1776). *The Wealth of Nations* (edit. 1805), vol. 1, p. 105.
[2] Hammond, J. L. and B. (1911). *The Village Labourer* (1925 edit.), p. 206.

From Adam Smith, say the Hammonds, the industrialists borrowed 'the general notion that perfect freedom was the best stimulus to production, and that all the apparent, or temporary, disadvantages resulting from uncontrolled competition would sooner or later be eliminated by the natural operations of economic forces'.[1] Burke[2] in 1795 restated a widely held philosophy to the effect that the interests of farmer and employees are so interwoven, that it is as much in the interest of the former, to treat the latter generously and wisely, as it is for him to feed and groom his horses; for ultimately the labour of man is that on which he is most to rely for the repayment of his capital. 'On the other hand, if the farmers cease to profit of the labourer, and that his capital is not continually manured and fructified, it is impossible that he should continue that abundant nutriment, and clothing, and lodging, proper for the protection of the instrument he employs.' As to the sharing of the advantages of the partnership, only reciprocal convenience can determine that. 'If the farmer is excessively avaricious, why so much the better—the more he desires to increase his gains the more interested is he in the good condition of those upon whose labour his gains must principally depend'—a philosophy which condoned the exploitation of children.

Borrowing again from the Hammonds, we come on a third philosophic stream. The French Physiocrats had discovered the principle expressed in the words of Turgot: 'In every sort of occupation it must come to pass that the wages of the artisan are limited to that which is necessary to procure him his subsistence, *Il ne gagne que sa vie?*' Hence cheaper food inevitably meant lower wages, and dearer food, higher wages. An effective charter of poverty. It was the logic of this conclusion which inspired Malthus's opposition to Young's and Eden's plans for simplifying and cheapening the dietary of the poor, by the introduction of the potato. Nevertheless, it was Malthus's principle of population, viz. that men tend to multiply much faster than do the sources of their nourishment, which, by making poverty inevitable, 'robbed it of its horrors to the rich'. From Ricardo the industrialists deduced that the only motive which operated in industry and commerce was self-interest—the law of supply and demand settling all else. Labour's share of the profit was determined, like the price of any article, by competition, with the added disadvantage that it inevitably gravitated towards the lowest level of subsistence. As the Hammonds point out, the views entertained by the employing classes did not fairly represent the true opinions of the great economists. It was not what Malthus and Ricardo taught, that mattered, so much as what lesser folk deduced from their teaching; not least of

[1] Hammond, J. L. and B. (1917). *The Town Labourer* (edit. 1936), p. 198.
[2] Burke, Edmund (1795). *Thoughts and Details on Scarcity.*

such deductions was the feeling that 'science seemed to put its seal on the irremediable poverty of the poor'.[1] This attitude of mind found expression in the terms which were current in speaking of the working people. Cobbett deplores the change in this respect which had taken place since his youth. People who were then proud to be regarded as 'the commons of England', were now the 'lower orders', 'the peasantry' and, he might have added, commonest of all, 'the labouring poor': as he says, they speak of them as if they were 'stock on the farm'.[2]

Philosophy may be a guide to action, but it may equally serve as a cloak to the expression of emotions, otherwise suppressed. From 1790 to 1815 the French Revolution and the Napoleonic wars had, between them, excited both fear and hatred of the masses of the people. Englishmen of all classes were horrified at the excesses of the revolutionaries, and alarmed at the imminent Napoleonic threat to this island. But greater than either, was the terror entertained by the upper, and perhaps still more by the middle classes, of a similar rising of our own lower classes. Anti-Jacobinism thus became acclimatized for many a long year in our midst, and reinforced the industrialist's philosophy of self-interest, by the genuine fear they now entertained for their own bodily safety. It proved moreover an effective protection to the employers from the attacks of the few sentimentalists who had resisted its infection. These reactions may explain much in the employers' relation with their workers, which to the present generation appears callous or cruel, no less than the complacency of those who, when the danger was past, heralded their slender schemes to relieve their underpaid labourers in terms such as the following:

To those whose labour is their only wealth, we surely owe two duties: first that of doing all we can, in our station, to find them useful employment, at such wages [8s. per week] as will enable them to provide against a time of sickness or infirmity, to them or their families; that *we* may thus teach *them* to become better subjects and better men in so doing, *each of their benefactors may hope for that blessing which is promised to him who 'careth for the poor'*.

The second duty was, through organized societies, to find a small sum of money to reward those whose good conduct throughout life might merit it—a gesture rendered the more important 'because of its being the public stamp of real *merit although found in humble station*'.[3]

With this we may close our survey of the economic and social conditions prevailing during the first half of the century, and return to the progress of the potato itself.

[1] Hammond, J. L. and B. (1917). Op. cit. pp. 202–4.
[2] Cobbett, W. (1832). *Political Register*, Dec. 22, vol. LXXVIII, p. 710.
[3] Almach, Barugh (1845). The Agriculture of Norfolk. *J. Roy. Agric. Soc.* vol. VI, p. 356. (Italics are mine R.N.S.)

The Progress of the Potato during the first quarter of the Century

Outside Lancashire and the North, the potato was almost unknown to the English countryside in the early years of the century and, where grown, it was in the kitchen garden only. On Trent-side it is recorded as a field crop in 1750, but was only esteemed as a preparation for wheat.[1] A 'good fat mould' and the 'cutting of the roots into several pieces',[2] was advised. Mortimer[3] recommends the potato as a kitchen-garden plant in preference to the Jerusalem artichoke, and suggests that this may be 'planted either of the roots or seeds, and may probably be propagated in great quantities, and prove good food for swine'. It would seem that neither of these authors wrote from personal experience.

The household accounts of a Suffolk family record that in 1709, 6½d. was paid for a peck of potatoes,[4] which is equivalent to something like 3d. per lb. in to-day's money and was obviously a luxury dish. Suffolk was one of the latest counties to raise potatoes as a customary crop.

In a book on the duties of the Lady of the Household, published about this time, she is advised to raise her potatoes in November and put them in her cellar.[5]

Richard Bradley, Professor of Botany at Cambridge, refers in several of his works to the potato. In the earlier ones he speaks disparagingly: 'Potatoes and Jerusalem artichokes are roots of less note than any I have yet mentioned, but as they are not without their admirers so I shall not pass by their cultivation.'[6] In his next, the possibility of discovering in the potato a cheap food for the labouring poor begins to attract him: 'Such land as is esteemed the worst will do well for these roots and considering the profit they bring to a family I wonder they are not more generally propagated in the poorer parts of the country.'[7] A year later he notes that these 'roots are planted in several parts of the country to very great advantage',[8] and in the same year in yet another book: 'It is a root of extraordinary use to mankind both for food and the making of starch, but however it happens, I know not, we don't find it cultivated in England except near London.'[9] Three years later Bradley adopts a more enthusiastic tone: 'It is a root of great use...serving very well in place of bread in some countries...is cultivated pretty plentifully about London...they are not got enough into the notion of the country

---

[1] Marshall, W. (1811). *Review of Reports*, vol. II, p. 445.

[2] *Dict. Rusticum Urbanicum et Botanicum* (1704). Paternoster Row: A. J. Churchill.

[3] Mortimer, John (1707). *The Whole Art of Husbandry*, p. 472.

[4] Halliwell, J. O. (1852). Op. cit.

[5] Evelyn, Charles (1717). *The Lady's Recreation*, p. 192.

[6] Bradley, R. (1724). *New Improvements in Planting and Gardening*, p. 300.

[7] Bradley, R. (1724). *A General Treatise of Husbandry and Gardening*, vol. III, p. 27.

[8] Bradley, R. (1725). *General Dictionary* (trans. of Chomel's *Dict. aeconomique*).

[9] Bradley, R. (1725). *A Survey of the Ancient Husbandry, etc.* p. 207.

people considering their profit.'[1] It is disappointing that in this, his last and most eulogistic reference, he advises that the tubers be planted in the garden in January or February, which would argue that he had no close personal experience of the plant.

The popular estimate of the potato at this time would seem to be that expressed in a contemporary book on Agriculture: 'Potatoes are generally thought an insipid root: but when they are cultivated in a good mixed soil, they are not without their admirers: the smaller roots and knots are commonly preserved for a succeeding crop.'[2] The wording of the last sentence suggests once more that the author had but a slight acquaintance with the plant itself.

The first quarter of the century had passed and there was still no outstanding progress to record in England south of the Trent. Popular opinion as to its merits may be gauged by a passage in *Pamela*: the heroine, faced by the threat of destitution, declares: 'Bread and water I can live upon, Mrs Jervis, with content. Water I shall get anywhere; and if I can't get bread, I will live like a bird in winter upon hips and haws, and at other times upon pig-nuts [*Conopodium denudatum*] and potatoes or turnips.'[3]

The London Market

According to Hindley,[4] the historian of the *Cries of London*, potatoes were hawked in the streets of the city in the reign of James I.[5] No authority is given, and it is more than probable that it was the sweet-potato which was being offered. Less equivocal is a plate in a collection of illustrated 'Cries', which Hindley thinks were printed in the reign of Charles II, depicting a woman with a basket of roots on her head, calling 'Potatoes, ripe Potatoes'. A further example of the kind is to be found in one of the Roxburghe Ballads whose date is said not to be later than 1700: it runs as follows:

> Here's Cucumbers, Spinnage and French Beans
> Come buy my nice Sallery.
> Here's Parsnips and fine Leeks
> Come buy my Potatoes too.

Here there can be no doubt that it is the domestic potato which is being 'called' in common with the everyday products of the local market-garden in the streets of post-revolution London.

We may with some assurance conclude that before the opening of the

---

[1] Bradley, R. (1728). *A Botanical Dictionary*. See 'Battatas'.
[2] Laurence, John (1726). *A New System of Agriculture*, p. 368.
[3] Richardson, S. (1740). *Pamela* (10th edit. 1775), vol. I, p. 99.
[4] Hindley, Charles (1881). *History of the Cries of London* (2nd edit. 1884), pp. 62–116.
[5] Coulter (1950, in a letter to Salaman) quotes R. Burton (1811, *The History of Ireland*, etc.) that boys in the streets ran after the coach of the Irish envoys to King James with potatoes on sticks, indicating, Coulter thinks, that potatoes were cheap and plentiful in London in 1687. – Ed.

eighteenth century the potato was well known and accessible to all classes of Londoners, though it had not as yet obtained a permanent place in the household of any one, and perhaps least of all in that of the artisan. For although 'it grows in vast plenty' as Salmon[1] says, it was still being sold in London at the time by the bushel only. Nevertheless, a reprint of Ray's synopsis[2] in 1724 describes the supply to London as copious. The potatoes for the London market were first raised in Ilford, Essex, and later at Plaistow and Wanstead, where the early enclosures allowed professional market-gardeners, mostly of Irish origin, to cultivate them on an ever increasing scale. 'By 1796 there were more than 1600 acres under potatoes in Barking, Ilford, Leyton, Wanstead and East and West Ham. In 1811 there were 420 acres in West Ham alone.'[3]

The industry originated as a luxury trade and long retained this character; so late as 1767 the crop was 'taken up in July, when they are not above one-fourth grown, they yield 40 sacks per acre [i.e. 2 tons per acre] in a medium and in money £25–£35 per acre, sometimes, which is very great'.[4] Maincrop varieties were also grown: in 1778 these were sold at between £4 and £5 per ton wholesale, a high price in the currency of those days.[5]

The retail price at that time was a little under $\frac{1}{2}d.$ per lb., and that of beef not more than $3\frac{1}{2}d.$ There was, in fact, a ratio of 8·5 to 1 between the price of these two foodstuffs; in 1939 the ratio between their retail prices was 18:1. That is to say, potatoes in the eyes of a working-class housewife seeking the best value for her money, were more than twice as expensive 170 years ago, as they were before the war.

It is obvious from the recipes in a well-known cookery book of the mid-century,[6] that potatoes were regarded with favour in a 'gentleman's' house, and treated with due respect. We have a long way yet to go before the potato attained its position in the 'joint and two veg.' phase of civilization.

Some twenty years later, one learns that 'in the neighbourhood of London so great a quantity is raised annually as to fill the markets even to profusion',[7] by which time it is probable that its use had spread to most classes of Londoners.

This would seem to be confirmed by the following doggerel from

[1] Salmon, W. (1710). Op. cit.
[2] Ray, John (1690). *Synopsis Methodica Stirpium* (ed. 1724), p. 265.
[3] Clapham, J. H. (1939). *Econ. Hist. Railway Age*, p. 228, from *V.C.H. Essex*, vol. II, pp. 474–7.
[4] Young, A. (1768). *Six Weeks' Tour*, p. 266.
[5] Mawe, T. and Abercrombie, J. (1778). *Universal Gardener*.
[6] Glasse, Mrs (1747). *The Art of Cooking made Plain*.
[7] Henry, David (1771). *The Practical Farmer or The Complete English Farmer*, p. 275.

a collection of *London Cries* issued in 1820;[1] an Irish colleen, pushing
a barrow of potatoes, is depicted, crying:

> Potatoes, three pounds a penny, Potatoes
> Augh fait, here's a kind hearted lass of green Erin
> Unruffled in mind, and for trifles not caring
> Who, trundling her barrow, content in her state is
> Still crying, three pounds for a penny Potatoes.

Progress in the Countryside

Outside this *enclave* but little progress had been made in the south
of England by the middle of the century, and Hale,[2] who thought that
the potato was far better fitted for field than garden cultivation, recommended that every encouragement should be given to farmers in the
neighbourhood of the big towns to grow them. Actually, the demand
from such centres, stricken with the birth pangs of the new industrialism,
was making itself felt. We hear of farmers in the neighbourhood of
Nottingham who were much interested in potato cultivation as early as
1738,[3] though another forty years were to pass before any material
advance had been made. There is reason to think that Bristol, the second
biggest city of those days in England, was not behind London, either
in regard to the raising, or the consumption of potatoes. In 1771 they
were selling at 5*d*. per peck, and a labouring family with two children
consumed on the average two pecks (28 lbs.) per week. In Oxford in
1745 they fetched 1*s*. per peck, but in 1761 they are quoted at 8*s*. per
bushel,[4] double the price.

At West Bromwich near Birmingham, the 1775 crop was so abundant
that potatoes were retailed at 2½*d*. to 4*d*. a peck; which being an unremunerative price, the growers reduced their acreages in the following
year.[5]

How little importance the potato had attained at the end of the first
quarter of the century may be gathered from the fact that Defoe in his
Tour of England (1724), though often mentioning the turnip, makes no
reference to the potato either as food or crop. Nor is there very much
more to chronicle in the next twenty-five years.

In Staffordshire at this time it was one of several crops specially
raised for the feeding of their much prized hogs.[6] But the same author

---

[1] Syntax, Samuel (1820). *Description of the Cries of London* (2nd edit. 1821), Fitzwilliam Mus. 12⁰, p. 10. St Paul's Churchyard: J. Harris and Son.
[2] Hale, Thomas (1756). *A Compleat Body of Husbandry*, p. 453. London.
[3] Deering, Charles (1738). *Catalogus Stirpium*, p. 208. B.M. 968, f. 13.
[4] Rogers, James (1902). *History of Agricultural Prices*.
[5] Young, A. (1776). *A Tour to Shropshire*, No. 14. *Scarce Tracts in Economics, etc.*
(1932), p. 141.
[6] Grant, Sir Archibald (1757). *The Farmer's New Year Gift*.

in another work dismisses them with the remark: 'Potatoes are good for none but swine and those they won't fatten.'[1]

In France, a guarded, if more appreciative, judgement was passed by Duhamel du Monceau[2] who thought they were excellent fodder and might be of value to men in time of scarcity, adding: 'After a little use, the taste becomes at least as agreeable as turnips and particularly if the potatoes are boiled with bacon and salt pork.'

We find Tull[3] experimenting with the potato as a horse-hoed crop in Berkshire. In Hertfordshire on the gravelly soils, it was raised in small quantities on a lazy-bed, made of furze in enclosed fields.[4] In the Home Counties generally, outside of parts of Essex, its culture was looked on askance, when it was not actually forbidden. The Duke of Buckingham's steward[5] considered that tenants should be forbidden to grow potatoes, except in small quantities for their private use, or if the tenants were allowed to grow them on the farm, they should pay a fine of £10 per acre; the same sum, it may be noted, as the Government is to-day paying farmers to grow them.

The operative clause appears to have met with widespread approval. In Durham seventy years later, complaint is made that most of the gentry insist on the inclusion of a like clause in their leases, notwithstanding that experience had shown that to ban the potato from the field, was as detrimental to good husbandry as it was inimical to the cause of the poor.[6]

Hale, in his *Husbandry*, remarks that he has only lately acquainted himself with the cultivation of the potato and is convinced that it is not suitable for the small beds of gardens, but it should be assiduously cultivated in the fields; more particularly 'it should be put in the hands of the farmer especially near big towns'.[7]

On the other hand, Phillip Miller,[8] one of the most eminent botanists and gardeners of his day, assures us that 'they are so generally esteemed as to be one of the most common esculent Roots now in use'. This contradiction may be explained by the fact that he had the gardens of the wealthier classes and the market-gardens in mind, for he adds that the 'quantity of them which are cultivated near London, I believe, exceeds that of any part of Europe'. Miller seems to have been unduly optimistic in view of the experience of Gilbert White[9] of

[1] Grant, Sir Archibald (1756). *The Practical Farmers' Pocket Companion*, p. 11.
[2] Miller, Phillip (1760). *The Elements of Agriculture*, vol. II, p. 187, from *Traite de la Culture des Terres*, 1754.
[3] Tull, Jethro (1733). *The Horse-Hoeing Industry*, p. 36.
[4] Ellis, W. (1732). *The Practical Farmer*, p. 62.
[5] Laurence (1727). *The Duty of a Steward to his Lord* (2nd edit.), p. 119.
[6] Forster, Rev. M. (1795). *Annals of Agric.* vol. XXIV, p. 89.
[7] Hale, Thomas (1756). *A Compleat Body of Husbandry*, p. 453.
[8] Miller, Phillip (1733). *The Gardener's Dictionary* (2nd edit.).
[9] White, Gilbert (1789). *Nat. Hist. of Selborne* (ed. 1900), vol. II, p. 122.

Selborne who began growing potatoes in 1758 and only succeeded in getting the village labourers to do the same, after years of encouragement, including the award of premiums. White was the first in this country to conduct experiments on the potato; over a number of years he tried the effect of various composts on cropping. Another missionary in the same field was Samuel Carr, a grocer of Colchester, who advocated the cultivation of the potato and the cause of the Sunday School with equal conviction.[1]

The coincidence of this period of stagnation in the potato's progress, with one of relative well-being and content in the lives of the workers, is no accident. The mass of the people, though poorly paid, were better off than they had ever been before; they could at least obtain an adequate supply of good food and maintain themselves and their family in what at that time counted as relative comfort. What need had they to adopt a foodstuff merely because they were told it was cheap and easy to produce?

The poor are invariably, indeed inevitably, conservative in their dietary habits; thus, when Mrs Austen, about the year 1770, advised a tenant's wife at Steventon near Basingstoke, to plant potatoes in her garden, the answer she received was: 'No, no, they are all very well for you gentry, but they must be terribly costly to rear.'[2]

The Advance of the Wheaten Loaf

To-day, all classes have become almost uncomfortably food-conscious, but that is due to propaganda, and the spread of hygienic teaching and practice by means of the School, the Press, and the B.B.C. A hundred years ago, or less, before the advertiser had fathomed our psychology, there were but two forces powerful enough to influence the people's dietary: poverty and unemployment could depress it, the desire to be as good as 'their betters', raise it. At the time of which we are speaking, i.e. about 1750, the pressure of the former was somewhat lightened, whilst the latter was instrumental in bringing about a change in the character of the daily bread eaten by the working people in the greater part of England other than the North. Here too, a change was taking place in favour of a wheaten loaf; Young in 1798 reports that 'the usual diet of labourers in Hull and its neighbourhood is wheaten bread, but since the great advance in the price of wheat, about two-thirds wheat and one-third rye: the latter is about half the price of the former. 'The cheapest sort of butcher's meat, potatoes and fish, the latter may be frequently bought on moderate terms.'

[1] Benham, Charles E. (1891). *A Biographical Index of Colchester*, p. 12. Colchester.
[2] Austen-Leigh, E. (1870). *A Memoir of Jane Austen*, p. 5.
[3] Young, A. (1798). *Annals of Agric.* vol. XXXI, p. 79.

Till the early part of the eighteenth century the workers south of the 'Coal Line'[1] had been content with a loaf of mixed rye and wheat, to which there might be added a not inconsiderable portion of barley meal. Those in the towns were the first to demand a pure wheaten loaf, to be followed before long by the agricultural labourers. By about 1770 the great majority of the population was entirely dependent on wheat for its bread. This had the support of Young, who in 1767 wrote: 'Rye and barley bread, at present are looked on with a sort of horror even by poor cottagers, and with some excuse, for wheat now is as cheap as rye and barley were in former times.'[2]

It was estimated in 1760 that there were 4,638,000 persons in England who lived on wheat and rye, and 1,362,000 on barley and oats.[3] Between then and the end of the century the consumption of wheat had greatly increased. Young, anxious to be on the safe side, thought that in England 2,000,000 persons, rather than the more likely figure of one million, would more than cover all the consumers of lenten corn, leaving a minimum of eight million to be maintained on wheat alone.[4]

Loss of the commons deprived many of the people of their poultry and eggs and, to a great extent of their home-cured bacon and, most serious of all, of their milk. When prices rose, the majority of the country's working people became increasingly dependent on white bread and cheese for their maintenance. The net result was a badly balanced, insufficient, and almost vitamin-free diet.

It must not be thought that this persistence of the people in the matter of the colour and composition of the loaf was dictated to any great extent by economic or hygienic reasons, for in fact it lent itself to neither; rather was it the outward evidence of a spiritual conflict, which had been operative throughout the ages. There is abundant evidence to show that white bread had always served as a token of class distinction, and was recognized as a mark of privilege. Its adoption by the working classes should be interpreted as evidence of an equalitarian spirit beginning to make itself felt throughout England. When a little later it came to be allied with tea-drinking, it conveyed a challenge to the accepted stigmata of social distinction and was deeply resented by many of the upper class. Doubt has been thrown by some writers as to the completeness of the conversion of the working classes in the eighteenth century to the use of the white wheaten loaf. None such was entertained by the numerous correspondents of the *Annals of Agriculture*. Only one eminent authority, Eden, was not entirely satisfied that the labourer lived 'wholly and

---

[1] See p. 484, n. 2.
[2] Young, A. (1767). *Farmers' Letters*, No. v (3rd edit. 1771), vol. I, p. 245.
[3] Smith, Charles (1766). *Three Tracts on the Corn Trade*. (See infra, n. 4.)
[4] Young, Arthur (1800). *The Question of Scarcity*, etc.
[5] Eden, Sir Frederick (1797). *Annals of Agric.* vol. XXIX, p. 5.

entirely on wheat'.[5] It may be said that by the year 1795, its supremacy, outside of the North, was for all practical purposes complete. It is necessary to emphasize this point because after 1770, as provisions began to get scarcer and dearer, and meat had all but vanished from their tables, it was white wheaten, and not a cheaper and coarser barley loaf, which together with cheese, constituted the staple food of the masses. Moreover, there was no going back, not even when the balance of fortune turned against them towards the end of the century. It was felt to be better to make use of the Irishman's potato, or even the coolie's rice, both the food of peoples regarded socially as little better than slaves, than return to a coarse and coloured loaf.

The Potato in England in the second half of the Century: Arthur Young's 'Tours'

It was about this time, namely between 1760 and 1769, that Arthur Young made his three famous Tours.[1] With their help we are able to get some idea of the state of the peasantry and the progress made in the cultivation and use of the potato.

In the counties of Hertford, Bedford, Huntingdon, Oxford, Nottingham and Northampton, he mentions potatoes but once, namely at Sandy in Bedfordshire, where they were raised with other market-garden stocks, but the area occupied by them was trifling as compared with that devoted to onions. It was only in Essex and Middlesex, namely at Ilford and Brentwood, that potatoes were raised in large quantities for the London markets. At first all the cultivation in these market gardens was done by spade with Irish labour, but in Young's time this had given way to the horse-drawn plough and hoe. Outside these areas there does not appear to have been any noticeable development of potato culture in the Home Counties. In Kent, at Bridge, about ten miles south of Canterbury, he saw two acres of land, and in East Sussex an acre, sown with potatoes; both were regarded as experiments. No potatoes are recorded as being grown in any of the East Anglian counties, Lincoln, Norfolk, Suffolk or Cambridge, but in regard to the latter, Young strikes a prophetic note. At Wisbech he found oat crops grown throughout a long succession of years, after which the land was allowed to go over to twitch and was grazed for some years before being ploughed. He condemns this 'amazing system of barbarism' and recommends a rotation in which potatoes should play a minor part. It is this minor role which in the next century was to become the dominant one in this part of East Anglia.

[1] Young, A. (1768). *A Six Weeks' Tour through the Southern Counties of England and Wales*; (1770). *A Six Months' Tour through the North of England*; (1771). *A Farmer's Tour through the East of England.*

In the south and west, Young did not go beyond Taunton: here too, potato culture was wanting. Only at Poole in Dorset did he find, or at least record, a field of 1½ acres under potatoes.

In the Midlands things were very little better, except for small plots on the western borders of Warwickshire and at Stone in Staffordshire. In Gloucestershire another writer[1] records the astonishment of local farmers when one of them ventured to put ¾ acre under potatoes.

When Young turned his steps to Yorkshire and the North, he found a very different state of affairs: the potato was frequently to be found in the workers' gardens, and not seldom on a considerable scale in the farmers' fields. It is particularly in the neighbourhood of the larger towns, in the North and West Ridings, rapidly developing as centres of industry, that the area under potatoes had recently attained a magnitude of any importance. In the district round Doncaster it was planted as a field crop in 1767, but the produce was fed to horses.

In Lancashire, as we have seen, the potato was already fully established. Indeed, it was thought to have attained a similar position to that acquired in Ireland. That may well be an exaggeration, but that it had overcome all opposition appears from the statement that it was already established in the open field in Lancashire—where such existed.[2] In Cumberland and Northumberland Young found that the labourers generally had their patch of potatoes, but there was no large-scale production. In Durham he does not record its presence as a growing crop.

Young only penetrated a few miles into Wales on this occasion, following the southern coast route of Monmouth and Glamorgan; everywhere he notes that potatoes are either grown or are on sale, confirming what has been recorded earlier.

In the Map (between pp. 495 and 496), the districts are indicated in which Young saw the potato growing as a crop, but this should not be taken as being more than a general guide to its distribution, for the map also shows that there were many places where Young had found it on sale in the markets or shops of the district although he did not record it as being grown locally.

It will be observed that the distribution both of the culture and consumption of the potato, so far as that is shown by its being on sale in market or shop in and about the year 1770, follows neither the disposition of industry, as then located, except to some extent in Yorkshire and the surrounding country, nor does it correspond to the density distribution of the population nor the location of soils particularly suited to its cultivation, as its absence in East Anglia and Lincolnshire proves. Nevertheless, this lack of co-ordination should not deceive us into

[1] Cox, H. (1846). On the Cultivation of the Potato. *J.R.A.S.* vol. VI, p. 345.
[2] Henry, David (1771). *The Complete English Farmer.*

imagining that its culture in any particular county was a matter of chance. On the contrary, it is not difficult to see that its distribution was influenced by some factor of importance which was not itself the outcome of existing economic demand. In the map, those areas which are shaded were at that time, either entirely or in the main, enclosed, the remainder of the country being for the most part under the open-field system. It is at once apparent that the potato, whether locally cultivated or appearing in the markets or shops, is far commoner in the enclosed- than in the open-field districts. In fact for every hundred miles traversed by Young in the open-field area, he met with potato cultivation in 1·2 places and found it on sale in the markets in 2·6 places, whilst in the enclosed area he found it cultivated in 2·2 places, and offered for sale in 4·2 places per 100 miles. In brief, Young's three Tours show that prior to 1770, the potato was almost twice as common in the enclosed parts of England as in those still under the open-field system.

Young[1] was obviously disappointed by the indifference, on all hands, to potato-growing, for he writes about this time that, wherever he went he found the labourers enjoyed some garden or plot with their cottage —what a splendid thing it would be were they to devote it to the potato— 'it would make excellent bread'.

In later years Young[2] made several more tours, but on a less extended scale. In that to Shropshire and the Midlands, undertaken in 1776, it is interesting to note that the farther he gets away from the Cambridge area, the more frequently he encounters the potato. At Newport Pagnell, Banbury, West Bromwich and Wolverhampton, potatoes were sold at low prices. In Shropshire itself, he finds all the cottage gardens filled with potatoes, and at Preston they had invaded the headlands of the fields. East Anglia, the greater part of which was still 'open' at the end of the century, was visited in 1784: throughout he records but one farmer who grew any potatoes, none were seen in cottage gardens.

Nathaniel Kent,[3] writing about this time, does not refer to the potato as a farm crop in England, though he states it is treated as such in Holland. He advises its use on light lands, and was one of the most powerful advocates of its cultivation by cottagers.

Even in the last decade of the century, when the prejudice against the potato had been largely overcome, the same contrast in distribution is to be observed. Thus in Eden's survey[4] of the people's dietary around the year 1794: of eighty-three localities mentioned in those parts of the country which were still in the main 'open', the potato was publicly

[1] Young, A. (1767). *Farmers' Letters*, No. v (3rd edit. 1771), vol. I, p. 205.
[2] Young, A. (1776). *Tour in England and Wales. London School Econ. Scarce Tracts*, No. 14, 1932.
[3] Kent, Nathaniel (1777). *Hints to Gentlemen*, pp. 68 and 211.
[4] Eden, Sir Frederick (1797). *The State of the Poor.*

marketed in forty-two, and formed one of the main articles of diet in twenty-five. Of eighty-six localities in the 'enclosed' districts, the corresponding figures were sixty-three and fifty respectively, showing that despite the steady infiltration of the potato in the twenty years which had elapsed since Young's tour, the same hindrance to its general adoption was still at work.

The primary reason for the disparity between the frequency of the potato in the open and enclosed parts of England is to be found in the established customs and restrictions of open-field husbandry. At the time of the Tours, little or nothing had been done to overcome these difficulties, although Young does note that in one district near York, he saw large quantities growing in the open field. When the economic demand for a cheap food became sufficiently insistent, the invasion of the open field by the potato was no longer delayed.

Cultivation of the Potato differs on either side of the Coal Line

Clapham[1] has pointed out that the course of the Rivers Trent, Soar, Avon and Severn coincides almost exactly with that of the western edge of the New Red Sandstone, and that all the out-cropping coal measures of England and Wales, except the small fields of Somerset, lie to the west and north of it.[2]

To this region, so rich in water power, coal and iron ore, all the large-scale power-driven factories characteristic of this period, were attracted. It had also been said of these parts as early as 1748 that 'provisions were cheaper, the poor more easily satisfied, and coals more plentiful', in which we are justified in seeing a reference to the potato.

The large factory phase of industry was, with the outstanding exception of the cotton mills which started as power factories north of this line, a two-way movement. Old-established industries such as the iron foundries of Sussex, died out in the south, only to be resurrected in Yorkshire and Wales. The woollen industries of the south-west and midlands suffered a like fate. Suffolk, once so wealthy as a result of its looms, now that these had migrated to Yorkshire, reverted to the beatitudes of Constable, and the cultivation of the simple rural life. In short, whilst an ever-growing industrialization was dominating the country north of the Coal Line, to its south, except in the great towns, the old industries were fast decaying.

This geographical trend in the development of the industrial revolution

---

[1] Clapham, J. H. (1926). *Economic Hist. of Modern Britain*, vol. I, p. 47.
[2] This line, which may be called the Coal Line, is shown in Map (between pp. 495 and 496). Its course is very similar to that described by Caird in 1850, dividing the high-wage northern from the low-wage southern district.

led to an increasing demand for the potato in the districts north of the Coal Line, where it already had become firmly established, whilst to the south of the line, its immediate effect was to throw a number of more or less destitute people back on to the land and stifle, for the time, such individual enterprise as might have led to a wider cultivation of the potato.

Although Adam Smith wrote in 1773 that 'the very general use which is made of Potatos in these Kingdoms as food for man, is a convincing proof that the prejudices of a nation, with regard to diet, however deeply rooted, are by no means unconquerable',[1] prejudice south of the Coal Line had by no means been dissipated at that date.

The fact that it was only at Sandy, in Bedfordshire, and in the London area, that Young found any potato-growing of note south of the Coal Line, is evidence that, except in the North, the potato had hardly begun to exert any noticeable influence on the domestic economy of the people. Indeed, were it not for the abundance of testimony of a like kind, one might think that it was Young's failure to observe, rather than the rarity of its cultivation, which explains his reticence. Nor was it that Young was blind to the value of the potato even at this date; indeed, he devotes an entire Letter, viz. No. xxvii, in the *Six Months' Tour*, to the subject of the potato. But the best he can then say for it is that it is a valuable 'ameliorating fallow crop' which can be highly profitable if well cultivated. He urges that there could be no greater agricultural improvement in three-fourths of England than its introduction into the crop rotations, itself evidence of how little progress the crop has made outside the remaining quarter of the country, by which he presumably means the northern counties. The reason Young gives for this neglect of what he considers so valuable a crop, is to be found in his summing up. 'The common objection to cultivating them in large quantities is the want of a market' which Young ascribes to the fact that they have no place in the domestic household, for elsewhere he remarks 'the object in cultivating potatoes is not Covent Garden but the food of cattle. The first is confined, but the latter universal'.[2]

It is doubtful whether at this time Young contemplated the raising of potatoes on areas of more than a few acres on any farm, for he continues to urge their cultivation by the spade. He recounts the experience of a Mr Ray of Tostock, near Bury St Edmunds, who prepared an acre for potatoes by trenching, and raised a crop of 600 bushels (15 tons) at a total cost of £13. 3s. 8d. which included the rent and a special rate for the fencing-in of the plot, presumably from the rest of an open field. Ray could find no ready market for his wares, and Young goes on to

---

[1] Smith, Adam (1776). *The Wealth of Nations* (5th edit.), p. 251.
[2] Young, A. (1771). *Eastern Tour*, vol. ii, p. 409.

say: 'however it may be in other counties, it is by no means a favourite food with the poor in this neighbourhood'.[1]

It is significant that at this date (1769) Young is not concerned about the potato as a food for the labourer and with wheat at 41s. a quarter, there was perhaps no reason why he should have been. It is as fodder for cattle and poultry that he recommends it, and he becomes almost lyrical in its praise when he describes his experiences and observations on the fattening of pigs with potatoes. The same is urged several times in his *Rural Economy*. How little it was grown south of the Trent, may be gathered from his suggestion that as an alternative to sowing headlands with corn, they might with advantage be planted with potatoes. But he adds, this must only be 'as a preparation for laying them down to grass'.[2] Even twenty years later, Young's ideas on the value of the potato were still fluid, for when in France in 1787, impressed by the cultivation and use of maize in the Garonne district, he proceeds to compare its value, as a human food, with that of potatoes. His conclusions, which from the context must be regarded as referring to the conditions prevailing in France, are not very different from those he, at this time, entertained of its use at home. 'For as to potatoes,' he says, 'it would be idle to consider them in the same view as an article of human food, which ninety-nine hundredths of the human species will not touch.'[3]

Outside the north and extreme west, where the potato was already established as a feature in the workers' food, the barriers of prejudice in the 1770's were only beginning to give way: it needed the pressure of want to bring about their final collapse, and for that it had not very long to wait. At Chippenham in the Wye Valley, it was regarded as a great concession should a farmer allow a favoured carter, or shepherd, to dig up the site of a thrashed stack and plant it with potatoes,[4] evidence that the generality of agricultural labour was prepared to adopt it as a cottage-garden crop. In Bedfordshire in 1766 crops of about one acre in extent were planted experimentally, with a view to cleansing the land; the Howard variety was grown around Cardington, as food for cattle and pigs,[5] and at Sandy it was raised as food for the market.

In Cambridgeshire, a county almost entirely unenclosed so late as 1794, the potato was unknown as a field crop, but it was freely grown in the cottage gardens, where, as the report says, it helped 'to contribute greatly to the sustenance of the poor'.[6]

---

[1] Young, A. (1768). *Six Weeks' Tour*, App., p. 373.
[2] Young, A. (1770). *Rural Economy*, p. 304.
[3] Young, A. (1792). *A Tour in France*, p. 350.
[4] Kilvert, Francis (1944). *Diary*. Jonathan Cape.
[5] Dossie, Robert (1768–71). *Memoirs of Agric.* vol. I, p. 358; vol. II, p. 292.
[6] Vancouver, Charles (1794). *General View of the Agriculture in the County of Cambridge*, p. 178.

In Cornwall and Devon, on the other hand, the potato had long since been grown in the gardens of both rich and poor.[1]

In Essex, which soon was to become the chief potato-growing county of the south, the large farmers were already devoting an hundred acres of their land or more to the crop; within the next ten years or so, most of them had trebled that area.

Common as the potato may have been in the Dorset labourer's cottage garden, it seems to have been less so in the gardens of the Great House; at least, so it would appear from the following incident. In 1795 William Wordsworth and his sister Dorothy became tenants of Racedown, the family mansion of the Pinneys. On leaving in the summer 1797, the poet wrote calling attention to the potatoes he had planted specially for his friend, son of the squire. The latter instructed his bailiff that 'when ripe, have them dug up and put away in my cellar'.[2]

The Potato as the Food for the Labourer

The period of relative well-being which the labouring classes had hitherto enjoyed, was gradually drawing to a close. With the opening of the last quarter of the century, clouds began to gather on the horizon. The American War of Independence, 1776–83, cut off our best market for hosiery and the Nottingham hosiery workers were thrown out of work.[3] A little later the spinning-jenny began to withdraw work from the cotton spinners, whilst it put increased work for a time into the hands of the hand-loom weavers. Labour began to move in volume from the land, as well as from Ireland, to the factories, and all the while the price of wheat, and with it the cost of living, was steadily rising.

The relation of wages to the rising cost of living, together with the increasing hazard of local unemployment and mounting poor rates, began to be the subject of serious concern to political economists of all shades.

Young, who generally displayed a fundamentally kind and sympathetic attitude to labour, typical of the best of his time and class, regarded the worker as an industrial tool, whose value was determined solely by the law of supply and demand; hence he had but little more sympathy for the labourer who had ideas of self-betterment, than for one who was lazy. The labourer was not to be robbed of such few rights as he had, but was not to be pampered or, still worse, made independent. Whilst he cannot be accused of desiring to lower wages, he was certainly alarmed at the prospect of their rising. When one remembers his slogan for the farmer: 'the magic of property turns sand into gold', one realizes

---

[1] Henry, David (1771). *The Complete English Farmer*, p. 275.
[2] Evans, Bergen, and Pinney, Hester (1932). *Rev. English Studies*, vol. VIII, No. 29.
[3] Felkin, W. (1867). *A History of Machine-Wrought Hosiery*, p. 116.

the extent to which class distinction had gone in the formation of what Disraeli so aptly described as the 'two nations'. To Young the acid test of successful husbandry was the rent, which improved land could demand; it was obvious that a successful farmer could and would pay an increased rent for improved land, and to do that, labour must be plentiful and cheap. In 1769[1] Young made a detailed study of the wages, food prices, and the size of farms throughout the entire country, and came to the conclusion that there was no consistent relation between them. That there should be no correlation between the rate of wages and the price of foodstuffs, made a great impression on him, and may be the explanation of why at this time he did not advocate the potato as a cheap food for the labouring poor. When nearly thirty years later, the price of foodstuffs soared, whilst wages scarcely increased, no one was more insistent in urging the wholesale use of the potato, as the mainstay of the working family's dietary.

Kent's[2] solution of the problem was unique in his day: he demanded a fair wage for the labourer commensurate with the enhanced profits which were being earned by the farmers and landlords; in addition, he advocated half-acre potato plots and some pasture for all cottages.

Adam Smith was convinced that the potato might, to a large extent, replace wheat as the mainstay of the poor, and estimated that an acre of land under potatoes would yield an equivalent in food to three acres of wheat, and would therefore maintain a much larger population. This justified him in concluding that 'the labourer being mainly fed on potatoes, a greater surplus would remain after replacing all the stock and maintaining all labour employed in cultivation. A greater share of the surplus too, would belong to the landlord. Population would increase and the rents would rise much beyond what they are at present.' In less than twenty years this prophecy was in a large measure fulfilled, but the prophet failed to realize that, whilst it would bring prosperity to the landlord, to the potato-fed labourer it was but another step backwards to serfdom.

Adam Smith was far from being unmindful of the well-being of the workers. At a time when the English upper classes were growing increasingly jealous of the slightest sign of independence, or luxury, on the part of the labouring poor, he laid it down, that it was a definite advantage to society that its workers should enjoy a high standard of living. 'No society', he said, 'can surely be flourishing and happy of which the far greater part of its members are poor and miserable. It is but equity, besides, that they who feed, clothe and lodge the whole body of the people should have such a share of the produce of their own labour,

---

[1] Young, A. (1769). *Six Months' Tour*, Letter XXIX.
[2] Kent, Nathaniel (1777). *Hints to Gentlemen* (edit. 1793), p. 236.

as to be themselves tolerably well fed, clothed and lodged.'[1] When some twenty years later the crisis came and the 'labouring-poor' were being coerced to mould their economy on a potato standard, the famous economist Malthus could in effect offer the workers no better comfort than the suggestion that were there but fewer mouths, there would be more food for each; and that there were too many, was no one's fault but their own.

Neither in England nor Scotland at this time was the progress of the potato such as might inspire even so prescient an authority as Adam Smith to foretell for it a great future; it may be that he was influenced rather by the role the potato was already playing in Germany. A series of bad wheat and rye harvests on the Continent had been followed by famine conditions in 1770. This was countered by so great an increase in the production of potatoes that, as one author says, it looked as if it might assume a similar role in Europe, as rice had for centuries done in China.[2] To many authorities the prospect of such a domination was sufficiently real, as to cause them to renew the old regulation, by which every commune was obliged to maintain a magazine of grain. Fortunately, the potato failed to attain so exclusive a position, though from then onwards it occupied an increasingly important place in the food of the people. How important may be gleaned from the fact that a few years later the War of the Bavarian Succession, 1778–9, commonly known as the 'Kartoffelkrieg', was brought to an end when the contending armies had consumed all the available potatoes in Bohemia.[3]

The New Systems at Work

Whilst the Industrial Revolution was gathering momentum, a revolution in farming methods, no less radical, was proceeding throughout the countryside. In so far as fresh lands were opened up to arable cultivation, better methods of husbandry employed, and new crops such as clover, sanfoin and, above all, turnips introduced, the effect on the agricultural labouring classes was all to the good. But the new crops could not be readily raised, nor the improved methods efficiently carried out in the open fields, controlled as they were, by age-old customs and the dictates of a village council. The free and unhampered action of a master farmer in complete control of the land was felt to be essential if new crops and rotations were to be introduced. It was a case of new wine in old bottles: the restrictions and regulations, essential to cultivation in the open field

---

[1] Smith, Adam (1776). *An Inquiry into the Nature and Causes of the Wealth of Nations*, p. 106 (1805 edit.).
[2] Hansen, Marcus (1940). *The Atlantic Migration*, p. 20.
[3] See chapter XXXII, p. 572.

were inimical to experimentation, and more particularly to the introduction of autumn crops. A rapidly growing population, and its increasing tendency to concentrate in towns, necessitated a more effective and economic method of food production. The open-field system was doomed: there was but one solution—the common fields must be divided and enclosed. Reference has already been made to earlier enclosures, but considerable as they were, there is reason to believe that as late as 1750 at least half of the English countryside was still in open field. In the latter quarter of the century, the enclosure movement once more gathered strength and in the early nineteenth century it swept forward like a tornado, destroying both the good and the bad in its progress. Before the next fifty years were past, most of the open fields as well as the commons, which from time immemorial had characterized village life throughout the greater part of England, had disappeared for ever. In the process, small owners, cottars, and those workers entitled to rights on the common, alike fared badly.

So much has been written concerning the gross injustice frequently amounting to fraud, with which many of the enclosure schemes were carried out, that it is not necessary here to enlarge further on that aspect of the matter. The important fact, that has too often been overlooked, is that the enclosures of the eighteenth and nineteenth centuries differed from all preceding, not so much in their character as in their volume and their tempo. They brought the medieval era to an abrupt end. A radical change had been effected in the course of a generation in the economic life of the majority of the labouring population, and, more particularly, in their relation to the land of their birth. Throughout the ages in the English countryside, there had been in action a reversible social-economic process by which the peasant sank to the status of a labourer, and the landless labourer became either a squatter on the common, or rose to be a holder of strips in the common field and once more an independent peasant. That is not to say that there had not been always a section of the population engaged in work as labourers on the land for others, but till now the majority of them cultivated small plots of land of their own and often maintained a few head of stock on the commons. Neither the smallholder working for himself, nor the part-time labourer who had his plot of potatoes and his rights of commons, could survive enclosure, even when such had not been unjust to his claims; for the smallholder could not afford to hedge and ditch the piece of land allotted him, nor the industrious labourer survive without the use of the common.

Enclosure brought to an end the century-old struggle—the attempt of the agricultural labourer to maintain some degree of independence. So long as a man could scrape together a living without devoting his entire labour to the farmer, there remained to him not only a feeling of independence, but the knowledge that it was still possible for him to remove himself to a higher grade of society.

With the spread of enclosure, the peasant-labourer vanished, the landless day-labourer remained; a result welcomed by farmer and landlord alike. Both have left it on record that in their opinion, independent labour would cripple the industry.

This amazing revolution of the social and economic life of rural England began at a time when there was neither social unrest nor shortage of foodstuffs. On the contrary, wheat was plentiful and cheap, and the lot of the agricultural worker better than it had ever been. Enclosure was agriculture's response to the demands of industry, reorganized on an increasingly capitalistic basis.

The abolition of the open field was inevitable. Had it been carried through with due regard to the rights and needs of the peasantry, had they received but a tithe of the consideration shown to the squire and the rector, the social history of the last 150 years might well have been a happier one.

Probably one of the greatest privations the worker suffered, second only to the loss of his land and his grazing rights on the commons, was the loss of his rights of turbary—the collecting of peat fuel from the wastes, and that of gathering rough timber for firing from the woods, matters never long absent from Cobbett's mind. From now on, the poor were dependent on water-borne coal for their fuel, the high price of which was to many prohibitive.

Another loss, though not universal, was that of the immemorial right of gleaning, by which the labourer's wife and children had in the past acquired most of the grain needed during the year for their poultry. The farmers with their fenced-in, well-cultivated fields, on which all rights of stubbling had been abolished, were all too frequently loath to allow in gleaners, who might perhaps help themselves to a little grain from the sheaves. Indeed, the gleaner came to be regarded even in the eye of the law, as a trespasser: such at least was the decision, reached by a majority, in the Court of Common Pleas in 1788.[1] It is not to be doubted that it was the ever-rising price of wheat which made many farmers less ready to spare that of which the poor had never been in so great a need. From the second half of the nineteenth century onwards, when the price of wheat had fallen, gleaning once more became general, and was regarded as a 'valuable privilege by the labourers' womenfolk'.

Henceforth, the economic path along which the agricultural worker wended his weary way, was a one-way track, eternally shadowed by poverty, whose monotony was only varied by sickness or crime, and whose latter stages led through the hated Union to a pauper's grave.

[1] Hammond, J. L. and B. (1911). *The Village Labourer*, p. 109. Longmans.

Before the century was out, the peasant's doom was finally sealed: the landless labourer had become the ideal tool for the new capitalistic phase of agriculture and, as such, landlessness came to be regarded by landowner and farmer as an indispensable attribute of the agricultural labourer.

Of the many debts we owe to Arthur Young, few outweigh that occasioned by the publication, under his editorship, of the *Annals of Agriculture*. From the forty-five volumes of this series we can, between the years 1784 and 1808, derive an almost day-to-day picture, as seen through the eyes of persons of every class and opinion, other than that of the labourer's, of the life and conditions of the agricultural and, to a lesser extent, of the industrial workers of Great Britain.

Between 1784 and 1794, we hear much more frequently than before, of usually small acreages of potatoes, planted in the fields, in an increasing number of districts, up and down the whole country; the crops of which were, in most cases, devoted to the fattening of bullocks and hogs. The potato had, moreover, been subjected to many and often well-designed trials, in all of which it had proved its worth. A beginning was now being made to use it as a means of improving the routine of husbandry; from many parts of the country there are recorded during this period experiments with the object of testing the worth of the potato as a fallow-cleaning crop, as a sequel to the artificial grasses, and as a crop suitable for drilling and horse-hoeing, thus allowing it to take its place in the four-course rotation which was becoming increasingly popular.

Apart from its use as a farm crop, in most counties, other than Suffolk and Norfolk, the majority of cottagers were now growing potatoes in their gardens. In the latter county, Coke had spent five years experimenting with the potato and persuading his tenants to make use of it: the only response had been that 'perhaps 't wouldn't poison the pigs'.[1] Better success awaited him when he allowed his cottagers to grow potatoes in his new plantations, a policy soon adopted by other landowners. Lord Clive, before a Select Committee, reports that both he and Coke found that it was good both for the trees and the men.[2] At Winsford, Somerset, owners desirous to convert the rough grass of the steep hillsides into good pasture, limed the land, and then let it free for two years to the labourers for potatoes. After this, it was laid down to grass, and its value rose from 5s. to 40s. per acre as a result.[3]

In some districts the potato had caught up with the position it held in Lancashire: more particularly was this true of Cornwall, where two

---

[1] Stirling, A. M. W. (1908). *Coke of Norfolk*, vol. I, p. 281.
[2] Report of Select Committee (1795). *Re-Cultivation of Wastes, etc.*, p. 61.
[3] Pusey, Ph. (1843). Agricultural Improvement in Lincs. *J. Roy. Agric. Soc.* vol. IV, p. 313.

crops a year were raised. In 1794 the winter crop fetched more than double that then obtaining in Cheshire. One does not hear of the early crop being exported to Exeter or Bristol or London, though it is probable some of it was. By 1830 'Cornish Earlies' were well established in Covent Garden.[1] Meanwhile, the people themselves had become enthusiastic potato-eaters. In the Isle of Wight, the cultivation of the potato had become general, and in Rutland great progress was reported. Suffolk, although at least half the county had been enclosed for centuries, held out then, and for many years to follow, against any change in the domestic economy of its workers. Even when in 1796 they were offered potatoes at 8d. per bushel, the workers of Clare rejected them although, as Ruggles, a Suffolk squire declared, they were such an excellent substitute for bread.[2] How strongly prejudice of this kind can become entrenched is shown in a letter received by Young in 1797 from Mr Hasfield of Wickhambrook, who writes:[3] 'The recommendation of the culture of potatoes from the Board of Agriculture has afforded me particular pleasure, the more perhaps, for its coincidence with the advice which I have been earnestly pressing upon my parishioners for nearly forty years, with as little effect as if it had been delivered from the pulpit.' This in a county where wages even in 1797 were only 1s. 4d. in winter and 1s. 6d. a day in summer. Young, in 1813, reports in much the same sense for Sussex, a county which had long since been enclosed, though here the potato was employed as fodder for cattle and hogs.[4]

The Struggle between the Wheaten Loaf and the Potato

From 1780 onwards the economic conditions of the agricultural workers, though definitely inferior to those obtaining twenty or thirty years earlier, were still endurable. The demand for a white loaf of bread throughout the greater part of the Midlands, the south and the west counties, had grown increasingly persistent; by 1784 it had, in conjunction with cheese, come to be the staple food in these parts of the worker and his family, replacing the meat and bacon which, a Sunday dish for the few, had become little more than a memory for the many.[5] In Lancashire, Durham and the North generally, the wheaten loaf was still regarded as a luxury. Elsewhere at this time the wheaten loaf was no longer seriously challenged by any other cereal, still less by the potato.

[1] Loudon, J. C. (1831). Encyclopaedia of Agriculture, p. 849.
[2] Ruggles, Thomas (1797). The History of the Poor, p. 384.
[3] Young, A. (1797). General View of the Agriculture of the County of Suffolk, p. 117.
[4] Young, A., Jnr. (1793). General View of the Agriculture of the County of Sussex (edit. 1813), p. 115.
[5] Traill, H. D. (1893-7), Social England, vol. v, p. 349.

Ultimately the popularity of the white loaf depended on its price, which was fixed annually by assize. The lowest price the quartern loaf reached between 1750 and 1764 was 4½*d*. in 1761; more usually it was in the neighbourhood of 6*d*. Between 1765 and 1795 with but an occasional exception, the price rose to 7*d*. or 8*d*. So much the labouring population was prepared to pay, however great the effort, and however tempting the relatively low price of barley and rye bread. The potato, where the supplies were of easy access, was a much cheaper food than either, but except where hunger dictated, domestic policy, prejudice and self-respect were more than enough to keep it at bay and the wheaten loaf in power. It was not long before this trial of strength was to be fought out.

The harvest of 1791 was an exceptionally good one; those of 1792 and 1793 were poor, those of 1794 and 1795 disastrous. Hence the year 1795 became in a sense a critical one for the working classes of Great Britain. It marked, to borrow a famous phrase, 'the end of the beginning', the end of that uneasy period which during the great changes in the social order induced by the industrial revolution and the increasing pressure of enclosures, had gathered sufficient momentum to constitute a definite challenge to the existing social order. An orderly change-over was only possible if the basic needs of the people in food, clothing, housing and fuel, were reasonably satisfied.

We have a remarkable picture of the daily life of the agricultural labourer prior to the critical year of 1795, from the hands of a Berkshire Rector.[1] The poor had taken to a wheaten loaf, he says, because it was much more abundant than in the past, when they had plenty of milk to wash down the coarser bread. The habit was encouraged by the rich because the demand increased rents. To-day 'the whole labouring people have neither meat nor cheese nor milk nor beer in sufficient quantities, they eat good bread where everybody else eats it'.[2]

To those who complain that the poor neglect potatoes either for themselves or their pigs, Davies replied: 'Though the potato is an excellent root, deserving to be brought into general use, yet it seems not likely that the use of it should ever be general in the country.' Wheat, he argues, is a much superior food. 'In richer counties the poor have neither the garden to grow it [the potato] nor milk to eat it with. This is due to engrossing, the little scrap of garden left to him he uses for a variety of vegetables, where buttermilk can be got, potatoes are eaten.'

---

[1] Davies, David (1795). *The Case of the Labourers in Husbandry*, pp. 34 ff.

[2] Trevelyan, G. M. [*England under Queen Anne* (Blenheim), p. 10], states that 'the people of England had acquired an invincible prejudice against eating any bread save wheat, even for purposes of poor relief under the Speenhamland system...that defiance of the national economy of our climate was achieved by large farming and the application of capital and capitalistic methods to the cultivation of the soil.'

His remarks on the growing use of tea shed further light on the current domestic economy. 'Why should such people, it is asked, indulge in a luxury which is only proper for their betters? As they can't get milk they take tea, where they have pasture for a cow, the commons are occupied by the rich whose cattle would starve out the poor man's cow even if he could afford to buy one. Beer, owing to the malt tax, is now too dear for the labourer', and he concludes: 'Tea drinking is not the cause but the consequence of the distresses of the poor.' The author's remedy is to raise wages and maintain them in relation to the price of wheat.

Up till now, the wages of the agricultural labourer, apart from piece-work and harvest, averaged about 7s. 6d. per week, the womenfolk and children still earned a few shillings at spinning, and between them they could just—and only just—make both ends meet. The price of bread in 1792 was 6½d. Ruggles,[1] the authority on the Poor Law, writes 'everybody knows that bread covers at least two-thirds of the expenditure on food'. Later in the same year he lays it down that a labourer's wage must be at least sufficient to maintain himself and his family, and must allow for something over. Evidently he has some doubts as to whether the existing wages did fulfil this condition; for were they not to do so, he continues, anticipating Malthus, then 'the race of such workers would not last beyond the first generation'. Notwithstanding the mounting poor rates, he concludes that 'in Great Britain the wages of the labourer seem to be evidently more than what is precisely necessary to bring up a family',[2] and that the price of corn must determine everything in regard to the economics of labour, a view which was held by many, including the leaders of the agricultural workers. Indeed, it was the failure to implement the lessons of this truism which not only determined the future of the potato in this country but influenced the whole course of our social history for the next fifty years.

Variations in the price of corn were not merely reflected but, in fact, magnified, in the price of the loaf, hence in considering the relation of wages to the acquisition of a working man's food, it is convenient to consider the price of the loaf rather than that of wheat.

Two other matters must be borne in mind. In the period under consideration, England had only just ceased to be an exporter of wheat, and no important article of food consumed by the working classes was introduced from outside our shores. The other, that communications were still bad, although the canals were beginning to exert an important influence on national transport; apart from that, and coastal sea-borne traffic, the inland carriage of corn was dependent on horse-drawn

---

[1] Ruggles, Thomas (1792). *Annals of Agric.* vol. XVII, p. 205.
[2] Ibid. p. 353.

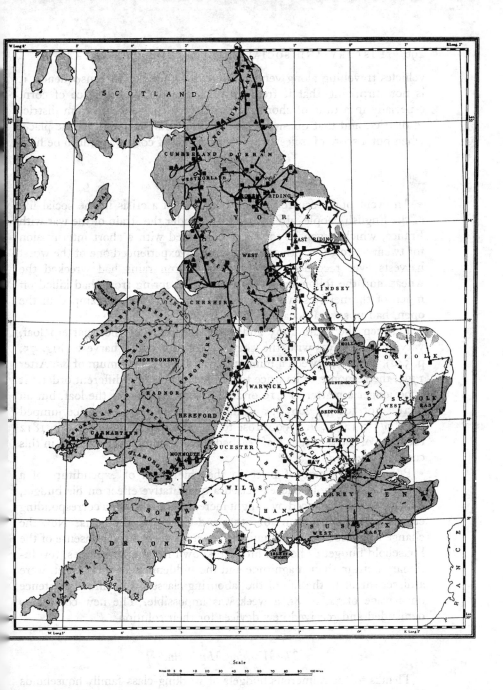

Scale

Miles 10 5 0   10   20   30   40   50   60   70   80   90   100 Miles

Map 2. The shaded portion represents that part of England and Wales in which more than half of the cultivated area was enclosed by the middle of the eighteenth century. The unshaded portion represents that part where the greater part of the cultivated area was still in open field. On the Map are also shown Arthur Young's three main tours, as well as his later excursion into Wales.

continuous heavy line ——————— represents the six months' tour undertaken in 1768.

broken line - - - - - - - - represents the six weeks' tour undertaken in 1767.

thin dotted line ··············· represents the Eastern tour undertaken in 1770.

heavy dotted line •••••••••• represents The Coal Line (see ch. xxv, p. 484).

The route across Wales from Milford Haven to Ross was traversed in 1776.

▲ indicates localities where potatoes were observed to be cultivated.

■ indicates the towns in which potatoes were offered for sale in the market.

vehicles travelling along very indifferent highways. In consequence, it is not surprising that it frequently happened that the price of corn, especially in a time of shortage, varied very considerably from district to district, and that quasi-famine conditions might obtain in one place, when but a score of miles away, a sufficiency of corn was still to be had.

The Critical Year, 1795

An event now occurred which precipitated a crisis in the social life of the English people, already suffering under the strain of the war with France, which began in 1793 and continued with a short intermission for twenty-two years. In 1794 the country experienced one of the worst harvests ever recorded. Continuous autumn rains had wrecked the wheat, and the following severe winter and spring frosts had killed off much of the newly sown corn, whilst potatoes, where clamped in the open, had in several localities, been frosted.

Between the years 1765 and 1794, the price of the quartern loaf, varying as always, with the character of the year's harvest (Fig. 75, p. 540), ranged between a minimum of 6d. and a maximum of 8d. After 1794, the response of its price to bad harvests is of a different order. It is no longer a matter of a 10 or 20% rise in the cost of the loaf, but an increase of 100%, 200%, and more. Thus in 1795 the price jumped from 7d. to 12¼d.; in 1799 it rose to 13d.; in 1801 to 15¾d.; and in 1812 the price of the quartern loaf reached the maximum ever attained in this country, viz. 17d.

Previously, change of price in the chief item of expenditure of a labourer's household had exercised a quantitative effect on his budget, which could be balanced by a slight increase of income or a corresponding contraction of expenditure on other and less essential objects. Now the change had assumed a qualitative character which made nonsense of the household budget as he had hitherto known it. The new prices, revolutionary both in their magnitude and the suddenness of their onset, were a direct threat to the life of the labouring classes. Continued existence on a wage of 7s. or 8s. a week was impossible. The new conditions demanded and received new devices for their solution.

The Working Man's Budget

Thanks to the numerous budgets of working-class family households Eden and others have bequeathed us, referring to times before, during, and after 1795, it is not difficult to form some picture of the immediate social and economic problems which now confronted the labouring classes.

A feature common to the great majority of the later budgets of this kind is that they are unbalanced. It has been suggested in the case of those presented by Eden that the 'statistics show in fact rather what the poor had been able to buy before the rise in prices than what they were actually getting in 1795 or 1796'.[1] Against this view is the fact that five Welsh budgets of 1788 also show substantial deficits.[2]

That the labourer had always been on the verge of bankruptcy was nothing new; that he had no reserves against sickness, the lying-in of his wife, or burials, was not regarded either by himself or his master as unjust; it had always been so. In the days before the enclosure movement, the inevitability of destitution had escaped him. There had been many ways by which a labourer might improve his income and supply the household larder; in any case he had not been haunted by that fear of unemployment, which enclosure and engrossment had converted into an imminent terror. But now it was no longer a question of being on the verge of bankruptcy—bankruptcy had reached his door and crossed the threshold. In its crudest and commonest form, every labouring man was offered the choice between starvation and the chronic pauperism of himself and family. This is more evident when we compare these budgets with similar ones referring to the 1760's. In these, bread accounts for 44% of total family expenditure and, after allowing for rent, clothing, sickness, etc., a surplus of about 8% of the total family income is left.[3]

But to return to the budgets, confining ourselves to those dealing with districts south of the Coal Line, there are two for the year 1789, in these no potatoes are bought but bread absorbs 60% of the weekly outlay. Two more refer to the years 1792 and 1793: in these, potatoes account for 4% and bread for 60% of the weekly income; four further budgets relate to the year 1795, the money spent on potatoes rises to 7%, whilst that on bread remains at the old figure of 60%. If bread remained a constant charge and potatoes an increasing one, an economy must have been made on some other item of the household expenditure. It is meat which has been sacrificed. In the 1789 budgets meat accounted for 12% of the income; in those for 1792 and 1793, 9%; whilst in the 1795 budgets the purchases of meat practically cease, accounting for only 0·08% of the weekly income.

It is interesting to compare these budgets with five from Wales for the year 1788.[4] These show that although the peasants in Denbigh and Monmouthshire consumed no wheat, they spent on barley meal exactly

[1] Cole and Postgate (1938). *The Common People*, p. 79.
[2] Dodd, A. H. (1933). *The Industrial Revolution in North Wales*, p. 420.
[3] Young, A. (1767). *Farmers' Letters*, No. v (3rd edit.), vol. I, p. 196.
[4] Dodd, A. H. (1933). Op. cit. p. 420.

the same proportion, viz. 60% of their income as the English did on wheat, 6% went on potatoes at a time when little or none was being bought by the agricultural labourers in England. The Welsh budgets show no outlay on meat. Milk however is of importance: on it 7% of the weekly income is spent as against 0·03%, the highest in any one of the English budgets.

These unbalanced budgets, brief records of hunger and anxiety, are evidence of the people's determination to adhere to a wheaten loaf against all odds. It was a struggle in which they could expect no help from any, outside their own class.

The discussion of the economic status of the worker has so far been centred around the agricultural labourers, who still greatly outnumbered the skilled artisans of the late eighteenth century. Low as the wage of the former was, it was paid at regular weekly intervals and was reasonably constant in amount; 'Hodge' at least knew how he stood. Very different was it with the industrialist, even when engaged in a relatively well-paid industry, under a good employer and in the more progressive districts. He suffered under two major disabilities: the one, that he, working mainly by the piece and in his own home, was never certain what his earnings would be, especially as he was expected to supply his own hand-tools, or purchase them from his employer on credit; and the other, that he was seldom paid at regular intervals. The whole situation is clearly illustrated in a recent publication describing from contemporary documents the relations which existed between the famous file manufacturer, Peter Stubbs, and his workmen. Settlements were only effected between them when a particular contract was completed; and then it was almost invariably the case that against earnings would be set off the payment of loans which the workman had secured from his employer. The loans were incurred because workmen were expected to finance the contract, including sometimes the raw material. Very rarely did they have sufficient cash to do this and at the same time support themselves and their families.

This state of affairs was by no means limited to the file trade: it was common in most manufacturing trades, notably among the nail-workers and the Sheffield plate-workers. Other industrial workers, especially the miners, suffered under the truck system, but the bane of the metal-worker was chronic indebtedness to his employer. So rare was it for the worker to be free of debt, that he automatically became economically tied to one employer. How firmly established was this system, may be seen from the fact, that even when Stubbs founded a factory in Warrington in 1803, the employees still failed to establish their independence. They borrowed from their employer 'not only to meet unforeseen emergencies, but also for current expenditure and it is difficult to imagine that debt did not spell poverty, at least intermittently'.[1] In short, the artisan, like the agricultural labourer, was rarely solvent, and when trade depressions set in, as they did in 1793, he was driven by the same economic pressure as the latter, to reduce his standard of living, which meant, amongst other things, a greater reliance on the potato for the support of his family.

War Favours the Potato's Progress

Nothing emerges more clearly from the writings of contemporary authorities, not excluding Arthur Young himself, that in their view the labourer had no right to any amenities he could not pay for. Few men of his time had more consideration for the working man than Kent, yet it is obvious that he instinctively regarded him as an almost distinct species, as compared to the gentry, and only entitled to a marginal type of existence. He introduces the chapter on the labourer thus: '*Thou shalt not muzzle the ox when he treadeth out the corn* is a divine law, figuratively signifying, that the poorer race of people, who are the instruments, by which the earth is cultivated, ought to enjoy a reasonable portion of its produce.'[2] And again, in relation to new cottages: it is essential that they should be simple and inexpensive and contain 'a warm, comfortable, plain room, for the poor inhabitants to eat their morsel in'.

Sacrifice was the order of the day, so long as it was confined to the labouring poor. Milk had already gone, meat had followed, and now the labourer was asked to surrender the last barricade, and substitute potatoes for his wheaten loaf.

The times were peculiar: the country was at war with revolutionary France, the landlords were doubling their incomes, the farmers making fortunes, and industry flourishing. What then, was to be the share of the labourer?

It would have seemed but natural that wages should have risen, if not proportionately, yet in some commensurate degree. But such was not the case. In the year 1800, the agricultural wage was still under 10s., and had only risen about 15% since 1790. It was evident that the labourer, whether agricultural or industrial, was to have no direct share in the spoils; yet the cost of living had far outstripped any rise in wages. How was the problem to be solved?

The farmers objected to raising wages, because of their oft-expressed fear that the labourer might become independent, and that wages, once increased, could never be reduced, should bad times supervene. The

---

[1] Ashton, T. S. (1939). *An Eighteenth Century Industrialist*, pp. 9 and 31. Manchester University Press.

[2] Kent, Nathaniel (1777). *Hints to Gentlemen* (edit. 1793), p. 208.

policy of both landlord and farmer then, and for the next forty years, was perhaps unconsciously influenced by the rising tide of anti-Jacobinism in England, which followed the September massacres. Be that as it may, there was undoubtedly a tendency to regard the labouring classes as potential rebels, and a deliberate attempt was made to retain them at the lowest economic level consistent with the execution of their work. If deficits there were, which could not be covered by the painful frugality of himself and his family, then his wage must be subsidized from the poor rate. That, in fact, was the solution adopted.

Speenhamland

The practice was not new, but it had never before been widely adopted, nor carried out in a logical manner. From now on, it was to acquire a quasi-official authority, by reason of the concise and definite character of the decisions reached at a certain meeting of magistrates held on 6 May 1795, in the Pelican Inn at Speenhamland in Berkshire. At this meeting, a clear-cut set of regulations was drawn up by which: 'When the gallon loaf of second flour, weighing 8 lb. 11 oz. [i.e. two quartern loaves] shall cost 1s., then every poor and industrious man shall have for his own support 3s. weekly, either produced by his own or his family's labour or an allowance from the poor rates, and for the support of his wife and every other of his family 1s. 6d.'[1] When the loaf reached 1s. 4d., the sums were to be 4s. and 1s. 10d. respectively. At this same meeting, it was laid down that the Justices, 'wishing, as much as possible, to alleviate the Distresses of the Poor with as little burthen on the occupiers of the Land as possible', recommended overseers to cultivate land for potatoes, and to give the workers a quarter of the crop, selling the rest at 1s. a bushel. They were also advised to purchase fuel and retail it at a loss.[1]

The new standard wage-plus-relief thus allowed 9s. a week for the maintenance of a wife and four children when the quartern loaf was 6d., and 11s. 4d. when it was 7d. Before the year was out, the price of bread was already double the minimum value on which these calculations were based—no happy augury for the future.

Except in the north, where the Speenhamland policy was only sparingly adopted, the consequences of that meeting of magistrates at a country inn were disastrous to the working classes, and not much less so to the welfare of the state as a whole. As an immediate result, the labouring classes were confronted with a policy of universal pauperism which, in combination with the law of settlement, and the 'roundsman' policy, differed little from slavery. From this degrading economic nexus it

[1] Hammond, J. L. and B. (1911). *The Village Labourer*, p. 163.

took the country more than forty years before it could even begin to free itself. During the whole of that period the country seethed with unrest, which from time to time was little removed from open revolution. The economic and political aspects of this period have been faithfully depicted by the Hammonds and many other distinguished economists and historians. We are concerned only with the influence this organized pauperism had on the spread of the potato as an article of diet in the home, and the effect of the potato regime on the economic status of the workers.

How far the potato was itself responsible for Speenhamland is no idle question. Had the magistrates not had some cheap alternative food in their minds, this scheme would have been unworkable. Barley, oats and potatoes were, as has been pointed out,[1] all available, but in the writer's opinion the cheapness of the potato no less than the dislike of the southerner for barley and oatmeal gave it a position of exceptional importance. Hitherto, as Ruggles[2] maintained, the economics of labour had been determined by the price of wheat; soon they were to be influenced by the abundance of the potato.

Lest it be thought that the views expressed above are exaggerated, it may not be amiss to quote a letter addressed by a farmer of Tuxford, Notts, to the Board of Agriculture in 1816, by which time the full fruits of the Speenhamland policy and the drive to the potato were being reaped:

In some parishes in the neighbourhood a number of labourers would be out of employment except by the following means: viz., The overseer of the parish to which they belong, calls a meeting of the inhabitants on the Saturday evening, at which meeting he puts up each labourer by name separately to auction and they have been let generally at 1s. 6d. to 2s. per week, the farmer or other person finding victual to the labourer for six days only. I was offered one of the labourers at 1s. 6d. p.w. but refused to take him; he was a stout able married man, 34 years of age; the family, if any, is of course supported at the expense of the parish. The superfluous labour of the parishes in which I hold land are apportioned and allotted to each farmer for a certain time, according to his rental and to his next neighbour afterwards around the parish: the farmer paying the labourer from 8d. to 1s. per day, and from 8d. to 1s. per day is given to him for the maintenance of himself and his family by the overseer of the poor.[3]

The General Reviews

The Board of Agriculture, then under the enlightened control of its founders, Sir John Sinclair and his energetic Chief Secretary, Arthur Young, were not altogether unprepared. They had caused a survey to

[1] Slater, Gilbert (1929). *The Growth of Modern England* (2nd edit.), p. 217.
[2] Ruggles, Thomas (1794). *Annals of Agric.* vol. XVIII, p. 205.
[3] Board of Agriculture (1816). *Agricultural State of the Kingdom...*, p. 250.

be made, county by county, of the agricultural and industrial state of the whole country. The majority of these reports, known as the *General Views*, were compiled in 1792 and 1793 and published in 1794 and 1795, they provided a picture—often, it must be said, scrappy and deficient— of the state of the countryside, the conditions of labour, and, incidentally, the progress of the potato, before the year of crisis.

Unfortunately the reporters of the *General Views* of 1794 do not shed much light on the subject of the potato in England or Wales. In the case of Oxford, Middlesex, Suffolk and Somerset, they made no mention of the crop, notwithstanding that in the last-mentioned county it had already established itself as an essential part of the people's daily food. In the northern counties, more especially Cheshire, Lancashire and Cumberland, its importance and popularity receive full justice.

In Wales the reporters generally refer to the potato as being in common use and cultivation, but fail to make clear the measure of its importance. A comparison of the English *General Views* with the contemporary reports from the Lowlands of Scotland, convinces one that whilst the use and cultivation of the potato in Lancashire and Cheshire may possibly have equalled that in Ayrshire and Fife, in the remainder of the English counties such fell far behind that prevailing generally in the Lowlands.

The main object of the survey had been to advance the enclosure policy, to which Arthur Young had devoted so much of his energies. A country engaged in war and becoming every day more industrialized, it was argued, needed abundant food, and food meant cereals; and these could be produced in greater quantity and at much less expense on enclosed fields. The criterion of success was held to be improved rental values which, indeed, were impressive. Had this been coupled with a corresponding increase in wages, the drear chapter in the history of British agricultural labour about to open, might well have been avoided. But Young was living in the eighteenth, not the twentieth century, nor should he be blamed for failing to recognize the existence of tendencies in the social organism whose effects were not clearly manifest till a later generation. Not least of these were the conflicting reactions of the different social classes to the potato. For example, Lancashire and the Isle of Wight are both dealt with in the *General Reviews*; though geographically poles apart, they had much in common, in both regions the soil was rich, the cultivation good and the farmers prosperous, yet the reactions we are considering were in the two areas diametrically opposed.

In Lancashire[1] where the potato crop, much of which was exported, was described as one of the most important crops raised in the county, the labourers lived on a generous diet of oatmeal, milk, cheese and meat,

---

[1] Holt, John (1794). *General View of the Agriculture of the County of Lancaster.*

with potatoes as an accessory food; wages were the highest in the kingdom. In the Isle of Wight,[1] on the other hand, the potato was not a field crop, nor was it cultivated by the farmers, but the 'labouring poor' all grew it in their cottage gardens, and subsisted almost entirely on its produce. Agricultural wages in the Isle were the lowest, and the hours of labour the longest, in all England; whilst cottage rents were, in the opinion of the reporter, too high and food too dear. The two examples illustrate how the potato, when raised as a commercial crop, and used as an accessory foodstuff, may have great economic and social value; whereas when used merely as the food of one class, and that the 'labouring poor', it automatically becomes an instrument of class exploitation—even when neither group is conscious of the part it is playing.

The Battle of the Loaf

The failure of the 1794 and 1795 harvests, and the consequent widespread distress, was countered by the Board of Agriculture by two measures, one official, the other unofficial. The first was the publication of a series of well-informed articles on the Cultivation and Uses of the Potato,[2] which advocated its adoption by the workers as a cheap substitute for wheat; the second, by the publication in the *Annals of Agriculture*, a journal edited by Arthur Young, of a Questionnaire which was sent to leading farmers, clergymen, and local magnates throughout the country, inquiring as to the conditions of the corn crops, potatoes in store, what substitutes were being or could be used for wheat, and the welfare of the labouring poor. Whilst the reports on the winter wheat were generally adverse, that on the state of the potatoes in store was generally good. Very significant was the fact that in the great majority of cases the correspondents pointed out that as the potatoes were stored away in the cellars of the house, they had come to no harm. The inference is clear, viz. that there were few large areas under potatoes, hence relatively few clamps were exposed to the frost, but of these several were destroyed. When a similar emergency occurred ten years later, we no longer hear of storage within the house, but only of field clamps.

The day of the potato had arrived, with the active assistance of those who genuinely desired to relieve the widespread distress of workers, rural and industrial, no less than of those whose main object was to keep down wages, even at the cost of increasing the already heavy Poor Rate. As a policy, the potato was in the mouths of all those who did not need it, whilst it had only just begun to reach the bellies of those who did.

[1] Warren, Rev. (1794). *General View of the Agriculture of the Isle of Wight.*
[2] Board of Agriculture (1795). Report Committee on Culture and Use of Potatoes.

The policy of the Board of Agriculture was simple and to the point: to persuade the people to substitute potatoes for bread in the widest sense. Its approach consisted in encouraging an extensive cultivation of suitable varieties such as the 'Champion' and 'Ox Noble', for use as a vegetable in the home, and that of the 'Yam' variety for cattle fodder. At the same time every effort was to be made to induce the people to incorporate potatoes in the loaf. The Board published detailed accounts of how such a loaf was to be prepared, and assured the public that 12 lbs. of potatoes when added to 20 lbs. of wheaten flour, would make 42 lbs. of excellent bread. Actually the suggestion was not new: twenty-five years earlier it had been pointed out in a popular book on farming that potatoes might be used instead of rye, adding prophetically 'of this discovery the poor may avail themselves in time of dearth'.[1]

The clergy, up and down the country, were invited to urge the incomparable advantage of such bread to their flock. This approach was seconded by correspondents all over the country who, in their turn, recommended every conceivable proportion of potato and flour, each of which was declared capable of producing the perfect loaf. Pitt himself advocated a loaf made of maize and potato, and held that it was very pleasant and nutritious.[2] Many of these enthusiasts tried out the potato bread on their immediate families; all but a few failed to induce the labouring poor of the district even to look at the new-fangled loaf. Out of the 104 answers from 98 different districts, to Young's Circular Letter, only seven correspondents[3] reported that any of their 'poor' had used potatoes in their bread, viz. at Dunmow, Essex; Sunderland, Ormsby and Asgarby, Lincolnshire; Frickley near Doncaster, Scarisbrook, Lancashire; and Middleton-Scriven, Shropshire. In none had the venture got beyond the experimental stage, nor is there any evidence to be found in later volumes of the Annals, that it ever did do so, except in Devonshire, where potatoes, prior to 1795, had been commonly incorporated in the loaf.[4]

It would be a mistake to look on this sudden enthusiasm for the potato as consciously cynical. Eden[5] reflects the outlook of the best minds of his time, as well as the actual change which was taking place in the dietary of the people, when he writes:

The Naturalists of Queen Anne's time would probably have been astonished to hear, what the Board of Agriculture mentions as a fact of the greatest

---

[1] Henry, David (1771). *The Complete English Farmer*, p. 275.
[2] *The Times*, 4 November 1795.
[3] *Annals of Agriculture*, vols. XXIV, XXV and XXVI, contain detailed answers to Young's Circular Letter of Enquiry from all parts of England.
[4] Board of Agriculture (1795). Report Committee on Culture and Use of Potatoes.
[5] Eden, Sir Frederick M. (1797). *The State of the Poor*.

importance, 'that potatoes and water alone, with common salt can nourish men completely'....Potatoes are perhaps as strong an instance of the extension of human enjoyment as can be mentioned; and progress which various districts have made in the cultivation of the valuable root, which may be aptly denominated 'the poor man's wants, the rich man's luxury'[1] [suggests] that in the course of a very few years, the consumption of potatoes in this Kingdom will be almost as general and universal as that of corn.

A prophecy which only just escaped being fulfilled.

In general, the attitude of the working poor was misunderstood by the majority of Young's correspondents: some considered it irrational and, what in their eyes, was a worse offence, unbecoming. The criticisms have the familiar eighteenth-century ring about them. 'The poor are too fine mouthed to eat inferior bread till imperious necessity compels them';[2] 'Our labourers reject anything but wheaten bread';[3] 'For tea the women insist on white bread, otherwise even rich families eat oat bread';[4] 'The poor eat as good flour as the gentlemen farmers do';[5] 'The flour must be divested of its bran and in a fit state for the most luxurious palate, or it is rejected not only by the affluent but by the extremely indigent'.[6] Finally, two opinions from Suffolk: the first, 'the poor will not eat potatoes if they can get anything else' comes from the foremost authority of his day on poor law affairs;[7] the second, 'I believe the daintiness of the poor has been the chief obstacle',[8] illustrates the gulf of ignorance which at this time so commonly divided the worker from the middle classes.

A minority of the correspondents shared the labourers' view, that white bread was not only more nutritious but, in fact indispensable, for men engaged in hard manual labour. 'The poor allege that as they live almost entirely on bread, they cannot perform their tasks without good bread.'[9] 'They have nothing but bread and they want the best.'[10] 'The principal food of the Poor is the whitest bread of which they eat but little else, and they must have it of the most nourishing kind.'[11]

The defence of the loaf was not confined to fine speeches. Food riots were widespread and were notable for the prominent part taken by the

[1] Somerville, William (1725). *Fable of the Two Springs.*
[2] Sheffield, Lord (1795). Bristol. *Annals of Agric.* vol. xxiv, p. 202.
[3] Bevan, S. (1795). Riddlesworth Hall, Norfolk. *Annals of Agric.* vol. xxiv, p. 172.
[4] Lofft, Capel (1796). Troston, Suffolk. *Annals of Agric.* vol. xxvi, p. 311.
[5] Poole, John (1795). Salehurst. *Annals of Agric.* vol. xxiv, p. 244.
[6] Majendie, Lewis (1795). Hedingham, Essex. *Annals of Agric.* vol. xxiv, p. 281.
[7] Ruggles, Thomas (1794). *Annals of Agric.* vol. xxiv, p. 138.
[8] Butts, Thomas (1794). *Annals of Agric.* vol. xxiv, p. 135.
[9] Wickens, John (1795). Blandford, Dorset. *Annals of Agric.* vol. xxiv, p. 31.
[10] Onley, Charles (1795). Stisted Hall, Essex. *Annals of Agric.* vol. xxiv, p. 49.
[11] Bernard, James (1795). Near Taunton, Somerset. *Annals of Agric.* vol. xxiv, p. 20.

housewives. Food shops were raided and the confiscated stores paid for at what they considered an equitable rate.[1]

The frontal attack made by the potato on the white loaf had been defeated, nor was its redoubtable opponent, the maslin loaf, any more fortunate. In only one district is it reported that the barley-wheat loaf had been reintroduced, whilst amongst those in which it had been current from time immemorial, several had already begun to yield to the lure of the white loaf. In Durham it was reported 'the poor will not eat good rye bread except under greatest necessity'.[2] The defence advanced by the workers for the privilege of eating the same bread as their betters, was not confined merely to refusing a substitute. At the risk of depriving themselves of essentials such as milk and meat, they persisted in buying or baking a white wheaten loaf, no matter the cost.

Not the least important, though generally unexpressed, motive underlying the determination shown by the poorer classes in this matter, was clearly and sympathetically stated by a City alderman, a few years later. 'If there was only one species of bread, of an inferior quality to the present consumed by *all* classes, the lower orders of the people in this metropolis would be satisfied with it. I think I should libel the people if I said they would not, provided they should be convinced of the necessity of such arrangements, and I much fear the necessity exists.'[3]

The attempt to substitute Potatoes for Bread

The battle of the white loaf was won in 1795, and the invasion of the potato in that particular sphere was not repeated for more than a hundred years. Nevertheless, potatoes did gain an entry to the bread of the nation, but on another basis. About the middle of the nineteenth century they were generally incorporated into the loaf with the object, not of saving flour, but of improving the flavour, moisture and keeping quality of the bread. The practice, still common, was a generation back almost universal amongst those who made their bread at home, as well as in the village bakeries. The quantity used was one part of raw potatoes to twenty of flour. The unpeeled potatoes were washed, boiled to a pulp, strained, and added to the dough. In recent times, electrically driven peelers and washers are employed which obviate the straining. The use of the potato in war as a constituent of the loaf, is considered in chapter XXXII.

The original fight was Parthian, the fruit of victory was less wheaten bread at a greatly increased cost. During all this time agricultural cash

---

[1] Hammond, J. L. and B. (1911). *The Village Labourer*, p. 96.
[2] Mowbray, A. (1795). Sherburn, near Durham. *Annals of Agric.* vol. XXIV, p. 91.
[3] Weston, Alderman (1800). *Annals of Agric.* vol. XXIV, p. 486. (The italics are mine—R.N.S.)

wages, as apart from relief from 'the poor's table', increased about 15%.

The struggle to retain the white loaf had been short and costly; it was but the opening phase of that waged for a decent standard of living for the labouring classes, which should be at least as good as that enjoyed prior to the last quarter of the century. In this long-drawn out campaign the potato played an ambiguous part, at best a dubious ally, more often an insidious enemy.

The people wanted bread, but bread was too dear to satisfy even their barest needs; meat and cheese had more than doubled in price; milk as a result of enclosures and loss of grazing rights was, in many parts of the country, unobtainable. Where were they to look for a bare sustenance? The potato was relatively cheap, easy to come by, and nutritious. Statesmen, landlords and clergy were at one in exhorting the workers to make use of it. Against its adoption were the facts that it was something new and therefore to be distrusted, but more particularly that it was the food of the immigrant Irish labourer, for whose mode of living the English worker had the greatest contempt. Was he also destined to sink to the same level, a question which in one form or another confronted an entire generation of workers, rural and urban alike.

Hunger being a harsh taskmaster, it was not long in breaking down such opposition as still existed in the countryside to the use of the potato as a vegetable, a far easier task than that of persuading the people to allow it to be substituted for wheaten flour in their bread.

A Shropshire correspondent, representative of many throughout the country, tells how the colliery workers consumed large quantities of grain, presumably leaving little for other classes of workers in town or country. Of the latter he says 'were it not for potatoes and with such wages many of the families must starve or come on the parish'.[1]

In order that the potato should take its place in the daily regime of the workers, it was necessary that the latter should either grow it themselves, or be able to buy it locally in sufficient quantities. We have already seen that south of the Coal Line and excluding the extreme west, the cottage potato plot was by no means general; its use, however, was growing. The replies to Arthur Young's inquiries which appeared in the *Annals of Agriculture* for 1795 and 1796 show that the distress of 1795 did much to extend the use of the potato. Such is confirmed by an article in *The Times* of 10 September 1795: 'From the apprehension of a second year of scarcity, potatoes have been everywhere planted and their produce has been generally great.'

Industrial workers were already in the habit of buying potatoes, retail, in the towns, though probably in no great quantity. A new departure

[1] Harries, E. (1795). *Annals of Agric.* vol. XXIV, p. 59.

was the purchase of potatoes by the rural workers; how common it was, it is difficult to say, but in the family budgets to which reference has already been made, a purchase of potatoes is recorded in almost all of those dating from 1795 onwards.

Although potatoes had been coming into England regularly for several years from Scotland, it is evident from the *Annals* that in 1795 the stocks of the country were insufficient to meet the sudden and unexpected demand: prices rose in some places to three times the normal; in others the overseers bought the local stocks and distributed them to the poor at from 1*s*. to 1*s*. 6*d*. a bushel, about half the normal price.

Where the potato was available in adequate quantities, it is reasonable to suppose that it gained an immediate and permanent foothold; where it was in short supply its progress was delayed indefinitely; as a correspondent from Felsted, Essex, writes: 'the addition of potatoes to the diet, unless in large quantities, is no good to the poor'.[1]

The 1795 crisis gave rise to a wave of propaganda in which the most distinguished men of the day took part: it was directed to the provision of a cheap substitute for wheat as a food for the poor. The Privy Council[2] in July appealed to all to abjure pies and puddings, to eat more vegetables, and to use household bread, part rye. No person, it held, should eat more than a quartern loaf a week. Carolina rice was recommended as food for the poor.[2]

In February an Order of Council prohibited all exports of grain or malt, and allowed all such to be imported, free of tax, until the sixth week after the commencement of the next session. The Order was prolonged by another issued on 29 July. Sir John Sinclair, as President of the Board of Agriculture, asked the Privy Council to recommend that bread should be made of all the produce of the grain; that less bread should be eaten and the deficiency be made up by eating vegetables [potatoes] and a proportion of meat and fish; that the quantity of corn given to animals should be diminished.[3] This did not receive the entire approval of the Privy Council, nor did a further application urging the approval for making a cheap soup by a German method.[4]

The Times in July of that same year, echoed the same hope, and proceeded to advise the poor to abstain from the Public House and to adopt the dietary of Lancashire with its mixed grained bread, and abundant potatoes and oatmeal porridge.[5] In two later issues it advocated the use of a soup for the poor, mainly composed of potatoes,[6] and Pitt's loaf

---

[1] Onley, Charles (1795). *Annals of Agric.* vol. XXV, p. 494.

[2] Traill, H. D. (1893–7). *Social England*, vol. V, p. 493. [The Record Office cannot trace this order.]

[3] Record Office. Communicated to R.N.S. 30 August 1944.

[4] Record Office (15 July 1795). P.C. I/27, A55.

[5] *The Times* (11 July 1795).   [6] *The Times* (10 October 1795)

of maize and potatoes which, it assures its readers, is pleasant and nutritious.[1]

An engagement was entered into by the members of the Privy Council[2] recommending their fellow subjects only to consume standard wheaten bread, and another addressed to the gentry by the Duke of Portland, to cut down their own consumption of white flour by one third, and reduce the oat rations in their stables.

They did not propose themselves to subsist on potatoes, all of which were to be put at the disposal of the poor. As alternatives, rye, barley, oats and, not least, imported rice, had all their supporters, but the potato was easily the favourite. The farmers, generally, responded to the call, so that even in Norfolk and Suffolk potato cultivation began to make some progress, whilst in Worcestershire the potato output was said to have been increased sixfold. From now on, it became common practice for farmers to put aside a portion of the field that was destined for their own potatoes, for the cultivation of those of their labourers, a practice which survives to this day.

It is not to be assumed that because in 1795 the barriers had begun to fall, that from then onwards the potato dominated the table of the 'labouring poor'. When in the following year bread fell nearly to its old figure it became, though for a very short time, once more the mainstay of the people. For more than thirty years, white bread and potatoes competed for the first place in the dietary of the nation, pride and tradition supporting the former, adverse economic conditions the latter.

The early association of a potato diet with the experience of acute economic distress, cannot have failed to create in the minds of both labourer and employer an unfortunate impression. The former regarding it as the diet of necessity, and a reminder of the injustice he felt himself to be suffering under; the employer all too frequently concluding that as the use of the potato had staved off the raising of wages, and as these were regulated by the bare cost of living, the new food by reducing this cost, should reduce wages in a similar manner. Already one hears of an employer near Bagshot remarking with satisfaction that wages were now 8s. per week, having only increased 1s. in twenty-five years, and that 'considering the use of potatoes and turnips, the labourer is better off than before'.[3] It is noteworthy that in his district, potatoes which had been 2s. a bushel before the crisis, were now selling at 4s. A similar though unconscious mixture of motives appears in a communication from the Incumbent of Gosfield, Essex:

Potatoes are in great use here, which necessarily lessens the consumption of bread, but unfortunately they have been greatly injured by frost. A School

---

[1] *The Times* (4 November 1795).   [2] Record Office (1 July 1795). P.C. I/27, A54.
[3] Leycester, Ralph (1795). *Annals of Agric.* vol. XXIV, p. 247.

of Industry, open every day in the week is supported here by the liberality of the Marquis of Buckingham: a breakfast and dinner are given to the children every Sunday: the breakfast is milk gruel and bread; the dinner meat soup thickened with potatoes and bread; besides a large quantity of potatoes boiled by themselves... *the children are thus habituated to the use of, and acquire a fondness for potatoes,* which is by no means checked by the parents in supplying them with food.[1]

In the last year of the century Pitt,[2] introducing his Bill to amend the Poor Law, gave a vivid description of the conditions of the labouring-poor with their miserable wages of 1s. 4d. in winter and 1s. 6d. in summer. He stated that when wheat is more than 60s. it is impossible for a labouring family to live on their earnings. Indeed, he went so far as to say that, unhelped, no labourer can support more than four children. This, from England's foremost statesman, must remove any doubt in our minds to-day, whatever it may have done in those of his contemporaries, that the condition of the great mass of the people was as dangerous as it was unhappy.

The five anxious years, which completed the century, witnessed a considerable advance in the progress of the potato as a field crop, and the increasing subjection of the 'labouring-poor' to its influence. To relieve distress in the towns, recourse was had to the methods which Count Rumford had recently perfected in Munich. There the poor were collected into vast workhouses and fed on soups, which contained a very high proportion of potatoes and a very low one of meat. Incidentally, the poor of Munich were still so prejudiced against potatoes that he had been obliged to keep their inclusion strictly secret.[3] In England, this method of dealing with a shortage of bread was not received with much enthusiasm by the poor. Rumford himself advocated big communal kitchens but, outside some of the workhouses, these do not seem to have been adopted. In Epping Workhouse they brewed a soup according to the following recipe: 4 lbs. of pickled pork, 6 stones of shins and legs, 6 lbs. of skibling (meat waste), 28 lbs. of potatoes, 20 lbs. of Scotch oatmeal, 2 lbs. of salt, 1 lb. of whole pepper and ¼ lb. of ground pepper, a dozen carrots and a handful of mint, to 56 gallons of water.[4]

The Epping soup was designed on more generous lines than was usual in such cases; nevertheless, if we take the most optimistic view of it and assume that all the ingredients were edible, that the meat contained no bone, and that there was no evaporation, it may be assumed that

[1] Thurlow, Rev. (1795). *Annals of Agric.* vol. XXIV, p. 149. [The italics are mine—R.N.S.]

[2] Young, A. (1799). *Annals of Agric.* vol. XXXIII, p. 621.

[3] Rumford, Count (1753–1814). *Collected Works,* vol. IV, p. 414.

[4] Beaton, T. (1799). *Annals of Agric.* vol. XXIV, p. 298.

a pint would contain something over 300 calories.[1] An average working-man would therefore need a gallon and a quarter per day, to maintain his strength. Some of the soups destined for the poor were almost worthless, and many were made from kitchen scrap and waste.[2]

Towards these concoctions Eden says the poor reacted with 'we will not be fed on meal and chopped potatoes like hogs'.[3]

More practical, and commoner, was the method adopted by some poor law authorities of giving relief in kind, including a large proportion of potatoes. In a Sussex parish, a family of eight which formerly were allowed one bushel of wheaten flour per week, now received two gallons of flour and 60 lb. of potatoes. The poor paid 1s. for the potatoes alone, and 6s. 2d. for the wheat, and the parish, instead of incurring an outlay of 15s. 4d. as heretofore, now spent but 8s. 3d.[4] Relief took various forms: the one most widely advocated and certainly the most successful, was that by which the 'poor' were encouraged to grow their own potatoes on land put at their disposal by the farmers or the overseers. At Chippenham, near Bath, 'They speak much of the importance of potatoes and assert that the poor in the scarcity [1795] must have suffered dreadfully but for that root.'[5]

Arthur Young had for some time achieved the position of philosopher and guide to the more intelligent section of the landed interests of his day. He had attained this position by reason of his enthusiasm, controlled by experiment, his conspicuous intellectual honesty, and his untiring industry. By birth and education a class-conscious country squire, by heredity and association an intellectual with a keen sense of social justice, his reactions to passing events have an exceptional value for us to-day.

Young, the landlord and patriot, horrified by the wasteful and slovenly methods, all too common amongst open-field farmers, plunged head-long into the campaign for enclosure. His passion for an efficient scientifically developed husbandry, which he was convinced was in the best interests of the nation as a whole, no less than in those of the land-lords and farmers, blinded him for many years to the injustices to the 'labouring poor', which this policy had so frequently brought in its train. The crisis of 1795 and the distress which ensued, reawakened Young's dormant humanitarianism. To retrace his steps, had he so desired, was impossible. It was essential to discover, if possible, a new foundation on which to rebuild the lost security of the landworker. His dream was to endow the agricultural worker with a good cottage and

[1] For this estimate I have to thank Dr R. A. McCance, who has given the matter his careful and expert consideration.
[2] Beaton, T. (1799). *Annals of Agric.* vol. XXVI, p. 215.
[3] Eden, Sir Frederick M. (1797). *The State of the Poor*, vol. I, p. 533.
[4] Sheffield, Lord (1797). *Annals of Agric.* vol. XXIX, p. 469.
[5] Young, A. (1798). Tour in South and West. *Annals of Agric.* vol. XXXI, p. 79.

three acres of land, by which he would ensure the economic safety of his family, through the raising of potatoes and the keeping of a cow. This policy was restated in 1885 by Jesse Collings, who had no need to call in aid the potato; the problem of the cheap loaf or its substitute for which it had been the specific, had ceased to be. The New World had at least redressed that particular failing of the old.

The first stirrings of the new policy are to be found in an article on The State of the Poor in his own county of Suffolk.[1] He found that the labourer preferred a crust of bread and a bit of cheese to any parish soup he might be offered. But what distressed him most, was that families on relief were still left half starved. 'Is this the way', Young writes, 'that English families should live, while England is annually boasted as the most prosperous country on earth? Do we merit the blessing of Divine Providence either at home or abroad, while we feed our poor in such a manner?'

After demanding public kitchens and the use of rice in all parochial distributions, Young returns to the charge: 'Our cottagers are without bedding, without fuel, unless stolen, and in many places inhabiting buildings, or rather ruins, which keep out neither wind nor rain...the whole is a disgrace to Christianity.'

In the same article he throws out the suggestion: 'The common lands should be served out to them [the labouring poor] and they would save themselves with potatoes and cow....A man with 10 children should have 4½ acres.' Young's anxiety as to the state of the poor appears a little later, when he notes how the poor still struggle to get white bread and advises that oats should no longer be fed to horses and that oat flour, potatoes and rice should be served to the poor as soup.[2] Here we find Young in line with official policy, though not with the spirit which inspired it.

A Committee of the House of Commons reported on 10 February 1800:[3]

Your Committee have heard with very great concern, that from the mistaken application of the charity of individuals, in some parts of the country, flour and bread have been delivered to the poor at a reduced price; a practice which may contribute very considerably to increase the inconveniences arising from the deficiency of the last crop; and they recommend that all charity and parochial relief should be given as far as is practicable, in any other articles except bread, flour and money, and that the part of it which is necessary for the sustenance of the poor should be distributed in soups, rice, potatoes or other substitutes...*if this regulation was generally adopted, it would not only, in a very great degree, contribute to economize at this time the consumption of*

[1] Young, A. (1795). *Annals of Agric.* vol. XXIV, p. 186.
[2] Young, A. (1794). *Annals of Agric.* vol. XXIV, p. 494.
[3] Report Committee. House of Commons, 1800. *Annals of Agric.* vol. XXXIV, p. 449.

flour, but that it might have the effect of gradually introducing into use a more wholesome and nutritious species of food than that to which the poor are at present accustomed.[1]

Here we have the formulation of a policy by the highest authority, designed permanently to reduce the standard of living of the working classes of the kingdom, by deliberately weaning them, in a season of distress, from a food proper to the upper classes, and enuring them to a subsistence level based upon the potato. For all the talk of 'soup, rice and other substitutes' meant in practice no more nor less, than the potato.

A Proclamation by the King issued on 3 December 1800 approached the subject from a different angle: if the well-to-do eat less, there would be more for the poor. Hence it called on farmers to reduce the consumption of bread in their families to one-third, desired that no one should consume more than one quartern loaf per week, nor make any pastry, and that the oat ration of pleasure-horses be reduced. Thus inspired, the inhabitants of the village of Kensington decided to abstain from pastry, placing greater reliance on potatoes.[2]

Young, realizing how the majority of the enclosures had succeeded in cutting the labourers off entirely from the land, when the Bill for General Enclosures came up for consideration on 5 December 1801, wrote: 'Take care of the interests of the poor: they will pay for wastes [in saving rates] treble the rent of all your other improvements put together [i.e. by growing potatoes on the commons and thus keeping the poor off the parish], and I had rather that all the commons of England were sunk in the sea, than that the poor should in future be treated on enclosing as they have generally been hitherto.'[3]

A little later he put his scheme for using the 'wastes' for providing the labouring poor with potato-ground into concrete form in the *Annals*. As an introduction, he advises his reader to visit the ale-house kitchen in an old enclosed parish and there he will hear all that he need know about the origin of poverty and the condition of the poor. The village labourers over their beer will enlighten him. 'For whom are they to be sober? For whom are they to save? Such are the questions for the parish. If I am diligent shall I have leave to build a cottage? If I am sober shall I have land for a cow? If I am frugal shall I have half-an-acre of potatoes? You offer no motives! You have nothing but a parish officer and a workhouse! Bring me another pot.'[4]

---

[1] Report Committee. House of Commons, 1800. *Annals of Agric.* vol. xxxiv, p. 449. [The italics are mine—R.N.S.]
[2] Cunningham, W. (1892). *Growth of English Industry*, vol. ii, p. 496.
[3] Young, A. (1801). *Annals of Agric.* vol. xxxvi, p. 214.
[4] Young, A. (1800). *Annals of Agric.* vol. xxxvi, p. 508.

Young never allowed the warmth of his feelings to obscure his appreciation of realities, or delay his passion for action. Three main issues presented themselves to him: What was the true cause of the rapid and alarming rise in the price of wheat; what could be done to allay the fears and suspicions of the people, and what remedy could be devised in the interest of the only sufferers—the 'labouring poor'. The result of his studies are embodied in a brochure, which is now very rare.[1] Young concluded that the rise in price followed a genuine shortage of stocks, consequent on the bad harvest of 1799, and that there was a deficiency of wheat stocks throughout the country of at least one-third. The suspicions, so widely held, that the mounting price was due to the manipulation of the market by gamblers, had no foundation in fact. The disaster was an Act of God and as such must be borne with patience and resignation by the 'poor'.

The remedy, Young concluded, must be sought by inducing the 'poor' to subsist on a cheaper food, and leave wheat to those who could afford it. To that end he wrote to a number of correspondents for their opinion as to whether any, or all of the following expedients could be of service. A Government bounty on the cultivation of the potato, the exclusion of the potato from the payment of tithe, and the devotion of the common lands to the use of the poor. The answers he received were too conflicting to be of much assistance; the only one which met with general approval was the freeing of the crop from tithe.

Young put forward a short- and a long-term policy: the public should be at once advised to remove the eyes of the potatoes before cooking, and save them for seed.[2] London alone, he assures us, wasted every day in its garbage, enough potato eyes to plant 30 acres of land.

The long-term policy rested, so to speak, on two legs: one, the weaning of the labouring class from wheat to potatoes and milk; the other, the rapid completion of enclosure by a simplified General Enclosure Bill, and the establishment of an agricultural bureau of statistics. The former was realized in a Bill in the following year; the latter had to wait another sixty years before any further approach to the subject was made.

It will be recalled that Nathaniel Kent had advocated holdings of three acres or thereabouts, for the use of labourers in 1777 (see p. 488). The idea had found at least a few stalwart supporters, Lord Winchelsea, Lord Carrington, the Earl of Yarborough, Sir Cecil Wray and Mr Chaplin:

---

[1] Young, A. (1800). *The Question of Scarcity Plainly Stated*. Macmillan.

[2] The idea that the excised eyes might be removed from the domestic potato, dried, and used as seed, had been suggested many times during the quarter of a century prior to Young's brochure, and had been put into practice in Nova Scotia. Experiments with such, as well as with peelings, are to be found in the literature of the time. Lately the idea has reappeared as a recent Russian discovery; in Canada the practice had been commercialized somewhat earlier.

all had put the scheme into practice on a generous scale on their estates in Rutland and Lincolnshire. In the 1795 crisis and later, the labourers on these estates proved to be immune to the distress around them. Thus encouraged, Young put forward a detailed scheme by which agricultural labourers should be equipped with a cottage, three acres of pasture for a cow, and an half-acre of land for potatoes.

With his accustomed honesty, Young leaves his readers in no doubt as to the motive which lay behind his proposals: 'The great object is by means of milk and potatoes to take the mass of the country's "poor" from the consumption of wheat, and to give them substitutes equally wholesome and nourishing and as independent of scarcities natural and artificial, as the providence of the Almighty will permit.' And to leave no loophole open as to the identification of the matter which is under the guidance of Providence, he adds: 'another method of obtaining the same object would be to pass an Act prohibiting parochial relief as far as subsistence was concerned in any other manner than by potatoes, rice and soup, not merely as a measure of the moment, but permanently.'

These proposals encountered the opposition of two of the dominant philosophers of the day: one, Young dismissed in his brochure in the following words: 'Adam Smith prevailed; political principles were thought more nourishing.' The other resulted in a polemic between himself and Malthus. The latter objected to Young's scheme on the ground that such a basis for subsistence would result in the degradation of the people, similar to that seen in Ireland, and to the lowering of wages. Moreover, such easy conditions would lead to early marriages, large families, over-population, and the inevitable Malthusian concomitant of vice and misery. Malthus concludes with two devastating criticisms: 'Is it not possible', he says, 'that one day the potato crop itself may fail?' He then records: 'When the common people of a country live principally upon the dearest grain, as they do in England on wheat, they have great resources in a scarcity; and barley, oats, rice, cheap soups and potatoes, all present themselves as less expensive yet at the same time wholesome means of nourishment; but when their habitual food is the lowest in this scale, they appear to be absolutely without resource except in the bark of trees like the poor Swedes.'

Malthus warns Young that inherent in his scheme lurks another danger—cheap feeding means cheap labour, and cheap labour points an easy route to the conquest of foreign markets, the capture of which means an opulent and luxurious nation. 'I should not envy', says Malthus, 'the feelings which could suggest such a proposal...nothing could be more detestable than the idea of knowingly condemning the labourers of the country to the rags and wretched cabins of Ireland for the purpose of selling a few more broad cloths and calicoes.'[1] A sequence of events closely parallel to those enunciated by Dr Paley, as being just those conditions 'most favourable to the population of a country and conducive to its general happiness', which he summed up as 'that of a laborious frugal people administering to the demands of an opulent luxurious nation'.[2]

Malthus's reaction to this, the teaching of one of the major lights of the Church, was very similar to that excited by Young's proposals. 'Nothing but the conviction of its being absolutely necessary, could reconcile us to the idea of ten millions of people condemned to incessant toil, and to the privation of everything but absolute necessaries, in order to minister to the excessive luxuries of the other million.'

Young[3] had no difficulty in finding a satisfactory answer to the main Malthusian argument, the danger of an increase in the ranks of the 'poor'. He pointed out that his proposal was to give the people sound and decent homes; experience had shown, over and over again, that an improvement in the amenities of the home invariably led to smaller, not larger families. Unfortunately, Young's cottage holdings never matured. The scheme was defeated by the land-hunger of the farmer and the timidity of the landlords, but his attempt to force the labouring poor on to a potato diet only just failed of success.

The controversy, though it led to no immediate result, has a unique value inasmuch as it reveals the attitude of mind of two men of outstanding integrity, intelligence and public spirit, to the most pressing social problem of their day. To both, the 'labouring poor' were so far removed from their own world as to be almost of another species of beings. It may be remembered that Kent frankly spoke of them as a 'race' whose existence, though essential to the body politic, did not entitle them to any control of their own welfare. Whether they were to be fed on wheat, or on potatoes, whether their wages were adequate, or not for their subsistence, were matters which had always been controlled by their employers. Now it had been revealed that there existed fundamental economic laws which providentially confirmed what might otherwise have appeared to be the arbitrary, not to say self-interested decisions of their betters. If so sensitive a man as Young was unable to free himself from the fetters of thought, imposed by the religio-philosophic doctrine of his day, we need not be surprised to find that the farmers and industrialists of England needed the best part of a century of economic

[1] Malthus, T. (1806). *An Essay on the Principle of Population* (3rd edit.), vol. II, pp. 460 and 482.

[2] Paley, William (1785). *Moral and Political Philosophy*. Ed. 1877, bk. IV, ch. XI, p. 182. London: W. Tegg.

[3] Young, A. (1804). *Annals of Agric.* vol. XXXI, p. 208.

strife before they began to realize that master and man might, after all, be equal partners in the struggle for existence.

Before leaving the eighteenth century, it would be well to get a bird's-eye view of what had been accomplished during the hundred years, to meet the nation's requirements in regard to its wheat supplies. A recent authority has summed up the situation: 'The area [under wheat] was enlarged by one-third, the total yield by approximately two-fifths, and, during the time the farmers took to secure this increment, the population had doubled, which at once removes any lingering doubt as to the reason why the export dwindled and importation became necessary.'[1]

In short, at the end of the century, the average man had at his disposal about two-thirds of the wheat that he had enjoyed at the beginning. Even had the distribution been equable, which was far from being the case, an additional source of food would have been necessary. War had checked the progress of industry; the great advancing wave of enclosures had brought displacement and unemployment to the agricultural labourer, and now it needed only the soaring price of bread, in the absence of imports, to convert unrest into disaffection. A disaffection which, during the next two decades, was prevented from assuming a revolutionary character, as much by the agency of a new and relatively cheap food, as by the Speenhamland wage-system or the threat of armed force. It was inevitable that the potato, whose worth had at long last been widely recognized, should have been called on to fill the gap in the nation's larder.

[1] Fussell, G. E. (1929). Population and Wheat Production in the Eighteenth Century. *The History Teachers' Miscellany*, vol. VII, p. 125.

CHAPTER XXVI

The Nineteenth Century and After

The Period of the Napoleonic Wars

From 1793 till 1815 this country, with a couple of short intervals, was at war with France, and between 1812 and 1815 with America also. During the whole of this period there were only two really good harvests, viz. those of 1796 and 1813; a further six which might be considered up to the average in yield, whilst seven of the remainder, those of the years 1795, 1799, 1800, 1809, 1810, 1811 and 1812, were more or less complete failures. During the war period imports of corn were small and extremely difficult to come by: in 1808 and 1809 we were driven to importing corn from France and the Netherlands. Scarcity, and still more, the fear of it, sent prices soaring: in 1800 it was that the Baltic might be closed, which drove the price of wheat up to 130s. a quarter; in 1812 it was the efficiency of the blockade, consequent on Napoleon's Berlin and Milan decrees, which forced the price up to 155s. Lord Ernle[1] points out that even had it been possible to obtain supplies the price would still have been very high, as the costs of transport and insurance alone, under war conditions, amounted to 50s. a quarter. This, and the high market values, put wheat on a price-plane on which the Corn Laws ceased to exert an influence.

Throughout most of the period there was a real though intermittent food shortage, the extent of which would be greatly exaggerated were it to be gauged by the high prices which reigned. On the other hand, these inflated prices, when reviewed in relation to the current wage, do afford a measure of the distress which had overtaken wage-earners throughout the entire country. In years when the home crop was deficient, as in 1799 and 1810, the distress of the labouring classes in some of the industrial districts often reached famine conditions, but this was not always due to the absence of food in the markets, and still less in the country, but to lack of sufficient cash wherewith to purchase it.[2]

The profits, no less than the pains of war, were very unequally divided: the farmer prospered exceedingly, the landlord, on a modest estimate, doubled his income, but the increase in the agricultural labourer's wage was in no way commensurate with his increased cost of living. It is true that there was no agricultural unemployment on the land; on the other hand, those valuable additions to his family's earnings,

---

[1] Ernle, Lord (1912). *English Farming* (5th edit. 1936), p. 269.

[2] In 1800, potatoes cost £15 per ton – thus dearer than flour (Salaman's manuscript note). – Ed.

whether won at the loom, by spinning or by carding, were fast disappearing with the migration of industry to the north, or its concentration in factories in the larger Midland towns.

We are told, however, that agricultural wages at this time went up about 100%, a statement which had the support of Tooke[1] and of Young,[2] who thought that between 1770 and 1810 such had occurred. It is notoriously difficult to estimate the value of a wage when, as frequently happened, it included, in addition to a cash payment, allowances in kind, the use of a potato-patch and occasionally cottage accommodation free of rent. I have failed to find evidence to substantiate the existence anywhere of such an increased agricultural wage. It is essential to distinguish between allowances and a cash wage. Had allowances and the like, in fact, increased substantially in value, it would have made no very great difference to the maintenance of a labourer's family south of the Coal Line. The reason for this view has already been discussed when dealing with the 'battle of the loaf', and the realization of its truth is vital to an understanding of the economic position of the labouring class of the nineteenth century. The landworker and the industrial hand were bread eaters, first and last, and the former only retreated from but never abandoned that position, even when the quartern loaf rose to 1s. 5d. and higher: he merely ate less of it, making up for the loss, as far as he could, with potatoes when he could get them. To live on bread, one must buy one's loaf with coin of the realm: harvest money, allowances of turnips, potatoes, or even a rent-free cottage, do nothing to alter the hard fact that the baker must be paid in cash each week, and the only cash available to the labourer now that he had neither pigs nor poultry to sell, was his weekly wage. That wage in most districts went up from 1s. 4d. to 1s. 6d. a day, and that not in all. An increase of 12½% in cash, against one of 200–300% in the cost of bread, was not calculated to keep the labourer in health. After 1811, cash wages went up again in some districts, but even so, they fell very far short of a 100% increase on the pre-1795 rate.

The following wage rates given in a *Report* published in 1816[3] seem to be a fair sample: Derbyshire, 2s. 6d. per day all the year round; Hampshire, 10s. to 15s. per week; Norfolk, 1s. 6d. to 2s. per day; Warwickshire, 12s. per week the maximum; Wiltshire, no figures given, but the labourer was stated to be worse off than before 1811 because of unemployment. These figures find support in a recent survey of the problem by two economists of standing. They admit the difficulty of

[1] Tooke, Thomas (1838). *History of Prices*, vol. I, p. 329.
[2] Young, A. (1815). *Enquiry into the Rise of Prices in Europe during the last twenty-five years*, p. 215.
[3] Board of Agriculture (1816). Replies to a Circular Letter, etc.

presenting a thoroughly satisfactory statement, but claim as a 'broad impression', the following:

At the time of the outbreak of the war with France in 1793, 9s. a week was a frequent agricultural wage in the Southern Counties, and 8s. in the North.[1] By 1810 about 13s. was being paid in the South and Southern Midlands, where the Speenhamland system was in force, whereas in the North, where the system did not exist, wages had risen as high as 15s., and in some places higher. In the West Riding, for example, 16s. 6d. was being paid in 1813.

Before the end of the war, agricultural wages had begun to fall, and by 1822–3 they were down to 8s. or 9s. in the Eastern Counties—the great wheat-growing area. In the South, except in Wiltshire and the West, where they were about 8s. 6d., they seem to have ranged from 10s. to 12s., and in the North to have fallen to 9s. to 10s. Thereafter they rose again in the North, to 12s. in Yorkshire and even 14s. in Lancashire, but changed little in the South until after 1834.[2]

The three bad harvests of 1809–1811, accompanied by the industrial depression consequent on Napoleon's decrees and the outbreak of war with America, combined to throw scores of thousands out of work all over the country, especially in the cotton and textile industries. Those that remained in work suffered heavy reductions in wages. The Nottingham lace-workers were fortunate if they earned an average of 7s. a week.

The historian of the hosiery trade[3] discussing the Luddite troubles, ascribed their cause to 'the hunger and misery into which the large portion of the fifty thousand framework-knitters and their families were fallen, and from which they never fully emerged for the following forty years. During that long interval, the average of the framework-knitters clear earnings by long hours of labour did not exceed six shillings a week.'

Unrest and violence, frequently mistaken by the governing classes for revolution, and generally treated as such, became rife throughout the industrial districts. In all cases, low wages, high taxation and excessive food prices were the basic causes of the trouble. The loaf was between two and three times its pre-war price, and every article of food, drink and wear, was taxed—except the potato. The majority of the industrial workers of England during the war years, whether on the land or in the factories, were on the verge of starvation, and in their necessity they turned more and more to the potato as a substitute for the bread and cheese, which had formerly been their mainstay. As Young said: 'Since

---

[1] In addition to substantial payments in kind (R.N.S.).
[2] Cole, G. D. H. and Postgate, Raymond (1938). *The Common People*, p. 198.
[3] Felkin, W. (1867). *A History of the Machine-Wrought Hosiery, etc.* p. 239.

the scarcities, hardly any object has occupied so much attention or any article of cultivation so greatly increased.'[1] At Croom in Worcester in 1801 he found the potato acreage had increased fivefold.[2]

Another advocate was Colquhoun,[3] whose enthusiasm permitted him to believe that the same number of people could be subsisted on a quarter of an acre under potatoes as on one acre under wheat. He urged that fish and potatoes should be combined in the people's dietary and is assured that an increase in the consumption of fish can already be recognized. It is, however, salt or 'corned' fish, already an established dish amongst the 'inferior classes' of Cornwall, which, in association with the potato, he thinks is becoming increasingly popular.

The Rumford soups played their part, too, in popularizing the potato, though not always with success; when the quota of meat was exiguous, that of the potato loomed too large. From Grimblethorpe, Lincs, a complaint to this effect reached the *Annals* in 1800.[4] In the absence of bread, it is potatoes which the people from now on demand with increasing vehemence. In Bristol the risings of 1812 were directed against the farmers, who were holding up their stocks of potatoes for higher prices. 'At Stockport on April 15th of the same year, the demonstrators entered the market, enquired the price of potatoes, considered them too dear, and threw them into the street.'[5] In the year 1811, and for at least twenty-three years later, the food of the working classes in the Manchester districts was confined to potatoes, porridge and some bacon.[6]

During the war there was not always enough potatoes to meet the new demand. The price of no other food varied locally and seasonally so much as did that of the potato. The lowest figure at this time, apart from specially designed poor relief prices, was 1s. a bushel. Two shillings was perhaps the average but 3s. and 4s. a bushel were not at all exceptional. The retail price in 1800 at Rochcliffe, Hants, was 7d. to 8d. for 18 lbs.; in big towns it must, later in the war, have been on a very much higher scale, seeing that the Luddite demonstrators asked for a reduction of current prices by 1d. per lb.[7]

A tragic picture of the time is recorded by the Hammonds: the scene was in the market at Manchester. A number of poor people seized a man's potatoes and compelled him to sell them at a lower price than the one

[1] Young, A. (1807). *General View, etc. Essex*, vol. i, p. 381.
[2] Young, A. (1801). *Annals of Agric.* vol. xxxvii, p. 465.
[3] Colquhoun, P. (1814). *Treatise on the Wealth, Power and Resources of the British Empire*, pp. 11–15.
[4] Scott, W. (1800). *Annals of Agric.* vol. xxxv, p. 441.
[5] Darval, Frank (1934). *Popular Disturbances and Public Order in Regency England*, p. 95.
[6] *V.C.H. Lancaster* (1908), vol. ii, p. 10.
[7] Cole, G. D. H. and Postgate, Raymond (1938). *The Common People* (ed. 1946), p. 187.

asked; amongst them was a woman: she was arrested, tried and hanged.[1] The price enforced by the mob was 8s. a load.[2]

Post-war Collapse

The long-sustained boom in prices which had done as much to enrich both farmer and landlord as it had to pauperize the labourer, drew to a sudden close. The first break in the run of prosperity was, curiously enough, the bumper harvest of 1813, which sent wheat down from 123s. 10d. to 67s. 10d. Between 1814 and 1816 the collapse continued and a Bill to bolster up prices by excluding imports till the home crop rose to 80s., was hastily passed.

The depression had shown itself first in the heavy-land corn-growing districts; before long it had spread to the grass and mixed farms. 'Bad seasons in 1816', says Ernle, 'created a temporary scarcity; the rise of wheat to the old prices aggravated rural distress... the potato crop which had recently become so important in England, failed.'[3] Rents were lowered, but not soon enough to forestall disaster; bankruptcies piled up and a great many farmers were obliged to give up their farms. Agricultural war economy had been reared on dear corn, and the industry found great difficulty in adjusting itself to the changed conditions. Recovery did not set in till about the time of Queen Victoria's accession.

The lot of the labourer was less dramatic. He had always been poor— now he was poorer; he had always expected to end his days in the work-house—now he became a pauper in the fullness of his strength. Before, he had eaten much bread, little potatoes, and washed both down with beer; now, he ate much potato, little bread, and washed both down with tea—when he could get it.

So great was the depression, the misery and the resentment of the agricultural labourers, that as time went on it became an easy matter to incite them to violence. But even so, it was not until the new thrashing machinery in 1830 had threatened to rob them of their winter work, that rick burning and the like under 'Capt. Swing', spread from one end of the country to the other and, despite the savagery of the punishment meted out to those who were caught, continued in a desultory manner into the 'hungry forties'.

Industry fared but little better. With peace came a short-lived boom, followed by a fall both in volume and value of exports, to a Continent which could not afford to pay for them. The American market, which

[1] Hammond, J. L. and Hammond, B. (1916). *The Skilled Labourer* (1925 edit.), p. 128.

[2] Slater, Gilbert (1932). *The Growth of Modern England* (ed. 1939), p. 231. [A load of potatoes may have been five bushels.]

[3] Ernle, Lord (1912). *English Farming* (edit. 1936), p. 323.

had absorbed half our exports, because of unwise speculation, failed also in 1819, with the result that unemployment and wage-cutting swept the factories. In the country districts, foremost amongst the sufferers were the hand-loom weavers who found their dual support in industry and agriculture cut from under them. The demand for cheap child labour was of all measures the most destructive of the workers' interests: it increased the number of the adult unemployed, whilst it destroyed the health and morale of the whole family. Possibly nothing did more to force the labourer on to a potato diet. In 1825 there was a recovery, but it was not sustained.

Not all trades and occupations shared in the general depression and much new enterprise found its expression in the thirty years which followed the peace. The canals, the railways, and the macadamized roads, are permanent witnesses of the feverish anxiety of our local industrialization. The vast increase in our exports and shipping witnessed to the fantastic accumulation of wealth in the country, and the new slum towns, to the degrading poverty of the majority of their population. Under such circumstances, it was not surprising that the potato met with little opposition on the part of the workers, nor that it acquired its nick-name, 'the root of misery'.

William Cobbett's Opposition

We have no figures to show how rapid was the spread of the potato, but it was sufficient to excite the serious attention of the political economists and arouse the fury of William Cobbett, whose views on the subject were already coloured by the picture of the Irish peasant, whom he regarded as little better than a slave, sharing hovel and potatoes with pig and poultry. He spoke of the potato as 'Ireland's lazy-root', or the 'root of extreme unction', and was ever ready to suspect that there was economic oppression when he encountered a labouring family making it the substance of their chief meal; nor was he always disappointed. In the West country he had found the potato used 'instead of bread to a very great extent' and had learnt from the Agricultural Committees that it was customary to allot the labourer a potato-patch in part payment of wages. Already in 1828 Cobbett had sensed the abyss which threatened the labourer should he allow the potato to displace wheat in his home. Such a change, he was assured, spelt revolution in the relation of master and man, and to suppose such possible was to renounce all confidence in the sanity of the labourer. As the years passed and the condition of the agricultural labourer worsened, Cobbett never tired of pointing out where the real danger lay.[1]

[1] Cobbett, W. (1828). *A Treatise on Cobbett's Corn*, p. 170.

Cobbett may have frequently allowed his heart to run away with his head, but he realized that manual labourers would not forsake bread, meat and cheese for potatoes, if they could possibly help it, but with the potato as such, he, as a sensible man, had no quarrel. He makes his position clear in a passage written in 1832 on his tour to the North.[1] Near Hexham, he observes, the potato may be seen in the cottage gardens, and goes on to explain that 'as garden stuff and used in that way, it is very good.....It is the using of it as a substitute for bread and for meat that I have deprecated it, and when the Irish poet, Dr Drennan '[1754–1820] called it "the lazy root" and "the root of misery", he gave it its true character.' He quoted the experience of the reforming baronet, Sir Charles Wolseley, in France, Italy and Germany, in support of his views, 'in whatever proportion the cultivation of potatoes prevails in these countries, in that same proportion the working people are wretched'.[2]

Ten years earlier, Cobbett had gathered the impression that the potato habit was on the wane. 'Englishmen seem to be on the return to beer and bread from water and potatoes'[3] he wrote; but events had not borne out his hope. However, to him should be given the credit of being the only public man of his time to proclaim openly the danger society incurred by forcing its workers to adopt a standard of living based on the potato. Equally to his credit was it, that in bread and beer he saw the labourer's chief weapon of defence.

A much more learned authority[4] than he had come to a very different conclusion: 'With the exception of wheat and rice, it is now certainly the vegetable most employed as the food of man; and it is probable that the period is at no great distance, when its extensive use will even place it before those which have hitherto been considered the chief staples of life.' If Sabine's prediction seemed in 1822 likely to be realized, then Cobbett deserves the greater credit.

Cobbett's views on the potato were not shared by the best informed agriculturists: one writes that 'potatoes as an article of human food are, next to wheat, of the greatest importance in the eye of the political economist'[5]—an appeal which must have enraged Cobbett, who however may have found consolation in the words used by Loudon who, after stating that an acre of potatoes returns more food than an acre of wheat, expresses serious doubts as to its 'great importance'. Its most important application, he admits, is as a human food, but there are drawbacks. They require a great deal of manure, are bulky to handle,

[1] Cobbett, W. (1830). *Rural Rides* (Everyman edit.), vol. II, p. 291.
[2] Ibid. pp. 291–2.
[3] Cobbett, W. (1821). *Cottage Economy* (edit. 1926), p. 49.
[4] Sabine, Joseph, F.R.S. (1822). On the Native Country of the Potato. *Trans. Hort. Soc.* vol. V, p. 257.
[5] Lawson, A. (1827). *The Farmers' Practical Instructor*, p. 255.

can only be freely sold when raised in the vicinity of great towns and hence are in most respects an unprofitable crop; concluding that: 'To the farmer the real criterion is the profit which potatoes will return in feeding beasts', and in this capacity the turnip and swede were in his opinion superior.[1] From which it would appear that the towns were now getting their potatoes from nearby farms, but that in the depths of the country the farmer was not greatly interested in the crop, a fact which is explained by the growth of the allotment movement.

How dependent on the potato the towns had become by the middle of the century was shown by the tragic effects of the 'Blight' on the health of the people. The mortality figures rose some 30%, scurvy once more was prevalent throughout Great Britain, and the slums of the great towns were packed with starving and diseased Irishmen.[2]

The Allotment Policy and Potatoes

The early nineteenth century saw the inception and development of labourers' allotments as a national economic policy. The object of the movement was to induce the 'labouring poor' to raise potatoes for their own subsistence, and by so doing, eschew the more expensive dietary based on the consumption of white wheaten bread. This it was hoped would enable them to exist in times of shortage without recourse to the raising of wages. Some landlords, like Mr Estcourt at Long Newnton, Wilts,[3] let allotments on a fourteen years' lease to labourers on condition that at least one quarter was planted with potatoes, and that they refrained from accepting poor law relief; his scheme, adopted by all the local workers, rescued the parish from misery and ruin. Not all reformers were so simple minded: one records the hope that potato allotments will eventually bring about a reduction in wages, a lowering of the poor rates, and the breaking in, at an early age, of the labourer's children to the routine of farm work.[4] In some districts there must have been a very real demand for potato land on the part of the workers: before 1818 we hear of the labourers in Bedfordshire digging up plots on the side of the road, in order to plant them for this purpose.[5]

So pressing had the demand for accommodation for potato raising become after the wars that the word 'allotment', during the first half of the nineteenth century, came to mean little more than a potato-patch.

[1] Loudon (1831). *Encyclopedia of Agriculture* (2nd edit.), Art. 5296.
[2] Morpeth, Lord. Election Address. *The Times*, 9 August 1847.
[3] Estcourt, Thomas (1802). *Annals of Agric.* vol. XLIII, p. 1.
[4] Crutchley, J. (1804). *Communication to the Board of Agriculture*, vol. I, pp. 93–6 and 221–36.
[5] Lords Commission on Poor Laws (1818). Q. 76 (Clapham's *Early Railway Age*, p. 121).

In later days the allotment was used for a wider assortment of vegetables; nevertheless, before the last war, probably half of the allotment ground in England was annually under potatoes. In the war period, this proportion was greatly exceeded.

Allotments were rarely more than an acre in area and were generally less; they could be hired for the year as a tenement, and were independent of the holder's home or place of work. In this sense the allotment differs both from a garden patch tied to a cottage, and from the accommodation land, which was frequently put at the labourer's disposal by the farmer for whom he worked. This latter might be so many yards of drill in the employer's own potato field, or a separate small plot of land within the same field or, not seldom, some odd piece of land which had not been brought into the year's cultivation, such as a rick plot, the corner of a field or, less commonly, the headland of a cornfield.

Originally the users were agricultural labourers, but after 1815 their ranks in the neighbourhood of the larger towns were often augmented by tradesmen and artisans.

There was a notable difference in respect to both tenure and usure, between an allotment and a potato-patch situate in the farmer's field. An allotment holder, though without the protection of an agreement, usually enjoyed a continuous tenancy. He held either under the local landlord, the tenant-farmer or, in later years, the parochial authority. In most cases he was free to cultivate the land as he pleased, and therefore enjoyed the full benefit of all the manure and cultivation he applied. It was otherwise when the farmer put land at his labourer's disposal. If it were some odd piece of land, it was generally lent free of charge, but if the potato-patch or allotment was in the farmer's field, a rent was charged and it was often complained that such might be four or five times that which the farmer himself paid to his superior landlord. When the labourer made use of a potato-patch in the farmer's field, whether free or not, it was part of the bargain that he should expend all his manure on it and keep it clean during the growing season.

In the first flush of enthusiasm it was thought that an allotment should be not less than an acre of arable land, but it was soon found that one-half or still better one-quarter of that size was adequate if the occupier was in full employment. Towards the end of the century allotments were rarely more than a quarter of an acre, and in recent times, as well as in the 1850's, an eighth of an acre was commonly regarded as adequate in the neighbourhood of towns.

Allotments did more than ease the labourer's food supply, a point to which we shall return; they provided one of the few channels into which the activities of such landlords, clergy and others who had a genuine regard for the welfare of the labouring class could be profitably directed, seeing that the obvious remedy, the raising of agricultural wages to a level compatible with a tolerable standard of life was excluded. It is noteworthy that in counties where wheat was the major crop, potatoes were but rarely grown in the field; but it is in just those districts that the cottages were most often bad and gardens lacking, so that allotments devoted to the potato became extremely popular. In fact until the potato restored the balance there was invariably less food available for the 'labouring poor' in those areas where most was raised for the well-to-do.

The spread of the allotment movement, as might be expected, was equally correlated with low-wage districts. These conditions were exemplified in Notts where, in 1846, allotments were abundant, especially on the estates of great landlords such as the Dukes of Rutland and Newcastle:[1] the latter alone provided 2,000 allotments for labourers on his estate. In Suffolk one finds the same thing: Sir Henry Bunbury[2] a great enthusiast, had more than 100 allotments on his estate at Mildenhall. He found at first that his tenant-farmers objected to give up land for the purpose, but later they approved and co-operated. On this estate, allotment holders were under a certain amount of kindly supervision; for a long time they grew only potatoes and wheat, but later beans were introduced in order to consolidate the land.

In much of the North, where wages were higher and living conditions better than South of the Coal Line, there was little demand for allotments by land workers, who were always provided with a potato-patch, or with potatoes themselves, as part wages; in Northumberland, however, there was a demand for allotments which was not fully satisfied.

Allotments were more general in those parts of the country where good gardens were scarce, as in Devon and Dorset; and vice versa. Hence in the West country generally, they were less common than in the Midland and Eastern counties where so many cottage gardens had been swept away by the enclosures.

Although the *General Report on Enclosures* (1808) had stated that where allotments existed the agricultural labourer was much better off,[3] the spread of the movement had been slow until, as a result of the agricultural revolt of 1830, it was jostled into activity. Three Acts of Parliament between 1819 and 1832 were passed, enabling overseers to acquire up to 50 acres of land for the purpose, but they were never seriously implemented. The development of the movement depended on the urgency of the local demand, and the degree to which the larger

---

[1] Carrington, R. W. (1846). The Agriculture of Nottinghamshire. *J. Roy. Agric. Soc.* vol. VI, p. 1.
[2] Bunbury, Sir H. (1845). The Allotment System. *J. Roy. Agric. Soc.* vol. V, p. 391.
[3] Dunlop, O. J. (1913). *The Farm Labourer*, p. 55.

tenants permitted an indifferent landlord to take action. By 1831 allotments must have been fairly numerous, for the *Poor Law Report* of that
year commends them for their assistance to the poor, but warns against
allowing them to exceed one-quarter acre in extent, and points out that
the landlords have found it very profitable to supply them.[1] In the
following decade progress was more rapid, and the 1843 *Report on
Allotments* was able to publish encouragingly on both their number and
condition.[2] The change was due to the cessation of out-door parish relief
after 1834 when, as one writer has it, the poor 'could dig and poach,
and by the aid of allotments they dug themselves into a potato standard'.[3]
While it is not possible to say that a 'potato standard' was actually
reached, the danger of such had been great, and was only averted by
larger supplies of cheap food from America.

   The progress of the movement certainly did correspond to an increasingly depressed living condition of the workers, both agricultural
and urban. In a letter written in 1831 by Thomas Postans to Sir Thomas
Baring, the writer refers to the state of the agricultural labourer of 1795:
when poor and ill nourished as he was, 'the value of potatoes was neither
so well known nor so highly appreciated as it is at present; and the idea
of subsisting on potatoes alone [as he was not far from being forced to
do] as an article of food, was not entertained by the labourers of England
[i.e. in 1795]...in times of stress, bread and water sustained him at his
last extremity'.[4]

   Caird[5] in 1850 seems to have taken the possession of an allotment by
the labouring man for granted, when he records that Oxfordshire farmers
still complained of them 'as injurious to the steady, industry of
the labourer and a heavy tax on themselves'. It is here, too, that he notes
that they are often given the worst land and are rented extravagantly.

   Farmers as a class disliked the allotment policy and were definitely
opposed to the larger sized ones, as they held that the more a labourer
was engaged on his own land, the less of his time and strength was he
likely to give to that of his employer. Towards the smaller allotment
their attitude varied with the economic circumstances of the time. In
the first quarter of the nineteenth century, when bread and other foodstuffs were so dear, they welcomed the allotment with its potato crop,
regarding it as a buffer against agitation for higher wages. In the 1860's
they were less warmly received, but so long as they did not exceed a
quarter of an acre in area, farmers were not actively opposed to their

[1] Dunlop, O. J. (1913). *The Farm Labourer*, p. 185.
[2] Venn, J. A. (1933). *The Foundations of Agricultural Economics*, p. 128.
[3] Fay, C. R. (1932). *Great Britain from Adam Smith to the Present Day*, pp. 123–4.
[4] Postans, Thomas (1831). A letter to Sir Thomas Baring at the present state of the
Agricultural Poor. London: Michael Stannton.
[5] Caird, James (1852). *English Agriculture*, p. 29.

use by the labourers.[1] To the potato-patches, they never raised any objection; indeed, they were assets, inasmuch as they brought manure and hand-cultivation to their fields, which outweighed any crop removed by the labourers.

Another frequently expressed objection to allotments by the farmer was the fear that the private use of land by the labourer might render him to some extent independent. The big farmers of the newly enclosed lands, in particular, were convinced that nothing could be more detrimental to their interests than that the labourer should have any means of subsistence, other than that offered by himself at a wage which he alone dictated.

More comprehensive was the objection raised at the vestry of Bishops Waltham, Hants, to Cobbett's suggestion that an acre of waste be granted to every married labourer. With the exception of the local schoolmaster, it was rejected by all as tending to make the men 'too saucy', that they would breed more children, and 'want higher wages'. The Hammonds point out that it was not the farmer only who opposed allotments, but also the local tradesmen, who feared they would lose customers.[2]

Nor were the landlords always well disposed. Disraeli's Lord Marney represented an influential if small, reactionary group in the 'hungry forties'. Asked whether a labourer could bring up a family on 8s. a week, he replied: 'Oh! as for that, they get more than that, because there is beer-money allowed, at least to a great extent among us, though I for one do not approve of the practice, and that makes nearly a shilling per week additional; and then some of them have potato grounds, though I am entirely opposed to that system.'[3]

Estimate of Area and Production

Exactly when the allotment system attained its maximum development in relation to the population it served is uncertain, but it was not far off that point in the 1850's. What is worthy of note is that it had by then achieved its main purpose, that of saving the agricultural and part of the urban labouring community from starvation during the worst times of scarcity and unemployment. What then was the measure of its help? No straightforward answer can be given, for the only acreage figures available refer to a period more than thirty years later, and the size of the agricultural labouring community, including its immediate dependents, must needs be deduced from the return of agricultural labourers in the 1851 Census. Notwithstanding these difficulties, a

[1] Cadle, Clement (1867). *J. Roy. Agric. Soc.* vol. III (2nd ser.), p. 122.
[2] Hammond, J. L. and B. (1911). *The Village Labourer*, p. 159.
[3] Disraeli (1845). *Sybil* (new edit. 1881), p. 126. Longmans, Green and Co.

reasonably reliable estimate can be made (see Appendix II). It would appear that at this period allotments accounted for about 49,000, potato patches 12,000, and cottage gardens 16,000 acres of land, all under potatoes. The crop derived from these three sources would furnish each man, woman, and child of the agricultural community in England and Wales with about 0·75 lb., 0·19 lb. and 0·25 lb. of potatoes respectively: that is, a minimum of 1 lb. 3 oz., each per day, of which some 14 oz. represents the contribution from the allotments.[1]

When one recalls that before the beginning of the century the consumption of potatoes per head of the agricultural working classes south of the Coal Line was so small as to be inconsiderable, it is evident that within half a century, a great change had come over the food habits of the people. The dominance of bread and cheese had perforce given way in large measure to a cheaper form of subsistence founded on the potato.

That the allotment's contribution to the family subsistence was a very real one, and probably more than the estimate which has been put forward, is supported by the reaction it caused amongst those who desired to see a betterment in the labourer's standard. It was not long before fear began to be expressed that the spread of allotments might, by their very success, lead to a lowering of wages, or at least prevent them from rising in harmony with the increased cost of living. Such views were logical enough, seeing that the system was primarily devised in order that the labourer might raise potatoes, a cheap food, for the maintenance of his family. Indeed, for the latter view there was ample ground for anxiety; for the former, the evidence was by no means so clear.

Towards the middle of the century, the question as to whether an extended allotment policy might not lead to lower wages, a debased standard of living and, ultimately, to the reproduction of the dreaded Irish scene in the English countryside, was never far from the minds of serious thinkers of all classes. Sir George Nicholls[2] who had devoted much study to the problem, voiced the fears of many, when he pictured the English labourer living nastily on a modicum of potato land. Caird[3] who combined the qualities of politician, sociologist and agriculturist, discussing the question of cheap food a few years later, is more explicit. 'Such cheapness', he writes, 'is a very different thing from forcing labourers on to a low potato standard—which debases all. There could be no greater evil befall the English agricultural labourer, than that any circumstance could compel him to depress his standard of comfort so far as to be content for his principal subsistence with the lowest species

---

[1] For the details of this calculation see Appendix II.
[2] Nicholls, George (1846). *J. Roy. Agric. Soc.* vol. VII, p. 1.
[3] Caird, J. (1852). *English Agriculture*, p. 518.

of human food in this country, the potato.' In a *Report* of 1867–8 a Nottinghamshire clergyman gave evidence that allotments delayed any rise of wage, a view the Commission thought to be well founded.[1] Millin,[2] touring the southern counties in 1891 came also to the conclusion that allotments kept wages down to the lowest subsistence level. In the same *Report*, evidence was given that in Dorset the men spent so much time on their half-acre allotments that it had caused a marked increase in child labour on the land, itself a potent cause of low wages. A further objection was that it tended to make the family far too dependent on the potato. The demand in this county for allotments had been so active that farmers were accused of charging exorbitant rents for their land. The farmers, on the other hand, complained that the movement had robbed them of their wonted supplies of manure.[3]

Some time after the middle of the nineteenth century, the area under allotments proper, i.e. excluding small-holdings, seems to have remained stationary, but towards the close of the century it increased once more, providing a potato area of about 60,000 acres, on the assumption that the average allotment was still one-quarter acre, half of which was under potatoes.

Even an extravagant use of allotments by the workers was not, in itself, enough to undermine the standard of living; nor, indeed, did the extensive use of the potato by the working classes, so long as there was a competitive market for their labour. In Cheshire, where only in one poor-law area out of twelve, was any kind of rate relief in aid of wages given, and that but sparingly,[4] potato-raising in allotment and garden was very popular. But it was just here that the use of a 'cowgate' was common, and the keeping of pigs general. It was here also that, when in 1845 potato-patches and allotments in the South and Midlands were rapidly increasing, the movement already had reached its zenith and was on the wane.[5]

It is scarcely to be doubted that the complex: allotments, a potato-ridden dietary and a sinking wage, ending in the lowest standard of life, only becomes effective in the presence of a further factor—economic or political oppression, exerted directly on the worker. No other factor in the daily life of the people during the first half of the nineteenth century could compete with the Speenhamland system, with its serf-like roundsmen and state-aided and controlled wage, in converting this otherwise harmless combination into a source of grave national danger.

During the two recent war periods, the number of allotments

---

[1] Dunlop, Jocelyn (1913). *The Farm Labourer*, p. 693.
[2] Millin, George (1891). *Life in Our Villages*. London: Cassell and Co.
[3] Dunlop, Olive J. Op. cit. p. 128.
[4] Palin, W. (1845). *J. Roy. Agric. Soc.* vol. LVII, p. 185.
[5] Clapham, Sir J. H. (1939). *The Early Railway Age*, p. 123.

increased enormously, though in the interval between them it had fallen sharply.

Wages of late years have risen rapidly and steeply, allowing the agricultural labourer to enjoy an incomparably higher standard of living than he has ever known, with the result that he can afford to buy what now he seems to be too lazy to grow. However that may be, there is fortunately no longer the urge of hunger, as of old, forcing him to raise potatoes by the sweat of his brow after his day's work is done. By 1887 'the demand from agricultural labourers for small allotments, fractions of an acre, used mainly for potatoes was nearly satiated',[1] states Clapham. To-day the demand appears to be rapidly declining, though that of the suburban dweller has more than made good the loss. In times of peace about 10% of the nation's ware potato supply is probably raised in gardens and allotments up and down the country.

There was a form of allotment, popular in Cornwall in the mid-nineteenth century, which had all the attributes of the Irish conacre (see p. 247). 'It is common practice for the farmer to let out portions of land to their labourers or to potato-jobbers, the farmer ploughing and manuring the land, and the latter finding and planting the seed and undertaking the subsequent cultivation and paying £5 to £7 per acre to the farmer for rent and taxes and his portion of the labour. Many industrious men have in this way gradually raised themselves to the condition of small farmers and have become the owners of several acres of land.'[2] A somewhat similar development took place in certain favoured areas of Lincolnshire and East Anglia where potato-raising became the mainstay of the smallholders and farmers occupying from one to fifty acres; especially was this the case around Chatteris in Cambridgeshire. In the Isle of Axholme it was by its means that the smallholder in the open-field successfully braved the agricultural storms of the 1890's. Generally, potatoes were found to be an unsuitable crop for the smallholder,[3] because he could not put his crop on the market as cheaply as could the owner of the large mechanized farms.

The Last Phase, Recession

From Cobbett's time onwards one hears much less of the potato, at least from its advocates: their work was done. During the 1840's and 1850's it was familiar in every home, and essential in most. Whilst the price of the loaf remained in the neighbourhood of 10d., and wages between 5s. and 8s. per week, its position was assured.[4] It is, however,

[1] Clapham, Sir J. H. (1938). An Economic History, vol. III, p. 108.
[2] Acland, Dyke Thomas and Sturge, W. (1851). The Farming of Somerset, p. 145.
[3] Levy, Hermann (1911). Large and Small Holdings, pp. 106-7.
[4] Osborne, S. G. Let the poor glean. The Times, 12 Aug. 1848.

a matter of surprise to find that in the 1870's and 1880's, when bread had fallen to 7*d*. and later to 6*d*. the quartern, how many homes in the country there were still, in which the potato was almost as important as the loaf in providing for their maintenance. Domestic histories which I have collected from my elderly friends amongst the working families of my home village[1] leave me in no doubt as to the facts. Three examples may suffice to illustrate how narrow was the threshold that lay between reasonable comfort and actual hardship; between using the potato as an accessory food and relying on it as the main support. All three families *A*, *B* and *C* consisted of highly respectable hard-working, sober folk, established for generations as farmworkers or local craftsmen in the district. In all, the husbands were farm hands earning in the late 1870's 7*s*. 6*d*. per week, though occasionally with extra work they might receive a little more, but their earnings never exceeded 10*s*. per week.

In family *A* there was no child of the marriage for twenty years, and it was not until 1868 that their only son was born. This lad in the early 1880's earned 1*s*. 3*d*. a week. The mother, a clever manager, baked her own bread, to which she added a small quantity of potatoes for its better flavour and keeping: she gleaned enough corn to supply nearly three-quarters of the flour needed for the year. The father was given a few rows in the field for potatoes, ready manured, by the farmer, and had in addition an allotment, one half of which was devoted to peas and green vegetables, the other to potatoes. From the produce of the allotment and by the purchase, on credit, of meal, they kept pigs, and never failed to enjoy a dish of bacon or pork every day of their lives. Potatoes were eaten at breakfast, dinner and supper, but they were not regarded as other than a welcome and additional item of food. They drank 'real' tea. Though they had little cash to spare, the family were never pinched for food, nor felt themselves dependent for their existence on the potato. Clothes and boots were their chief difficulty: boots were hand-made and paid for by instalments. They were never in debt, and the father before his death had put by £60 for his old age.

In family *B* there were thirteen children. The earnings of the father were 13*s*. in 1868 but this, with the fall in the price of wheat, dropped to 12*s*., and in the 1870's to 10*s*. per week. As the sons grew up, they helped whilst they lived at home, to maintain it. The wife baked her own bread and she, too, added potatoes to the dough. She was a very active gleaner, and in one year collected as much as fourteen bushels of barley and three of wheat. In this home the potato was the staple food and in a very real sense their life-line; they ate few green vegetables but in winter, parsnips and swedes were a welcome change. The mother bought two pennyworth of scrap meat each week: with

[1] Barley, Hertfordshire.

this and a few small pieces of pork she made potato pies for the men to take to the field. Butcher's meat was eaten only once a week. Breakfast, dinner and tea consisted of potatoes, with 'tea' made from boiling water and burnt crusts, a very common substitute at that time. On Sundays she provided her household, which in the 1880's consisted of four grown men besides the young children, with a good meat dinner which cost her 2s. 6d. They had both garden and allotment, and kept a pig. Most of the carcass was sold to pay for the fodder, which they had had on credit, the remainder was salted and retained for use at home. The provision of clothes and boots for the family was an exhausting problem, and had it not been for a kindly farmer's wife who gave them her worn garments, the girls would have fared very badly. The family economy of the household remained as described till the beginning of the twentieth century, when the children had grown up and scattered. It is well to record that, hard as were the conditions under which this large family was raised, and dependent as they certainly were on the potato for their subsistence, every member, *pace* Goldwin Smith,[1] has been a credit to both parents and country.

Families *A* and *B* may be regarded as examples of the two extremes of the economic scale. Family *C* with six children may be looked on as nearer the normal for those less sophisticated days. As regards social position, work and wage, and the high character of the parents, there is no difference between them and families *A* and *B*. The mother was 'a famous gleaner', and by her needle earned a few shillings a week, as well as making and mending the clothing of her family. They made their own bread, but did not add potatoes to the dough. Breakfasts for six days of the week were either milk with bread, which had first been soaked in boiling water to prevent its absorbing too much milk, or toast and butter; on Sundays they had fried potatoes. Dinner consisted of potatoes, with an occasional pudding made with raisins, and a supper of bread and cheese. The father's dinner eaten in the field was a potato pie with an ounce of meat in it. On Sundays they all had some butcher's meat. They kept a pig, fed on potatoes from the allotment, selling more than half the carcass, and pickling and smoking the remainder. Clothing and boots were in this, as in the other families, the outstanding problems. Any of these histories would fit perfectly in Flora Thompson's sketch of north-east Oxfordshire in the nineties.[2]

As wages rose and food cheapened, with the opening of the twentieth century, the potato habit gradually weakened, and its place in the dietary of the landworkers became only little more important than that which

[1] Smith, Goldwin (1883). *Nineteenth Century* (16 June).
[2] Thompson, Flora (1939). *Lark Rise*. Guild Book No. 223, 1946. Oxford Univ. Press.

it occupied in the households of the rich. One can still find, however, amongst the older generation in the countryside those who, maintaining the usage of their youth, consume about 2 lbs. of potatoes daily. As one man remarked recently to the author, he 'never felt he had had a meal if there weren't plenty of potatoes to go with it'.

In urban districts, reliance on the potato by the poorer class of artisans ceased much earlier than in the countryside. In the towns there was to be found a large range of cheap foods. The rural districts have, till very recently, been at a disadvantage because of lack of accessibility to these same supplies. Prior to the war of 1914–18, it was the writer's experience that in the village of Barley in Hertfordshire, fish only arrived twice a week; colonial meat was not sold by the local butcher; there was no delivery of milk, which could only be procured by the courtesy of such farmers as might be able to spare it; oranges were rare, and bananas almost unknown. Yet this village was a good deal better off than many in the neighbourhood.

Seebohm Rowntree's studies of the social economy of the working classes in York in the years 1899[1] and 1936[2] respectively, show clearly that the cheapening, no less than the greatly enlarged choice of food-stuffs induced by Free Trade, whether produced at home or imported, profoundly affected the position which the potato had acquired in the economy of the working-class home. In the 1899 account, the family budgets of working-class homes, whether above or below the poverty line, show that potatoes were regularly consumed at the midday meal only in the poorer homes, and that they were occasionally used as an additional supper dish in the homes of those better off.

In 1936 the analyses of the food supplies of four groups of artisans, the very poor, the poor, those who were just solvent, and those who were comfortably well off, are set out in Table II, p. 536. From this it appears that the potato no longer is acting as a buffer between the impact of high food prices and low wages. No more potatoes and very little more bread were eaten by the poor of York in 1936 than by their better-off colleagues. What happened was that the poor economized mainly on sugar, milk, eggs, green vegetables and fruit. From a nutritional point of view their fathers had been far better off when they made good their deficiencies with the potato, for in 1936 the poor were not only short of calories but also of vitamins. The disuse by the poorer classes of the potato as their chosen defence against want, rather than want itself, is probably the major factor involved in the reduced consumption of potatoes *per capita*, which has been so notable a feature during the last fifty years. These are the reactions to be expected in times of

[1] Rowntree, B. Seebohm (1901). *Poverty, a Study of Town Life*, p. 195. Longman.
[2] Rowntree, B. Seebohm (1941). *Poverty and Progress*. Longman.

peace, with markets open to the foodstuffs of the world. Let these markets be restricted by tariffs or, more particularly, by war, then the demand for potatoes to make good the deficiency is, as recent experience has shown, more clamant than ever.

Table II. *Consumption of certain foods per man per week*

Group	Full cream milk	Skim con-densed milk	Full cream milk per child under 14	Skim milk per child under 14	Butter	Mar-garine	Lard suet and drip-ping	Meat	Fish	Eggs	Bread flour and tea-cakes	Fresh fruits	Potatoes	Other vege-tables	S
	Pints	Equiv. to pints	Pints	Equiv. to pints	Oz.	Oz.	Oz.	Lb.	Lb.	No.	Lb.	d.	Lb.	d.	
I	1·80	0·65	3·28	0·87	2·6	4·5	4·6	1·52	0·32	1·99	5·15	0·97	4·52	1·87	
2	2·51	0·44	3·49	0·34	5·5	3·8	5·0	1·94	0·27	2·99	5·13	3·63	4·50	3·08	
3	2·90	0·20	4·54	0·22	5·9	2·3	5·6	2·04	0·45	3·94	4·81	3·64	4·80	2·78	
4	4·02	—	6·77	—	8·8	3·0	4·8	2·00	0·52	4·89	4·64	5·48	3·95	4·10	

[From Seebohm Rowntree's *Poverty and Progress* (1941), p. 195. By kind permission of the author and Messrs Longmans, Green and Co.]

CHAPTER XXVII

The Relation between Potato and Bread Consumption in a Rapidly Growing Population

An attempt to deal with the problem to which this chapter is dedicated on a statistical basis, presents many difficulties, to overcome some of which the discussion has been limited territorially to England and Wales. Even so, the obstacles due to the paucity of figures prior to 1866 make the attempt not merely hazardous, but one open to serious criticism. It is for this reason that the manner in which the various curves have been constructed, and the data on which they are based, have been given in full in the Appendices. In this chapter it will be assumed without further argument that the resultant graphs are substantially accurate, or rather, are a near approximation to the truth, and that to draw general conclusions from them is justifiable. (See Appendix III.)

Fig. 73 (p. 538), *ABCD*, represents the total acreage in England and Wales under potato cultivation from 1770 to 1939, and curve *EFGHIJ*, the population in millions of England and Wales.

It will be observed that the rise from a very small, though quite uncertain, initial acreage in 1770 to that of 1795, the year of crisis, is rapid, and continues so from thence onwards till 1814, when we have a reasonably reliable estimate in the neighbourhood of 200,000 acres. From that point, the rise is again steady and sharp to 1838, another datum year; between 1814 and 1838 the area under potatoes had been almost doubled. From 1838 to 1866 when the official returns commence, progress is still rapid, there being a further increase over 1838 of about 33%. From then onwards, the two late war periods excepted, the acreage increased somewhat rapidly, reaching the half-million mark in 1872.

The rapid growth of potato acreage during the hundred years, from its humble beginnings in 1770 to a maximum of half a million acres in 1870, stands in strong contrast to its fate after that date. After reaching the maximum, potato production attained a stage of equilibrium which has lasted, recent war years excluded, for over seventy years.

From 1870 onwards, it is obvious that either the urge which had forced the people to adopt the potato had ceased to operate, or, alternatively, the force was still in action but other foodstuffs had been adopted, thereby relieving the pressure on the potato as a buffer against want. It was this latter which provides us with the more correct explanation.

This conclusion follows, indirectly, from a comparison of the acreage curve with that representing the growth of the population. The two curves follow a very similar course between 1810 and 1870, but from then on they part company; the potato acreage no longer expands *pari passu* with the number of mouths to be fed. As there was no potato famine to account for the divergence, it is obvious that foods of other kinds, viz. imports of wheat, meat, butter, etc., were reaching the people.

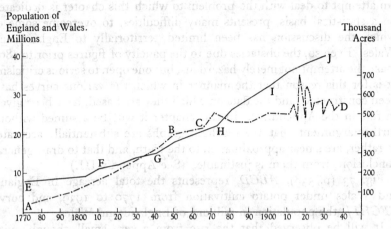

Fig. 73. Curve *ABCD* represents the acreage under potatoes in England and Wales, in hundred-thousand acres. That between *A* and *C* is based on deductions from contemporary estimates. That between *C* and *D* is based on official estimates. Curve *EFGHIJ*, represents the population of England and Wales. That between *F* and *J* is based on census returns. That between *E* and *F*, on estimates from Ernle's *English Farming, Past and Present*, 1936.

There is no need to stress again the intimate relation between the use of bread and the adoption of the potato as a human food. It remains, however, to compare the relative supplies of wheat and bread with the growing area under potato cultivation, and observe the sequence of events.

An effort has been made to compute the amount of wheat, including imported flour, available to every individual in England and Wales, whether home-grown or imported, between the years 1770–1910. There are many difficulties to be overcome, and no high degree of accuracy can be assumed. The method of obtaining these figures, with full details of the adjustments which were necessary, will be found in Appendix IV. The calculated weights in pounds available per diem are shown in Fig. 74, *EFGH* (p. 539), together with the curve of potato availability *A–D*. These curves do not represent the amount consumed by the average individual, but that quantity which was available for all purposes per head of the population.

Examination of the two curves in Fig. 74 demonstrates that, as wheat availability sank in the early nineteenth century, potato availability rose in an equal degree, until the lowest point of the wheat curve, which was reached in 1850, nearly coincided with the highest point of that of the potato. Conversely, the sinking of the potato availability curve during the second half of the nineteenth century, coincides with the recovery of wheat availability. There is, however, a certain lack of parallelism

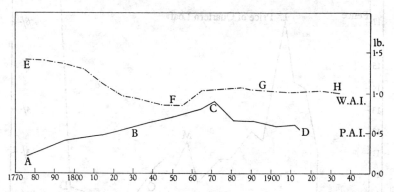

Fig. 74. Curve *ABCD* represents the daily quantity in pounds, of potatoes available per head of the population in England and Wales, i.e. the P.A.I. (See Appendix III.) Curve *EFGH* represents the daily quantity in pounds, of wheat available per head of the population in England and Wales, i.e. the W.A.I. (See Appendix IV.)

after 1840. The potato acreage, instead of sinking again in harmony with the rise of wheat availability, maintained its maximum till 1870. This lag between the two curves, suggests that there were other factors at work, and for their discussion we must turn to Fig. 75 (p. 540).

In Fig. 75 are shown the potato availability curve *FGHIJ* once more; the curve *KLMNO* which represents the five-year average price of the wheaten quartern loaf, and the curve *ABCDE* which represents the average daily wage of the agricultural workers, deduced from Ernle's averages for the four regions of England.

Comparing the first two curves, it appears that in the interval between the years 1770 and 1840 there is a close parallelism between potato availability and the high price of the quartern loaf; the dearer the loaf, the more potatoes were grown; to make this more evident, the number of loaves which the average daily cash wage of the agricultural labourer could purchase is shown at the base of the graphs.

The lag between the rapid fall in the price of the loaf and the far less dramatic reduction in the per-head consumption of the potato is doubt-less, in part, due to the conservative habits of the working classes in respect to their diet; this, however, is certainly not the whole explanation.

The wages of the agricultural labourer fell heavily between 1870 and 1900, a fact which reacted immediately on his standard of life—as many elderly people in the countryside to-day well remember. It was not on bread that the country labourer economized, for that was cheap

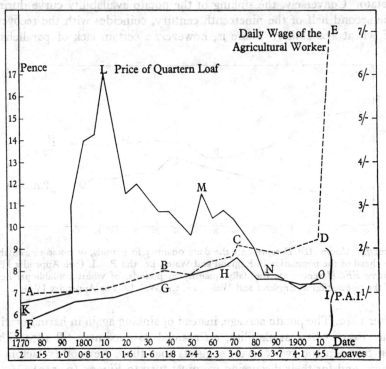

Fig. 75. Curve *ABCDE* represents the daily average wage in shillings of an agricultural labourer from 1770 to 1920. From Ernle's *English Farming, Past and Present*, 1936. Curve *FGHI* represents the average consumption in England and Wales, of potatoes per head of population, in decimals of 1 lb. weight, i.e. the P.A.I. The part of the curve *FG* has no statistical basis, that of *GH* is based on contemporary estimates and deductions from the same, and that of *HI* is based on official statistics. Curve *KLMNO* represents the five-yearly average price of the quartern loaf. The numbers below, viz. 2·0, 1·5, 1·0, 0·8, etc. represents the number of quartern loaves an agricultural labourer could purchase with a day's cash wage.

enough; it was by cutting down his supplies of milk and meat to a minimum, whilst maintaining or increasing the home-grown potato ration, that he contrived to bring up his family. The period between 1870 and 1900 was one of great difficulty for the agricultural worker, and not much less so for the majority of unskilled workers everywhere. When they did succeed in carrying on without public assistance, it was only because they abandoned all provision for sickness and old age.

Those who have intimate knowledge of the workers on the land and in the towns will realize that it was not until after the beginning of the twentieth century that they enjoyed enough food of all kinds, to say nothing of the most elementary amenities—clothing, heating, lighting— to satisfy what to-day would be regarded as essential requirements, and at the same time ensure health and contentment in the home. That point was not reached until the daily wage would purchase at least four quartern loaves; and it was only then that the demand for the potato began noticeably to fall off.

We may now look at the potato problem from a somewhat different angle. Fig. 73, E–J (p. 538), shows how steadily and rapidly the population increased during the nineteenth century. It was not surprising that home-grown wheat supplies were insufficient to maintain the people on the same standard that they had enjoyed in 1770. Prices were bound to rise, but that they soared to fantastic heights was not due to shortage, so much as to panic, and, to some extent, manipulation by interested parties.

A definite shortage there was in 1795, but after that year it was not severe; indeed, it would be a misreading of the facts were we to conclude that the rapid rise of the potato acreage was due entirely to wheat shortage during the Napoleonic wars. Some deficiency there was, but unequal division between the different classes of society consequent on inflated prices was a far more potent factor in producing a picture of shortage and want. This would appear from the following consideration. In 1775 wheat availability was 1·8 lb. per head, at which time an agricultural labourer could buy a couple of wheaten loaves with his daily cash wage; in 1800, although the availability had only sunk to 1·6, he could buy no more than three-quarters of a loaf; in 1810, although wheat availability was still standing at 1·6 lb. per head of the population, yet after fifteen years of hunger and distress, not rarely accompanied by riot, the agricultural labourer's daily wage only sufficed to purchase a single loaf. It was not till after 1860 that his wage was sufficient to purchase as much bread—should he desire to do so—as he could have afforded to do a hundred years earlier.

The analysis of the economic situation, which allowed of the successful invasion by the potato of the Englishman's home, suggests the conclusion that, if the breach in the traditional habits of the labourer was effected through a genuine, though temporary, shortage of wheat in 1795, its further success was due to the policy which demanded a high price for wheat to please the farmer and landlord, and denied a commensurate wage to the labourer with which to buy this, his essential food. Such a policy, though fundamentally unsound, could only be effected if an alternative and cheaper food could be found for the poor.

The history of the first half of the nineteenth century would seem to prove, beyond a doubt, that it was the potato which fulfilled this role, and that without it, the economic policy, which was content to let the 'devil take the hindermost', would have collapsed, almost before it had got under way.

How far such a policy was the outcome of conscious design has already been discussed; what is important is that it was adopted, and that by the use of the potato it did, in fact, enable the workers to survive on the lowest possible wage. It may be that in this way the potato prolonged and encouraged, for another hundred years, the impoverishment and degradation of the English masses; but what was the alternative, surely nothing but bloody revolution. That England escaped such a violent upheaval in the early decades of the nineteenth century, and more than once we were within an ace of such disaster, must, in large measure be placed to the credit of the potato.

CHAPTER XXVIII

The Potato in Tristan da Cunha

A Parallel and a Contrast

There is another island, as different as it is distant from Ireland, where the potato has also played a commanding role in the lives of the people, though under different circumstances and with different results.

Tristan da Cunha is an island, lying in the South Atlantic on lat. 37·6. It has an area of 45 square miles but only a very small part of it, that along the north-west coast, is fit for habitation.

The island, which takes its name from its discoverer, the Portuguese Admiral, Tristan da Cunha, is the largest of a small group of volcanic islets, lying half-way between the Cape of Good Hope and Rio de Janeiro. Occasional, though shortlived and unsuccessful attempts to create settlements, were made in 1656 by the Dutch, and a few years later by the English East India Company. In 1775, William Bolt of Amsterdam floated a company to exploit the island, but this effort suffered a similar fate, and he and his company left da Cunha in 1781. Ten years later, a Captain Patten and his crew spent seven months on the island and cultivated a few vegetables; it is doubtful whether the potato was one of them, for only cabbage, turnip and lettuce are mentioned.

Between 1810 and 1815 a serious attempt at settlement was made by three men who cultivated vegetables and planted potatoes. In 1816 the British Government took over the island, partly because it was being used as a place of call for water and vegetables by hostile American cruisers, and partly because it was thought that it might be used as a base for parties attempting to rescue Napoleon from St Helena. It was at this time that William Glass, his wife and two children and two other men, settled permanently on the island and were joined later by a few others who had been shipwrecked. To these latter there were brought a half-dozen coloured women from St Helena. This, then, was the foundation stock of the human population of Tristan da Cunha, with but an occasional addition from outside, notable amongst whom was the Italian family of Repertto, who now, in the third generation, are the foremost citizens of the settlement.[1] This small group has peopled and cultivated the island, whose population to-day numbers close on 200 persons. It should be noted that despite the very mixed racial and national origin of the families which go to make up the community, owing to unselected inbreeding, no cleavage based on racial origins has survived.

[1] Branders, J. (1940). *Tristan da Cunha.* Allen and Unwin.

The health of the islanders has always been remarkably good; indeed they themselves are apt to boast that none die except by accident or of old age.[1] It is, however, their dental health which of late years has won for them a certain notoriety. In 1926 no caries was observed in the teeth of any of the island youth below the age of 20; only 1·6% of those between 20 and 44, and but 6·5% amongst all over that age showed any sign of decay.[2] In 1938 a careful scientific survey showed that the dental ,condition, though still exceptional, was not quite so good. But even so, half the population exhibited no caries at all and in the remainder the damage was generally limited to one tooth, and that not severe.[3] The change was found to be correlated with an increased supply of imported wheaten flour and a lesser consumption of potatoes during the previous five years. Whilst the relative immunity to dental caries is in the main to be ascribed to the small part played by cereals in the islanders dietary, it is equally evidence of the fact that potatoes, however great their consumption, have no ill effect on the teeth. It is of interest that cleaning of the teeth is neither taught nor practised.

The islanders have always enjoyed an abundance of fish, the eggs of the molly-hawk and penguin, fat young molly-hawks, a good supply of cow's milk, of which, however, they consume less per head than is drunk in Norway, and a restricted supply of beef and mutton, notwithstanding the large head of cattle and sheep running semi-wild over the rough island grazings.

Their diet, so long as it is drawn from these sources, could be regarded as rich in fats, proteins, vitamins A, B_1, D and E, as well as minerals such as calcium, iron and phosphorus. Lacking, however, is a supply of vitamin C and the energy-producing carbohydrates. Although the island has an excellent water-supply, there were no indigenous fruits or vegetables, except the wild cranberry. The settlers raised carrots, turnips, onions and cabbages in their gardens, but before long they came to place reliance entirely on the potato for their carbohydrate supply and, unconsciously, for that of vitamin C as well. Indeed, it may be said that from 1810 till to-day the potato has dominated the domestic economy of the islanders' lives. As early as 1852 the greater part of their cultivated area was under potatoes. Unsuccessful efforts have been made to raise wheat, but the very high rainfall, the strong winds and the invasion of the island by rats, following a shipwreck on the coast about the middle of the nineteenth century, has rendered cereal raising impossible, and more than once has threatened the potato crop itself.

[1] Gane, Douglas (1932). *Tristan da Cunha*, p. 139. Allen and Unwin.
[2] Marshall, E. H. (1926). A Visit to Tristan da Cunha. *Brit. Dent. Journ.* vol. XLIV, p. 1099.
[3] Christopherson, Erling (1940). *Tristan da Cunha, the Lonely Isle*. London: Cassell.

Indeed, so serious was the infestation that after a severe storm in 1885, in which many of the male population lost their lives, their former leader and minister, Dodgson, offered to return to the island and organize the import of a supply of potato ware, as the rats had destroyed many of the seed potatoes. In August 1886 Dodgson arrived and found ninety-seven souls on the island, that much of the potato crop had been destroyed, but that there were still 600 bushels left for use as seed.

The fact is, the islanders have only two sources of carbohydrates, home-grown potatoes, and such flour, biscuits and sugar as they can barter, or receive as gifts from passing ships. In the latter decades of the nineteenth century, when the whalers were active in this part of the South Atlantic, as well as such sailing vessels as still crossed the oceans, ships would frequently put in for water and potatoes, which the Tristanites exchanged for flour and sugar. But not all the sailing ships or the less powerful steamers which desired to stop off the island were able to do so, as the coast is extremely dangerous and exposed to very high winds from which there is no harbour of any kind in which to shelter. Hence it often happened that the islanders would pull out in their canvas covered dinghies, only to find that the ship with its coveted supplies of flour and sugar had sailed away.

During the years 1907–9, Katherine Barrow visited the island and has recorded her experiences.[1] The islanders, she reported, have always enjoyed abundant protein and fat supplies in the fish they catch and the young of the eaglets which they consume, but it is the potato which is the main plank in their dietary. During her stay they were fortunate in receiving enough flour to allow of a distribution of 68 lbs. per head per year, which may be compared with the pre-war consumption in this country of 280 lbs. of wheaten flour. In some years they have no cereal food at all. Sugar is always scarce; tea, coffee and salt frequently absent from their diet for months on end. Soap is a luxury more often than not wanting in the home.

In the early decades of this century, whalers and sailing ships had almost ceased to frequent these waters and only an occasional steamship called at the island.

Since 1932 there has been an appreciable increase in the supplies of sugar and flour but even so, the standard is very far removed from that to which we are accustomed.[2] Prior to the war of 1939–45, the Admiralty took steps to maintain communications and bring to the island some of the amenities of European life.

The da Cunha potato crop has other enemies besides the rats; blight is often serious, much damage is done by the high winds, and still

[1] Barrow, K. M. (1910). *Three Years in Tristan da Cunha.*
[2] Barnes, H. N. V. (1937). *Brit. Dent. Journ.* vol. LXIII, p. 86.

more by the larvae of a moth; hence its cultivation demands the utmost attention from the inhabitants and the neglect of his potato-patch at once lowers a man in the esteem of his fellows.[1]

A scientist who visited the island in 1938[2] states that fish and potatoes are the two staple foods, and of the latter 25–30 bushels per annum, i.e. 3·8–4·6 lbs. per day per individual, is considered an adequate quantity, but that in bad years, such as 1932, many households fell far short of this. The fish supply is from 259–392 g. per day per household.

The more intimate structure of the community has not been described in much detail. The number of persons was 95 in 1909, 163 in 1932 and 188 in 1938, evidence that the community is anything but decadent. Although the land as a whole is held and worked in common, the potato-patches are strictly individual, and only revert to the community if their enclosing walls are allowed to decay. Money, i.e. a coinage, does not exist, but the equipment of the homes varies with the industry and, to some extent, with the tradition behind the man and his wife. The building of new homes and the recovery of land is undertaken com-munally. There is no landlord class, but all according to our standards are poor, though some may have more cows and sheep than others. This has not led to any stratification of their society. There is but one school and one church. Crime is practically unknown whether of violence or fraud, nor does one hear of domestic discord. Such govern-mental authority as there is, is entrusted to the male population only.

In so far as their dependence on the potato and the large quantities they consume is concerned, the people of Tristan da Cunha closely resemble the Irish of the mid-nineteenth century; but there the analogy ceases. In the one case the potato has been a major factor in the degrada-tion and misery of the people, in the other it is merely a rather over-worked article of diet, the cultivation of which, so far from inducing anti-social repercussions, has done much to encourage the energy and self-respect of the individual whilst tending to conserve a uniform structure in the social organism.

In Ireland it became the weapon of defence of a conquered people against their masters, as well as the instrument by which the latter achieved the most complete exploitation of the workers. In this sinister capacity it proved an efficient instrument, whilst the age-old cleavages, racial, religious and social, offered an ideal field for its use.

---

[1] The trouble was observed by the Norwegian Scientific Expedition, 1937–8. The caterpillar belongs to the *Agrotis* group of moths and can be controlled by D.D.T. The ravages on the island coincide with the use of sheep manure instead of kelp, and the almost complete suppression of the island thrush by rats. See Broekhuysen, G. J. and Macnae, W. The Potato Caterpillar Pest, etc. *Nature, Lond.*, 7 Aug. 1948, p. 225.

[2] Sognnaes, R. F. (1941). *J. Dental Research*, vol. xx, p. 303. London: Skeffington and Sons.

CHAPTER XXIX

The Potato in St Helena

St Helena[1] offers yet another, and possibly a unique, example of the manner in which the potato may exert an influence on the economic development of an isolated group of people. Though bearing a superficial resemblance to the roles it played in Ireland of the eighteenth century and in Jersey of to-day, the use of the potato in St Helena took on a distinctive character in response to the peculiar social environment which evolved in the island.

When discovered by Admiral de Nova in 1502, the island was uninhabited both by man and the higher animals. For close on a hundred years it served the Portuguese and Spanish as a place of call, at which their homeward-bound galleons bringing rich cargoes from India and the Spice Islands, might take on board supplies of fresh water and such food as the island could afford. In accordance with their usual practice, the Portuguese stocked the island with cattle, goats, fruit trees and green vegetables, so that when visited by Linschoten[2] in 1589, it seemed to him and his scurvy-ravaged crews, a 'veritable heaven on earth'.

Except for a few of the more seriously sick, whom the Portuguese usually left behind, to be picked up by the next year's fleet, and a handful of escaped slaves, the island remained uninhabited, and to the outer world unknown.

The visit of Thomas Cavendish in 1588, on his return journey round the world, brought this phase of the island's history to a close. Armed English and Dutch merchantmen alternately, soon rendered the island unsafe for others, and the Portuguese abandoned it before the end of the century. Capt. Kendall, commanding one of the three of the first ships to be sent to India by the East India Company, visited the island in 1593 on his return from the Cape of Good Hope. He had on board fifty sailors sick with scurvy, all of whom made a rapid and complete recovery whilst on the island. He was soon followed by Capt. Lancaster[3] who found great store of birds and fish, hogs, oranges and lemons, but expressed the quite definite opinion that the island was 'no earthly paradise'.

---

[1] The author has benefited very much from the study of Mr Philip Gosse's book, *St Helena* (Cassel, 1938), which has proved a most useful guide to further research.

[2] Linschoten, J. H. van. *His discourse of Voyages into the East and West Indies* (edit. 1598), chapter 94, p. 173.

[3] Lancaster, Sir James (1593). Hakluyt Soc. Ser. II, vol. LXXXV (1940), pp. 16, 119 and 139.

For the next forty years St Helena was practically a no-man's land, until its seizure by the East India Company put it in the possession of England. Their hold on the island, however, was disputed by the Dutch, and it was not until 1667 that the Company firmly established themselves and obtained a charter from Cromwell, investing them with full sovereign powers over the island with a specific purpose—'for refreshing of their servants and people on their return homeward'.

In 1659 the Company sent out Capt. Dutton as Governor, and at the same time Capt. Bowen of the *London* was instructed to call on the outward journey at St Iago in the Cape Verde Islands, and there procure 'planton rootes [=plantain], cassandra sticks [=cassava], large yams [=*Dioscorea alata*], potatoes and bonavist [=*Dolichos*], pease, gravances [=chick pea, *Cicer arietinum*], and beanes of all sorts, oranges and lemons', and, finally, but not least, half-a-dozen slaves.[1] In the same year, another vessel from England brought stores from home and made purchases on the Guinea coast of further supplies, including yams, potatoes and more slaves.

Prior to 1659, no new foodstuff seems to have reached the island; this may be gathered from the fact that Peter Mundy,[2] who paid two visits there, in 1638 and in 1656, records the presence of the same collection of plants, fruits and the like, as Linschoten had done more than forty years previously.

Unconsciously the Company had, by its introduction of the potato and the yam, laid the foundation for a revolution in both the internal and external economy of the islanders. The yam supplied the food on which the slaves were maintained, and it was they who were employed in raising the potatoes whose sale to the visiting ships supplied both an income to the white planters, and a ready reason for demanding an ever increasing supply of black labour.

Once more we are confronted with the old question: was it the sweet-potato, *Ipomoea batatas*, or our potato *Solanum tuberosum*, which Dutton acquired? Inasmuch as no visitors to the island prior to Dutton make any mention of potatoes, it is to be presumed that neither species was growing on the island. The places of origin, St Iago and the Guinea Coast, and the fact that the sweet-potato is to-day one of the principal crops of the Cape Verde Islands, inclines one to the view that it was the sweet-potato.

Nor does the fact that arrack was distilled from these 'roots' militate against this suggestion, for a drink known as 'Mobbi', made from the sweet-potato, was popular at this time in the Barbadoes.[3] Sweet-potatoes

[1] Gosse, Philip (1938). *St Helena*, p. 46.
[2] Mundy, Peter (1638). Hakluyt Soc. Ser. II, vol. XLVI; (1656), vol. LXXVII.
[3] Verney (1925). *Memoirs of the Verney Family*. Entry of 10 February 1639.

were certainly grown on the island, but when they were introduced, if not in 1659, cannot now be determined. In a rare *Flora*[1] of 1825, sweet-potatoes are recorded as *Convolvulus batatas*, and Melliss[2] in 1875, under the same name, includes two varieties which he says are both consumed by the inhabitants and sold to the ships. Both authorities refer to the common potato, *Solanum tuberosum*, of which Melliss says many varieties are raised.

It is difficult to assess the degree to which the culture of the sweet-potato attained prior to 1728, the year in which we know for certain that the common potato was introduced from Ireland.[3] But from that time onwards, it is this latter which took the lead and before long became one of the most important products raised in the island. A surprising entry in the Melliss book refers to *S. commersonii* as a wild plant of St Helena. *S. commersonii* is a native potato of South-American swamps and is nowhere cultivated or eaten.[4]

In 1666 the Sieur de Rennefort[5] visited St Helena and, in the narrative of his travels, records his admiration for the abundance of vegetables and fruit grown there; in his list no mention occurs of either the sweet or other potato, or the yam, which suggests that the recent introduction had not as yet assumed any considerable importance, although by 1671 Barlow[6] called attention to the large quantities of potatoes which were being raised. A merchant who called at the island in 1703, after describing the fruits growing there, continues: 'and all manner of garden trade common to us, besides planting of potatoes and yams, a large thick root...tasting between a potato and an artichoke bottom'.[7] By the end of the year he landed at Cork and writes of the potatoes without indicating any difference between them and those he encountered at St Helena. Unfortunately, nothing can be deduced from the fact that he is addressing his friends in England, for they, in 1703, might be as familiar with the imported *Ipomea batatas*, or sweet-potato, as with the home-grown *Solanum tuberosum*. One can only conclude that Rogers's reference could be interpreted as referring to the latter.

Both the potato and the yam flourished exceedingly, as indeed did oranges, lemons and bananas, but unfortunately the rats from the ships, and the goats left by the Portuguese, found the island no less to their taste. During the next 200 years, the islanders' domestic food economy was largely determined by the extent to which these two pests could be kept under control.

[1] Boyd, J. (1825). *Flora*, p. 4. *St Helena*.
[2] Melliss, J. C. (1875). *St Helena*, pp. 304 and 309.
[3] Gosse, Philip (1938). *St Helena*, p. 164, quoting from official record.
[4] The recording of *S. commersonii* seems to have been one of Melliss' errors (Q. Cronk, *pers. comm.*). – Ed.
[5] Rennefort, S. de (1688). *Histoire des Indes Orientales*. Paris.
[6] Barlow, Edward (1671). *Journal* (edit. Basil Lubbock 1934), p. 199.
[7] Rogers, Francis (1703). *The Journal of* (edit. Bruce S. Ingram, 1936). Constable.

All doubt as to the nature of the potato is removed after the year 1728, when one learns that owing to the suppression of the distilleries, the red-skinned potato hitherto grown had been neglected, and that a new Irish stock of seed was introduced.

As the sweet-potato grown on the Guinea Coast in 1749 was a red-skinned variety,[1] it is probable that the earlier potato of St Helena was *Ipomoea batatas*, and that it was only after 1728 that the common potato was introduced.

Cereals, other than a few attempts on a small scale to grow rice and some maize, were not raised before the nineteenth century, when a small quantity of barley was grown, not as a foodstuff, but with a view to supplying the local brewery. The European settlement was dependent for its wheat and flour on ships coming from England, and the slave population, so far as it was given cereal food, on rice from India; in fact an order was issued in 1659 by which every Company's ship was obliged to land at least one ton of rice when calling at the island for water and stores. A later order, ensuring that every ship touching at Madagascar must deposit one slave at St Helena, went some way to cancel out any advantage conferred by the former.

The potato, whose cultivation soon exceeded that of all other food-stuffs, with the possible exception of the yam, seems to have been regarded at first as a food for the European settlers and their slaves, rather than the subject of sale or barter with the ships.

In 1679 it is reported that the plague of rats so harried the growing crops of potatoes that they were found to be too precious to be fed to slaves; a cheaper and more abundant substitute was found in the yam, which henceforth became the staple food of the slave and poorer popula-tion. Europeans generally found the yam too unpleasant for their use, but by prolonged boiling, it lost its acidity and became sufficiently palatable to be accepted on occasion.

Home consumption of potatoes was not limited by its use as a vegetable for the officers and well-to-do: before long it was employed in the manufacture of arrack. Stills sprang up everywhere, and drunkenness became, and remained, one of the most serious troubles amongst all classes of the island's population. Indeed, it was the chief cause of the frequent mutinies of the garrison troops which punctuated the history of St Helena, no less than of the almost unbroken succession of worth-less chaplains under which the island suffered during the eighteenth century. One excuse for the inordinate consumption of potato-arrack was the plea that it was a sovereign cure for the alleged ill effects of eating yams. So great did the evil become that an order was issued by the London headquarters in 1701, demanding the suppression of all

---

[1] Arkstee and Merkus (1749). *Allgemeine Historie der Reisen*, vol. III, p. 244.

stills. This, however, seems to have been a very difficult task. How difficult may be gathered from the letter of Governor Pyke, dated 7 March 1711, in which he says: 'We have been in a very bad condition for want of liquor upon the island. We have not had a drop of strong liquor in your [the Company's] store this month. There is no living in this hilly country and drink nothing but water.'[1] The Directors informed Governor Pyke of their astonishment at the quantity of arrack consumed, and flatly declared that in their opinion, 'the people have grown sottish'. A little later, Governor Pyke admitted to the Directors that 'the miserable devastation formerly made by distilling arrack from potatoes is too sensibly felt now by every one in the place. Their waste and destruction of wood was so great that if they had not been hindered from distilling, the island would have been entirely barren before this time'. He followed this up with further efforts to close down the stills, and imposed a tax on imported spirits.

The Governor's enthusiasm for temperance, however, could not withstand the popular demand, which found ready support from the medical profession, for on 8 May 1717 Pyke writes to the Directors: 'The physical people we sometimes converse with [i.e. the ship surgeons], tell us that strong liquor is necessary to all people who have no other bread but these watery roots [i.e.'yams'], and we also find it so—wherefore though we shall encourage temperance and sobriety as well by our example as precept, yet it is vain to dissuade the use of arrack among these people who prefer it to the choicest wines.'

To understand how it came about that the potato acquired so important a place in the economy of St Helena, we must consider for a moment the social basis on which the economic life of the islanders was built up. From the beginning of its history, St Helena was a revictualling station, and as such it served the East India Company's ships returning from China and the East via the Cape of Good Hope. It was to safeguard the depot, and not from any imperial motive, that a garrison was maintained there. That the island happened to serve as a place of detention for Napoleon, and later for the Boer prisoners, was a tribute to its isolation, not to its strength.

The arrival of a ship was an event which at all times brought everybody to Jamestown, the capital. Capt. William Dampier[2] in 1691 records that 'their plantations afford potatoes, yams, and some plantains and bananas', and remarks how 'they all flock to town when ships arrive and buy what they want and sell their produce'. As time went on, other than the Company's ships, 'interlopers' as they were termed, both British and

[1] Janisch, H. R. (1885). *Extracts from the St Helena Records*. For the correspondence between the governors and directors see pp. 95, 113, 122, 138 and 146.

[2] Dampier, William (1691). *Voyages* (edit. J. Mansfield, 1906), vol. I, p. 526.

foreign, found it convenient to anchor off Jamestown and purchase water and stores, though at prices considerably higher than those paid by the Company's ships. The Company, having as its first interest the welfare of its own fleet, was content throughout its tenure of the island, to maintain the station on an uneconomic basis. Its water and fresh stocks of food were in the nature of an insurance against the losses by scurvy, which were so heavy and costly a drain on their resources of man-power. Stores of all sorts were sold to the islanders, often at under cost and never much above, and every assistance was given to the planters who, in return, were obliged to sell their stocks of fresh beef and mutton at a low fixed figure, viz. 25s. per cwt. dead weight, to the Company's ships. Against this, the island planters were encouraged to raise potatoes and green vegetables, which were eagerly sought after by the ships, and for which there was an open market.

How much the potatoes were prized, may be gauged from a passage in Nicol's *Journal*, 1788. The captain of his ship presented Governor Skottowe with a number of empty bottles and in return was given potatoes which, Nicol says, were 'a valuable present to us'.[1]

During most of the island's history, there was an unrestricted, though not strictly a free market for potatoes. Producer-rings and the use of barter allowed the farmers to overcome all attempts at controlling the price of potatoes for export, and ensured the planters handsome profits.

It was not to be expected that the business methods of the St Helena merchants should be of a high standard. They had but one market in which they could make cash purchases or from which they could acquire commodity goods, namely, that offered by the ships. The ships, in their turn, had but one source from which to procure fresh food for the homeward journey, namely the planters.

These factors would of themselves have ensured high prices, but others tended to give the market a speculative and unhealthy character. The stocks of potatoes, never very large, might in any season, owing to tempestuous weather and the ravages of the rats, be considerably reduced, whilst the number of calling ships fluctuated widely.

The position will be appreciated from the following episode, recounted by Governor Beatson[2] who was anxious to put down profiteering. It happened about the year 1810: 'One of the potato farmers some time ago, assured me he had lost 500 bushels (worth at that time about £200) which had rotted, as there was no demand for them. I did not pity him because if he had been in the habit of feeding his servants and cattle at that time in the manner here proposed, or of lowering and suiting his prices to the market, such a loss could never have happened.'

---

[1] Nicol, John (1822). *Life and Adventures* (edit. 1937), p. 124.
[2] Beatson, A. (1816). *Tracts relative to St Helena*, p. 12.

Beatson's point of view is thrown into strong relief when we compare the prices current for potatoes and yams respectively. Throughout the eighteenth and nineteenth centuries the recorded price of yams remained constant at 6s. per cwt., whilst that of potatoes never sank below 8s. 6d., was commonly 16s., and during the Napoleonic era rose to 24s. per cwt. —and by reason of barter methods, to still higher figures. In the official returns for 1851, the market price of potatoes is quoted as between 13s. and 18s. per cwt.—evidence of the brisk demand which the 800 to 1,000 ships calling annually at that time, made on the resources of the island.[1]

The business of the island farmer was a gamble, in which his slickness as a dealer far outweighed his skill as a producer. It was a gamble, moreover, which from about 1760 to 1850 offered rich returns to the very few who eventually obtained control of the greater part of the island's arable land.

If the market for the potato was anomalous, the machinery of production was no less peculiar. The amount of arable land available was never more than about 2,000 acres, and less than 200 of that was under potatoes, the most lucrative crop. Cultivation until 1824 was effected by slave labour, using until the beginning of the nineteenth century nothing more advanced than spade and pickaxe. The exploitation of slave-labour was encouraged by the Company, and endorsed by the planters who were for ever demanding further importations of slaves, and the extension of the area under yams, on which they were almost wholly subsisted.

Drunkenness, as we have seen, was rife in all classes. The garrison soldiers, for the most part untrained, were idle, driven to drink and never far removed from mutiny. Discipline, such as it was, was maintained by flogging and the torture of the wooden horse.

Although contemporary historians plead that the treatment of slaves was better in St Helena than elsewhere, the extracts of the actual procedure of the courts[2] during the eighteenth and nineteenth centuries, and the gross brutality of their sentences, fail to bear this out. The anomalous character of the market, and the exorbitant prices which the potatoes commanded when the number of ships needing revictualling was large, seem to have made the planters peculiarly callous as to the welfare of their slaves. Although they valued their labour at between 1s. 6d. and 2s. a day, at a time when the British agricultural labourer was obliged to be content with no more than 1s. to 1s. 2d., they did nothing to make their lives bearable, or to encourage them to increase their output. It is not too much to say that throughout most of the eighteenth century the upper classes, both civil and military, were in

[1] St Helena. Almanac and Annual Register, 1851.
[2] Janisch, H. R. (1885). *Extracts from the St Helena Records.*

a chronic state of fear of reprisals either from their slaves, the garrison soldiers, or both, which may perhaps explain the senseless brutality with which they were often used. This had not always been the case: in 1683 the Governor assured the Board of Directors that if 600 whites could keep 50,000 blacks in subjection in Barbadoes, they in St Helena should have no reason to fear any trouble. But as the demand for the planters' produce, and more especially for their potatoes, grew, so it would seem did the exploitation of their slave-labour become more oppressive.

Several governors, and in particular Governor Beatson (1808–13), made determined attempts to introduce new crops and improved methods; it was he who was responsible for introducing the plough for potato-cultivation and for stepping up the yield per acre to as much as 16 tons per annum. But there was little inducement to create new industries, raise other crops, or adopt improved methods so long as the Company was prepared, no matter what it cost them, to maintain the station for the provision of their ships.[1]

In 1802, Lord Valentia[2] visited the island and commented on the enormous prosperity of the farmers, who could grow three crops of potatoes a year on the same ground, 'and an acre producing on an average 400 bushels' [= 10 tons], which they sold to the ships at 8s. a bushel. The truth was that by the beginning of the nineteenth century, the farmers operating in an exclusive market, had created a ring and maintained prices, not only of potatoes, but all other commodities, at the highest level. Turkeys, which flourished on the island, were sold at £2. 2s., ducks at 8s., fowls at 5s., potatoes at 8s. a bushel, and a single cabbage at 1s. 6d. So high was the cost of living to those visiting St Helena, that it was recorded by James Prior that the common seamen could not afford to buy anything more than a few potatoes and wild water-cress.[3]

There is no doubt that at such remunerative prices, the consumption of potatoes by the islanders themselves was very restricted. Earlier, when there had been a shortage of rice and flour, which was not infrequent, the loss had been made good by an increased use of potatoes, but in 1812, when a similar crisis arose, the garrison, no longer accustomed to potatoes, refused to accept them and a mutiny ensued. As a matter of fact the price which the ships' pursers at that time were prepared to pay for potatoes was so high, often amounting to 12s. a bushel, that rather than sell them at lower prices on the island, farmers, as Governor Beatson complains, frequently allowed them to rot in the ground.

---

[1] Beatson, A. (1816). *Tracts relative to St Helena*, p. 12.
[2] Valentia, Lord (1809). *Voyages and Travels*.
[3] Prior, Sir James (1819). *Voyage along the Eastern Coast of Africa*, p. 86.

The quantity of potatoes sold to the ships between 1802 and 1813, averaged 6,000 bushels p.a., which represents a cash value of at least £3,000 p.a. This may seem a small sum to-day, but in a community which, prior to the arrival of Napoleon, scarcely numbered 3,000, of which about half were slaves or black free-men, and more than a quarter garrison and civil servants, it represented an important part of that revenue of the island, which was not the property of the Company.

The heyday of the island's economic history coincided with the residence of Napoleon, 1815–21. Prices soared and the minimum price for potatoes was 8s. a bushel for use on the island, the same as the official price for sale to the ships, nearly three times the figure they fetched in the large towns of England. Such high prices seem to have prevented the poorer classes using potatoes at all, for when Darwin[1] visited St Helena in 1836, he noted that the mass of the people were extremely poor and lived on rice and salt meat, both of which were imported and dear. It was in this year that the British Government took over control of the island. Martin[2] in the following year, whilst complaining of the high price of foodstuffs including potatoes at 4s. a bushel and yams at 6s. a cwt., records that potatoes have largely replaced yams, and that whilst they were formerly bartered, they now find a ready sale with the ships. Forty years later, the area under yams (*Dioscorea alata*) was inconsiderable.[3] The reduction in price was due to the withdrawal of most of the garrison, following the death of Napoleon. The replacement of the yam by the potato was doubtless the result of the abolition of slavery, when the blacks could no longer be forced to eat a food which had always been distasteful. About this time, St Helena exported potatoes to the Cape; the trade, however, was brought to a close when a tax of 2s. per 100 lbs. was imposed by the Cape Government.

Between 1830 and 1835, the average quantity of potatoes brought to market in Jamestown seems to have been about 4,000 bushels p.a., of which 3,200 were sold to the ships calling at the island:[4] if we may assume that a bag of potatoes contained two bushels.

Towards the end of the third quarter of the century, St Helena began to lose its unique position as a revictualling station for ships returning from the East. The number of ships calling by the middle of the century had reached to close on 1,000 a year; by 1870 it had sunk to 677, and from then on, the decline quickened. Increased tonnage of ships, the use of steam power, and the introduction of refrigeration, gave the

[1] Darwin, Charles (1845). *Journal of a Voyage round the World* (edit. 1889), p. 355.
[2] Martin, R. M. (1837). *History of the Falkland Islands, St Helena, etc. Brit. Colon. Lib.* vol. x, p. 26.
[3] Melliss, J. C. (1875). Op. cit. p. 338.
[4] Martin, R. Montgomery (1837). *History of the British Possessions in the Indian and Atlantic Oceans*, p. 205.

shipping of the world an increasing independence. The final blow to the island's life followed the use of the overland Syrian route to India, whilst the opening of the Suez Canal in 1869 before long completed the diversion of the Indiamen from the Atlantic and Cape route.[1]

For a few years there was a revival in the island's economic life, with the coming of General Cronje and his fellow Boer prisoners in 1900, but with their return to the Cape, the island and its potatoes were no longer in request. The garrison was finally removed in 1907, with the result that potato-growing, as indeed most other of the island's activities, reached its lowest level. In 1936 the working classes were living mainly on imported rice.

Before the war of 1939–45, an attempt was made to create an industry in new potatoes for export to England, which gave promise of success, but that, like so many of the island's economic ventures, notably whaling and fibre-growing, has been thwarted by forces beyond the control of its inhabitants. A similar fate overtook the promising industry which grew up between the wars, based on the cultivation of Madonna lilies which, in view of the disease prevalent in Japan, bid fair to obtain a firm foothold in the English market. There is only one industry left which flourishes on the island, and that is the sale of its stamps to the philatelists of the world.

That the potato failed to maintain its position as one of the chief commodities of the islanders is, in the main, due to the fact that it was grown for the foreign, not the home market. Of late years, the arable land has passed into the hands of three large owners who devote their land to the cultivation of New Zealand flax (*Phormium tenax*), so that there are but few small-holders left who might raise potatoes for their own and their neighbours' use.[2]

The part played by the potato in St Helena was twofold: it served at first as a cheap food for the slave population until it was replaced by a still cheaper substitute, the yam. Later, and for the best part of 200 years, the position was reversed: it was not the worker who fell victim to the potato, but the rich merchantman who was forced to purchase it at an exorbitant price. The effect so precarious a monopoly had on the planter and his slave labourer was, as we have seen, detrimental to the latter whilst it lasted, and fatal to the former when it ceased.

[1] The potato in the Chatham Islands played a similar role *vis à vis* the whalers and others who frequented those parts (Mrs C. E. Richards) (Salaman's manuscript note, but without further reference). – Ed.

[2] This industry has now failed (Cronk, *pers. comm.*). – Ed.

CHAPTER XXX

The Potato in Jersey

The island of Jersey has won for itself a position so unique as regards the potato, that it is desirable that the development and the consequences of this association should be studied. Largest of the Channel Island group, Jersey has a long and unchequered history, during which its cultural life received a double enrichment consequent on its intimate relationship with both England and France.

The structure of its society has for centuries been stable: a landed peasantry below, and a feudal aristocracy above. A small middle-class, amongst whom we must reckon that considerable body of naval and military officers and officials, who for many years now, have been in the habit of spending their retirement in the island.

The peasantry, who have always enjoyed a reputation for their hard-work and frugality, have for the last 200 years at least, enjoyed a relatively high standard of living. In the seventeenth century, the turnip and parsnip were introduced: both have played an important part in the life of the islanders. The former supplied winter feed for their stock, and led to the establishment of the famous and jealously guarded herds of island cattle; the latter, for some generations, dominated the domestic economy of the people: they were eaten abundantly in the home, as well as being fed to the hogs. Parsnip-fed pork has been claimed as the finest in the world.

Apart from their participation in husbandry, the womenfolk of the island had built up a flourishing industry in knitted hose, known as Jersey 'stocks', which were in great demand in the English market.[1]

In the eighteenth century, the chief export product of the island was grain, which was shipped to Spain, but its cultivation fell off and much of the arable land, in about the middle of the eighteenth century, was given over to the planting of orchards. From then until the end of the Napoleonic wars, all other crops were relegated to a second place.

Jersey claimed to produce more and stronger cider to the acre than any other place in the world. We are not told whether it was all for home consumption, but from Camden's[2] account it would appear that it, too, was in large measure exported to Spain.

The use of Vraic, or sea-weed, as a manure, is an immemorial custom; on it has rested very largely the prosperity of the people, and never more

---

[1] Camden, William. *Britannia* (Gough's edit. 1789), vol. III, p. 749.
[2] Ibid.

so, than when its use was devoted to the potato crop. Vraic, cut and collected on the shore, is brought inland, dried, stacked and thatched ready for use in the spring and summer. Besides such treatment, it had always been customary to keep a Vraic fire burning continuously, both within doors for domestic purposes, and in the yard. The ash, a valuable source of potash, was frequently sold, or bartered for grain—one-quarter of ash for one-thirteenth of a quarter of wheat.

With the spread of the orchards, the demand for labour in the Merchant Navy, and the falling off of grain cultivation in the later decades of the eighteenth century, Jersey's prosperity began for a while to wane.

The most widely grown vegetable in the island during the eighteenth century was the parsnip: it was sown in the orchards as well as in the fields. About 1740 the potato was introduced into Jersey, but it was not till some forty years later that it invaded the fields. From that moment, the predominance of the parsnip was threatened and, before long, over-come; nor was it only the parsnip which was forced to retire in face of the potato: the orchards, too, began to recede till, by 1880, they had ceased to exist as an industrial feature.

The potato from the very start had neither popular prejudice nor the imposition of the tithe with which to contend. Within the first decade of the nineteenth century, Jersey was exporting 'Earlies' to London, a trade which rapidly expanded. In 1809 the export amounted to 849 tons; in 1811 to 1,400 tons, and in 1832 to 8,000 tons.[1] At the same time, the practice of growing a second crop of potatoes on the same ground was instituted; nor was evidence of organization lacking in those early days, for we find that a practice of lifting by contract, by which labour took a tenth of the crop, was already in force. At this time, the surplus of the potato crop was exported to Guernsey and Portugal. A hundred years later, it is this latter country which is sending early potatoes to England.

The policy which has culminated in successfully converting the island into a vast market-garden for the production of early potatoes and late season tomatoes, must be put to the credit of the Royal Jersey Horti-cultural Society which was founded in 1833. On 7 December of that year, the following resolution was recorded:[2]

That the hogshead of Potatoes presented by Sir Isaac Coffin be (with the exception of a small lot to be given to Mr Saunders to try an experiment with) divided into two parts; one part to be taken charge of by Col. Le Couteur and the other by Mr Charles Bertram of Grouville and that these two gentlemen

---

[1] Marquand, J. le (1939). Communicated to R.N.S.
[2] Shepherd, H. G. (1934). *One Hundred Years of the Royal Jersey Agric. and Hortic. Soc.* 1833–1933, p. 8. Jersey: J. T. Bigwood.

divide their respective lots into other two parts, one of each to be planted according to the plan recommended by Mr Knight and the other according to the mode practised in Jersey.

The Jersey farmers had much to learn, and many painful failures to experience, before they won their place in Covent Garden as one of the largest producers of early potatoes. Actually, it was the Guernsey Horticultural Society, founded a little earlier than that of Jersey, which first pointed the way, in its *Report* for 1836:[1]

It would be desirable to obtain potatoes of very early habits raised from seed, so as to enable this Island to supply the first demands of the London Market, which the climate might very well admit; early potatoes frequently selling at from one to two shillings the pound in Covent Garden Market, when in great plenty here.

The possibilities of early potato cultivation as the Island's Industry seem here to be brought to the notice of farmers for the first time.

In 1838 the Jersey Society warned their members that the island's potatoes did not approach in earliness or quality the best in Covent Garden. To bring about an improvement, they decided to import two new varieties, 'Phillip's Red', and a seedling of Andrew Knight's; with what success, is not recorded. But, from now on, it is abundantly clear that the islanders were moulding their whole agricultural system so as to fit it for the production of early potatoes for export to London.

In 1841 we hear of the manufacture of specially designed ploughs to deal with the extension of Jersey potato-farming: one, a very heavy, deep-trenching plough, worked communally with six to eight horses, and the other a light one designed for planting potato seed.[2]

The Jersey potato industry received a great stimulus in 1844 by the importation of guano, the pungency of whose aroma, it is said, filled the growers with expectation; unfortunately, in the following year the crops were cut down by the new disease, the Blight, *Phytophthora infestans*, whose devastation was by some accredited to the action of the guano.

Blight has, ever since, proved a serious obstacle to the island's potato trade; in 1858, it is complained that the trade had wellnigh suffered an eclipse, and that the crop returns were but one-third of their former volume. It was not Blight alone, which was to blame, but the much older enemy, 'Curl'.

It is evident that the growers were confronted with still another

---

[1] The Guernsey Hortic. Soc. *Annual Report* for 1836.
[2] Le Couteur, J. (1841). On the Great Jersey Trench Plough. *J. Roy. Agric. Soc.* vol. VIII, p. 47.

trouble: blame was rightly placed on the varieties which, it may be presumed, were infected with this virus disease. Once more the Society urged its members to concentrate on the earliest possible varieties, to discard all foreign markets, and to devote their whole energy to the capture of Covent Garden.

From now on, there seems to have been a recovery, and exceptionally good returns, at high prices, are recorded for 'First Earlies' in 1861, namely six tons per acre, and £25 per ton. In that year, the total crop of the island was 3,920 tons and was sold at an average price of £8 per ton. The potato continued to spread, and the orchards to retreat: in 1872 an effort was made to revive the latter, but it does not appear to have met with any success. In 1876 Jersey began to send potatoes to Hull as well as to London, and its total export now reached 23,000 tons and was valued at £230,000.

In 1886 Jersey potatoes suffered a reverse owing to a glut in the London markets, and the producers were correspondingly depressed. The Society's Committee expressed its anxiety at the pursuance of a policy which put all their eggs into one basket:[1] 'The Committee therefore would earnestly ask the Farmer if he is acting wisely in trusting almost entirely to such an expensive and precarious crop as the Potato.' And the Committee itself supplies the answer: 'The results of this year offer the reply: It has attained undue limits; it has been unprofitable.'

The islanders, however, were not to be daunted, and they continued on their course with increased vigour. The major effort of the Jersey potato farmers was directed towards combating the Blight, which they did by liberal spraying with Bordeaux Mixture and, in recent years, by burning off the tops with sulphuric acid. The introduction of new varieties was suggested as a further means of combating the disease, and trials for this purpose were instituted. No effort was spared to maintain the fertility of the soil and great quantities of the best artificials, in addition to farm-yard manure, were used. The high level of cultivation attained, allowed of a follow-on crop with tomatoes in suitable places, the harvest of which is now only second in importance to that of the potato.

As regards new varieties, it is a remarkable fact, that only very few have ever succeeded in holding their own in the island for any length of time. The outstanding example is that of 'International Kidney', raised by Robert Fenn, and introduced into the island by Hugh de la Haye in 1878 under the name of 'Jersey Fluke'. It is on this variety, and on the island-grown seed of the same, that the subsequent fortunes of the Jersey potato trade have been built.

Since 1906, Jersey has had to face the competition of the St Malo

[1] Shepherd, H. G. (1934). Op. cit. p. 65. Jersey: J. T. Bigwood.

growers, a fact which stimulated all concerned, to greater efforts, and led to the creation of an efficient scientific advisory staff to guide the industry and help it solve the complex phytopathological problems, which, to-day, so often determine the difference between failure and success.

Reference has been made to the failure of the crop in 1886; similar set-backs occurred before, and more were to follow. On most of these occasions there were serious doubts as to the wisdom of encouraging so exclusive an industrial system. It is of interest to compare the experience of Jersey with that of other parts of the United Kingdom in which the potato assumed a position of outstanding importance in the economy of the people.

In Ireland, as in the Highlands of Scotland, a somewhat similar question had been asked many a time, but the reason for posing it had been an entirely different one. In Jersey the question could be reduced to the simple problem of commercial expediency. There had never been the remotest suggestion that the potato was undermining the morale of the people, lowering their standard of living, inducing early marriages, or creating an excess of poverty-stricken labourers. The obvious distinction between the two cases, namely that the Irish fed almost exclusively on their potatoes, whilst the Jersey folk exported all but the surplus for others to feed on, is, however, not sufficient to explain the difference between the social and economic circumstances of the two people. The Jersey peasant had always lived uncommonly well, long before the potato had assumed so important a place in the economy of the island. Home-baked bread, unlimited butter, and a rich soup made of fish, potatoes, peas and parsnips, formed the usual daily diet; meat was eaten but sparsely, and cheese not at all; sugar and tea, being both untaxed, were plentiful.[1]

And now that the potato had come, the economy of the home-life was not affected. The peasantry, with their age-old rights in the use of the soil and in the control of affairs, notwithstanding a certain feudal atmosphere, which still remained, were proof against such misuse of the potato as had occurred in Ireland and the Highlands. There, the potato, in its capacity as a cheap food, had been ruthlessly employed as an instrument of exploitation, in a society bereft of its right in the soil and without any political power by which to protect their interests. The failure of the potato in Jersey meant a commercial crisis over a short period; in Ireland and the Hebrides, a collapse of society.

Before the War of 1914–18, the Jersey trade had reached its apogee. The combination of a first-class husbandry, and highly efficient labour,

---

[1] Quayle, Thomas (1815). *General View, etc., of the Islands on the Coast of Normandy*, p. 210.

working in unison with a perfectly organized transport, had succeeded in establishing a sure market for their produce throughout England, and, generally, an adequate livelihood for all engaged. The area in Jersey under potatoes covered sixteen of the fifty-four square miles which make up the total surface of the island. The 1919 crops sold for a million pounds; in the 1930's prices dropped, but the tonnage had increased; before the War of 1939–45, 55,701 tons were exported, and £585,887 received in exchange. In 1939 Jersey headed the list of importers of early potatoes with 67,738 tons, followed by Spain with 14,700, and the Canary Isles with 6,900 tons.

It is with regret that one has to end this account with the statement that, during the occupation by the enemy, the Colorado potato-beetle established itself in several of the fields, and the island's export trade to England is for the time in abeyance. The campaign against this pest in both 1945 and 1946 was so successful that its final elimination in the near future is confidently expected.[1]

---

[1] In the compilation of this chapter, I have relied on three main sources:

(1) Simpson, D. and Small, T. (1938). The Potato Industry in Jersey. *Empire J. Exp. Agric.* vol. VI, pp. 95–100.

(2) Shepherd, H. G. (1934). *One Hundred Years of the Roy. Jersey Agric. and Hortic. Soc 1833–1933.*

(3) Quayle, Thomas (1815). *The General View, etc., of the Islands on the Coast of Normandy.*

CHAPTER XXXI

The Industrial Uses of the Potato

by W. G. Burton

The adoption of the potato as a major source of food—as in the bleaker parts of the Andes of South America, and in Ireland not very long after its introduction into Europe—caused its two principal disadvantages to become apparent. First, although it was a well-balanced foodstuff, its content of water was such that a great bulk of it was required. Secondly, as we have seen, its storage-life was comparatively short, and the wastage, particularly towards the end of the storage period, was great, even when the tubers were sound and free from disease.

In both properties mentioned above—bulk and storage-life—the potato was much inferior to grain, which it had partially replaced, and efforts were made very early in its history to dry it, mainly with a view to its preservation. This method of extending the storage-life was common to most of the more impermanent foodstuffs—meat, fish, milk, butter, fruit—and the preparation and properties of the earliest forms of dried potato of which we have any record have already been described (Chapters II and III). In Europe, experiments on various types of dried potato were made in the latter half of the eighteenth century,[1] partly with a desire to increase the usefulness of the tubers as ships' provisions. In England, a Dr Cuthbert Gordon in 1786 'produced, at a highly respectable meeting of the Subscribers to the British Society for extending the Fisheries and improving the Sea Coasts, a specimen of flour or meal, that keeps sound for any length of time, (being impervious to the air), made of potatoes, which together with the bread made thereof, is grateful to the taste, a wholesome and nutritious food, and in all respects much to the satisfaction of every one present'.[2] Whether it would have been to the satisfaction of the people who were intended partly to subsist on this flour—the settlers who it was proposed should be introduced into the partially depopulated Highlands of Scotland—we do not know. The next time we hear of potato-flour in the British Isles, it is recommended as a means of reducing the loss of the potato crop in Ireland in 1845,[3] but if used at all it was only to a slight extent. In the War of 1914–18, dried foods of all kinds, and particularly dried potato, were manufactured

---

[1] Parmentier, A. A. (1781). *Recherches sur les végétaux nourrissans, qui, dans les temps de disette, peuvent remplacer les alimens ordinaires....* Paris.

[2] Fraser, R. (1794). *General View of the County of Cornwall.* London.

[3] Large, E. C. (1940). *The Advance of the Fungi.* London: Jonathan Cape.

for the use of the combatants, mainly because such foods could readily be transported, stored, and prepared for use under field conditions. They disappeared from the scene as soon as hostilities ceased, and the partial famine in Europe abated, leaving a legacy of great distrust, more especially of any form of dried vegetable. Quite considerable quantities of potatoes continued to be made into potato-flour both for stock feeding and for human consumption on the continent of Europe, and to a much smaller extent in this country and in the United States, but dehydration of potatoes, in forms other than flour, lingered on only on a small scale and for special purposes. There seems to have been little attempt either to control the quality of the products, or to investigate the forms of deterioration to which they might be subject. Nevertheless the memory of the potential usefulness of dehydration survived, and the War of 1939–45 saw a great expansion of the industry. The bulk of the Allied production was manufactured in the United States, but almost 100,000 tons (representing some 500,000–600,000 tons of raw potatoes) of dried potato of all types were made in Great Britain for stock-feeding, as well as for human consumption. The dried potato was produced in various forms—potato-flour prepared from either raw or cooked tubers, dried strips of potato, 'riced' potato, and mashed-potato powder. The potato-flour was produced mainly for stock-feeding, and the bulk of it was made by drying slices of raw potato in sugar-beet pulp driers or similar plants and then grinding them to a flour. The high temperatures employed in such driers both char the material and gelatinize the starch. The potato strips were partially cooked before drying to inactivate the enzyme systems—which would otherwise have caused discoloration during preparation and reconstitution—and were dried at a low temperature to avoid charring,[1] while riced potato[1] and mashed-potato powder[2] were produced from fully cooked and mashed potato. The three last-mentioned forms of dried potato were all intended to replace fresh potatoes in the diet. They were 'reconstituted' by the addition of water, followed by cooking if necessary, to give products resembling—and in some cases practically indistinguishable from—freshly cooked potatoes.

Apart from a longer storage life, the main advantage of dried, as compared with raw, potatoes in time of war lay in their superior packing density. The approximate volumes of dried or raw potatoes sufficient

[1] Wager, H. G., Tomkins, R. G., Brightwell, S. T. P., Allen, R. J. L. and Mapson, L. W. (1945). The drying of potatoes. *Food Manuf.* vol. xx, pp. 289–93, 321–5, 367–71.

[2] Barker, J. and Burton, W. G. (1944). Mashed potato powder. I. General characteristics and the 'brush sieve' method of preparation. *J. Soc. chem. Ind.* vol. LXIII, pp. 169–72. Burton, W. G. (1944). Mashed potato powder. II. Spray-drying method. *J. Soc.chem. Ind.* vol. LXIII, pp. 213–15. Rendle, T. (1945). The preservation of potatoes for human consumption. *Chem. Ind. Rev.* 1945, pp. 354–9.

to provide a ton of cooked potatoes are as follows: fresh tubers (allowing a 25% peeling loss), 73 cu. ft.; dried strips, 30 cu. ft.; riced potato, 30 cu. ft.; mashed-potato powder, 8 cu. ft.

The nutritive value of reconstituted dried potato differs from that of the freshly cooked tubers mainly in so far as it is affected by the actual drying processes. These do not affect the value of the products as sources of calories or nitrogen, but they may cause large losses of vitamins. Vitamin C, of which the freshly harvested potato is a useful source, is present in reconstituted riced potato or mashed-potato powder to the extent of some two-thirds of that present in comparable freshly cooked potato[1] while reconstituted potato strips contain only 15–20% of the vitamin C in freshly cooked potato.[2] Raw potatoes, of course, lose much of their vitamin C during storage, as may dried-potato products, though at a slower rate in a temperate climate; the nett result being that after storage for, say, six months in this country, riced potato and mashed-potato powder will probably contain more vitamin C than would a sample of the potatoes from which they were produced.

Although, given proper conditions, the storage life of dried-potato products may be several years, they are subject to serious deterioration unless care is taken. Charring may occur if they are stored at tropical temperatures, the development of the brown colour and 'burnt' taste being the more rapid the higher the moisture content of the dried potato.[3] Normally this is of the order of 6–8%, but it may be much more if the products are kept in a humid climate in containers which allow equilibration to occur between their contents and the atmosphere. Under such conditions mould growth too may occur.[4] Unless they are stored in an inert atmosphere such as nitrogen—which is not the normal commercial practice—the vitamin C contained in dehydrated potatoes may, as mentioned above, be oxidized during storage, particularly if the storage temperature and the moisture content of the product are high.[5] Other

---

[1] Barker, J. and Burton, W. G. (1944). Mashed potato powder. I. General characteristics and the 'brush sieve' method of preparation. *J. Soc. chem. Ind.* vol. LXIII, pp. 169–72. Wager, H. G., Tomkins, R. G., Brightwell, S. T. P., Allen, R. J. L. and Mapson, L. W. (1945). The drying of potatoes. *Food Manuf.* vol. XX, pp. 289–93, 321–5, 367–71.

[2] Ibid.

[3] Tomkins, R. G., Mapson, L. W., Allen, R. J. L., Wager, H. G. and Barker, J. (1944). The drying of vegetables. III. The storage of dried vegetables. *J. Soc. chem. Ind.* vol. LXIII, pp. 225–31. Burton, W. G. (1945). Mashed potato powder. III. The high temperature browning of mashed-potato powder. *J. Soc. chem. Ind.* vol. LXIV, pp. 215–18.

[4] Burton, W. G. (1945). The storage life of a sample of potato-flour produced from potato slices dried in a sugar-beet factory. *J. Soc. chem. Ind.* vol. LXIV, pp. 85–6.

[5] Tomkins, R. G., Mapson, L. W., Allen, R. J. L., Wager, H. G. and Barker, J. (1944). The drying of vegetables. III. The storage of dried vegetables. *J. Soc. chem. Ind.* vol. LXIII, pp. 225–31.

oxidative changes occur at low moisture contents, particularly in mashed-potato powder, giving rise to 'off' flavours.[1]

Although the potato was first eaten in this country as a luxury, when it became established as a popular food it was mainly as a cheap source of calories and bulk—in fact as a substitute for bread when the cost of the latter was prohibitive to the poorer sections of the population. It is as this cheap source of food that the potato has retained its place, and even so, when Orr carried out his survey in 1926–35[2] about 10% of the population consumed less than the average amount of potatoes because of poverty. Against this background it may seem doubtful to what extent dried potatoes will find a place in normal times. If they are to be satisfactory, they can only be produced from good quality potatoes, and the saving on the cost of raw tubers is thus only such as results from buying a large bulk. The preparation and cooking, in that they are done on a large scale, may well be cheaper than the 'boilings of the pot, . . . the labour, . . . the time, . . . the peelings and scrapings and washings' condemned by Cobbett in his *Cottage Economy*; but the carefully controlled drying and the packaging must make dried potatoes more expensive to the housewife than the freshly cooked tubers, even disregarding overhead costs and profit. It seems probable, therefore, that the main peacetime use of dried potato will be in restaurants and the like, where ease of storage and convenience in preparation are of more importance than an increase in cost.

In addition to being used for the production of dried potato, potatoes find a use on a small scale in the canning industry, and in the manufacture of potato crisps. The nutritive value of canned potatoes is much the same as that of the freshly cooked tubers, though they may contain rather less vitamin C.[3] Potato crisps are an excellent source of calories, mainly because they are dried by the frying process and absorb a large amount of fat. Weight for weight, they are more than seven times as good a source of calories as boiled potatoes, but their high cost relegates them to the category of luxuries rather than foodstuffs. They retain about half the vitamin C present in the raw tubers.

So far, we have been concerned only with the use of the potato, as such, in the food industries. A high proportion of the world production of potatoes—possibly higher than that devoted to human consumption—is used as food for stock. This use developed as soon as potatoes were

---

[1] Burton, W. G. (1945). Mashed-potato powder. III. The high temperature browning of mashed potato-powder. *J. Soc. chem. Ind.* vol. LXIV, 215–18.

[2] Orr, J. B. (1936). *Food Health and Income*. London: Macmillan.

[3] Olliver, M. (1936). The ascorbic acid content of fruits and vegetables with special reference to the effect of cooking and canning. *J. Soc. chem. Ind.* vol. LV, pp. 153–63. Zilva, S. S. and Morris, T. N. (1938). Vitamin C in canned meat and vegetable rations and in canned potatoes. *Rep. Food Invest. Bd., Lond.* 1938, pp. 222–3.

generally cultivated, and the county agricultural surveys and the agricultural society publications of the end of the eighteenth century contain numerous references to experiments on the most advantageous ways of using them. Werner[1] stated that in Germany over 38% of the crop was used for stock-feeding, compared with some 30% used for human consumption. In general, on the continent of Europe, some 20-50% of the potato production is normally fed to stock,[2] while in Eire, almost 60% of the potato production is used for stock-feeding.[3] In England and in the United States, on the other hand, the use of potatoes as stock food is not nearly so important as their use for human consumption.

Raw potatoes tend to cause scouring and should not be fed to pigs or poultry. Cooked potatoes have a laxative effect but may be fed with advantage to all stock. As in the case of potatoes for human consumption the main disadvantages of potatoes as stock food are their bulk and the inevitable loss on storage. In addition there is the necessity of cooking them before they are fed to certain classes of stock, which, though not regarded as a disadvantage in human food, may well be such in stock food. The disadvantage of the bulk of potatoes may be illustrated by the fact that the raw or cooked tubers, because of their high content of water, are equivalent in nutritive value (disregarding the vitamins) to only a fifth to a quarter of their weight of, for example, barley or maize meal.

Losses during storage may be considerably reduced if the potatoes are ensiled; silage made from cooked potatoes, or from the raw sliced tubers with the addition of fermented maize meal, may be fed to all classes of stock.[4] Such silage will keep in condition for at least eighteen months and it forms an excellent means of preserving potatoes on the farm, particularly as damaged or partly blighted tubers may be included without risk of rotting. Silage is equivalent in nutritive value to a similar weight of freshly cooked tubers and thus, although it has a long storage life, it shares with the latter the disadvantage of being bulky.

As mentioned above, considerable quantities of potatoes are dried for stock-feeding. If it is to be fed to stock which cannot eat raw potatoes, the dried potato must be produced either from raw tubers in such a way that the starch is gelatinized by a high drying temperature, or from cooked potatoes. The value of potato-flour for stock-feeding is roughly

[1] Werner, H. (1930). *Der Kartoffelbau* (9th edit. revised by K. Opitz). Berlin: Paul Parey.

[2] Yates, P. L. (1940). *Food Production in Western Europe.* London: Longmans, Green and Co.

[3] Kennedy, H. (1941). The importance of the potato (Broadcast Talk). *J. Dep. Agric. Eire*, vol. XXXVIII, pp. 15-19.

[4] Wallace, J. C. and Thompson, J. K. (1931). Potato silage. *J. Min. Agric.* vol. XXXVIII, pp. 909-13.

equivalent to that of an equal weight of barley or maize meal, although it is not comparable as a source of vitamins, and thus cannot, for example, be substituted for maize meal in the diet of young chicks.[1] Clearly the cost of transport, drying, and milling, plus the overhead costs and profit of the drying firm must make potato-flour more expensive than an equivalent weight of raw potatoes. How far it would normally pay the farmer to purchase potato-flour rather than to store the potatoes on the farm, preferably as silage, would depend upon the extent to which this greater price (due allowance being made for the cost of storage on the farm, and of cooking if necessary, and for losses during storage) was offset by the greater convenience of a concentrated feeding-stuff.

The potato is a source of nitrogen, vitamin C, and starch, of which the latter forms by far the greater part of the dry matter of the tuber. Because of this it is natural that some attention should have been paid to the possibility of using the potato as a source of starch for industrial purposes. In industry the starch may be used as such, or it may be used as raw material for the production of substances such as alcohol. In either case the advisability or otherwise of using potatoes provides an interesting economic problem. Because of its high content of water the potato is, weight for weight, a much poorer source of starch, of which it contains on the average some 15–20%, than the cereals, which may contain from 50 to 80%. On the other hand the yield of potatoes, in a suitable climate, is so much greater than that of cereals that the yield of starch per acre is very much greater from potatoes than from any other source. Thus if from force of circumstances or on grounds of national economy it is impossible or inadvisable to import more efficient raw materials, and necessary to make the most efficient use of the land available, potatoes may be the best source of starch in temperate regions. Also in countries where farm-labour is comparatively cheap, and the climate suitable, the price of potatoes may be sufficiently low for it to be more profitable to the manufacturer to use them rather than raw materials richer in starch but more expensive. A brief outline is given below of the various products which can be produced from potatoes, with a few of their possible uses.

Starch is extracted by breaking the cell walls, either mechanically or by digestion with Bacillus felsineus, washing the starch free of cell débris and then drying it. Potato-starch is particularly suitable for sizing paper and textiles, and is the type of starch most frequently used for finishing fine cotton goods, but it may be put to many other uses. Newkirk[2]

[1] Common, R. H. and Bolton, W. (1944). Dried-potato products and nutritional encephalomania in chicks. Nature, Lond. vol. CLIII, pp. 744–5.
[2] Newkirk, W. B. (1939). Industrial use of starch products. Industr. Engng. Chem. (Ind. Edn.) vol. XXXI, pp. 153–7.

summed the matter up by saying that there were a few cases in which starch from one particular origin supplied some requirement more satisfactorily than other starches, for example, the use of potato-starch for sizing, mentioned above, and of tapioca or sweet potato-starch in making postage stamp adhesives, but that even in these cases acceptable products could be made from starch of any origin. The choice really depended upon the availability and price of the various types of starch in the country in which the factory was operating.

Starch has an obvious use in the food industry as a major constituent of various compounded pudding mixtures, pie fillings, soup powders and substitutes for custard powder. There are many other uses[1], particularly for pre-gelatinized starches, ranging from the production of moulded articles such as dolls' heads, to forming the foundation of poster paints, and from uses as an agent for settling suspended slimy materials in mine waters to employment as the adhesive constituent of sand moulds for the production of castings. Various forms of oxidized starches are included in printing inks for cotton and linen goods.

Dextrins and British gums are produced by roasting acidified starch. They are used as adhesives, for sizing textiles, and as constituents of textile printing inks.

Dextrose and commercial glucose are prepared by the acid hydrolysis of starch, the extent to which the hydrolysis is completed, and the degree of purification later attempted depending upon the prospective uses of the product. Commercial glucose is used in tanning, and in the food industry, while pure dextrose may be used in the preparation of pharmaceutical products.

Alcohol may be prepared by the fermentation of a cooked mass of potatoes by yeast, followed by distillation. The alcohol so produced normally contains a higher proportion of fusel oil than that derived from other sources such as molasses. Jacobs,[2] assuming an 85% plant efficiency, stated that nearly 23 U.S. gallons of alcohol could be produced from a short ton (2000 lb.) of potatoes, this comparing reasonably well with the yield from sugar-cane, apples or grapes (c. 14–15 gal./ton) and from other root and tuber crops such as sugar-beet (c. 22 gal./ton) and Jerusalem artichokes (c. 20 gal./ton); but unfavourably with the yield from sweet potatoes (c. 34 gal./ton), raisins, blackstrap molasses and cereals (c. 70–85 gal./ton). On the other hand, on the basis of average yield of alcohol per acre the potato (averaging 178 gal./acre) is surpassed only by sugar beet (averaging 287 gal./acre) and sugar cane. Thus, as in the case of starch production, the value of the potato as a source of

---

[1] Ibid.

[2] Jacobs, P. B. (1939). Alcohol from farm products. *Industr. Engng. Chem.* (*Ind. Edn.*) vol. XXXI, pp. 162–5.

alcohol may be very different when regarded from the point of view of the most efficient employment of an acre of land or from the point of view of a manufacturer wishing to produce alcohol from the smallest bulk of the cheapest raw material. It would seem that the use of potatoes for alcohol would be worthwhile only in countries where the potato gives good yields and where there is no cheap supply of molasses or grain for industrial purposes. In such countries the relative merits of sugar-beet and potatoes as raw material would still have to be considered carefully. In assessing the merits of the potato it should be remembered that by growing varieties with a high content of dry matter, under optimum conditions for yield, their value as a source of alcohol might be increased considerably above any estimate based on the average figures given by Jacobs. Assuming a plant efficiency of 85%, the figures for yield and percentage content of starch published by Drew and Deasy[1] would indicate a potential production, in Ireland, of some 350 British gallons per acre in normal years, rising to as much as 470 gallons/acre under exceptionally favourable conditions. In one year of their experiments the potential yield from one variety they studied was nearly 33 gal./ton, though in this case the yield of alcohol per acre would not have been exceptional—some 380 gallons.

As might be expected from the different economic factors involved, the extent to which the potentialities of the potato as a source of alcohol have been exploited varies considerably in the different potato growing countries. In the United Kingdom and the United States such a use of the potato is negligible. In Eire there has recently been a little production of alcohol from potatoes[2] though the possibility of using them was considered as long ago as 1917. On the continent of Europe on the other hand, alcohol production is important. Werner[3] mentioned the annual peace-time use in Germany of $1\frac{1}{2}$ million tons of potatoes for alcohol production, a proportion of which quantity would be used for the manufacture of liquor, such as Schnaps; while in Russia, Barron[4] stated that alcohol, produced from potatoes, was used on a large scale as a starting point in the production of synthetic rubber.

Acetone may be produced by the bacterial fermentation of starch-containing vegetable products such as maize. As in the case of alcohol production, potatoes, though a less efficient raw material, can be used,

[1] Drew, J. P. and Deasy, D. (1939). Potato growing in Ireland with particular reference to production for industrial purposes. *J. Dep. Agric. Eire*, vol. XXXVI, pp. 205–29.
[2] Ibid.
[3] Werner, H. (1930). *Der Kartoffelbau* (9th edit. revised by K. Opitz). Berlin: Paul Parey.
[4] Barron, H. (1943). *Modern Synthetic Rubbers* (2nd. edit.). London: Chapman and Hall.

and acetone has been produced from them to some extent in Germany and also, at the beginning of the War of 1914–18, in this country.

To conclude: some branches of the crop drying and food industries have developed from attempts to remove the chief disadvantages of the potato—namely, its bulkiness and its impermanence. The importance of potato drying and canning varies considerably in different parts of the world. In the British Isles and the United States of America such uses of the potato were slight before the War of 1939–45, and their magnitude in the future cannot yet be assessed although, in Great Britain, mashed potato powder is being manufactured on a large scale. Where price is not a serious consideration, the reduced bulk and weight, and the extreme ease with which a dish can be prepared, may make such products welcome to restaurateurs and to the housewife who has no domestic help. On the continent of Europe the use of potato-flour was common even in peace-time, but nevertheless only some 1·5% of the German crop was dried.[1]

The potato provides a readily obtainable but uneconomic source of starch or the products which may be produced from starch. Its disadvantages as such (due to the high proportion of water it contains) are partially offset—though not from the manufacturers point of view—by the fact that, in temperate climates, it yields more starch per acre than any other crop. The importance of this latter varies with the economic conditions peculiar to the different countries, and the availability of alternative raw materials. In the British Isles and the United States of America the potato has been almost disregarded as a raw material, but it is extensively used in Russia and continental Europe. It should be noted, however, that the amounts of potatoes used in industry are of a different order of magnitude to the quantities used for food. Of the world's production of potatoes a greater proportion is probably used for stock-feeding than for any other single purpose, closely followed by the proportion used for human consumption. An analysis of the normal peace-time uses of the German potato crop[2] showed that less than 7% was used for distilling, starch manufacture and drying, compared with 10% wasted and nearly 70% used for human consumption and stock-feeding, practically all the remainder of the crop being kept as 'seed'.

[1] Werner, H. (1930). Op. cit.
[2] Ibid.

CHAPTER XXXII

The Potato in War-Time

War in an island community such as ours, so long as the country itself was not overrun, could hardly fail to act as a stimulus to increased production of home-grown food. During the Napoleonic wars the necessity of producing more wheat hastened on the enclosures, and improved the husbandry of the country. But unfortunately, in the absence of all controls, it led to such an inflation of wheat prices, that the masses were driven not merely to consume potatoes as a substitute for bread but, in the end, to accept it permanently as one of the chief sources of nourishment. Hence it is that whilst the acreage under potatoes increased considerably during the war years, it increased very much more in the subsequent decades.

On the Continent, prior to the Napoleonic wars, there is evidence that the potato occasionally influenced either directly or indirectly, the conduct of the late eighteenth century campaigns.

It was during the Seven Years War, 1756–63, that Parmentier, who was in the French Army in Hanover, first met the potato. He had become, for the fifth time, a prisoner of war in the hands of the Prussians, and having only potatoes to live on, he appreciated to the full their value as a food. Indeed, without them, he tells us, he could scarce have survived.[1] It was his war experiences, which inspired him to work for the reintroduction of the potato into France. During the wars of the Revolution, Parmentier redoubled his efforts to popularize its cultivation, and in most of the departments his efforts, which received the fullest support from the National Convention, were crowned with success.

Fifteen years later, in 1778, Frederick the Great attacked Austria, and for two years Europe was once more plunged into war, the War of the Bavarian Succession. This campaign is commonly spoken of as the 'Kartoffel Krieg', or 'Potato War', the reason for which will appear directly. The campaign from the start was indecisive. Frederick invaded Bohemia by way of the town of Nachod, and his and the Austrian armies eventually faced each other on the upper Elbe, in the neighbourhood of Königgratz. Although Prussian troops under Prince Henry threatened the Austrian flank, Frederick, partly owing to shortage of supplies, and partly because of the strength of the Austrian position, determined that the campaign, as he had conceived it, could not succeed. 'Both the Prussian and the Austrian armies thenceforth confined themselves to the

[1] Roze, E. (1898). *Hist. de la Pomme de Terre*, p. 162.

"potato-war"—that is, they consumed the resources of the enemy's country, till the cold weather set in and forced them to terminate their inglorious campaign by evacuating Bohemia.'[1]

There is a notable difference between the part played by the potato here, and that in Cromwell's campaign in Ireland. In the latter, the invader planned to chastise and overawe a peasant people, by means of harassing bands after the chief urban centres had been subdued, as the result of decisive engagements. When such tactics were pursued, the potato proved a source of strength to the enemy, for the scattered lazy-beds of potatoes still remained intact and at the disposal of the peasantry. But when encamped armies deliberately establish themselves in a countryside, the potato crop proves a ready and easily gathered source of supply for a commissariat operating on a large scale.

In the Bohemian campaign, the part played by the potato was essentially a passive one, and its chief interest for us lies in the evidence it affords of the wide extent of potato cultivation in that part of Europe twenty years and more before it had attained any comparable development in England south of the Trent.

The two great World Wars present new features in regard to the feeding both of combatant and non-combatant. The submarine and aeroplane have radically altered the character of war; the struggle has spread from the field of battle to every home in the lands of the combatants, however distant; indeed, as we have learned to our cost, its destructive force respects no boundary, whether of friend or foe. In the early days of the War of 1914–18, this truism was by no means generally recognized, and its lesson had to be painfully learnt, even by those in control.

At the outbreak of war in 1914, although everybody in England was aware that we were importing four-fifths of our cereals and two-fifths of our meat, no preparations had been made to expand home-production. At that time the aeroplane was a minor and almost negligible source of food destruction; it was the submarine which was the potential and, as it proved later, the most dangerous weapon directed against our food supplies. In the first year, the shipping losses were not very severe and did little to disturb the complacent attitude of the authorities or of the public. No steps of any kind were taken till April 1915, when the losses at sea began to look rather more serious, but all that was done was to appoint a strong committee under Lord Milner, to consider means for increasing home-production 'on the assumption that the war may be prolonged beyond the harvest of 1916'. In an interim report, it was suggested that a minimum price for wheat should be guaranteed for four years, that statements as to the arable areas of the United Kingdom in

[1] *Cam. Mod. Hist.* (1909), vol. VI, p. 706.

1875 and 1914 respectively, be prepared and communicated to district committees set up by the County Councils, and that the district committees should report on the willingness and capacity of the local farmers to co-operate.

Nothing further was done till December 1916 when, in addition to the disappointment caused by a disastrous harvest, the shipping losses of the previous twelve months made it abundantly clear that the danger of starvation at home was as great, or greater, than that of defeat in Flanders. In the interests of the army in the field, the countryside had been denuded of labour and horses; steam-tackle had been demobilized; the accessory trades, even that of the blacksmith, were closed down or brought to a standstill; to which must be added an acute shortage of potash and phosphate fertilizers.

The first step was to set up the sixty-one executive war committees recommended by the Milner Committee; this was followed by the creation of a Food Production Department of the Ministry of Agriculture. This new body had wide powers which it used with outstanding ability. It could, and did, supply seeds of all kinds, fertilizers, horses, tractors, as well as directing labour. It had power to fix the prices of all farm products and the price of labour; and, finally, it had compulsory powers in respect to the cultivation of the land.

At last the campaign for increased production at home got under way. Its task was indeed a hard one: the wheat area had fallen by 600,000 acres since 1913, and that under potatoes had been stationary for many years. The authorities, the farmers, and, not least the public, threw themselves wholeheartedly into the fight to raise more food. Whilst the main advance was based on the plough, and the conversion of grassland to tillage, the use of the spade was not ignored. Allotments sprang up everywhere and all classes, in town and country, took their share in their cultivation. The number in the country of such allotments, mostly ¼ acre in size, rose during 1917 and 1918 from 54,000 to 140,000 in England and Wales. By 1918, our home-grown food, both cereal and potatoes, had increased by over 50%. However, not all of this was gain: had the grasslands been retained as pasture we should have had some 100,000 tons more of beef. Against that, the country had an annual increase of nearly 4,000,000 quarters of corn, and 1½ million tons of potatoes. See Table III.

At this time the convoy system had gone far to control the submarine menace; still, a programme for the conversion of a further 1,000,000 acres from grass to arable was prepared for 1919, but this, after the collapse of the German front, was cancelled.

Between December 1916 and the harvest of 1918 an increase of about 1,700,000 acres under cereals and 170,000 acres under potatoes had been added to our arable cultivations. The latter, as it does not include the new allotments, does not represent the full increase of new land under potatoes. These, which were largely devoted to potato-raising, may be regarded as accounting for a further area of about 20,000 acres, making an increase of 190,000 acres under potatoes in England and Wales, or 41% over the pre-war acreage, as compared with a corresponding increase of 30% in the acreage under cereals.

Table III. *England and Wales*

Crops	1918	Increase		Percentage of increase	
		Over 1916	Over 1904–13	Over 1916	Over 1904–13
		1916	1904–13	1916	1904–13	1916	1904–13

Crops	1918	1916	1904–13	Over 1916	Over 1904–13	Over 1916	Over 1904–13
		(In thousands of quarters)					
Wheat	10,534	6,835	6,653	3,699	3,881	54	58
Barley	6,085	5,181	6,212	904	−127	17	−2
Oats	14,336	10,411	10,572	3,925	3,764	38	36
Mixed corn	620*	—*	—*	620	620	—	—
Beans and peas	1,328	1,122	1,529	206	−201	18	−13
Total	32,903	23,549	24,966	9,354	7,937	49	32
		(In thousands of tons)					
Potatoes	4,209	2,505	2,643	1,704	1,566	68	59

* Mixed corn is shown separately in 1918. In previous years it is shown under wheat, barley, or oats. (From Ernle. Op. cit. p. 407.)

It is of interest to compare the difference between the war agricultural policy of 1914–18 with that pursued during the Napoleonic wars just a hundred years back. In both the objective was the same—the production at home of more bread, or its equivalent. In the earlier period the task was technically much easier because we were accustomed to feed ourselves entirely off our own land; the countryside was fully equipped with man and horse-power, and the task of increasing supplies could be materially assisted by the cutting down of avenues of waste, such as the use of corn in distilleries, of starch as hair-powder, and the excessive use of corn to the large population of luxury horses. But, as Lord Ernle[1] points out, there was a deeper and more significant difference between the two periods: in the Napoleonic period the consumer was not considered at all; in the War of 1914–18 he was the focus around which the whole food production plan was designed. It was a distinction which epitomizes a century's march towards democracy. In the earlier period the stimulus of production was the high prices which the farmer secured in return for his effort; in the latter the Government relied, and not in vain, on the farmers' patriotism, and far less on the material reward.

[1] Ernle, Lord (1912). *English Farming* (ed. 1936), p. 400.

In the War of 1939–45 the same principles held good, but the technique was improved and the scope of the undertaking extended. The administration realized, and the figures of the previous war proved, that the potato was hardly second to wheat in its value as a war-time food; but its control in the interests of the public as a whole presented greater difficulties. The problem has been very clearly put by Beveridge:[1]

As a producer of problems for Food Controllers, the potato has no rival in the vegetable or the animal world. With average crops it yields a much higher food value per acre than any cereal, and is therefore attractive to administrators who have just learned about calories. But the advantage is diminished by the greater cost of production and the labour involved. Still more is it affected by the highly speculative nature of the crop, and the difficulty either of making good a shortage by importation or of finding markets for a surplus. Owing to its very variable crop, its limited storage life, its susceptibility to disease and its relative large bulk, it is subject to great variations of price. With the potato we are back in the period before international trade; its prices rise and fall precipitously, as did that of wheat in the Middle Ages.

The major administrative troubles in connection with the potato in 1917 arose owing to an unusually heavy crop; special methods were necessary to deal with it. The fixing of minimum prices was not difficult in face of a glut, but the disposal of the surplus was another matter. In October 1917, the Ministry were forced to buy up the entire crop and resell it to the dealers at fixed prices, which varied both with the variety and the district. The retail prices were equally controlled, at 1*d*. and 1¼*d*. per lb. The scheme, though very difficult and somewhat costly to the taxpayer, was a great success, for it encouraged both a larger area under potatoes and heavier yields as a result of more intensive cultivation.

The potato acreage in the United Kingdom rose from 1,170,000 acres (the average of 1904–13) to 1,380,000 in 1917, and 1,510,000 in 1919; the tonnage which had averaged 6,540,000 before the war, fell at the end of 1916 to 5,470,000.

Just at the moment when our food stocks were at the lowest, the farmers, no less than the owners of gardens and allotments, replied to this challenge with so good a will that by 1918 the harvest returns showed a crop of 9,220,000 tons.

In view of the difficulties of controlling a crop so liable to gluts, so difficult to store for any length of time, and so costly to transport, it was not surprising that when the farmers asked for the government control to be extended into 1919 they were met with a polite but firm refusal. Indeed, control of the potato can only be prolonged beyond a period of

---

[1] Beveridge, Sir William H. (1928). *British Food Control*, pp. 153 and 161. Oxford Univ. Press.

crisis if provision is made to deal with gluts by methods which would convert the excess tubers into some processed material such as flour, dried matter for cattle-food, alcohol, or the like. And when such has been done the problem of the economic disposal of such products under peace-time conditions still remains; notwithstanding, it is interesting to note that the country looked to the potato to eke out its bread shortage, and not to rye, whose acreage of 50,000 remained practically unaltered during the war years.

The potato's role in the War of 1914–18 can best be gauged from the official figures showing the weekly average individual consumption before and during the war; these figures include the potatoes used in the making of the National loaf:

	1909–13	1914	1915	1916	1917	1918
Weekly consumption in lbs. per head of population	3·67	4·29	4·44	4·07	3·84	5·26

The War of 1939–45 found us little, if any, better prepared on the Food Front as far as supplies were concerned, than we were in 1914. But technically, administratively and, if one may use the term in this relation, spiritually, we were much better equipped. Not only had we the experience of 1917–18 behind us, but we knew that the enemy's attack on our shipping would be an all-out one from the start.

In the War of 1914–18 the main effort had been directed towards the recovery of the lost acreage under wheat, and it was rather later that it was realized that the potato might fill the gap more economically, seeing that one acre under potatoes will, on a conservative estimate, feed at least four times as many persons as one acre under wheat. Now, all looked with confidence to the potato to safeguard the nation's larder.

In the United Kingdom the potato had been employed almost exclusively as a crop for the table, hence we could not do, as was commonly done on the Continent, switch over the potatoes grown for industrial purposes, for use as human food. It was obviously necessary to extend to the utmost the acreage under potatoes.

From the outset the supreme importance of the food supply was recognized, and a Ministry of Food was set up. Its functions were to regulate, in the widest sense, all supplies, whether home-grown or imported, from the country of origin or our own fields, till they reached the table of every citizen. Nor did its duty end there; it had not only to find the food, but to see that it was equally distributed at prices which would allow everyone to acquire an adequate supply.

To determine what was an adequate dietary, what its caloric value, its vitamin content, its palatability, its keeping-qualities, its behaviour during transport and, not least, its accessibility, were but some of the hundred and one problems which the Ministry of Food, in conjunction with the Ministry of Agriculture, had to face and attempt to solve. That the country was fed adequately, the health of the civilian and military population maintained under conditions of unimaginable danger and difficulty, at a level considerably higher than the poorer classes had ever enjoyed in peace-time, was a triumph of which this country may be justly proud.

Whilst it would be out of place to attempt to tell, even in outline, the tale of how the task of feeding the nation was carried out during the war-years, one cannot recount the part taken by the potato in isolation, for there was throughout a close relation maintained between the supplies of the chief feeding-stuffs—bread, meat, potatoes, sugar and fats. The position of the country as regards its cereal supplies before the war was the same as that prior to the last: we still grew but one-fifth of our requirements. Against that, practically all our potatoes, other than a small import of luxury early potatoes, were raised within the British Isles. But inasmuch as the population of the country had increased whilst the potato acreage had at best remained constant, the average consumption per head of population was falling, as it had been doing for a generation. The experience of the War of 1914–18 was firmly implanted in the official mind. 'In 1917 it was only because we had a good stock of potatoes in hand, that we survived the critical U-boat peril.'[1]

In the War of 1939–45 our food imports were in danger from the beginning, and our losses due to submarine attacks very serious during the first four years. The shortage was met, as before, by ploughing up grasslands, and concentrating on cereals, potatoes and sugar-beet; the difference between the two war efforts was one of degree rather than of kind. This war saw 5 million acres of additional land put under the plough in England and Wales, of which about 1½ millions were devoted to wheat, ½ million to potatoes, and 70,000 to sugar-beet, in the first two cases an increase of just on 100%, notwithstanding the loss of the early potato crop from the Channel Islands, and in the last, an increase of 25%.

The actual increase of crop was greater than that dictated by the acreage owing to the improved cultivation of the land consequent on the mechanization of the industry.

The policy of the Government was to regard potatoes as the main reserve for calories, necessary for the maintenance of the day-to-day output of human energy, replacing imports and acting throughout as a substitute for bread.

Potatoes were controlled centrally by a body, known as the Potato and Carrot Division, of the Ministry of Food under Capt. Sir John Mollett, and production was directed peripherally by the War Agricultural

[1] *Land at War* (1944), p. 35. London: Stationery Office.

Executive Committees throughout the country. The pressure of the war, transmitted as it was to these local bodies of farmers and experts, led to potatoes being grown in districts where the farming population had never raised a tuber outside their kitchen gardens. They were grown, and that with success, on land which in normal times would have been regarded as either too heavy or too light, or deficient in humus, and, above all, they were raised with a minimum of farmyard manure and insufficient dressings of fertilizers, notwithstanding that such supplies as there were, were directed primarily to the potato and beet crops. The factor which converted what, twenty years ago, might well have been failure into more or less complete success, was the latent fertility of the soil, brought into action by deep ploughing and efficient cultivation, consequent on the use of the tractor.

The plan of the Ministry in respect to the potato, was to guarantee a market for the entire crop, but in order to encourage farmers to make the best of the poorer soils they gave a bonus of £10 per acre to all producers of an acre and over, balanced, to some extent, by a reduction in tonnage price of approximately 30s. Prices were fixed at every stage of the potato's progress from the field to the consumer. To encourage consumption, an elaborate campaign was maintained which began by fixing the retail prices with the help of subsidies at levels low enough to make the potato the most welcome, as well as the most available, foodstuff to the housewife, and thereby persuade her to substitute potatoes for bread.

Propaganda by speech, poster, cartoon and reasoned article in the Press followed; all adopted the same policy. A few examples will suffice: in Pl. XXII, fig. 76, Lord Woolton, the Minister of Food, speaks; in fig. 77 it is his Ministry, and in fig. 78 the Press endorses their messages by means of cartoons. In addition, pamphlets and booklets of useful recipes for potato dishes were put on sale at every bookstall. Perhaps the most effective weapon used by the Ministry of Food was the early morning talks on the B.B.C. by the artistes 'Gert and Daisy' (the Misses Elsie and Doris Waters), who combined humour and good sense in a manner rarely, if ever, equalled.

Sales by growers were made chiefly to licensed buyers, but the Ministry of Food bought the farmer's potatoes in the clamp in order to secure a guaranteed market and a stock of good keeping types for an end of the season reserve. The relative proportions between the tubers fit for table use, those for seed, and the chats destined for fodder, were regulated by means of orders issued from time to time defining the size of mesh to be used in the riddles employed in the sorting machines for the different classes of varieties.

To make the crop spread more evenly over the year, the digging of early varieties was, at the writer's suggestion, delayed so that heavier crops might accrue, a procedure which added over a quarter of a million tons to our total annual supply.

As time went on the Ministry kept an increasingly tight control on the 'earlies' in Cornwall, the Scilly Isles and the Tamar Valley; it took over all the stocks grown on areas of a $\frac{1}{4}$ acre and over. The plan of delaying lifting 'earlies', already referred to, was later extended to the maincrop varieties so as to prevent immature stocks, particularly those of 'King Edward' and 'Majestic', being put on the market as 'earlies' in order to obtain the higher price. The sale of varieties was staggered throughout the season in accordance with their maturity and in relation to their keeping qualities. This latter measure allowed of the best keeping varieties such as 'Arran Peak' and 'Arran Consul' being held over for use at the end of the season, before the new potatoes reached the market.

Transport by road and rail was severely restricted, and instead, much use was made both of canal and marine services. In 1944, when transport was taxed to the utmost by the large-scale movements of men and munitions, an Order was made by which the United Kingdom was divided into twenty-four divisions, and only by special licence could potatoes be shifted into certain specified areas.

Damage by frost was another difficulty which caused considerable loss, due in the main to the shortage of tarpaulin coverings for the trucks, and straw with which to insulate the sacks. Although the authorities took such steps as were possible, the losses in 1943 were often heavy. Dry rot, following the rough handling often experienced under the strained transport conditions was, at one time, a source of serious trouble.

Notwithstanding that the objective was to get potatoes to the people in as large a bulk as possible, yet the Ministry went to great lengths to study the wishes and prejudices of the trade. The most elaborate price regulations were devised in order to give due preference to potatoes coming off the different types of soil: limestone, red soils, skirtlands, and the like. These, again, differed according to the variety grown; the following were regarded as the best varieties: 'King Edward', 'Gladstone', 'Red Skin', and 'Golden Wonder' and, in consequence, commanded higher prices throughout. Actually, the difference in price between such, and more productive varieties, as 'Majestic', was not so great as in pre-war days; the consequence was, that under the Order the heavy yielders were more favoured. The list is of interest because, although there is no sound evidence that any of these, with the possible exception of 'Golden Wonder', is better in taste than 'Majestic' or 'Arran Peak', it does correspond to a certain pattern of popular taste.

As has been pointed out, one of the most difficult features of an efficient control of potatoes is the economic disposal of a surplus. This problem was approached by the Ministry in two ways. They made use of the sugar-beet factories for the conversion of potatoes into dried meal for cattle, and they created some twenty specially designed potato factories in the chief producing areas. These latter turned out a more refined product, mainly in the form of dried, high quality strips, which were sent overseas for the use of the Forces.

A good overall picture of the control can be obtained from the monthly figures for 1944 and 1945, recording the quantity at the disposal of the Ministry, and the amount consumed as food:

	1944		1945	
	Total disposals	Food	Total disposals	Food
	(In thousands of tons per week in Great Britain)			
Jan.	127·4	123·8	111·6	109·0
Feb.	134·0	128·5	141·8	136·3
March	136·0	129·3	120·0	115·0
April	129·6	122·4	121·0	117·8
May	118·5	111·8	105·5	101·5
June	111·8	103·0	84·3	83·5
July	103·0	95·2	97·0	92·6
Aug.	93·5	93·0	100·3	95·3
Sept.	103·3	103·0	113·3	106·0
Oct.	110·2	109·6	104·6	101·6
Nov.	113·8	113·0	120·5	110·0
Dec.	117·3	115·8	122·3	107·5

From the above it will be seen there was very little surplus for purposes other than human consumption.

When such surplus was destined for fodder purposes it was 'denatured' by the addition of a little dyestuff which discoloured the skin of the tuber; it was then sold at a reduced price to stock-owners through the recognized trade channels.

Table IV, which gives the acreage under potatoes each year in England, Wales, Scotland and Northern Ireland respectively, shows how, within five years, it was doubled. The output was even more than doubled: improved husbandry in the country generally, thanks to the War Agricultural Executive Committees, and the extended use of fertilizers, resulted in an increase in the average output from 6·7 to 7·0 tons per acre.

Table IV. *The acreage under Potatoes to the nearest* 1000 *acres*

	1939	1940	1941	1942	1943	1944	1945
England	438	515	729	836	890	913	918
Wales	17	22	48	63	67	67	64
Scotland	134	157	189	218	236	239	226
Northern Ireland	115	137	157	187	197	198	190
Great Britain	704	831	1123	1304	1390	1417	1398

Such was the achievement; the means by which it was achieved may be briefly epitomized as follows.

The Department of Potatoes and Carrots had to adjust supplies and distribution in such a manner as to neutralize both gluts and scarcities of the potato crop itself. It had to work through the established channels of the wholesale and retail trades with the least possible friction, and hold a just balance between them and the public. It had to meet the requirements of the seed trade and, at the same time, in order to make sure of the next year's crop, insist that only high quality seed was planted throughout the country. It had to watch for the spread of disease in the crop, supply the growers with the necessary safeguards and the machinery with which to apply them. It had to ensure that every ton of surplus stocks should be used to eke out the feeding-stuff of pigs and poultry. All these considerations needed to be so co-ordinated that the ultimate object, viz. the harbouring of our wheat resources, and the offering to the public of an adequate supply of an acceptable substitute, was attained. A test of the Department's efficiency may be found in the fact that each season's crop was, in fact, disposed of. There was no annual carry-over of stocks.

Potato control was but one of many excursions into the realms of bureaucratic control which the war forced on a public which, by age-old tradition, was hostile to, and distrustful of, such methods. Of this particular venture it may be said that it achieved a measure of success which it is difficult to believe could have been attained by individual initiative, however well intentioned.

PLATE XXII

Fig. 76. Lord Woolton's appeal for greater production of and use of the potato. *The Times*, 5 December 1942.

Fig. 77. 'Eat more potatoes instead.' *The Times*, 14 January 1943.

Fig. 78. 'Eat potatoes.' *Daily Express*, 18 January 1943.

PLATE XXIII

Fig. 79. Cascrome from Loch Uiskevage, Benbecula

Fig. 80   Fig. 81

Fig. 80. Crocan of wood, for digging potatoes and lifting
sea-weed. From Benbecula.

Fig. 81. Crocan of iron, potato digger, early nineteenth century.
From South Uist.

PLATE XXIV

Fig. 82. A spirally twisted scythe blade, mounted on handle, for cutting potatoes for cattle-feed.

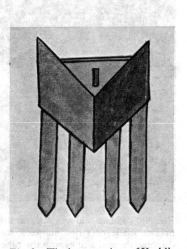

Fig. 83. The bottom piece of Yeald's hoe, for lifting potatoes, with its double mould-board and forward projecting prongs. *The Culture and Use of the Potato*, Board of Agriculture, 1795, p. 40.

Fig. 84. Three-row P. G. M. potato planter.

PLATE XXV

Fig. 85. Potato plough, tractor drawn, with broad flat share, and double breasts made of strips allowing soil to drop through the slats; tail prongs disperse the soil and expose the tubers.

Fig. 86. Potato digger, spinner type, tractor drawn. The horizontal share passes below the tubers, loosening the soil. The spinner revolves behind, its free pendulous tines strike the raised soil, pushing the tubers out to the right. The power is transmitted from the driving wheels.

PLATE XXVI

Fig. 87. Potato harvester: Johnson. A digging-share raises the potatoes on to a front elevator web, separating the soil and passing the tubers to a second web which transfers them to a crosswise conveyor elevator which drops them into a trailer.

Fig. 88. Potato elevator digger: by John Deere, U.S.A. A broadshare passes below the tubers, pushing the soil and tubers on to a moving elevator web of metal rods mechanically agitated; the soil falls away, the tubers pass to a second moving web, which deposits them in an even row.

PLATE XXVII

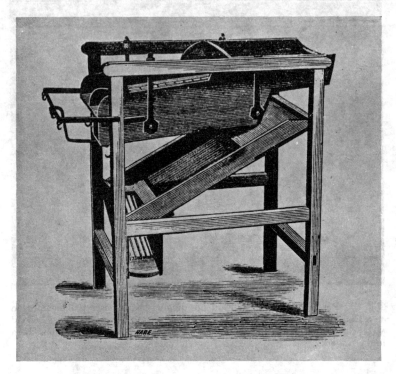

Fig. 89. Cooch's potato separator, 1885 model.

Fig. 90. Cooch's motor-driven potato sorter, 1944 model.

PLATE XXVIII

Fig. 91. Still life. By Vincent van Gogh. Painted at Nuenen, 1885.

CHAPTER XXXIII

The Implements of Production, and their Relation to the Economics of the Crop

The tools by which our staple food crops are sown, cultivated, and finally harvested, are obviously amongst the most important of human devices, whether for war or peace, for it is ultimately by their means that control over the environment is won and maintained. Whilst their development and efficiency may have little or no relation to the intellectual or spiritual development of the people who use them, they may yet afford us a valuable measure of the tension which is never altogether absent between the size of the human group and the volume and quality of its available supplies of food. When and where such tension is at its lowest, as in a tropical and humid country, then the cultivators' tools are not only simple, but may persist unaltered over long intervals of time. If conditions are such as to increase that tension, whether it be by the introduction of some practice such as vaccination which induces a material increase of population, or by the occurrence of some epidemic disease such as the Potato Blight, causing a decrease of supplies, then an effort to improve both the methods and tools of agriculture, or a mass migration to a more generous habitat, will ensue.

Examples of tools which have undergone an ordered development through the ages are the digging-stick and the sickle, each of which is still with us in its simple and almost elementary form, as the hedger's sickle, and the gardener's dibbling-stick. Both, however, have undergone so intensive a development that their descendants, the mower and the mechanical grab, show no outward signs of their ancestry. In all cases the motive underlying the progressive development of our agricultural tools is similar, namely, the necessity to do the like amount of work at a greater speed, or, what is much the same thing, to cause the same amount of work to be done by a lesser number of people.

Sometimes the transition is brought about by the discovery and use of new material: the sickle, originally made of flint or stone, is, with the discovery of metal, later made of bronze, and finally of iron. By this means it has become a much more competent and serviceable tool, but it is still a sickle, and does not represent any new idea.

In much the same way the wooden digging-stick, and its immediate shovel-like developments (Pl. XVI, figs. 40 and 41), have become transformed into our common garden spade and fork. A more important step forward was taken when the iron sickle, still a one-handed tool, enlarged and remounted, was converted into a scythe. The progress effected by such a change is not to be measured by the ingenuity of the underlying idea, or the mechanical dexterity of its manufacture, but rather by the economic development that followed in its train.

In a recent lecture it was pointed out[1] that an active worker with the scythe could cut down a couple of acres of corn in the same time as another with a sickle would take to reap at most a quarter of the same amount. Before the scythe, in its turn, was replaced by modern machinery, there was developed in relation to it an adjustment so simple that its high significance has scarcely been recognized. A light wooden cradle was attached to the blade and handle, which allowed a uniform quantity of the crop at each swing of the scythe, to be deposited in an orderly way along the track pursued by the reaper. This is but one example of many of those anonymous contributions to social progress which creep almost imperceptibly into our midst and which, after a period of dormancy, undergo so intensive and varied a development that the world is apt to forget their humble origin, and to fail to recognize in those marvels of ingenuity, the mower, the binder, and, finally, the harvester, its lineal descendants. Each of these tools outstrips its predecessor in economic worth in exactly the same manner as the scythe did the sickle.

It is commonly accepted that the use of roots as a foodstuff preceded the cultivation of plants propagated by sowing; hence as might be expected, the tools by which their cultivation was effected, would be of the simplest. In the digging-stick, used by the pre-Incan Peruvian for planting his potatoes, and in similar tools used by early man in all parts of the world, we see the original form of all the spade family of tools. In the *taclla* of Peru (Fig. 46, p. 48), and the *cascrome* of the Scotch Highlands (Pl. XXIII, fig. 79), we see examples of its early development into a more effective and economically valuable instrument.

The potato arrived in Western Europe at a time when agricultural methods in England, and above all in Holland, were undergoing a very lively development. In England this was characterized by the change over in many parts of the country of the common open arable field to the enclosed farm units, the recovery and enclosure of much waste-land, and an intensive development of sheep culture. In Holland, the leading agricultural country of the world, emphasis was laid on the intensive cultivation of a greater variety of vegetable crops and, above all, on the inclusion of clover and turnips into the farm rotation. Great as were the economic changes involved in the tenure and management of the land, no corresponding development in the character of the agricultural tools

---

[1] Davies, Cornelius (1944). Harvesting Machinery. *Proc. Inst. of Brit. Agric. Engineering*, vol. III, pp. 64–76.

which even the best agriculturist of the day had at his disposal, had been effected.

Throughout the Tudor and Stuart periods it was the tempo rather than the volume of national life which was quickened. The feverish spirit of the Renaissance showed itself in the daily life of the people by a demand for better housing and furnishing, higher quality and more varied clothing, and a richer and more abundant diet. Industry had taken on not merely a new life, but a new form. Capitalism, whatever may be thought of it to-day, was at that time an inspiring and fructifying force, improving the technique and enlarging the scope of national and international trade and finance. The people of this country enjoyed a larger, richer, more varied and dynamic life than they had previously experienced, but this was not accompanied by any outstanding increase in their numbers. The intake of assart or waste-lands, and the enclosure of the open field, so far as they had proceeded, still allowed for an ample supply of food for all, and left a surplus for export.

There was as yet no strong urge to increase the yield per acre, nor to economize on the quantity of labour employed. What enclosures did was to save time and allow the same number of persons to do more effective work.

It was not till the following century that, under the inspiration of Jethro Tull (1674–1741), our methods of cultivation were radically amended; old instruments were greatly improved, and a new one, the seed drill, invented. But perhaps the most important of all was his introduction of the practice of the horse-hoeing of crops which, though first applied to the turnip crop, was later to assume as important a role in the cultivation of the potato. Both Tull's improvement of the farmers' mechanical tools, and Bakewell's that of his animals the sheep, the ox, and the horse, were coincident with and introduced by the new type of industrial activity, which found its chief expression in the large-scale mechanization of the spinning and weaving of wool, linen, and later of cotton,[1] all of which were in process of ceasing to be home industries and were being transferred to large power-driven factories in the towns and larger villages. The development of the provincial towns, in association with the practice of vaccination and the recent introduction of improved water supplies and drainage, evoked an unprecedented increase of the population, which necessitated a vast increase in the supply of foodstuffs.

In the agriculturally advanced countries there was no field cultivation of the potato till about the middle of the eighteenth century, nor for the next fifty years did its cultivation assume any great dimension, although it had, during the interval, enjoyed all the improvements of technique

---

[1] The cotton industry from its inception was conducted in factories.

which by then had become incorporated into the general practice of farming. It was not till towards the close of the last century, when the demand for a cheap food for the industrial labourer rang out from every side, that tools specially designed for its cultivation made their appearance.

The relation of agricultural methods to economic demand can be followed in its simplest form by studying the manner in which the potato crop was handled in Ireland, the Western Highlands and the Lowlands of Scotland respectively. In Ireland the potatoes were raised in the lazy-bed, a method admirably suited to the soil conditions and the circumstances which dominated the individual subsistence agriculture practised by a peasantry who had no outlet for their products beyond their immediate homes. So long as such conditions obtained, the lazy-bed and a simple spade were all that were necessary. Nearer the towns, where a market for potatoes existed, the lazy-bed was gradually replaced by the drill method.

In many isolated parts of western Ireland the lazy-bed system still holds sway, but both in the north and the south wherever the industry has taken on an industrial character, whether it be for the provision of ware to the towns, or the export of first-class 'seed' abroad, the methods of cultivation, though frequently hampered by the small size of the enclosed fields of a previous generation, have become modernized and improved *pari passu* with the growing demand of the new markets. So effective has been this new economic stimulus that the more favoured districts of Ireland in their agricultural technique are in no way behind that of the best potato-growing areas of England and Scotland.

In Scotland the relation between the volume of the demand for the produce and the development of the tools wherewith it is produced are seen to particular advantage, owing to the sharp contrast existing between the conditions geographical, social, economic, and even racial, of Highland and Lowland respectively.

In the Highlands of Scotland the potato was accepted, under what may not unfairly be described as duress, and grown exclusively as a subsistence crop by each family. Hence potato plots were small, frequently on poor soil, generally irregular in shape, and often broken up by the intrusion of rocky boulders. The lazy-bed system was the commonly adopted method of cultivation. Use was made of the primitive foot-plough, or Cascrome[1] (Pl. XXIII, fig. 79). Wooden harrows with horn tines were used for breaking up the clods, but neither hoeing nor cleaning of the growing crop were customary in the Highlands prior to 1845. Harvesting was undertaken with a simple wooden hook, or Crocan (Pl. XXIII, fig. 80). In the nineteenth century this was replaced by a similar instrument made of iron (Pl. XXIII, fig. 81), a definite advance in technique from what Andrew Lang has not inappropriately called the

---

[1] A letter from Sir Hugh Rankin to R.N.S. in 1949 states that the Cascrome was still in use in Shetland in 1938 to the exclusion of all horse-drawn or mechanically driven implements (Salaman's manuscript note). – Ed.

'wooden age' of Highland culture. Another hand-made tool found at this period amongst the small-holders of the Celtic fringe of Britain was one designed to cut the raw potato tubers into small segments, preparatory to feeding them to stock and poultry. It consists of the blade of a scythe coiled on itself, and mounted on a long handle (Pl. XXIV, fig. 82). Its occurrence in the early nineteenth century is probably bound up with the widespread cultivation of the yam potato, the crop of which was devoted entirely to the feeding of cattle and horses.

In the Lowlands, at the end of the eighteenth century, spade culture, as well as the lazy-bed system, were to be found alongside the more efficient method of planting in drills, the latter, however, predominating where there was a market outlet to a neighbouring town. In some counties, such as Dumfriesshire and Kirkcudbrightshire, an export trade to Bristol was already in being, and it is here that better tillage prevailed. The cultivation of the potato in the immediate neighbourhood of the lesser towns of the Lowlands was in the main conducted on small plots of land and most of it by spade labour. The custom by which tradesmen and town workers hired plots from neighbouring farmers, up to an acre in extent, on which they grew their own potatoes, helped to perpetuate spade labour because the sum of individual crops reduced the volume of the wholesale demand, and with it the necessity of large-scale field culture. As far as one can discover, not even in the best cultivated parts of the Lowlands were implements specially designed for potato-raising in use during the first decade of the nineteenth century, although it is possible that such may have been the case in districts in close proximity to Glasgow and Edinburgh, where a considerable acreage was devoted to the production of potatoes for the markets of these two cities.[1]

Later in the nineteenth century, the advantage of a change of seed from Scotland, as a means of combating the ravages of the 'Curl', was recognized, and as a result a very important industry, both in seed and ware potatoes, was created in the richest lands of the South and East Lowlands. It is here that some of the best examples of potato cultivation, including the use of the most modern methods, are to be seen.

In England, agricultural methods and implements, by the end of the nineteenth century, had reached not only a higher development than elsewhere, but one more in harmony with the ever-expanding economic opportunities of the time.

It was not long before the demand for potatoes in the towns, especially in London, necessitated field cultivation. Sowing was carried out by planting in the furrow and ridging up with the plough, and the crop was raised by hand with a fork. The Napoleonic wars induced a greatly increased price of wheat and a corresponding demand for a

[1] *The London Chronicle* of 1766 mentions that a Mr Randall of York has produced a special plough for sowing and covering potato tubers (Salaman's manuscript note). – Ed.

cheaper substitute, the potato. It was now that a plough with a double mould-board was used for clearing out furrows and was found of great service both in the sowing of the tuber and again in the autumn, when it reopened the ridges for their harvesting, leaving the potatoes exposed and ready for picking up by hand. Another type of plough, constructed by Mr Yeald of Herefordshire, and used by him prior to 1795, is probably the first tool designed exclusively to deal with this crop. Yeald's implement[1] was a plough mounted on a pair of fore wheels and furnished with a wide double moulding-board made of a metal sheet bent at right angles, with the angle projecting; attached to the base of this board were four strong prongs which entered the ground in front of the mould-board and below the level of the tubers, throwing them up against the board, which dispersed them to either side. The plough was drawn by three horses or four oxen. Fig. 83 (Pl. XXIV) represents the essential lifting unit. Developments of this kind of lifter continued steadily, and in 1829 the Royal Agricultural Society awarded a prize of £5 for a paddle-plough for raising potatoes.

Similar methods are followed to-day on farms where the area under potatoes is limited to a few acres, except that the double-breasted ridging plough used in harvesting is fitted with prongs projecting backwards instead of continuous mould-boards, so that much of the earth falls between them.

In recent years this method of raising the crop has been mechanized. Ploughs of a like kind, originally drawn by horses, are now used behind a tractor whose greater speed much increases their efficiency (Pl. XXV, fig. 85). Although this method of raising the crop is probably the safest, inasmuch as it causes less bruising of the tubers, it is not to-day much used on the great potato farms of East Anglia, or in the potato areas of Eastern Scotland, because it tends to re-bury many of the tubers, a proportion of which get left behind, whilst at the same time it calls for more labour in the gathering of the crop.

During the recent war years (1939–45), two new factors have come to play a dominant part in the methods of potato cultivation. One is the enormously increased power now available to the farmer following the replacement of horses by more and more powerful tractors; the other, which has played the greater part in the determination of the type of tool to be used, is the unprecedented rise in the wages of the agricultural labourer, which, notwithstanding the government bonus on the acreage under potatoes, is out of all proportion to the wholesale price of the potato. Whilst the one allows the farmer a greatly extended choice in the type and capacity of his implement, permitting him to put far larger

[1] Board of Agriculture (1795). Report Committee on Culture and Use of Potatoes, p. 40.

quantities of his land under potatoes, the other narrows that choice to one which will consume the least manpower extended over the shortest time. To meet these new conditions there are now on the market planting machines such as that shown in Fig. 84. The mechanical planters have not as yet attained much support in this country because it is doubtful whether, on balance, they are really more economical than well-trained and organized labour gangs following on furrows drawn by the double-breasted potato plough, with the seed tubers arranged for them in trays or baskets at suitable intervals.

The harvesting of the crop on the large potato farms, however, is becoming more strictly mechanized every year. For this purpose we have two types of machine. The earlier and still the most widely used is the Spinner, introduced about 1860, in which a lifting share raises the potatoes by cutting the soil beneath them, behind which is a spinning-wheel, from which depend loosely hanging tines which act as a kind of flail, driving the potatoes out of the loosened earth and throwing them to one side. There are many varieties of Spinner: one of the more usual is shown in Fig. 86 (Pl. XXV). The drawbacks to this type of machine are twofold: it tends to bruise the tubers, especially on heavy land, and it scatters them over an unnecessarily wide surface, and thus calls for more labour than does the mechanical lifter. This latter machine consists essentially of a wide rather flattened share which passes below the potatoes in the ridge and pushes them on to an elevator belt made of transverse steel rods about an inch apart, which, whilst being continually rocked, carries tubers, earth and stones, up an inclined plane, during which the soil and smaller stones fall to the ground, whilst the tubers pass to a second web of rods which effects a further separation and finally drops them in a narrow concentrated row on the ground. These machines (Pl. XXVI, fig. 87) are extremely effective on the lighter types of land where there are not too many stones, but they cannot be used when the ground is too moist, as they tend to get clogged with the sticky soil.

In America, this type of lifter is sometimes fitted with a further elevator web of rods which raises the tubers from the end of the first and deposits them through a hopper into sacks or an accompanying lorry (Pl. XXVI, fig. 88). This type of machine is still faced by the difficulty of separating stones from tubers, other than by hand labour, travelling on the lifter. A later development is a lifter with an adjustment to deflect the potatoes into a smoothed depression made by a 'smoother-plough' attached to the lifter which leaves the tubers in a neat row ready to be picked up by hand.

On our most advanced potato farms in the Fen country, the economic balance between labour costs and the choice of machinery has to be very closely considered. For example, on one of the most outstanding group of farms where 1300 acres of potatoes are raised annually, the choice between the spinner and the lifter becomes a serious matter. On the one hand the labour charge for picking up the tubers in the trail of a spinner is 5s. per acre higher than doing the same behind a lifter; on the other, if the weather turns wet, the lifter must be idle and the spinner, if possible, used. In practice, farmers seem agreed that for large acreages the lifter, in the long run, is the more economic implement, even if the weather is such as to put it out of action from time to time.

Once the crop is gathered and stored in field clamps, the construction and character of which have not materially varied during the last hundred years, it remains to be prepared for market, whether as seed or ware. The procedure is to open the clamp at one end and shovel the potatoes out and pass them over a 'riddle', i.e. a sieve, or series of sieves, which will allow the large tubers to pass out at one exit into sacks as ware, a second grade from another as seed, and a third, the smallest size, as 'chats', which are generally fed to pigs.

In recent years, the main steps in the process have been mechanized, and effective machines are on the market for this purpose. The first of its kind was introduced into this country in 1885 by Henry Cooch of Northampton, and the same firm are responsible for the most up-to-date types of sorters now on the market. Fig. 89 (Pl. XXVII), represents the earliest machine: it needed two men, one to fill the hopper at the right-hand end, the other to work the oscillating frame and pick out the damaged or diseased tubers as they passed over the riddle in front of him. Two men could then handle between 25 and 30 cwt. of potatoes per hour. Fig. 90 (Pl. XXVII), illustrates the latest type: it is driven by an internal combustion engine and consists of a hopper and elevator on the left, a pair of riddles in the middle, one to hold back the ware and let through the seed-size tubers, and one beneath it to hold the seed and let the chats out through a hopper seen near the middle. At the other end the ware and seed are discharged on to an elevator composed of moving rollers which turn the tubers over and over, and allow of damaged ones being removed. The elevator is divided longitudinally so that the ware can pass up one side and the seed the other; at the end of both are attachments for bags into which the tubers are discharged. This type of sorter requires one man to load, another to look after the bags and a third, if circumstances demand, to remove damaged tubers. Such a machine dealing, as it does, with six tons of potatoes in an hour, affords a striking illustration of the advance in saving of both labour and time that has overtaken an industry which started and for so long remained one worked throughout by hand.

A seemingly paradoxical position has been reached, for whilst the potato lends itself more readily than any other foodstuff to small-scale cultivation in garden and allotment, where it makes an exceptionally heavy demand on labour, it is equally well suited to cultivation on the largest possible scale, and is being produced both here and in America under conditions allowing of the most advanced mechanization and a consequent economy of labour. Both these methods have been exploited to the full in the war years. We are witnessing, by the latter method of production, a drastic reduction relative to the acreage employed, in the number of man-hours actually consumed in the raising, whilst by the former the enormous cost of labour is lost sight of because so much of it is contributed by the consumer-grower and his family, whose recompense is not only the material one arising from an increase to their own larder, but the knowledge that their efforts have contributed towards the national struggle for survival and victory.

CHAPTER XXXIV

The Potato in the Realm of Art

In an earlier chapter it has been shown how the pre-Inca Peruvian artists made full use of the potato as a motif in their remarkable sculptured pottery; in Europe it aroused no corresponding reaction. It came too late to take its place in the still-life pictures by the greatest seventeenth-century Dutch artists, who could find beauty and inspiration in the common products of the kitchen garden. Better has it fared at the hands of the craftsmen who fashioned the utensils more directly concerned with its use; there, at least, can be found evidence of the artistry which, in the pre-mechanical age, rarely failed to manifest itself, even in the most prosaic walks of life.

It was not till our own times that the potato found an artist who could read the riddle which its massive simplicity hides from those whose appreciation is engendered by colour and form alone. It needed the penetrating vision of Vincent van Gogh to discover the symbolic message of the potato, and by so doing give the Doctrine of Signatures a new and far truer significance.

Van Gogh spent the years 1883–5 at Neuenen, a district of Holland, flat and canal riven, a land of marsh and mist. Here he found a peasantry, simple and hard-working, whose men and women-folk lived in the closest harmony with the soil and its fruits. For people such as these, van Gogh had an intuitive and sympathetic understanding. With the instinct of genius, though almost unconsciously, he grasped the reality of the sway which the potato, the dominant subject both of their culture and their diet, had come to exert over the peasant household.

In those years at Neuenen, van Gogh painted a large number of pictures dealing with peasant life and work, both in the fields and the home. The majority of the outside studies are concerned with men and women planting, hoeing or harvesting the potato, whilst those indoors, besides studies of heads, deal in the main with women sitting in their simple homes, peeling potatoes. Not content with that, van Gogh painted at least four important still-life pictures entirely devoted to the potato, and others in which it was included with the equally homely cabbage.

All of this was but preparatory to the creation of the outstanding masterpiece of this period of the artist's activity; in 1885 he completed his famous picture 'The Potato Eaters' (see Frontispiece). In this van Gogh would seem to sum up the gamut of his reactions to peasant life, whilst demonstrating in the clearest manner, those of the peasant to his immediate environment, including his diet.[1]

Fortunately we have van Gogh's own comment on the picture: 'I have tried', he writes to his brother, 'to make it clear how those people, eating their potatoes under the lamplight, have dug the earth with those very hands they put in the dish, and so it speaks of *manual labour*, and how they have honestly earned their food.....All winter long I have had in hand the threads of this tissue, and have searched for the definite pattern, and though it has become a tissue of a rough and coarse aspect, nevertheless the threads have been selected carefully and according to certain rules.'[2]

The same spirit may be recognized in the potato still-lifes. Of one such (Pl. XXVIII, fig. 91) he writes: 'I mean to express the material in such a way that they become heavy, solid lumps, which would hurt you if they were thrown at you.'[3]

Here may be the explanation of why van Gogh did, and the old Masters did not, use the potato. The latter were seeking to express beauty in colour and form; the former, a symbol of man's struggle to wrest a living from the soil.

Once more we must turn to Ireland to study the earliest treatment of the potato and the simplest method of preparing and serving it as a food.

The Irish peasantry in the past, no less than to-day, wisely refrained from peeling their potatoes; in the countryside, apart from occasionally adding boiled mashed potato to the dough in making bread, they employed but one method of preparation, boiling. From its first entry into the country till the end of the last century, the peasantry had but one utensil for cooking the tubers, the cauldron.

The cauldron, of which a series is shown in Pl. XXIX, fig. 92, is a vessel with an age-long history; originally made of pottery, it was in use as early as 1500 B.C. Bronze forms occur a thousand years later, and persisted into the sixteenth century, when iron finally replaced the nobler material. The cauldron is essentially a circular pot, provided with two side-handles and three legs, and designed either to be hung above an open fire, or set directly over the hot ashes, and thus is peculiarly adapted to an open turf fire. Cauldrons vary in size but the majority are about 12–15 in. in their greatest diameter. The style of structure and ornamentation has remained remarkably consistent, so that it is

[1] Van Gogh painted three versions of this theme, that belonging to Mr V. W. van Gogh, has with his permission been reproduced as the frontispiece to this work: another version is in the possession of the Rijksmuseum Kröller-Müller, Otterlo, Holland.

[2] Van Gogh, Vincent (1927). *Letters to His Brother*, vol. II, Letter no. 404, p. 482.

[3] Loc. cit. vol. II, Letter no. 425, p. 532. Three versions of this picture were painted by van Gogh. Of these, one is the property of Mr V. W. van Gogh, and the second is in the possession of the Rijksmuseum Kröller-Müller, Otterlo, Holland.

extremely difficult to date an Irish cauldron with any degree of accuracy, and even the modern machine-made cauldrons closely follow the traditional pattern. To-day their use is confined to the smaller households, where Estyn Evans speaks of them as being an indispensable feature in the peasant home. The beauty and simplicity of design which characterizes the series of cauldrons is evidence of the importance which the vessels had attained in the households of the people. When the potato reached the Irish people, there was no need to fashion a distinctive vessel for its use; rather the potato gave a new lease of life to a primitive utensil in which art and function had found so happy a union.

In the homesteads of the more substantial farmers, the advent of more up-to-date stoves, and the use of oil, has brought about the eclipse of the cauldron which, replaced by saucepans and the like, is frequently to be seen on the rubbish-heap in the corner of the farm-yard.

Once cooked, the potatoes were 'served' by the simple method of tumbling them out on to a shallow wicker basket, or tray, called a 'skeehogue', which allowed any excess of water to drain away; here, too much skill and not a little art is displayed (Pl. XXIX, fig. 93). In Ireland they use a minimum of water in which to boil the potatoes, hence one is not surprised to learn that up till fairly recent times, there being no tables in the huts of the peasantry, the family sat in front of the fire, with the 'skeehogue' on their knees, and ate their potatoes without the aid of knife or fork. When the potato was mashed, wooden beetles of varying shape and design (Fig. 94, p. 595) were used, as well as an iron tool which looks more formidable than useful.

Ireland was ever the land of anomalies and contrasts. Whilst the common folk lived like Pacific islanders, the gentry of Dublin pursued a life of leisure, culture and extreme elegance. At no time was this more in evidence than during the eighteenth century, in the second quarter of which the character of the furniture in vogue amongst the aristocracy underwent a change which, beginning slowly, before long developed into one of those tidal waves of fashion, which from time to time affect the upper classes. About the year 1715, mahogany timber began to be imported from San Domingo and Cuba, when it was promptly employed by the cabinet-makers of the day for the construction of tables, chairs, commodes and the like, replacing the French furniture then in vogue, as well as the fine old Jacobean oak pieces which had been handed down from previous generations.

In England, the new and stately homes which were being built both in town and country by the Adams brothers offered an harmonious setting for the type of furniture which Chippendale, Sheraton and Hepplewhite were perfecting, and for the superb carvings with which

Grinling Gibbons had earlier embellished both furniture and fixtures. The new style in house design was welcomed in Dublin and coincided with the creation of the fashionable residential quarter of Merrion

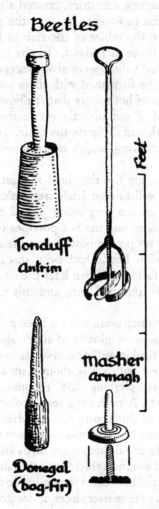

Beetles

Tonduff
Antrim

masher
armagh

Donegal
(bog-fir)

Feet

Fig. 94. Beetles for the mashing of potatoes.
From *Irish Heritage* (1942), p. 72.

Square and Fitzwilliam Street. The Anglo-Irish of Dublin were amongst the first to fill their new homes with mahogany furniture which, made in Ireland, reached a very high level in craftsmanship.

A feature of the mahogany furniture was the high polish given to it in order to bring out the beauty of the grain of the wood. To maintain the polish it was not only necessary to treat it from time to time with a suitable polishing material but, above all, to avoid any contact with hot surfaces, hence the use of mats and damask table-cloths. The potato, in relation to the new furniture, created a special problem.

In the first half of the eighteenth century the potato, though still a comparative stranger on the tables of the rich in England, was a long-established denizen on those in Ireland. In the houses of the rich and middle classes the cooked tubers were always served in a wooden bowl, or mazer, which might be furnished with silver mountings; but such is the latent heat of a mass of hot tubers that the bowl would soon become uncomfortably hot and if put directly on to the polished mahogany would destroy the polish and disfigure the table. To avoid this, the bowl was supported on a metal ring, which raised it several inches above the surface of the table.

Another method of using the ring held at least in some households. Col. B. G. Berry, the well-known Irish archaeologist, informs me that as a child he remembers the ring being placed on the table, its base filled with a folded napkin, and the hot potatoes placed in the ring and resting on the napkin, no pot or bowl being used. This practice only came in after the wooden bowls had been discarded; with them the rings went also out of fashion. When later the rings returned to favour, there were no bowls to put on them, and this unorthodox method of use crept in.

All these dish rings, which seem to have been made in Dublin between about 1760 and 1808, were originally of silver and highly ornamented. They were usually elliptical in outline and wider in each dimension below than above. The greatest width was about 8 in. and the height 3–4 in. Use was made of both piercing and repoussé work to obtain the highest decorative effects. After having seen probably all the rings which exist, in the Museums of this country and of Ireland, one can say with some assurance that none bear designs which are in any way suggestive of the potato. The more usual themes are birds and cattle, and scrolls of flowers, often displayed around a shield with the family coat-of-arms. The finest specimens are dated between 1760 and 1780 (Pl. XXX, figs. 95–97). Many of the silver rings are masterpieces of design (Pl. XXX, fig. 97 and Pl. XXXI, fig. 98), and far more restful and satisfying than the magnificent but over-decorated example shown in Figs. 95 and 96 (Pl. XXX). About the latter date, rather simpler rings were made, both in silver and Sheffield plate: the latter never achieved the elaboration of the best silver ones, but many exhibit a very delicate if restrained design, with pierced ornamentation. It would have been easy to give examples of more elaborate Sheffield rings than those shown in Figs. 99 and 100 (Pl. XXXI) which have been selected as being the simplest and perhaps the most effective of their kind so far encountered. Rings of a similar shape, and destined for the same purpose, are said to have been made of glass, but so far I have failed to find an example. Mr Sinclair of Belfast, an expert on these matters, writes that he has only seen one genuine glass 'ring': it was the same shape as the silver ones, but was perfectly plain, with a deep turn-over rim both top and bottom. Other pieces, sometimes highly cut, are often offered by dealers as potato rings, but they are merely stands for glass bowls.

The wide range exhibited, both in regard to style, extravagance of design and material, and their apparently exclusive use in Ireland, adds additional strength to the view that they were intended in the first place for the potato bowl, and it is not surprising that they are always known in Ireland as 'potato rings'. Jackson[1] objects strongly to the use of this term, and claims that they should only be spoken of as 'dish rings'. The *Oxford Dictionary* supports his view. Nevertheless, it is as 'potato rings' that they have been known in Ireland and as such have been described in catalogues and the like for at least sixty years, and probably much longer.

In the well-known series of *London Cries*, published about 1813, there is one plate devoted to the seller of Hot Roast Potatoes. Beneath it occur the lines:

Flowery Ware—All Hot!
Here's taters hot, my little chaps,
Now just lay out a copper,
I'm known up and down the Strand,
You'll not find any hotter.

The hawker of hot potatoes, with his gothic-fronted oven, heated with coke and mounted on a two-wheeled barrow, with great brown and crusted tubers impaled like the heads of traitors on its triangular spikes, could be found during the winter months as late as the beginning of this century, crying his hot potatoes at such crowded centres as Marble Arch, Oxford Circus and Piccadilly, and many a time have I bought and enjoyed one. If in those days you were accompanied by a lady, and the weather was cold, it was ten to one that the hawker would suggest that you should buy one for the lady to put in her muff to keep her hands warm, and they were invariably welcomed. It should be remembered that at that time most women carried a muff slung from the neck, and within them some would secrete special slow combustion charcoal cylinders contained in metal holders which, when ignited, imparted a welcome warmth to the hands on a frosty day. This cheery merchant of the street went out of business, as the muff went out of fashion in London, at the beginning of the first great war: may both return!

---

[1] Jackson, C. J. (1911). *History of English Plate*, vol. II, p. 935.

This talk of muffs and hot potatoes may serve both as introduction and excuse for an excursion into a hobby of the author. Some twenty years ago, a friend presented the writer with a Staffordshire ware model of a potato (Pl. XXXII, fig. 101) about 7 in. long and 3½ in. broad, with a hollow spout at one end, 1½ in. long, leading into the interior, which holds about ¾ pint of fluid. The tuber was well moulded and furnished with deep eyes. The suggestion was made that it was probably intended for use as a gin flask.

I have long searched for similar Staffordshire ware throughout most of the Museums of England, Ireland and Scotland, and have found but eleven specimens, of which one in the Fitzwilliam Museum, Cambridge, bore the date 1827. In the Brighton Museum there are eight such flasks and two more are in the National Museum, Dublin. Five more have been seen in antique shops; all sixteen were of the same general type and size as shown in Fig. 101, though each differed somewhat in shape and colour. One day when visiting the Wine Merchants, Messrs Berry Bros. of St James's Street, London, I saw a collection of old bottles and flasks. Amongst them I noticed several Staffordshire potato bottles, which Mr Berry had collected on the assumption that they were gin flasks. Permission was most generously given me to examine them and obtain a photograph of each. There were eleven specimens in all: nine conformed in contour and size to the former series, though again there were lively differences in the moulding, colour and glaze of each; indeed no two of these Staffordshire ware potato bottles have so far proved to be identical in shape, much less in colour. Two of the Berry collection call for comment (Pl. XXXII, figs. 102 and 103). Both are realistic and highly artistic productions, the one of a 'lumper' potato, and the other of one of those 'monstrous' tubers particularly common in deep-eyed varieties which, owing to secondary growth, acquire a bizarre shape. Two flasks in the Brighton collection are unglazed, one in its entirety, the other with the exclusion of the neck. The unglazed surface enhances the air of reality, but must have seriously impaired their use as a container of fluid of any kind.

Doubts had already arisen in my mind as to the purpose of these potato bottles: their large size and extremely bulky and clumsy shape seemed to make them peculiarly unfitted for use as hip flasks for spirit. And in any case, why the potato? What intimate relation existed between the potato and any of the ardent spirits popular in the late eighteenth and early nineteenth centuries? None could be found, and had there been such, it seems unlikely that such characteristic bottles would have escaped Hogarth's eagle eye, but in none of his pictures in which gin-drinkers and the like are so vividly portrayed is there a sign of one.

The discovery of the two specimens illustrated in Figs. 102 and 103

PLATE XXIX

Fig. 92. Irish cauldrons: Front row: left to right: 1, Locality unknown; 2, Locality unknown; 3, Bofeenaun, Co. Mayo; 4, Locality unknown. Back row: left to right: 1, Locality unknown; 2, Locality unknown; 3, Type in present-day use.

Fig. 93. Potato skips, or skibs. Front row: left to right: 1, Locality unknown; 2, Ballyglunin, Co. Galway; 3, Dowra, Co. Cavan; 4, Inishmore, Aran, Co. Galway; Back row: left to right: 1, Ennistymon, Co. Clare; 2, Cape Clear Island, Co. Cork; 3, Co. Fermanagh.

PLATE XXX

Fig. 95. Dish ring, silver; $8\frac{1}{4} \times 7\frac{1}{2} \times 3\frac{3}{4}$ in.
Dublin, c. 1750–60.

Fig. 96. Dish ring, silver; diam. $8\frac{1}{4}$ in. Maker: Isaac D'Olier,
c. 1760, Dublin.

Fig. 97. Dish ring, silver; $7\frac{3}{4} \times 7 \times 3\frac{3}{4}$ in. Maker: William
Townsend, 1760–70, Dublin.

PLATE XXXI

Fig. 98. Dish ring, silver; 6⅞ × 6¾ × 2⅜ in. Maker: John Hamilton, 1745, Dublin.

Fig. 99. Dish ring, Sheffield plate.

Fig. 100. Dish ring, Sheffield plate; 8 × 7 × 3⅝ in.

PLATE XXXII

Fig. 101. Potato pot, Staffordshire ware; blue, glazed; $7 \times 3\frac{1}{2} \times 2\frac{1}{2}$ in.

Fig. 102. Potato pot, Staffordshire ware; dull grey and brown, glazed; $6 \times 4\frac{1}{4}$ in.

Fig. 103. Potato pot, British ware; cream glazed; $7\frac{1}{4} \times 5$ in.

Fig. 104. An earthenware cup in the shape of a potato tuber.

(Pl. XXXII), whose shape precludes their use as pocket flasks, convinced me that they were, in fact, artificial 'hot potatoes'. The bottles, filled with hot water or hot sand and closed with a cork, might have been carried in the muff or pocket, and because of their thick earthenware walls, would have retained their heat for several hours. If this explanation is correct, and the absence of any other model, vegetable or animal, renders it probable, it follows that the real hot potato must have been used for the purpose of keeping the hands warm prior to the last quarter of the eighteenth century, the period to which most authorities attribute the earliest of these Staffordshire bottles. It is evident from their rarity that their use was neither general nor persistent. Some of these flasks are so big and clumsy that it is unlikely that they were intended to be anything but ornaments for the cottage mantelpiece, a possibility supported by the existence of a whole series of hollow flasks of similar ware but of a rather later period, representing such diverse objects as mermaids, jack-boots, field-marshal batons, and the heads of generals and other famous personages.[1]

The Brighton collection also contains an earthenware cup of a blueish white colour which, modelled in very thin ware, represents half of a potato cut transversely and its contents removed; the eyes are skilfully modelled with sprouts beginning to emerge (Pl. XXXII, fig. 104). As the 'cup' cannot stand, its use if other than ornamental, seems dubious. There is no clue as to its age but it may be assumed to be of the same period as that of the flasks.

Before closing this chapter, reference should be made to the possibility of using the potato as an ornamental plant. The early European varieties bore abundant flowers and Rudbeck[2] in 1658 described the potato as equally suitable for the flower border as the table. It will be remembered that in order to popularize the potato, Louis XVI accepted a bouquet of potato blooms from Parmentier, and Marie Antoinette wore one in her hair. In my genetic cultures I have frequently raised varieties which by the abundance and beauty of their flowers would have pleased the most eclectic of gardeners.

---

[1] Mayhew, the first editor of *Punch*, states that in 1861 there were some 300 street potato-vendors, each selling about 1½ cwt. daily between mid-August and the end of April. The variety used was the mealy 'French Regent' costing 5s. 6d. per cwt. The tubers were bought as often to warm the hands as to be eaten. Mayhew, Henry (1861). *London Labour and London Poor*, vol. 1, p. 173. London: Griffin Bohn and Co. The hot-potato merchant was still common in my youth.

[2] Rudbeck, Olaus (1658). *Catalogus Plantarum*, pp. 38 and 44. Upsala.

EPILOGUE

If for any reason, good or bad, conscious or otherwise, it is in the interests of one economically stronger group to coerce another, then in the absence of political, legal or moral restraint, that task is enormously facilitated when the weaker group can either be persuaded or forced to adopt some simple, cheaply produced food as the mainstay of its subsistence. Experience shows that this course inevitably results in a lower standard of living. The lower that standard, the easier is the task of exploitation and the nearer will the status of the weaker class approximate to serfdom. The potato, being the cheapest and one of the most efficient single foods man has as yet cultivated in the temperate zones, lends itself readily to the task of solving labour problems, along certain well-defined lines, in a society which, for any reason, is already stratified into social classes. Whenever, therefore, the potato wins an important, and still more, a dominant position in the dietary of the people, it behoves us to ask ourselves the question: What part is it playing in the economic scheme, and what is the risk society is taking in encouraging or suffering a continuance of the same?

The potato can, and generally does, play a twofold part: that of a nutritious food, and that of a weapon ready forged for the exploitation of a weaker group in a mixed society.

It is obvious that if a foodstuff is to be used as an instrument of exploitation, the more valuable and acceptable it is as a food, the more effective will it be. Hence the richer nature's gift, be it potatoes, rice or maize, the more extreme the contrast between its dual activities, feeding and exploiting.

In a society, wedded to the doctrine of *laisser-faire*, the problem of coercing the politically weaker labourer in the interests of the politically protected employer, was simple, given a suitable instrument with which to bring it about.

The course of events is well illustrated in eighteenth-century Great Britain: the employing class desired cheap labour; wages, in the absence of any protective mechanism, were determined in the main by the labourer's cost of subsistence; a potato dietary was capable of reducing that cost to the lowest level. Hence, it was to the employers' interests to urge the use of the potato on the worker, which he did directly the cost of subsistence called for an increased wage. It may be that it is seldom a cheap food has been designedly forced on European workers, with a view of lowering their wages, but the potato has certainly been used, and that of set purpose, with the view of preventing them from rising.

Other factors there are—competition for labour, freedom or otherwise of communication, doctrines whether religious, racial or national, tending to the greater or lesser stratification of society—each of which can exert an influence on the application and efficiency of the instrument of exploitation, of which the potato affords an extreme example.

In the rare case of a society such as that of Tristan da Cunha, where there are no economic motives for the exploitation of one group or class over another, or alternatively, where the society has always been classless, the almost exclusive use of the potato has had no evil social effect. Similarly, where, as in the Channel Islands, potatoes are raised in great quantities for export, in the economic interest of the great majority of the community, there need be no adverse social repercussion.

A different type of situation to either of the above developed during the latter part of the eighteenth and the first half of the nineteenth centuries in the Lowlands of Scotland and the northern counties of England. In both these regions the potato had been long established as an article of the people's daily food and had reduced their cost of living. But here its influence as an agent of exploitation was, at an early stage, largely neutralized owing to the competition of the mines and ironworks for labour. Nevertheless, the potato by its cheapness, as well as its nutritious qualities did, unknown either to worker or employer, effectively prevent any pronounced rise of wage in either the Lowlands or the north of England in the time of the corn shortage at the end of the eighteenth century. The danger of a potato economy was there, but it only showed itself when local industry as a whole was temporarily paralysed by the collapse of foreign markets after the French wars.

When absence of competition is associated with a high degree of isolation, as it was in the Highlands of Scotland, then the potato can be, and in fact did become, the perfect instrument of exploitation, an exploitation so ruthless that it ended in the emigration of the greater part of the local working population. When later the Highlands were developed in the interests of grouse-shooting and deer stalking, exploitation of labour as such ceased; but the low standard which had been acquired in the early nineteenth century remained, and can be seen to-day amongst the remnant which has not found employment as gillies or the like.

In Ireland, where at the advent of the potato, native society was already hopelessly disintegrated, it met with no resistance and became in the shortest possible time the food of the people. In an environment poisoned by religious jealousies, undermined by political dissension, where industry was hamstrung at the dictate of an alien power, all the factors were to hand which made it inevitable that the use of the potato, cheapest of foods, would reduce the standard of living to the lowest level ever attained in Europe. After proving itself the most perfect instrument for the maintenance of poverty and degradation amongst the native masses, the potato ended in wrecking both exploited and exploiter.

Thus man's wisdom, or his lack of it, alone decides whether even the richest of nature's gifts shall serve as a blessing or a curse. It is but a league that separates the mountains of Gerizim and Ebal.

APPENDIX I

Failures of the Potato Crop in Ireland

Failures of the potato crop, no less than their attendant effects on the welfare of the Irish people, may be conveniently divided into two classes. The first includes those cases where the potato plant fails to grow at all, those where the plant grows but does not thrive, producing but an indifferent crop of tubers and, lastly, those where the tubers are for some reason destroyed. The second class includes those cases where the fault does not lie primarily with the potato, but with the cereal crops, the failure of which, with the consequent shortage of bread-corn, necessitates the untimely consumption of those other articles of food which may be kept in store.

In Ireland, both classes of failure are represented, and their social repercussions were intimately related. If it was the potato that failed, there was at once an urgent demand in the autumn for corn—mostly oats; generally speaking, the peasant had but a very limited supply of corn, as he only grew enough to afford an occasional oatcake and that modicum of meal he needed to tide him over the two or three 'hungry months' of late summer. If, for want of potatoes, he consumed his oats, he could procure no more, having no cash resources, and famine conditions arose in the first month or two of the following year.

If, on the other hand, it was the corn harvest which failed, then there was no bread or meal for his use during late autumn, winter and spring, and a heavier call was necessarily made on his store of potatoes, with the result that they were consumed probably by the end of the spring of the next year, and he was left without food supplies of any kind at all till the late autumn, when the new crop of potatoes were ready to dig. Sometimes the cottier might have a patch of early potatoes in addition to his main crop, which might be dug in July, but this was not common; early varieties were not generally grown by the peasantry, for they looked for large crops and cultivated heavy cropping, late, coarse varieties, such as the 'Lumper'.

The Table which follows records the recurrence of Crop Failures and, in some cases, their economic effects, but, unfortunately, very little reliable information as to their causation. In some, this is clear enough: very severe frosts killed the growing plants, or froze the tubers in the ground or, not infrequently in the clamp, a testimony to the inefficiency with which these latter were often constructed. It is very probable that several of the 'failures' were due to dry rot (*Fusarium caeruleum*) in the

Failure of the Potato Crop in Ireland

Year	Predisposing factors	Contemporary description	Possible cause	Distribution	Social and economic consequences	Authority	Date	Reference
1724–5	Very severe weather	Failure of corn crops, due to 'blight'	Unknown	General	Price of barley rose to 400%, oatmeal to 200%. Distress of peasantry due to premature consumption of potatoes	Lloyd-Dodd, F. T. *Irish Census**	1942 1851	MSS. article loaned to R.N.S. Part v, p. 120
1726–9	Floods followed by frosts	Failure of corn crops	Unknown	General	Winter stocks of potatoes consumed two months earlier than usual. Thousands died of famine which lasted till 1729 and inspired Swifts' *Modest Proposal*	Boulter, Archbp. Jones, M. G. *Irish Census*	1728 1935 1851	*Letters*; vol. I, p. 226 *The Charity School Movement.* Camb. Univ. Press Op. cit. p. 120
1739	Very severe frosts in early November, continued throughout the winter	Failure of potato crop by frost and rotting	Freezing of tubers in the ground and subsequent bacterial infection	General, but worse in the north	300,000 persons said to have perished, i.e. one fifth of population. More distress in the north. Shortage of food continued throughout 1740 and 1741	Wilde, Sir Will. R. O'Rourke, J. Trevelyan, Ch. Sir *Irish Census*	1858 1875 1880 1851	*Proc. Roy. Irish Acad.* vol. VI, pp. 356–63, *Hist. Great Famine*, p. 102. Dublin *Irish Crisis.* Macmillan Op. cit. p. 124
1740–1	As in 1739, but followed by drought in summer	Failure of potato crop in store and poor growth of new crop	Shortage of seed and drought	General, but especially severe in Dublin area	Memorial of the famine of 1741 erected on hill at Killiney. A third of the cottiers in Munster said to have perished	Ball, F. E. O'Brien, G.	1902 1918	*Hist. County Dublin.* Dublin *Econ. Hist. Ireland Eighteenth Century*, p. 108. Dublin Op. cit. p. 125
1756–7	Very wet season	Failure of potato and corn crops, especially the latter	Secondary rot of tubers in store	General	Large numbers said to have died of famine. The Viceroy, Duke of Bedford, sanctioned £20,000 for relief	*Irish Census* Lecky, W. O'Brien, G. Anon.	1851 1892 1918 1836	Part v, p. 241 *Hist. of Ireland*, vol. I, p. 468 Op. cit. p. 105 *Commercial Restraint of Ireland.* Quoted from Lewis (1836) *Irish Disturbances*, p. 438
1765–6	Very wet early season followed by drought	Failure of potato crop through drought and subsequent frost in clamps	Drought and shortage of seed	General	Owing to shortage of potatoes, corn rose to exorbitant price. Government bought and distributed corn to the poor. Exports of corn and use of same in distilleries forbidden	Wilde, Sir Will. R. Lloyd-Dodd, F. T. O'Brien, G. *Irish Census*	1858 1942 1918 1851	Loc. cit. Loc. cit. Op. cit. p. 104 Op. cit. p. 143

Year	Weather / Season	Failure of potato crop	Cause	Extent	Distress	Source	Years	Reference
1769–70	Very wet early season followed by drought	Failure of potato crop	Drought and 'curl'	General	Widespread distress. Exports of food continued on a large scale	Lloyd-Dodd, F. T. *Irish Census*	1942 1851	Loc. cit. Op. cit. p. 146
1777–8	Bad weather, heavy rains in June	Failure of both potato and corn crops	Unknown	General	Considerable distress especially in Dublin area	Dunlop R. *Irish Census*	1910 1851	*Camb. Modern Hist.* vol. XII, p. 76 Op. cit. p. 149
1779	—	'Black Rot'	?Bacillary Rot	Northern counties	Not serious	Wilde, Sir Will. R. *Irish Census*	1858 1851	Loc. cit. Op. cit. p. 150
1784	Late autumn frost and heavy snow in January	'Spuggour', i.e. soft potatoes	Freezing of tubers and secondary rots	General	Great increase of emigration to America. Distress great	Wilde, Sir Will. R. *Irish Census*	1858 1851	Loc. cit. Op. cit. p. 150
1795	Cold spring followed by very wet and warm summer	Failure of potato crop	Poor growth and attacks of *Botrytis cinerea*	Unknown	Other vegetables failed and fruits went mouldy	Wilde, Sir Will. R. *Irish Census*	1858 1851	Loc. cit. Op. cit. p. 153
1800	Very severe drought	Partial failure of potatoes and corn crop	Lack of growth	Local	The yield of wheat and oats only half of the normal. Similar conditions prevailed in England	Wilde, Sir Will. R. *Irish Census*	1858 1851	Loc. cit. Op. cit. p. 159
1801	Severe drought	Partial failure of potato crop	Lack of growth	General	Starvation and scurvy amongst the poor	Wilde, Sir Will. R. *Irish Census*	1858 1851	Loc. cit. Op. cit. p. 160
1807	Severe frost in November and throughout winter	Half of crop destroyed	Freezing of tubers and secondary rots	General	Distress greatest in Galway and Limerick	Wilde, Sir Will. R. *Irish Census*	1858 1851	Loc. cit. Op. cit. p. 168
1809	Dry spring and early summer	'The Curl'	Probably Leaf Roll	Dublin area	Distress but no famine	Wilde, Sir Will. R. O'Brien, G.	1858 1921	Loc. cit. *Econ. Hist. Ireland from the Union to the Famine*, p. 227. Longmans
1811	Excessive rain	Partial failure	Secondary rots	Local	Food prices high	*Irish Census*	1851	Op. cit. p. 169
1812	Unknown	The early varieties failed	Probably dry-rot and scarcity of seed	Unknown	No serious famine	Wilde, Sir Will. R. *Irish Census*	1858 1851	Loc. cit. Op. cit. p. 170
1816	A backward spring and a very wet summer and autumn	Tops blackened, plants died down and smelt	Possible attacks by *Botrytis cinerea*	Very poor crop General	Distress general except in Belfast area	Wilde, Sir Will. R. *Irish Census* Quinn, D.	1858 1851 1942	Loc. cit. Op. cit. p. 175 Personal communication

* *Irish Census for the Year 1851*, pt. v, vol. I. Table of Deaths: article 'Epidemics', Report of Commissioners, 13, xxx, 1856.

Year	Predisposing factors	Contemporary description	Possible cause	Distribution	Social and economic consequences	Authority	Date	Reference
1817	Early drought followed by very wet autumn	Rot in the clamps. Failure of oat crop	Possibly bacterial rots	General	Following shortage of 1816 crop. Famine conditions ensued; typhus epidemic broke out. A wave of evictions followed	Wilde, Sir Will. R. Bridges, J. H. / Irish Census	1858 1888 / 1851	Loc. cit. *Two Centuries of Irish History*, p. 266. Kegan Paul Op. cit. p. 177
1821	Frosts in the spring, a dry summer and a very wet autumn	Rotted both in the field and in the clamp	Probably dry-rot of seed and bacterial rot of crop	South of line from Bay of Donegal to Youghal	Deaths from starvation in Clare. Government failed to provide potatoes or oats. Great scarcity of seed potatoes, much disorder. Government voted £500,000 and public subscribed £250,000 for relief	Wilde, Sir Will. R. Hansen, M. L. / *The Times* Bridges, J. H. *Irish Census*	1858 1940 / 1822 1888 1851	Loc. cit. *Atlantic Migration*, p. 116. Harvard Univ. Press April 27 Op. cit. p. 275 Op. cit. p. 188
1825	Early rains followed by summer drought	Partial failure of potato crop	Lack of growth	Local	Distress serious but not so severe as in 1821/2	Wilde, Sir Will. R. *Irish Census*	1858 1851	Loc. cit. Op. cit. p. 205
1829	Very wet autumn	Damaged crops especially potatoes	Damage by rain and wind	General	In some localities, famine conditions	Wilde, Sir Will. R. *Irish Census*	1858 1851	Loc. cit. Op. cit. p. 206
1830	Severe storms	Damaged crops especially potatoes	Rain and wind	Local	Famine in the west, especially on coasts of Mayo, Galway and Donegal	Wilde, Sir Will. R. *Irish Census*	1858 1851	Loc. cit. Op. cit. p. 206
1831	Severe storms causing very late planting	Damaged crops	Probably dry-rot	Widespread but uneven	Government voted £74,000 for relief in the west. Large sums collected for same purpose in England and Ireland	Trevelyan, Sir Ch. *Irish Census*	1880 1851	Loc. cit. Op. cit. p. 208
1832	Good growing season	Failure	Probably dry-rot of seed	General, and also in England and America	Failure heaviest in Connaught and Munster. £311,000 subscribed for relief and £15,000 devoted to emigration to Cape of Good Hope	Wilde, Sir Will. R. Trevelyan, Sir Ch. *Irish Census*	1858 1880 1851	Loc. cit. Loc. cit. Op. cit. p. 211
1833	Heavy rains in summer	Disease thought to be the 'Curl' also some disease of tubers. Potatoes in the clamps affected	Probably dry-rot of seed and Black-leg *B. atrosepticus* of growing crop	General	Increased emigration to to U.S.A.	Wilde, Sir Will. R. *Irish Census*	1858 1851	Loc. cit. Op. cit. p. 212
1835–7	Unknown	Partial failures	Unknown	Chiefly in the west	Unknown	Wilde, Sir Will. R. Trevelyan, Sir Ch.	1858 1880	Loc. cit. Loc. cit.

Year	Season	Crop failure	Cause	Distribution	Distress / relief	Authority	Date	Reference
1839	Excessively wet season	Failure of potato crop. Black Rust attacked crop on 27 August	Probably an attack by fungus *Botrytis cineria*	General, also in Hebrides and New England, U.S.A.	Price of corn and potatoes rose to great height. Relief organized by Capt. Chads, R.N. for the government	Wilde, Sir Will. R. Trevelyan, Sir Ch. *Irish Census*	1858 1880 1851	Loc. cit. Loc. cit. Op. cit. p. 220
1840	Very wet season	Failure of the potato crop	Probably an attack by *B. cineria*	Chiefly in Leinster and Munster. Widespread in Germany	Great distress in Abbeyleix, Cashel and Waterford areas	Wilde, Sir Will. R. *Irish Census*	1858 1851	Loc. cit. Op. cit. p. 141
1841	Wet season especially from August onwards	'Dry gangrene' of potatoes, poor cereal crop	Bacterial rot	Mostly in the west	Distress not severe	*Irish Census*	1851	Op. cit. p. 225
1842	Very wet summer	Partial failure of potato crop and inundation of fields	Secondary rots. Late crops were good	Chiefly in the south	Government subscribed £3,448 to Relief Funds. Elsewhere food abundant and prices low	*Irish Census* Trevelyan, Sir Ch.	1851 1880	Op. cit. p. 228 Loc. cit.
1845–7	Dull moist summer	Destruction more or less complete of crop in 1845 and 1846 'Blight'	*Phytophthora infestans*	General and throughout Western Europe	Described in chapters XVI and XVII	See chapter XVI		
1879	Wet summer	Failure of potato crop due to 'Blight', only 25% of crop saved	Infection by *P. infestans*	General	Much distress all through 1880. £250,000 collected for relief. No deaths from famine. Chief need was for fresh seed, which was provided	Anon. Tuke, J. H. Lough, E.	1881 1880 1896	*The Irish Problem.* London: Ward Lock *Irish Distress.* London: Ridgway *England's Wealth and Ireland's Poverty.* Fisher Unwin
1883	Unknown	Scarcity of potatoes	Infection by *P. infestans*	Mainly in the west	Reports of distress exaggerated. Need for new seed genuine	Maurice, Col.	1886	*Letters from Donegal,* p. 69. Macmillan
1886–91	Unknown	Failure of potato crop	Infection by *P. infestans*	General	Much distress amounting in some cases to famine conditions. Seed potatoes distributed	Lough, E.	1896	Loc. cit.
1894	Unknown	Failure of potato crop	Infection by *P. infestans*	Unknown	Much distress, often severe. Seed potatoes distributed	Lough, E.	1896	Loc. cit.

seed. In only one case is 'Curl', i.e. the virus disease causing Leaf Roll, or possibly the 'Y' virus producing Leaf Drop Streak, declared to be the cause of the trouble. It is probable that this was a local failure, for virus infections to-day are practically confined to the eastern districts of Ireland, especially to the county of Dublin.

In 1816 the growing plants were said to fail and blacken, the dead haulms to smell like frosted plants. It is dangerous even to hazard a suggestion as to the causes of the troubles, seeing how scanty is our information, but a bad outbreak of *Botrytis cineria* in 1816[1] was not improbable, whilst in 1833, the trouble may have been due to Black-leg.

Extreme wet weather in late summer and autumn seem to have been a not infrequent cause of rotting of the tubers, an event which was to be expected in those parts where drainage of the land was wanting, and water-logging of the fields common.

Although some of the failures, such as that of 1739, induced a devastating famine and great loss of life in some measure comparable to that following the attacks of Blight in 1845 and 1846, it is improbable that the others were either so general or so severe.

[1] Pethybridge, G. H. (1916). *Investigations on Potato Diseases*. Dept. Agric. and Tech. Instruction, Dublin, pp. 17–22.

The number of persons, including agricultural labourers, their wives and children working on and maintained off the land, in England and Wales in 1851

I am indebted to Dr D. V. Glass of the Population Investigation Committee for a reconstruction from the 1851 *Census Returns* of the approximate number of persons—men, women and children, which made up the agricultural labouring population. Glass has deduced a multiplier, viz. 3·816 which, applied to the various categories of male labour over twenty years of age, should give the approximate population. The categories are:

Outdoor agricultural labourers approximately		725,000
Shepherds	„	10,000
Indoor agricultural workers	„	43,000
	Total ...	778,000

Applying the multiplier, the estimated population will be 2·969 million or, say, 3 million persons.

The Total Potato Acreage

Whilst there are no statistics embracing the *total* acreage under potatoes in Great Britain, we have to-day two distinct official estimates which go a long way towards meeting this deficiency.

1. *The Potato Marketing Board Returns.* Since the year 1934, the Board has registered all areas under potatoes, exceeding one acre.

2. *The Ministry of Agriculture Returns.* For England and Wales, together with that of the Board of Agriculture for Scotland, since 1866.

Both returns have concerned themselves with agricultural holdings of one acre and over. The record includes all areas of potatoes over ¼ acre in extent. Private gardens and allotments are not deemed to be 'holdings' for this purpose, and are in consequence not included in either return.

There are, therefore, two gaps in the records to be filled. One, which we may call 'A', between the two official estimates, which can be directly ascertained by simple subtraction, and the second, 'B', between the Returns of the Ministry and the total area grown under all conditions.

The difference referred to as 'A', represents those lands under potatoes which are less than one acre and over ¼ acre in area, and which are neither allotment nor garden crops. The 'A' cultivations are therefore field-grown plots, on farms on which potatoes are a relatively unimportant crop, grown for domestic use and the supply of fodder. It is not surprising, therefore, to find that the extent of the 'A' area has been remarkably constant over the six years prior to the War of 1939–45, during which the Potato Marketing Board's records have been in force. With but trifling variations, the total 'A' area annually under potatoes is 70,000 acres. (See Fig. 105.)

The second gap in the estimates, referred to as 'B', covers the area under potatoes grown in gardens and allotments and small patches of land, and can only be estimated indirectly. In official circles it is generally assumed that the gardens and allotments of Great Britain account for something over 50,000 acres. A comparison of the Ministry's *Returns* over sixteen years prior to 1939, for the potato acreages of England and Wales and Scotland respectively, shows that the two stand in a fairly constant relationship of 3·4 to 1. This simple relationship, however, cannot be applied to the 'B' area, because gardens and allotments are far more common in England and Wales than in Scotland; it is thought that a proportion of 4 or 5 to 1 would probably be a closer approximation to the truth. On this basis, the estimate of 50,000 acres might be divided as to 40,000 in England and Wales, and 10,000 in Scotland. In my opinion, however, these figures are too low.

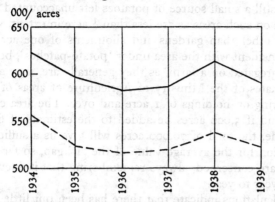

Fig. 105. The upper curve represents the area of potatoes grown annually in England, Scotland and Wales, in thousands of acres as recorded by the Ministry. The lower curve represents the acreage for the same, of all cultivations of an acre or more in extent, as returned by the Potato Marketing Board. Reproduced with permission from the Potato Marketing Board's *Miscellaneous Publication*, no. 6, after completion of the data for 1939.

In the year 1886, Major Craigie[1] estimated that there were in England and Wales

    (1) Allotments   389,000
    (2) Cottage gardens   257,000
    (3) Field potato-patches   93,000

It is suggested that the following estimates held true for that date, viz.

    (1) Allotments considered to be $\frac{1}{4}$ acre in size
    (2) Cottage gardens ,,   ,, $\frac{1}{8}$,,
    (3) Field-patches   ,,   ,, $\frac{1}{8}$,,

Of these, one-half of (1) and (2), and all of (3) would be under potatoes, i.e.

    Allotments   389,000 × $\frac{1}{8}$ acres, say 49,000⎫
    Gardens   257,000 × $\frac{1}{16}$,,   16,000⎬ 65,000
    Potato-patches 93,000 × $\frac{1}{8}$,,   12,000⎭

              Total acres   77,000

Another estimate for the 'B' acreage, is based on the quantity of seed employed for planting potatoes in private gardens, allotments, etc., which is estimated at 75,000 tons. Such should suffice for an area of

[1] Venn, J. A. (1933). *The Foundations of Agricultural Economics*, p. 138.

75,000 acres, of which on a 4·5:1 ratio 63,000 acres would fall to England and Wales, and 12,000 acres to Scotland; for convenience, we may regard the quota for England and Wales as 65,000 acres.

There is still a small source of potatoes left unaccounted for: that is, those raised on such areas as are less than ¼ acre in extent, which occur in holdings other than gardens and allotments of one acre and over. It is not coincident with the area under 'potato-patches', because when they are aggregated on a farm, as they generally are, they are included in the estimates of the Ministry of Agriculture of areas of ¼ acre and over, occurring on holdings of 1 acre and over. The area concerned is not large, and if 5,000 acres be added to the estimate of 65,000 acres already made, the total of 70,000 acres will give us a sufficiently close approximation for the average value of the 'B' gap, so far as England and Wales are concerned, always remembering that it fluctuates somewhat from year to year.

These calculations indicate that there has been but little variation in the 'B' area since 1886; indeed, war periods apart, there is reason to believe that the 'B' area has remained fairly stable for nearly a hundred years. The allotment movement was reaching its apogee in the 1850's; after the Crimean War, the price of wheat assumed a permanently lower level as compared with prices ruling in the first half of the century. The combined effect was gradually to slacken the demand for home-grown potatoes, and with it that for further garden and allotment accommodation.

Prior to 1814, we have no data on which to base any estimates of the potato acreage of England and Wales. We know, however, that by 1795, in the north of England, and Wales, it was an established food amongst the working classes; hence it would probably be safe to assume that the total area was not less than 100,000 acres, and that in 1775 it was not much more than half this amount, viz. 50,000 acres.

In 1814, and again in 1838, we have estimates of the acreage in Scotland, viz. 80,000 and 140,000 acres respectively. The earliest official records of the potato areas in England and Wales and Scotland respectively, bear to each other a ratio of about 2·5:1. This would allow of an English acreage of 200,000 in the year 1814, and 350,000 in that of 1838. The official return for 1866, however, is only 355,417; which would imply that in eighteen years the English and Welsh areas under potatoes had only increased by 5,000 acres, which is obviously untenable. It would be wiser to reduce the 1814 and 1838 ratios to 2:1, especially in view of the fact that Scotland was a potato-growing country some fifty years earlier than the major part of England.

In 1851 Caird[1] estimated that in England and Wales 2,116,750 acres

---

[1] Caird, Sir James (1852). *English Agriculture*, p. 522.

were devoted to turnips, mangolds and potatoes. How these crops were apportioned, he does not tell us, but from what we know of the popularity of the turnip in those days, it might be assumed that there were not less than five times the area devoted to turnips and mangolds as to potatoes. This would give an area of 350,000 acres. This total bears a reasonable relation to the official estimates for 1866 and is possibly not far wide of the correct figure.

In Fig. 73, p. 538, these various estimates are combined in the form of a graph *ABCD*.

Having obtained an approximate estimate of the gradual growth of the acreage under potatoes, we can now get some idea of the amount available, per head, per day, of the population. To obtain this figure, the available crop has been calculated on the assumption that there would be at least six tons per acre which would be fit for human consumption. It is not of course assumed that all of this was necessarily consumed in the home, but only that it was available if necessary. The quantities thus ascertained do, as a matter of fact, tally closely with the official estimates of consumption. The figures so obtained are given below, and are embodied in the curve *ABCD*, Fig. 74, p. 539:

	Potato acreage	Population of England and Wales	Daily consumption of potatoes in pounds per head of population
1775	50,000	c. 8 millions	0·25
1795	100,000	c. 9 millions	0·40
1814	160,000	11·5	0·47
1838	280,000	16·5	0·62
1851	350,000	18·0	0·07
1866	425,000	21·0	0·80
1871	513,000	22·0	0·90
1881	460,000	26·0	0·64
1891	463,000	29·0	0·65
1901	517,000	32·0	0·58
1911	499,000	36·0	0·60
1914	532,000	36·5	0·53

The figures in the column on the right, may be called the Potato Availability Index or P.A.I.

Wheat Availability

Population Figures. From 1801 use is made of the official census returns. Prior to 1800 the estimates of the population of England and Wales as set out in Ernle, p. 266, have been adopted. For the year 1740 the figure of 6,500,000 has been used, being the mean of the three estimates recorded.

The population in Scotland in 1755 has been taken as 1,265,380, as estimated by Alexander Webster.

The population of Ireland prior to 1845 does not concern the calculation under consideration, but subsequent to that date we have the census returns.

Wheat: Home Supplies

England and Wales. Official statistics date from 1866; prior to that, we are dependent on estimates of the acreages under this crop. The figures for the period have been borrowed from Ernle, pp. 266–7. In 1771 Arthur Young estimated the wheat acreage of England and Wales as 2,795,808, and in 1808 W. Comber put it at 3,160,000 acres. These, as well as the official returns of the wheat acreage, have been converted on the basis of three-quarters to an acre, at $4\frac{1}{2}$ cwt. per quarter to a total tonnage. The conversion rate is probably too low for the last fifty years commencing 1889, but as home supplies played an ever-decreasing role during the period, the effect on the W.A.I. will be but slight. The total figure for home supplies has been reduced by 10% each year, to allow for seed requirements.

Great Britain and Ireland. Up to the year 1921, i.e. prior to the creation of the Free State and Northern Ireland Governments, 100,000 tons of wheat has been added to the annual total crop of England and Wales, to allow for the slight production of wheat in Scotland and the limited crop in Ireland. After that date, no alteration has been made, but the allowance of 100,000 tons has been retained as full cover for the production of wheat in Scotland and Northern Ireland.

Prior to 1846 Ireland exported wheat to England on a small scale; in 1896 she was importing wheat. It should be said that in the period prior to 1921 the acreage under wheat in the Irish Free State was under 25,000 acres. In Scotland Sir John Sinclair says that in 1814 the acreage was 140,095, probably the highest reached; between 1924 and 1938 it averaged 70,000 acres.

The number of Wheat Consumers in Great Britain and Ireland

Wheat imports into Great Britain began to be of increasing importance from the beginning of the nineteenth century. They were distributed throughout the length and breadth of the country and our statistics tell us nothing as to where and in what proportion in Great Britain they were consumed. It is necessary, therefore, to regard them as a pool from which all could draw and then, on the basis of other information, estimate that proportion of the population in each part of the kingdom which consumed wheat.

It has been assumed that the entire population of England and Wales are 100% wheat eaters. This is, or rather was, an over-statement in respect to the northern rural population, but as it was here that industrialization spread most rapidly, and with it grew up an ever-increasing number of workers who demanded wheat, the error introduced by this assumption is not very great, or rather it was soon wiped out.

It is in respect to Ireland and Scotland that difficulties arise. In regard to the former, no account of the Irish population in their capacity as wheat eaters has been taken till after the attack of potato blight in 1846. The small number of wheat-eaters prior to that date may be assumed to have consumed their own home-grown supplies. After 1847 the Irish people began to be eaters of wheat; the change, however, was a slow one, and in order to allow for it, the following reductions of the Irish census figures have been made in order to arrive at the number who may be considered to have been wheat-eaters:

From 1766 to 1846	100% reduction
„ 1847 „ 1870	66% „
„ 1871 „ 1899	50% „
„ 1900 „ 1921	33·3% „

In Scotland the problem is slightly different: the Highlanders may be disregarded altogether as wheat-eaters; the proportion of the total Scotch population occupying these parts ranged from $\frac{1}{7}$ in 1801 to $\frac{1}{6}$ in 1831, $\frac{1}{8}$ in 1861, $\frac{1}{11}$ in 1891, $\frac{1}{14}$ in 1911, and $\frac{1}{17}$ in 1936. In the lowlands, oatmeal, an important factor in the people's food, is still much eaten. In order to arrive at a workable estimate of the amount of wheat consumed in Scotland, the population may be regarded as being but three-quarters of its actual amount, but that all of the reduced number are full wheat-eaters. In other words, the census returns for Scotland have been cut down by one-quarter.

Below are given, over a number of years, the estimated tonnages of the total wheat supplies of the United Kingdom, including home-grown and imported grain and flour. The population figures are shown in gross, with the reduction applicable for each year.

The wheat availability $= \dfrac{\text{Total tonnage}}{\text{Population of wheat-eaters}}$. This latter figure is converted into pounds by multiplying the former figure by the factor 100/166. This gives the Availability Index (W.A.I.) or the amount in pound weight of wheat available per day to each individual of the population.

The curve *EFGH* (Fig. 74), represents the variation in the index figure from 1775 to 1925.

Date	Imports in million tons	Home produce plus 100,000 tons, less 10 % for seed, in million tons	Population of Great Britain and Ireland in millions	Deduction in respect to Scotland in millions	Deduction in respect to Ireland in millions	Population of wheat consumers	W.A.I.	W.A.I. ten-year average and equivalent in pounds per day
1932	5·85	1·17	47·3	1·25	0	46·05	1·55	
1931	6·7	1·08	46·0	1·25	0	44·75	1·8	1·6 = 1 lb.
1930	6·0	1·13	45·8	1·2	0	44·6	1·6	
1929	6·4	1·26	45·7	1·2	0	44·5	1·75	
1928	5·8	1·26	45·5	1·2	0	44·3	1·8	
1927	6·25	1·43	45·3	1·2	0	44·1	1·7	
1926	5·8	1·35	45·1	1·2	0	43·9	1·6	
1925	5·45	1·35	45·0	1·2	0	43·8	1·6	1·70 = 1·03 lb.
1924	6·65	1·35	44·7	1·2	0	43·5	1·8	
1923	5·8	1·44	44·6	1·2	0	43·4	1·7	
1922	5·7	1·67	44·5	1·2	0	43·3	1·7	
1921	5·1	1·99	44·3	1·1	0	43·2	1·64	
1920	6·3	1·44	47·2	1·1	1·4	44·7	1·7	
1919	4·8	1·8	47·0	1·0	1·3	44·7	1·5	
1918	5·2	2·12	46·8	1·0	1·3	44·5	1·7	
1917	5·5	1·58	46·7	1·0	1·3	44·4	1·6	
1916	5·65	1·58	46·5	1·0	1·2	44·3	1·6	
1915	5·2	1·8	46·0	1·0	1·2	43·8	1·6	
1914	5·7	1·53	45·8	1·0	1·5	43·3	1·7	1·67 = 1·01 lb.
1913	6·15	1·53	45·7	1·0	1·5	43·2	1·8	
1912	6·15	1·53	45·5	1·0	1·6	42·9	1·8	
1911	5·55	1·58	45·3	1·0	1·6	42·7	1·7	
1910	5·9	1·53	45·0	1·0	1·6	42·4	1·7	
1909	5·65	1·53	44·3	1·2	1·5	41·6	1·7	
1908	5·4	1·53	44·0	1·2	1·5	41·3	1·7	
1907	5·85	1·49	43·7	1·1	1·3	41·3	1·8	
1906	5·6	1·47	43·5	1·1	1·3	41·1	1·7	
1905	5·7	1·46	43·0	1·1	1·3	40·6	1·8	
1904	5·9	1·44	42·7	1·1	1·3	40·3	1·8	1·72 = 1·03 lb.
1903	5·8	1·44	42·3	1·1	1·3	39·9	1·8	
1902	5·4	1·30	42·0	1·1	1·3	39·6	1·7	
1901	5·0	1·3	41·7	1·1	1·3	39·3	1·6	
1900	4·9	1·44	41·3	1·1	1·3	38·9	1·6	
1899	4·85	1·51	41·0	1·1	2·0	37·9	1·7	
1898	4·65	1·53	40·5	1·1	2·2	37·2	1·7	
1897	4·4	1·58	40·2	1·0	2·1	37·1	1·6	
1896	4·9	1·62	40·0	1·0	2·1	35·9	1·8	
1895	5·35	1·67	39·5	1·0	2·1	36·4	1·9	
1894	4·8	1·71	39·3	1·0	2·1	36·2	1·8	1·76 = 1·04 lb.
1893	4·7	1·78	39·0	1·0	2·1	35·9	1·8	
1892	4·75	1·8	38·5	1·0	2·1	35·4	1·9	
1891	4·4	1·8	38·2	1·0	2·1	35·1	1·8	
1890	4·16	1·99	38·0	1·0	2·3	34·7	1·8	
1889	3·95	1·99	37·5	1·0	2·3	34·2	1·7	
1888	4·0	1·96	37·4	1·0	2·4	34·0	1·8	
1887	4·0	1·98	37·0	1·0	2·5	33·5	1·8	1·8 = 1·05 lb.
1886	3·35	2·05	36·8	0·9	2·5	33·4	1·7	
1885	4·15	2·06	36·5	0·9	2·5	33·1	1·9	

Date	Imports in million tons	Home produce plus 100,000 tons, less 10 % for seed, in million tons	Population of Great Britain and Ireland in millions	Deduction in respect to Scotland in millions	Deduction in respect to Ireland in millions	Population of wheat consumers	W.A.I.	W.A.I. ten-year average and equivalent in pounds per day
1884	5·3	2·11	36·0	0·9	2·5	32·6	1·7	
1883	4·25	2·15	36·0	0·9	2·5	32·6	1·9	
1882	4·05	2·16	35·5	0·8	2·7	32·5	1·9	1·8 = 1·05 lb.
1881	3·50	2·24	35·2	0·9	2·5	31·8	1·8	
1880	3·4	2·28	35·0	0·9	2·6	31·5	1·8	
1879	3·65	2·34	34·5	0·9	2·6	31·0	2·0	
1878	3·0	2·37	34·0	0·8	2·5	30·7	1·8	
1877	3·18	2·43	33·7	0·8	2·6	30·4	1·8	
1876	2·6	2·48	33·0	0·8	2·6	29·6	1·7	
1875	2·95	2·52	32·8	0·75	2·6	29·4	1·9	
1874	2·47	2·61	32·5	0·7	2·6	29·2	1·7	1·8 = 1·05 lb.
1873	2·57	2·68	32·0	0·7	2·6	28·7	1·8	
1872	2·35	2·7	31·5	0·7	2·6	28·2	1·8	
1871	2·25	2·89	31·2	0·7	2·6	27·9	1·9	
1870	2·35	2·73	31·0	0·6	2·7	27·7	1·9	
1869	2·25	2·7	30·6	0·7	3·6	26·3	1·9	
1868	1·8	2·66	30·3	0·7	3·6	26·0	1·7	
1867	1·95	2·60	30·0	0·7	3·6	25·7	1·8	
1866	1·48	2·59	29·7	0·7	3·6	25·4	1·6	
1865	1·3	2·57	29·5	0·7	3·6	25·2	1·5	
1864	1·45	2·52	29·2	0·7	3·6	24·9	1·6	1·7 = 1·03 lb.
1863	1·56	2·52	29·0	0·7	3·6	24·7	1·7	
1862	2·5	2·51	28·7	0·7	3·6	24·4	2·0	
1861	1·85	2·48	28·5	0·7	3·6	24·2	1·8	
1860	1·6	2·46	28·3	0·6	3·6	24·1	1·7	
1859	1·0	2·43	28·2	0·6	4·0	23·7	1·4	
1858	1·15	2·43	28·2	0·6	4·0	23·6	1·5	
1857	0·88	2·41	28·1	0·6	4·0	23·5	1·4	
1856	1·15	2·37	28·0	0·6	4·0	23·4	1·5	
1855	0·7	2·35	28·0	0·6	4·0	23·4	1·3	
1854	0·95	2·34	27·8	0·6	4·5	22·7	1·5	1·4 = 0·85 lb.
1853	1·25	2·24	27·7	0·6	4·5	22·6	1·5	
1852	0·85	2·35	27·5	0·6	4·5	22·4	1·4	
1851	1·2	2·30	27·3	0·6	4·5	22·2	1·6	
1850	1·07	2·25	27·1	0·6	4·7	21·8	1·5	
1849	1·07	2·25	27·1	0·6	4·7	21·8	1·5	
1848	0·67	2·23	27·1	0·6	4·8	21·7	1·35	
1847	0·95	2·19	27·0	0·6	4·8	21·6	1·5	
1846	0·55	2·16	27·0	0·6	4·8	21·6	1·25	
1845	0·2	2·16	19·05	0·6	—	18·45	1·3	
1844	0·32	2·16	19·03	0·6	—	18·43	1·35	1·4 = 0·85 lb.
1843	0·2	2·14	19·0	0·6	—	18·4	1·3	
1842	0·65	2·10	18·8	0·6	—	18·2	1·5	
1841	0·65	2·10	18·5	0·6	—	17·9	1·5	
1840	0·5	2·1	18·3	0·6	—	17·7	1·5	
1835	0·44	2·05	17·4	0·6	—	16·8	1·5	1·5 = 0·9 lb.
1825	0·3	2·01	15·0	0·5	—	14·5	1·6	1·58 = 0·95 lb.
1815	0·11	2·0	12·0	0·5	—	11·5	1·8	1·8 = 1·05 lb.
1805	0·14	1·94	10·0	0·3	—	9·7	—	2·14 = 1·3 lb.
1795	0·02	1·99	9·2	0·3	—	8·9	—	2·26 = 1·36 lb.
1785	0·81	1·8	9·0	0·3	—	8·7	—	2·3 = 1·4 lb.
1775	0·02	1·71	8·5	0·3	—	8·2	2·34	2·1 = 1·3 lb.
1765	—	1·62	6·5‡	—	—	6·5	—	2·5 = 1·5 lb.

* The following figures represent the average for the decades 1830–8, 1820–9, etc., as the exact figures for imports over these periods are unknown. Estimates of imports are founded on the extrapolation of the curve whose values at its beginning in 1815 and end in 1840 are known.

Wheat availability in pounds per day per head of population

	1835	1825	1815
	0·9	0·95	1·09

† These import figures are derived from Ernle, p. 266.
‡ England and Wales only.

The Potato in the Early Herbaria

Whilst this work was in the press, my friend Dr J. G. Hawkes discovered two Herbarium specimens of the common potato, *S. tuberosum*, in the Vaillant Collection now in the Muséum National d'Histoire Naturelle, Paris. Sebastian Vaillant died in 1720, so that these specimens may be regarded as dating from about the end of the seventeenth century. Both specimens, that is to say their leaves and stems, can be referred without hesitation to Group IV of the *S. andigenum* series (see chapter v, Figs. 53 and 54).

Thanks to Mr S. Savage, and the generosity of Prof. Binz of Bâle, I have succeeded in acquiring a photograph of Gaspard Bauhin's original herbarium specimen of the potato, which he described in his *Phytopinax* (1596). The leaf formation conforms closely to the type shown in Fig. 52 and can therefore be regarded as an example of Group III of the *S. andigenum* series. A photograph of another early herbarium specimen prepared by Joachim Burser (1583–1639) has come into my possession through the good offices of Dr Uggla of Uppsala: it also can be ascribed to Group III of the series. Indeed it may well be derived from the same variety as Bauhin's, a suggestion made the more probable by the fact that these two eminent botanists were at one time close colleagues.

Following up this line of research, I have since discovered ten more examples of similar Herbarium material in England. Nine of these specimens were collected in the latter half of the seventeenth century and all of them can confidently be regarded as being more or less typical specimens of the Group IV type of foliage, and in respect of the character of their foliage, distinct from the types grown in this country to-day. One of these herbarium specimens, which cannot be exactly dated but which from the character of the paper on which it is mounted and the writing of the name *Battatas* appears to be somewhat later in date would appear to belong to the first half of the eighteenth century. However this may be, its leaf character, whilst distinguishing it from all the others, unites it to the majority of our common domestic types. Although not an extreme example, it clearly conforms to the Group V type of foliage.

There would seem therefore to be no doubt that the type of potato plant which reached Western Europe at the end of the sixteenth century must have been much like the types we now know were common in

England prior to the latter half of the seventeenth century. In other words, the newcomers were examples of those types of *S. andigenum* we have designated as belonging to Groups III and IV.

In the eighteenth century, when potato cultivation became more general and selection for better cropping and earlier varieties began to be practised, a change of leaf type was brought about. This change was not intentional, but followed inevitably from the fact that in order to attain the above two desirable characters, a large area of chlorophyll-containing leaf surface was essential. This latter has been achieved by an enlargement in the overall size of the leaf and more particularly by a widening of the individual folioles, which leads to their overlapping. Associated with this, a richer development of secondary folioles is common, which converts the 'open' leaf of the early immigrant potato plant into the 'closed' leaf exhibited by the majority of our present-day varieties.

An account of these early Herbarium specimens will be published shortly in the Journal of the Linnean Society by Dr J. G. Hawkes and myself.[1]

[1] Salaman, R. N. and Hawkes, J. G. (1949). The character of the early European potato. *Proc. Linn. Soc.*, vol. 161, 71–84. – Ed.

BIBLIOGRAPHY[1]

ACLAND, DYKE THOMAS and STURGE, W. (1851). *The Farming of Somerset* (Murray, London) 532

ACOSTA, JOSÉ DE (1590). *Natural and Moral History of the Indies* (trans.; Hakluyt Soc., 1880) 28, 92, 102

ADAIR, COL. R. A. (1886). *Ireland and her Servile War* (Ridgway, London) 340

ADAM, JAMES (1789). *Practical Essays on Agriculture* (London) 235

ADLER, NATHAN, Chief Rabbi. *Sermon delivered in the Great Synagogue* 24 March 1847 (Sherwood, Gilbert and Piper, London) 314

ALBERTUS MAGNUS, Bishop of Ratisbon (1193–1280). *De Vegetabilibus, c.* 1256 (ed. 1867; Berlin) 74

ALISON, WILLIAM PULTENEY (1847). *Observations of the Famine of 1846–47* (Blackwood, Edinburgh) 377

Allotments, Report on (1843). *Parliamentary Papers* (London, 1843) 528

ALMACK, BARUGH (1845). The Agriculture of Norfolk. *J. Roy. Agric. Soc.* vol. VI 473

ANDERSON, ADAM (1764). *History of Commerce* (London) 434

ANDERSON, JOHN (1827). *The State of Society and Knowledge in the Highlands of Scotland* (W. Tait, Edinburgh) 352

ANGLO HIBERNICUS (1847). *Letter to Lord John Russell by Anglo Hibernicus* (Cleaver, London) 313

Annals of Agriculture (ed. A. Young, 1795–6) 462, 479, 492, 503–4, 507, 510–13, 516, 521

ANON. (1757). *Letters from an Armenian in Ireland to his friends at Trebisond* attributed to R. Hellen (London) 248

ANON. (1847). The Yield of Irish Tillage Crops. *J. Dept. of Agric. and Tech. Inst., Ireland*, vol. XXI (reprinted 1921) 248

ANON. (1848). *History of Youghal*, attributed to Samuel Hayman (John Lindley, Youghal) 155

APULEIUS PLATONICUS. *Herbarium* 75 *See also* ARBER, A. 38–41

ARBER, AGNES (1938). *Herbals* (Cambridge Univ. Press) 74–6, 84–5, 88–9, 93–5, 111

ARBLAY, MME D'. *See* BURNEY, FRANCES

Archaeologia, vol. XIII 439 n.

ARCHDALL'S ed. of *Lodge's Peerage of Ireland* (Dublin, 1789) 155

ARGYLL, 8TH DUKE OF (1883). *Crofts and Farms in the Hebrides* (Douglas, Edinburgh) 384

ARKSTEE and MERKUS (1749). *Allgemeine Historie der Reisen* 550

ARMSTRONG, ROBERT A. (1825). *Gaelic Dictionary* (London) 139

ARRIAGA, PAUL JOSEPH DE (1562). *Extirpación de la Idolatría de los Indios del Peru* (Lima, 1920) 8, 28

ASHTON, T. S. (1939). *An Eighteenth Century Industrialist* (University Press, Manchester) 499

AUSTEN-LEIGH, E. (1870). *A Memoir of Jane Austen* (Bentley, London) 479

BACON, FRANCIS (1627). *Sylva Sylvarum* (Will. Lee, London) 432, 443

BAGWELL, R. (1885). *Ireland under the Tudors* (Longmans, London) 149

[1] The page numbers cited here refer to this book and not to the bibliographic references themselves. – Ed.

BAINES, EDWARD (1836). *History of the County Palatine and Duchy of Lancashire* (Fisher, London) 451

BAKER, W. F. (1941). A Seventeenth-Century Harvest Account Book. Lecture to Cambridge Antiquarian Soc. 465

BALL, F. E. (1902). *History County Dublin* (Athers, Dublin) 604

BANDELIER, ADOLPH (1910). *Islands of Titicaca and Koati* (Hispanic Soc., New York) 8, 26, 28, 30, 33

BANKS, SIR JOSEPH (1800). A Breviary touching the order and governments of a nobleman's House. *Archaeologia*, vol. XIII 439

BANKS, SIR JOSEPH (1805). *Trans. Hort. Soc.* vol. I 429

BARKER, J. and BURTON, W. G. (1944). Mashed potato powder. I. General characteristics and the 'brush sieve' method of preparation. *J. Soc. Chem. Ind.* vol. LXIII 564-5

BARLOW, EDWARD (1671). *Journal* (ed. Basil Lubbock; Hurst and Blackett, 1934) 549

BARNES, H. N. V. (1937). *Brit. Dent. Journ.* vol. LXIII 545

BARRON, H. (1943). *Modern Synthetic Rubbers* (2nd ed.; Chapman and Hall, London) 570

BARROW, K. M. (1910). *Three Years in Tristan da Cunha* (Skeffington, London) 545

BAUDIN, L. (1929). *C.R. l'Acad. Sci. Morales et Politiques* 43

BAUHIN, GASPARD (1596). *Phytopinax* (Basle) 66, 84-5, 91, 93, 94, 618

BAUHIN, GASPARD (1598). *Matthiolus's Commentary on Dioscorides* (ed. G. Bauhin, 1598; Frankfurt-a-M.) 91-2, 344

BAUHIN, GASPARD (1620). *Prodromos Theatri Botanici* (Frankfurt-a-M.) 66, 83-5, 91, 94, 104, 108

BAUHIN, GASPARD (1623). *Pinax Theatri Botanici* (Basle) 84-5

BAUHIN, GASPARD (1658). *Theatri Botanici* (König, Basle) 84

BAUHIN, JEAN (1651). *Historia Plantarum Universalis* (ed. by Chabrey, Yverdon) 64, 66, 84, 95, 97, 104, 108, 344

BAXTER, RICHARD (1611). *The Poor Husbandman's Advocate* (ed. F. Powicke, 1926; *Bull. Rylands Lib.* vol. X, no. I) 464

BEALE, JOHN (1664). MSS. v. B i: Royal Society 409, 433, 440

BEALE, JOHN (1663). Boyle MSS. v. Miscellaneous: Royal Society 448

BEALE, JOHN (1672-5). *Phil. Trans.* (1672-3, 1675) 226, 449

BEALS, C. (1934). *Fire on the Andes* (Lippincott and Co., Philadelphia) 8

BEATON, T. (1799). *Annals of Agric.* vols. XXIV, XXVI 510, 511

BEATSON, A. (1816). *Tracts relative to St Helena* (Booth, London) 552, 554

BECKMANN, JOHN (1780-1805). *A History of Invention* (Bohn's 4th ed. 1846; London) 441

Belfast Magazine (1825) 223

BENHAM, CHARLES E. (1891). *A Biographical Index of Colchester* (Colchester) 479

BENZONI, GIROLAMO (c. 1565). *History of the New World showing his travels from 1541-1556* (Venice, 1565; Hakluyt Soc. 1857) 126

BERGEN, FANNY (1899). *Animal and Plant Lore* (Boston) 118

BERGZABERN, JACOB DIETRICH (Tabernaemontanus) (1588). *Neuw Kreuterbuch* (Frankfurt-a-M.) 77

BERNARD, JAMES (1795). Near Taunton, Somerset. *Annals of Agric.* vol. XXIV 505

BESLER, BASIL (1613). *Hortus Eystettensis* (Nuremberg) 112

BEVAN, S. (1795). Riddlesworth Hall, Norfolk. *Annals of Agric.* vol. XXIV 505

BEVERIDGE, WILLIAM H, LORD (1928). *British Food Control* (Oxford Univ. Press) 576

BEVERIDGE, WILLIAM H, LORD, AND OTHERS (1930). *Prices and Wages in England* (Longmans, London) 439

BICHENO, J. E. (1830). *Ireland and its Economy* (John Murray, London) 200

BLYTH, WALTER (1652). *The English Improver Improved* (London) 445

Board of Agriculture (1816). *Agricultural State of the Kingdom* 501

Board of Agriculture (1816). *Replies to a Circular Letter, etc.* 519

Board of Agriculture (1795). *Report Committee on Cultivation and Use of Potatoes* 417, 503–4, 588

BOSWELL, JAMES (1785). *Journal of a Tour to the Hebrides* (6th ed.; Clarendon Press, Oxford) 345, 348

BOSWELL, JAMES (1791). *Life of Dr Johnson* (ed. 1901; Dent and Co., London) 355

BOULTER, HUGH, Abp Armagh (1770). *Letters* (Faulkner, Dublin) 252, 604

BOURGCHIER, SIR H. (1623). Advertisements for Ireland. Repr. *J. Roy. Soc. Antiq. Ireland* (1923) 224

BOYD, J. (1825). *Flora* (St Helena) 549

BOYLE, ROBERT. Boyle MSS., Roy. Soc. 227, 448

BOYLE, ROBERT. Roy. Soc. Letter Books, vol. I 238

BRADDON, ELIZ. (1881). *Asphodel* (Maxwell, London) 140

BRADLEY, R. (1728). *A Botanical Dictionary* (Woodward, London) 475

BRADLEY, R. (1725). *General Dictionary* (trans. of Chomel's *Dict. aeconomique*; London) 474

BRADLEY, R. (1724). *A General Treatise of Husbandry and Gardening* (London) 474

BRADLEY, R. (1717). *New Improvements in Planting and Gardening* (4th ed. 1724; London) 474

BRADLEY, R. (1725). *A Survey of Ancient Husbandry* (London) 474

BRANDERS, J. (1940). *Tristan da Cunha* (Allen and Unwin, London) 543

BRANDRETH, B. *J. Nat. Inst. Agric. Bot.* vol. IV 407

Breviary (A). *See* BANKS, SIR JOSEPH (1800)

BRICEGNO, DIEGO DÁVILA (1586). *Relac. Geográf. d. Ind.* Quoted from E. Heckel, *Ann. de la Faculté des Sciences de Marseilles*, 1906, tome XVI 126

BRICEGNO, DIEGO DÁVILA (1586). Descripción y Relación de la Provincia de los Yauyos. *Relac. Geográf. de Indias* (publ. 1881, Madrid) 143

BRIDGES, J. H. (1888). *Two Centuries of Irish History* (Kegan Paul, London) 274, 280, 606

British Museum, Harleian MSS. no. 157 441

BROCKBANK, REV. THOMAS. *Diary and Letter Book* (Chetham Soc.; n.s. 1930) 452

BROEKHUYSEN, G. J. and MACNAE, W. (1948). The Potato Caterpillar Pest, etc. *Nature, London* 546

BROILI (1921). Mitteilungen der Biologisch. *Reichsantalt. f. Land. u. Forst-wirtscht.* Ht. XXI 178

BROWN, PETER HUME (1911). *History of Scotland* (3 vols.; Cambridge Univ. Press) 389

BRUFORD (1935). *Germany in the Seventeenth Century* (Cambridge Univ. Press) 115

BRUSHFIELD, T. N. (1898). Raleghana. *Trans. Devonshire Assoc.* vol. XXX 148

BRYCE (1888). *Two Centuries of Irish History* (Kegan Paul, London) 267

BUNBURY, SIR H. (1845). The Allotment System. *J. Roy. Agric. Soc.* vol. V 527

BURGOYNE, SIR JOHN (1847). *The Times* (6 Oct.) 303

BURKE, EDMUND (1795). *Thoughts and Details on Scarcity* 472

BURKILL, I. H. (1938). The contact of the Portuguese with African food plants.... *Proc. Linn. Soc.* (Sess. 150) 138

BURNEY, FRANCES (MME D'ARBLAY). *Dairy and Letters* (1778–1840), 7 vols., publ. 1842 (Colbourn, London) 140

BURTON, ROBERT (1621). *The Anatomy of Melancholy* (Edward Shilleto, London, 1893) 113, 429

BURTON, W. G. (1944). Mashed potato powder. II. Spray drying method. *J. Soc. Chem. Ind.* vol. LXIII 564

BURTON, W. G. (1945). Mashed potato powder. III. The high temperature browning of mashed potato powder. *J. Soc. Chem. Ind.* vol. LXIV 565–6

BURTON, W. G. (1945). The storage life of a sample of potato-flour produced from potato slices dried in a sugar-beet factory. *J. Soc. Chem. Ind.* vol. LXIV 565

BUTLER, W. F. (1913). Policy of Surrender. *J. Roy. Soc. Antiq. Ireland,* vol. XLIII (p. 123) 194

BUTTS, THOMAS (1794). *Annals of Agric.* vol. XXIV 505

CADLE, CLEMENT (1867). *J. Roy. Agric. Soc.* vol. III 529

CAIRD, SIR JAMES (1852). *English Agriculture* (Longmans, London) 528, 530, 612

CAIRNES, JOHN ELLIOT (1873). *Political Essays* (London) 266

Camb. Mod. Hist. (1909). Vol. VI (Cambridge Univ. Press) 573

CAMDEN, WILLIAM (1586). *Britannia* (ed. 1610; London) 224

CAMDEN, WILLIAM (1789). *Britannia* (Gough's ed.; T. Payne and Son, London) 224, 557

CAMERON, JOHN (1883). *Gaelic Names of Plants* (Edinburgh) 139

CAMERON, JOHN (1912). *The Old and the New Hebrides* (Cameron, Kirkcaldy) 352

CAMPBELL, JOHN (1774). *A Political Survey of England* (London) 364, 370

CAMPBELL, JOHN (1900). *Superstitions of the Scotch Highlands* (Glasgow) 376

CAMPBELL, W. J. (1928). The Scottish Seed Potato Trade. *Scot. J. Agric.* vol. XI 405

CARDAN, JEROME (1557). *De Rerum Varietate* (Basle) 102, 126, 145

CARLYLE, THOMAS (1843). *Past and Present* (2nd ed. 1858; London) 323–4

CARMICHAEL, ALEX. (1928). *Carmina Gadelica* (Edinburgh) 137

CARR, F. C. (1901). *Handbook of Administration,* 1801–69 (ed. 1901; London) 296

CARRINGTON, R. W. (1846). The Agriculture of Nottinghamshire. *J. Roy. Agric. Soc.* vol. VI 527

CASTELLANOS, JUAN DE (1886). *Historia del Nuevo Reino de Granada* (Madrid) 36, 102, 126

CASTLEHAVEN, LORD (1680). *Memoirs* (James Touchet) (H. Brome, London) 152

CATHCART, E. P. (1933). Unpublished material, quoted by T. P. McIntosh 407

CAULDFIELD, RICHARD (1878). Ed. *Council Book of the Corporation of Youghal* (Billing and Sons, Guildford) 225

Census. *Report of the Census Commissioners* (1841) 279, 287

Census. *England & Wales* (1851) 609

Census of Ireland (1851) 304, 315, 604–7, 609

CHABRAEUS, DOMINICUS (1666). *Stirpian Incones et Sciagraphia* (Geneva) 97

CHAMBERS, E. K. (1923). *Elizabethan Stage* (ed. 1923; Oxford) 426

CHAPMAN, GEORGE (1611). *May Day* (ed. by C. W. Dilke, *Old English Plays,* 1814–15; London) 427

CHICK, HARRIETTE (1940). Nutritive Value of the Potato. *Chemistry and Industry* 124

CHRISTOPHERSON, ERLING (1940). *Tristan da Cunha, the Lonely Isle* (Cassell, London) 544

CIEZA DE LEÓN, PEDRO DE (1550). *The War of Quito* (Madried, 1886; trans. C. R. Markham, Hakluyt Soc., 31, 1913) 126

CIEZA DE LEÓN, PEDRO DE (1553). *The Chronicle of Peru* (trans. Markham; Hakluyt Soc. 1864) 27, 36, 91, 92, 102

CLAPHAM, SIR J. H. (1944). *The Bank of England* (Cambridge Univ. Press) 298-9

CLAPHAM, SIR J. H. (1926). *An Economic History of Modern Britain: The Early Railway Age* (ed. 1939; Cambridge Univ. Press) 276, 322-3, 418, 476, 484, 525, 531

CLAPHAM, SIR J. H. (1938). *An Economic History of Modern Britain: Machines and National Rivalries* (Cambridge Univ. Press) 532

CLAPHAM, SIR J. H. (1932). *An Economic History of Modern Britain: Free Trade and Steel* (Cambridge Univ. Press) 420

CLODE, CHARLES (1875). *Memorials of the Guild of Merchant Taylors* (London) 441

CLOS (1874). *Quelques documents pour l'histoire de la Pomme de Terre* (quoted from Roze) 109

CLUSIUS, CAROLUS (1576). *Rariorum aliquot Stirpium per Hispanias observatoarum historia* (Antwerp) 68

CLUSIUS, CAROLUS (JULES CHARLES DE L'ECLUSE) (1601). *Historia* (*Rariorum Plantarum Historia*) (Antwerp) 66, 84, 88, 89, 92, 93, 95, 430

COBBETT, WILLIAM (1821). *Cottage Economy* (Peter Davies, London, 1926) 464, 524, 566

COBBETT, WILLIAM (1832). *Political Register*, vol. LXXVIII (London) 473

COBBETT, WILLIAM (1830). *Rural rides* (ed. 1912; Dent, London) 149, 524

COBBETT, WILLIAM (1828). *A Treatise on Cobbett's Corn* (W. Cobbett, London) 523

COBO, BERNABÉ (1653). *Historia del Nuevo Mundo* (ed. Marcos Jiminez de la Espada, 1890-5; Seville) 103, 143

COLE, G. D. H. and POSTGATE, RAYMOND (1938). *The Common People* (ed. 1946; Methuen, London) 299, 497, 520-1

COLES, WILLIAM (1657). *Adam in Eden* (London) 112, 232, 444

COLQUHOUN, P. (1814). *Treatise on the Wealth, Power and Resources of the British Empire* (London) 521

Commercial Restraint of Ireland, quoted from Lewis, Sir G. Cornewall (1836) 604

COMMON, R. H. and BOLTON, W. (1944). Dried-potato products and nutritional encephalomania in chicks. *Nature, London*, vol. CLIII 568

Complete Farmer or Dictionary of Husbandry (1st ed. 1766; 3rd ed. 1777; London) 255-6

COOK, O. F. (1918). Foot Plow Agriculture in Peru. *Ann. Rept. Smithsonian Inst.* 46

COOTE, SIR CHAS. (1809). *Stat. Survey of County of Armagh* (Dublin Society, Dublin) 278

The Cork Examiner (25 May 1936) 152-3

Cork Historical Journal 152

The Cottage Gardener, 30 Sept. 1852 165

County Histories of Scotland (1897). Vol. IV, *Inverness* 367

COURTOIS-GÉRARD (?1894). *Du Choix et de la Culture des Pommes de Terre* (Paris) 144

COWAN, JOHN MACQUEEN (1938). *The History of the Royal Botanic Garden, Edinburgh.* Notes from the Roy. Bot. Gardens, Edinburgh, vol. XIX 344, 345

COX, H. (1846). On the Cultivation of the Potato. *J. Roy. Agric. Soc.* vol. VI 482

CROKER, J. W. (1808). *A sketch of the state of Ireland.* Publ. anonymously; reprinted 1822 (John Murray, London) 279

CRUTCHLEY, J. (1804). *Communication to the Board of Agriculture* 525

CULLUM, SIR THOMAS GERY (*c.* 1775). MSS. Diary, Nat. Lib., Aberystwyth 413, 416

CUNNINGHAM, W. (1892). *Growth of English Industry* 513

CURTLER, W. H. R. (1908). *Victoria County Histories, etc., Lancaster* 455

CURWEN, J. C. (1818). *State of Ireland* 282, 286

CUVIER, LEOPOLD (1813). *Éloge de Parmentier* (quoted from Roze) 114

DAMPIER, WILLIAM (1691). *Voyages* (ed. J. Mansfield, 1906; Grant Richards, London) 551

DARVAL, FRANK (1934). *Popular Disturbances and Public Order in Regency England* (Oxford) 521

DARWIN, CHARLES (1845). *Journal of a Voyage round the World* (ed. 1889; Ward Lock and Co., London) 555

DAVIDSON, W. D. (1933). History of Potato Varieties. *J. Dept. of Agric., Eire* 161

DAVIDSON, W. D. (1939). Famous Potato Raisers. *J. Roy. Agric. Soc.* vol. C 168

DAVIDSON, W. D. (1936). The History of the Potato and its Progress in Ireland. *J. Dept. Agric., Eire,* vol. XXXIV 148, 223, 226

DAVIDSON, W. D. (1928). The Rejuvenation of the 'Champion'. *Proc. Dublin Roy. Soc.* vol. II 176

DAVIES, CORNELIUS (1944). Harvesting Machinery. *Proc. Inst. Brit. Agric. Engineering,* vol. III 584

DAVIES, D. J. (1933). *The Economic History of South Wales* (University Press, Cardiff) 412, 416

DAVIES, DAVID (1795). *The Case of the Labourers in Husbandry* (Bath and London) 494

DAVIES, W. M. (1935). *Annals of Appl. Biol.* vol. XXII 182

DAVIES, WALTER (1810). *General View of Agriculture in North Wales* (London) 410, 413

DAVIES, WALTER (1814). *A General View of the Agriculture, etc. of South Wales* (London) 414

DAWSON, THOMAS (1596). *The Good Huswife's Jewell* (London) 424, 444

DEERING, CHARLES (1783). *Catalogus Stirpium* (Nottingham) 477

DEFOE (1706). *Letter to Harley.* Nor. Hist. MSS. Comm. Portland Papers 353

DEFOE, DANIEL (1724). *A Tour through the Whole Island of Great Britain* (ed. G. D. H. Cole, 1927; Peter Davies, London) 461, 477

DEKKER, THOMAS (1612). *If it be not God, the Devil is in it* (ed. John Pearson; Covent Garden, 1873) 426

DEKKER AND OTHERS (1621). *The Witch of Edmonton* (Mermaid Series, ed. Ernest Rhys, 1887; Vizetelly, London) 436

DE LEEUW (1935). *Crossroads of the Caribbean Sea* (Julian Messner, New York 6

Destitution of the Highlands (1848). Statement issued by the Committee of the Free Church 374

DE VELASCO, JUAN (1789). *Historia del Reyno de Quito.* In TERNAUX–COMPANS (HENRI). *Voyages, Relations et mémoires originaux, etc.* (Paris) 27

Devon Commission (1845) 286–7

Dictionarium Rusticum Urbanicum et Botanicum, 1704 (A. J. Churchill, London) 465, 474

Dictionnaire des Sciences Naturelles, 1816–45 (61 vols.; Paris) 135

DIETSCHY, H. (1944). *Acta Tropica* 32

DIETSCHY, H. Die Heilkunst in Alten Peru. *Ciba Zeitsch.* 43

DINELEY (DINGLEY) THOS. (1675–80). Observations made on his Tours in Ireland and France, 1675–80. *J. Roy. Soc. Antiq. Ireland* (1870) 229

DIOSCORIDES (1st cent. A.D.), *De Materia Medica Libri Quinque* 74–5

DISRAELI (1845). *Sybil* (new ed. 1881; Longmans, London) 529

DISRAELI, BENJAMIN (1926). *Tancred* (Bradenham ed.; Peter Davies, London) 297

DODD, A. H. (1933). *Industrial Revolution in North Wales* (Univ. Press, Cardiff) 411, 415, 417, 420, 497

DODOENS, REMBERT (1554). *Cruydeboeck* (Jan van der Loe, Antwerp) 77, 79–80

DODOENS, REMBERT (1583). *Pemptades* 78

DODOENS, REMBERT (1644). *Cruydt Boeck* (ed. B. Moretus) 66, 95

DONALDSON, JAMES (1794). *General Views, County Elgin* 390

DONOVAN, EDWARD (1805). *Excursions through South Wales* 417

DOSSIE, ROBERT (1768–71). *Memoirs of Agriculture* (3 vols.; London) 162–3, 486

DRAKE, Sir FRANCIS (1628). *World Encompassed.* (Hakluyt Soc. 1854) 147

DREW, J. P. and DEASY, D. (1939). Potato growing in Ireland with particular reference to production for industrial purposes. *J. Dept. Agric., Eire,* vol. XXXVI 570

DRIVER, C. M. and HAWKES, J. G. (1943). Photoperiodism in the Potato. *Imp. Bur. Pl. Breed. & Genetics* 62, 67

DRUCE, G. C. *Pharmaceut. J.* (1899) 90

DRUMMOND and WILBRAHAM (1939). *The Englishman's Food* (Jonathan Cape, London) 434–5

DUFFERIN, LORD and BOYLE, HON. G. F. (1847). *Narrative of a Journey from Oxford to Skibbereen* (Parker, Oxford) 301

DUGUID, JULIAN (1931). *Green Hell* (Jonathan Cape, London) 7

DUNLOP, OLIVE JOCELYN (1913). *The Farm Labourer* (Fisher and Unwin, London) 527–8, 531

DUNLOP, R. (1910). *Camb. Mod. Hist.* vol. XII (Cambridge Univ. Press) 304, 605

DUNTON, JOHN (1699). Some account of my Conversation in Ireland. Repr. in Appendix B, letter 4, of MacLysaght's *Irish Life in the Seventeenth Century,* 1939 (Dublin) 231

DURANTE, CASTORE (1584). *Herbario Nuovo Venezia* (quoted from Laufer) 129

DUTTON, HELY (1808). *Stat. Surv. of the County of Clare* (Dublin) 278

EDEN, SIR FREDERICK (1797). *Annals of Agric.* vol. XXIX 480

EDEN, SIR FREDERICK (1797). *The State of the Poor* 362, 366, 417, 438, 441, 452, 465, 483, 497, 504, 511
ELLENBY, C. (1946). *J. Min. Agric.* vol. LIII 187
ELLIS, W. (1733). *The Practical Farmer* 478
ELLY, SAMUEL (1848). *Potatoes, Pigs and Politics* (Kent and Richards, London) 290, 299, 321
Enclosures, General Report on (1808) 527
Encyclopaedia Britannica (3rd ed. 1797) 356
Encyclopaedia Britannica (14th ed. 1929, vol. XVII) 297
Encyclopédie, La Grande (1st and 2nd ed, 1777; Paris) 114–15
ENGEL, SAMUEL (1762–84). *Biographie Universelle* (Nouvelle ed.; t. 12ᵐᵉ, 1855; Paris) 115
ENGEL, SAMUEL (1777). Author of article 'Pomme de terre' in the 1777 edition of *La Grande Encyclopédie* 135
ENGELS, FREDERICK (1892). *The Condition of the Working Class in England in 1844* (London) 323, 325
ERNLE, LORD (1912). *English Farming* (5th ed. 1936; Longmans, London) 197, 438, 467, 470, 518, 522, 575
ERNLE, LORD (1923). *The Land and its People* (Hutchinson, London) 434, 470, 614, 617
ESTCOURT, THOMAS (1802). *Annals of Agric.* vol. XLIII 525
EVANS, BERGEN and PINNEY, HESTER (1932). *Rev. English Studies*, vol. VIII 487
EVANS, E. ESTYN (1939). *Geography* (March) 194
EVANS, E. ESTYN (1942). *Irish Heritage* (Dundalgan Press, Dundalk) 191, 197, 199, 203, 219, 232–3, 253
EVANS, J. (1812). *The Beauties of England and Wales* 411, 415
EVANS, NESTA G. (1936). *Social Life in Mid-Eighteenth Century Anglesey* (Cardiff) 414
EVELYN, CHARLES (1717). *The Lady's Recreation* 345, 474
EVELYN, JOHN. *Diary* (ed. Wheatley, 1879) 445
EVELYN, JOHN (1664). *Sylva* (4th ed. 1745) 160
EVELYN, JOHN (1664). *Sylva. Tena. Pomona acetaria and Kalendarium Hortense* 345, 446

Facts from Fisheries (Waterford, 1848) 301
FAY, C. R. (1932). *Great Britain from Adam Smith to the Present Day* (Longmans) 397, 528
FELKIN, W. (1867). *A History of Machine-Wrought Hosiery* (Longmans, London) 487, 520
FENTON, RICHARD (1804–13). *Tours in Wales* (Bedford Press) 410
FEUERBACH, LUDWIG (1862). *Sämmtliche Werke* (ed. 1911) 338
FISHER, JOSEPH (1862). *How Ireland may be Saved* (Ridgway, London) 322
FLETCHER, JOHN (1637). *The Elder Brother* 428
FLETCHER, JOHN (?1623). *Love's Cure or the Martial Maid* (ed. Alex. Dyce; London, 1846) 432
FLETCHER, JOHN (1617). *The Loyal Subject* 428
FORBES, JOHN (1852). *Memorandum made in Ireland* (Smith Elder, London) 327
FORSTER, JOHN (1664). *England's Happiness Increased* (London) 409, 448
FORSTER, REV. M. (1795). *Annals of Agric.* vol. XXIV 478
FRANCK, H. A. (1917). *Vagabonding down the Andes* (Appleton, New York) 8, 9

FRASER, R. (1801). *Survey of County Wicklow* 200

FRASER, R. (1794). *General View of the County of Cornwall* (London)　563

FRAZER, SIR J. G. *Golden Bough* (1911) (enlarged ed.; Macmillan, London)
49, 118

FROUDE, J. A. (ed. 1881). *The English in Ireland* (Longmans, London)　243

FROUDE, J. A. (1879). *History of England* (Longmans, London)　206, 209–12,
217

FUESS, W. (1935). Die Urheimat der Kartoffel. *Die Ernährung der Pflanze*,
Bd. XXXI　114, 146, 437

FULLARTON, COL. (1793). *General View of Agriculture, County Ayr*　391

FUSSELL, G. E. (1947). *Old English Farming Books* (Crosby Lockwood and Son,
London)　438

FUSSELL, G. E. (1929). Population and Wheat Production in the Eighteenth
Century. *The History Teacher's Miscellany*　517

FYFE, J. G. (1942). *Scottish Diaries and Memoirs* (Mackay, Stirling)　376, 384,
389–91

GALT, J. (1821). *The Annals of the Parish* (Blackwood, Edinburgh)　387

GALT, J. (1821). *The Ayrshire Legatees* (Blackwood, Edinburgh)　395

GANE, DOUGLAS (1932). *Tristan da Cunha* (Allen and Unwin)　544

GARCILASO DE LA VEGA (1609). *Royal Commentaries* (transl. Hakluyt Series,
1869–71)　8, 46, 127

Gardeners' Chronicle　173, 291, 467

GARNETT, THOMAS (1800). *Observations on a Tour through the Highlands*
(London)　362

GARNIER, RUSSELL MONTAGUE (1895). *Annals of the British Peasantry* (Sonnen-
schein, London)　121, 367

GASKELL, E. C. (1857). *The Life of Charlotte Brontë* (ed. 1924; John Grant,
Edinburgh)　325

General Views (1794–5)　501–3

General Views, Berkshire　467

GERARD, JOHN (1596). *Catalogue* (London)　77–8, 84, 144, 146. Critical ed. by
B. Jackson (1876)　79

GERARD, J. (1597). *The Herball* (London)　51, 66, 78, 146, 430, 435

GERARD, J. (1633). *The Herball* (T. Johnson's ed.; London, 1633)　95, 108, 344

GIBAULT, G. (1912). *Histoire des Légumes* (Libraire Horticole, Paris)　105

GLASSE, MRS (1747). *The Art of Cooking made Plain* (London)　476

GODKIN, JAMES (1870). *Land War in Ireland* (Macmillan, London)　277,
306, 313

GÓMARA, LÓPEZ DE (1552). *Historia General de las Indias*　91, 92, 102, 126

GONNER, E. C. K. (1912). *Common Land and Enclosure* (Macmillan, London)
467

GOOCH, G. P. (1907). *Camb. Mod. Hist.* (Cambridge Univ. Press)　269

GOOKIN, VINCENT (1655). *The Great Case of Transplantation* (London)　227

GORDON, ABERCROMBY (1798). *The Statistical Account of Scotland* (Edinburgh)
365

GOSSE, PHILIP (1938). *St Helena* (Cassells, London)　547–9

GOUGH, G. C. (1919). Wart Disease of Potatoes. *J. Roy. Hort. Soc.* vol. XLV　172

GRAHAM, CUNNINGHAM (1922). *Conquest of New Granada* (Heinemann,
London)　36

GRAHAM, HENRY GREY (1906). *The Social Life of Scotland* (A. and C. Black,
Edinburgh and London)　357, 390

Grand (Le) Herbier (c. 1500) (Paris) 75
GRANT, SIR ARCHIBALD (1757). *The Farmer's New Year Gift* 477
GRANT, ARCHIBALD, SIR (1756). *The Practical Farmer's Pocket Companion* (Aberdeen) 391, 453, 478
GRANT, I. F. (1924). *Everyday Life on an old Highland Farm*, 1769–82 (Longmans, London) 349–50
GRANT, REV. JOHN (1794). *The Statistical Account of Scotland* (Edinburgh) 351
GRATTAN, HENRY. *Speeches*. (ed. by his son, 4 vols.; London) 249, 250
GRAY, HOWARD LEVI (1915). *English Field System* (Harvard University Press) 411
GRAY and TRUMBULL (1877). *Amer. J. Sci.* vol. LXIII 83
GREEN, ALICE STOPFORD (1909). *The Making of Ireland* (Macmillan, London) 215–16
GREEN, THOMAS (1816). *Universal Herbal* 446
GREENE, ROBERT (1592). *A Disputation betweene a Hee Conycatcher and a Shee Conycatcher, whether a thiefe or a whore, is most hurtful in cousanage to the Commonwealth* 426
GREG, ROBERT HYDE (1842). Scotch Farming in the Lothians. *Manchester Guardian* (9 Sept. 1842) 404
Grete Herball, The (1526) 75
GRIEVE, M. (1931). *A Modern Herbal* (Jonathan Cape, London) 119
GRIFFIN, GERALD (1827?). *The Half Sir* (ed. 1857; Duffy) 279
GROSE (1785). *Dict. of the Vulgar Tongue* 140
GUBERNATIO, A. DE (1882). *La Mythologie des Plantes* (Paris) 118
GUEDALLA, P. (1926). *Notes to Disraeli's Tancred* (Bradenham ed.) 297
Guernsey Hortic. Soc. *Annual Report* (1836) 559
GUNTHER, R. W. T. (1922). *Early British Botanists* (Oxford) 98, 105

HACKBARTH, J. (1935). Versuche ü. Photoperiodismus bei südamerikanischen Kartoffelklonen. *Züchter*, VII 62
HALE, THOMAS (1756). *A Compleat Body of Husbandry* (London) 477–8
HALLIWELL, J. O. (1852). *Some Accounts of a Collection of several Thousand Bills, etc. of the Archer Family* (Richard, London) 465, 474
HAMILTON, E. (1934). American Treasure and the Price Revolution in Spain, 1501–1650. *Harvard Economic Studies*, vol. XLIII 143
HAMILTON, H. (1945). '*Monymusk*' *Papers* (Edinburgh Univ. Press) 391
HAMMOND, J. L. and B. (1917). *The Town Labourer*, 1760–1832 (ed. 1936, Longmans, London) 325, 472–3
HAMMOND, J. L. and B. (1916). *The Skilled Labourer* (1925 ed.; Longmans, London) 522
HAMMOND, J. L. and B. (1911). *The Village Labourer* (1925 ed.; Longmans, London) 471, 491, 500, 506, 529
HANSEN, MARCUS (1940). *The Atlantic Migration* (Harvard Univ. Press) 317, 489, 606
HARIOT, T. (1588). *A Briefe and True Report...etc.* (De Bry, 1590; Frankfurt) 82
HARLAND, J. (1866). *Collecteana relating to Manchester* (Chetham Soc.) 453
HARLOW, V. T. (ed. 1932). *Raleigh's Last Voyage* (Argonaut Press, London) 151
HARRIES, E. (1795). *Annals of Agric.* vol. XXIV 507
HARRISON, WILLIAM (1577). *A Description of England, Britain, etc.* Ed. Frederick Furnivall. New Shakespeare Soc. 1877 (Trübner, London) 78, 88, 156, 424, 434

HARTLIB, S. (1651). *Legacy of Husbandry* (London)   436, 438

HAUDRICOURT, ANDRÉ and HÉDIN, LOUIS (1943). *L'Homme et les Plantes Cultivées* (Paris)   132

HAWKES, ARTHUR J. (1940). Early Cultivation of the Potato in Lancashire. *Notes and Queries* (7 Dec.)   451

HAWKES, J. G. (1946). Potato Bolters. *Nature*, London, vol. CLVII,   68, 375–6

HAWKES, J. G. (1944). Potato Collecting Expeditions in Mexico and South America. *Imp. Bur. Pl. Breed. & Genetics*, Cambridge   53, 63

HAYES, RICHARD (1937). The German Colony in County Limerick. *North Munster Antiq. J.* vol. I   340

HAYMAN, REV. SAMUEL (1848). The Handbook for Youghal. *Annals of Youghal* (3rd ser., 1852; Youghal)   155

HAYMAN, REV. SAMUEL (1856). Ecclesiastical Antiquities of Youghal. *J. Roy. Soc. Antiq. Ireland*, vol. IV   151

HEAD, SIR FRANCIS (1826). *Journey across the Pampas, etc.* (4th ed. 1846; (John Murray, London)   70

HELLEN, ROBERT (1757). *Letters from an Armenian in Ireland* (London)   248

HENNESSY, SIR JOHN POPE (1883). *Sir Walter Raleigh in Ireland* (Kegan Paul, London)   149

HENRY, DAVID (1771). *The Practical Farmer, The Complete English Farmer*   105, 416, 452, 476, 482, 487, 504

HENZE, GUSTAVE (1886). *Notice sur l'Introduction et la Propagation de la Pomme de Terre en Europe et en France* (Paris)   144

HEPBURN, G. BUCHAN (1794). *General View of Agriculture, East Lothian* (Edinburgh)   391

HEPBURN, LORD (1808). *Communication to the Board of Agriculture*   132, 389, 405

Herbarius, The Latin (1484)   75

Herbarius, The German (1485)   75

HERRERA, ANTONIO DE (1601). *The General History of the Vast Continent and Islands of America* (trans. Stevens, 1725)   103, 126

HEYWOOD, THOMAS (1633). *The English Traveller* (Mermaid Series, 1888)   431

HICKSON, M. (1884). *Ireland in the Seventeenth Century and Massacre of 1641* (Longmans, London)   220

HINDLEY, CHARLES (1881). *History of the Cries of London* (2nd ed. 1884)   429, 475

History of Lancashire (1881) (Historical Publishing Co.)   454

History of Youghal. See ANON. (1848)

HOGELAND, J. (1601). See CLUSIUS, CHARLES (1601)

HOLT, JOHN (1794). *General View of the Agriculture of the County of Lancaster*   502

HOOK, SIDNEY (1936). *From Hegel to Marx*   338

HOPPE, T. B. (1747). *Kurzer Bericht von denem Knottlichten und essbaren Erdaepfeln* (Wolfenbüttel)   187

HORE, HERBERT FRANCIS (1858). *Ulster J. Archaeol.* vol. VI   236

Hortus sanitatis (1491), Moguntia   75

HOUGHTON, J. (1699). *Collection of Letters*, 15 December (Bradley's ed. 1727)   148–9, 235, 455

HOWE, DR WILLIAM (1665). Mathias de L'Obel, *Stirpium, illustrationes* (London)   94

HOWELL, JAMES (1654). *Familiar Letters* (ed. Joseph Jacobs, 1890)   431–3

HRDLIČKA, A. (1918). *Bull. Bur. Amer. Ethnol.*   31

HUME, MARTIN (1906). *Sir Walter Raleigh* (Fisher and Unwin, London) 149, 151
HUNTER, A. (1777). *Georgical Essays* (London) 454
HUTTON, J. H. (1943). *Folk Lore*, vol. LIV 26

Indian J. Agric. Sci. vol. VIII 177
INGELEND, THOS. C. (*c.* 1560). *The Disobedient Child* (London) 332
Irish Poor Commission (1835). Selection from the Evidence 276, 284
Irish Problem, The (Anon. 1881; Ward Lock, London) 607

J. C. (1852). *Cottage Gardener* (p. 408) 165
JACKSON, C. J. (1911). *History of English Plate* 597
JACKSON, R. WYSE (1941). *Scenes from Irish Clerical Life* (Z. M. Ledger, Limerick) 198, 220, 239
JACOBS, P. B. (1939). Alcohol from farm products. *Industr. Engng Chem.* (*Ind. Edn.*), vol. XXXI 569
JANISCH, H. R. (1885). *Extracts from the St Helena Records* 551, 553
JOHNSON, G. W. (1829). *A History of English Gardening* 434
JOHNSON, SAMUEL (1775). *Journey to the Western Islands of Scotland* (Oxford ed., 1924) 348, 354
JOHNSTON, JAMES F. W. (1845-6). *The Potato Disease in Scotland* (W. Blackwood, Edinburgh) 375-6
JOHNSTON, THOMAS (1923). *History of the Working Classes in Scotland* (Forward Publishing Co., Glasgow) 360
JONES, CLARENCE (1928). Agricultural Regions of South America. *Econ. Geog.* vol. V (Clark Univ., Concord, N.Y.) 37
JONES, EVAN J. (1928). *Some Contribution to the Economic History of Wales* (London) 412
JONES, FRANCIS (1940). A Squire of Anglesey. *Trans. Anglesey Antiq. Soc.* 414
JONES, M. G. (1935). *The Charity School Movement* (Cambridge Univ. Press) 604
JONSON, BEN (1601). *Cynthia's Revels* (Marlowe Society) 427
JONSON, BEN (1598). *Every Man out of his Humour* (Marlowe Society) 427
J. Cork Hist. and Archaeol. Soc. vol. XXVI (1920) 152
JOYCE, PATRICK WESTON (1903). *A Social History of Ancient Ireland* (Longmans, London) 217
JOYCE, T. A. (1920). *Catalogue of an Exhibition of Indigenous American Art* (Burlington Fine Arts Club, London) 14-16

KAMES, LORD (1776). *The Gentleman Farmer* (Edinburgh) 362
KENNEDY, H. (1941). The importance of the potato (Broadcast Talk). *J. Dep. Agric. Eire*, vol. XXXVIII 567
KENNEDY, PAT (1875; first written in 1856). *The Banks of the Boro* (Macmillan, London) 121
KENT, NATHANIEL (1777). *Hints to Gentlemen* (ed. 1793; London) 462, 483, 488, 499
KERN, FRANK D. Visiting Venezuela. *Scientific Monthly* (Feb. 1937) 144
KILVERT, FRANCIS (1944). *Diary* (Jonathan Cape, London) 486
KIRKPATRICK, F. A. (1935). Letter to R. N. S. 36
KIRSCHOFFER, G. (1806). *Communication to the Board of Agriculture* 405
KNIGHT, THOMAS ANDREW (1807). *Trans. Hort. Soc.* vol. I (1815) 164

KNIGHT, THOMAS ANDREW (1810). On Potatoes. *Trans. Hort. Soc.* (2nd ed.) 292

KRICHAUFF, HON. T. E. (1896). The Tercentenary of the Introduction of Potatoes in England. *J. Roy. Hort. Soc.* vol. XIX 441

LAMPITT, L. H. and GOLDENBERG, N. (1940). The Potato as Food. *Chemistry and Industry*, vol. LIX 122, 125; and The Nation's Food, 1946. *Soc. Chem. Ind. Lond.* 125

Lancashire Man, A (1795). *Ann. Bot.* vol. XXIV 452

LANCASTER, SIR JAMES (1593). Hakluyt Soc. ser. II, vol. LXXIV (1940) 547

Land at War (H.M. Stationery Office, London, 1944) 578

LANG, ANDREW (1898). *The Highlands of Scotland* (Blackwood, London) 364

LANGHAUS, DANIEL (1768). *L'Art de guérir soi-même* (2 vols.; quoted from Roze, p. 146) 114

LARGE, E. C. (1940). *The Advance of the Fungi* (Jonathan Cape, London) 171, 291, 293, 563

LATOCNAYE, DE (1796). *A Frenchman's Walk through Ireland* (trans. J. Stevenson, 1917) 340

LAUFER, BERTHOLD (1938). The American Plant Migration, Pt. 1, The Potato. *Field Mus. Nat. Hist.* vol. XXVIII (1) 128, 135

LAURENCE, EDWARD (1727). *The Duty of a Steward to his Lord* (2nd ed.; London) 478

LAURENCE, JOHN (1726). *A New System of Agriculture* (London) 475

LAWSON, A. (1827). *The Farmers' Practical Instructor* 524

LECKY, W. (1892). *A History of Ireland* (Longmans, London) 269, 305, 604

LE COUTEUR, J. (1841). On the Great Jersey Trench Plough. *J. Roy. Agric. Soc.* vol. VIII 559

LEIGH, ROBERT (1684). An Account of Ye Towne of New Rosse. *J. Roy. Soc. Antiq. Ireland* (1858; vol. V, p. 466) 236

LENNARD, REGINALD (1932). English Agriculture under Charles II. *Econ. Hist. Rev.* vol. IV 449

LEVER, TRESHAM (1942). *The Life and Times of Sir Robert Peel* (Allen and Unwin, London) 297

LEVY, HERMANN (1911). *Large and Small Holdings* 532

LEWIS, SIR GEORGE CORNEWALL (1836). *Local Disturbances*. Rept. Irish Poor in Great Britain (Dublin) 270, 604

LEYCESTER, RALPH (1795). *Annals of Agric.* vol. XXIV 509

Limerick Chronicle (1845) 294

LINKE, LILO (1944). *Andean Adventure* (Hutchinson, London) 6, 45

LINNE (1939). *Nature, London* 3

LINSCHOTEN, J. H. VAN (1595). *His discourse of Voyages into the East and West Indies* (Engl. trans. 1598; Hakluyt Soc. 1885) 546

LINTON, RALPH (1945). *The Science of Man* (Columbia Univ. Press) 45

Lismore Papers, vol. I 152–3

LLOYD, SIR J. E. (1935). *A History of Carmarthenshire* 412

LLOYD-DODD, F. T. (1942). Land Tenure. MSS. 270, 604, 605

L'OBEL, MATHIAS DE and PENA, P. (1570). *Stirpium adversaria nova* (London) 79

L'OBEL, MATHIAS DE (1581). *Plantarum seu stirpium historia* (Antwerp) 95

LODGE, JOHN *Peerage of Ireland* (Archdall's ed.; Dublin, 1789) 155

LOFFT, CAPEL (1796). Troston, Suffolk. *Annals of Agric.* vol. XXVI 505

London Cries (1813). Sam Syntax's A description of the Cries of London as they are daily Exhibited in the Streets (2nd ed. 1821; Harris and Son, London) 597

LONGFIELD, ADA K. (1929). *Anglo-Irish Trade in the Sixteenth Century* (Routledge, London) 195, 214

Lords Commission on Poor Laws (1818) 525

LOUDON, J. C. (1831). *Encyclopaedia of Agriculture* (2nd ed.; London) 222, 493, 525

LOUGH, E. (1896). *England's Wealth and Ireland's Poverty* (Fisher and Unwin, London) 331, 607

LOVELL, ROBERT (1659). *The Complete Herbal* (1st ed. 1659, 2nd ed. 1665; Oxford) 109

LYONS, SIR HENRY (1944). *The Royal Society* (Cambridge Univ. Press) 447

MACADAM, ALEX. (1794). *Statistical account of Scotland* 365

McBRIDE (1921). *The Agrarian Indian Communities of Highland Bolivia* (Oxford Univ. Press, New York) 33

McCARTHY, JUSTIN (1880). *A History of our Own Times* (Chatto and Windus, London) 296

MACCULLOCH, JOHN (1824). *Highlands and Western Isles*. Letters to Sir W. Scott, 1811 (Longmans, London) 348, 367

MACDONALD, ALEXANDER (1741). *Gaelic Dictionary* 354

MACDONELL, G. P. (1888). Part author of *Two Centuries of Irish History* (Kegan Paul, London) 317, 327, 329

McINTOSH, T. P. (1927). *The Potato* (Oliver and Boyd, Edinburgh) 344, 441

McINTOSH, T. P. (1943). The Potato Industry in Scotland. *Scot. J. Agric.* vol. XXIV 404, 407

McINTOSH, T. P. (1933). Report on the Marketing of Potatoes in Scotland. Dept. of Agric. for Scotland (1933) 407

MACINTYRE, REV. JOSEPH (1793). *The Statistical Account of Scotland*, vol. VIII (Edinburgh) 365

MACKAY, W. (1911). *Industrial Life in the Highlands. Leabhar a' Chlachain* (Robert Maclehose and Co., Glasgow) 354

MACKENZIE, AGNES MURE (1940). *The Kingdom of Scotland* (W. Chambers, Edinburgh) 361

MACKENZIE, W. C. (1911). *The Social Life of the Community. Leabhar a' Chlachain* (Robert Maclehose and Co., Glasgow) 354

MACKENZIE, REV. WILL. (1795). *The Statistical Account of Scotland*, vol. XVI (Edinburgh) 363

MACLEOD, DONALD (1945). Letter to R. N. S. 354

MACLEOD OF MACLEOD, FLORA (25 March 1944). Letter to R. N. S. 377

MacLYSAGHT, ED. (1939). *Irish Life in the Seventeenth Century* (Longmans, London) 229, 231, 237

McMANUS, M. J. (1939). *Irish Cavalcade, 1550–1850* (Macmillan, London) 217

MacSKIMIN, SAMUEL (1676). *History of Carrickfergus* (ed. 1811; Belfast) 225

MAGAZINI, FATHER (1623). *Dell' Agricultura Toscana* 146

MAJENDIE, LEWIS (1795). Hedingham, Essex. *Annals of Agric.* vol. XXIV 505

MAJOR, HENRY (1815). *Observations Demonstrative of the Necessity of Ireland's Welfare, etc.* (Dublin) 273

MALPEAUX (1899). *Culture de la Pomme de Terre* (Masson et Cie, Paris) 144

MALTHUS, T. R. (1806). *An Essay on the Principle of Population* (3rd ed. London) 373, 516

MALTHUS, T. R. (1820). *Principles of Political Economy* 343, 470

MANGELSDORF, P. C. and REEVES, R. G. (1939). The origin of Indian Corn and its relatives. *Bull. Tex. Agric. Exp. Sta.* 4, 5

MANSERGH, NICHOLAS (1942). *Britain and Ireland* (Longmans, London) 276

MARKHAM, GERVASE and MACHIN, LEWIS (1608). The Dumbe Knight. *Dodsley's Old Plays* (1825) 428

MARKHAM, GERVASE (1615). *The English Huswife*, 1631 and 1660 (London) 432

MARSHALL, E. H. (1926). A Visit to Tristan da Cunha. *Brit. Dent. J.* vol. XLIV 544

MARSHALL, WILLIAM (1811). *Review of the Reports of the Board of Agriculture* (London) 322, 474

MARSHALL, WILLIAM (1794). *General View of the Agriculture of the Central Highlands* 364

MARSHALL, WILLIAM (1788). *The Rural Economy of the Midland Counties* (London) 160

MARSTON, JOHN (c. 1630). *Histrio-Mastix*, Richard Simpson's *School of Shakespeare*, vol. II, 1878 (Chatto and Windus, London) 426–7

MARSTON, JOHN (1599). *The Scourge of Villanie*, Satyre III (ed. J. O. Halliwell, 1856) 426

MARTIN, MARTIN (1697). *Roy. Soc. Trans.* vol. XIX 354

MARTIN, MARTIN (1703). *A Description of the Western Islands of Scotland* (Andrew Bell, London) 353

MARTIN, R. MONTGOMERY (1837). *History of the British Possessions in the Indian and Atlantic Oceans* (Whittaker, London) 555

MARTIN, R. MONTGOMERY (1837). *History of the Falkland Islands, St Helena, etc. Brit. Col. Lib.* vol. X 555

MARTYR, PETER (1516). *De Orbe Novo* (trans. Paul Gaffarel, 1907) 131

MASON, A. E. W. (1941). *Life of Drake* (Hodder and Stoughton, London) 147

MASSINGER, PHILIP (1632). *A New Way to Pay Old Debts* (ed. *Great English Plays*, 1928; Gollancz, London) 429

MASSINGER, PHILIP (1629). *The Picture* (ed. W. Gifford, vol. III) 431

MATHEW, FATHER (27 July 1846). Letter published in Parliamentary Papers. Quoted from O'Brien 300

MATTHIOLUS, P. A. (auct. G. BAUHIN) (1598). *Opera quae extant omnia.* Frankfurt-on-Main 76–7, 91–3, 344

MAURICE, COL. (1886). *Letters from Donegal* (Macmillan, London) 607

MAWE, T. and ABERCROMBIE, J. (1778). *Universal Gardener* (London) 476

MAXWELL, CONSTANTIA (1940). *Country and Town in Ireland under the Georges* (Harrap, London) 259

MAXWELL, CONSTANTIA (1923). *Irish History from Contemporary Sources* (London) 151

MAY, ROBERT (1665). *The Accomplisht Cook* 443

MAYHEW, HENRY (1861). *London Labour and London Poor* (Griffin, London) 599

MEDSGER, O. P. (1939). *Edible Wild Plants* (New York) 1, 83

MELLADO (1854). *Diccinario Universal* (Madrid) 145–6

MELLISS, J. C. (1875). *St Helena* (Reeve, London) 549, 555

MERCER, WILLIAM (attributed to 1675). *The Moderate Cavalier* 237

MEREDITH, GEORGE. *Diana of the Crossways* 295

MERRETT, CHRISTOPHER (1667). *Pinax rerum naturalium Britannicarum* (London), 97–8, 409

METRAUX, ALFRED (1943). The Native Tribes of Eastern Bolivia and Western Matto Grosso. *Bull. Bur. Amer. Ethn.* 6, 7

MILL, J. S. (1821) *The Elements of Political Economy* 334

MILLER, PHILLIP (1760). *The Elements of Agriculture*, from *Traite de la Culture des Terres* (1754) 478

MILLER, PHILIP (1724). *The Gardener's Dictionary* (2nd ed. 1733; Rivington, London) 161, 478

MILLIN, GEORGE (1891). *Life in our Villages* (Cassells, London) 531

MISSON, FRANÇOIS (1697). *Memoirs and Observations, etc.* (trans. W. Ozell, 1719; London) 135, 219

MOFFETT, THOMAS (?1595). *Health Improvement.* Corrected and enlarged by Christopher Bennet, London, 1665) 430

MOLINA, CRISTÓBAL DE (1573). *An Account of the Fables and Rites of the Incas* (trans. Clement Markham; Hakluyt Soc., vol. XLVIII, 1873) 102, 127

MOLINA, IGNATIUS (1787). *History of Chile* 128

MOLL, HERMAN (1724). *New Description of England and Wales* 414

MONARDES, NICHOLAS (1571). Trans. by Jhon Frampton, 1577, under the name *Joyfull newes out of the newe founde world*... (Tudor Translation Series, 1921) 77

MONTELL, GÖSTA (1929). *Dress and Ornaments in Ancient Peru* (Oxford Univ. Press) 25

MONTGOMERY, SIR HUGH (b. 1633). Montgomery MSS. (ed. J. Hill, 1869; Belfast) 222-3

MOORE, REV. GILES (1848). *Journal and Account Book of Rector of Horstead Keynes. Sussex Archaeological Collection* 120, 437

MORISON, ROBERT (1680). *Plantarum Historia Universalis* (1658), *Catalogus Horti. Botan. Oxon.* 445

MORISON, ROBERT (1699). *Plantarum Historia Universalis*, vol. 2 (Oxford) 98

MORPETH, LORD (1847). Election Address. *The Times* (9 Aug. 1847) 525

MORRIS, MRS HELEN (1938). *Soyer, The Portrait of a Chef* (Cambridge Univ. Press) 312

MORTIMER, JOHN (1707). *The Whole Art of Husbandry* (London) 160, 474

MORYSON, FYNES (1617). *Itinerary*, 1617 (ed. 1907; Glasgow) 218

MOWBRAY, A. (1795). Sherburn, near Durham. *Annals of Agric.* vol. XXIV 506

MÜLLER, K. O. (1930). *Angewandte Botanik.* Bd. XII 178

MUNDY, PETER (1638). Hakluyt Soc. ser. II, vol. XLVI; (1656), vol. LXXVI 548

MUNSTER, JULIUS (1846). *Die Frankheiten der Kartoffeln* (Berlin) 114

MURPHY, PAUL, PROFESSOR (1936). Report of Speech in the *Weekly Irish Times* (April 26) 148

MUSTEL, G. F., LE CHEVALIER (1767). Address to the Roy. Soc. Agric. Rouen. *Abst. Rev. Hort. Suisse* (1942) 123

NEWKIRK, W. B. (1939). Industrial use of starch products. *Industr. Engng Chem.* (*Ind. Edn.*), vol. XXXI 568

NICHOLLS, SIR GEORGE (1846). On the condition of the agricultural labourer. *J. Roy. Agric. Soc.* vol. VII 530

NICHOLLS, SIR GEORGE (1841). *The Farmer's Guide* (Dublin) 286

NICHOLSON, ASENATH. *Ireland's Welcome to the Stranger* (ed. 1844; Gilpin, London) 315

NICOL, JOHN (1822). *Life and Adventures* (ed. 1937; Cassells, London) 552

NICOLAUS DAMASCENUS. *De Plantis.* Latin ed. E. N. F. Myers, 1841 (Leipzig) 74

NIVEN, N. (1846). The Potato Epidemic, etc. A Letter to the Duke of Leinster (J. McGlashan, Dublin) 119, 316

NORDEN. *Survey of Wrexham* (1620) 410
Notes and Queries (1887) 451; (1940) 451
Nurseryman and Seedsman (1922) 173 n.

O'BRIEN, GEORGE (1921). *Econ. Hist. of Ireland, from the Union to the Famine* (Longmans, London) 247, 266, 283, 289, 300–1, 304, 306–7, 315, 605

O'BRIEN, GEORGE (1918). *Economic History of Ireland in the Eighteenth Century* (Maunsel, Dublin) 250, 264, 273, 335, 604

O'BRIEN, GEORGE (1919). *The Economic History of Ireland in the Seventeenth Century* (Maunsel, Dublin) 193, 218–19

O'BRIEN, GEORGE (1940). *New Light on Emigration* (Harvard Univ. Press) 322

O'BRUADAIR (1674). *Cuippead Cluany ap & pobony* (ed. Father McErlean, *Irish Texts*, Pt. II, p. 67) 229

O'FAOLAIN, SEAN (1942). *The Great O'Neil* (Longmans, London) 205, 213, 218

O'FAOLAIN, SEAN (1940). *An Irish Journey* (Longmans, London) 314

OLDYS, W. (1736). Life of Sir Walter Raleigh. Preface to Raleigh's *History of the World* 149–50

OLLIVER, M. (1936). The ascorbic acid content of fruits and vegetables with special reference to the effect of cooking and canning. *J. Soc. Chem. Ind.* vol. LV 566

OLLIVER, M. (1941). Paper read before the Food Group of the Soc. of Chemical Industry 129

ONLEY, CHARLES (1795). *Annals of Agric.* vol. XXV 508

ONLEY, CHARLES (1795). Stisted Hall, Essex. *Annals of Agric.* vol. XXIV 505

ORMOND, EDWARD (1887). Editor, *Armiston Memoirs* (1748) 389

O'ROURKE, JOHN (1875). *History of the Great Irish Famine* (McGlashan and Gill, Dublin) 253, 299, 300, 304, 307–11, 326, 604

ORPEN, GODDARD (1903). Raleigh's Home at Youghal. *J. Roy. Soc. Antiq. Ireland*, vol. XXXIII 150

ORR, J. B. (1936). *Food, Health and Income* (Macmillan, London) 566

ORWIN, C. S. and C. S. (1938). *The Open Fields* (Clarendon Press, Oxford) 201, 468, 470

ORWIN, C. S. (1929). *Reclamation of Exmoor Forest* (Clarendon Press, Oxford) 326

OSBORNE, S. G. Let the Poor Glean. *The Times* (22 Aug. 1848) 532

OVERBURY, THOMAS (1613–73). *Characters* 437

OVIEDO Y VALDES, G. F. (1557). *La Historia general y natural de las Indias* (ed. 1851; Madrid) 131

PAGE, FREDERICK (1943). *Notes and Queries* 389

PALEY, WILLIAM (1785). *Moral and Political Philosophy* (ed. 1877) 516

PALIN, W. (1845). *J. Roy. Agric. Soc.* vol. LVIII 531

PALMER, ALFRED NEOBARD (1883). *The Town, Fields and Folk of Wrexham* (Henry Gray, Manchester) 410

PARKER, CHARLES STUART (1929). *Encyclopaedia Britannica* (14th ed.), vol. XVII 297

PARKER, MATHEW (1504–75). *A proper Newsbook of Cookery* (ed. Frances Frere) 440

PARKER, W. H., SALAMAN, R. N. and BRANDRETH, B. *J. Nat. Inst. Agric. Bot.* vol. III 407

PARKINS, J. (1846). *Gardeners' Chronicle* 290

PARKINSON, JOHN (1629). *Paradisi in Sole Paradisus Terrestris* (London) 66, 93, 95, 105–6, 438; (2nd ed. 1656) 94

PARKINSON, JOHN (1640). *Theatrum botanicum. The Theater of Plants* (London) 94–5, 344

PARMENTIER, A. A. (1781). *Recherches sur les végétaux nourrissans, qui, dans les temps de disette, peuvent remplacer les alimens ordinaires* (Paris) 563

PARMENTIER, A. A. (1789). *Sur les Pommes de Terre* (Paris) 162

PAYNE, ED. J. (1892). *History of the New World* (Clarendon Press, Oxford) 26

PELLEW, GEORGE (1888). *In Castle and Cabin* (Putnam's Sons, New York) 328–9

PENNANT, THOMAS (1772). *Tour in Scotland and voyage to the Hebrides* (1776 ed.) 363, 370

PENNEY, NORMAN (1920). *The Household Account of Sarah Fell* (Cambridge Univ. Press) 451

Penny Encyclopaedia (1833–43) 451

PETER, REV. ALEX. (1793). *The Statistical Account of Scotland*, vol. IX (Edinburgh) 399

PETHYBRIDGE, G. H. (1916). *Investigations on Potato Diseases.* Dept. Agric. and Tech. Instruction, Dublin 608

PETHYBRIDGE, G. (1940). *The Potato Blight. Roy. Cornwall Polytechnic Soc.* vol. IX 292

PETTY, SIR WM. (1691). *Political Anatomy of Ireland* 219, 227–8

PHILLIPS, EDWARD (1658) (4th ed. 1678). *A New World of English Words, or a General Dictionary* (London) 433

PHILLIPS, HENRY (1822). *History of Cultivated Vegetables* (London) 119, 441

PICTON, J. A. (1903). *Memorials of Liverpool* (Gilbert and Wallesley, Liverpool) 453

PINK, JAMES (1879). *Potatoes and How to Grow Them* (Crossley Lockwood, London) 146, 358

PINKERTON, W. Ploughing by Tail. *Ulster J. Archaeol.* (o.s.), vol. VI 197

PLANK, J. E. VAN DER (1946). Origin of the first European Potatoes and their Reaction to Length of Day. *Nature, London*, vol. CLVII 63

PLATT, SIR HUGH. *The Floraes Paradisi.* Editions 1608, 1653, 1675 (London) 438

PLATT, SIR HUGH (1594). *The Jewell House of Art and Nature* (P. Short, London) 438

PLAUTUS, *Menaechmi* (trans. W. W. 1595) 426

PLAYFAIR, JAMES (1797). *The Statistical Account of Scotland* (Edinburgh) 371

POLO DE ONDEGARDO, J. (c. 1560). Report (trans. C. R. Markham; Hakluyt Soc. 1873) 126

POMA DE AYALA, FELIPE GUAMÁN (c. 1613). *Nueva Corónica y Buen Gobierno* (ed. P. Rivet, Inst. d'Ethnologie; Paris, 1936) 47, 127

POOLE, JOHN (1795). Salehurst. *Annals of Agric.* vol. XXIV 505

Poor Law Report (1831) 528

PORTA, GIAMBATTISTA (1588). *Phytognomonica* (Naples) 111

POSTANS, THOMAS (1831). A letter to Sir Thomas Baring on the present state of the Agricultural Poor (Michael Stannton, London) 528

PRAIN, SIR DAVID (1923). The Story of some common Garden Plants. *Trans. South Eastern Union Scientific Soc.* 134

PRENDERGAST, J. (1922). *The Cromwellian Settlement* (Mellifont Press, Dublin) 226

PRESTON, GEORGE (1716). *Catalogue of Plants* (Moncur, Edinburgh) 345

PRIOR, SIR JAMES (1819). *Voyage along the Eastern Coast of Africa* (Sir R. Phillips and Co., London) 554

PUSEY, PH. (1843). Agricultural Improvements in Lincs. *J. Roy. Agric. Soc.* vol. IV 492

PUTSCHE, C. (1819). *Versuch einer Monographie der Kartoffelen* (Weimar) 145, 149, 164

QUAYLE, THOMAS (1815). *General View, etc. of the Islands on the Coast of Normandy* (Macmillan, London) 561–2

QUELCH, MARY T. (1941). *Herbs for Daily Use in Home, Medicine and Cookery* (Faber and Faber, London) 110

Querist, The (1753) 253

QUINN, D. (1942). Note of a conversation with, 19 July 605

RAMSAY, JOHN (1888). *Scotland and Scotsmen in the eighteenth century* (ed. A. Allardyce; Blackwood) 360, 392

RATHLEF, H. (1932). Die Stammtafeln des Weltsortiment der Kartoffel. *Kühn-Archiv*. Bd. XXXIII 166

RAWSTOYNE, L. (1848). *The New Husbandry* (Preston) 452

RAY, JOHN (1686). *Historia Generalis Plantarum* (London) 77, 98

RAY, JOHN (1690). *Synopsis Methodica Stirpium Britannicarum* (ed. 1724; London) 476

REDDICK, D. (1939). *J. Heredity*, vol. XX 157–8

REES, THOMAS (1815). *The Beauties of England and Wales* (London) 415, 417

REID, JAMES (1697). *Husbandry anatomized* (Edinburgh) 345

REID, JOHN (1683). *Scots Gardener* (Edinburgh) 344

REID, THOMAS (1823). *Travels in Ireland* (Longmans, Hunt, London) 251, 278, 283–5

RENDLE, T. (1945). The preservation of potatoes for human consumption. *Chem. Ind. Rev.* (1945) 564

RENNEFORT, S. DE (1688). *Histoire des Indes Orientales* (Paris) 549

RENNIE, ROBERT (1796). *The Statistical Account of Scotland*, vol. XVIII (Edinburgh) 390

Report of Select Committee of the House of Lords on the Collection and Payment of Tithes in Ireland (1831–2) 249

Report of Select Committee (1795). *Re-Cultivation of Wastes, etc.* 492

Report Committee. House of Commons, 1800. *Annals of Agric.* vol. XXXIV 512–13

Report on Select Farms (1840). *British Husbandry* 359, 368

Report of Departmental Committee on Deer Forests (Scotland, 1919) 358

Report on the Failure of the Potato Crop and Conditions of the Poorer Classes in the West of Ireland (16 Feb. 1891; Dublin) 330

Report Select Committee on Potato Crop (1880) 168

Report to the Board of Agriculture (1795), *on the Curl* 390

RICHARDSON, S. (1740). *Pamela* (10th ed. 1775) 475

RITCHIE, REV. GEORGE (1840). On Cross and Burness. *New Statistical Account of Scotland* (Blackwood, Edinburgh) 373

ROBERTSON, GEORGE (1763–1832). Diarist. *See* FYFE, J. G.

ROBERTSON, JAMES (1794). *General View of the County of Perth* (London) 365

ROBERTSON, JAMES (1808). *General View. Inverness* (London) 371

ROBINSON, LENNOX (1932). *Three Homes* (Michael Joseph) 272

ROBINSON, URSULA (1941). *Nature, London*, vol. CXLVII 125

RODERICK, JOHN (1725). *English-Welsh Dictionary* 410
ROGERS, FRANCIS (1793). *Journal* (ed. Bruce Ingram; Constable, London, 1936) 247, 549
ROGERS, JAMES EDWARD THOROLD (1902). *History of Agricultural Prices* (Oxford) 439, 477
ROGERS, JASPER W. (1847). *The Potato Truck System of Ireland* (James Ridgway, London) 293
ROLAND, EUGENE. *Flore populaire* 118
ROUTH, SIR RANDOLPH (1846). Memorandum to Commissionary-General Hewetson, Commissariat Series. Quoted from O'Rourke, J. 307
ROWLANDSON, THOMAS (1846). The Agriculture of North Wales. *J. Roy. Agric. Soc.* vol. VII 420
ROWNTREE, B. SEEBOHM (1901). *Poverty, a Study of Town Life* (Longman, London) 535
ROWNTREE, B. SEEBOHM (1941). *Poverty and Progress* (Longman, London) 535-6
Royal Society. Boyle MSS. (1695) 227, 448
Royal Society. Letter Book, vol. I 238
Royal Society, 1662. Miscellaneous Papers of Council, etc. 228
Royal Society. Manuscript Journal (1693) 153, 188
ROYER, JOH. (*c.* 1651). Beschreibung des Furstlich Braunschweigischen Gartens in Hessen... 1607-1651. (Quoted from Feuss, *Die Ernahrung d. Pflanze*, 1935) 114
ROZE, E. (1898). *Hist. de la Pomme de Terre* (J. Rothschild, Paris) 59, 83, 85, 108-9, 114, 572
ROZE, E. (1896). Les deux premières variétés de la Pomme de Terre. *Journal de la Société nationale Horticulture de France* (3e Série, T. XVIII, pp. 146-53) 100
RUBNER, M. (1918). *Arch. Anatomie Physiol.*, *Abt. Physiologie-Jahg.* 124
RUBNER, M. and THOMAS, K. (1918). *Abt. Physiologie-Jahg.* 124
RUDBECK, OLAUS (1658). *Catalogus Plantarum* (Upsala) 599
RUGGLES, THOMAS (1792-4). *Annals of Agric.* (London) 495, 501, 505
RUGGLES, THOMAS (1797). *The History of the Poor* 493
RUMFORD, COUNT BENJAMIN THOMPSON (1753-1814). *Collected Works* (ed. G. E. Ellis, 5 vols.; Boston, U.S.A.) 115, 510
Rural Cyclopaedia (1850) 451. *See* WILSON, J. M.
RUSKIN, JOHN (1869). *Queen of the Air* (London) 119
RUSSELL, JAMES. *Diary. See* FYFE, J. G. 391
RUSSELL, P. (1769). *England Displayed* 415
RUSTON, A. G. WITNEY DENIS (1934). *Hooten Pagnell* 468
RYE, GEORGE (1730). *Consideration on Agriculture* (Dublin) 161

SABINE, JOSEPH, F.R.S. (1822). On the Native Country of the Potato. *Trans. Hort. Soc.* (London) 524
SADLER, MICHAEL (1828). *Ireland, its evils and their remedies* (London) 277
SAFFORD, W. E. (1925). The Potato of Romance and of Reality. *J. Heredity* vol. XVI 39, 144, 147-8, 157
SAFFORD, W. E. (1925). *J. Heredity*, vol. X 35
SAFFORD, W. E. (1917). Food Plants and Textiles of Ancient America. *Proc. Nineteenth Internat. Congress of Americanists* 18, 19
St Helena. Almanac and Annual Register (St Helena, 1851) 553
SALAMAN, R. N. (1939). Deformities and Mutilations of the Face as Depicted in the Chimu Pottery of Peru. *J. Roy. Soc. Anthrop. Inst.* vol. LXIX 31

SALAMAN, R. N. (1922–37). *Gardeners' Chronicle* (London) 173, 177
SALAMAN, R. N. (1938). *Indian J. Agric. Sci.* vol. VIII 177
SALAMAN, R. N. (1928). The Inheritance of Cropping in the Potato. *Zeitschrift f. induktive Abstammungs-und Vererbungslehre* (1928) 62
SALAMAN, R. N. (1923). *J. Genetics* (vol. I) 177; (vol. XIII) 174
SALAMAN, R. N. (1937). *J. Roy. Hort. Soc.* (vol. LXII) 23; (vol. LXV) 109
SALAMAN, R. N. (1946). *J. Linn. Soc., Bot., London*, vol. LIII 56, 57
SALAMAN, R. N. (1910). Male Sterility in Potatoes. *J. Linn. Soc.* vol. XXIX (London) 159
SALAMAN, R. N. (1936). Master's Lect. *J. Roy. Hort. Soc.* vol. LXII 68
SALAMAN, R. N. (1926). *Potato Varieties* (Cambridge Univ. Press) 160, 162, 170
SALAMAN, R. N. (1940). Why Jerusalem Artichoke? *J. Roy. Hort. Soc.* vol. LXV 121, 134, 223
SALAMAN, R. N. and LESLEY, J. W. (1920). The Inheritance of an Abnormal Haulm Type. *J. Genetics*, vol. V 82
SALAMAN, R. N. and LESLEY, J. W. (1921). *Rept. Internat. Potato Conf.* (Horticultural Soc., London) 174
SALMON, WILLIAM (1710). *The English Herbal* (London) 98, 106, 188, 224, 476
SANDEMAN, CHRISTOPHER (1939). *A Forgotten River* (Clarendon Press, Oxford) 9
SANDERS, T. W. (1905). *The Book of the Potato* (Collingbridge, London) 345, 439
SANDERS, T. W. *Encyclopaedia of Gardening* (21st ed. 1934; Collingbridge, London) 145
Scotland. New Statistical Account of (1840–5) 373–4, 390–1, 403
Scotland. The Statistical Account of (1791–7) (Edinburgh) 355–6, 358, 364–5, 368–9, 370–1, 382, 388, 390–1, 392, 393, 396, 397, 399, 400
SCOTT, W. (1800). *Annals of Agric.* vol. XXXV 521
Scottish Economic Committee on the Highlands (1938) 361, 363
SCROPE, GEORGE POULETT (1849). *Some notes of a Tour in England, Scotland, etc.* (John Ridgway, London) 378
SCROPE, GEORGE POULETT (1849). Letter to the *Morning Chronicle*. Publ. as a pamphlet, *Some notes on a Tour in England, Scotland and Ireland* (John Ridgway, London) 379
SCROPE, GEORGE POULETT (1834). *Letters to Lord Melbourne*. Quoted from G. O'Brien (1921). *Econ. History of Ireland from the Union to the Famine* 283
SCROPE, GEORGE POULETT (1847). *Reply to Archbishop of Dublin* (Ridgway, London) 313
SELKIRK, EARL OF (1805). *On Emigration and the State of the Highlands. Observations on the Present State of the Highlands* (ed. 1806; Constable and Co., Edinburgh) 366, 372
SENIOR, NASSAU WILLIAM (1867). *Journals of Ireland* 325
SERRES, OLIVIER DE (1600). *Théâtre d'Agriculture et Mesnages des Champs* (ed. 1619; Paris) 66, 86–7
SHAKESPEARE, WILLIAM. *Merry Wives of Windsor* 425, 436; *Troilus and Cressida* 425
SHEFFIELD, LORD (1795). *Annals of Agric.* vol. XXIX 511
SHEFFIELD, LORD (1795). Bristol. *Annals of Agric.* vol. XXIV 505
SHEPHERD, H. G. (1934). *One Hundred Years of the Roy. Jersey Agric. and Hortic. Soc. 1833–1933* (J. T. Bigwood, Jersey) 558, 560, 562
SHERRINGTON, SIR CHARLES (1946). *The Endeavour of Jean Fernel* (Cambridge Univ. Press) 31

SIGERSON, G. (1871). *History of Land Tenure and Land Classes in Ireland* (London) 192

SIMINGTON, ROBT. (1942). Eire. Tithe Applotment Books of 1834. *J. Dept. Agric. Eire*, 1942, vol. XXXVIII 282

SIMPKINSON, JOHN NASSAU (1860). *The Washingtons*, App. A (2) (Longmans, London) 439, 444

SIMPSON, D. and SMALL, T. (1938). The Potato Industry in Jersey. *Empire J. Exp. Agric.* vol. VI 562

SINCLAIR, SIR JOHN (1812). *An Account of the System of Husbandry in Scotland* (Edinburgh) 368, 396

SINCLAIR, SIR JOHN (1814). *General Report of the Agricultural State and Political Circumstances of Scotland* 365

SINCLAIR, SIR JOHN (1795). *General View. Northern Counties* (London) 381

SINCLAIR, SIR JOHN (1796). *The Statistical Account of Scotland* (Edinburgh) 358

SKEENE, WILLIAM F. (1880). *Celtic Scotland* (David Douglas, Edinburgh) 360

Sketch of the State of Ireland, Past and Present, A. See CROKER, J. W.

SLATER, GILBERT (1920). *The Growth of Modern England* (2nd ed.; Macmillan, London) 501, 522

SLOANE, DR (1693). The Origin of the Irish Potato MSS. *J. Roy. Soc.* (6 Dec.) 188

SMEE, ALFRED (1846). *The Potato Plant* (Longmans, London) 291

SMITH, ADAM (1776). *Wealth of Nations* (ed. 1805) 471, 485, 489

SMITH, CHARLES (1746). *The Ancient and Present State of the County and City of Waterford* (Dublin) 150

SMITH, CHARLES (1750). *The Ancient and Present State of the County of Cork* (Dublin) 150

SMITH, CHARLES (1760). *Three Tracts on the Corn Trade* (London) 480

SMITH, GOLDWIN (1883). *Nineteenth Century* (16 June) 534

Society of Friends. Relief Committee of, Trans. (1846-7) 300, 306

SOGNNAES, R. F. (1941). *J. Dental Research*, vol. XX (Skeffington and Sons, London) 546

SOMERVILLE, WILLIAM (1725). *Fable of the Two Springs* 505

SOYER, ALEXIS (1847). *Charitable Cooking, or the Poor Man's Regenerator* (Hodges and Smith, Dublin) 312

SPEED, ADOLPH (1659). *Adam out of Eden* (London) 445

SPEED, JOHN (1611). *Historie of Great Britaine* (3rd ed. 1632) 195

SPENSER, EDMUND (1596). *View of the Present State of Ireland* (ed. W. L. Renwick, 1934; Eric Partridge, London) 193

STANHOPE, PHILIP H., EARL (1888). *Notes of Communications with the Duke of Wellington*, 1831-56 (World Classics, 1938; Oxford) 320

State Papers (Ireland), 1600-1 219

STEVENS, JOHN (1689-91). *Journal* (ed. R. Murray; Oxford, 1912) 229, 237

STEWART, COL. DAVID (1822). *Sketches of the Character etc. of the Highlanders of Scotland* (Constable, Edinburgh) 352, 358, 361, 363

STIRLING, A. M. W. (1908). *Coke of Norfolk* (London) 492

STONE, THOMAS (1794). *General View of the Agriculture of the County of Bedford* (London) 467

STUART, REV. PATRICK (1796). *The Statistical Account of Scotland*, vol. XVII (Edinburgh) 350, 369

SUTHERLAND, JAMES (1683). *Hortus Medicus Edinburgensis* 344

SWANTON, JOHN R. (1911). *Bull. Bur. Amer. Ethn. Soc.* no. 43 26

SWIFT, JONATHAN (1765). *Considerations about maintaining the poor* (Temple Scott's ed. 1908; London) 265

SWIFT, JONATHAN (1729). *A Modest proposal* (Temple Scott ed.; London, 1908) 252, 604

SWIFT, JONATHAN (1727–8). *Short view of the State of Ireland* (Temple Scott ed.; London, 1908) 251

SYNGE, J. M. (1907). *The Arran Islands* (London) 118

Synonyms. Annual Report on Synonyms. *N.I.A.B. Journal* (Heffer, Cambridge) 173

SYNTAX, SAMUEL (1820). *Description of the Cries of London* (2nd ed. 1821), Fitzwilliam Mus. (J. Harris and Son, St Paul's Churchyard) 477

TABERNAEMONTANUS, J. (1590). *Eicones. See also* BERGZABERN, J.

TAYLOR, JOHN (*c.* 1621). *Collected Works*, 1630 (The Spenser Society, Manchester, 1868). The Goose Fair at Stratford, Bow. The Thursday after Whitsuntide 430

TEBBUTT, C. F. (1941). *Bluntisham cum Erith* (St Neots) 469

TELLO, J. (1922). *Prehistoric Peru, Inter-America* 4, 21

TENNYSON, ALFRED (1875). *Queen Mary* 240

THEOPHRASTUS (b. 370 B.C.). *Enquiry into Plants* (Engl. trans. by Sir Arthur Hort; London, 1916) 91

THOM, ALEX. (1729). *Tracts on Ireland* (Dublin, 1860). *An Essay upon the Trade of Ireland* (1728) 231, 265

THOMPSON, FLORA (1939). *Lark Rise.* Guild Book, no. 223, 1946 (Oxford Univ. Press) 534

THOMSON, J. (1800). *General View of the Agriculture of the County of Fife* (Edinburgh) 394

THURLOW, REV. (1795). *Annals of Agric.* vol. XXIV 510

TIGHE, W. (1802). *Statistical Observations relative to the County of Kilkenny* (Dublin Society, Dublin) 271

The Times 158, 287, 295, 303, 504, 507–9, 525, 606

TOMKINS, R. G., MAPSON, L. W., ALLEN, R. J. L., WAGER, H. G. and BARKER, J. (1944). The drying of vegetables. III. The storage of dried vegetables. *J. Soc. Chem. Ind.* vol. LXIII 565

TOOKE, THOMAS (1838). *History of Prices* 519

TOWNSHEND, DOROTHEA (1904). *The Life and Letters of the Great Earl of Cork* 150

TOWNSHEND, REV. HORATIO (1815). *General and Statistical Survey of the County of Cork* (Duckworth, London) 162, 276

TRADESCANT, J. (1656). *Catalogus Plantarum* 437

TRADESCANT, JOHN, JUN. (1656). *Musaeum Tradescantium*, or a collection preserved in South Lambeth near London (Nathaniel Brooke, London) 160

TRAILL, H. D. (1893–7). *Social England* (6 vols.; London) 493, 508

TREVELYAN, SIR CHARLES (1848). Irish Crisis. *Edinburgh Review*, vol. CLXXV 1848 and Macmillan, London 1880 289, 298–300, 303, 306, 312, 604, 606–7

TREVELYAN, G. M. *British History in the Nineteenth Century, 1782–1901* (Longmans, London) 295

TREVELYAN, G. M. (1930). *England Under Queen Anne* (Longmans, London) 461, 494

TREVELYAN, G. M. (1944). *English Social History* (Longmans, London) 386

TREVELYAN, G. M. (1926). *History of England* (Longmans, London) 388, 457–8

TRYON, THOMAS (1683). *The Way to Health* (London) 113, 446

TRYON, THOMAS (1688) (Phylotheus Physiologus). *Monthly observations for the Preserving of Health* (London) 446

TSCHIFFELY, A. F. (1933). *Southern Cross to North Pole Star* (Heinemann, London) 47

TSCHUDI, J. J. (1891). *Beiträge zur Kenntniss der alten Peru* 32

TSCHUDI, J. J. (1846). *Reiseskizzen aus den Jahren, 1838–42* (St. Gallen) 28, 35, 128

TSCHUDI, J. VON (1847). *Travels in Peru, 1838–42* (D. Bogue, London) 8, 26

TUKE, J., JUN. (1794). *General Views of the Agriculture of Yorkshire* (Macmillan, London) 405

Tuke (James) Fund (1883). *Emigration from Ireland, Second Report* (Nat. Press Agency) 330

TUKE, J. H. (1880). *Journal. Irish Distress and its Remedies. A Visit to Donegal and Connaught* (Ridgway, London) 326, 607

TULL, JETHRO (1733). *The Horse-Hoeing Industry* (London) 478

TURNER, WILLIAM. *The Nature of Herbs* (1551 ed.; London) 177; *A New Herbal* (1568 ed.; London) 77

TYSSEN-AMHERST, The HON. ALICIA (1894). *The Feate of Gardening*, by Master Ion Gardener, *c.* A.D. 1445 (*Archaeologia*, vol. LIV, pp. 157–72) 434

ULLOA, GEORGE and ANTONIO (1760). *Voyage to South America* (2nd ed.; London) 34

VALENTIA, LORD (1809). *Voyages and Travels* (3 vols.; London) 554

VANCOUVER, CHARLES (1794). *General View of the Agriculture of the County of Cambridge* (London) 469, 486

VAN GOGH, VINCENT (1927). *Letters to His Brother* (Constable, London) 593

VARGAS, C. (1936). *El Solanum tuberosum* (Lima) 48

VARLEY, C. (1770). *A New System of Husbandry* (3 vols.; York) 253

VAUGHAN, W. (1608). *Golden Grove. See LLOYD, J. E.*

VÁZQUEZ DE ESPINOSA, ANTONIO (*c.* 1628). Compendium and description of the West Indies (1942) (trans. C. U. Clark). *Smithsonian Miscell. Collect.* No. 102 44, 48, 50, 103

VENN, J. A. (1933). *The Foundations of Agricultural Economics* (Cambridge Univ. Press) 528, 611

VENNER, TOBIAS (1620). *Via Recta ad Vitam Longam* (London) 93, 104, 424, 429

VERNEY, MARGARET, LADY (1925). *Memoirs of the Verney Family* 548

VERNEY, MARGARET, LADY (1930) *Verney Letters* (Longmans, London) 459

Victoria County History, Lancaster (St Catherine's Press, London, 1908) 521

VROLIK, G. (1846). *Observations et Expériences relative à la Maladie des Pommes de Terre* (Amsterdam) 290

WAGER, H. G., TOMKINS, R. G., BRIGHTWELL, S. T. P., ALLEN, R. J. L. and MAPSON, L. W. (1945). The drying of potatoes. *Food Manufac.* vol. XX 564–5

WALKER, JOHN (1808). *Economical History of the Hebrides* (2 vols.; Edinburgh) 358

WALLACE, J. C. and THOMPSON, J. K. (1931). Potato Silage. *J. Min. Agric.* vol. XXXVIII 567

W. R. *Wallography, a mighty lover of Welsh or the Briton Described* (1682) (London) 409

WALTON, CLIFFORD (1894). *History of the British Standing Army* (Harrison and Sons, London) 119

WARD, EDWARD (1699). *A Trip to Ireland* (attributed to Ward), ed. H. Thoyer, *Facs. Text. Soc.* (Columbia Univ. Press, 1933) 231

WARD, EDWARD (1707). *Wooden World Dissected* (4th ed. 1749) and Reprint 1929, p. 79 (London) 452

WARING, ELIJAH (1850). *Recollections and Anecdotes of Edward Williams* (London) 416

WARNER, REV. RICHARD (1798). *A Second walk through Wales* (2nd ed. 1800; Bath) 412–13

WARREN, REV. (1794). *General View of the Agriculture of the Isle of Wight* 503

WEAVER, THOMAS (1654). *Songs and Poems of Love and Drollery* 239

WEDGE, THOMAS (1794). *General View, etc.* Chester (London) 453

WERNER, H. (1930). *Der Kartoffelbau* (9th ed. revised by K. Opitz; Paul Parey, Berlin) 567, 570–1

WESLEY, JOHN (1756). Entry in his *Journal* (6 Jan.) (publ. 1827, 4 vols.; London) 340, 389

WESTON, ALDERMAN (1800). *Annals of Agric.* vol. XXIV 506

WESTON, SIR RICHARD (1591–1652). *Discourses of the Husbandrie used in Brabant and Flanders in the Year 1645* (London) 196–7, 438

WHEATLEY, HENRY B. (1877). Note on Norden's 1593 Map of London in Furnivall's ed. of Harrison's *Description of England* 78

WHITE, GILBERT (1789). *Nat. Hist. of Selborne* (ed. 1900; Fremantle, London) 464, 478

WICKENS, JOHN (1795). Blandford, Dorset. *Annals of Agric.* vol. XXIV 505

WIGHT, W. F. (1917). Origin, Introduction and Primitive Culture of the Potato. *Proc. Pot. Assoc. America* (1916) 63, 128

WILDE, W. R. (1858). *Proc. Roy. Irish Acad.* vol. VI 253, 604–7

WILDE, SIR WILLIAM R. (1856). Introduction and time of the general use of the Potato in Ireland. *Proc. Roy. Irish Acad.* vol. XI (ser. A) 226, 238

WILLIAMS, E. (1816). *Cambria Depicted* (London) 417

WILSON, J. DOVER (1922). Introduction to Shakespeare's *Measure for Measure* (Cambridge Univ. Press) 425

WILSON, JOHN MARIUS (1849–51). *Rural Cyclopaedia* (Fullarton, Edinburgh) 358, 451

WOODS, MRS CLARENCE. *High Spots on the Andes* (Putnam, N.Y.) 29, 39

WOOTON, A. C. (1910). *Chronicles of Pharmacy* (Macmillan, London) 112

WORLIDGE, JOHN (1699). *Compleat System of Husbandry* (Samuel Speed, London) 450

WORLIDGE, JOHN (1669). *Systema Agriculturae* (London) 450

WORLIDGE, JOHN (1688). *Systema Horticulturae* (T. Burrel and Co., Housman, London) 409

YATES, P. L. (1940). *Food Production in Western Europe* (Longmans, London) 567

YOUNG, A. (1798–1804). *Annals of Agric.* 462, 479, 492, 503–4, 507, 510–13, 516, 521

YOUNG, A. (1771). *A Course of Experimental Agriculture* (London) 468

YOUNG, A. (1771). *Eastern Tour* 485

YOUNG, A. (1815). Enquiry into the Rise of Prices in Europe during the last twenty-five years. *The Pamphleteer*, vol. VI (London) 519

YOUNG, A. (1767). *Farmers' Letters* (2 vols.; 3rd ed. 1771; Strahan, London) 480, 483, 497

YOUNG, A. (1771). *A Farmer's Tour through the East of England* (London) 481

YOUNG, A. (1807). *General View of the Agriculture of Essex* (Richard Phillips, London) 521

YOUNG, A. (1804). *General View of the Agriculture of Hertfordshire* (Board of Agriculture, London) 469

YOUNG, ARTHUR (1809). *General View of the Agriculture of Oxfordshire* (Board of Agriculture, London) 468

YOUNG, A. (1797). *General View of the Agriculture of the County of Suffolk* (Macmillan, London) 493

YOUNG, A. (1800). *The Question of Scarcity Plainly Stated* (Macmillan, London) 480, 514

YOUNG, A. (1770). *Rural Economy* (T. Becket, London) 486

YOUNG, A. (1770). *A Six Months' Tour through the North of England* (Dublin) 481, 488

YOUNG, A. (1768). *A Six Weeks' Tour through the Southern Counties of England and Wales* (Strahan, London) 415, 476, 481, 486

YOUNG, A. (1776). *Tour in England and Wales*. London School Economics, Scarce Tracts, no. 14 (1932) 483

YOUNG, A. (1792). *A Tour in France* (Bury St Edmund's) 486

YOUNG, A. (1780). *A Tour in Ireland* (London) 202, 249, 253, 257, 259, 262, 340

YOUNG, A. (1776). *A Tour to Shropshire*. London School Economics, Scarce Tracts, no. 14 (1932) 477

YOUNG, A. (1776). *Tour in Wales*. London School Economics, Scarce Tracts, no. 14 416

YOUNG, A. JUN. (1793). *General View of the Agriculture of the County of Sussex* (ed. 1813; London) 493

ZEDLER, J. H. (1735). *Lexicon* 134

ZEDLER, J. H. (1744). *Lexicon Universalis* (Leipzig) 114

ZEDLER, J. H. *Lexicon Universalis*, 1732–1750 (Leipzig) 136

ZILVA, S. S. and MORRIS, T. N. (1938). Vitamin C in canned meat and vegetable rations and in canned potatoes. *Rep. Food. Invest. Bd.*, London, 1938 566

ZWINGER (1696). *Neu Vollkomen Kraüter-Buch* (Basle) 98

INDEX

Prices, speculation in potato seed, 169–70
Priest, Dr, 78–80
Prince Edward Island:
potato in, 372
Scottish settlement (1802), 372
Principles, four, of nature, 75
Privy Council, food campaign (1795), 508
Propaganda in war-time, 579
Propagation by seed. *See* Seed
Protein content, 122–5
Prussia, potato and scrofula, 115
'Puffe, great', species of *Lycoperdon*, 131
Puma, 7
pottery design. *See* Pottery
Puno region, Lake Titicaca, 38
Puppets, ceremonial, maize and coca, 28
Purpura, following Irish famine, 304
Putsche, Dr Carl (1819), 164
Pycnocomon, Pyconoconium, of Dioscorides, 93, 97
Pyke, Governor (1711), 551
'Pyttatws', Welsh term for potato, 410

Quanjer, 179
Quechuan, list of diseases, 32
names for potato, 63, 128
Quemotte, term for potato in Vosges, 132
Quesada, Gonzalo Jiménez de (1536–7), discovery of the potato, 36
Quinn, D. (1942), 604
Quinoa, Chenopodium quinoa, 5, 11, 91
beer from, 13
Quipu system, 43, 45
Quito, 92
Cieza's account of the potato at, 91
potato as food in, 103

Rachitic, anti-, vitamin D, 124
Railway development, in relation to potato famine, 309
Irish labour for, 325–6
Rainfall, Ireland, 189
Raleigh, Sir Walter:
character and events of his life, 148–9, 151–2
potato:
introduction of, 55, 145, 149–50, 153, 156–7, 222
planted at Youghal, 146
Raleigh legend concerning, 142 *et seq.*
Raleigh's agent, Hariot, and, 146
Sir Robert Southwell's statement concerning, 153
the gardener story concerning, 146–8, 150
Virginia and the, 82–3, 148, 153

Southwell family, relations with, 154
tobacco, introduction of, 150
Youghal, connection with, 150
Ramsay, John, 392
Ramsden and Appleyard, Messrs, 184
Ravius, introduction of potato to Spain, 145
Ray, Mr, of Tostock, 485
Ray, John, 77, 85, 98
Rees, Principal J., 411 n.
Reform Bill (1832), 419
Reinvigoration of stock, 165
Renaissance, spirit of, 585
Rennefort, Sieur de, 549
Repertto, family of, 543
Revolution or reform, 458
Rheumatism, potato protection from, 118
Riboflavin, 123
Ricardo, Antonio, 128
Ricardo, David, doctrines of, 472
Rice, 188, 512
'Riced' potato, 564
Rickets, 356
Riddell, Sir James, of Strontian, 376
Riddle, crop grading, 590
Rings, dish-rings, in Ireland, 596–7
Roanoke, 82
colony at, 148
Robinson, firm of, 298
Rochdale, Yorkshire, 454
Rochcliffe, 521
Rondelet, Guillaume, 88
Root cultivation, 5
Rose, 125
Rot, in potato clamps, 604–6
crop failures due to, 605–7
dry-rot, 171, 605
Roxburgh Ballads, 475
Royal Horticultural Society, Committee on names, 173
Royal Society, committee on potato cultivation (1662), 447
Rumford, Count, soups introduced by, 115, 510, 521
Rundale system, Ireland, 194–6, 198–202
Runrig system, 195, 349, 358, 376, 379, 386–7, 392, 397–8, 413
Rural workers, use of potatoes by (1795), 508
Ruskin, John, views against the potato, 112, 119–20
Russell, Lord John:
attitude towards railway development project, 309
Corn Laws, letter to *The Times*, 295
government and resignation (1845), 295
speech on Irish famine (1847), 311